BEE 

ERIC HUGHES, Ed.D., University of Washington, is Associate Professor of Physical Education and Gymnastic Coach at the University of Washington. He previously taught and coached at Bemidji State Teachers College in Minnesota and the University of Illinois. Dr. Hughes has been Past Chairman of the Pacific Northwest AAU Gymnastics Committee, Vice-President of the National Association of Gymnastic Coaches, Gymnastic Coach of the Year for the Western United States in 1963 and 1965, and Coach of the United States National Team (Men and Women) that toured Russia, Poland, and Czechoslovakia in 1961. He is chairman of the gymnastic committee for People-to-People Sports Committee, Inc. Dr. Hughes is the author of *Gymnastics for Girls—A Competitive Approach for Teacher and Coach* (published by The Ronald Press Company).

GYMNASTICS FOR MEN

A Competitive Approach for Teacher and Coach

ERIC HUGHES
UNIVERSITY OF WASHINGTON

THE RONALD PRESS COMPANY • NEW YORK

7MP

Library of Congress Catalog Card Number: 66–21863
PRINTED IN THE UNITED STATES OF AMERICA

Preface

When gymnastics is taught as a competitive sport in a manner similar to other physical education activities, it has proved to be very popular. Instead of presenting skills individually, this book offers every stunt as part of a routine. Teaching gymnastics in this way is more meaningful to students and much more interesting.

This text is designed to be a complete guide for the gymnastic teacher and coach. Physical education teachers cannot be expected to be experts in all activities, but even a teacher with little gymnastic background can have a successful gymnastic unit if he follows the procedures outlined in this text. He does not have to spend considerable time planning and selecting stunts to be taught. If the students are beginners, no matter what their age, they should start with Routine I in each event. When a complete routine has been presented, the teacher does not have to constantly remind students what stunts should be practiced. Students can quickly memorize the sequence (or they can refer to routines posted in the gymnasium or locker room) and therefore need little direction as they have an understandable goal toward which they can strive. This makes the teacher's job much easier. As soon as students have accomplished the first routine, Routine II should be taught to provide another goal.

This method of presenting gymnastics is a practical one that has proved to be successful with children eight years of age to young men in college. It is especially valuable for teachers who do not feel they have the knowledge to guide students in the formation of optional routines and for teachers who have large classes and do not have the time to give individual guidance to each student. After students have had sufficient background, there is no reason why they should not be given an opportunity to form optional routines. It has been found, however, that most beginning and intermediate students waste so much time trying to compose exercises of their own that they accomplish very little in the time available in a physical education class.

Students enjoy gymnastics when the methods suggested in this text are used. When a complete exercise has been learned, they get a real feeling of accomplishment. They have something to show for their efforts, something that will be remembered.

A book such as this could not be written without the help of many individuals. Special thanks are due to: my wife, Jean, for her patience and understanding as well as for her assistance in the preparation of the manuscript; Gary Finne, Mike Flansaas, and Gene Jensen for their help in demonstrating stunts and spotting methods; and Ione Nelson for the illustrations.

ERIC HUGHES

Seattle, Washington
July, 1966

Contents

GYMNASTICS FOR MEN

1

Introduction

PURPOSE OF THIS BOOK

This book is intended to be used as a complete syllabus or teaching guide for the physical education teacher and team coach. It is designed for use in junior high school, high school, and college, but some of the material included might be used in elementary schools.

The method of presentation suggested is designed to make gymnastics a more popular activity in our curriculum. For years gymnastics has been taught to half interested students who lacked real enthusiasm. In carefully analyzing the situation two major weaknesses were found in the method of presentation used by the vast majority of physical education teachers—(1) lack of variety in teaching techniques and class organization; and (2) insufficient use of the competitive element.

This book suggests a variety of teaching techniques and stresses that gymnastics is a competitive sport and should be taught as a competitive sport by the physical education teacher as well as the coach.

Our American way of life is competitive. Adults compete in business, in politics, for offices in civic clubs, and for jobs. Students compete with each other for academic grades, for student offices, for roles in plays, and in music, art, and debate contests. Most activities taught in our physical education program are also of a competitive nature. All of the more common sports, whether team, dual, or individual, involve some form of competition. In volleyball and softball, teams play against each other and scores are kept. In tennis and badminton individual players compete. In golf and archery scores are kept, and this score is compared with a previous score or with scores made by others. In track and field and swimming, races are held between class members.

During a teaching unit of almost every sport except gymnastics the students compete on a team or against another individual many times during the unit. Furthermore, in most activities, "playing the game" is a part of every class period. In many cases, because of the interest factor a class is permitted to play the game even though it is not really ready for a competitive game situation.

Of course, physical educators concentrate on teaching skills, but they do not devote a whole unit, or seldom even an entire class period, to this. Even in lead-up drills the competitive element is frequently used. In volleyball, for example, each squad is placed in a circle and competes to see which group can keep the ball in the air the longest by passing it back and forth between squad members. In basketball, dribbling relays or shooting contests are held. Similar examples could be presented for every sport. The same type of techniques can be used in gymnastics so that competition can be introduced after only a few class periods of instruction.

For almost every activity in our physical education program there is a standard set of rules available. Physical educators believe that it is desirable to use standard rules and to use standard equipment (balls of a certain size, nets of a certain height, courts of regulation size). Of course, these rules are sometimes modified for inexperienced students or for younger children, but generally teachers follow the rulebook and emphasize the importance of the rules. But this is seldom done in gymnastics. Very few teachers teach this sport according to the rules. In fact, many are unaware that there are rules for gymnastics and that specific events are included in the sport. Many teachers who keep up to date in other activities and adopt rule changes immediately are years behind the times in gymnastics.

Teachers who teach every other sport as a competitive activity with standard rules forget about competition and rules when they come to their gymnastics (or tumbling) unit and devote the entire unit to the teaching of individual skills or stunts. The only common technique of a competitive nature used in gymnastic teaching in our schools today is the stunt checkoff list. This enables the individual to compete indirectly against other members of the class. It is a good technique but it is not enough. No wonder gymnastics is not so popular as other sports in our schools.

Competition, of course, is not the only answer to successful gymnastic teaching. A gymnastic unit, or for that matter any other unit, is not likely to be successful unless the teacher organizes the unit and daily lessons thoroughly and teaches with enthusiasm.

Because of the method of presentation this book is of special

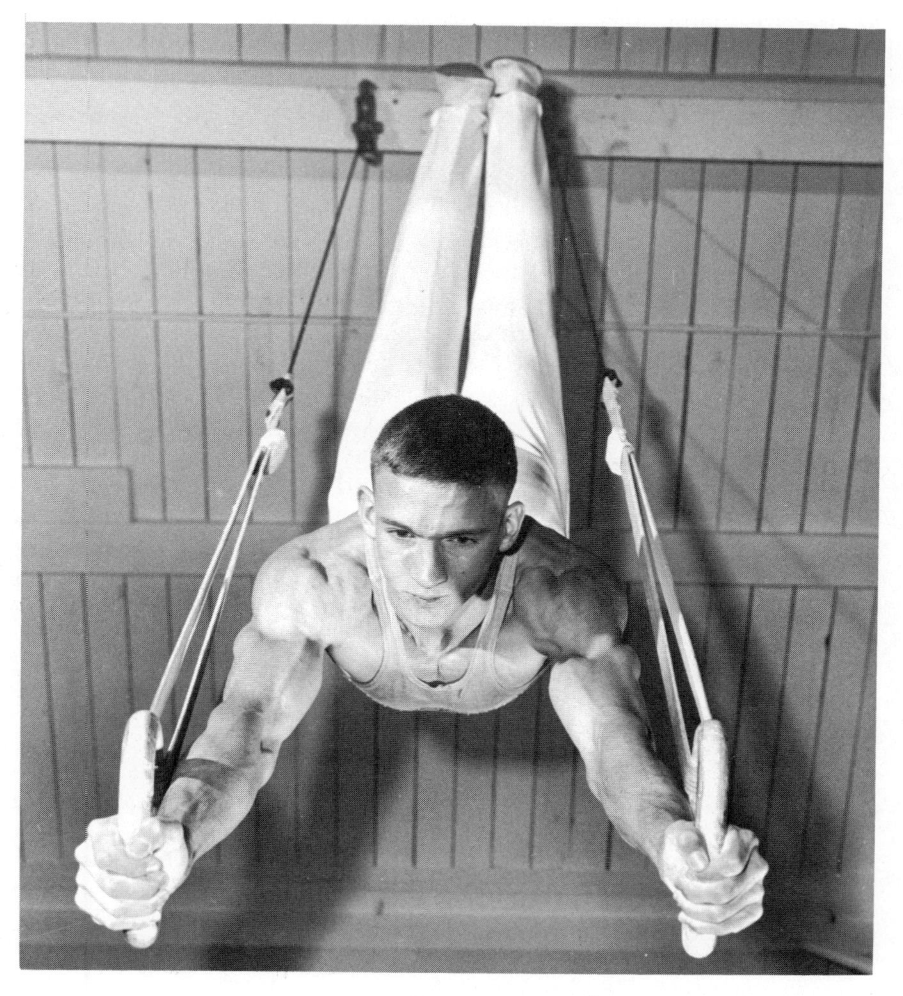

University of Washington News Service photo

Brian Sternberg Holding a Handstand on the Rings. Brian was one of the most promising athletes ever to attend the University of Washington until an injury interrupted his career at the end of his sophomore year in 1963. He had attained the ultimate in the sport of track and field—a world record. His record of 16 feet 8 inches in the pole vault was an amazing feat for a youngster of nineteen. Brian was a good all-round performer in the sport of gymnastics and also outstanding on the trampoline. He performed several different types of double twisting fliffis and a quadruple twisting back somersault.

value to coaches and intramural supervisors whose specific goal is to prepare gymnasts for competition against other individuals and teams. Many physical educators, although they have included gymnastics in their curriculum, have hesitated to include the sport in their extracurricular program because of insufficient knowledge about aspects of competition. This book provides a complete guide for the coach. It is hoped that many athletic directors and school administrators will be stimulated to add gymnastics to their extracurricular program now that this guide is available.

The United States is a little behind some other countries in international gymnastic competition. Unless we provide team competition for our boys at the junior and senior high school levels we will continue to take a back seat to other more interested and progressive countries that do have well-organized competition for their young people. Developing gymnasts of Olympic caliber is not an important objective of a competitive gymnastic program in our schools, but it is an objective that should be given some thought. Americans have dominated most international sport competitions in the past but in recent years have been beaten quite consistently in some sports by the Russians and by other smaller nations. This has hurt our cause considerably in our cold war struggle and defense of our beliefs and ideals. Every American citizen, especially physical education teachers, should be concerned about this situation.

NOMENCLATURE

The most common terms needed for a working knowledge of gymnastics are defined and included in a glossary at the end of the book. In some cases terms that apply only to one event will be explained in the chapter devoted exclusively to that event.

Two very broad and general definitions are appropriate in this chapter:

Gymnastics is a competitive sport in which individuals or teams compete by performing routines—either prescribed, optional, or both—in the following eight events: floor exercise, side horse, rings, long horse, parallel bars, horizontal bar, trampoline, and tumbling. In recent years there has been a trend to eliminate events. In some parts of the country rope climb and flying rings might be added to the list of events given in the definition, but they are not generally included. The tumbling event has also been eliminated from some competitions, but it is still a part of most competitions in the United

States. A definition of gymnastics is included to emphasize that gymnastics is a *competitive sport with a definite list of events* and *specific rules* just as are basketball, swimming, tennis, baseball, etc. In the past the term gymnastics was used to refer to all the activities performed in a gymnasium. More recently it was used to refer to a group of activities such as formal calisthenics, Indian club swinging, and marching drills, as well as the heavy apparatus activities. These old definitions should give way to the modern one presented here.

Tumbling is one of the eight gymnastic events. The conduct of the event and the type of stunts used will be explained in Chapter 2 on tumbling. A partial definition is included at this time to clarify that "tumbling" and "gymnastics" are not synonymous terms and that gymnastics is a much broader term than tumbling. Many teachers name their unit "tumbling" when they actually are teaching much more than this. Others entitle their unit "tumbling and gymnastics." The use of tumbling in this way is not necessary because the sport of gymnastics includes tumbling. In some schools the tumbling event is the only event taught. In this case it is acceptable to call the unit "tumbling."

GYMNASTICS IN THE PHYSICAL EDUCATION CURRICULUM

There are so many sports and recreational activities available that it would be impossible to teach them all each year. Some activities should be taught only at the junior high school level, some only in senior high school. Because of limited time some sports can only be included in one grade and must then be replaced by another sport in the next grade. For example, soccer might be taught in the seventh grade, touch football in the eighth grade, and speedball in the tenth grade for the first six weeks of each year.

Many physical educators believe that track and field and gymnastics are basic activities that teach skills of running, jumping, throwing, and body control that are used in all other sports and in the activities of daily living and that, for this reason, it is advisable to include these two activities in every year.

In the more progressive schools the time allotment for gymnastics has been increased in recent years and is still being increased. Because of the great physical benefits to be derived from gymnastics it is believed that from one sixth to as much as one quarter of the school year should be devoted to this sport. As the normal school year is 36 weeks in length this means that the gymnastic unit should be from six to nine weeks in length.

At the junior high school level and above most students are physically able to participate in all events, but many teachers believe that only four events—tumbling, floor exercise, trampoline, and vaulting—should be taught to children below thirteen years of age. Certainly the other events should be used with caution. Stunts have to be selected carefully and rules have to be modified to make the activity suitable for youngsters who lack strength. Young children are better able to perform on the horizontal bar and rings, which use many hanging positions, than on the parallel bars and side horse, which use chiefly supporting positions. Even the parallel bars and side horse, however, can be adapted for use in primary grades by selecting stunts in which free support is not needed, or kept to a minimum. Stunts should be emphasized in which the performer sits on the equipment and bears part of the body weight on the legs. If this is done, children will become accustomed to the apparatus and gradually develop the strength that is necessary for regular gymnastic work that requires many free support positions.

CHAPTER ORGANIZATION AND CONTENT

Each of the eight gymnastic events used generally throughout the United States is dealt with in a separate chapter of this book. For each event, except vaulting, the stunts described are included as part of a routine or exercise (see definition). If the reader wishes to locate a specific stunt in a book such as this, he must refer to the index or to the abbreviated routine descriptions that appear in each chapter. There are five routines for each event. Number I is very simple. The skills included can be learned by students of just average ability in just a few class periods. Routine II in each chapter is composed of a combination of beginning and intermediate skills. Routine III includes quite a few intermediate skills that are considerably more difficult than those in the first two routines and might be too difficult to present to all students in a physical education class. This routine would be a presentable one for a boy to use in his first year of gymnastic competition. Routine IV in each chapter includes many advanced skills that would provide a real challenge for the better students in a physical education class. This routine is one that might be used by a competitive gymnast of average ability. Routine V is designed for the advanced performer competing on a high school or college team. It is not as difficult an exercise as would be used by a top college performer, but nevertheless a gymnast who can master the last exercise in any chapter can certainly be classed as an excellent performer in that event.

METHOD OF TEACHING ROUTINES

If students do not have text books themselves, copies of the routines should be made available to them. Routines should be posted in the locker room and in convenient places around the gym. A good idea is to have the routines printed on large cards or posters that can be tacked onto the gym wall. Making the information available will greatly increase interest and speed up learning. Students, of course, must be taught proper terminology so that they can read and understand the exercises. In most junior high schools only two routines in each event need to be posted; in senior high schools three are probably sufficient for physical education class purposes.

A suggested method of presenting these routines to a class is as follows:

1. Demonstrate the Entire Routine. If the teacher is unable to demonstrate himself, the routine should be taught to a skillful student ahead of time so that he can demonstrate it for the class. If this technique is used, class members can see how the stunts flow together and form a mental picture of the entire routine. This establishes a goal for which they can strive.

2. Present Each Stunt Separately. Each stunt should be demonstrated and explained separately even though several stunts may be taught on the same day. The stunts do not have to be taught in the order in which they appear in the routine. The easy ones should be presented first and the harder ones later. Considerable time should be devoted to the practice of individual stunts before they are combined.

3. Divide the Routine into Parts for Practice. These parts should be made up of three to five stunts. A routine of ten stunts might be divided into parts as follows: Part 1—Stunts 1, 2, 3, and 4; Part 2—Stunts 4, 5, 6, and 7; and Part 3—Stunts 7, 8, 9, and 10. The overlapping of the parts is important. If routines are divided in this way, each stunt can be practiced in the way it must be performed in the full-length routine, that is, immediately following the previous stunt.

4. Practice the Entire Routine. After each stunt has been learned and the parts of the routine have been practiced until they can be reasonably well performed, students should spend a good part of their time performing the routine as a whole. When this stage is reached, another demonstration of the entire routine by an expert performer is a good technique to use.

CLASS ORGANIZATION

ORDER OF EVENT PRESENTATION

The easiest type of class to teach is one in which the entire class performs the same activity. If the students have absolutely no background in gymnastics, it is very desirable to introduce one event at a time and have the entire class spend a day or two practicing the same event. This method can usually be used for tumbling, floor exercise, and sometimes for vaulting but can not be used in most schools for the other events because of equipment shortage.

Tumbling is the best event to present first because it provides a background for all other events. An entire class can be kept busy on just a few mats. Many stunts can be practiced across the mats. Other stunts can be executed easily on a single mat placed lengthways so that an entire squad can work successfully with each member taking his turn on one mat. Of course, for the practice of routines several mats will have to be placed together.

Floor exercise is another activity in which a very large group can participate at the same time. The event requires a reasonable amount of floor area but absolutely no equipment except a few mats on which some stunts can be learned before they are tried on the bare floor. This event utilizes many tumbling stunts and other movements and positions that can be performed crossways on a mat.

The long horse vaulting event can be presented to an entire class in many schools. Vaulting is usually taught to beginners on a cross horse or broad horse rather than a long horse. Because performance in this event moves rapidly and, because it involves considerable running, students get much activity in a short period of time. For these reasons squads can be larger for the practice of vaulting than for other events. Many schools have both a long horse (side horse with pommels removed) and a "box horse" or "Swedish box." Some schools also have a buck horse. With three vaulting horses a small-sized class can be kept busy practicing the one event. If the class is larger, other equipment can be modified to serve very successfully as vaulting horses. A tumbling mat can be placed across a set of parallel bars lowered and adjusted to a narrow width. This piece of equipment, often called an elephant, serves very well as a vaulting horse. A small sturdy table with a tumbling mat placed across it can also be used for vaulting practice. A girls' balance beam padded with a tumbling mat is long enough to serve as two or even three horses so that two or three squads can practice on the same piece of equipment. An ingenious instructor can improvise other equipment that can be used successfully as a vaulting horse. Take-off boards are not essential for the teaching of beginning vaulting.

The other gymnastic events are very difficult to teach individually to an entire class unless a great deal of equipment is available. The usual way of presenting the other events is to have them all a part of the same class. Tumbling, floor exercise, and vaulting, although they may be presented separately, can also be combined with the other events. If this is done, there would be eight different activities going on in the same class with a squad assigned to each event. This method of organizing a gymnastic class is certainly nothing new or different as many physical education activities are taught in this manner.

Teaching a unit in gymnastics to a beginning group might be approached in this way:

1. Teach tumbling to the entire class for one or more class periods.
2. Teach floor exercise to the entire class for one or more class periods.
3. Teach vaulting to the entire class for one or more class periods, utilizing improvised equipment as vaulting horses. This step can be omitted if equipment is not available.
4. Divide the class into the number of squads desired for the rest of the unit and establish the same number of squad stations. There may, of course, be two or three stations for the same activity. Locate squad stations so that each squad will get practice on all three events as it rotates from one to another.
5. Add the trampoline, horizontal bar, parallel bars, rings, and side horse one at a time for the next five class periods in place of some of the tumbling, floor exercise, and vaulting squad stations.

The method of presentation suggested above need only be used in teaching a group with little or no previous gymnastic experience. In schools that have a gymnastic unit each year this method might be used in the seventh grade in junior high school and the first year of senior high school. In the other years all events might be started on the first day of the gymnastic unit and the class divided immediately into the number of squads desired. The first few days can be devoted to a review of material learned the previous year.

SIZE OF SQUADS

When gymnastic classes are divided into squads, it is advisable to keep the squads as small as possible. Three to five in a squad is a good number for most events. In some events the best number to have in a squad is two—one performer and one spotter. For other events, for reasons that will be explained later, it is best to have more than two in a squad. Five, or at the most six, to a squad is a maximum for effective teaching. Rather than increase the number in a squad, if the class is large, the teacher should increase the number of groups. Remember students learn primarily by "doing," not by standing and waiting for a turn.

Let us assume that we have a class of twenty-four students, who have had a little previous gymnastic experience, in a school that is equipped with a box horse, horizontal bar, trampoline, parallel bars, and ample tumbling mats for floor exercise as well as tumbling. In this case the class could be divided into six squads of four students. If there are more than twenty-four in a class, in this particular school, four students could be assigned to another section of tumbling mats and four more to another floor exercise practice station. A class of 32 has now been assigned to eight squads at eight separate practice stations. To take care of a larger class a girls' balance beam (or two tables covered with a mat) could be utilized as a vaulting horse for two more squads. One more tumbling and one more floor exercise station could be established for two more squads. Forty-eight students have now been assigned to twelve squads. By increasing the squad size from 4 to 5 a class of sixty has been accommodated. One can see that a very large class can be taught without making the squads too large and without utilizing a great amount of equipment. Considerable improvisation should be done before squads are increased to over five members.

The example above is used to show what might be done in a particular situation. The ring event and the side horse event are not mentioned. These, of course, should be included if at all possible. As a school is able to purchase more equipment, all events should be provided for; in fact, two pieces of most equipment are needed for maximum teaching effectiveness. It is very desirable to have both a low and a high horizontal bar available at all times so that the one bar does not have to be adjusted during a class period. Time used to adjust equipment is time taken away from practice. The availability of high and low rings and high and low parallel bars also increases teaching effectiveness. Of course, if extra sets of equipment are available, double the number of squads can be accommodated or double the number of individuals can be assigned to the same squad that has both a high and a low piece of equipment for its use.

Many activities of a gymnastic nature, although not gymnastic events, may be used in a gymnastic unit and may serve as a squad station. Examples of these are: double tumbling and balancing, climbing ropes, horizontal ladders, springboards, trampolets, etc. In schools where there is a minimum of gymnastic equipment other activities may be conveniently combined with the sport of gymnastics. A set of barbells would serve well as an extra squad station. Punching bags, heavy or light, would accommodate another squad. Rope skipping also would fit well with a gymnastic unit.

SQUAD ORGANIZATION

The division of the class into squads is an important function in class organization. It is desirable to individualize instruction to let all students progress as much as possible. If this principle is followed, students must be grouped into squads by ability for gymnastics so that each group can proceed at its own pace. Because of the safety factor it is especially important to group by ability in gymnastics. If a single group varies greatly in ability, a poor student might be tempted to try a difficult stunt that is being learned by a more proficient student in his group.

If grouping is done only by ability, it creates certain problems. Often students in one group will vary greatly in size. It is less convenient for students of different heights to work on the rings, horizontal bar, parallel bars, and vaulting horse. It is time-consuming enough to adjust equipment for each squad let alone to adjust it for individual members of a squad. It is also difficult for students of greatly different shoulder widths to work at the same time on the parallel bars. It creates a serious problem if there is one individual considerably heavier than the other members of his squad as the light students might be physically incapable of spotting the heavy boy. For these reasons it is wise to group primarily by ability but also to consider body height, width, and weight. This can be accomplished by having two squads of superior ability, two of average ability, and two of low ability. One squad at each ability level should be composed of the larger students while the other squad at each level should be composed of the smaller students.

Each squad should have a squad leader who is responsible for the effective functioning of his squad. The partner method of organization can also be used within the squad structure. While one student performs a stunt or routine, his partner can spot and offer advice and criticism. *It is very essential in a gymnastic class that spotting techniques be taught to all students as each stunt is taught. Everyone in the class—not just the squad leaders—should be a spotter.*

LENGTH OF ASSIGNMENT TO EACH SQUAD STATION

During each class period squads should be moved or rotated from one event to another. The amount of time spent on each event will vary depending on the age, the physical condition, and the ability level of the group. Younger children because of their interest span should be moved more often than older students. Those in poor physical condition have to be rotated rather often. Beginners should be moved more often than advanced performers as they tend to lose interest quickly. For most classroom situations the time spent at one squad station should range from ten to twelve minutes for beginning or younger groups and from twelve to twenty minutes for older or more advanced groups. However, in schools where the physical education period is very short these suggested time limits should be reduced slightly. At a team practice session of one and one-half hours in length a group of advanced performers might spend as much as thirty to forty-five minutes on one event. It is not essential that each squad gets practice on each piece of equipment every class period. If a complete rotation can not be made in one class period, squads should be started from the point that they ended on the previous day.

PLACEMENT OF EQUIPMENT AND ORDER OF EVENTS

The placement of equipment on the gym floor should be planned carefully so that the class can function efficiently and so that one squad does not interfere with another. Some equipment can not be moved because it fastens into permanent floor plates on the floor or hangs from permanent brackets on the ceiling. Other squad stations should be planned around these permanent ones. Events that are hard on the hands should not be too close together in the order of rotation. Students should not be moved directly from one supporting event to another or from one hanging event to another. Events that use primarily the legs, such as trampoline and vaulting, should not follow each other. Because of the similarity of tumbling and floor exercise these events should be separated by another event. Events that are particularly demanding on upper body musculature such as rings and parallel bars should be separated by another event. It is very difficult to plan the order of rotation to satisfy all these requirements, but if equipment is located to give variety as a squad is moved from station to station most of the requirements will be automatically satisfied.

ECONOMY OF TIME

Although economy of time is important for all academic teachers and in teaching all activities in physical education, it is especially important in the gymnastic unit because of the amount of equipment involved and the number of skills to be taught. Most sports have a limited number of skills which are practiced over and over to gain the desired proficiency. Take volleyball, for example. Few teachers teach over ten separate volleyball skills and most limit their instruction to six, seven, or eight skills. In gymnastics probably ten skills are taught in each of the eight events in a single unit and many of these skills are more complicated than those required in other sports. Many beginning teachers of gymnastics have had the experience of moving the equipment into position, adjusting it, placing the mats in position, giving instruction in a number of events, and then looking at their watch to find that it is time to move the equipment off the floor and dismiss the class. Instructors must remember that students learn primarily by "doing" and that as much time as possible in every class period should be reserved for practice. This means that the class has to be well organized so that time for roll call, equipment-moving, equipment-adjusting, instruction, and squad rotation is kept to a minimum.

From experience it has been found that teachers should not attempt to give instruction in more than three events and probably only in two events on the same day. The normal procedure is to give all instruction immediately after roll call while the class is still together in an organized group. Following the instruction they are assigned to their first squad station and for the rest of the period are rotated from event to event. If equipment has to be moved on and off the floor, special assignments should be made. One method that works well is to have the same squad responsible for moving the same piece of equipment out each day but to have each squad responsible for moving the piece of equipment off the floor that they were working on at the end of the period. The established assignments at the beginning of the period contribute to economy of time in getting started, while the variety at the end of the period contributes to breadth of knowledge in handling equipment.

VARIETY IN LESSON PLANS

For effective teaching the normal pattern of instruction should be changed occasionally to give variety. Some form of competition should be a part of almost every class period. Various forms can be used to stimulate interest. Other techniques that can be used to give variety to the class are as follows:

1. Play follow the leader in each squad. In this game the leader performs a stunt and then everyone tries it. Those who miss a stunt are moved to the end of the line. When the squad is rotated to the next event, the individual immediately behind the leader becomes the leader for that event. Players should be of approximately equal ability or this could be a dangerous game. Even with equal ability groups, careful spotting is necessary.
2. Play "add-on" in each squad. In this game the first boy performs a single stunt. The next boy does that stunt and adds one more. The third player adds one more and so on. The game is a test of memory as well as physical ability. Those who miss are dropped from competition. Some provision, of course, should be made to keep those who have been eliminated active in some other way.
3. Hold tumbling relay races. Relays should be held only occasionally as sloppy execution often results from trying to hurry. They should be used with caution as certain stunts become very hazardous when done hurriedly. The type of relay usually used is to have the first boy in each line perform a certain stunt such as a cartwheel, a forward roll, or an animal walk down the row of mats and then run back and touch the next boy in line. A better type of relay is to have the first boy in each line run to a mat located at the other end of the gym, turn and face his squad, and then execute a single stunt, such as a headstand or a headspring, and then run back to touch the next boy. If the stunt is missed, penalties can be imposed such as crawling back or hopping back on one leg. By making players run beyond the mat and turn before executing the stunt they are slowed down so that the stunt can be executed with a minimum of danger. Imposing a penalty if the stunt is missed encourages proper execution.
4. Have a free choice day so that students can spend all their time on one or two events of special interest to them. A variation of this is to have free choice for the last ten or fifteen minutes of the class period. Some method of adjustment must be used if too many individuals select the same event.

5. Have a pyramid-building day. Two or more squads should be combined for this activity. Pyramids can be planned by the instructor or by a leader assigned for each group. After time for practice each group in turn can demonstrate their pyramids to the rest of the class.

6. Have a related activity day. Although most of the time devoted to gymnastics should be spent on the events included in the rules, there are other activities that are worthwhile and fun for students of all ages. There are dozens of two- and three-person tumbling and balancing stunts that can be taught. Springboard or mini-tramp tumbling is also a good activity.

7. Include gymnastic "circuit training" as a part of some class periods. Examples of items that might be incorporated in the circuit are: ten pull-ups on the horizontal bar, climb a rope, half-lever for ten seconds on the floor parallel bars, five skin-the-cats on the rings, hold a back bend (bridge) on the tumbling mats for ten seconds, hold a handstand against the wall for thirty seconds, ten dips on the parallel bars.

8. Have an "achievement board" with appropriate names given to the various levels of achievement. Those who accomplish the easiest list of stunts might be called the "shooting stars"; those who accomplish the next list the "junior varsity." The next level might be called the "varsity" and the top level the "professionals." There should be a bulletin board on which is displayed the names of the individuals who have reached the various levels of achievement.

9. Plan a demonstration. An excellent method to stimulate interest and to give variety to one or more class periods is to work toward a gymnastic exhibition or demonstration for a school assembly, basketball half-time, P.-T.A. program, or some other function. This might mean the introduction of clowning, synchronized performance, pyramid building, or specialty stunts using tables, chairs, or other novelty equipment. It might also give some students an opportunity to get experience with musical background, specialized lighting, or preparing costumes. Students can be involved in a number of ways other than as performers.

COMPETITION IN PHYSICAL EDUCATION CLASSES

This section could very well be included as a section under the previous heading "Class Organization," but because of its importance it is being presented separately.

There are many forms of competition that can be used in physical education gymnastic classes to stimulate interest in the activity. Most of these suggestions can be used in beginning classes as well as in advanced classes. Some can be used throughout the class period as a part of the daily activity. Some are best when used at the end of the period during the last five or ten minutes. Some are appropriate for the whole class; some are best used within a single squad.

1. Put the best performer at the front of the line after the performance of each stunt. If a record is kept of the number of times a player has been at the head of the line, this form of competition becomes more interesting as a squad champion can be decided at the end of the class period. Good squad leaders are needed to make this technique work well.

2. Select the best performer in each squad to compete against the best performer in other squads. This competition could be in the performance of a single stunt rather than a routine. The technique does not have to be restricted to the best in the squad. The second best performer could be chosen from each squad to represent their squad in competition in another stunt, and still another person chosen to compete in a third stunt. If the best in each squad is chosen, however, a class champion can then be selected for each stunt. This adds interest to the competition.

3. Use checklists of stunts. Students compete to see who can accomplish the greatest number of stunts. Checklists can be of a permanent type that are posted on the wall throughout the entire gymnastic unit or one that is used for a single day, with a new list being introduced another day.

4. Have a "record board" for such things as:

a. Number of pull-ups
b. Handwalking for distance (or handstand for time)
c. Number of consecutive swivel hips on the trampoline
d. Greatest distance from take-off to landing on the straddle vault over the horse
e. Number of muscle-ups on the rings
f. Number of handstand dips on the low parallel bars
g. Rope climb for time with or without the use of legs

5. Have a ladder tournament board for each event. Permit challenges at any time or designate certain days as challenge days. The teacher or a group of student judges can determine the winner and whether there should be a change in order on the ladder.

6. Hold intersquad competition. One of the best forms of competition to use in a gymnastic class is team competition between

two or more squads. The whole class does not have to be involved every day, but probably the most effective way to use this form of competition is to have the whole class compete during the last ten or fifteen minutes of each class period. This is much the same technique that is used in teaching other physical education activities—the first part of the period being devoted to practice of skills and lead-up drills and the last part of the period being devoted to "playing the game."

If classes are divided into squads of equal ability, the squads can be assigned in any way for competition. If squad assignments are made according to ability, the best two squads should be assigned to compete against each other, the third and fourth squads should compete, and so forth. It is not advisable to use too much of any class period in this way. Competition in one or two events is sufficient to introduce the competitive element and to get the desired effect.

It is not necessary to have four judges, a score keeper, or other officials for this intraclass competition. One student official can serve as announcer, scorekeeper, and judge for each contest. In a class of eight squads, as four contests are going on at the same time, four officials are needed. These officials might be squad leaders, the better performers in the class, or class members who are injured and not able to take part in the activity on that particular day. All class members should have an opportunity to act as an official sometime during the unit.

Full length routines do not have to be used for this type of competition. Competition can be held using single stunts, abbreviated routines, or full length optional or prescribed routines.

The best way to determine the winner in intraclass competition is to match each boy against a boy in the other squad. The competitors do not compete for a score out of ten, as in normal gymnastic competition, but try to beat their opponent. Teams should alternate performers. After the first boy in each squad has performed, the student judge awards a point to the boy who did the best. The next two boys then compete and a point is awarded to the best performer. After all squad members have competed in this way, a team score can be determined for that event.

If the official is efficient and competitors are ready when it is their turn, two squads of four or five members each can complete competition in one event in just a few minutes.

7. Hold an official gymnastic meet. A good culminating activity for a gymnastic unit is to hold an official gymnastic meet during the last class period. Students should be assigned as competitors,

officials, and coaches. If the class is large, it might be best to divide it into two separate groups and conduct two meets simultaneously. The organization of this type of meet is explained in Chapter 10.

GRADING IN PHYSICAL EDUCATION CLASSES

The biggest part of the grade for a gymnastic unit, if this book is used as the guide for instruction, should be awarded for the performance of the routines taught. Certainly the major part of any grade in physical education should be awarded for the ability to play the game. Learning skills is of little value unless they can be used successfully in a game situation. Similarly, being able to perform difficult stunts does not mean very much in gymnastics unless they can be performed in a complete exercise. Performing an exercise is "playing the game of gymnastics." This does not mean that a checklist of stunts can not also be used for grading purposes. Everyone in the class might be tested on Routine I in each chapter and then extra credit given for students who have learned stunts from Routine II or who can perform the routine in its entirety. It is a good practice, in order to encourage initiative and creativeness, to also give extra credit for an optional routine composed by the student. The grading system should be planned to encourage students to progress and learn the next routine, or stunts from it, or to prepare one of their own. If everyone is graded only on a simple required routine, the difficulty element, which is an important factor in scoring gymnastics, has been omitted.

A knowledge test should be given for the gymnastic unit if it is a practice to do this in other physical education activities. This test should include items on: how stunts are performed, spotting techniques, safety precautions, rules, and care of equipment.

Any other factors that are considered in awarding a grade should be minor in comparison with those mentioned. The effect of absenteeism, tardiness, cleanliness, and so forth on the grade should be determined by general philosophy and policy of the school. Improvement is another factor that might be given minor consideration, but the author is opposed to this practice of awarding physical education grades. If the school has not determined a policy in this respect, the individual teacher must decide his own philosophy.

It is reasonable to expect that junior high school students can accomplish the first routine in each chapter and that high school students can accomplish the second one if they have had experience in junior high school. This depends, of course, on the length of class periods, the length of the units, and whether gymnastics is offered each year. Until it is analyzed, it might seem that one routine is very little to accomplish in three years of junior high school. When you consider, however, that one routine in seven events plus several vaults over the horse totals approximately sixty different stunts, it sounds like a great deal to achieve. If you consider that, in order to learn some of these stunts, it is necessary to go through several lead-up drills, it takes on still greater proportions. If the second routine is required in senior high school, almost two hundred different stunts will have been learned if the lead-up stunts are also included. The accomplishment of routines I and II might be minimum requirements established by junior and senior high school teachers, respectively. The better students should be able to accomplish much more, however; thus provision must be made in the grading system that encourages more advanced routines to be learned. College teachers will have to set their goals depending on the gymnastic background of the students that enroll. If the secondary schools do a good job, the third routine is probably within the reach of most college students.

SAFETY

1. Inspect equipment regularly. Check floor plates, and the overhead fittings of all suspension equipment. Check all bolts for tightness and ropes for dangerous wear (especially ropes on spotting belts). Check parallel bars for cracks.

2. Have enough mats to provide adequate padding. This means double thickness for many stunts. Arrange the mats around the equipment to assure maximum safety. Do not allow mats to overlap so that there is a ridge or uneven surfaces on which to land. Place mats over the equipment while certain stunts are being learned.

3. Use gymnastic chalk (magnesium carbonate) to keep hands dry and thus minimize slipping for events that require a hand hold or grasp. Chalk or resin might also be used for the feet in events like tumbling, floor exercises, and vaulting.

4. Provide the best possible situation for the activity. Remove hazardous objects. Avoid distractions such as loud yelling at the time difficult stunts are being performed. Keep bouncing balls out of the area. Do not permit horseplay.

5. Lower equipment whenever possible for teaching new stunts

in order to minimize the danger from falls, to enable the spotter to work more effectively, and to give the performer confidence.

6. Emphasize spotting. Teach every student how to spot. Spotters must learn and practice spotting of easy stunts in order to become effective spotters for more difficult stunts.

7. Determine the condition of the students at the start of the activity. Gradually increase the amount of work and the ruggedness of the activity. The instructor or coach should watch for signs of fatigue and stop practice on dangerous stunts when fatigue begins to set in.

8. Make sure that students warm up before trying difficult stunts or those that require considerable stretching.

9. Follow an intelligent progression in teaching. Make sure students have skill equal to the task assigned. Overlearning fundamentals is extra insurance. Only present the more difficult routines to the better students. This means that students probably should be grouped into squads by ability rather than by age, size, year in school, or by some other method of classification.

10. Develop a confident but not cocky attitude in students. Encourage courage but discourage foolish displays of daring. Students should be taught to use discretion and intelligence and not to try stunts beyond their ability.

11. Organize and supervise classes carefully. The problem of whether to permit unsupervised extracurricular use of gymnastic equipment must be solved within each school. In schools where safety rules are emphasized in physical education classes unsupervised extracurricular use is often permitted.

CARE OF HANDS

The hands, for many individuals, determine the length of the practice session. Because many hours must be devoted to gymnastics, if an individual expects to become a top performer, the care of the hands also determines whether a boy will become an expert gymnast. Even students in a gymnastic class, although it is of short duration, can develop very sore hands unless they take care of them. Some general hints can be given for hand care.

1. Use hand protectors or guards for practice on the horizontal bar, rings, and parallel bars.

2. Keep the horizontal bar, rings, parallel bars, and side horse pommels sanded free of caked chalk during workout sessions.

3. Stop practice when the hands have taken all they can stand. Stopping before a blister is formed or before the skin tears will permit more work the next day. Some gymnasts work on the pieces of equipment that are hard on the hands only every other day, but some prefer to distribute the wear on the hands evenly.

4 a. A beginning gymnast whose hands are soft should keep them out of water as much as possible and use one of the commercial products that toughen skin. He should avoid any oily hand creams that will soften the skin.

4 b. Most advanced gymnasts who spend many hours on the equipment develop hands that are too hard. Because of the friction to which the hand is exposed the skin builds up on the palm and becomes very thick. Soaking the hands in hot water after a workout and using a lubricant that will soften the skin and make it more pliable are solutions in this case. Most gymnasts have to shave the callouses with a razor blade or sand them with a file, sharpening stone, or piece of sand paper. A thick ridge of skin will catch on the bar and tear off.

5. If a tear does occur, care should be taken to prevent infection and then before the hand is used again the thick ridges of skin around the tear should be trimmed off so they do not catch on the bars. The raw patch should be kept lubricated with skin cream to prevent cracking.

6. If the hand blisters but does not tear, drain the blister. The loose skin will protect the flesh underneath and permit more use. Eventually the loose skin will have to be removed. The raw patch is then treated as a tear.

EXHIBITIONS

A whole text could be devoted to this subject. Although this book stresses competitive gymnastics, the author also believes in other related activities and in "show gymnastics." Exhibitions help sell the program and raise the status of the teacher in the school and community. Gymnastics is one of the best activities in our program to use in exhibitions for assemblies, P.-T.A. meetings, and other school and community functions. Exhibitions have much the same value as competitions. They help motivate the students participating and also increase interest in the activity among other students in the school. An excellent exhibition can be put on with students of just average ability from a physical education class if the demonstration is planned carefully. If the school administration will not include interschool competition, the next best thing to stimulate the better performers is an exhibition team or club. Boys with special ability and interest should be given an opportunity to participate in gymnastics as an extracurricular activity and have the thrill of performing for an audience if they are deprived of the opportunity of team competition. With our present emphasis on physical fitness it seems especially appropriate to offer considerable extracurricular, as well as curricular, gymnastic activity. Exhibitions are a vital part of the overall gymnastic program.

Some suggestions that will improve the quality of exhibitions are as follows:

1. Plan the show for the audience.
2. Select stunts and routines that can be performed smoothly and gracefully and not ones that are too difficult for the participants.
3. Use uniforms and special costumes.
4. Have musical accompaniment if possible.
5. Use special lighting if possible.
6. Impress upon the participants to smile and appear as if they are enjoying the presentation.
7. Practice the entrances and exits as much, or more than, the show itself.
8. Plan the sequence of acts carefully to give variety. Start with something fast-moving. Save the best until toward the end. Include many people in the last act. Try to incorporate novel ideas to add interest throughout the program.

SELECTION OF EQUIPMENT

Until recently, our American gymnastic equipment companies did not produce satisfactory equipment. Competition with excellent European equipment has resulted in United States producers coming out with new designs and producing modern, serviceable apparatus of excellent quality. In spite of this some schools are still purchasing outdated equipment because of lack of knowledge on the part of administrators and even physical education personnel.

Many school districts insist on purchasing from the lowest bidder. Sometimes a physical education teacher is prevented from getting the equipment he desires because of this rule even though he knows the differences that exist in equipment. This practice is especially unfortunate in the purchase of gymnastic equipment because much of it does not wear out and therefore will have to be used much longer than most other sports equipment.

This does not mean that the most expensive equipment should always be purchased. Some inexpensive equipment is very usable, although the lasting quality might not be as great as higher priced equipment. Even homemade equipment can be very satisfactory. For example, a vaulting box is a very satisfactory substitute for a long horse until funds are available for the purchase of the official horse. Suggestions for the construction of homemade equipment are included in each chapter.

Good equipment is available. Physical education personnel should be sure that they get it. Some of the things that have to be considered are as follows:

1. In most cases equipment should be purchased that meets official specifications. Some exceptions are given below.

2. Rings, horizontal bar, side horse, and parallel bars should be adjustable to low heights for teaching purposes. Parallel bars should also be adjustable to narrower widths for smaller students than the minimum width specified by the rules. These suggestions probably will mean the modification of official specifications. If possible it is advantageous to have a regulation set of equipment and a second set that will adjust to lower heights or narrower widths.

3. Equipment should be easy to adjust so that it can be done quickly. This item is not quite the same as item two. The point that is being stressed above is that "equipment should be adjustable" while the point that is being made now is that "it must be able to be adjusted quickly and easily." No matter how carefully a teacher plans and even though equipment of two different heights is available, there always seems to be some adjustment of equipment necessary during a class period. For economy of time the adjustment should be a simple procedure.

4. Equipment should be easy to move, especially in schools where there is no gymnastic area and equipment has to be moved on and off a multipurpose area. Normally light-weight equipment is easier to move than heavy equipment, but even heavy equipment can be moved easily. Roller carts with large wheels are usually better than ones with small wheels. Rubber-covered wheels that do not mark the floor are better than metal wheels.

5. Equipment should be stable. The only two pieces that usually give difficulty in this respect are the side horse and long horse. Occasionally trouble is experienced with parallel bars. (Uneven parallel bars that the girls use cause great stability problems.) If equipment is heavy in weight, little movement occurs during use, but, of course, then there is more difficulty in moving it from place to place. Equipment with a wide base is more stable than equipment with a narrow base. The American-style horse with two vertical uprights from the base to the top section is more stable than

the European style with four legs. For stability the European style must be fastened to a floor plate by a chain and turn-buckle that is attached to the undercenter section of the horse.

6. It is difficult to recommend what type of mats to buy. From the statements made below the individual purchaser will have to determine what type of mat to purchase for his school.

a. Large mats are more stable (do not slip on the floor during use) but are harder to move and harder to store.
b. Thick mats provide more protection but are more expensive, heavier, and harder to move. If thin mats are purchased, a double thickness will have to be used for many activities.
c. Most tumblers prefer hair-filled mats for tumbling, but the rubber or ensolite mats provide better protection around the apparatus.
d. Most tumblers prefer canvas-surfaced mats because of the nonskid surface, but canvas is difficult to keep clean. Plastic-covered mats or rubber mats can be easily cleaned.
e. Rubber mats are lighter and easier to move than hair-filled mats with canvas or plastic covers but do not last as long.

CARE OF EQUIPMENT

This is not meant to be a complete list but rather a few important suggestions. Other suggestions about equipment for each event are given in the individual chapters. Gymnastic equipment is expensive and thus should be treated properly. Most equipment, even with very little care, will last almost indefinitely, especially if it does not have to be moved around too much. Some equipment, or parts of equipment, need special care to prolong its life.

1. The most important factor in care of equipment is to move it as little as possible or, if it has to be moved, to move it carefully. Moving equipment on and off the floor wears it out far faster than the actual use of the equipment for gymnastics. Students should be taught how to move and adjust equipment properly.

2. Mats need more care than the other equipment. They should be cleaned several times a year or every few weeks if they are used extensively. Rubber mats or plastic-covered mats may be scrubbed with soap and water. Canvas-covered mats should be vacuumed and cleaned with rug or carpet cleaner so that they do not get too wet. When being moved, light mats should be carried. Carrying heavy mats usually does more damage than dragging them, as the handles are not strong enough to stand the weight of the mat and often tear off. Care should be taken not to drag mats over sharp

objects, such as bolts on the base of equipment, or to scrape them against horizontal bar cables, or against the edges of doors if they have to be moved in and out of a storeroom. If canvas- or plastic-covered mats are torn, they should be mended immediately before the damage increases. Mats often have to be retufted as the tufts pull loose. Rubber mats can be repaired by filling small holes and tears with a special material provided by the company. The whole mat can also be repainted with special paint to renew the surface. When rubber mats get in really bad condition, a plastic envelope can be purchased for them. Several years' more use can be obtained when they are covered in this way.

3. The trampoline bed should be cleaned once or more a year. It can be scrubbed with soap and water while it is in place (care should be taken not to get rubber springs wet) or it can be removed and washed in a washing machine. Occasionally beds need to be returned to the factory for resewing. The wear on rubber springs should be distributed equally to prolong their life. The point of greatest wear is where the rubber cable goes through the eyelet that attaches the spring to the frame and bed. This point of wear can be shifted every month or so without removing the spring by merely rotating the rubber cable slightly. The trampoline should be folded and unfolded carefully so as not to damage the frame.

4. The leather on the side horse and long horse should be cleaned and lubricated several times a year. It can be cleaned with ordinary saddle soap or, better yet, with a solution of two tablespoons of oxalic acid in a gallon of water. When the leather dries, neat's-foot oil is used to lubricate it and keep it pliable.

5. Rings, pommels, parallel bars, reuther boards, or any other equipment that is made from laminated wood should be kept dry and away from any dampness. These items are expensive and can be ruined if they get wet.

6. All movable parts on the parallel bars, horses, horizontal bar, and ring attachments should be lightly oiled every few months.

7. Heavy shoes should not be permitted on any of the equipment or mats. This applies to rubber-soled basketball and tennis shoes as well as street shoes.

START YOUR PROGRAM NOW

If the physical education teacher waits until he feels fully prepared and qualified to teach gymnastics before introducing it into the program, he will never start the activity. None of us feels completely qualified in this sport. There is so much to learn and such a variety of skills involved that only a few teachers will ever become experts in all phases of the activity. That is what makes it so interesting. There is a challenge for all. Teachers are always learners in this sport, more so than in other activities. They should read as much as possible, attend clinics and workshops, enroll in university summer school courses, order films occasionally, and attend gymnastic competitions to increase their knowledge of the activity.

Teachers do not have to wait until they have equipment to start gymnastics. Everyone would like to have all regulation equipment, but remember—tumbling mats are all that is necessary for a satisfactory program. A little improvisation or construction of equipment will enable those with initiative to get a program into low gear. A reasonably good unit can be taught including only tumbling, floor exercise, and vaulting over a table over which a mat has been draped. Do not be content for long with this minimum program but get out of low gear and into second gear by constructing several pieces of equipment as suggested in chapters that follow. The final step is regulation equipment for a highly geared program.

Teaching gymnastics is a real challenge and very interesting. It is a rugged, demanding, and exciting sport that develops the physical and mental qualities that we admire in our youth. Gymnastics is a popular activity in many countries in the world. It can become popular in this country, too, if it is presented in the right way. Our young people need this type of activity; a physical education program is not complete without it.

2

Tumbling

Tumbling is taught as a physical education activity in almost every civilized country in the world. It is undoubtedly the most important of all our gymnastic activities. It can be performed indoors on mats or out-of-doors on the lawn, in the park, or on the beach. It is a natural activity for children. Children make up stunts and try to tumble even though they have never been exposed to the activity. It is an excellent background activity for the other gymnastic events and for other sports. Although tumbling takes more strength than many of our popular sports, it does not take a great amount of strength and so is suitable for almost every boy from kindergarten through college.

Tumbling has many values. It develops the basic physical qualities of agility, flexibility, balance, power, strength, and endurance. Timing and coordination are also developed. A tumbler learns to fall properly and how to control his body. One of the greatest values of this activity is the development of courage and self-confidence in activities where falls, body contact, or any type of unusual movement is involved.

A large class can be taught by one teacher in a relatively small area. As tumblers become more advanced, however, they need a longer row of mats and more running space. Series in Routines I require a row of mats 30 feet long. Forty feet of mat is needed for Routines II and III. Routines IV and V require 40 to 50 feet of mats. This does not mean that mats need to be placed in 30- to 50-foot sections for every class period. Most of the stunts can be taught on a single 5′ x 10′ mat. Many stunts can be taught with students working across a 5′ x 10′ mat. If this is done, three or four students can work on a single mat.

It is much better to keep the students active on a small mat area than to have them standing in a line waiting for their turn on a long row of mats. Several times during a tumbling unit, or possibly for a short time during every class period, the mats should be placed in 30- or 40-foot sections so that students may perform their entire routines after they have learned the individual stunts in the routines.

Tumbling is a common and popular competitive gymnastic event. This is true throughout the world, even though it is not a competitive event in the Olympics or in other international competition. It is a competitive event for both boys and girls in the United States and Canada. In Sweden and in many other foreign countries, it is a competitive event for children and young men and women in junior competitions. In Germany double-tumbling (two-people) competition is sometimes held.

In 1964 the N.C.A.A. rules committee dropped tumbling from college competition. This step was criticized by a great majority of the college coaches themselves. Many thought eliminating the event might have an influence on high school rules. Fortunately, this has not happened as yet. Tumbling should continue to be included in all high school and younger competition. It is an especially important event for developing gymnasts.

RULES

Tumbling rules for competition are brief and uncomplicated. Rules call for a minimum mat length of 60 feet, a width of 5 feet, and a thickness of 2 to 4 inches. The mats should be tied together and have a firm and nonslippery surface. When space permits, more than 60 feet of mats is suggested. A performer may utilize more area than is covered by mats by going off the end of the mats to obtain a running start or by tumbling off the end of the mats during one of his series. It is considered poor form, however, and points are deducted by the judges, if he touches the floor on either side of the mat. A competitor may leave the mats to perform certain stunts or routines on the floor if he prefers.

The tumbling event is limited to a maximum of four "trips down the mat" or series of not more than one and one-half minutes' total duration. (In some competition the maximum duration of the tumbling event is two minutes.) The one and one-half minute time limit includes the rest periods between the trips. Overly long rests, not commensurate with the difficulty of the contestants' routines, are penalized by the judges. As long as the performer begins his run for his last trip before the one and one-half minutes are up, he is given credit for the whole trip. Warning times are usually given the competitor during his resting periods at the end of the mat.

There is little information in the rules about what stunts should be included or about how the four trips should be composed. This means that a competitor has free rein in selection and composition of his particular routine or exercise. Over a period of years several practices have become generally accepted, however, and should probably be considered by the competitor and coach. Only fast-moving stunts are considered as tumbling stunts. Front or back walk-overs, for example, are not considered tumbling stunts. (These stunts can be used in the floor exercise event.) Routines should be continuous without stops or pauses. Both front (forward roll, front handspring, front somersault) and back (back roll, back somersault, back handspring) tumbling should be included in the complete competitive exercise. Some teachers say side tumbling (cartwheels and side somersaults) should also be included, but this is not a generally accepted belief. It is general practice to have one or more trips combining forward, backward, or sideward moving stunts. Examples of these are included in all routines in this chapter. Another unwritten rule accepted in most competition, and which the author believes should be adopted officially in the rules , is the elimination of the "interrupted" or "double-barreled" trip down the mat. Some competitors perform a short trip and then, finding considerable mat left, take another run and perform another short routine or single stunt as they leave the mat. This should be counted as two trips or penalized as a major break as in other gymnastic events. A trip once started should be continuous. Extra steps in the middle of a routine should always be considered as a break and penalized by the judges.

ABBREVIATED ROUTINE DESCRIPTIONS

I. A. Forward roll, forward roll, jump half-pirouette, backward roll, backward roll.
   B. Forward roll with a walkout, cartwheel, cartwheel, forward roll.

II. A. Roundoff, backward roll, backward extension roll, backward roll, backward extension roll.
   B. Cartwheel, cartwheel, forward roll walkout, roundoff, backward extension roll.

III. A. Headspring, forward roll, headspring, forward roll, headspring.
   B. Roundoff, backward roll, backward extension roll, fish flop, squat-through, snap-up.

C. Front handspring, forward roll, headspring, forward roll walkout, cartwheel.

IV. A. Front somersault, headsprings in series.

B. Roundoff, back handspring, backward extension roll, fish flop, squat-through, snap-up.

C. Front handspring walkout, cartwheel, roundoff, back handspring walkout with half turn, handspring, headspring.

V. A. Roundoff, series of back handspring, tuck-back somersault.

B. Front handspring, front somersault walkout, roundoff, back handspring walkout with half-turn, front handspring.

C. Roundoff, back handspring, whip-back somersault, back handspring, back somersault.

D. Roundoff, back handspring, back somersault with a full-twist.

I. BEGINNING ROUTINE

SERIES A

1. Forward Roll (Fig. 2–1). From the standing position the performer bends forward at the waist and reaches for the mat with hands shoulder width apart (1). The arms actually lower the body to the mat. The chin is placed on the chest and the legs give a little

Fig. 2–1. Forward Roll.

push (2). The back of the head contacts the mat, then the back of the shoulders. As the shoulders make contact with the mat, the hands are taken off the mat and grasp the shins to pull the body and legs into a tight tuck position (3). An alternate method is to reach forward as far as possible on each side of the legs as the hands are taken off the mat. The head and shoulders should be kept forward at this point to aid in rolling to the feet (4).

Teaching Techniques. This stunt should be taught from a squat position before being taught from a stand. If a boy has difficulty rolling in a straight line or in getting his head tucked under so he can start to roll, have him straighten his legs somewhat in the squat position, thus raising his hips higher. If he has trouble rolling all the way up to the feet, have him get down on his back on the mat and practice rocking back and forth in the tuck position grasping the shins. Emphasize a tight tuck and a forward lean of the head and shoulders. It is easier to roll to the feet if the knees are together and the feet wide apart with the toes turned out. This is considered poor form but might be suggested to boys who are having considerable trouble.

SPOTTING. Most students will not need to be spotted for the forward roll but it is wise to be cautious. One hand can be used behind the head to aid in tucking the chin on the chest. The other hand can be placed under the abdomen or in front of the hips to help start the forward motion and to bear some of the tumbler's body weight. The spotter should be down on his knees on the mat close to the performer. Make sure that all boys learn how to spot and get practice in spotting. If they learn how to spot the simple stunts, they will then be better able to spot the difficult ones.

2. Forward Roll. The second forward roll in this routine is exactly like the first except that it starts from a squat position instead of from a stand and therefore is easier.

3. Jump Half-Pirouette (Fig. 2–2). This is nothing more than a jump in the air with a 180 degree turn so that the tumbler lands facing the opposite direction. As the second forward roll is completed, the legs should be straightened rapidly. A high jump should be encouraged to give "life" to the routine. Reaching with the arms straight above the head will give extra height and probably result in a better half-pirouette. The head should look in the direction of the turn but should be kept in an erect position. Looking down at the mat usually results in landing off-balance.

Fig. 2–2. Jump Half-Pirouette.

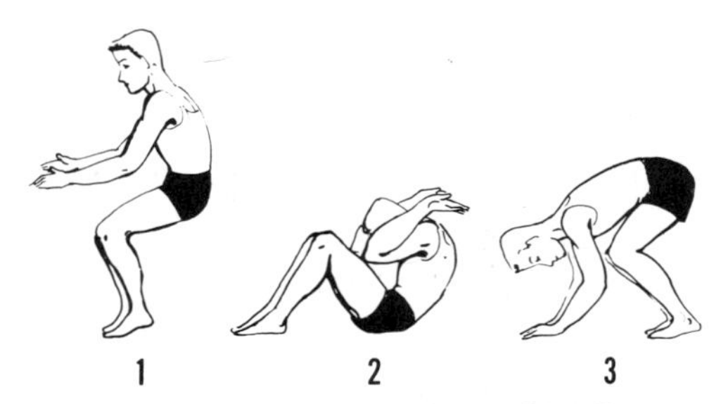

Fig. 2–3. Backward Roll.

4. Backward Roll (Fig. 2–3). Upon landing from the half pirouette, the performer leans backward and bends the knees rapidly (1). As the point of the buttocks makes contact with the ground, the chin should be forward on the chest and the hands should reach over the shoulders with palms up and thumbs toward the ears (2). The hands will make quicker and better contact with the mat if the elbows are kept well forward in front of the body. The chin should be kept on the chest and the knees close to the chest throughout the roll. As the hands make contact with the mat, the arms push to help lift the head off the mat. The roll is completed by straightening the knees slightly and reaching for the mat with the feet (3). A common mistake is to land on the knees or on the entire lower leg. This is caused by straightening at the hips rather than at the knees in completing the roll.

Teaching Techniques. This stunt should be taught first from a squat position with the hands on the mat well in front of the body. A good technique is to practice reaching over the shoulders while in a stationary squat stand to make sure that the hands are in the right position before attempting the roll. The first movement should be to rock forward onto the hands before pushing backward onto the buttocks. Another technique is to lie on the back and rock back and forth in a tuck position with the knees close to the chest. The hands should make contact with the mat over the shoulders each time that the performer rolls back onto the upper back. This drill is completed by rolling all the way over to the feet as in the regular backward roll.

Spotting. Spot every student at first. For heavy boys place a spotter on each side. Make sure everyone learns the spotting technique and gets practice in spotting. The spotter should lift some of the performer's weight as the stunt is being learned. This can be done by standing and reaching over the buttocks of the tumbler with one hand on each hip or by kneeling beside him and lifting with one hand under the hip or front of the thigh. The spotter should not push on the lower back of the tumbler to help him over as this often results in injury to the neck.

5. Backward Roll. The second backward roll is the same as the first except that it starts in the squat position and therefore is easier.

SERIES B

1. Forward Roll Walkout (Fig. 2–4). A forward roll with a walkout is started exactly the same as a regular forward roll. The only difference is that at the completion of the roll only one leg is kept tucked while the other is extended forward (1). The weight of

Fig. 2–4. Forward Roll Walkout.

the body, therefore, is first placed on the bent leg, and then as this leg is straightened it shifts forward to the other leg (2). The purpose of a walkout forward roll is to permit a more fluid movement into the next stunt of the series when the next stunt is one that is executed with a one-foot take-off.

2. Cartwheel (Fig. 2–5). As the walkout forward roll is completed, the tumbler will be in a semistanding position with the feet quite wide apart (1). Either foot can be forward, but the description here will be given with the left foot forward. The left hand is placed in the center of the mat about a foot or two in front of the left foot. The head should be kept up (chin off the chest). There should be a push first off the right foot and then off the left foot (2). As the left foot pushes, the right hand reaches for the center of the mat slightly more than shoulder width from the left hand. This first part of the cartwheel actually is a sideward kick into a handstand (3). As the motion continues, the right foot reaches for the center of the mat. This is accomplished by bending at the waist (4). If enough momentum is started on the take-off, the left

Fig. 2–5. Cartwheel.

foot will follow and can also be placed in the center of the mat a few feet from the right foot so that the performer ends in a standing position facing the side of the mat.

TEACHING TECHNIQUES. Start teaching the cartwheel facing the side of the mat with the feet quite wide apart and the arms stretched to the side. A rock to the right precedes a cartwheel done to the left. It helps many students to place a tumbling slipper or some other small object on the left side of the mat in a position that will be about equal distance between the hands as the cartwheel is executed. The eyes should be kept on this object throughout the stunt. If a student has considerable trouble with the cartwheel, have him try it to the other side. This might solve the problem. Draw a chalk line down the center of the mat so that hands and feet can be aimed for this line. Suggest to those who have trouble that the cartwheel be started from a partial squat position and finish in a partial squat position. The legs can gradually be straightened as the performer "gets the feel" of the stunt. A student who has trouble with the finish of the cartwheel should be supported in a handstand. He can drop the right foot from this position close to the right hand and then take a quarter turn to the left and thus "get the feel" of the finish of the stunt.

SPOTTING. The spotter stands behind the performer and reaches for the performer's right hip with his left hand and the left hip with his right hand. The performer can be guided through the cartwheel in this way. At the start of this spotting technique the spotter's arms will be crossed with the left over the right. When the performer is in the handstand position, the arms will be in a normal position. As the cartwheel is completed, the arms will again be crossed with the right over the left.

3. Cartwheel. The second cartwheel is the same as the first except that it starts from a standing position facing the side of the mat.

4. Forward Roll. Following the second cartwheel in this series there is a quarter twist on the right foot as it touches the mat. The movement continues forward on the left foot and the roll is done in the same direction as the rest of the stunts in the series.

II. LOW INTERMEDIATE ROUTINE

SERIES A

1. Roundoff (Fig. 2–6). The roundoff is one of our most important tumbling stunts as it is used to start most backward moving routines, even at the advanced level. The purpose of the stunt is to change forward run to backward movement. It is very similar to the cartwheel and yet quite different. The roundoff may be done to either side but is described only to the right in this series.

The stunt starts with a run and a hop on the right foot with the left foot raised very slightly forward. The arms should also be raised to about face height. It is important to maintain a forward lean of the body at this time (1). If the arms are raised higher than the face or if the forward leg is raised too high, there is a tendency for a beginner to lean backward. The left foot, or forward foot, is placed on the mat as the body bends forward at the waist and the hands reach for the center of the mat (2). Both

Fig. 2–6. Roundoff.

hands reach for the mat at the same time; however, the left hand will make contact first. The fingers of the left hand point toward the left side of the mat while the fingers of the right hand point slightly backward in the direction of the run. The right hand is placed about a foot from the left hand and either straight ahead or slightly to the left of the left hand. It is very important that the entire body be facing in the direction of the movement until the actual reach for the mat. At this time the upper body will start to twist. It is also important that both hands reach for the center of the mat and not be placed out to the left side of the mat. The right foot is thrown overhead followed by the left foot, which pushes vigorously off the mat. The head should remain up—that is, chin off the chest. As the feet pass vertically over the hands and head, the feet come together (3). The body executes a quarter turn during the first part of the roundoff and then another quarter turn as the body is rapidly flexed to snap the feet to the mat (4). At the time the feet are snapped down, there is a vigorous push from the fingers and shoulders. The feet usually make contact with the mat so that they are in front of the center of gravity. The body is, therefore, off-balance backward (5). This is true when a roll or a back handspring follows the roundoff but not when a back somersault is the next stunt.

2. Backward Roll. The backward roll has already been described in Routine I–A.

3. Backward Extension Roll (Fig. 2–7). This stunt is a backward roll to a momentary handstand followed by a rapid snap-down to the feet. It should be taught to beginners using the same start as a regular backward roll; however, when it has been learned, it is usually started from a stand with a straight leg sit-down. To fall

Fig. 2–7. Backward Extension Roll.

backward from a stand with a straight leg the body should lean sharply forward from the waist. The hands may be placed beside the hips with the fingers pointing toward the toes to catch part of the weight, but this is not necessary if the body is leaning well forward (1). As the weight rolls backward and the back of the head contacts the mat, the performer is in a pike position with the legs straight (2). From this position the body is rapidly extended and the feet are pushed toward the ceiling (3). There must be a hard push off the mat with both the hands and the head. Most teachers do not emphasize the head push enough. When the handstand position is reached (4), the feet are snapped toward the mat with a rapid flexing at the hips. At the same time there should be a vigorous push from the shoulders and fingers so that momentarily both the hands and the feet are off the mat (5).

SPOTTING. It helps some students to have a spotter stand beside them as they roll, grasp the near thigh, and lift the legs to the handstand position. This will aid the student to "get the feel" of the rapid extension.

TEACHING TECHNIQUES. The finish of the stunt may be practiced separately by kicking to a momentary handstand and practicing the snap-down and the shoulder push from this position.

4 and 5. Backward Roll and Backward Extension Roll. The two stunts that complete this routine have already been described—the backward roll in Routine I–A and the extension roll immediately above.

SERIES B

Cartwheel, cartwheel, forward roll with a walkout, roundoff, backward extension roll.

The five stunts included in this trip down the mat have been previously described. They are combined in a slightly different way, however, in this series. The first cartwheel should be done from a run with a skip takeoff similar to the roundoff in Routine II–A. The roundoff in this routine is not done with a run but is executed immediately after the forward roll with a walkout.

III. INTERMEDIATE ROUTINE

SERIES A

1. Headspring (Fig. 2–8). The headspring starts with a short running approach and a two-foot takeoff (1). Do not allow stu-

Fig. 2–8. Headspring.

dents to use a one-foot takeoff for a headspring as it changes the entire technique of the stunt and it becomes more like a handspring with bent arms than a headspring. The performer leans forward from the waist and places the hands on the mat about shoulder width apart. The front part of the head (approximately the hairline, not the forehead) is also placed on the mat slightly in front of the hands. The tumbler then jumps or pushes from both feet into a pike position with the legs straight and the feet slightly lower than the hips (2). In this pike position there is a slight fall off-balance before any leg motion starts. This is a very important part of the headspring (3). After the center of gravity has moved well beyond the points of support, the legs whip hard in a rotary movement and the arms push hard off the mat (4). In this first headspring in the series the legs will have to be bent a little on the landing so that the performer can proceed quickly into the next stunt (5). An arched back landing (used in the third headspring of the series) is considered better form, however, and should be emphasized in teaching.

Teaching Techniques. Roll a mat loosely so that it will form a flat surface on the top. This rolled mat should be about a foot high. Students place their hands and head on this mat in learning the headspring. The extra height makes it easier to get to the feet. As the performer becomes more proficient, the height of the rolled mat can be reduced gradually until the headspring can be performed on the level mat.

Spotting. Two spotters sit facing each other on this rolled mat. The performer places his hands and head on the mat between the spotters. The spotters place one hand on the performer's forearm and one under his upper back. The hand on the forearm protects the spotters from flying arms and also enables the spotters to control the landing. The hand under the upper back does most of the lifting. It is a good technique for the spotters to assist students who are having trouble with slow motion headsprings. The hand closest to the performer is placed on the leg, the other under the upper back. The performer can thus be held in a pike position. The fall off-balance can be initiated and controlled by the spotters. At the right point in the fall off-balance, the hand on the leg can initiate the whipping motion of the performer's legs and then quickly shift to the performer's forearm.

2. Forward Roll. Previously described in Routine I–A.

3. Headspring. This second headspring in this series is done exactly as the first. It is a little more difficult to do a headspring immediately after a forward roll than it is to do one from a running approach. Because there is not as much forward motion, there is a tendency for students to start the whipping motion of the legs too soon, before the body has fallen off-balance in the pike position. There is also a tendency to place the hands too close to the feet. This usually results in the head being tucked under too far so that the weight is on the back of the head. As the performer completes the forward roll, he should reach well forward with the hands and make sure the front of the head is placed on the mat.

4. Forward Roll. Previously described in Routine I–A.

5. Headspring with Arched Landing (Fig. 2–9). This is approximately the same stunt as the previous two headsprings in this series; however, as the tumbler gets better, one change can be made. If he whips the legs hard and pushes hard with the hands, it is possible to come to a stand with the feet and legs together and the hips forward so that the landing will be in an arched position with the hands above the head. It is hard to do another stunt im-

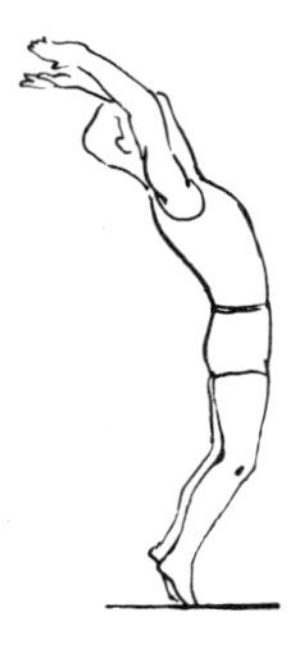

Fig. 2–9. Headspring with Arched Landing.

mediately following a landing in this position, but it is a very good landing to use for the last headspring in a series. This type of landing should be emphasized when teaching the headspring. If spotters are used to give an assist during the learning process, most students can accomplish an arched back landing.

SERIES B

1, 2, and 3. Roundoff, Backward Roll, and Backward Extension Roll. The first three stunts in this routine have been described previously in the chapter. The last three stunts are new, however, and are explained below. The reader should note that there are actually three backward rolls in this series. The first is a regular tucked backward roll, the second an extension roll finishing with a snap-down to the feet, and the third an extension roll that ends with a chest roll-down.

4. Fish Flop (Fig. 2–10). Fish flop is the common name given to a backward extension roll that is completed with a chest roll on the mat instead of with a snap-down to the feet. The first part of the stunt is done exactly the same as the backward extension roll. When the handstand position is reached, the performer quickly bends the arms and lowers the chest to the mat (1, 2). If the body remains in a good arched position, a smooth roll-down can be executed from the chest, to the abdomen, to the legs (3). As the chest roll is completed, the upper body will rock up off the mat (4). The arms are straight in this position and support the weight of the upper body.

Fig. 2–10. Fish Flop.

TEACHING TECHNIQUES. Do not insist that a beginner get all the way to the handstand before lowering the chest to the mat. The stunt can be executed if the arms are straightened just enough to get the head through. In fact, if the head is twisted to the side a little, it can be executed without the head being lifted off the mat. Do not encourage this type of fish flop, however, but instruct the performers to push with the hands and get as high as possible.

SPOTTING. Stand on the side of the performer and as the chest is lowered to the mat reach under the thighs with one arm and lower the performer to the mat. The spotter does not have to grasp the performer in any way. The legs of the performer merely lie across the arm of the spotter during the chest roll.

5. Squat-Through (Fig. 2–11). The squat-through starts from a front leaning rest or push-up position (1). As the chest roll is completed, the performer springs off the lower legs and feet and quickly brings the knees up toward the chest so that the body can pass between the arms in a tucked position (2a). Flexible students can squat through the arms in this manner to a sitting position on

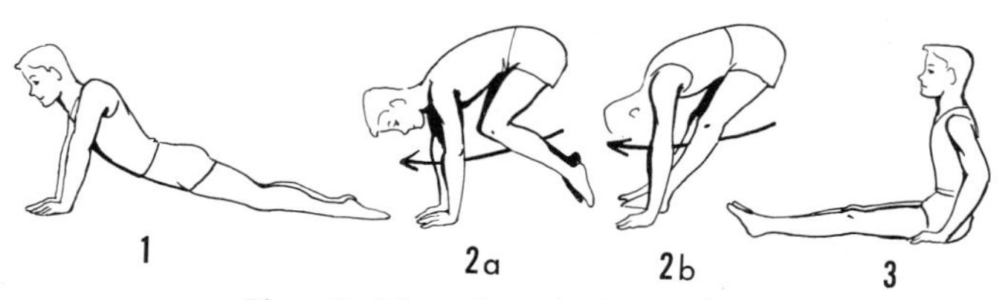

Fig. 2–11. Squat-Through.

the mat without raising their hands off the mat and without bending their legs. This is called a stoop-through (2b). Other students, however, will have to give a good push upward with the hands in order to raise the shoulders enough to permit the legs to squat through the arms. The squat- or stoop-through ends in a sitting position on the mat with the legs straight out in front and the trunk vertical (3).

6. Snap-Up (Fig. 2–12). This stunt is often called a neck spring or a kip-up. It starts from a sitting position with the legs straight out in front and the trunk vertical (1). The first part of the stunt is similar to a backward roll except the legs are kept perfectly straight. The performer rolls onto the back of the neck and the hands reach over the shoulders to make contact with the mat. The hips should be raised high off the mat with the thighs directly

Fig. 2–12. Snap-Up.

above and close to the face in a tight pike position (2). The tumbler immediately starts to roll or rock back in the opposite direction maintaining the tight pike position with the legs straight (3). This rock back is very important. After the hips have moved about six inches, the kipping motion starts. This consists of a rapid extension of the body and a hard push with the hands (4). The legs actually go through a rotary movement–up, out, and then down. They should be straight during this kipping motion. It makes it much easier to get to the feet if the knees are bent on the landing and the feet placed quite far apart with the toes turned out (5a). As the learner gets better, he can try to keep his legs together and straight and come to a stand with an arched back and arms above the head (5b). This second method is considered much better form and should be emphasized in teaching.

Teaching Techniques. Do not let students start the snap-up from a lying position on the mat with the hands already in position for the push. It might seem easier from this position, but the rhythm and timing of the stunt are lost if this is permitted.

Some students find it hard to get the idea of keeping the buttocks off the mat in the snap-up. To correct this the leg motion and landing position can be practiced alone without any arm push and without the head and shoulders leaving the mat. The roll into the pike position, the slight rock back in this position, the body extension with the rotary leg motion, and the placement of the feet for the landing can all be practiced in this drill. At the completion of this practice drill the feet are on the mat, the legs are bent at the knees, and the body is arched from the knees to the shoulders with the hips in the air well off the mat.

SPOTTING. This is a difficult stunt to spot successfully. The spot is used as an assist in learning the stunt as there is no real need to spot from a safety standpoint. The spotter kneels beside the tumbler as he rolls back onto his shoulders and places one hand under his lower back and one hand under his upper back. An assist can be given with both hands at the time of the kipping motion.

SERIES C

1. Handspring (Fig. 2–13). The handspring starts with a run and a skip takeoff, the same as that used for the roundoff. The performer hops on the right foot, with the left foot raised slightly in front. The arms are raised forward to about face height and the body maintains a forward lean (1). As the hands reach forward

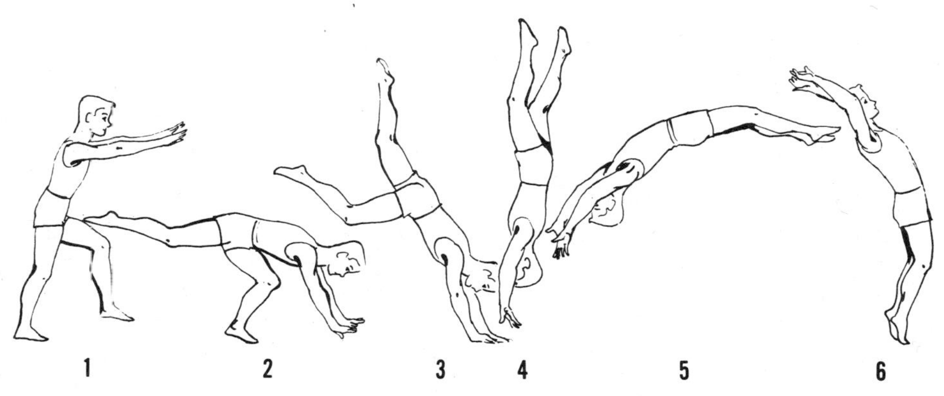

Fig. 2–13. Handspring.

for the mat, the left foot makes contact with the ground and the right foot is thrown up over the head. The hands are placed on the mat shoulder width apart about two feet in front of the left foot. The arms should be perfectly straight and the head back (chin off the chest) with the eyes focused on a spot on the mat about a foot in front of the hands (2). About the time the hands make contact with the mat, or maybe slightly before they touch the mat, the left foot thrusts vigorously off the mat and follows the right foot overhead (3). As the legs reach the handstand position, the hands leave the mat and the feet continue their circling arc over to the mat (4, 5, 6). This is described as a push in most texts but is actually more of a rebound off the hands, with the push from the fingers and the thrust from the shoulders being secondary in importance. If the approach and first part of the handspring are executed correctly, the hands will remain on the mat only a fraction of a second. The rebounding effect will be lost entirely if the arms are bent or if the shoulders are allowed to get in front of the hands when the hands are on the mat (see Fig. 2–14). At the time of the rebound off the mat the lower arms, upper arms, and trunk should

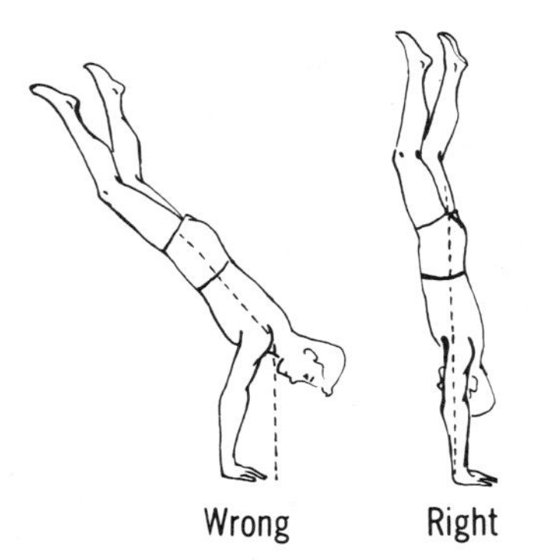

Fig. 2–14. Handspring Shoulder Position.

form a straight line with the shoulders extended as far as possible. A performer who gets a good rebound off the hands will be able to complete the handspring in an arched or straight body position on the feet. Beginners will not be able to get enough lift off the hands and will have to bend at the knees on the landing. Even with beginners, however, an arched body landing should be emphasized and practiced, so that a bend at the knees and hips does not become a permanent bad habit. In a good handspring the head will be slightly back on the landing and the arms will be above the head.

Teaching Techniques. a. Have students practice the approach and kick to the handstand position without going over. A partner can stand in readiness to catch the back of the thighs as the handstand position is reached and to push the performer back to his feet. This technique teaches the performer to keep the shoulders above the hands and the arms straight.

b. Have students practice the approach and kick as if to do the handspring but just before the vertical position is reached to rebound off the mat and hop forward a foot or two with the hands. The vertical position is never quite reached and the feet drop back to the mat without completing the handspring. This teaches the rebound off the mat with the hands remaining in contact with the mat for only a fraction of a second.

c. The hands may be placed on a rolled mat to give a little extra height as the handspring is learned. This technique makes the finish of the handspring easier but the start more difficult; as it sometimes brings about bad habits, it should be used cautiously.

d. On no condition allow students to place their hands on the floor and arch over another kneeling student. This technique is used by some teachers, but it teaches bad habits such as tucking the head on the chest and staying too long on the hands.

e. Boys with flexible shoulders often leave one hand on the mat much longer than the other. To correct this fault the spotter on this side should lift hard under the upper back to make sure that both hands come off the mat at the same time.

SPOTTING. This can be done by placing the performer in a hand belt or by two boys grasping hands or holding a towel under the small of the back of the performer as he executes the handspring. Probably the best method is to have two spotters kneel one on each side of the spot where the hands will be placed. The spotter's hand nearest the performer as he approaches is placed on the lower arm while the other hand is placed on the upper back. The hand under the back does most of the lifting.

2. Forward Roll. This stunt was described in Routine I–A.

3. Headspring. This stunt was described in Series A of this routine.

4 and 5. Forward Roll Walkout and Cartwheel. The last two stunts in this routine were explained in Routine I–B.

IV. LOW ADVANCED ROUTINE

SERIES A

1. Front Somersault. The term flip is a common substitute for somersault that is accepted by most authorities.

The front somersault starts with a hard run, a low hurdle, and two-foot takeoff. The hurdle should be an extension of the run rather than a jump. The body is almost vertical with the head up at the time of takeoff. The feet should be slightly ahead of the center of gravity. This position of the feet will help change the

Fig. 2–15. Front Somersault.

forward run to an upward movement for a good high somersault.

There are three common arm movements used for the front somersault. As these are difficult to describe, they are presented in the form of a drawing (Fig. 2–15; 1a, 1b, 1c).

In 1a the arms reach up and then pull forward into the tuck. In 1b, the elbows lead and the motion of the arms is backward and then upward and forward. In 1c, the arms lift up and then pull forward and downward into the tuck. Whatever method is used, the arms must be coordinated with the takeoff to provide height and forward spin.

After the takeoff the head tucks forward onto the chest and the hips lift hard backward and upward (2, 3). The legs are bent and a tuck position is assumed (3, 4). In arm motion "a" and "c" the hands almost always grab the shins in the tuck position, but in arm motion "b" they probably will not make contact with the legs. It is hard to explain exactly when to open out of the tuck for the landing. The tumbler can not see the ground but must time the opening of the tuck (5).

Teaching Techniques. Teach the stunt first on the trampoline. If a trampoline is not available, teach it off a spring board or from a reuther board.

Spotting. The front somersault will require very careful spotting. A handbelt may be used but if the front somersault has been learned on another piece of equipment, a good hand spot should be sufficient. The hand closest to the performer as he approaches is placed under the stomach or hips to give spin and lift. The other hand is placed under the neck or upper back. Extra mats should be used to provide a soft landing area. If plenty of mats are available, they can be stacked quite high, or rolled, to provide an exceptionally high and soft area and then spotting is not quite so essential.

2. Headsprings in Series. The headspring was described in Routine III, pages 39–40.

Headsprings done one after the other are a little more difficult than those done singly as they were in the previous routine. A series of headsprings should be done quite quickly to be impressive; the performer has to think a little quicker and work a little harder. When one does several headsprings in a row, the knees have to be bent on the landing of each except the last in the series, which can be completed with an arched back. The number of headsprings in the routine can be left up to the individual tumbler, but there is not much point in doing more than four.

SERIES B

1. Roundoff. This stunt was described in Routine II, pages 37–38.

2. Back Handspring (Fig. 2–16). This is undoubtedly the most important tumbling stunt in advanced competition. It is the stunt that separates advanced and intermediate tumblers. The body should be well off-balance backward for the back handspring. This means that the legs have to be cut under the center of gravity on the snap-down from the roundoff. The back handspring should be taught first from a stationary standing position and not following a roundoff.

Teaching Techniques. The tumbler stands erect with arms raised forward to shoulder height and palms down (1). The first movement is to swing the arms downward and backward and to bend the knees. The body should remain almost vertical. In this position the tumbler is off-balance and would fall on the mat if he tried to stop (2). It is a mistake to carry the knees forward so that an on-balance position can be maintained. It is also a bad mistake to lean forward from the waist rather than maintain an almost vertical body position. The first part of the stunt can be practiced by placing a chair in the right position to support the weight in this off-balance position. A partner's knee will serve the same purpose as the chair. A partner might also stand directly behind the performer and support the weight by placing a hand on the performer's back as this first movement is practiced. Another common mistake

Fig. 2–16. Back Handspring.

is for the performer to sit too low so that the buttocks almost scrape the ground. The thighs should form an angle of about 30 degrees or 35 degrees with a horizontal line drawn through the knees. From this position the arms are swung vigorously upward and backward and as they reach the vertical position the head is also thrown backward very rapidly (3). About the same time, the legs straighten quickly and thrust away from the mat and the chest and stomach arch up toward the ceiling (4). The feet leave the ground just slightly before the hands make contact with the mat (5). At the time the hands contact the mat, the body is still in an arched position with the hips thrust forward and the legs trailing (6). It is a common mistake to start flexing at the waist, or the knees, too soon in an attempt to get the feet over to the mat. After a fraction of second delay in this arched position with the hands on the mat the body is quickly flexed at the waist and the feet snapped down to the mat (7, 8). There is also a thrust from the fingers and shoulders to lift the upper body away from the mat.

It is a good technique for students who lack flexibility to practice backbends each practice session before trying back handsprings. It is necessary for other students to practice the leg drive alone. This is done by having them swing their arms above the head and jump upward and backward from the off-balance position without executing the back handspring.

Another teaching technique for the back handspring is illustrated in the first two photos on page 51. This is a partner activity that can start very slowly and can gradually be increased in speed to give the tumbler the "feel" of the back handspring. Photo 1 shows the starting position. In Photo 2 the hands are just reaching the mat. This is an especially valuable drill to teach the tumbler to trail his legs in an arch and not to start piking for the snap-down too soon. Notice that the spotter in the second photo has his hand on the performer's legs to prevent him from piking too soon.

The first two photos illustrate a partner drill used during the early stages of learning a back handspring. The technique might also be used later to help correct the mistake of flexing at the waist too soon for the snap-down to the feet. The second two photos show two different methods of hand spotting for a back handspring.

SPOTTING. The best way to spot a beginner for a back handspring is to put him in either an overhead safety belt or a hand belt. A belt suspended from pulleys is an essential piece of equipment for teaching advanced trampoline work and a very desirable piece of equipment for teaching advanced tumbling, especially if heavy students are to be spotted. A light person can easily spot a heavy individual with an overhead safety belt. The correct way to use a hand belt is to hold the ropes behind the tumbler with one hand very close to his waist. When the back handspring is attempted after a roundoff, the two spotters must run with the tumbler on his approach. The ropes must be wound one-half turn around the performer's waist so that they will unwind as the roundoff is executed. Two towels placed one in front and one behind and then twisted together will serve the purpose of a hand belt. After the back handspring is partially learned, other methods of spotting can be used. One method is to have two boys grasp hands or hold a towel behind the performer so that when he does the back handspring they can lift under the small of his back. Another method is to have two students kneel, one on each side of the performer, and lift under the lower back. Refer to photo 3 on page 51. This method is usually used after the stunt has been practiced in the belt but before the boy is quite ready to do it on his own. It may be used, however, if the spotters are strong and competent, much earlier in the learning process. Still another method of spotting a back handspring is to have one spotter kneel directly behind and place both hands on the performer's lower back. The back handspring is executed directly over one of the spotter's shoulders as illustrated in photo 4 on page 51. In this position the spotter is able to provide a great amount of help.

3. Back Extension Roll. This stunt is described in Routine II–A.

4. Fish Flop, Squat-Through, Snap-Up. These stunts are described in Routine III–B.

SERIES C

Front Handspring Walkout, Cartwheel, Roundoff, Back Handspring Walkout with Half Turn, Handspring, Headspring. There are no new stunts in this series, but the combination of stunts is quite difficult, especially the transition from the back handspring to the front handspring. The walkout landing (Fig. 2–17) for the front handspring is also fairly difficult and requires some explanation. Before attempting a walkout or stepout landing, the tumbler should be

Fig. 2–17. Walkout Landing.

able to execute a high handspring to a landing with the legs straight and the body vertical. Once this has been learned, the walkout is accomplished by spreading the legs slightly before the landing so that one foot touches the mat just before the other. It is important to keep the hips forward and the landing leg almost straight.

If the hips are flexed or the knee of the landing leg is bent, it takes a very strong leg to bear the weight. Usually this will result in the leg bending still further as the foot makes contact with the mat. It is not only very poor form, but it also becomes almost impossible to execute another handspring if the knees or hips bend too much. A spotter should be used to lift under the performer's back when the walkout handspring is being learned, even though the performer can execute a good handspring with a two-foot landing.

As the cartwheel is completed, there has to be a quarter turn and pivot on the first foot that touches so that the performer is facing in the right direction for the roundoff. It takes considerably more leg strength to do a good back handspring after a roundoff that follows several other stunts in a series than after one that is the first stunt in a series.

The start of the back handspring is the same as previously explained (see Routine IV–B). The finish, however, is different. Instead of snapping both legs down together, one leg is snapped down ahead of the other. The right leg is first in this description. As the right leg is snapped down, a turn to the left is started. When the right foot touches the mat, the turn is continued with a pivot on the foot so that a 180° turn is completed. The weight of the body quickly shifts from this right foot to the left foot, which is placed on the mat about two feet in front of the right foot.

In this position the performer is ready for a front handspring (Routine III–C). This handspring is much more difficult than the one previously explained as it has to be done from almost a stationary position. The last stunt in the series, the headspring, should be completed with legs together and back arched.

This routine will take considerable practice before it can be executed as a continuous series with a reasonable amount of speed. Remember, all tumbling series should be continuous and fast. The other routines described up to this point can be executed without much practice once the stunts have been learned. This series, however, even though the stunts have all been completely learned, will still cause trouble for the tumbler. Considerable practice will have to be devoted to the transitions between the stunts.

V. ADVANCED ROUTINE

SERIES A

1. Roundoff and a Series of Back Handsprings. Neither of these stunts is new. Back handsprings in series, however, are much more difficult than a single back handspring. The most important thing when doing this stunt in series is to snap the feet down so that they land in front of the center of gravity when they touch the mat. This means the body will be off-balance backward. This is true for the landing of the feet on the roundoff as well as the back handsprings. At the time the hands contact the mat they also should be cut under the shoulders so that the arms are at least vertical. Actually it might be better if the hands are cut under so that the arms are slightly beyond the vertical position. Fig. 2–18 illustrates this position. Good shoulder flexibility will make the position much easier to attain. Students should practice rocking back and forth in the back bend position and do other shoulder flexibility exercises if they lack this quality.

Fig. 2–18. Back Handspring Shoulder Position.

Back handsprings should cover quite a bit of distance. It is hard to say how much distance because of differences in body size and in back and shoulder flexibility. Back handsprings should also be fast and lively. A performer should be able to bounce up in the air as he lands, or work quickly into another back handspring. Sometimes, however, if too much speed is attempted, the back handsprings will become too low, the tumbler will get on balance and the series will bog down. Back handsprings should not be too high but should be high enough so that both hands and feet can be cut under the center of gravity so that each stunt is started with the tumbler off-balance backward.

Another very important thing in a successful series of back handsprings is to let the legs trail or hang behind the chest and stomach. The snap-down to the feet should be accomplished with a hard flexion at the waist with almost a straight leg rather than with the knees leading in a bent leg position. Starting the flexion at the waist too early, especially if the knees are also allowed to bend, is a very bad mistake and makes a good fast series of back handsprings almost impossible.

2. Tuck-Back Somersault (Fig. 2–19). The new stunt in this series is the back somersault. There are several types of back somersaults that can be done—the tuck back, the whip-back, and the layout. In this routine the tuck back is used. The layout, which is described later as a lead-up for the full-twisting back somersault, would be a good substitute. The whip-back is not a good type of somersault to use as the last stunt in a series.

On the back handspring prior to the somersault the legs should not be snapped down under the center of gravity but rather snapped down slightly behind this point. This will result in the backward motion being converted into upward movement for a high back somersault (1). In the tuck-back the arms lift straight up in the air or even stop slightly before they reach the vertical position. The arms in this type of somersault help give height but do not contribute to the spin. The turning motion comes from a chest lift or backward lean of the upper torso and head. The body should remain almost vertical at the time of the takeoff; that is, the center of gravity should be allowed to shift only slightly behind the feet. The backward lean should definitely come only from the upper torso and not from the waist (2). As the height of the jump is reached, the knees pull up rapidly to the chest in a tight tuck and the hands grasp the shins in this position (3, 4). The spin is started with the body stretched and long. When the knees pull up

Fig. 2–19. Tuck-Back Somersault.

into a tuck, the radius is shortened. The spinning motion therefore speeds up around the axis of rotation. As the somersault is completed, the tuck is released and the body straightened for the landing (5).

TEACHING TECHNIQUES. This stunt can be taught much easier on the trampoline and then transferred to the tumbling mat. Although it is probably harder to do from a standing position than after a back handspring, it should be practiced first from a stand. Another student can give an assist by lifting under the feet of the performer. The boy giving the lift sits in a straddle position on the mat and places his hands, palms up, on the mat. The performer stands on this boy's hands and is assisted by a lift at the time of the spring from the mat. A circular arm motion is recommended for a tuck-back when it is practiced from a stand. The arms are swung down the sides and then up the front of the body for the lift. The biceps, or front of the arm, should lead as the arms reach up above the head.

SPOTTING. An overhead safety belt or a hand belt should be used in teaching the back somersault. When the tumbler first comes out of the belt, he should be spotted carefully by hand. The spotter lifts under the lower back to contribute, if necessary, to both the height and spin.

SERIES B

Front Handspring, Front Somersault Walkout, Roundoff, Back Handspring Walkout with a Half-Turn, Front Handspring. There are no new stunts in this routine, but the combination results in a more difficult series than any of the previous ones.

The front handspring followed by an immediate front somersault is an extremely difficult combination. It is made more difficult by requiring a walkout landing for the somersault. The front handspring must be a high one with the body in a straight and approximately vertical position on the landing. If the legs and body are straight a rebounding effect will be the result and the somersault will be high. If the body is leaning backward too much on the landing, the somersault will be low and will not spin very fast. If the body is leaning forward too much on the landing (usually the result of a delay after the landing), the somersault will also be low but it will spin quite fast. The arm lift for the somersault is similar to the first one described for the front somersault in Routine IV, Series A. The arms lift in a single, continuous upward and then forward motion and must be timed perfectly with the rebound from the handspring.

The walkout landing for the front somersault should not be attempted until a good two-foot landing can be accomplished. The step-out should first be practiced on the trampoline and then following a somersault done off a reuther board or spring board. This will result in a higher somersault and make the walkout easier. The somersault must be slightly overspun so that the body is leaning a little forward on the landing. If this is not done it will be very difficult to make this routine flow continuously and rapidly beyond this point.

The tumbler should be placed in a hand belt when the handspring–front somersault combination is learned. The spotters run with him and give a little assistance on the handspring and then must be ready for a considerable lift on the somersault. A hand spot can be used after the combination has been partially mastered. The spotter stands at the point of the landing for the handspring and lifts with one hand under the stomach or hips and with the other hand under the upper back.

SERIES C

Roundoff, Back Handspring, Whip-Back Somersault, Back Handspring, Tuck-Back Somersault. This combination is usually referred to as "back alternates." The only new stunt in the series is the "whip-back" somersault. Whip-backs are the best type of somersault to use in the middle of a tumbling series as they can be executed quickly without slowing down the tempo of the series.

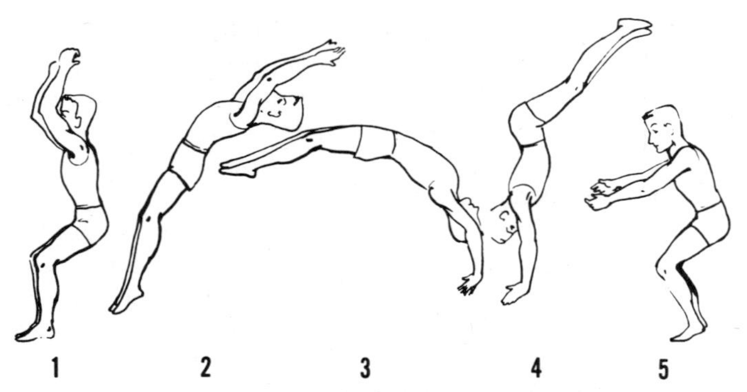

Fig. 2–20. Whip-Back Somersault.

The whip-back (Fig. 2–20) is a low somersault that does not require as much leg power as a tuck-back. It is really just a back handspring done a little higher than usual in which the hands are unable to reach the mat. The placement of the feet on the landing of the back handspring preceding the whip-back is the same as if another back handspring is to follow, that is, they are cut under so as to have the center of gravity behind the feet (1). The arm throw, the off-balance position, and the leg drive are all the same as for a back handspring. It can be noted by the illustration that, unlike for the tuck-back, the entire body leans backward on the take-off (2). As the feet leave the ground the arms, head, and upper body continue to pull backward and the legs are allowed to trail so that the body is momentarily in an arched position in the air (3). This is the secret of a good whip-back. The body stretches in an arch and then immediately starts to pike to get the legs over to the mat (4). If the full stretch in the arched position is not reached, most of the whipping effect will be lost. The body is piked for the landing with the legs cut under the center of gravity so that another back handspring can be executed without loss of speed in the series (5).

Teaching Techniques. Teaching a whip-back too soon often develops bad habits in the performance of back handsprings and tuck-back somersaults. A high back handspring or a tuck-back that has too much backward body lean might be the results. Teachers should be aware of this and present the whip-back with caution. The whip-back can be practiced readily on the trampoline or immediately from a roundoff. The fast stretch in the arch followed by a rapid pike can be practiced by lying backward and balancing in an inverted arched position on a side horse. From this position the head and feet are dropped simultaneously so that an exaggerated arch results from which the legs are rapidly piked up and over to a standing position facing the horse.

SPOTTING. The spotting for a whip-back is the same as for a tuck-back.

SERIES D

Roundoff, Back Handspring, Back Somersault with a Full-Twist. The only new stunt in this series is the full-twisting somersault. Until the twist is learned this trip can end with a "layout" somersault. The tumbler must master a layout somersault before attempting the full-twist. The layout is described as a teaching technique.

For the full-twisting somersault (Fig. 2–21) the arms lift almost straight above the head and quite wide apart. The upper body leans well back, but the hips are kept forward so that the center of gravity is only slightly behind the feet. The twist is started before the feet leave the mat by turning the head, shoulders, and trunk slightly in the desired direction (1). The twisting motion started in this way will continue in the air especially if the body is kept straight so that the radius around the longitudinal, or twisting axis, is kept as short as possible. After the arms lift high and wide above the head, they are wrapped in close against the chest. In a twist to the left the right arm is thrown across the front of the head in a straight position and then the elbow bends and the arm folds in to the chest. The left arm throws backward with the elbow bending in close to the left side (2). The straight body position with the

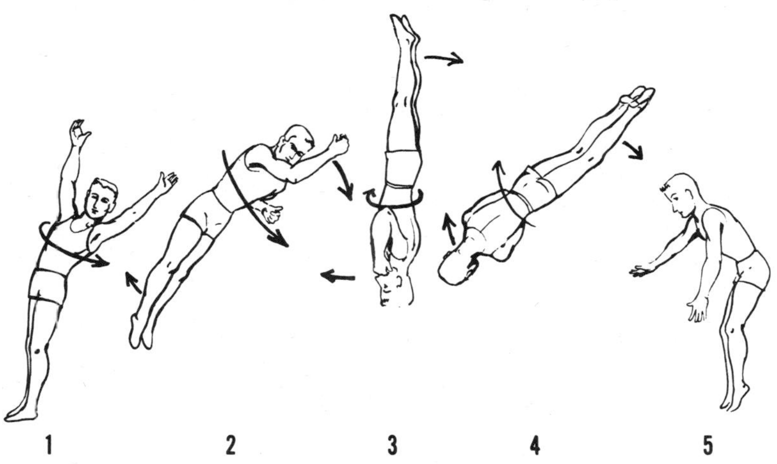

Fig. 2–21. Full-Twisting Back Somersault.

arms wrapped in close is maintained (3) until the twist and the somersault have been almost completed (4). Then the arms are extended out to the side to stop the twist and the body pikes ready for the landing (5).

TEACHING TECHNIQUES. The full-twist can be learned much easier on the trampoline than on the tumbling mats. Refer to Chapter 5 for more information. The layout somersault is a prerequisite on the tumbling mats. It can also be learned much easier on the trampoline. On the snap down from the back handspring the leg placement for the layout is the same as for a tuck-back because height is needed for this type of somersault. The upper body is leaned backward but to prevent the center of gravity from shifting backward too much the hips are kept well forward. The arms lift upward and backward as for a whip-back and then stretch out to the side away from the body. A hard chest and stomach lift and a strong backward pull of the head, shoulders, and arms are essential for a layout somersault. The arched position is maintained as long as possible, but the body must be piked slightly for the landing.

SPOTTING. The best way to spot a full-twisting somersault is with the tumbler in a twisting belt. Refer to Chapter 5 for more information about twisting belts. Because a reasonably long run is required to perform a roundoff, back handspring, and a full-twisting somersault, two spotters must run with the tumbler during his approach and series of stunts. If a twisting belt is not available, a regular belt can be used, but the ropes must be wrapped one and one-half times around the waist of the performer at the start so as to unwind as he does his roundoff and back somersault with a full-twist. A traveling overhead belt is now used by many coaches. This is exactly the same overhead spotting device described in Chapter 5 except that the pulleys are hung from a second set of pulleys that run on two tightly stretched cables. This permits the pulleys to move with the tumbler so that the supporting points remain directly above him at all times.

3

Floor Exercise

This event has been known by several different names in recent years. Until only a few years ago it was called "free exercise" and prior to that it was called "free calisthenics." In some countries it is known as "free standing exercise" or simply "free standing."

Because floor exercise requires no equipment other than a few mats, it can be a part of almost every school's physical education program. It should be started at the same grade level as tumbling and can be presented as soon as a few basic tumbling stunts have been learned. Most eight-year-olds are ready to learn simple floor exercise routines and many children even younger than this can benefit from exposure to the activity.

A description of the tumbling stunts that have been included in Chapter 2 is omitted in this chapter. For convenience a page reference is given for each. In two or more places in each routine, the word "run" has been used. The run should be very short as the rules say unnecessary running steps should not be taken. In most cases two or three steps followed by a skip are all that are needed. Five steps should be considered the maximum.

RULES

The floor exercise area is 12 x 12 meters, or 39′ 4½″ square. The exercise, which has a time limit of 50 to 70 seconds, must include alternating elements of suppleness and strength, held positions, balances, kips, jumps, and handstands. It must be composed with shifts in different directions to form a harmonious and rhythmic "whole." Repetitions, unnecessary running steps, and transitions and poses that are too simple should be avoided.

As with most gymnastic events the rules are not fully descriptive. A few remarks regarding customs, and the modern trend, are necessary for a complete understanding of the event. A great amount of tumbling is included; in fact, it is the backbone of the routine. The rules do not specifically indicate this by their reference to kips and jumps. Modern exercises must give the impression of being continuout and have very few holds. A great amount of emphasis is placed on a harmonious and rhythmic combination of movements. A few years ago it was considered necessary to cover the entire floor area but now this is not emphasized as long as the composition involves movement in several different directions.

A typical composition follows the following outline:

1. A series of tumbling stunts used as a "mount"
2. Transition movements to a strength stunt
3. A series of tumbling stunts
4. Transition movements to a flexibility stunt, and/or a balance, and/or another strength stunt
5. A series of tumbling stunts used as a "dismount"

In "2" and "4" several individual tumbling stunts or short tumbling series are often used as transitions. Some gymnasts vary this pattern by opening with one or two individual stunts of great difficulty, or of an "eye-catching" nature, before the first series of tumbling.

The N.C.A.A. rules now specify that a mat should be provided to cover the floor exercise area so that top quality tumbling can be included. The F.I.G. rules do not require floor padding but its use is recommended by the international technical committee and, therefore, in all important international competitions a mat or carpet is used.

VALUES

In the opinion of the author floor exercise is the best gymnastic event. The following points are presented to support this:

1. It requires no equipment so can be performed almost anywhere, indoors or out. Because of this it is a good extracurricular and "carry-over" activity.
2. It provides great opportunity for self-expression and creativeness. Even with required exercises students can develop different techniques of performing transitions between stunts. As soon as they have had enough background, they should be encouraged to create their own exercises.
3. It requires and develops a greater variety of physical qualities than any of the other events, or for that matter, any of our modern sports. All of the basic physical qualities—strength, flexibility, agility, balance, power, speed, and endurance—are needed.

TEACHING SUGGESTIONS

There is considerable difference of opinion regarding the use of "required" or "optional" exercises for class purposes. The author will readily admit that asking students to compose their own routines is sounder educationally than forcing them all to perform the same exercise. It has been found, however, that with inexperienced

University of Washington News Service photo

Jim David Performing an Inlocate Handspring in Floor Exercise. Jim executes this from a squat position following a forward roll and completes it in a side splits with his trunk resting on the floor between the legs. The position might also be held as a balance or be completed to the feet rather than to the splits. Jim placed second in tumbling in the National A.A.U. meet in 1962 and 1963. In 1964 he was second in the N.C.A.A. meet. He placed third in floor exercise in the 1965 N.C.A.A. meet. Jim was Conference champion of the Athletic Association of Western Universities in floor exercise during his three years of varsity competition.

gymnastic teachers and inexperienced students, and this includes the great majority of teachers and students in the United States, little progress is made if compulsory routines are not used as examples and guides.

Most beginning and intermediate students will not work on their own unless they have a complete routine to practice. There does not seem to be the incentive to learn individual stunts in this event as in some of the others. When they have a required routine, most students will continue to practice even though the instructor is not in direct supervision.

In spite of this, to stimulate creativeness, students should be encouraged to compose their own exercises. They may also be permitted to modify the required routine by adding stunts or changing the connecting moves slightly. Many teachers use required routines but permit the opening and closing tumbling series to be selected by the student.

After presenting the entire routine to a class, most of the stunts can be practiced individually across a mat five feet wide. By using this technique a high percentage of the students can be kept busy at the same time. After most of the stunts have been accomplished the continuity of the exercise must be learned on a row of mats. The best way to proceed at this point is to start with about three stunts. After everyone in the squad has tried these, another stunt is added and everyone takes his turn again. The stunts are added in this way, one at a time, until the whole routine is performed. If the routine is long, it is better to learn it in "halves," in this manner, and then put the two halves together. During this type of practice, those waiting for a turn should be either trying to memorize the exercise by watching the performer or they should be practicing on the floor stunts that do not require a mat.

All of the routines in this chapter can be practiced with very minor modifications on a single row of mats. In most cases, if transition moves are executed so that they involve exactly a 180° turn it is possible to do the next series of stunts in the reverse direction down the mat. Even expert gymnasts develop sore spots and bruises when they practice too much on the floor. Therefore, during most training sessions it is recommended that a row of mats be used for the practice of routines.

I. BEGINNING ROUTINE

As a beginning routine is normally performed on mats, this routine is designed to go forward and backward in a straight line. The

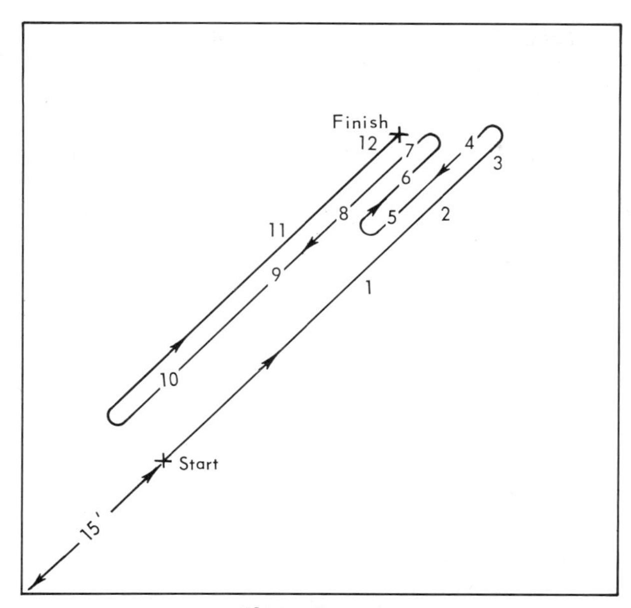

Floor Pattern.

stunts represented by numbers 2, 3, 4, 5, 6, 7, and 8 are performed on the same floor area but in order to show the turns and the direction of the movement it appears as if they shift to the left. The routine will require about 30 feet of mats if the initial run is only about ten feet long. If it is performed in a regular area it may start almost anywhere in the area as there is little chance of running out of room. In the above pattern it starts about 15 feet from one corner facing the corner diagonally across the area.

ABBREVIATED DESCRIPTION

1. Run, diving forward roll
2. Swedish fall
3. Squat, or stoop, through to rear support
4. Turn to front support
5. Forward roll to a sitting position with the legs straight and lower the head to the knees (HOLD)
6. Backward roll to a wide straddle stand with the trunk bent forward
7. Press to a headstand (HOLD)
8. Roll forward to the feet from the headstand
9. Cartwheel
10. Step forward and pivot 180°
11. Run, diving forward roll
12. Arched jump

DETAILED DESCRIPTION

1. Run, Diving Forward Roll (Fig. 3–1). This is done exactly the same as a regular forward roll except that there is more spring from the legs and a forward reach with the hands. The feet actually leave the mat before the hands touch the mat (1). In this po-

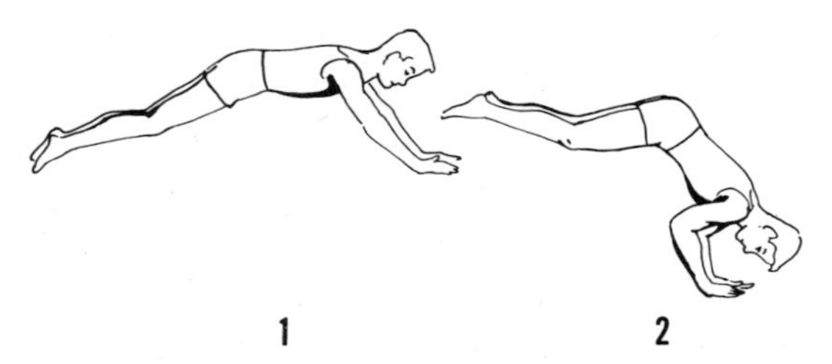

Fig. 3–1. Diving Forward Roll.

sition in the air the legs should be straight and together with the toes pointed. The head remains back with the eyes watching the mat as long as possible (2). If the head is tucked too soon, the performer will drop hard onto the upper back and will receive a jar.

Fig. 3–2. Swedish Fall.

2. Swedish Fall (Fig. 3–2). Following the diving roll the gymnast comes to a stand, stretches as tall as possible, and then falls forward with a straight body (1). As the upper body approaches the floor, the hands reach out and catch the body weight and one leg is raised (2). The chest is lowered to an inch or two off the mat and the raised leg is lifted high in the air so there is an arch from the head to the toe (3). This position should not be held but merely shown momentarily before the arms are straightened and the leg lowered. In this position the body sags at the hips and the head is raised (4).

TEACHING TECHNIQUES. One lead-up that may be used is to fall forward, catching the weight with the hands, and then lower to a prone position with the entire body and both legs resting on the mat. The next step is to prevent the body from making contact but to leave both feet on the floor. A third step is to raise the leg and lower the chest from a push-up position and thus practice the last part of the Swedish fall movement without dropping from a stand.

3. Squat- or Stoop-Through to Rear Support (Fig. 3–2). This must be timed with the finish of the previous stunt. The hips sag in an arch and then are immediately raised in the air. The feet push off the floor and the legs are squatted (1a) or stooped (1b) through

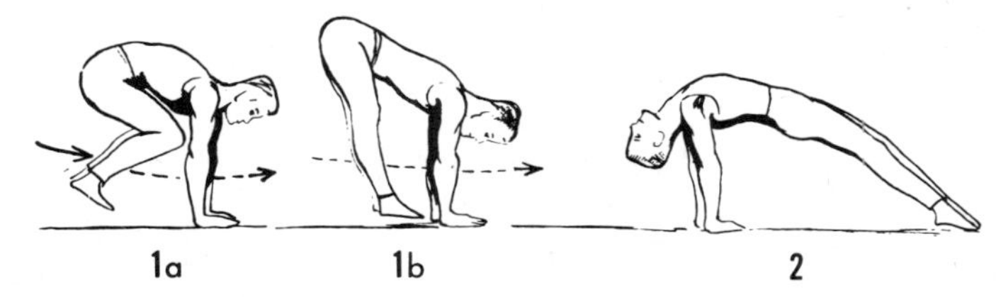

Fig. 3–3. Squat- or Stoop-Through to Rear Support.

between the arms to a rear support position with the hips raised in an arch and the head back (2). Flexible students will be able to leave their hands on the ground during the movement, but others will have to thrust off the floor in order to get their legs through.

TEACHING TECHNIQUES. The movement should be practiced first to a squat stand between the arms and then to a sitting position. The rear support position with hips high and head back should be practiced without any preliminary movements.

4. Turn to Front Support (Fig. 3–4). This is a very simple turn in which one arm thrusts off the floor as the weight is shifted to the

Fig. 3–4. Turn to Front Support.

other arm. The body remains straight as the weight is supported on one arm and one foot (1) during the turn from the rear support to front support (2).

5. Forward Roll to Sit and Lower Head to Knees (Fig. 3–5). From the front support the hips sag (1) and then are raised quickly in the air as the feet push off the floor. The arms are bent and the head is tucked onto the chest (2). The thrust from the feet push

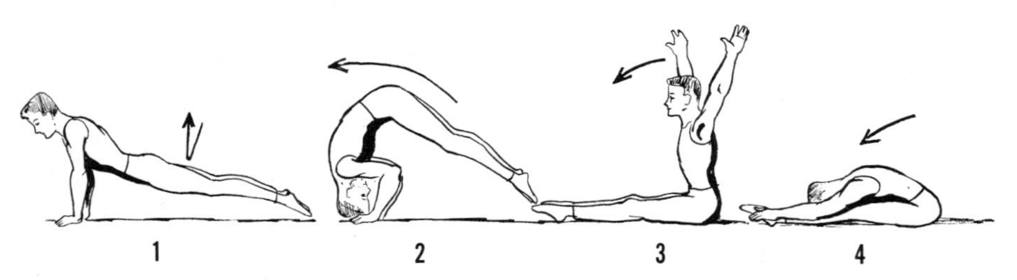

Fig. 3–5. Forward Roll to Sit and Lower Head to Knees.

the hips forward over the head in a forward roll. The legs are kept straight during the slow rolling movement to a sitting position (3). From the roll the arms circle upward, forward, and downward. The head and chest are lowered forward to touch the legs, if possible, and this position is HELD for at least two seconds (4). This is the first held position in the routine. Up to this point everything should have flowed rhythmically and harmoniously.

TEACHING TECHNIQUES. The biggest problem with this stunt will be to develop the flexibility to lower the chest to the legs. This will take weeks of practice for most students to stretch the hamstring muscles of the back of the legs and to develop the necessary trunk flexion. Most students will be able to accomplish this position if they persevere with forward flexion exercises. It is recommended that slow movements be used rather than hard bobbing movements. A partner can be used to push down slowly and easily on the upper back to aid in the gradual stretching process.

6. Backward Roll to a Straddle Stand (Fig. 3–6). The backward roll starts from the previous flexibility position by sitting up rapidly and leaning backward (1). The backward roll continues by raising the legs with knees straight, tucking the head, and reaching over the shoulders with the hands (2). As the arms push and lift the head off the floor, the legs are spread wide apart to finish in a wide straddle stand. The trunk is arched and raised to slightly above horizontal with the arms out to the side (3). This position is held

Fig. 3–6. Backward Roll to a Straddle Stand.

by some gymnasts but it should not be, as the rules definitely state "simple poses (holds) should be avoided."

TEACHING TECHNIQUES. The ordinary backward roll is a lead-up. Students who have trouble getting over to the feet may bend the legs at first, or spread them apart early in the roll to shorten the radius. The straddle stand allows for the demonstration of flexibility as did the previous stunt. For practice, students may assume the position and stretch by sliding their feet wider and wider apart. The hands are kept on the floor during this practice to support some of the body weight.

SPOTTING. A spotter, kneeling beside the learner, may need to assist by lifting with one hand under the shoulder during the backward roll.

7. Press to Headstand (Fig. 3–7). The hands are placed back on the floor almost immediately from the wide straddle stand position. They should be slightly wider than shoulder width with the fingers pointing forward and spread apart. The closer the hands can be placed to the imaginary line drawn between the feet the easier the "press" will be. The front part of the head (but not the

Fig. 3–7. Press to Headstand.

forehead) is placed on the floor about a foot in front of the hands. Tell older students that the hands and head form an equilateral triangle; younger students that the head is like the third leg of a three-legged stool (1). From this position the hips are raised slowly (no kick off the floor) by pushing hard with the arms until the center of gravity is over the points of support (2). From this position the legs are raised overhead and at the same time slowly closed together. The balance should be held in a slight arch with the weight primarily on the front of the head but not completely removed from the hands (3). There are only two held positions in this routine. This is the second one and it should be HELD for at least two seconds.

TEACHING TECHNIQUES. There are several easier methods of getting into a headstand that should be mastered before trying this one. The three presented are about of equal difficulty and all require the same placement of the hands and head so this will not be repeated.

1. Start from a position with the hips and one leg raised as close to the vertical headstand position as possible and then kick off the other leg and raise it to the first leg.
2. Start from a tight tuck position with the feet as close to the hands as possible, raise the hips so that the center of gravity is almost over the points of support by pushing slightly off both feet, then uncurl the legs slowly to the balance position.
3. Start from a tripod balance with the knees resting on the back of the upper arms and uncurl the legs slowly to the arched position.

SPOTTING. A spotter stands beside the performer to catch the legs as they are raised and to assist him in reaching the balance. Slow learners might need to have their legs lifted to the balance to give them the "feel" of the position. They are more likely to make a real attempt to reach the balance themselves after experiencing it. Students who always tuck their head and roll may be prevented from doing this by placing the spotter directly behind the performer with one foot under his shoulder and the lower leg against his upper back. From this position the spotter can prevent the head from tucking, the back from rounding, and can assist in getting the performer's hips up by pulling them into position. Students who have to be assisted to get up to the balance will probably need assistance also in lowering the feet to the floor.

8. Roll Forward to Feet from a Headstand (Fig. 3–8). This stunt is harder than one might think. In order to get a smooth and continuous movement to the feet the first step must be to fall off-balance

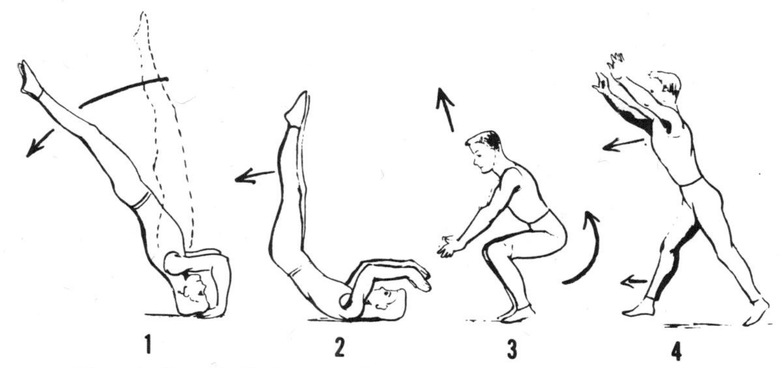

Fig. 3–8. Roll Forward to Feet from a Headstand.

in a straight body position (1). The hands thrust off the mat and the body starts to pike (2). The legs are drawn into a tuck at the last instant so that the roll can finish on the feet (3). As the feet contact the mat the legs should be straightened immediately. The arms raise forward and upward and one step is taken forward in preparation for the cartwheel (4).

9. Cartwheel. Refer to Chapter 2, pages 35–37.

10. Step Forward and Pivot (Fig. 3-9). This is a connecting move rather than a stunt. Connecting moves are extremely important in floor exercise as, unless they are learned smoothly and gracefully, they can spoil the general impression of the whole exercise. As the second foot—we will assume it is the left foot in this routine—contacts the floor on the completion of the cartwheel (1), the body turns 180° to the left and the right foot is brought forward in a long walking step (2). The turn to the left is continued on this step and then is completed by pivoting on the right foot as the

Fig. 3–9. Step Forward and Pivot.

left leg is raised forward (3). The step forward and pivot, combined, bring about a change of direction of 180° in the pattern of the routine, although if you consider that the cartwheel started facing to the side the turn involves a total of 270°.

11. Run, Diving Forward Roll. Refer to page 66.

12. Arched Jump (Fig. 3–10). This stunt is used to give the impression of height to the finish of the exercise. As the roll is com-

Fig. 3–10. Arched Jump.

pleted the gymnast springs into the air off both feet and arches his back. The legs should be together, the head back, and the arms obliquely sidewards and upwards (1). On the landing the knees are bent, the trunk leans forward slightly, and the arms maintain their same position (2). This landing position is held momentarily to show control and balance before assuming the normal standing position.

II. LOW INTERMEDIATE ROUTINE

This routine may follow the floor pattern diagrammed at right or be performed in a straight line forward and backward on a row of mats. If a row of mats are to be used, the pivots after stunts numbered 5 and 12 should involve a 180° turn instead of only 90°. If the initial run is not over 15 feet, the routine can be performed on about 35 feet of mats. The pattern diagrammed starts about 10 feet from the top left hand corner of the area and a few inches in from the sideline.

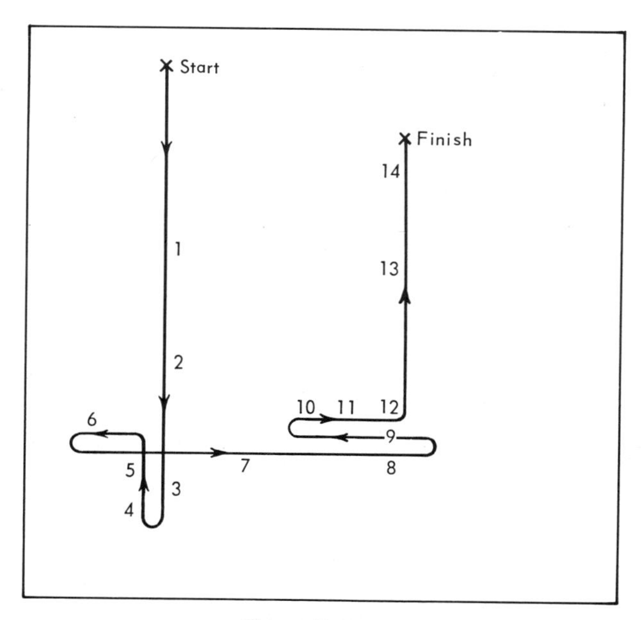

Floor Pattern.

ABBREVIATED DESCRIPTION

1. Run, roundoff
2. Backward extension roll
3. Backward roll to the shoulders with the body vertical, then piked with the feet touching the floor over the head, then vertical again
4. Roll forward to a squat on the left leg with the right leg extended forward
5. Three single leg circles (pinwheels) counterclockwise and pivot 90° to the left on the left leg to a stand
6. Step onto the right foot and pivot 180° to the left.
7. Step forward on the left leg and tour jeté, pivot 180° to the left on the landing leg
8. Forward roll to a V sit (HOLD)
9. Lower legs, bob head forward to the knees, backward roll to a chest roll down
10. Press a headstand (HOLD)
11. Roll forward to the feet from the headstand
12. Step forward on the right foot and pivot 90° to the left
13. Run, roundoff
14. Straddle jump touching toes

DETAILED DESCRIPTION

1. Run, Roundoff. Refer to Chapter 2, pages 37–38.

2. Backward Extension Roll. Refer to Chapter 2, pages 38–39.

3. Backward Roll to the Shoulders (Fig. 3–11). This stunt starts like a backward extension roll with a straight leg sit-down. The hands are used to catch part of the body weight (1). The roll continues backward to the upper back but the hands and arms remain on the floor (2). The backward movement is stopped momentarily by extending the body vertically (3). The legs are then lowered to a sharp pike position so that the feet touch the floor over the head (4). The body is immediately extended again vertically (5). This whole stunt should be combined into a flowing, rhythmic series with none of the positions being held.

Fig. 3–11. Backward Roll to the Shoulders.

TEACHING TECHNIQUES. The position with the body extended vertically may be practiced by bracing the hands under the back as indicated by the dotted lines in the third illustration of Fig. 3–11. This is the common position used for the inverted "bicycle-pedaling exercise."

4. Roll Forward to a Half-Squat, Right Leg Extended Forward (Fig. 3–12). This stunt should be connected to the previous one, as a part of one continuous, rhythmic movement. As the hips approach the floor in the forward roll, the left leg is bent (1) so that the movement ends in a half-squat on the left leg with the right leg extended forward. The hands shift forward and are placed on the floor about a foot in front of the left toe (2).

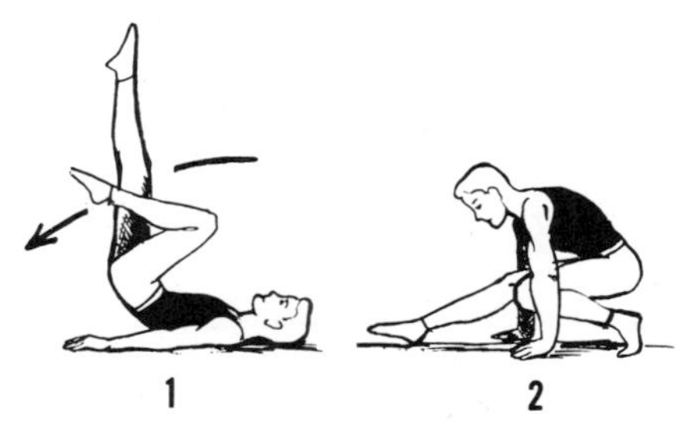

Fig. 3–12. Roll Forward to a Half Squat, Right Leg Extended Forward.

5. Single Leg Circles (Pinwheels) (Fig. 3–13). The pinwheels should be started immediately upon reaching the half-squat position. The right foot makes a complete counterclockwise circle with the left foot approximately the center of the circle. The right leg should remain perfectly straight throughout the whole movement. It first circles under the left hand, which must be raised momentarily (1), and then continues backward under the left foot. During most of the circle almost all of the body weight is supported by the left leg but at this time it is shifted forward momentarily onto both hands so the left foot can jump over the right leg (2). As the circle continues the right hand is raised so that the leg can pass underneath (3). In this routine three circles are executed. As the right leg circles forward on the third circle, the left leg is straightened and the body pivots 90° to the left on the left leg with the right foot in the air (4).

Fig. 3–13. Single Leg Circles (Pinwheels).

Teaching Techniques. During the learning process it is much easier to start pinwheels with the circling leg extended backward or to the side.

6. Pivot 180° to the Left (Fig. 3–14). The previous stunt, this one, and the one to follow must all be combined as one movement. As the previous stunt is completed, the gymnast steps forward onto the right foot (1), pivots 180° to the left on it, and then raises the left leg momentarily off the floor (2).

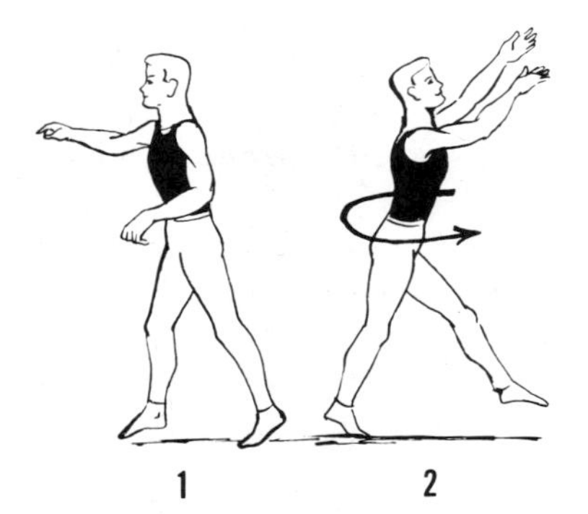

Fig. 3–14. Pivot 180° to the Left.

7. Tour Jeté (Fig. 3–15). A tour jeté, by definition, is a leap off one foot with a half turn in the air to a landing on the other foot. In this routine the left foot is placed forward on the ground and the right leg is swung vigorously forward and upward (1). The leap off the left leg is timed with this leg swing and a hard arm lift

Fig. 3–15. Tour Jeté.

upward (2). A half-turn to the left is completed in the air to a landing on the right foot. As the foot contacts the ground, the turn to the left continues with a 180° pivot on the right foot (3). The turn is stopped at this point, but the movement continues in the same direction by stepping forward on the left leg (4).

8. Forward Roll to a "V" Sit (Fig. 3–16). The step after the tour jeté is used to slow down the forward movement. The forward roll must be executed slowly as it does not continue to the feet but stops part way through. The roll starts like any forward roll except that the takeoff is from one foot in this exercise (1). After the arms

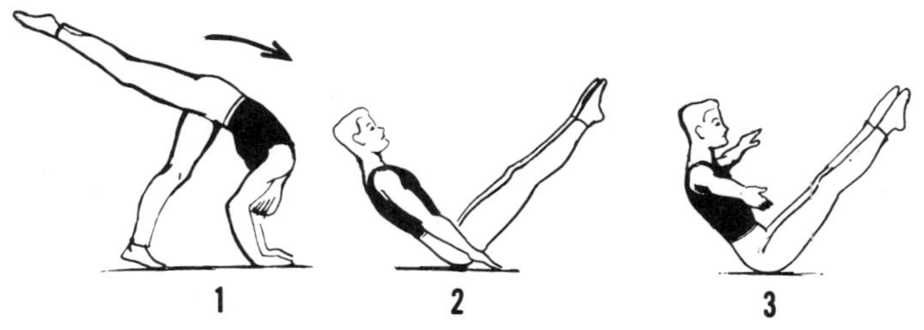

Fig. 3–16. Forward Roll to a "V" Sit.

have served the purpose of lowering the head and shoulders to the floor, the hands are shifted forward to the floor again to stop the rotation before the legs contact the floor (2). The legs are kept straight throughout the roll. Once the motion has been stopped the arms may, or may not, be taken off the floor and held out to the side in a horizontal position (3). HOLD this "V" sit for at least two seconds.

9. Backward Roll to Chest Roll Down (Fig. 3–17). This stunt is started by lowering the legs to the floor from the "V" sit and then bobbing forward with the trunk until the chest touches the legs.

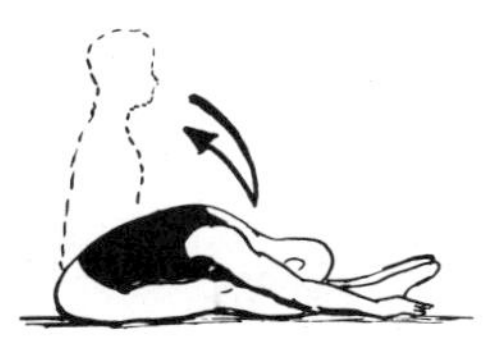

Fig. 3–17. Bob Preceding a Backward Roll to Chest Roll Down.

This position is not held as it was in the previous routine. The bob forward is used to develop momentum for the backward roll that is executed exactly as a "fish flop," or chest roll down, as described in Chapter 2, page 42.

10. Press to Headstand (Fig. 3–18). A press to a headstand was included in Routine I, but this press is different and harder. It starts from a push-up position, the position in which the chest roll down ended (1). The press starts by bending the arms and placing the front part of the head on the floor in front of the hands. The legs are drawn slowly forward and the hips are raised by pushing hard with the arms (2). As the hips are raised high enough so that the center of gravity is almost over the points of support, the legs are raised slowly to the head balance (3). The balance should

Fig. 3–18. Press to Headstand.

be HELD for at least two seconds. The teaching techniques and spotting are the same as described in Routine I, pages 69 and 70.

11. Roll Forward to Feet from a Headstand. This stunt is executed in the same way as described in Routine I, pages 70–71, Fig. 3–8.

12. Step Forward and Pivot 90° to the Left. As the roll is completed to the feet, the performer steps forward on the right foot, pivots 90° to the left, raises the left leg horizontally forward, and lifts the arms sideways to about shoulder height. This is the same connecting movement illustrated in Fig. 3–9 except that the turn is only 90° instead of 180°.

13. Run, Roundoff. Refer to Chapter 2, pages 37–38.

14. Straddle Jump Touching Toes (Fig. 3–19). The roundoff preceding this should be fast and lively so that a good high rebound results. In the air the legs are straddled and raised forward and upward to a horizontal position. The trunk leans forward and the hands reach for the toes (1). From this position the legs are lowered quickly for a stationary balanced landing with the knees bent and the arms horizontally to the side (2).

TEACHING TECHNIQUES. This leap in the air can be practiced on the trampoline or from a stationary standing position.

Fig. 3–19. Straddle Jump Touching Toes.

III. INTERMEDIATE ROUTINE

This routine may follow the floor pattern diagrammed or be performed forward and backward in a straight line on a row of mats by making two minor adjustments. To stay in a straight line Stunt 3, the roll forward to the knees, should be done without the quarter

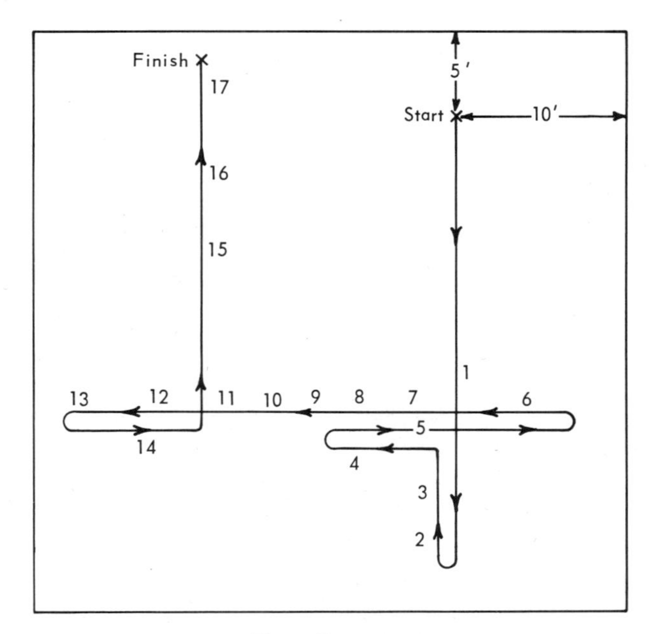

Floor Pattern.

turn to the left, and Stunt 14 should be done with a 180° turn instead of only 90 degrees. If the opening run covers no more than 15 feet, this routine can be performed on a 40′ row of mats. To follow the floor pattern given the gymnast starts by walking about five feet into the area with the boundary line on his left approximately ten feet away.

ABBREVIATED DESCRIPTION

1. Run, front handspring, diving forward roll
2. Pivot 180° to a Swedish fall, lower the leg, and straighten the arms
3. Forward roll from the push up position with a quarter-turn left to the knees
4. Headspring from the knees
5. Backward roll to a chest roll down to a knee stand
6. Press to a handstand with bent arms and bent legs (HOLD)
7. Roll forward from the handstand to the feet
8. Scissor kick
9. Front-scale (HOLD)
10. Kick to momentary handstand
11. Forward roll from the handstand to a half-lever (HOLD)
12. Snap up (or kip up), diving forward roll
13. Straddle jump touching toes
14. Backward roll to momentary handstand, step down with the left foot then the right foot, pivot 90° to the right
15. Run, roundoff
16. Half-pirouette
17. Headspring

DETAILED DESCRIPTION

1. Run, Front Handspring, Diving Forward Roll. Refer to Chapter 2, pages 45, 46, and 47 and to page 66 of this chapter.

2. Pivot 180° to a Swedish Fall. As the forward roll is completed the gymnast stands up rapidly and pivots 180° on one foot. The pivot is started before the performer reaches a balanced standing position so that the Swedish fall becomes part of the pivot. The fall itself is performed in the same manner as described in Routine I, page 66, with one leg raised, the back arched, the head up, and the arms bent so that the chest almost touches the floor. From this position the arms are straightened and the leg lowered to the front support position.

3. Forward Roll from Front Support with a Quarter-Turn to Knees (Fig. 3–20). If the hips are permitted to sag rapidly into an arched position (1), the reaction will be for them to rebound upward. As

Fig. 3–20. Forward Roll from Front Support with a Quarter-Turn to Knees.

this occurs the feet thrust off the floor, the hips are raised in a pike, the arms are bent, and the head is tucked for a forward roll (2). The legs are kept straight during the first part of the roll, but as they approach the floor they are bent and the knees allowed to drop sideways to the mat, to the left in this routine (3). The roll is not completed to the feet, as is usually done, but to the insteps, lower legs, and knees. The arms reach forward at about shoulder level during the second part of the roll (4).

4. Headspring. This stunt is described and illustrated in Chapter 2, pages 39–41. In this routine it starts from the knees so is somewhat harder. Because of this the first part of the headspring will probably be in slow motion. The rapid body extension and arm thrust will be the same as usual, however. Actually, in this routine the headspring does not have to be completed to a balanced landing as the next stunt, which is a backward roll, can be executed even though the headspring finishes in a slightly off-balanced position.

5. Backward Roll, Chest Roll Down to a Knee Stand (Fig. 3–21). The headspring preceding should be completed in an arched position if possible so that this stunt can start with a straight leg sitdown. The first part of the stunt is the same as a backward exten-

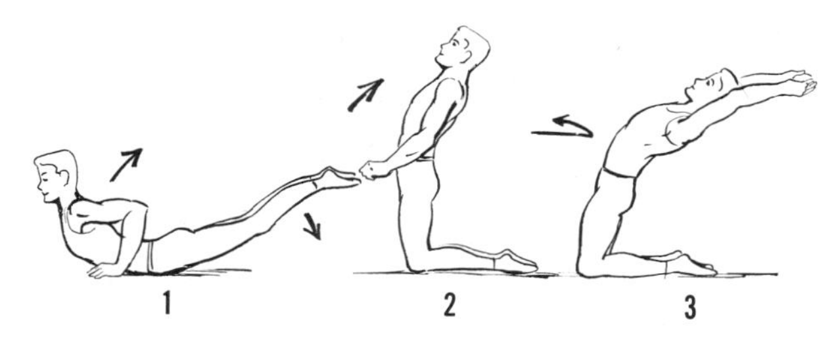

Fig. 3–21. Backward Roll, Chest Roll Down to a Knee Stand.

sion roll, pages 38–39, and the fish flop, pages 42 and 43. As the chest roll down is completed, the back must arch a great deal and the hands must thrust hard off the floor (1). If the momentum from the roll down and the thrust off the floor are both sufficient, and if the knees are bent as they contact the floor, this movement should end in a knee stand (2). In this knee stand the arms are raised overhead and the body is arched backward (3).

Teaching Techniques. This stunt definitely requires back flexibility. Pushing up into a "bridge" will help develop this quality. The last part of the stunt can be practiced separately, starting from a rocking motion in a prone position on the mat. As the student rocks back and forth, the arch can gradually be increased and the arm thrust can be practiced until he can rock all the way to the knee stand.

6. Press to a Handstand with Bent Arms and Bent Legs (Fig. 3–22). From the knee stand the gymnast bends forward and places the hands on the mat close to the knees and slightly wider than shoulder width with the fingers pointing forward and spread (1). The press starts from this position. The arms are bent to approximately a right angle and the hips are raised in the air with the legs curled in close to the body (2). When the center of gravity moves forward over the point of support, the legs are gradually uncurled to

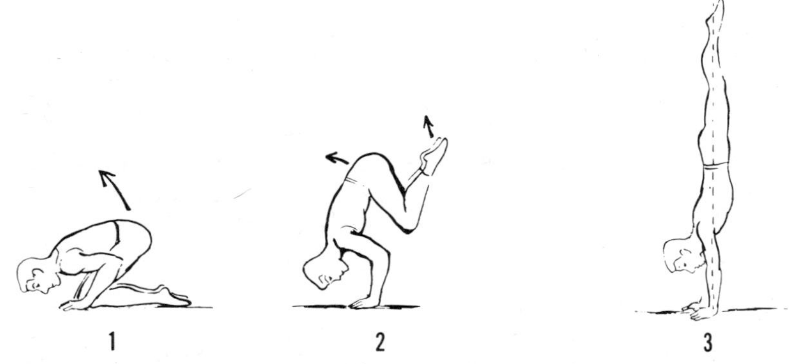

Fig. 3–22. Press to a Handstand with Bent Arms and Bent Legs.

the handstand position (3). There should be very little arch in the hand balance and the shoulders should be fully extended so that there is almost a straight line through the arms and upper body. The head should be back but not in an exaggerated position and the eyes should look at a point slightly in front of the finger tips. The handstand is HELD for at least two seconds.

TEACHING TECHNIQUES. Several different types of headstand presses should precede the handstand press in the teaching progression. Before learning to "press" to a handstand the student should learn to balance in the handstand position. The handstand may be practiced by kicking up into the position from one foot, with a spotter aiding or with the feet resting against a wall. The press to a handstand from a tip-up balance, or frog balance, with the knees resting on the upper arms, is an easier press than the one used in this routine and should be the first type of handstand press attempted by students.

Students should be taught how to control a balance once the position has been reached. An overbalance is counteracted by pushing with the finger tips and forcing the head backward while an underbalance is controlled by lowering the head and rocking onto the heels of the hands. The arms might also have to be bent to help control the underbalance but this could develop into a bad habit and should not be used unless absolutely necessary.

In this routine the press can be made easier for the beginner by straightening the legs and raising the hips before the insteps are removed from the floor. This places the center of gravity in a position almost over the point of support before the press starts. The legs should be bent again as soon as the feet leave the floor. At the start of the press it is very important, as was mentioned earlier, to place the hands close to the knees rather than reaching forward for the hand placement.

7. Roll Forward from a Handstand to the Feet. This stunt is so similar to the roll forward from a headstand to the feet that it will not be described or illustrated. Refer to Fig. 3–8 in Routine I. During the first part of the stunt, in which the body is allowed to fall off balance, the arms bend and the head starts to tuck so that the back of the head can be lowered to the mat to start the roll.

8. Scissor Kick (Fig. 3–23). As the gymnast rolls to a standing position from the handstand, a step forward is taken with either leg. In this routine it will be described with the left leg forward. The right leg and both arms swing vigorously forward and upward (1). At the top of the leg swing the left leg springs off the floor (2). The right leg then starts downward as the left leg is raised forward and upward. The legs pass each other in a scissoring mo-

Fig. 3–23. Scissor Kick.

tion somewhere in the air as the arms swing sideward and downward (3). The landing is on the right leg (4). This movement is similar to the old-fashioned "scissors" used in high jumping.

9. Front Scale (Fig. 3–24). The movement after the scissor kick is forward with a step onto the left leg. The weight is placed onto this leg as the trunk leans forward and the right leg raises back-

Fig. 3–24. Front Scale.

ward. The arms at this time are close to the sides of the body (1). The trunk and leg motion continues until a horizontal position is reached with a slight arch from the head to the right foot. The supporting leg, which may have been very slightly bent at the start, is now perfectly straight. During this movement the arms circle downward, forward, and upward until they are held obliquely forward in approximately a horizontal position (2). This position is HELD for at least two seconds.

TEACHING TECHNIQUES. This movement should be practiced over and over until it can be done with control. Far too often a nearly perfect performance in other respects is weakened by an unsteady scale. It may be practiced, in part, by starting from a hand and knee position on the floor. One leg and the head are raised so that there is an arch from head to foot and then the arms are also raised. This is called a knee scale. To aid in practicing the regular scale the hands may be rested on the edge of a table, or the trampoline, or supported by a partner's hands. The scale may also be done facing a wall so the finger tips can be placed on the wall. These techniques are used to eliminate the problem of balance so that the student may concentrate on attaining the correct body position.

10. Kick to a Momentary Handstand (Fig. 3–25). From the scale the trunk is lowered and the right leg raised so that the hands can be placed on the floor close to the left foot in the position described previously for a handstand (1). The arched position from the head to the right foot should be maintained if possible, but probably the body will have to be piked slightly and the support leg will have to be bent. The arms are kept perfectly straight, the head is back, and the shoulders lean forward over the hands. It takes only a very small push off the left leg to raise the body to a handstand from this starting position. The right leg reaches the handstand position almost immediately after the left leg pushes off the floor. As the left leg is raised to join the right leg, the shoulders shift backward over the points of support. In the balance the body should be in a slight arch with almost a straight line formed between the arms and trunk (2). As the previous handstand in this routine was held, and because the following stunt is also a held position, this handstand should not be held. There should be a momentary pause, however, to indicate control. The modern trend is for few complete stops in an exercise.

Fig. 3–25. Kick to a Momentary Handstand.

11. Forward Roll from a Handstand to a Half-Lever (Fig. 3–26). This is a similar movement to the forward roll to "V" sit, Fig. 3–16, which also involves a stop in a balance position before the roll is completed. From the handstand the arms are bent and the head tucked so that the shoulders and upper back can be lowered to the floor. The legs are dropped backward in a pike so that the center of gravity moves only very slightly forward in the direction of the roll (1). As soon as the weight rests on the upper back, the hands are shifted to a point on the floor almost under the hips. By the time the roll has progressed to the buttocks the finger tips and thumbs have been placed on the floor (2). As the legs continue downward toward the mat and the upper body moves forward to a vertical position the arms straighten and lift the buttocks off the floor so that a half-lever, or "L" lever, is held on the thumbs and finger tips (3). The feet and legs should not make contact with the floor but should remain in the air as the buttocks are lifted off the ground. This position should be HELD for at least two seconds.

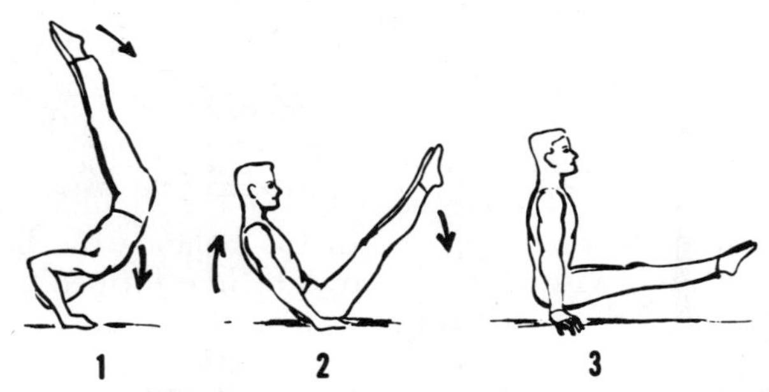

Fig. 3–26. Forward Roll from a Handstand to a Half-Lever.

TEACHING TECHNIQUES. The half-lever should be practiced by pushing up from a sitting position on the floor to develop the finger, arm, and abdominal strength necessary to execute the stunt from a forward roll. It may also be practiced on the floor parallel bars. It is easier for some students in this way because the bars may be gripped tightly to aid in holding the position. To make the half-lever easier during practice, one or both legs may be bent so that the abdominal muscles can be gradually strengthened to permit the straight leg "L" position. One of the most common mistakes in performing the half-lever in this particular routine is to roll forward too fast so that the feet hit the floor before the buttocks are lifted off the ground. A partner may be used to assist in slowing down the roll so that the "L" lever can be accomplished as described.

12. Kip-Up (or Snap-Up), Diving Forward Roll. The buttocks and legs are lowered to the floor from the half-lever and then the kip-up is executed as described in Chapter 2, pages 43–45. Refer also to page 66 for the diving forward roll.

13. Straddle Jump Touch Toes. This stunt has already been described in Routine II, pages 78–79, where it was used as the last stunt in the routine. In this routine the spring for the jump comes immediately as the legs are straightened from the previous forward roll and, on the landing from the straddle jump, the performer immediately sits back off balance for the following stunt.

14. Backward Extension Roll, Step Down, Pivot 90° to the Right (Fig. 3–27). The first part of this stunt is exactly the same as the backward extension roll included in Chapter 2, pages 38–39. From the handstand position (1) the feet are lowered quickly to the floor

Fig. 3–27. Backward Extension Roll, Step Down, Pivot 90° to the Right.

one at a time, first the left and then the right (2). As the right foot touches the floor, the weight is placed on it and the performer pivots 90° clockwise. The left leg raises forward and the arms raise sideways to about shoulder height (3).

15. Run, Roundoff. Refer to Chapter 2, pages 37–38.

16. Half-Pirouette. This is nothing more than a half-turn in the air as the gymnast rebounds from the roundoff. It should be as high as possible with the body straight and the arms stretched above the head. This is included to give the impression of height to the dismount series.

17. Headspring. As the performer lands out of the half-pirouette he bends forward quickly into the headspring. The headspring is the same as the one described in Chapter 2, pages 39–41, although it is somewhat more difficult because of the preceding combination of stunts. It should be finished in an arched back landing.

IV. LOW ADVANCED ROUTINE

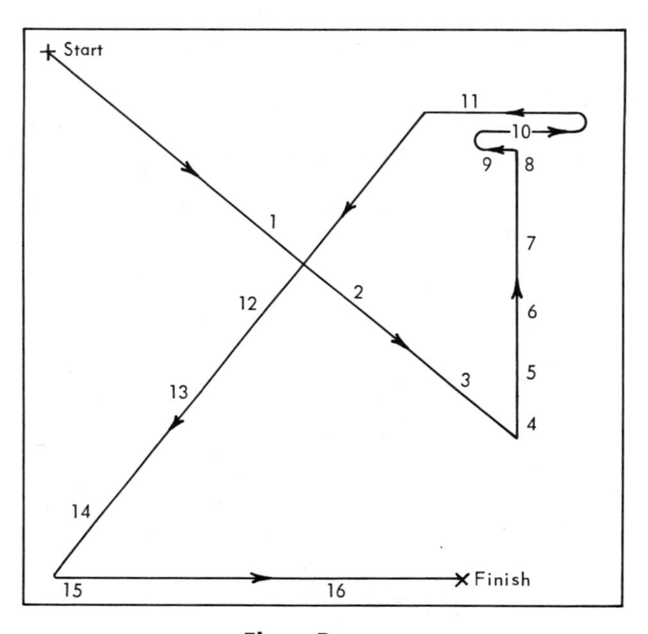

Floor Pattern.

The floor pattern diagrammed works very well when this exercise is performed in a regulation area. It would be very easy to go out of bounds during the opening series or during the series that starts with a front somersault if the approach runs are too long. Neither of these should be over 15 feet. Three to five steps are all that are really needed. The exercise starts in one corner with the first series moving along a line slightly to the left of the diagonal. This routine may also be performed on a row of mats for practice purposes. By pirouetting in the first handstand and by making adjustments in the number of degrees of turn in other places the exercise can easily be performed forward and backward along one straight line.

ABBREVIATED DESCRIPTION

1. Run, handspring with a step out, followed by another handspring step out (left leg forward)
2. Cartwheel off the left foot
3. Side scale on the left leg (HOLD)
4. From the scale, kick to a momentary handstand with a one-eighth turn to the left
5. Roll forward from the handstand to a straddle stand with the trunk bent forward
6. Press a handstand with straight arms and straight legs (HOLD)
7. Lower the head to the floor, headspring, diving forward roll
8. Swedish fall, turn 180° to splits (HOLD)
9. Neck spring with a half-twist to a front support position
10. Move the left leg forward to a half-squat, two and a half pinwheels to a rear support
11. Backward roll to a momentary handstand, step down one foot at a time, pivot 135° to the right
12. Run, front somersault, diving forward roll
13. Step forward, leap to a handstand, and jump forward in the handstand position
14. Straight leg forward roll
15. Step forward and pivot 135° to the left
16. Run, roundoff, back handspring, arched jump

DETAILED DESCRIPTION

1. Run, Handspring Walkout, Handspring Walkout. Refer to Chapter 2, pages 52–53. In this routine the landing is on the right leg with the left leg forward in both handsprings.

2. Cartwheel. The cartwheel is also described in Chapter 2, pages 35–37. As the left foot steps forward out of the second handspring walkout, it is used as the takeoff foot for the cartwheel. The left hand is placed on the floor first, followed by the right. The landing is first on the right leg then the left with the arms stretched overhead.

3. Side Scale (Fig. 3–28). As the left leg contacts the floor on the landing from the cartwheel, the weight is placed on it but the toe of the right foot maintains contact with the ground momentarily to aid in control of the balance. The left leg may be slightly bent at this time (1). The trunk is leaned to the left, the left leg is straightened, and the right leg is raised (2). The left arm remains stretched above the head but the right arm is lowered to the left passing in front of the face, then backward and upward until it

Fig. 3–28. Side Scale.

rests along the right side of the body. This whole body movement is to the side and stops when the trunk and right leg are approximately horizontal. Actually the head and foot should be slightly higher than the hips (3). The right hip remains high so that the line between the hips is vertical rather than horizontal. The side scale should be HELD for at least two seconds.

TEACHING TECHNIQUES. The front scale, pages 84–85, is much easier so can be used as a lead-up. When learning the side scale, the hand that is stretched above head may be placed on a table, trampoline, in a partner's hand, or against the wall to provide stability as the correct position is practiced. The common mistake is to allow the right hip to rotate downward into a front scale position rather than keeping it directly above the left hip.

4. Kick Sideward to a Momentary Handstand (Fig. 3–29). This movement from the side scale to a handstand is very similar to the first part of a cartwheel. The right leg is raised, the upper body is

Fig. 3–29. Kick Sideward to a Momentary Handstand.

lowered, the left leg is bent slightly, and the left hand reaches for the floor as if for a cartwheel (1). Just before the left hand contacts the floor, the left leg thrusts the hips and right leg upward and over the left hand to a handstand position (2). In this routine the right hand is not placed in continuation of the line of movement, as is usually the case, but off at a slight angle so that one-eighth of a turn to the left is executed during the kick to the handstand. It would be very difficult to hold this balance, but fortunately a held position is not called for in this exercise. The performer should stretch momentarily to a tall handstand position and then immediately fall forward to start the next stunt.

5. Roll Forward from a Handstand to a Straddle Stand (Fig. 3–30). As considerable speed needs to be developed for this forward roll, the gymnast should start to fall off-balance in a straight body position. The arms bend slightly and the head is lowered between the

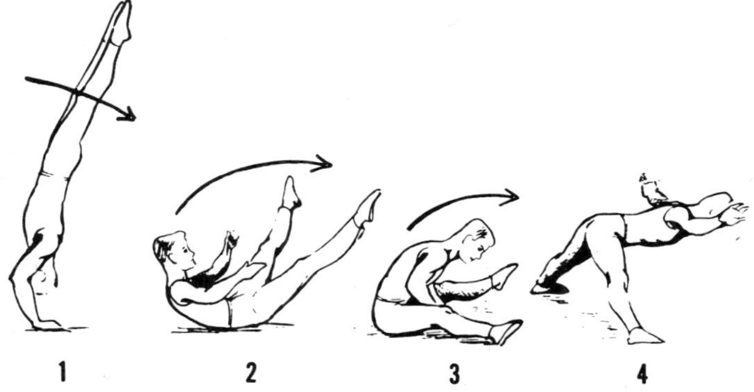

Fig. 3–30. Roll Forward from a Handstand to a Straddle Stand.

arms (1). As the fall progresses, the body is piked to start the roll and then during the roll the legs are spread wide apart (2). The critical point in this stunt is reached just as the heels contact the floor. At this time the head and upper body pike forward rapidly and the hands, which were shifted during the roll to a position by the crotch, thrust off the floor from between the legs (3). The legs are kept perfectly straight during the entire movement, which finishes in a straddle stand with the body bent forward and the arms sideways at about shoulder height (4).

Teaching Techniques. The finish of this stunt is the same as a straddle leg forward roll. The straddle leg roll should be learned first. It starts from a straddle stand and finishes in a straddle stand. The method of execution and the critical timing point are the same as described above. Flexibility is essential. The performer must be able to spread the legs quite wide apart, but even more important, he must be able to flex the body into a tight pike position. Flexibility exercises must be practiced to develop these qualities.

6. Press a Handstand with Straight Arms and Legs (Fig. 3–31). This stunt is similar to the bent arm bent leg press included in Routine III. It is officially rated as a more difficult press than the

Fig. 3–31. Press a Handstand with Straight Arms and Legs.

previous one, although for some quite flexible individuals it is often easier. From the straddle stand the hands are placed on the floor only slightly in front of the toes and then the shoulders are leaned well in front of the hands (1). The combination of the hand placement and the shoulder lean places the center of gravity almost over the points of support at the start of the movement (2). The shoulders are shifted back over the hands as the hips are raised during the press. Keeping the legs spread wide apart until the hips are raised quite high will also help to keep the center of gravity above the point of support. The legs are raised to the vertical position and then joined together to complete the press to the handstand (3). This handstand should be HELD for at least two seconds.

TEACHING TECHNIQUES. A prerequisite for this stunt is a well-controlled handstand. The bent arm press is also used as a lead-up. The most important things to learn are the shoulder lean and the straight arm position. This can be practiced with the legs in a tucked position thus making the press easier. Similarly, a straight leg position can be practiced during the press without keeping the arms straight. Students who have wrists that lack flexibility might have to turn the fingers out to the side as the hands are placed on the floor. This will permit a better shoulder lean but will make the balance harder to hold as the press is completed.

SPOTTING. A partner can assist in the learning of this stunt by standing directly behind the performer and placing his leg so that the performer's shoulder can be leaned against it. He then helps pull the performer's hips up into position.

7. Headspring, Diving Forward Roll. From the handstand the arms are bent so that the front part of the head can be placed on the floor slightly in front of the hands. The legs are lowered to at least a right angle pike and maybe slightly tighter. In this position the weight is allowed to fall off-balance and the headspring is executed as described in Chapter 2, pages 39–42. Also refer to Chapter 3, page 66, for the diving forward roll.

8. Swedish Fall, Turn to Splits (Fig. 3–32). The Swedish fall, or prone fall with the arms bent and one leg raised, is executed exactly as described in Routine I, pages 66–67. In this routine the right leg is raised (1). As the arms are straightened, the raised leg is swung forward counterclockwise (2) and placed on the floor almost directly in front of the hands (3). The trunk is turned to the left as the leg moves forward so that by the time the crotch has been lowered into the splits the body has made a 180° turn and is facing the

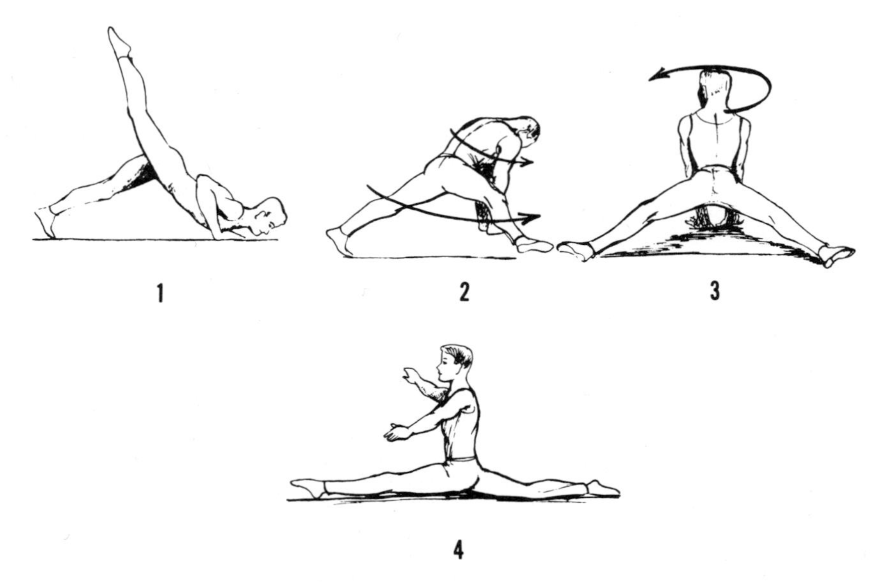

Fig. 3–32. Swedish Fall, Turn to Splits.

opposite direction from the one in which the prone fall was started. In the splits the arms are raised to the side about shoulder height (4). This position is HELD for at least two seconds and is the third, and last, hold in this exercise.

TEACHING TECHNIQUES. Almost everyone can learn to do the splits, but it takes considerable perseverance for some. Failure to stretch each day will probably result in the splits never being learned. Gradual daily stretching is necessary but trying to progress too fast will actually slow down the learning process. Practice starts by sliding the feet farther and farther apart from a standing position. During this learning process part of the weight can be supported on the hands as the crotch is lowered toward the floor.

9. Neck Spring with Half-Twist to Front Support (Fig. 3–33). From the splits the trunk is turned 90° to the right and the hands are placed on the floor in front of the crotch. The hips are gradually raised and the feet drawn toward each other (1). As the hips get higher (2), the legs are placed together and the head is tucked under so that the weight rests on the back of the head and shoulders (3). From this tight pike position the hips are permitted to rock forward a short distance as in the regular snap-up. (Refer to Chap-

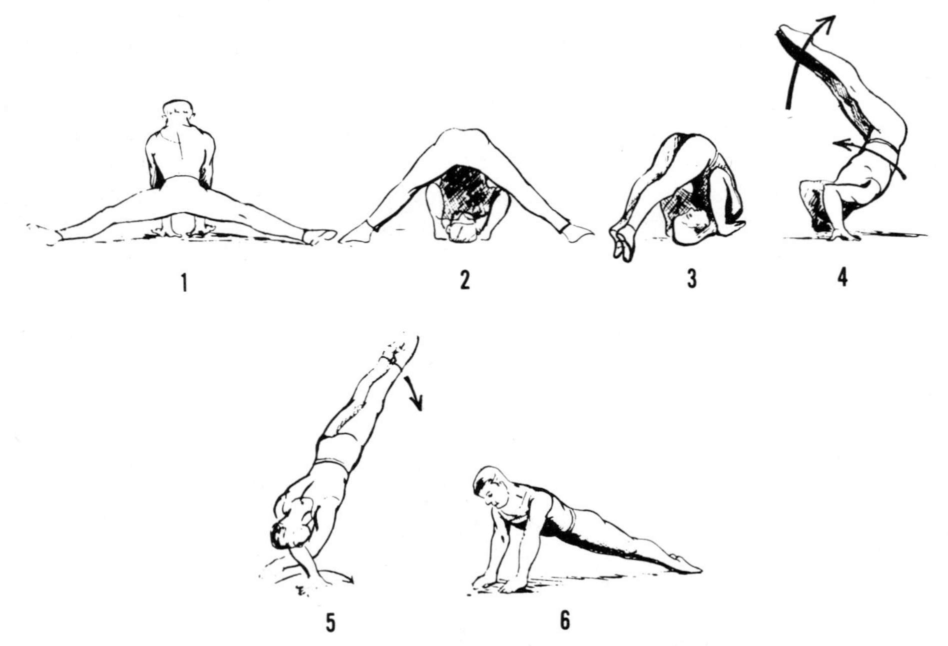

Fig. 3–33. Neck Spring with Half-Twist to Front Support.

ter 2, pages 43–45.) Before they have progressed very far the kipping motion starts. The body extension is directed straighter in the air than for a regular snap-up. This is essential so that sufficient time is given to complete the half-twist before the feet drop to the mat. The twist starts at the same time as the kipping motion by pushing harder with one hand and by rolling the hips over (4). If the body extension was directed high enough and if the twist was executed quickly (5), the feet will drop to the mat with the body in a push-up position. The hands have to be quickly shifted as the twist is executed (6). Upon the completion of this stunt the performer has made another 180° turn.

TEACHING TECHNIQUES. The snap-up is a good lead-up for this stunt but not necessarily a step that must be accomplished before the half-twist is tried. A soft mat should be used during the learning stages and at first the stunt should be practiced from a sitting position with a partial backward roll to the kip position. It is much easier to keep the hips high, where they should be, when practiced in this way. The most common mistake, especially when done from a forward roll as in this routine, is to let the hips roll forward too far and be too low when the body extension starts. Some students accomplish this stunt much quicker when they are told to think of it as a "shoot to handstand with a fast half-pirouette and then a straight body fall to the floor" than when they think of it as a "kip-up with a half-twist."

SPOTTING. A spotter can aid very easily in this stunt. If the twist is to the left, the spotter stands by the performer's right side, reaches over the top of him while he is in the tight pike position, and grasps both of his thighs. The direction of the extension and the half-twist can both be easily controlled by lifting and turning the thighs. The legs can also be lowered to the floor to prevent possible injury to the toes and feet.

10. Pinwheels to a Rear Support (Fig. 3–34). As the feet drop to the mat following the previous stunt, the hips should sag and then immediately be raised upward again. Both feet spring off the floor as the hips are raised. The left leg is bent and drawn forward to a half-squat position while the right leg is raised backward and upward (1). The pinwheels, or single leg circles, which have already been described and illustrated in Routine II, page 75, start from this position with the right leg circling forward in a counterclockwise direction. In this routine two and one-half pinwheels are executed. As the right leg starts forward after completing two full

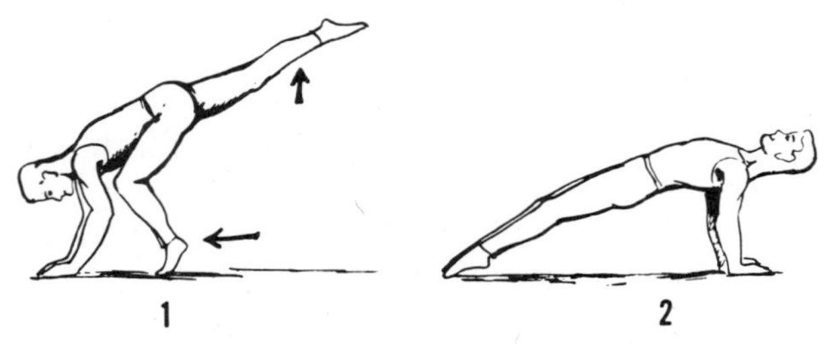

Fig. 3–34. Pinwheels to a Rear Support.

circles most of the weight is shifted to the left arm as the right leg passes under the right arm (2). The left leg pushes vigorously off the floor and both legs are thrust forward into a rear support (3).

TEACHING TECHNIQUES. At first the kip-up with a half-twist should be omitted so that the movement from the front support to the pinwheels can receive the performer's complete concentration. The combination of the kip-up with half-twist and the immediate movement into the pinwheels is a very difficult one and will have to be practiced a great deal to develop continuity.

11. Backward Extension Roll, Step-Down, Pivot 135° to the Right. This same combination is included in Routine III, Fig. 3–27, except that there is a 135° pivot in this routine instead of only 90°.

12. Run, Front Somersault, Diving Forward Roll. Refer to Chapter 2, pages 47–49, for the front somersault and to Chapter 3, page 66, for the diving roll.

13. Leap to a Handstand and Jump Forward in a Handstand Position (Fig. 3–35). This can be a very spectacular stunt if executed well. The gymnast should come to his feet quickly after the diving forward roll and take one step forward with either foot (1). He then springs forward off this foot and dives to a handstand (2) (3). If the arms are kept straight and the shoulders extended, he will rebound forward a foot or two to another handstand (4). Actually, neither handstand is held. The first one should be slightly underbalanced and, because the legs are probably moving faster than the shoulders during the rebound, the second one might very well be slightly overbalanced.

TEACHING TECHNIQUES. Practice for this stunt should start from a standing position with a very small leap into the first handstand. The distance and height can gradually increase. Only after considerable practice in this way should it be tried following a diving

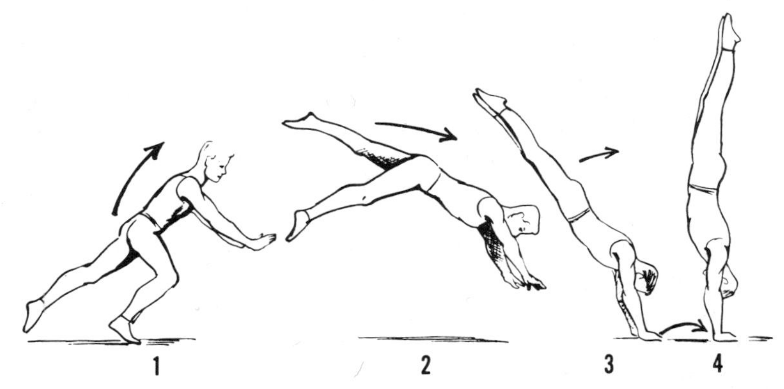

Fig. 3–35. Leap to a Handstand and Jump Forward in a Handstand Position.

roll. The stunt that follows, in this routine, is a forward roll. During the learning process the roll out of the second handstand can be started early as a safety measure.

SPOTTING. A spotter should stand on the side of the performer as he leaps forward and watch for too much of an overbalance. This can be prevented by reaching in behind the legs in the handstand position.

14. Straight Leg Forward Roll (Fig. 3–36). This stunt follows the same principles as the straddle leg forward roll that was performed from a handstand earlier in this routine (Fig. 3–30), but the legs are kept together in this roll. The roll is started as the performer falls forward out of the handstand. The head is tucked and the body is piked (1). As soon as the weight is on the back, the hands are shifted quickly to a position on each side of the hips. As the roll

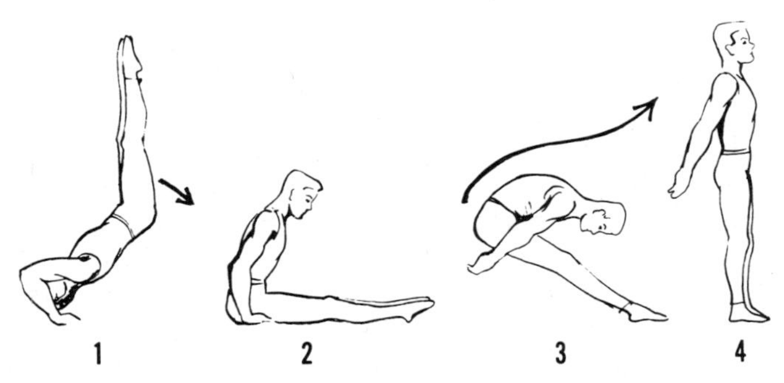

Fig. 3–36. Straight Leg Forward Roll.

progresses to the point where the feet contact the floor, the hands must thrust off the floor from their position by the hips, and the head and upper body must be whipped forward rapidly into a tight pike (2). Students who possess a reasonable amount of flexibility will be able to roll to the feet with perfectly straight legs (3). As the center of gravity shifts forward over the feet, the body is straightened to a vertical position (4).

TEACHING TECHNIQUES. Straddle leg forward rolls from a straddle stand to straddle stand are the best lead-up. Next, the straight leg roll with the legs together should be practiced from a standing position rather than from a handstand. Considerable push can be given from the feet to develop momentum when it is done in this way. Before some students will be able to accomplish this stunt, they will have to develop better trunk flexion and longer hamstring muscles on the back of the thighs.

15. Step Forward, Pivot 135° to the Left. This stunt should be quite familiar by this time as it has been included several times previously. In this case the step forward is with the right foot and the pivot is to the left. The left leg may, or may not, be raised forward before starting the run for the dismount. As it is the second time in the routine that this connecting move has been used, probably it is best to place the left foot alongside the right and then to raise onto the toes of both feet before the dismount run.

16. Run, Roundoff, Back Handspring, Arched Jump. The roundoff and the back handspring are included in Chapter 2, pages 37–38 and 49–52. The arched jump was illustrated in Routine I of this chapter, Fig. 3–10.

V. ADVANCED ROUTINE

The length of the run needed for the tumbling series that start with Stunts 1, 8, and 15 might change the floor pattern diagrammed considerably. Those requiring more than five steps for these series might have trouble staying in-bounds and may have to vary the pattern somewhat. To perform this routine forward and backward in a straight line so that it may be performed on a row of mats involves only a few minor adjustments. A quarter-pirouette in the handstand, Stunt 5; a change in the amount of pivot in Stunt 7; and a forward roll to the knees without a quarter-twist, Stunt 12; will bring about the change in pattern.

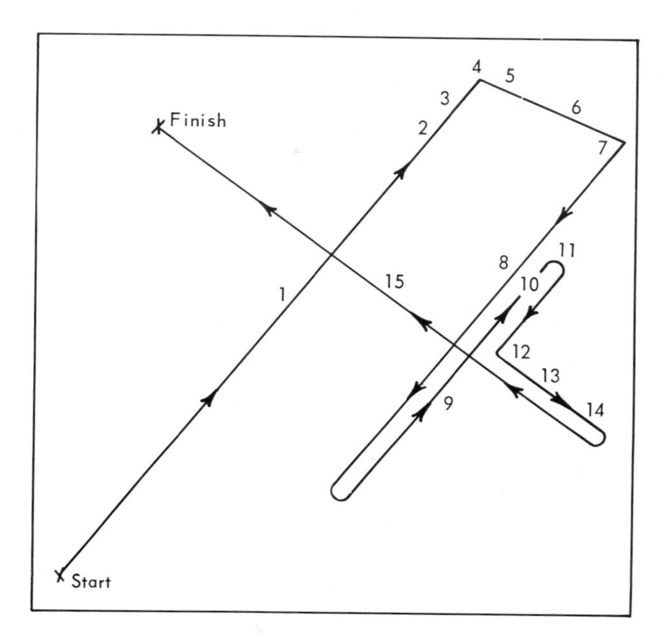

Floor Pattern.

ABBREVIATED DESCRIPTION

1. Run, front handspring, front somersault, diving forward roll
2. Headspring to sitting position with legs straddled, lower chest to floor (HOLD)
3. Turn the trunk 90° to the left to the splits
4. One-arm elbow lever on the right arm
5. Press a handstand (HOLD)
6. Straight leg forward roll
7. Step forward with the left foot, pivot 90° to the right
8. Run, roundoff, back dive with a half-twist to a forward roll, headspring
9. Back handspring step out with half-turn, front handspring
10. Step forward, hop with a half-turn to a front scale (HOLD), return to a stand
11. Back handspring, straddle jump touch toes, headspring
12. Forward roll with a quarter-turn left to the knees
13. Chest roll, 180° turn to another chest roll ("Lind")
14. Squat through to a sitting position, "Valdez" to momentary handstand, lower legs to stand
15. Run, roundoff, back handspring, back somersault

DETAILED DESCRIPTION

1. Run, Front Handspring, Front Somersault, Diving Forward Roll. The combination of the front handspring and front somersault is included in Chapter 2, pages 56 and 57. In this routine, however, the landing for the somersault is on two feet rather than one foot.

2. Headspring to Straddle Seat, Lower Chest to Floor (Fig. 3–37). The start of this stunt is no different from a regular headspring (1), but the body extension during the kipping motion is never quite completed and during the latter stages the legs start to straddle (2). The heels make contact first (3) and then the buttocks drop to the floor a fraction of a second later as the upper body

Fig. 3–37. Headspring to Straddle Seat, Lower Chest to Floor.

bends forward rapidly. This forward body movement prevents a jar as the buttocks contact the floor. The trunk continues forward until the chest and face rest on the floor. The arms stretch sideways and also rest on the floor (4). Some performers grasp their feet to help hold their trunk down and also to help hold the legs in a wide straddle. This is a flexibility pose and should be HELD at least two seconds.

TEACHING TECHNIQUES. This stunt, as a good number of floor exercise stunts, should be learned on a tumbling mat. If a double thickness of mat is used and if the student can execute a good headspring, there should be no problem with the headspring to the straddle seat as it is not a difficult movement. The problem will be to accomplish the flexibility position that follows. It will take practice day after day for some gymnasts to develop the required flexibility. A partner may aid by pushing down easily on the upper back during practice periods. If this position can not be held, it would be wise to bob forward as low as possible and then immediately shift into the splits, that are to follow, and hold them instead.

Fig. 3–38. Turn Left to Splits.

3. Turn Left to Splits (Fig. 3–38). From the straddle seat the trunk is raised to a vertical position and turned 90° to the left at the same time. The position of the legs and feet do not change, except to be spread farther apart. One or both hands might have to be placed on the floor in front of the crotch to support weight during this change of position; however, a really flexible individual can make the shift without the hands by taking a little bounce upward as he raises the trunk and turns to the left. To vary this split from the one in the previous routine the right hand is placed on the floor by the crotch and the left arm raised above the head. In this exercise the splits should not be held but demonstrated only momentarily as they are preceded by a held position as well as being followed by one. Refer to pages 93 and 94 for teaching techniques.

4. One-Arm Elbow Lever (Fig. 3–39). From the split the trunk is turned to the right and the right hand placed on the floor in a position that enables the right elbow to be placed on the abdomen just in front of the right hip (1). The trunk is leaned forward over this hand and the hips are raised (2). The legs are gradually drawn together as the back is arched into the elbow lever position (3). This position should be held momentarily to demonstrate control before starting the next stunt.

TEACHING TECHNIQUES. A two-arm elbow lever, with both elbows resting in the abdomen, can be used as a lead-up stunt. The

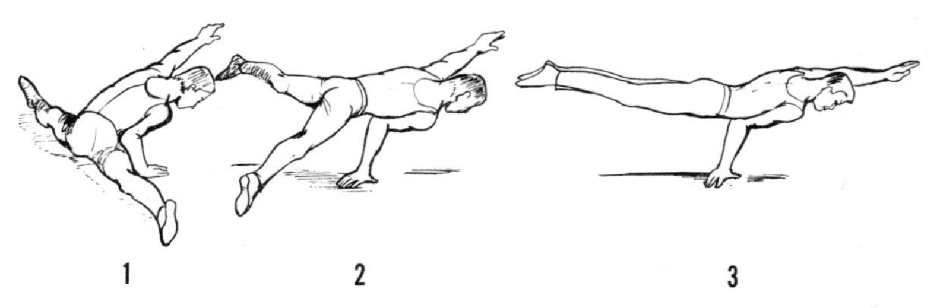

Fig. 3–39. One-Arm Elbow Lever.

one-arm elbow lever is learned from a kneeling position with both hands on the floor. The right hand is placed close to the knees so the right elbow can rest on the abdomen. The left hand is placed about two or three feet in front of the knees and is kept on the floor as the legs are raised so that it can be used to aid in the balance. It can be raised a few inches off the floor but kept ready to be placed back if needed. In the routine, when the elbow lever is performed from the splits, the left hand may also be placed on the floor, if it is needed. However, it is best to perform the stunt without the aid of the left hand, if possible.

5. Press to a Handstand from an Elbow Lever (Fig. 3–40). From the elbow lever the body is turned to the right, the legs are raised, and the left hand is placed on the floor ready for a handstand (1). The press is done with a straight body but is much easier than most

Fig. 3–40. Press to a Handstand from an Elbow Lever.

straight body presses because the hardest part, raising the body from a horizontal position to an angle of about 45°, is accomplished while the abdomen is still in contact with the elbow. From this point to the handstand there is no substitute for muscle power. As the legs are raised (2), the arms are gradually straightened until the handstand position is reached (3). The balance is HELD for at least two seconds.

TEACHING TECHNIQUES. The best way to practice this press is from a chest roll on a mat. Momentum can be built up by rocking back and forth or from a forward chest roll from a kneeling position. Because the upward movement of the legs and lower body is started from a rolling movement on the mat, the press is much easier. The hands are placed down one on each side of the hips and thrust upward as the legs and hips leave the mat. If the back is arched a great deal during the press, it also makes it easier, but as the press is completed the body should be stretched into a straighter line for the balance. A partner may be used to assist by lifting under the thighs or hips as the press is being learned.

6. Straight-Leg Forward Roll. This stunt was included in the previous routine, pages 97–98.

7. Step Forward, Pivot 90° Right. This connecting move, used to change direction, is used by almost all gymnasts. It is described in Routine I, pages 71 and 72.

8. Run, Roundoff, Back Dive with a Half-Twist to a Forward Roll, Headspring (Fig. 3–41). The roundoff and headspring are both included in Chapter 2, pages 37–38 and 39–41. The back dive with a half-twist is the new stunt in this combination. It starts from the rebound out of the roundoff, and the higher it is done the prettier it will look. The starting movement is much like a throw for a high back handspring out of a roundoff. The twist starts immediately as the arms swing upward and backward and the hips thrust upwards (1). If executed with lots of height, the twist should be almost completed at the top of the arc (2) so that the gymnast can concentrate on finishing with a smooth forward roll to the feet (3) (4).

TEACHING TECHNIQUES. Start from a stand on a mat and leap backward into the forward roll by executing a good part of the twist while the feet are still on the mat. Gradually increase the amount of spring, the arm swing, and the upward hip thrust, and gradually decrease the amount of twist started while the feet are on the floor. After it has been learned from a stand, it can be tried after a roundoff with several extra thicknesses of mats being used.

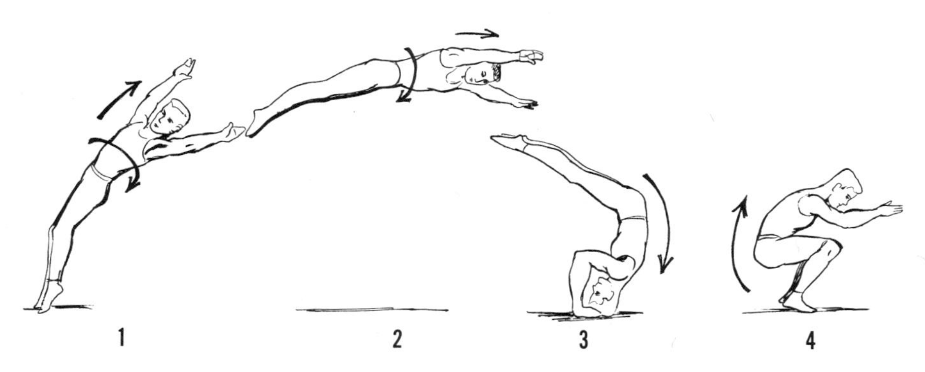

Fig. 3–41. Back Dive with a Half-Twist to a Forward Roll.

SPOTTING. The spotter must spot carefully and be ready to follow the gymnast through the stunt. He stands on the side away from the twist and supports under the hips during the first part of the dive to aid in the upward hip thrust and to be sure the center of gravity is carried over far enough so that the head can be tucked for the roll. Serious neck or back injuries may be caused if the roll is attempted without the hips or legs being high in the air. The spotter also watches for an overspin and reaches in behind the legs to prevent a painful landing on the back.

9. Back Handspring Step Out with Half-Turn to a Front Handspring. The preceding headspring could be finished with an arched back and the arms straight above the head. This position is shown momentarily and then the knees are bent for the start of the back handspring. Both the back and front handsprings are included in Chapter 2, pages 49–52 and 45–47. The connecting move between them is also described on page 53.

10. Step Forward, Hop with a Half-Turn to a Front Scale (Fig. 3–42). As the front handspring is finished there is a step forward on the left foot. The right leg swings forward and upward and the trunk leans backward (1). As the leg reaches the horizontal position, the left leg springs off the floor (2) and the trunk quickly rolls over to face the floor. This is a very quick half-twisting motion that is completed in a front scale position on the left leg with the arms stretched forward (3). The scale is HELD for at least two seconds and then the leg is lowered and the trunk raised with the arms vertically above the head. The back is momentarily arched in this standing position before proceeding to the next stunt (4).

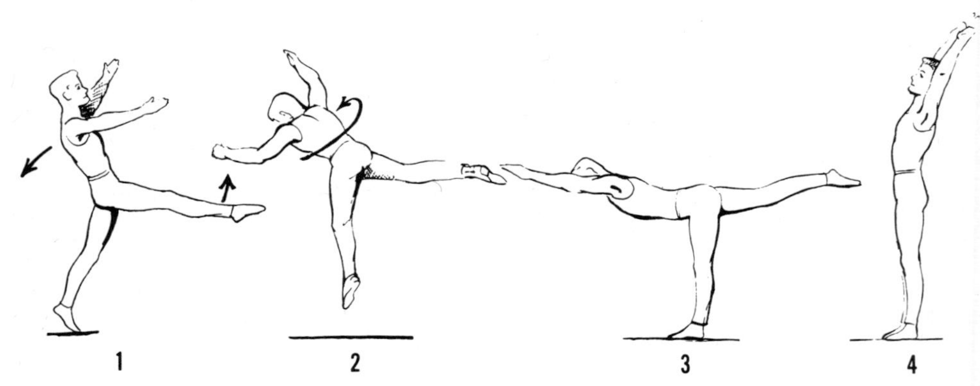

Fig. 3–42. Step Forward, Hop with a Half-Turn to a Front Scale.

TEACHING TECHNIQUES. A step that should be used as a progression between a front scale and this stunt is a "step forward, *pivot* with a half-turn to a front scale." In this lead-up everything is done in the same way except the left foot never leaves the ground but pivots during the half-turn.

11. Back Handspring, Straddle Jump Touch Toes, Headspring. This series involves backward movement, vertical movement, and then forward movement. The three stunts are meant to be put together using a rapid pace and with the straddle jump as high as possible. All three stunts have been described previously. Refer to Chapter 2, pages 49–52 and 39–41, and to the Routine II in this chapter, pages 78–79.

12. Forward Roll with a Quarter-Turn Left to the Knees. Refer to Routine III, pages 80–81, for this stunt.

13. Chest Roll, Half-Turn to Chest Roll, "Lind" (Fig. 3–43). This stunt is named after a former University of Washington gymnast, Alf Lind. The chest roll starts from an exaggerated arch in a knee stand (1). The hands are placed on the floor, one on each side of the hips, during the roll down (2). As the legs and hips start their upward motion the arms push hard and then one is placed flat on the floor (3), thus permitting the shoulder to be tucked under and the head to be turned to the side (4). A quarter-twist results and as the motion continues the points of support change from the hands

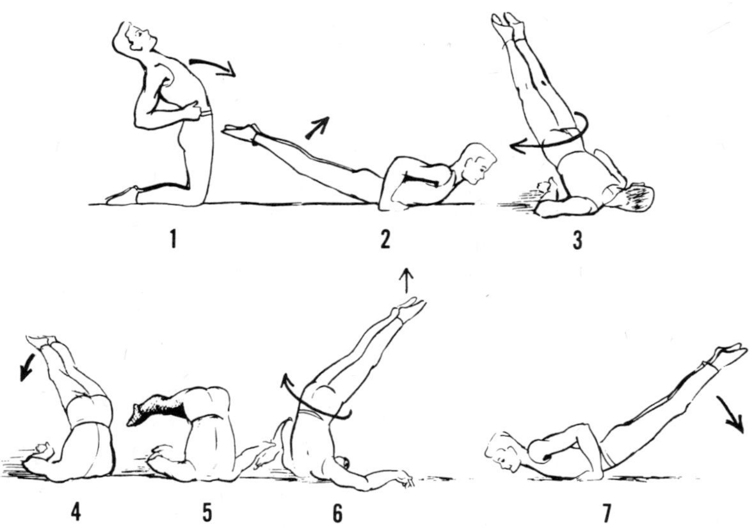

Fig. 3–43. Chest Roll, Half-Turn to Chest Roll, "Lind."

and the chest to the back of the shoulders and the head. At this time the legs drop in a pike but the hips remain high (5). The legs are then thrust upward and the body twisted another quarter-twist (6) so that the weight shifts from the back of the shoulders to the chest for another chest roll down facing the opposite direction from the first one (7). If the right shoulder tucks under after the first chest roll, the left shoulder will tuck under to complete the half-turn for the second chest roll.

Teaching Techniques. This stunt does not take a great amount of physical skill, but it does require a little mental analysis. Some students learn it in a few tries, others will have to be "man-handled" through it until they get the "feel" of the stunt. A partner stands on the right side of the gymnast if the right shoulder is to be tucked under. As the legs raise in the first chest roll, the spotter grasps both legs. He can aid in lifting the legs during the chest roll, initiate the turn, force the legs down in the pike at the appropriate time, raise them again as the second chest roll is started, and slow down the second chest roll to prevent a hard landing. Actually, the spotter can "man-handle" the performer through several slow motion "Linds" until the stunt has been learned.

14. Squat-Through to Sit, Valdez to Momentary Handstand (Fig. 3–44). Refer to Chapter 2, page 43, for the squat-through to a sitting position. In the sitting position the left hand is placed on the floor behind the left hip with the fingers pointing backward, the left leg is bent, and the right arm is held forward at shoulder height (1). The Valdez, which is a kick-up backward to a handstand, starts from this position. The body is flexed forward and the right arm lowered to develop momentum for the stunt. The right leg is then swung upward as the left leg drives hard off the floor (2). The right arm swings upward and then is placed on the floor for the handstand. The left hand pivots 180° on the floor during the movement and ends in the handstand position. The legs are brought together in the air as the body arches up to the handstand (3) (4). The handstand is shown momentarily to demonstrate control and then the legs are lowered slowly in a pike to a stand (5) (6).

Teaching Techniques. An easier but similar stunt that may be used as a lead-up is a kick-up to handstand from the same starting position but using a cartwheel-like motion instead of a back bend motion. This does not take as hard a kick, does not require as much back arch, and is not as blind a stunt as the Valdez. In this lead-up the handstand ends at a 90° angle from the starting position.

Fig. 3–44. Valdez to Momentary Handstand.

SPOTTING. A spotter stands on the straight leg side and grasps this leg as it swings upward. He can aid the gymnast in reaching the handstand or prevent a fall if the stunt is not completed. The spotter plays an important part in the learning of the Valdez.

15. Run, Roundoff, Back Handspring, Back Somersault. This is a very common "dismount," or closing tumbling series, for advanced floor exercise work. The gymnast should summon all his reserve energy and strive for a fast series, a high back somersault, and a balanced landing. These stunts are all included in Chapter 2, pages 37–38, 49–52, and 55–56.

4

Vaulting

The official name for the vaulting event is the "long horse vault." The activity of "vaulting," however, is done over many different types of horses and pieces of equipment. Beginners and intermediates do most of their vaulting over a horse placed crossways. "Vaulting" was considered to be a better title for this chapter than "long horse vault" because as much of the chapter deals with cross horse vaulting as with long horse vaulting.

In the other gymnastic events, as a student becomes more skilled, he progresses to new stunts that are more difficult; that is, he is taught entirely new and different stunts. In vaulting, however, the advanced gymnast performs most of the same vaults that are taught to beginners and intermediates. In this event, rather than introducing entirely new and different stunts, the difficulty of the activity is increased by raising the height of the horse, by changing the type of takeoff board, by using a long horse instead of a cross horse, or by executing the vault in a more spectacular manner.

Vaulting should be one of the first activities to be included in the gymnastic program. The only prerequisite is a basic background in tumbling. Because it takes little upper body strength, and for that matter little lower body strength if a springboard is used, it can be taught to young children. Most eight-year-olds are ready to learn vaulting skills. Older boys who lack upper body strength are more likely to be successful in this event than in most of the others. Because success is important in maintaining interest, this is another reason for introducing the event early. Vaulting is fun. Whereas some students must "learn to like" other events, almost everyone likes to vault the first time they try it. This is still another reason for starting vaulting early. A joyful experience early in the exposure to a new activity is important in bringing about a lasting love for the activity.

VALUES

This is the only event in which a series of stunts can not be performed. In this respect it is a less desirable event than the others but in some respects it has more to offer. Vaulting contributes to the cardiovascular condition of the students if they are kept busy running back and forth rather than standing waiting for a turn. The activity may be likened to a series of wind sprints followed by a high jump or broad jump. The explosive effort needed to propel one's body over the horse develops the basic physical quality of "power." Daring and self-confidence are also developed as students progress from the simple to the more spectacular and dangerous skills.

SAFETY

Only a few of the more important safety precautions are mentioned in this chapter. For other general safety practices the reader should refer to Chapter 1.

1. Mats should be placed so as to cover the entire area where a performer "might" land, not only the area where he is "supposed" to land. A double thickness of mats is very desirable to provide added protection in case of a fall as well as to provide added padding for all landings. The continued jar of the landing often causes leg problems that can be prevented by having adequate padding.
2. Because this event requires a fast run and a much larger area than most gymnastic events it is important to keep the approach area clear. Students working on other events close by should be cautioned not to move into the vaulting area.
3. Spotting is especially important for this event. In other events the dismount usually needs the most careful spotting. In vaulting every stunt is a dismount. Because there is more horizontal movement in vaulting than for most stunts performed in other events, the spotter must be trained to move with the performer as he spots.

RULES

Each gymnast may take two vaults in competition. Both are scored but only the better score counts. The second vault must be taken immediately after the first and may be the same vault or a different one. In the finals of important international meets each competitor must do two different vaults and may have two trials at each one.

Evaluation of the vault begins the moment the reuther board or horse is touched. The gymnast may run around the board and horse once without it counting as a try. A second pass in this way counts as a trial. The board may be placed at any distance from the horse.

Each vault is diagrammed in the rule book and must be executed as diagrammed. Difficulty ratings are also awarded each vault. Vaults not listed must be evaluated by each judge using similar listed ones for comparison. To be classed as a vault there must be a support of one or both hands on the horse. The rule book also designates where the hands are to be placed for each vault. They are listed as either far end or near end vaults. In two cases, one or both hands may be placed in the center section of the horse but, in both cases, the vault involves a turn, and one hand must also be placed on the far end. If the hands are placed too far down the horse for a near end vault or not far enough for a far end vault, the score of the vault is reduced. The horse is divided into five zones as diagrammed in Fig. 4–1. A full point is deducted if any part of the hand protrudes into the bordering zone and two full points if any part of the hands touch the center zone.

The angle of the body above the horizontal at the time of the hand touch is specified in the rules for some far end vaults. For a full score the angle must be at least 30° above the horizontal (Fig. 4–2).

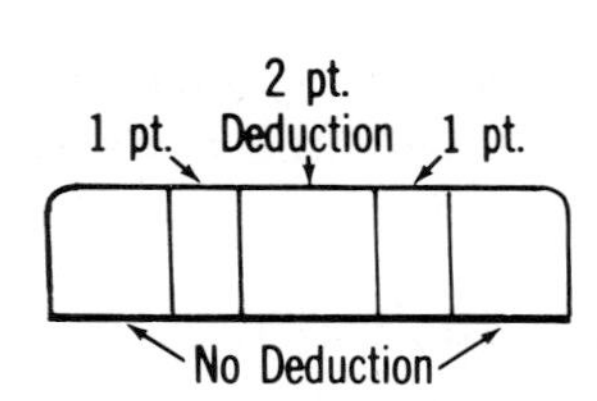

Fig. 4–1. Long Horse Hand Placement Zones.

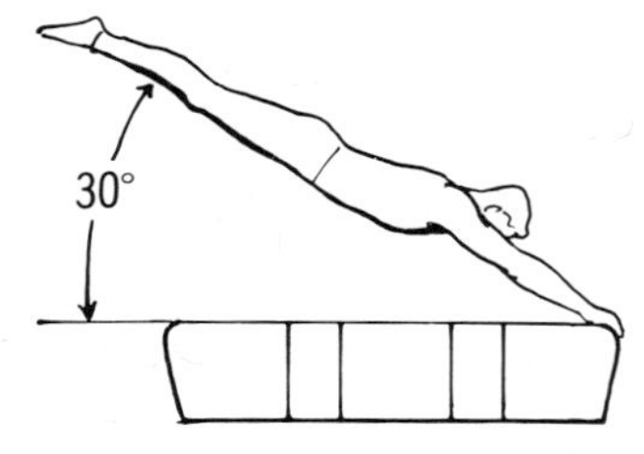

Fig. 4–2. Body Angle at Time of Hand Contact.

PARTS OF A VAULT

A vault is usually divided into parts for discussion purposes. The normal divisions are:

1. Approach and take-off — These are sometimes separated.
2. Pre-flight or on-flight
3. Hand contact
4. After-flight or off-flight

(3 and 4: These are sometimes considered together as the after-flight is a direct result of the hand touch.)

5. Landing

APPROACH AND TAKE-OFF

The run should be much like a broad jumper's approach. The arms should be carried fairly high and pump like a sprinter's during the run. The approach should be long enough to develop almost maximum speed. About nine-tenths maximum speed is used by most good vaulters although this might vary somewhat with the vault. The speed of the run is the biggest single factor in determining the distance the vault covers. A system of check points to aid in hitting the right takeoff point is necessary. Some vaulters use two marks, some one, some just measure the distance from the board to their starting point. The same number of strides should be taken for each approach. The strides should be rhythmical, without hitch steps or hesitations. The speed should build up to the desired speed (approximately nine-tenths maximum) several steps prior to the takeoff so that the last few strides are of equal speed. During most of the run the gymnast concentrates on the board and takeoff spot, but during the last few strides he should be able to shift his concentration to the takeoff itself, and to the horse, as major adjustments should have been made by that time. No major adjustments should ever be made just prior to the takeoff. It is better to run by the board and horse than to do this. Major adjustments should never be necessary if the approach distance has been measured and the approach run is rhythmical each time.

The last stride before the takeoff is known as the hurdle. It should be a continuation of the run—that is, it should be low and long rather than high and short as off a diving board. This will ensure that the full speed of the run is converted to upward movement. The balls of both feet should contact the board for the takeoff at the point of maximum spring. As takeoff boards differ, even though they look alike, the gymnast should experiment to determine the point on the board that gives maximum lift. The angle of the body lean and the position of the feet in relation to the center of gravity at the time of takeoff largely determine the height of the pre-flight. If the body leans well forward, the pre-flight will be low, if it is almost vertical the pre-flight will be high. If the feet are behind the center of gravity, the vault will be lower than if they are directly below or ahead of this point. The arm movement is very important on the takeoff. Just before the last stride both arms start to "cock," that is, they swing backward behind the hips and slightly out to the side. As both feet hit the board the arms are well back behind the body in the "cocked" position ready to swing vigorously forward and upward to contribute to the takeoff lift. Last, but not least, is the spring from the legs. This comes from an ankle, knee, and hip thrust. The takeoff is on the balls of the feet even though the heels might also momentarily make contact with the board.

To summarize, the following factors contribute to a good takeoff.

1. Speed of run and hurdle
2. Resiliency of the takeoff board
3. Position of feet in relation to center of gravity and/or body lean
4. Arm thrust
5. Leg spring

PRE-FLIGHT

The pre-flight is dependent upon the takeoff, as of course is the whole vault. It differs markedly for near-end and far-end vaults and also for the different types of far end vaults as can be seen by Fig. 4–3.

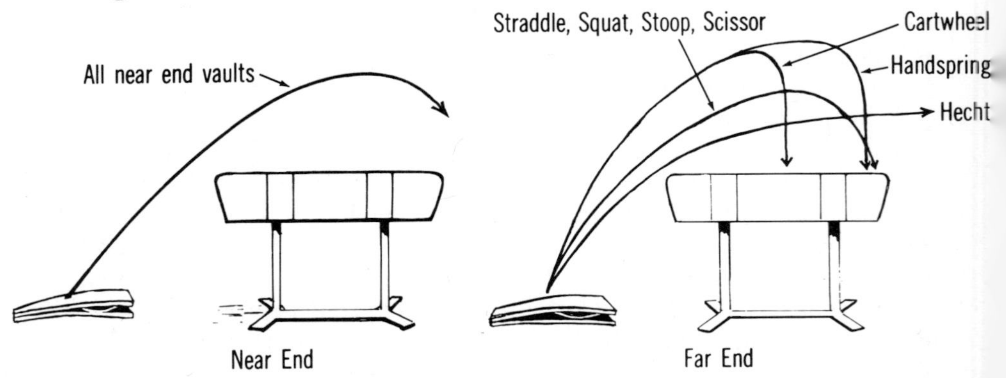

Fig. 4–3. Preflight Paths.

The board is placed quite a distance from the horse for near end vaults. This results in a long but low pre-flight. Far end vaults should have both a high (except for the hecht) and a long pre-flight. The board is usually placed much closer to the horse for far end vaults; however, in spite of this, the pre-flight is longer because it includes the length of the horse as well as the distance from the board to the horse.

HAND CONTACT

The hand contact is momentary and should be thought of primarily as a "rebound" rather than a push. There might be a shoulder thrust, a finger push, a body whip, or a hip lift but all these things are secondary to the rebound at the time of hand contact. In all vaults, except the headspring, the arms should be kept rigidly straight. In all far end vaults, except the headspring, the line through the arm and trunk should also be straight for maximum rebound. The hand contact results in either a change in direction of the flight, or a change in body position, or maybe both. It is largely responsible for the height of the after-flight although other factors also contribute to this. The key words regarding the hand contact are straight arms, momentary, and rebound. The angle of the body in relation to horizontal and the straightness of the line through the arms and trunk are also key factors for some vaults.

AFTER-FLIGHT

The after-flight should be both long and high. The speed of the run is the biggest factor in distance, the hand contact the biggest factor in height. Near end vaults will probably have greater after-flight than far end vaults. There must always be a slight arch of the body during the after-flight. This is usually called a "stretch," rather than an arch, when referring to vaulting.

LANDING

The landing should be on the balls of the feet, in balance, and with good posture. The knees and hips should bend, but not too much. The body leans forward slightly but the back remains straight and the head up. The arms should be stretched out to the side, preferably above shoulder height, and straight. Because there is usually forward movement as well as downward movement at the time of the landing, the feet are thrust forward of the center of gravity as they approach the ground. The amount of forward movement must be judged accurately to determine how far forward to place the feet to bring about a controlled landing with no foot movement after contact with the mat. The gymnast should always return to a standing position with good posture before walking away from the equipment.

EQUIPMENT

HORSES

There are several different horses that can be used for class purposes. Other devices may also be used as substitutes.

1. Long Horse (Fig. 4–4). The official long horse has four legs and a padded wooden top covered with leather. For stability it should be fastened to a floor plate by a chain and turn-buckle that

Fig. 4–4. Long Horses.

is attached under the center section. In the United States most manufacturers use a heavier base for their long horse. Although this base does not meet official specifications, it results in a far more stable horse. The top of the horse is 63 to 64 inches long and 53 inches high.

2. Side Horse. A side horse, with the pommels removed, can be used for vaulting by placing it either crossways or lengthways. Actually a side horse and a long horse are exactly the same piece of equipment except for the pommels. Vaulting should not be done over a pommel horse as this teaches a very bad habit of grasping and maintaining the hand contact too long. The hand contact should be a rebound off a flat surface and should not involve gripping an object like a pommel.

3. Box Horse (Swedish Box). This is an excellent substitute for the regulation long horse for class purposes and for exhibition vaulting. Refer to the section on "homemade equipment" for specifications. It is inexpensive, stable, and light in weight and therefore very highly recommended as a piece of school equipment. It also serves a double purpose as a spotting table for horizontal bar, parallels, and rings.

4. Buck Horse. This horse is exactly the same as a regulation horse except that it is shorter in length (usually about 18 inches). It is of some use in a school situation as an instructional piece of equipment, especially for small children, but is expensive and certainly not as usable as a long horse or box horse. It should only be purchased if there are ample funds for "extras."

5. Vaulting Table (Fig. 4–5). This is a good piece of equipment for instructional purposes and for exhibition vaulting. It may also

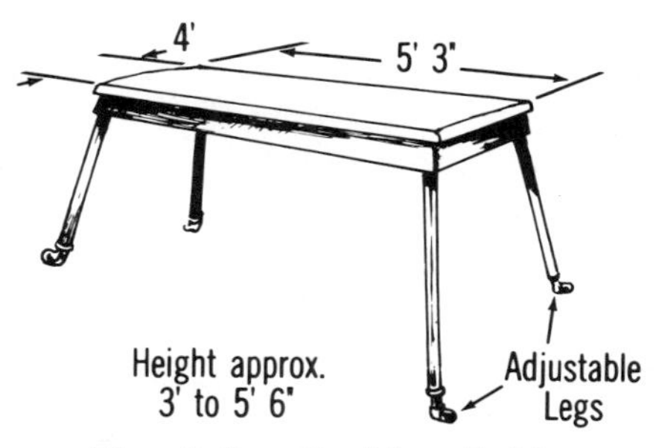

Fig. 4–5. Vaulting Table.

be used as a spotting table for horizontal bar, parallels, and rings. It is not quite as usable, considering all aspects, as a box horse but is a valuable "extra" for any school.

6. Elephant. This is the name given to a set of parallel bars when a mat is draped over the bars and they are used for vaulting. Hair-filled mats are much better for this purpose than rubber mats. It is a good substitute for a horse especially if a piece of heavy plywood is placed across the bars and fastened to them before the mat is draped over the top. This gives a solid surface and prevents the mat from sagging between the bars when the vaulter places his hands on it. The bars may be adjusted to any desired height. This is a good piece of equipment for exhibitions although it can only be used as a cross horse. Parallels are long enough so that for class or exhibitional purposes two students may vault side by side at the same time.

7. Balance Beam. A girl's balance beam with hair-filled mats draped over it will serve as a makeshift vaulting horse for instructional purposes. It is long enough for three vaulters to vault side by side at the same time. Although it will not go high enough for experienced vaulters, it is very useful for beginners and smaller children.

8. Desk or Table. Any strong desk or table may be used as a makeshift horse by draping a mat across it. With improvised equipment like this vaulting can be a part of every school's program. The table will last much longer if cross braces are fastened between the legs.

TAKEOFF BOARDS

There are several different types of takeoff boards that can be used for vaulting.

1. Reuther Board (Fig. 4–6). The reuther board, recently developed in Germany, is halfway between a spring board and the old-fashioned beat board. It is now the official board used for men's and women's competition and, because of this, is an essential piece of equipment for all schools.

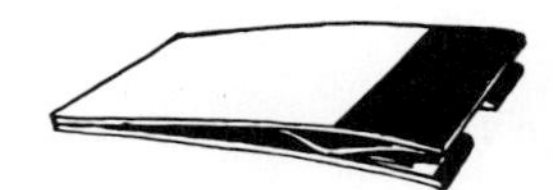

Fig. 4–6. Reuther Board.

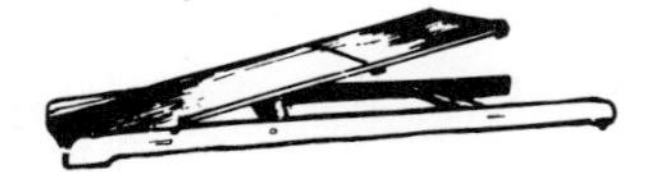

Fig. 4–7. Gymnasium Spring Board.

2. Spring Board (Fig. 4–7). The gymnasium spring board has been a fairly standard piece of equipment for many years. It is a valuable teaching aid for all levels of ability especially for younger children. It is often used in conjunction with a high horse for exhibition vaulting. Vaulting with a spring board is more fun than with a reuther board. If fun is an objective of the program, this piece of equipment certainly has a place.

3. Trampolet or Mini-tramp (Fig. 4–8). This piece of equipment seems to be replacing the gymnasium spring board. It is used for the same purposes as a spring board.

Fig. 4–8. Trampolet.

4. Beat Board. The old-fashioned beat board is nothing more than an inclined plane for takeoff purposes. It is very stiff and gives little or no spring. A more flexible board of similar design can be made very easily and will serve as an excellent substitute for a reuther board. Refer to the section on "homemade equipment" for specifications.

5. A take-off board is not essential. The least expensive substitute for a reuther board is the floor itself.

HOMEMADE EQUIPMENT

Vaulting should not be excluded from a school's program because of lack of regulation equipment. There are two excellent pieces of equipment that can be made easily and inexpensively that do the job just as well.

A box horse can be made of ⅜-inch plywood and 2-inch x 2-inch braces according to the dimensions in Fig. 4–9. The length and width of the top surface is the same as an official long horse.

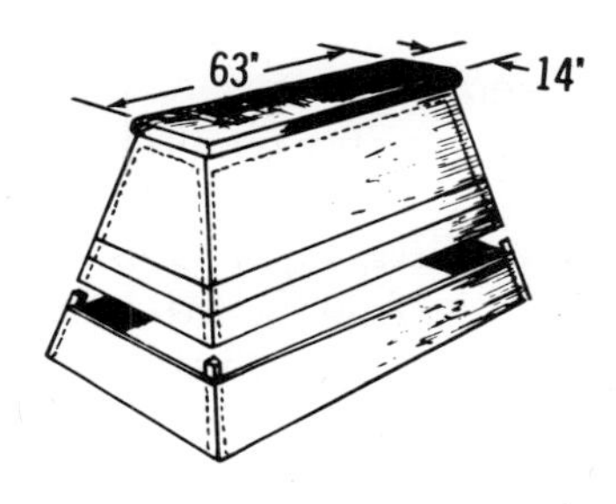

Fig. 4–9. Box Horse.

Top section: 37 inches high. Used for young children and for learning many vaults. The top is padded with approximately 1 inch of top quality felt and covered with canvas or a heavy non-slippery plastic material.

Second section: 8 inches high. Used for most high school vaulting and for more advanced gymnasts while learning many vaults.

Third section: 8 inches high. The top three sections make a horse 53 inches high, the regulation height of a long horse.

Bottom section: 12 inches high. May be added to give an extremely high horse for exhibition vaulting with a trampolet or spring board.

The dotted lines indicate 2" x 2" braces inside the four vertical edges and underneath the top section.

These braces must protrude above each section about 3 inches to fit into the section above.

A beat board with the approximate spring of a reuther board may be made out of a piece of top quality plywood 2 feet wide and 3 feet long. The thickness should be between ⅜ inch and ½ inch depending on the weight of the vaulters. The plywood is fastened

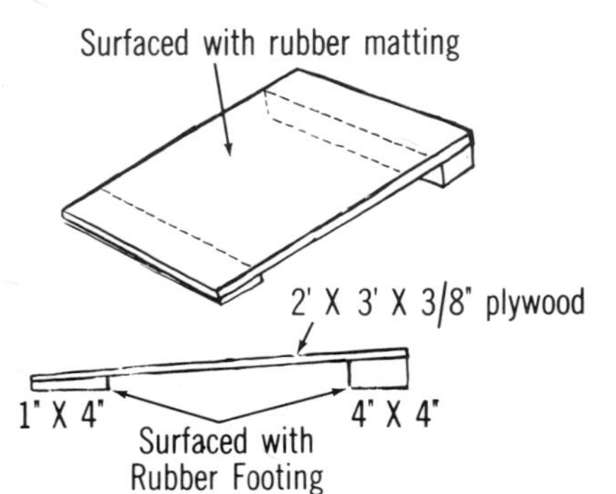

Fig. 4–10. Beat Board.

to a piece of 4″ x 4″ at one end and a 4″ x 1″ at the other end. Both of these pieces of lumber must have had their top surfaces planed to the correct angle for the slope of the board. The top surface of the entire board should be covered with a thin ribbed rubber matting. The two surfaces that rest on the floor should also be covered with rubber footing. Refer to Fig. 4–10.

EXHIBITIONS

It was stated in Chapter 1 that the purpose of this book was to stress the competitive gymnastic events. Vaulting is such a good activity for exhibitions, however, that it seems appropriate to make just a few remarks about exhibition vaulting in this chapter.

To make vaulting more interesting and spectacular for the average audience two things need to be done. First, the height of the horse should be increased, which means a spring board or mini-tramp must be used. Second, the activity should be given continuity by having the vaulters run very close together so that someone is in the air over the horse at all times. With practice vaulters are able to approach the horse about three steps apart. This means on the landing they must get out of the way very quickly. By making no modifications other than these two, vaulting becomes a good spectator activity.

By introducing several novelty ideas a vaulting demonstration can be made even more interesting. Most of these ideas can be used with both a cross horse and a horse placed longways. Have students sit or lie on the horse so that the vaulters place their hands on the shoulders or back of these individuals. The number of individuals on the horse can be gradually increased. A variation of this is to have one student sit on the near end of a long horse so that vaults can be executed over him to the far end without touching his back. Have some vaults over the cross horse, such as the squat, stoop, or hecht, performed through a "window." Two students stand facing each other, one on each end of the horse, and grasp hands to form the window frame. Novelty stunts can be used in exhibitions that are not actually vaults. Examples are: a diving roll, a front somersault over, a jump on to a stand and a back somersault off, and handwalking the length of a long horse with a straddle cut-off dismount. Another feature that adds to the impression of continued movement is to have each vaulter execute a diving roll immediately upon landing from each vault. Many vaults can be performed at an angle over a cross horse. The first vaulter vaults straight ahead, the next angles to the left, the next to the right, the next straight ahead to start the cycle again. Three landing mats, of course, must be used with the two side ones placed at about a 45° angle from the center one.

TEACHING SUGGESTIONS

It is possible to teach vaulting to an entire class by using improvised equipment. A checklist of equipment that may be used and the number of squads that can be kept busy on each is given below.

Equipment	Number of squads
Long horse (crossways)	1
Box horse	1
Buck horse	1
Vaulting table	1
Elephant	2
Balance beam with mats draped over it	3
Ordinary table or desk with a mat draped over it	1
TOTAL	10

It has been stated previously that squad size can be larger for vaulting than for most gymnastic events because it is a fast moving activity. Six to ten in a squad is about right. With the equipment suggested above, a class of 100 can be taught vaulting quite effectively. By adding more tables the number can be increased. Remember that takeoff boards are not essential for beginning or intermediate classes.

In most situations vaulting will be taught in conjunction with other gymnastic events. Two squads may be assigned to each vaulting station without overcrowding if the squad size is between three and five as was recommended in Chapter 1. When the signal is given to rotate to the next squad station, one squad moves and the other stays and is joined by a new squad.

It is recommended that the following steps be followed in teaching vaulting:

1. The approach and takeoff from a spring board.
2. Vaulting over a cross horse with a spring board.
3. The approach and takeoff from a reuther board, or beat board.
4. Vaulting over a cross horse with a reuther board or beat board.
5. Vaulting over a horse placed longways from a spring board.
6. Vaulting over a long horse with a reuther board or beat board.

The divisions are not as clear cut as they appear, however, as some easier vaults may be introduced on the long horse before more difficult ones are taught on the cross horse. Also, easy vaults may be attempted from a reuther board before more difficult ones are tried off a spring board. Some teachers use spring boards very sparingly, more as a teaching technique for some vaults rather than as an activity included for its own values and enjoyment. When spring boards or mini-tramps are used, the hurdle prior to the takeoff must be higher than described earlier in this chapter for a reuther board takeoff. Most beginners, especially smaller children, will have to take one step on the spring board prior to the hurdle. No matter what stage of vaulting is being taught, it is always wise to start with the horse quite low and then increase the height as the students become more proficient.

The parts of a vault can be practiced individually:

1. The approach and takeoff, of course, is the obvious one.
2. The pre-flight may be practiced for some vaults without completing the vault especially when using a cross horse. As soon as the hands contact the horse, the vaulter drops back down on the takeoff side of the horse.
3. The body angle at the time of the hand contact can be practiced on a tumbling mat by jumping into the correct position. This drill can also be used on the long horse by jumping from a stand on the near end to the correct position on the far end.
4. The stretch during the after flight can be practiced by jumping from a stand on the horse to the floor.
5. The landing is also practiced by simply jumping from the horse to the mat.

Another good teaching technique is to concentrate on one phase of the vault and to hold competitions between squad members on this phase only. Length of pre-flight makes a good contest. Start with the board close and gradually move it back so students are taking off as far from the horse as possible. Another contest can be held to see who can get the highest body angle at the time of the hand contact. This teaches students to raise their feet high during the pre-flight. After-flight contests for distance force students to concentrate on this important phase of the vault. It is also a "fun" activity that builds interest. A landing contest can be judged as a regular gymnastic competition with a ten-point maximum. The squad leader can be used to score the landings of the other squad members considering the stability, posture, arm and head position, and general impression.

VAULTS INCLUDED

	Cross Horse	Long Horse	
I. Beginning	1. Squat-on jump-off 2. Squat 3. Straddle	1. Squat-on straddle-off 2. Squat-on squat-off	
II. Low Intermediate	1. Stoop 2. Front 3. Flank 4. Rear	1. Squat-on stoop-off 2. Squat-on headspring off	
		Far End	*Near End*
III. Intermediate	1. Headspring 2. Cartwheel 3. Handspring 4. Handstand quarter-turn	1. Straddle 2. Headspring	
IV. Low Advanced		1. Squat 2. Stoop 3. Handstand quarter-turn	1. Straddle 2. Squat 3. Squat-stoop 4. Scissors
V. Advanced		1. Scissors 2. Cartwheel 3. Stoop half-turn 4. Handspring 5. Hecht	1. Stoop 2. Pike handspring (Yamashita)

I. BEGINNING VAULTS

A beginner should know what is involved in a properly executed vault. Things such as straight arms, a momentary hand touch, and the rebound should be stressed right from the start. He should also be told that the pre-flight should be long and high, that the body should be at a high angle at the time of hand touch, and that there must be a stretch during a long and high after flight. If he understands these things, he will be able to progress toward them even though they are not stressed in beginning vaulting.

CROSS HORSE VAULTS

1. Squat-On, Jump-Off (Fig. 4–11). This is not a true vault, as the feet are placed on the horse, but it is an important lead-up for all vaults. About the time the feet leave the board the hands are placed on top of the horse about shoulder width apart. The arms should be straight (1). The legs are tucked up immediately to a squat position on the horse (2). There should be no pause here by rather an immediate jump forward and upward to an arched position in the air with the arms above the head (3). The landing is on the balls of the feet. The ankles, knees, and hips all bend. The trunk is also bent slightly forward but the back remains straight

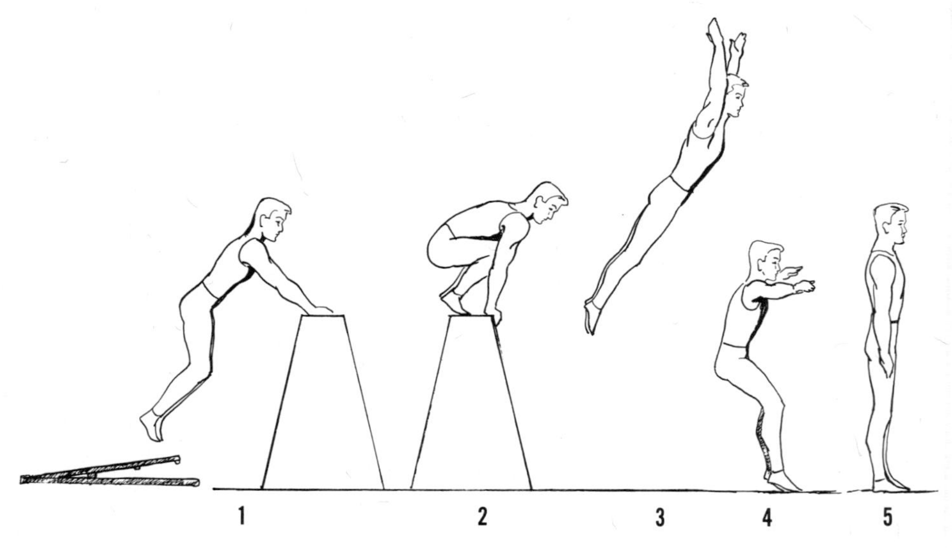

Fig. 4–11. Squat-On, Jump-Off.

with the head up. The arms may finish in a variety of positions but most gymnasts will land with them sideways and slightly above shoulder height (4). This is the landing position for most vaults. From this position the body is straightened and the arms are lowered to a normal stand (5).

TEACHING TECHNIQUES. Practice this skill in two parts, stopping in the squat stand before jumping off.

SPOTTING. One spotter stands on the takeoff side and places one hand on the upper arm and lifts with the other under the back of the thighs. Another spotter stands on the dismount side and actually leans his side against the horse as he reaches across with both hands to grasp the upper arm in a mixed grip. During the early stages this grip can be maintained as the performer jumps off, but as he jumps higher it will have to be released during the jump. The spotter steps sideways with one or more long sliding steps and follows the performer to the landing. The arm can be grasped again at this time if necessary, or the spotter can wrap his arms around the chest of the performer, to ensure a balanced landing.

2. Squat (Fig. 4–12). About the time the feet leave the board the hands are placed on the horse (1). The knees are drawn up to the chest and the arms thrust downward and backward. As the center of gravity passes over the horse, the hands come off. The tuck position is maintained until the feet clear the horse (2), then the body is stretched and the head raised (3). The landing is the same as described for the squat-on jump-off (4).

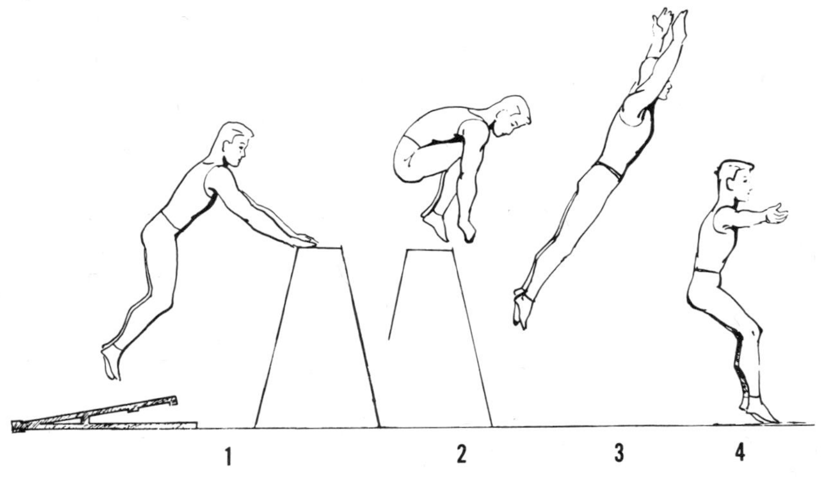

Fig. 4–12. Squat Vault.

Teaching Techniques. The previous vault, the squat-on jump-off, is the only necessary lead-up.

Spotting. Two spotters spot in exactly the same way as for the squat-on jump-off. The spotter on the landing side can, and should, maintain the grasp on the upper arm throughout the whole vault.

3. Straddle (Fig. 4–13). This vault is the same in principle as the squat vault except the legs are straddled wide apart as they pass over the horse instead of being tucked between the arms. The knees should stay straight.

Fig. 4–13. Straddle Vault.

Teaching Techniques. A leap-frog over another student is a lead-up. If a buck horse is available, the straddle vault can be learned very easily over it. It is easier than the previous two vaults when done over a buck. The first step on a cross horse is to straddle up to a stand on top of the horse and then to jump off. When the complete vault is tried, the student should be instructed to raise the head quickly as the hands leave the horse. There is a tendency to nose dive into the mat if this is not done because the hips have to be raised high in order for the feet to clear the horse.

Spotting. During the learning process, when the feet are being placed on the horse, the spotter stands directly in front of the performer and grasps both his upper arms. When the complete vault is tried, he moves slightly to one side and grasps the upper arm on that side in a mixed grip. He maintains the grip until the landing. No spotter is used on the takeoff side for the straddle vault.

LONG HORSE VAULTS

1. Squat-On Straddle-Off (Fig. 4–14). This is not a true vault but rather a lead-up for ones to come later. The squat on the near end of the horse is exactly the same as the squat on the cross horse already described (1). There should be no pause in this position. From the squat there is a spring forward and a reach with the arms to the far end of the horse (2). The arms press downward and backward and then are lifted off the horse as the legs are straddled and the head raised (3). The remainder of the vault is the same as previously described (4) and (5).

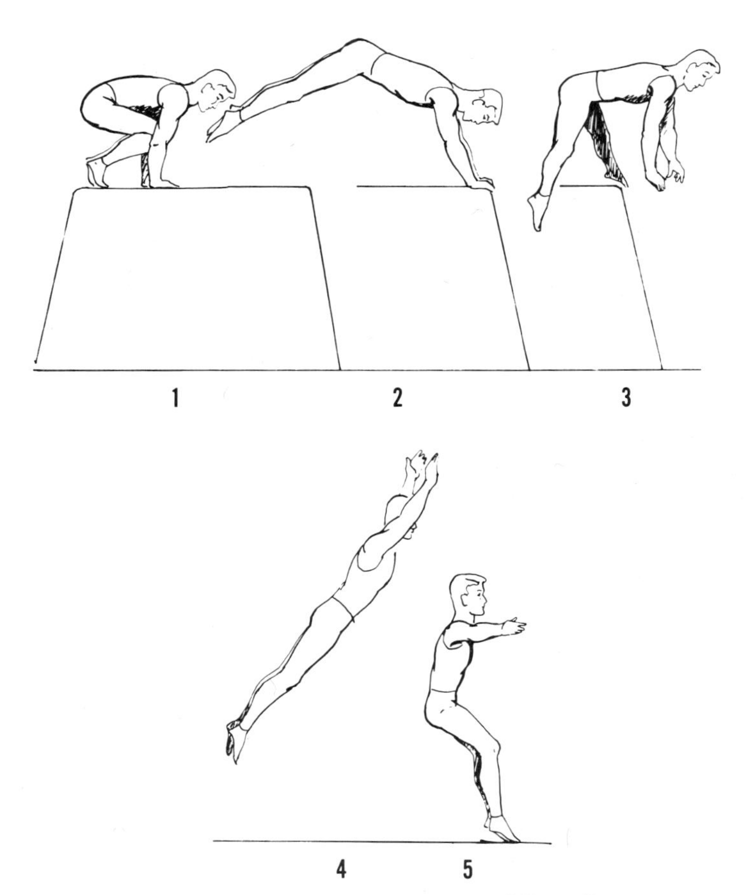

Fig. 4–14. Squat-On, Straddle-Off.

Teaching Techniques. The only lead-up that is necessary is to do the vault in two parts with a pause between the squat-on and the straddle-off.

Spotting. One spotter stands at the near end of the horse and helps the performer get up by lifting under the back of the thighs with one hand and helps him maintain balance by grasping his upper arm with the other hand. Another spotter stands with a wide straddle stance about level with the far end of the horse. He grasps the performer's upper arm in a mixed grip as the hands are placed on the end of the horse and follows the performer to his landing. The spotter must be quick to shift the weight in the straddle stance from the foot closest to the horse to the one away from the horse. He must also be ready to take an extra step if necessary to stay with the performer.

2. Squat-On Squat-Off. This is exactly the same as the squat-on straddle-off except that the legs pass between the arms during the second part of the vault. Refer to the previous vault for technique of performance, teaching methods, and spotting. This squat-off is somewhat more difficult than the squat over the cross horse as the arms have to be placed close together because the horse is only 14 inches wide on top.

II. LOW INTERMEDIATE VAULTS

At the beginning level there was no emphasis on pre-flight, on obtaining a high body angle at the time of hand contact, or on after-flight. At this level these things should be stressed and considerable time should be spent practicing them while reviewing the squat or straddle vaults. In fact, as much time should be spent improving the various parts of the vaults already learned as in learning the new ones. Refer to the teaching suggestions presented earlier in this chapter for suggestions.

CROSS HORSE VAULTS

1. Stoop (Fig. 4–15). The stoop vault is similar to the squat vault except that the hips are raised higher and the legs are kept straight. Students should be told to get some free flight between the takeoff and the hand contact at this ability level. The board should be moved back a little so that there has to be a reach for the horse (1). The hips start to raise immediately after the takeoff

Fig. 4–15. Stoop Vault.

and at the time of hand contact they are well above the head (2). The pike also starts at the time of the takeoff, but the legs do not whip through between the arms in a tight pike until after the hands rebound off the horse (3). The performer should try to stretch the body before the landing, but at the low intermediate level most students will not accomplish this (4). The landing is the same as previously described (5).

2. Front (Fig. 4–16). This is the first vault in which the legs are raised high over the head and so is a lead-up for cartwheel and handspring vaults. There must be a hard run and vigorous takeoff. During the pre-flight the legs are raised high and the body makes a quarter-turn (1) so that the hands may be placed on the horse with one at the front edge and one at the far edge. At this time the body should be slightly arched with the legs almost directly over the shoulders and hands (2). The shoulders are then thrust sideways and upward away from the horse (3) as the feet drop to the mat (4). If the turn has been to the left, the landing will be with the left side of the body nearest to the horse (5). The head stays back during the entire vault.

Teaching Techniques. The first step in learning the front vault is to execute it in a pike position and in two parts by resting the feet on the end of the horse and then jumping off. The next step is to vault over the horse in a pike position. The hips are gradually straightened in subsequent attempts until the vault can be per-

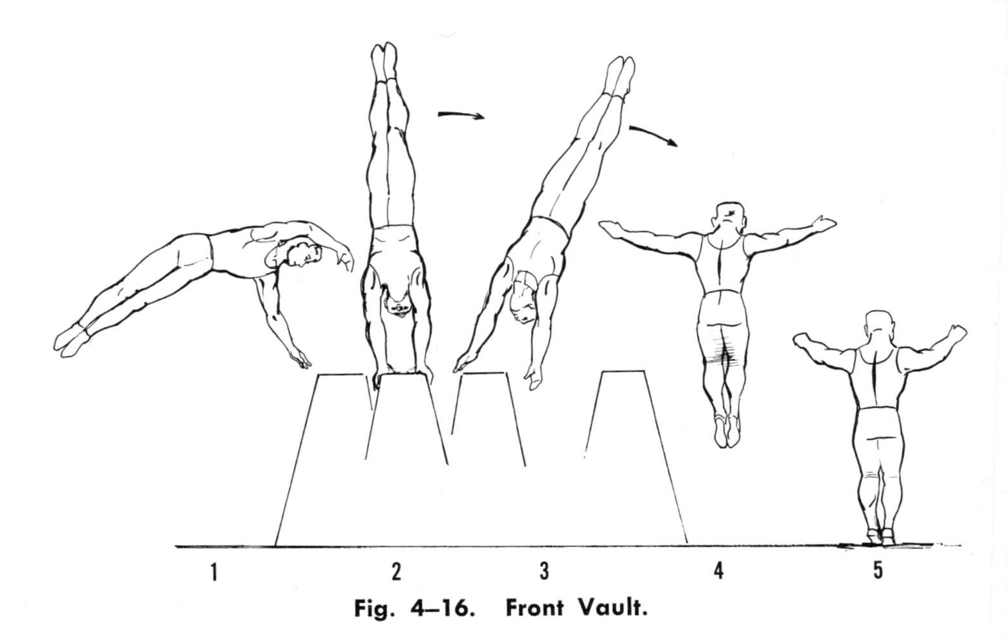

Fig. 4–16. Front Vault.

formed with the body remaining almost straight from the takeoff to the landing.

SPOTTING. The spotter stands on the landing side of the horse and grasps the upper arm to pull the shoulders away from the horse and to ensure a balanced landing. The spotter must know in which direction the vault is to be executed so that he does not get hit by the performers' legs.

3. Flank (Fig. 4–17). Most cross horse vaults can be considered lead-ups for long horse vaulting, but this one can not be done over the long horse. It bears a closer relationship to several dismounts off the pommel horse than it does to other cross or long horse vaults. Immediately after the takeoff the hips are raised in a pike and both the hips and the legs are moved slightly to the side (1). Not too much sideward movement occurs, however, until the time of hand contact. The legs then lift rapidly sideward and upward (2). At this time the body is still in a pike but, as one hand lifts off the horse so that the body can pass over, the hips are thrust forward into an arch (3). The second hand then pushes off the horse and the gymnast drops to a landing with the back to the horse (4).

Fig. 4–17. Flank Vault.

Teaching Techniques. Two lead-ups may be used. In the first the vault is executed in two parts with the feet being placed on the end of the horse. In the second the pike position is maintained throughout the vault.

Spotting. One spotter can be used on the takeoff side of the horse to lift under the hips. Another spotter on the landing side grasps the upper arm nearest to him to pull the vaulter forward and to make sure he lands in balance. Both spotters must be away from the direction of the leg movement.

4. Rear (Fig. 4–18). This vault is not done over the long horse but is a good lead-up for pommel horse work. The takeoff is much like any other vault and both hands are placed on the horse in the usual way. At this time the legs are raised to the side and the body makes a quarter-turn outward (1) so that the rear of the body is toward the horse. One hand is lifted off the horse so that the hips can pass over. The buttocks should be close to the top of the horse and the feet high in a pike (2). As the forward momentum carries the body over the horse, the support arm thrusts off and the other hand is placed back on the horse for the landing with the side of the body toward the equipment (3).

Teaching Techniques. Start from a stand on the takeoff board and jump to a sitting position on the horse with the legs stretched along the top. Continue through the movement of the vault by sliding over to a stand on the far side. One of the common mis-

Fig. 4–18. Rear Vault.

takes in this vault is to raise the hips too high as for a squat, straddle, or stoop. The buttocks should remain low on the pre-flight and should barely miss the horse as they pass over. On the other hand the feet should be raised as high as possible so that the body is in a tight pike as it passes over the horse.

SPOTTING. The spotter stands on the landing side of the horse and grasps the upper arm nearest to him. During the learning process he stops the performer from falling over the horse as he jumps to a sitting position. When the complete vault is tried, he pulls the vaulter over the top and assists during the landing. The spotter must be away from the direction of the leg movement.

LONG HORSE VAULTS

1. Squat-On Stoop-Off. This is a progression of the squat-on squat-off. As the stoop has already been described as a vault over the cross horse, it will not be repeated. Learning the stoop in this way, from a position on the horse, is an important step in learning the regular stoop vault, which comes later in the chapter.

2. Squat-On Headspring Off. There is discrepancy between the placement of this headspring in the low intermediate level and the tumbling headspring at the intermediate level. Although the "headspring vault" is probably easier, the author believes that the "headspring" should be presented first on the tumbling mats. As tumbling is presented first in the order of events, a class could very well reach the third level in tumbling before reaching the second level in vaulting. If the headspring stage has not been reached in tumbling, the headspring vault should be omitted. This vault does not need to be described or illustrated, as the squat-on is exactly the same as previously described in this chapter and the headspring is almost the same as in Chapter 2, pages 39–41. If the headspring is done in exactly the same way as on the tumbling mats, the performer will overturn and fall forward on his face because of the extra height. To compensate for the extra height there must be either a less vigorous arm push and body extension or this push and extension must be directed more vertically so that they contribute more to height than to forward rotation.

SPOTTING. It is wise to have two spotters put each student through several slow motion headsprings before they try it at normal speed. The spotters stand one on each side of the horse and, at the start of the headspring, hold the performer's legs in a tight pike position with one hand. As the fall off-balance occurs, this hand shifts to the wrist and the other hand lifts under the upper back. The grip on the wrist is maintained until the landing so as to prevent an over spin.

III. INTERMEDIATE VAULTS

At this level considerable practice is needed on the squat, straddle, and stoop vaults over the cross horse with the board placed a good distance from the horse. The body angle at the time of hand contact should be gradually increased until it is at least 30° above horizontal. This is done in preparation for the first vaults to be done over the horse placed longways.

CROSS HORSE VAULTS

1. Headspring. The headspring is executed in much the same way as in tumbling. The hands and front part of the head are placed on the horse. The hips lead with the legs straight and in a reasonably tight pike position. The fall off-balance is very important. If the body extension comes too soon, the student will fall back down on top of the horse or may even fall on the takeoff side. The arm push and body extension should be directed more vertically, however, than in the headspring on the tumbling mats because, if this is not done, the student will overturn and fall forward on his face.

TEACHING TECHNIQUES. It might be wise to remind the teacher at this time that, at first, vaults should be learned over a low horse.

This was stated in the introductory part of the chapter but has not been repeated for each vault. The headspring partially should be learned on the tumbling mats before being tried over the horse. It is wise to have two or more spotters put each student through several slow motion headsprings before they are tried at normal speed.

Spotting. One or two spotters stand on the takeoff side to aid in getting the hips in the air and to be sure that the legs are in a tight pike position. They lift under the upper thighs with one hand and grasp the lower leg with the other. One or two spotters also stand on the landing side and lift with one hand under the upper back and grasp the wrist with the other hand. This hand maintains contact until the landing to prevent a possible over spin.

2. Cartwheel (Fig. 4–19). The cartwheel starts just as the front vault with a fast run and a vigorous takeoff (1). During the pre-flight the legs are raised high and the body makes a quarter-turn so that the hands may be placed on the horse with one at the near edge and one on the far edge. The legs are together at the start of the vault and remain together throughout. This is a major difference between the cartwheel vault and the cartwheel as done in tumbling or floor exercise. As the handstand position is reached,

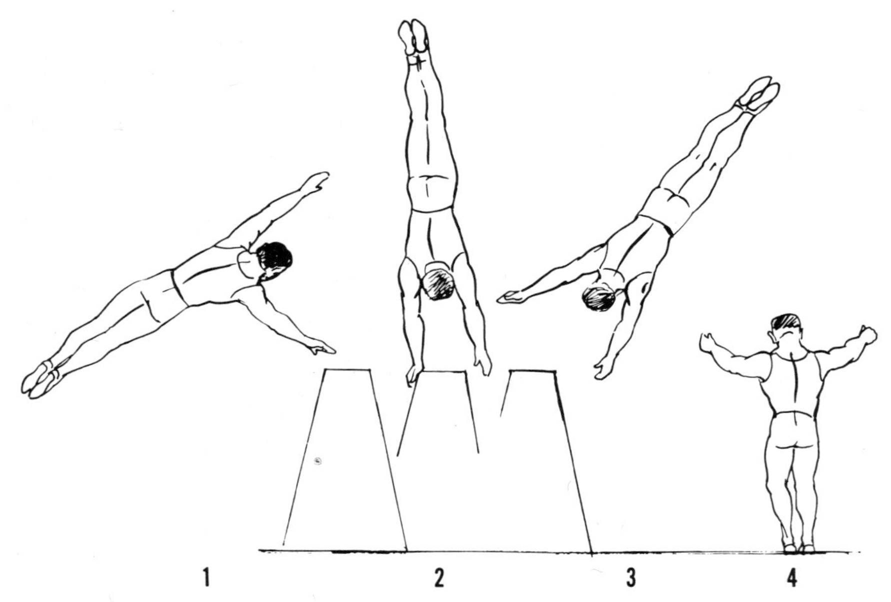

Fig. 4–19. Cartwheel.

halfway through the vault, the body should be slightly arched with the feet directly over the hands and shoulders (2). There should be a rebound off the horse resulting in a high, as well as long, after-flight (3). The cartwheel finishes in a landing with the side of the body to the horse (4). The head should remain back during the entire vault. The forward movement of the upper body continues in most vaults after the feet touch the ground. As the movement is to the side in the cartwheel, the feet must be placed out to the side rather than directly under the head on the landing. The center of gravity shifts over the feet after the landing.

TEACHING TECHNIQUES. The cartwheel on the ground is a prerequisite. The finish of the cartwheel vault can be practiced by standing on top of the horse at one end and executing a cartwheel off the other end to the floor. The horse should be turned lengthwise or the mat should be shifted around to the end for this lead-up. A low horse should be used so that the spotter can work effectively.

SPOTTING. The spotter stands as close to the horse as possible. He must know the direction in which each student faces for the cartwheel so as to place himself on the back rather than the stomach side of the performer. One hand is placed on each side of the rib cage to support the performer from the time his hands touch the horse until the landing.

3. Handspring (Fig. 4–20). For a good handspring there must be a fast run and a hard takeoff (1). The pre-flight should be high enough so that the body can be straightened well before the hands touch the horse. To reach this position the legs are lifted quickly overhead from the takeoff. The weight should drop down on the horse from above rather than push into the horse. This means that the body should be approximately vertical as the contact is made (2). If the arms are kept perfectly straight and if the shoulders are extended so that the line through the arms and trunk is a straight one, at the time of contact there will be a rebound off the horse that will result in a long and high after-flight (3) (4). The landing is with the back to the horse (side stand rearways) and with the arms high (5). The head should stay slightly back during the entire vault.

TEACHING TECHNIQUES. The handspring on the floor is a prerequisite. Many other vaults such as the headspring, front vault, and cartwheel provide a background for the handspring in one way or another. Using a springboard to give better pre-flight and to aid in raising the legs quickly over the head from the takeoff is an

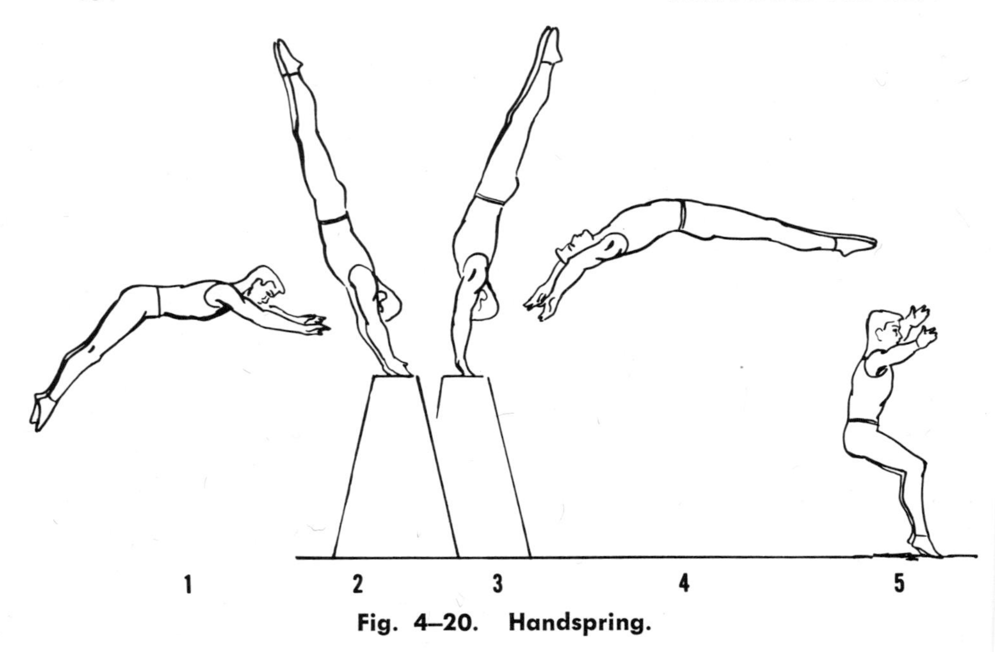

Fig. 4–20. Handspring.

especially good teaching technique for the handspring. A low horse should also be used as the stunt is learned. The finish of the handspring can be practiced from a standing position on the horse placed lengthwise. The student should concentrate on the straight line through the arms and trunk at this time. Most of the common mistakes are caused by a poor takeoff and a low pre-flight. This will probably result in: 1) the shoulders being ahead of the hands at the time of contact, thus breaking the straight line through the arms and trunk; 2) resting the hands on the horse for too long a time during the vault; and 3) bending the arms. These faults will all result in a poor after-flight.

Spotting. Two spotters should be used one on each side of the horse. The one on the takeoff side is used more as a teaching aid than as a safety precaution. During the early learning stages he stations himself to the side of the vaulter and lifts under the hips and thighs to bring about a high, straight body pre-flight. As the pre-flight gets higher, he can stand directly between the board and the horse so that the vaulter has to go right over his head. He then lifts on both hips as the vaulter goes over the top of him. The spotter on the landing side places one hand on the wrist and lifts with the other hand under the upper back. The grip on the wrist is maintained until the landing to prevent a possible overspin.

4. Handstand Quarter-Turn (Fig. 4–21). This vault is often called a handstand pivot cartwheel and is a combination of the last two vaults—the cartwheel and the handspring. The takeoff and pre-flight are the same as for the handspring but not necessarily quite as high (1). The hand contact should be made on the near edge of the horse with the body approaching a handstand position (2). One hand is immediately taken off the horse and placed down again on the far edge of the horse in line with the other hand (3). From this point to its conclusion the vault resembles a cartwheel. The hand on the near edge is raised (4) and the vaulter drops sideways to the mat to land with the side of the body to the horse (5).

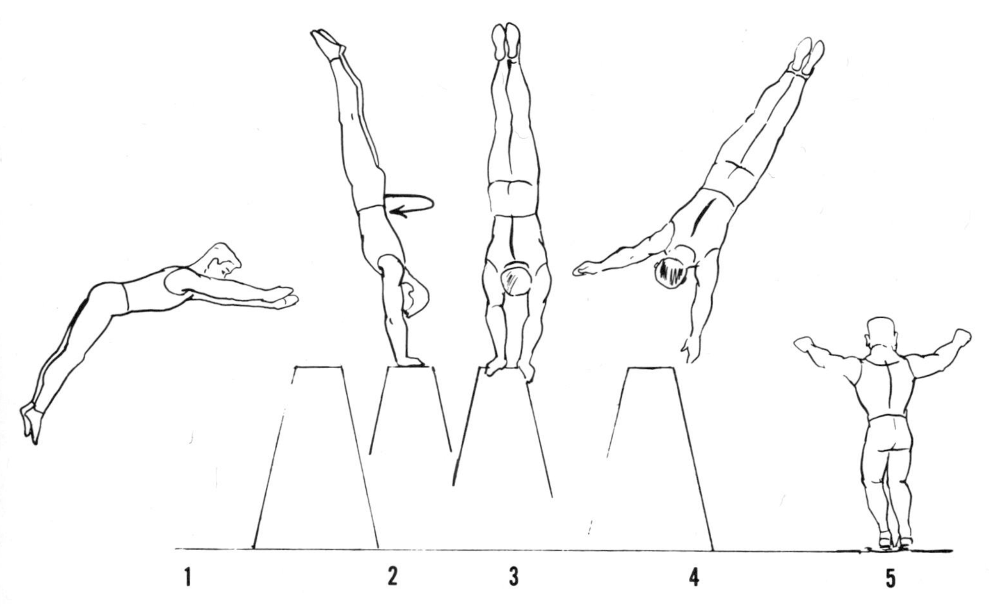

Fig. 4–21. Handstand Quarter-Turn.

Teaching Techniques. The hand change can be practiced by kicking to a handstand on the floor or on a slightly higher surface such as a rolled mat. Both the hand change and the finish of the vault can be practiced by kicking to a handstand from a standing position on a horse placed longways.

Spotting. The spotter on the takeoff side spots as for a handspring while the one on the dismount side spots as for a cartwheel. Refer to these two vaults for the description of the techniques.

LONG HORSE, FAR END VAULTS

According to the rules each vault over the long horse has a difficulty rating ranging from 7.50 points to 10.0 points. This rating is given for each vault throughout the rest of this chapter.

It might be wise to review the parts of a vault at this time, especially the approach and takeoff, as many of the techniques become more important when long horse vaulting is started. Refer to the introductory part of the chapter for this information. To make the change from the cross horse to the long horse less severe the horse may be lowered or a spring board may be used to provide extra spring.

1. Straddle (7.50 points) (Fig. 4–22). This is usually the first single contact vault to be attempted over the long horse. The student will probably have to take a longer and faster run than he has used for the cross horse vaults. From the takeoff the vaulter reaches for the far end of the horse and raises the feet quickly upward (1). At the time the hands contact the horse the body angle should be at least 30° above horizontal. The vaulter should strive to establish a straight line through the arms and body at the time of contact (2). This will result in a good rebound off the horse. If this straight line is not attained, the performer will have to compensate by pressing hard downward and backward with the arms. After the rebound off the horse, which drives the upper body up-

Fig. 4–22. Far End Straddle.

ward and the legs downward, the body is piked momentarily to facilitate the return of the feet to the floor (3). When the end of the horse is cleared, the body is stretched to a slight arch (4) and then quickly piked again for the landing with the back to the horse (5). As the forward movement continues even after the feet touch the ground, the legs must be placed in front of the center of gravity on the landing so that the balance can be controlled as the weight moves forward over the feet.

TEACHING TECHNIQUES. The squat on straddle-off should be practiced with special emphasis on getting the high body angle at the time of hand contact. Students can progress slowly into the straddle-over by leaping to a straddle seat about the middle of the horse and gradually leaping farther and farther down the horse until it can be cleared. Another method that can be used is to place one hand about the center of the horse and take one or two running steps with the hands along the top of the horse as the vault is executed. During both of these methods of learning the vault, care should be taken not to get the arms caught between the legs and the horse. This often causes injury to the hands and wrists. If the vaulter has learned to vault with the board placed a long way from the cross horse, lead-ups for the far end straddle might not be necessary as he might already be getting sufficient pre-flight to clear the long horse.

SPOTTING. The spotter stands about two feet from the end of the horse and very slightly to the side. He should be in a wide straddle stance reaching forward to grasp the upper arm of the vaulter as soon as possible. The spotter can help to pull the beginner over the horse and can aid during the landing. He should be quick to move with the vaulter during the after-flight by shifting the weight from the near foot to the far foot in the straddle stance or by taking several sliding steps away from the end of the horse.

2. Headspring. This is probably the easiest vault to do over the long horse although it takes more courage than some of the others. It is not rated according to difficulty in the rule book but is usually given the same rating as the straddle—7.50 points. Except for the longer pre-flight this vault is no different from the headspring over the cross horse. The squat on headspring off is also a lead-up. The hands and head should be placed in the far zone of the horse for a good vault but during the learning process may be placed farther back. It can be quite dangerous if the head placement is not at least two-thirds of the way down the horse, however, because the after-flight may be so short that the vaulter's back will hit the horse. The spotting is the same as for the previous headsprings. The two spotters stand, one on each side of the horse close to the far end.

IV. LOW ADVANCED VAULTS

LONG HORSE—FAR END VAULTS

1. Squat (8.0 points) (Fig. 4–23). The same principles apply to this vault as for the straddle but the legs pass between the arms in a tuck after the hand contact instead of to the outside of the arms. As can be seen by comparing Fig. 4–23 with Fig. 4–22, the only difference is in Step 3. The spotting methods are the same as for the straddle. The squat over the cross horse and the squat-on squat-off over the long horse are both lead-ups.

Fig. 4–23. Far End Squat.

2. Stoop (9.50 points) (Fig. 4–24). This is another vault that is identical to the straddle in principle. The only difference is the position of the legs during one short phase of the vault, as can be seen in Fig. 4–24. In the stoop vault the legs are brought between the arms with straight knees. This means that the rebound must be greater than for the straddle or squat to bring about a higher after-flight and thus permit the feet to clear the end of the horse.

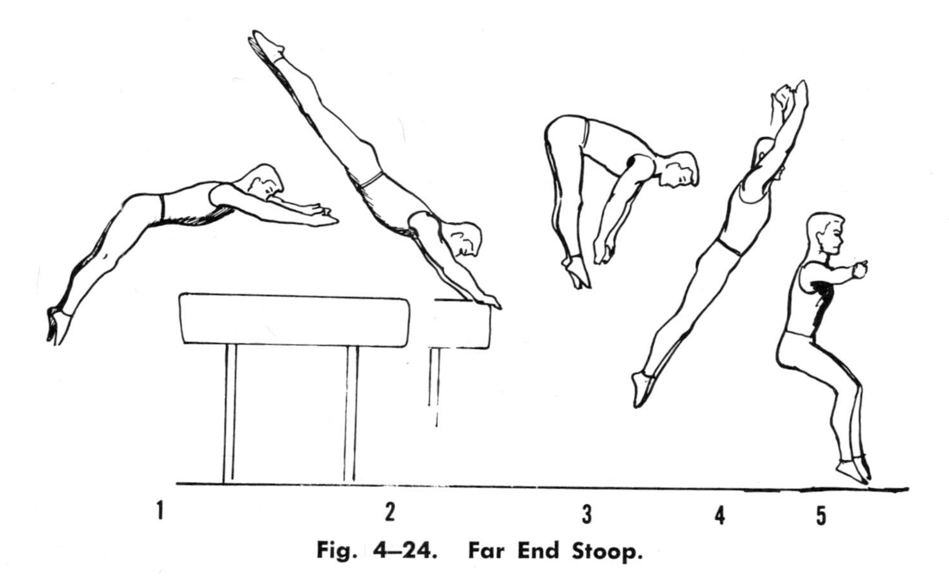

Fig. 4–24. Far End Stoop.

The stoop is considerably more difficult than the other two vaults because of this. The spotting methods are the same. The stoop over the cross horse and the squat-on stoop-off over the long horse are the lead-ups.

3. Handstand Quarter-Turn (9.0 points). This vault is the same as already described over the cross horse, page 135. The pre-flight ends in a handstand position in the center of the horse. After the quarter-turn one hand is placed on the end of the horse for the cartwheel off. The teaching techniques and spotting methods are the same as for the vault over the cross horse.

LONG HORSE—NEAR END VAULTS

Before students start on near end vaults it is advisable to review the parts of a vault with emphasis on how each differs from the equivalent part of a far end vault. The squat vault should be reviewed over the cross horse, using a long and low pre-flight and striving for as long an after-flight as possible. A rope can be stretched across the landing mat at a point equivalent to the length and height of a long horse. If this rope can be cleared by the vaulter in a squat position, he proves to himself that he is ready for near end vaults. The board is usually placed much farther from the horse for near end vaults than for far end vaults. This brings about a better body angle for a good rebound off the near end of the horse. If all other factors remain the same, a board placed close to the horse will bring about a high but short after-flight and a board placed a great distance from the horse will bring about a long and low after-flight.

1. Straddle (7.50 points) (Fig. 4–25). The vaulter runs fast and takes off with more of a forward body lean than for far end vaults. The arms are kept straight at the time of contact with the horse to bring about a good rebound. The arms also press downward and backward as they leave the horse (1). The body is straight, or maybe very slightly piked, at the time of the hand contact but immediately after goes into a slight arch with the legs straddled (2). The feet will undoubtedly be below the top of the horse during the after-flight. The body is piked slightly before the landing and the feet are placed well forward of the center of gravity (3).

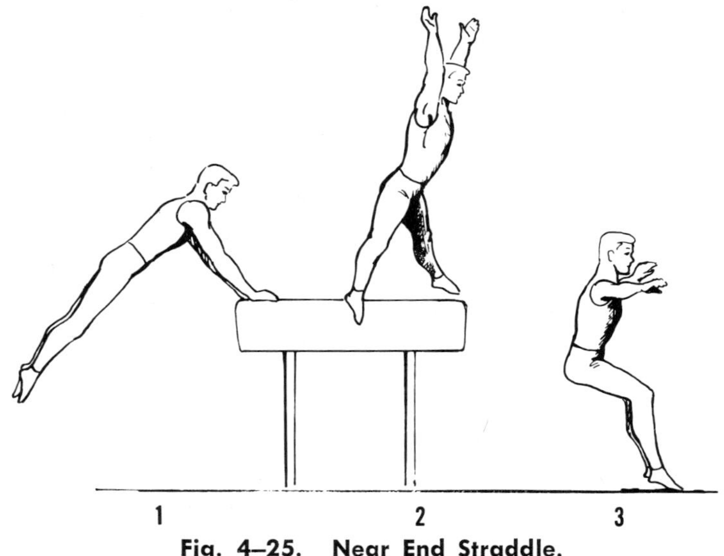

Fig. 4–25. Near End Straddle.

TEACHING TECHNIQUES. Some students progress into the near end straddle by placing the hands in the center of the horse at first and, as they continue to practice, they gradually place them closer and closer to the near end. Others find it best to learn the vault by placing one hand close to the near end and taking one or two running steps with the hands along the top of the horse as they straddle over. Still another method that can be used during the learning process is to use a double contact with the hands, one on the near end as in the regular near end straddle, and another farther down the horse. All three of these techniques might be explained so that the student can choose the one that seems best for him. Care should be taken not to catch the hands between the horse and the legs as this often causes injury to the hands or wrist.

SPOTTING. It is very difficult to spot near end vaults. The spotter stands a few feet beyond the far end of the horse and reaches forward to grasp the upper arm of the vaulter as soon as possible to help pull him over the end of the horse and to assist with the landing.

2. Squat (8.0 points) (Fig. 4–26). The approach and takeoff are the same as for the near end straddle. The vaulter reaches for the near end of the horse and tries to get a good rebound off the horse by hitting with straight arms. He should also give a downward and backward press with the arms as the hands contact the horse (1). In near end vaulting the run and takeoff are largely responsible for the length of the vault while the hand contact is largely responsible for the height attained during the vault. The legs start to draw up between the arms in a tuck position during the pre-flight but do not reach a tight tuck until the vaulter is directly above the horse during the after-flight (2). As soon as the far end of the horse is cleared, the body stretches into a slight arch (3) and then is quickly piked again for the landing with the back to the horse (4).

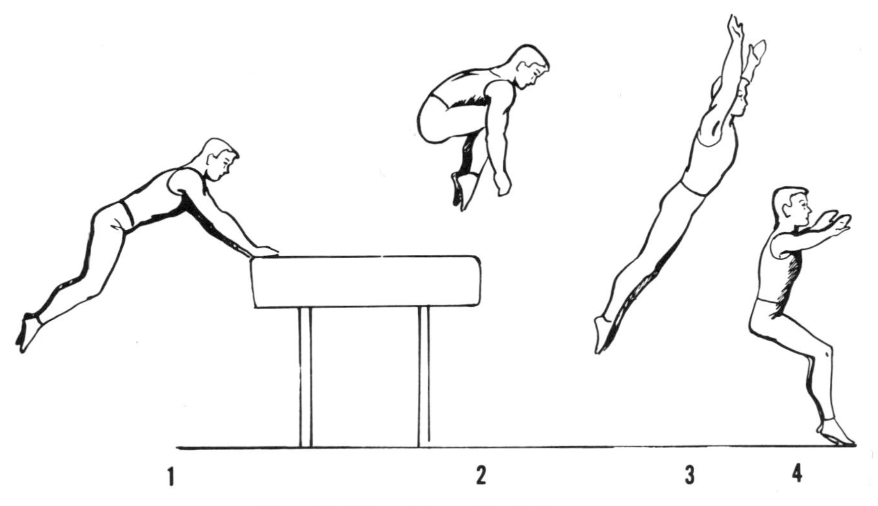

Fig. 4–26. Near End Squat.

TEACHING TECHNIQUES. The learner can progress gradually into the near end squat by doing a squat-on and jump-off. For some students this develops into a squat-on with a few short running steps on top of the horse before the jump-off. Even after the complete near end squat is attempted, the feet may be placed down on top of the horse at the last minute if the vaulter can see that he will not clear the horse.

SPOTTING. The spotter stands a few feet beyond the far end of the horse and grasps the upper arm of the vaulter as soon as possible to assist with the landing and to guard against a fall if the feet catch on the end of the horse.

3. Squat-Stoop (9.0 points) (Fig. 4–27). This vault is very little different from a near end squat vault but is somewhat more difficult. It is often called a squat extension. It starts exactly like a squat (1) (2) but shortly after the hand touch, while directly over the horse, the legs are straightened into a stoop position (3). This

Fig. 4–27. Near End Squat-Stoop.

stoop position is held until the end of the horse is cleared and then the vault is finished, as most other vaults, with a body stretch (4) followed by a controlled landing, in balance, with the back to the horse (5). It is spotted in the same manner as the near end squat.

4. Scissor (9.0 points) (Fig. 4–28). This vault is seldom seen in competition. It starts with a regular approach and takeoff but

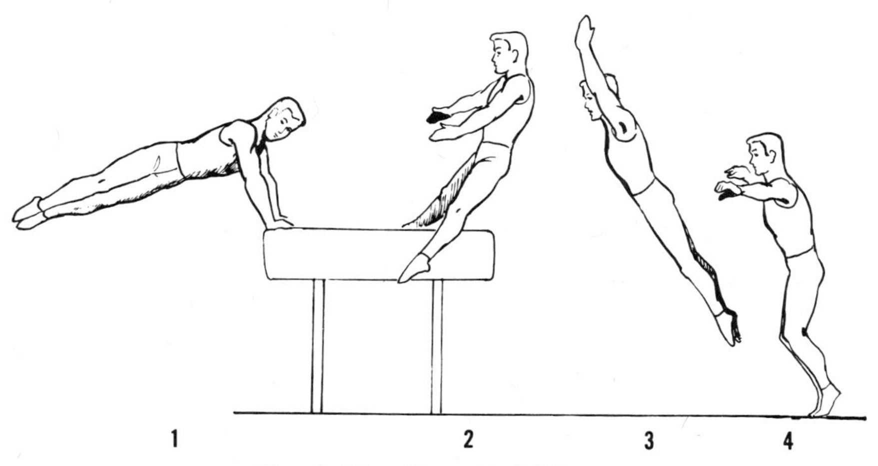

Fig. 4–28. Near End Scissor.

then the legs and hips start to twist slightly during the pre-flight. As the hands contact the near end of the horse, the arms should be straight for a good rebound. At this time the arms also press downward and backward with one arm pushing harder than the other to start a twist of the upper body (1). The half-twist is completed almost immediately after the hand contact and the legs are straddled so that most of the after-flight is in a straddle position with the back leading (2). The body is in a pike at this time. The feet may be above the top of the horse or below it with one on each side. Sometime before the landing the body should be stretched to a slight arch (3) and then piked again for the landing. As the movement is backward in this vault, the feet should contact the mat behind the center of gravity so that a balanced landing will result (4).

Teaching Techniques. The scissors should first be tried over a buck horse if one is available. Another step in the learning process is to scissor to a straddle sitting position on top of the horse. The distance can gradually be increased until the horse can be cleared. This is a somewhat painful process but, nevertheless, many gymnasts have learned the scissors in this way.

Spotting. The spotter stands directly off the far end of the horse and places both hands on the performer's back as he clears the end. He must be quick to step back after making contact so as to aid, but not be in the way of, the performer as he lands.

V. ADVANCED VAULTS

LONG HORSE, FAR END VAULTS

1. Scissor (9.8 points) (Fig. 4–29). The far end scissors start with the same approach, takeoff and pre-flight as the straddle, squat, and stoop from the far end (1). The body angle at the time of hand contact should be at least 30° above horizontal (2). As the vaulter rebounds off the horse, the legs straddle and the body twists

Fig. 4–29. Far End Scissor.

(3). This is a much faster twist than the one for the scissors from the near end. It is completed quickly so that the body can pass over the end of the horse in a rear straddle position (4). The body is stretched, as usual, during the after-flight and then piked again for the landing (5). The teaching techniques and spotting are the same as for the near end scissor.

2. Cartwheel (9.8 points) (Fig. 4–30). There are only minor differences between this vault and the cartwheel over the cross horse. The first hand may be placed anywhere on the horse but is usually placed approximately at the center. The second hand must be placed in the end zone for maximum score. Refer to pages 132–33 for a detailed description of this vault. The teaching techniques and spotting methods presented earlier will also apply to a cartwheel over the long horse.

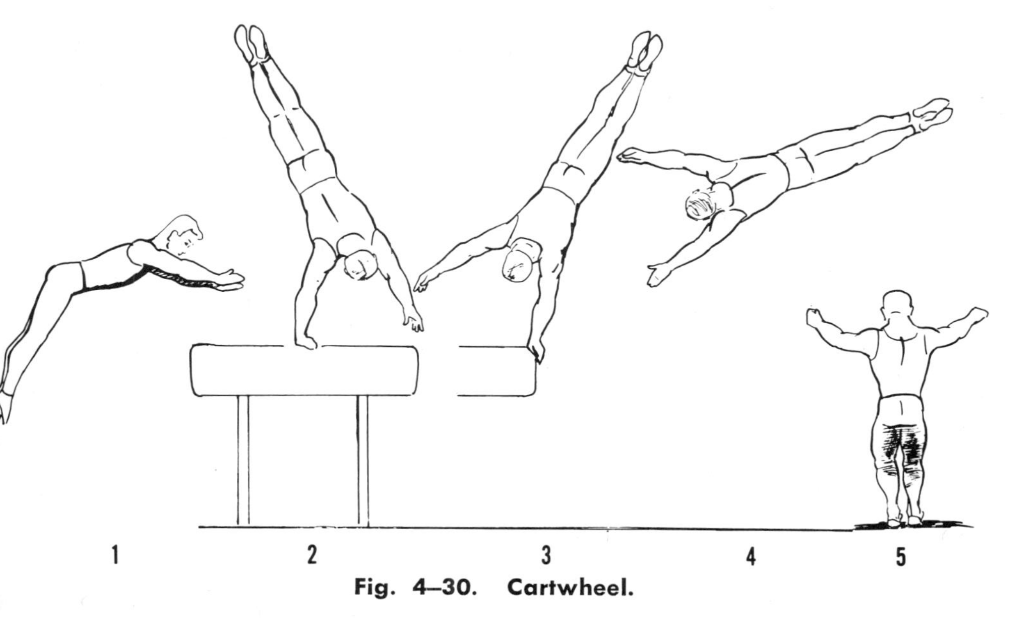

Fig. 4–30. Cartwheel.

3. Stoop Half-Turn (10.0 points) (Fig. 4–31). This vault is seldom used in competition because it is difficult to get a good landing on a vault that ends with backward movement. The stoop half-turn is the same as a regular stoop until the time of hand contact (1). The half-twist starts from the hand contact position. As the

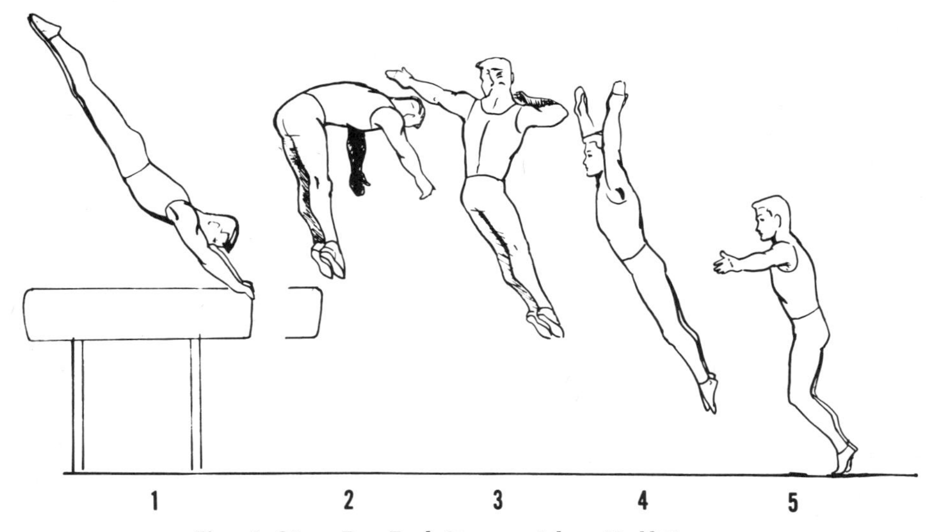

Fig. 4–31. Far End Stoop with a Half-Turn.

vaulter rebounds from the horse, he thrusts harder with one hand and starts to twist the head and upper body as the legs are piked between the arms (2). The twist will speed up as the body starts to straighten (3). The half-twist should be completed in the air as the body reaches the fully stretched position (4). The landing is with the front of the body toward the horse (5). The feet must be placed behind the center of gravity as they contact the mat to bring about a balanced position at the finish of the vault.

TEACHING TECHNIQUES. This vault may be practiced over a cross horse even though it has not been included in this chapter as a cross horse vault. It may also be practiced from a squat on the near end of the horse. The landing can be practiced by jumping off the end of the horse with a half-pirouette.

SPOTTING. The spotting is the same as for both the scissor vaults.

4. Handspring (10.0 points). As this vault is identical to the handspring over the cross horse, it will not be described or illustrated again. The teaching techniques are also the same. The only difference is the spotting. A spotter is not used on the takeoff side of the horse but the one on the landing side spots in the same manner as described previously. Refer to pages 133–34 in this chapter.

5. Hecht (10.0 points) (Fig. 4–32). This is sometimes called the swan vault and uses an entirely different prinçiple from the vaults already described. The board is usually moved slightly farther from the horse than for other far end vaults. The takeoff is much the same but the legs are lifted only slightly above horizontal during the pre-flight. The rules specify that the body must be above horizontal but do not require a 30° angle for this vault. Immediately before the hand contact the upper body is lowered quickly, which establish a reasonably straight line through the arms and trunk (2) to bring about a good rebound. Some vaulters arch immediately after the hand contact but another method is used by most to add a little extra height to the after-flight. If the hands drive into the end of the horse, the action of the rebound will force a slight pike to develop and convert more of the forward movement to upward movement than will be done with an immediate arch (3). From this slight pike the head and chest are raised into the arch that is held for the remainder of the after-flight (4). The body is piked again just prior to the landing and the feet are thrust well

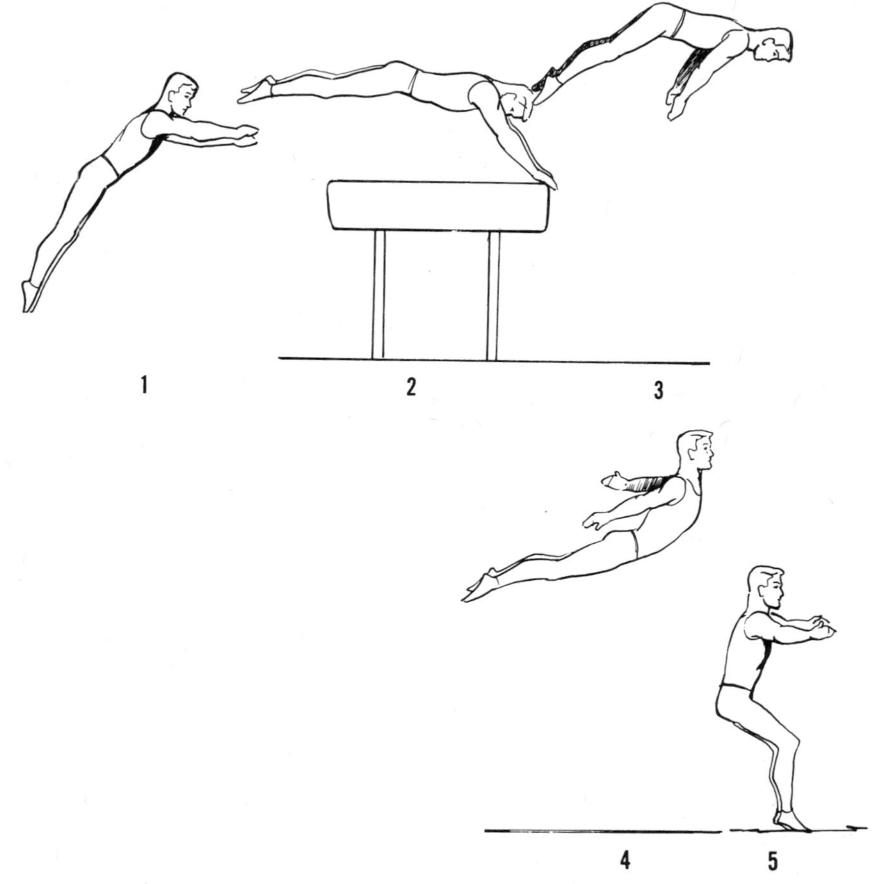

Fig. 4–32. Far End Hecht.

forward of the center of gravity as there is considerable forward movement on the landing of this vault (5).

Teaching Techniques. Although this vault was not listed as a cross horse vault in this chapter, it can be learned over the cross horse. Apart from this there are no good lead-ups or teaching techniques for the hecht.

Spotting. The spotter stands several feet from the end of the horse and slightly to the side of the path of flight. He reaches across the chest of the vaulter with one arm to lift the upper body and permit the feet to drop to the mat.

LONG HORSE, NEAR END VAULTS

1. Stoop (10.0 points) (Fig. 4–33). This vault is so similar to the near end squat and the near end squat-stoop that it does not need to be described. The only difference is that the legs are kept straight during the entire vault.

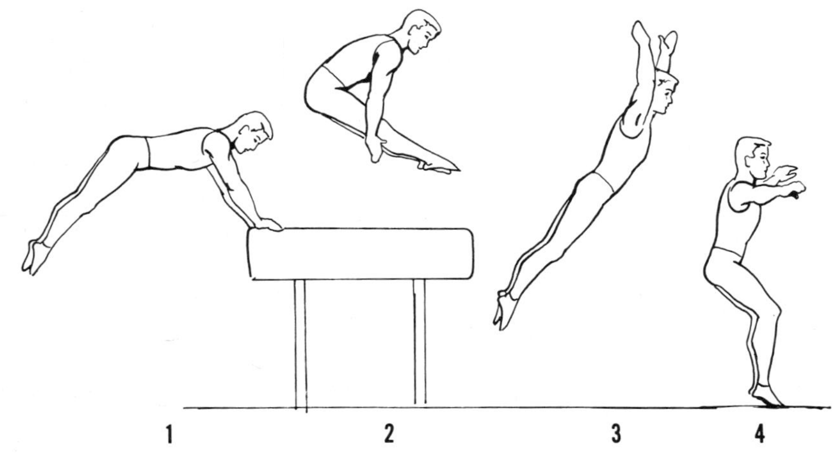

Fig. 4–33. Near End Stoop.

Teaching Techniques. The stoop over the cross horse and the squat-on stoop-off are both lead-ups. If the near end squat has been learned the gymnast should be ready to attempt this vault without any other teaching techniques.

Spotting. Spotting is the same as for the near end squat.

2. Pike Handspring or Yamashita (10.0 points) (Fig. 4–34). This vault, named after a famous Japanese gymnast, has become very popular, even though it was introduced quite recently. The take-off is much the same as for any other near end vault, but during the pre-flight the hips are raised so that at the time of hand contact the body is in a definite pike. The head should be back, the arms straight, and the shoulders behind the hands at the time of contact (1). This position will result in a good rebound off the horse and a high after-flight. The pike becomes quite pronounced during the after-flight (2), but when the end of the horse is cleared the body is stretched (3) prior to the landing, which is much the same as for a regular handspring (4).

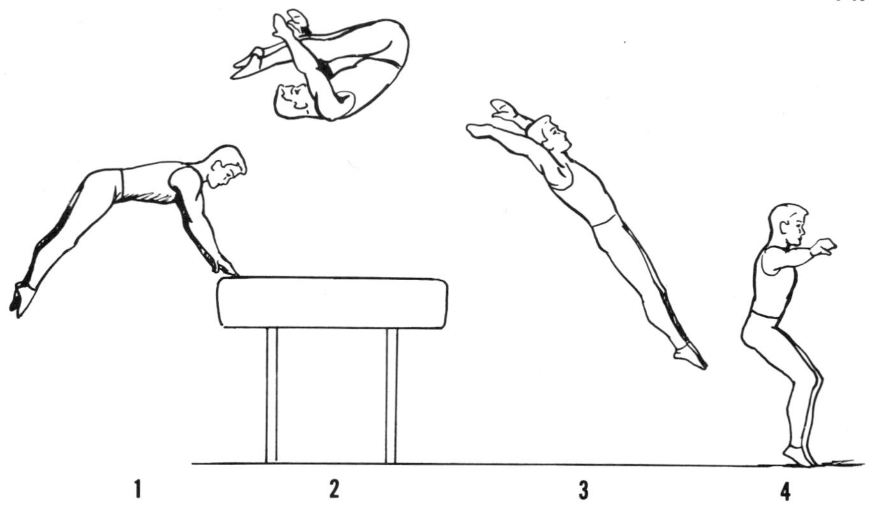

Fig. 4–34. Near End Pike Handspring or Yamashita.

Teaching Techniques. This vault is first learned over a cross horse. A rope can be held across the landing mat to indicate where the end of a long horse would be. If this rope can be cleared, the vaulter is ready to try the stunt over the long horse.

Spotting. One spotter stands beside the horse toward the far end in readiness to push under the vaulter's back if there is danger of his hitting the end of the horse. Another spotter stands several feet from the end of the horse to aid in the landing. He can reach across the performer's chest with one arm to prevent an overspin or lift under his back with the other arm to prevent an underspin.

5

Trampoline

There are many different versions of the origin of the trampoline. The dictionary defines "trampoline" as an exhibition on stilts. "Trampolin" in Spanish means "diving board." The idea for the modern trampoline probably came from aerial performers doing tumbling stunts in their safety net after dismounting from their trapeze.

Whatever the history may be, the modern trampoline, the piece of equipment as we know it today, has been developed in the United States in very recent years. Trampolining is the only gymnastic event that is truly American. The trampoline was first manufactured in quantity in 1937 by George Nissen of Cedar Rapids, Iowa. The trampoline event was first officially introduced into men's collegiate competition in 1948 and into A.A.U. competition in 1954. Since the Second World War the activity has grown greatly in popularity throughout the United States and Canada. The equipment is now manufactured in Europe and Japan and is rapidly growing in popularity throughout the world. The trampoline is not a recognized international gymnastic event, however, for either men or women and has never been an event in the Olympic Games. International competition has been held on the trampoline, but this competition has had no direct relationship to the sport of gymnastics and is instead conducted as a separate sport.

The trampoline has done a lot for the sport of gymnastics in our country. It appeals to younger children. Thousands of boys and girls have first become interested in the trampoline and later this interest has carried over to the other events.

At the time of writing there is another term being used for "trampolining." In the Amateur Athletic Union Rule Book it is known as "rebound tumbling." This term was also used in the collegiate rules for a period of two years. Teachers should be familiar with the term "rebound tumbling" as many written sources use this rather than "trampolining."

VALUES

Trampolining develops timing, coordination, a sense of balance, and control of the body in the air. The trampoline is also an excellent event for developing cardiovascular and respiratory fitness. It looks easy when you watch someone else bounce, but actually it takes considerable energy and good conditioning to bounce continuously for a period of just a couple of minutes. Trampolining is primarily a lower body activity. More can be accomplished in this event, than in the other five events, by the boy who lacks upper body strength, or by the boy who is overweight and can not handle his weight in the other events.

The trampoline can be used as a training aid for other gymnastic events. Many tumbling stunts, floor exercise movements, and dismounts from the other equipment can be taught first on the trampoline. The trampoline can also be used in teaching diving or as a conditioning activity for skiers or other athletes. Probably one of the greatest values of trampolining is the indirect value resulting from the enjoyment of the activity. It is fun to bounce. Students can relax, forget their worries, bounce their cares away, and thus improve their mental health.

SAFETY

Trampolining is somewhat dangerous, but so are many other physical education activities such as swimming and skiing. Automobiles are potentially far more dangerous than trampolines. With proper instruction and emphasis on safety procedures it can be made relatively safe. Most of the general safety procedures mentioned in Chapter 1 apply to the trampoline. Some of these should be re-emphasized when instruction in this event is given. The following points are the most important:

1. Do not allow any horseplay, especially horseplay that involves more than one on the trampoline at a time. This does not mean that two people cannot bounce at once. Instruction should be given in double bouncing. However, this text does not include this phase of trampolining.
2. A performer should never work out alone. A spotter is essential for many stunts. The spotter should be on the end of the trampoline, either in front of, or behind the performer, depending on the stunt. It might be wise to require two spotters at all times—one at

each end—so that the performer can execute stunts facing either direction. For extra safety a spotter might be placed on each side of the trampoline as well as on the ends, but spotters are seldom needed on the sides.

3. Encourage controlled bouncing. Excessively high bouncing should be forbidden.
4. Teach students how to get on and off (especially off) the trampoline. Do not let them bounce from the trampoline to the floor until they have reached the expert level. The hands should be placed on the frame of the trampoline when climbing off.
5. Do not allow inexperienced boys to use the trampoline unless supervised. Perhaps it should be kept locked and made available outside of class only to those who are well qualified.
6. Probably the most important safety precaution is to follow the right progression of stunts. Students should be taught to progress slowly, to overlearn fundamentals, and to try new stunts only when they are positive that they are ready for them. They should progress especially slowly and demand careful spotting when the somersault stage is reached.
7. Teach the technique of stopping the bounce or "killing the bounce" by flexing the knees upon contact with the bed. A performer should learn to judge when the center of gravity is not over his feet on a landing and use this technique of "killing the bounce" to prevent flying off onto the floor.
8. Frame pads are a necessity. They should be inspected regularly to see that they are securely fastened and cover all the metal frame.
9. Give instruction in unfolding and folding the trampoline. Many students have been injured because teachers have failed to do this and the trampoline has unfolded on them as they are setting it up or putting it away.

TEACHING TECHNIQUES

There are several general teaching hints that will help to make trampoline instruction successful. Assign three, or at the most five, students to a trampoline. Students who are waiting their turn should spot and learn by watching others perform. Performers should be limited in time, or in number of bounces, or number of stunts tried, each time they get on the trampoline. When this "time limit," "bounce limit," or "stunt limit" is completed, they should quickly climb off. The next student in line should be ready to climb or roll on just as quickly.

Before teaching stunts on the trampoline a beginner must learn a controlled bounce. A performer bounces with the feet about shoulder width apart for lateral stability. The feet may be brought together in the air and the toes pointed, but this should not be stressed for the beginner as he has enough to think about without this. The toes contact the bed first, but the heels also make contact, and the knees bend slightly as the performer sinks into the bed. The knees straighten vigorously on the rebound from the bed. The arms go through a circular motion during the bounce. They lift up the front of the body and reach overhead on the upward flight and move downward laterally, or out to the side of the body, during the downward flight. This circular motion is made with the arms relaxed and slightly bent and should not be exaggerated. The eyes look at the frame on the end of the trampoline. A performer should try to do all his bouncing on, or near, the center cross on the bed and should always face the end, not the side, of the trampoline.

RULES

Trampoline rules are in the process of change at the time this book is being written. The U.S.G.F., A.A.U., and high school rules in many states stipulate a routine of at least ten and not more than twelve contacts with the bed after the start of the first stunt. This rule was used by the N.C.A.A. for several years. College rules have recently been changed so that the trampoline rules parallel, in many respects, the rules for other gymnast events. This is a step in the right direction and one that will probably be adopted for general use in all competition in the near future. According to N.C.A.A. rules the exercise is composed of one sequence of at least eleven principal parts. The length of the routine is measured in "parts" rather than "bounces" or "contacts with the bed" and has a minimum number but not a maximum number just as the other events. A reasonable number of preparatory bounces are permitted before the start of the exercise.

Other requirements in the N.C.A.A. rules are:

1. All exercises must begin and terminate on the trampoline. This is unlike other apparatus in which there is a mount and dismount.
2. The last landing in the series must be on the feet, in a stationary position, in balance.
3. If a competitor touches the springs, or frame, or is assisted by a spotter he loses one full point.
4. There must be spotters on the sides and ends of the trampoline.
5. The area surrounding the trampoline must be covered with mats for a minimum of five feet.
6. Forward and backward somersaults and forward and backward twisting somersaults must be included.

7. Some part of the body other than the feet must contact the bed during the series. This means that there must be a stomach, back, seat, or knee landing in the exercise.

In this chapter the first three routines do not have eleven parts. They all have at least eleven contacts with the bed after the start of the first stunt but in many cases an extra bounce is "written into" the routine. Counting the parts has been done very generously. For example, the "swivel hips" has been counted as two parts instead of one; one part for the first seat drop and one part for the half-twist to second seat drop. In returning to the feet from any of the other landing positions it has been counted as a part if a twist, or some other reasonable complicated movement, is incorporated but otherwise it has not been counted.

As stated above, some extra bounces have been included by design in these routines. Until the routines have been completely mastered some other extra bounces might be needed but they should not be taken unless absolutely necessary as they are considered a fault, or break in the routine, and are penalized severely by the judges.

ABBREVIATED ROUTINE DESCRIPTIONS

I. Half-pirouette to front drop, feet, knee drop, feet, seat drop, half-twist to feet, full-pirouette to feet, seat drop, half-twist to seat drop, feet, back drop, feet (8 parts)

II. Half-twist to back drop, half-twist to feet, straddle touch toes to feet, front drop, half-turntable to front drop, feet, back drop, front drop, feet, back drop, pull-over to feet (9 parts)

III. Back somersault, seat drop, full-twist to seat drop, feet, back drop, half-twist to back drop (cradle), half-twist to feet, tuck bounce to feet, back somersault, seat drop, feet, front somersault (10 parts)

IV. Layout back somersault, baroni, back somersault, front one-and-one-quarter somersault, feet, three-quarter back somersault, front drop to back drop, half-twist to feet, seat drop, half-twist to seat drop, feet, back one-and-a-quarter somersault, pull-over to feet (11 parts)

V. One-and-a-half twisting front somersault, back somersault, baroni, back somersault, full-twisting back somersault, back somersault, three-quarter back somersault, cody, back somersault, baroni, back somersault, double back somersault (12 parts)

I. BEGINNING ROUTINE

1. Half-Pirouette to Front Drop (Fig. 5–1). This is a beautiful stunt if done high off the bed in an arched position all the way. It is a combination of two stunts that must be learned first—the half-pirouette and the front drop. Both of these skills are explained in detail under teaching techniques. As the performer leaves the bed he leans backward, looks over one shoulder, and starts to twist the upper body in the same direction (1). The hips are used as a pivot point with the legs being raised and the upper body lowered (2). The arms are usually kept out to the side like the wings of a bird

Fig. 5–1. Half-Pirouette to Front Drop.

during this stunt rather than being raised above the head as in the half-pirouette. The landing on the bed is the same as for a regular stomach drop (3). The performer has now turned 180° and is facing the opposite direction. To get back to his feet he pushes with the hands and forearms, raises the head, and pulls the feet back under the hips as he rebounds from the bed (4).

Teaching Techniques. The prerequisites for this stunt are the half-pirouette, the hand-knee drop (which is a prerequisite for the front drop), the front drop, and the half-pirouette to a hand-knee drop.

a. Half-Pirouette. A pirouette is nothing more than a half-turn in the air with the body vertical. As the performer leaves the bed, the head and upper body start to turn to the left (or right).

The arms lift in the normal way but continue to a position straight above the head so that they are a continuation of the longitudinal axis of the body as the height of the bounce is reached. The head should be erect. Looking down at the bed on a pirouette will usually result in landing off-balance. When the half turn has been completed, the arms go out to the side to stop the twisting motion.

b. HAND-KNEE DROP (DOGGIE DROP). As the performer leaves the bed, he leans forward so as to land in a hand and knee four-point position. The back should be horizontal, the head up slightly, and the weight equally distributed on the hands and lower legs.

c. FRONT DROP. As the performer leaves the bed, the hips are used as a pivot point. The legs are raised to the rear and the upper body is lowered forward. The hips should land approximately on the takeoff point. The palms of the hands, forearms, lower chest, abdomen, and thighs should contact the bed simultaneously. In this position the head should be up with the eyes focused on the end of the trampoline. To get back to the feet the performer pushes with the hands and forearms, raises the head, and pulls the feet back under the hips as he rebounds from the bed.

There are several teaching techniques necessary for the front drop. The first step is to lie flat on the bed and assume the prone position described above. The next step is to do the front drop immediately after a hand and knee drop. The body and head are in the right position in the hand and knee drop so that the only movement involved is to straighten the legs and reach forward slightly with the arms in order to drop to the prone position. The next step is to stand on the bed with the knees slightly flexed and bend forward at the waist so that the trunk is horizontal. From this position the learner springs slightly off the legs, raises them backward and lands in the front drop. A common mistake on the front drop is to dive forward. In lead-ups it should be stressed that the hips drop straight down and land on the bed immediately under their starting position.

d. HALF-PIROUETTE TO HAND-KNEE DROP. This stunt, which is the final step in the progression, needs no explanation. It is a combination of "a" and "b."

2. Knee Drop (Fig. 5–2). The performer returns to the feet after the first stunt in the routine. Following this foot landing the lower legs are raised backward for a landing on the knees, shins, and insteps. The knees should be slightly apart for balance. The trunk

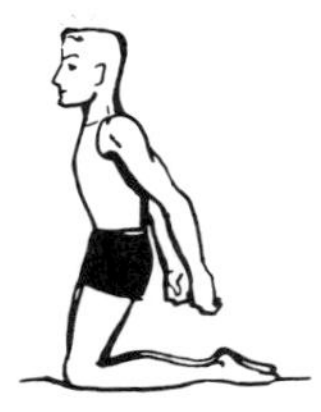

Fig. 5–2. Knee Drop.

should remain vertical with the back straight or very slightly flexed. If the back is arched on the landing, there is a tendency for the hips to snap further forward. This seldom results in injury, but it can be momentarily painful. If the hips are flexed too much, there will be very little rebound. The arms go through the same motions as during a regular bounce. This has already been explained in the introduction of this chapter. The head should be kept erect with the eyes focused on the frame at the end of the trampoline.

TEACHING TECHNIQUES. The stunt should be learned with a very low bounce.

3. Seat Drop (Fig. 5–3). Following the knee drop the performer returns to the feet (1). As he leaves the bed again, the body leans slightly backward and the legs are raised forward in a pike position (2). The landing on the bed is with the legs straight forward, the trunk slightly behind vertical, the head erect, and the hands on the bed slightly behind the hips with the fingers pointing toward the toes (3). As the performer rebounds from the trampoline, the hands give a push from the bed, the trunk is leaned forward, and the legs are pulled backward under the body.

Fig. 5–3. Seat Drop.

TEACHING TECHNIQUES. This stunt should be learned with very little bounce.

4. Seat Drop Half-Twist to Stand (Fig. 5–4). As the performer rebounds to the feet following the seat drop (1), a 180° turn is made so that he lands on the feet facing the opposite direction. This is the same movement as the half-pirouette except that it starts from a seat drop instead of from the feet. As the performer rebounds from the bed, the arms lift above the head and the head and upper body start to twist to the right (or left) (2). The legs are pulled back under the body, but by the time they reach the vertical position the half-twist has been completed (3).

Fig. 5–4. Seat Drop Half-Twist to Stand.

TEACHING TECHNIQUES. Before trying the seat drop half-twist to feet the performer should do a quarter-twist several times and end facing the side of the trampoline.

5. Full-Pirouette. The full-pirouette is a 360° twist or turn in a vertical position. The half-pirouette is a lead-up stunt. More twist has to be started as the performer rebounds from the bed than in the half-pirouette and the arms must remain over the head, in extension of the long axis of the body, a little longer. It is very important to keep the head erect. If the eyes look down at the bed before the twist is completed, it usually brings about a bend at the waist and this in turn results in an off-balance landing. The entire body must remain vertical throughout the stunt.

6 & 7. Seat Drop Half-Twist to Seat Drop (Swivel-Hips) (Fig. 5–5). Following the pirouette another seat drop is executed. The swivel

Fig. 5–5. Seat Drop Half-Twist to Seat Drop (Swivel Hips).

hips is actually a half-pirouette done from seat to seat rather than from feet to feet. On the rebound from the seat drop (1) the arms push off the bed and lift above the head, the head and upper body start to twist to the left (or right) with the head looking over the left shoulder (2), the legs are pulled back directly underneath the body to a vertical position (3). The twist continues and the legs are raised forward again (4). The stunt is completed in another seat drop (5).

TEACHING TECHNIQUES. The first lead-up stunt is a seat drop quarter-twist to a stand on the bed facing the side of the trampoline. The next is a seat drop half-twist to a stand facing the opposite direction. This stunt has already been described earlier in this routine. The most common mistake in learning the swivel hips is to swing the legs around to the side in a horizontal plane rather than to lower them to a vertical position. By using these two lead-up stunts this mistake will never develop.

8. Back Drop (Fig. 5–6). The performer returns to the feet following the seat drop half-twist to seat drop (1). The last stunt in the routine is the back drop. On the rebound from the bed the performer leans backward and raises the legs forward (2). The landing on the bed is on the flat of the back from the shoulder blades to the buttocks. The legs should be straight and form an angle of 60° to 80° with the bed of the trampoline. The head should be forward with the chin almost on the chest and the arms out to the side for balance (3). The elbows should be kept off the bed. It is a common mistake to drop the arms back to protect one-

Fig. 5–6. Back Drop.

self. This does not aid in any way and usually results in skinned elbows. Because the legs are in front of the contact point on the landing, as the performer rebounds from the bed the weight of the legs will help turn the body forward and bring the performer back to his feet. A little movement of the hips forward will also facilitate a return to the feet (4, 5).

TEACHING TECHNIQUES (Fig. 5–7). The performer should first become familiar with the landing position by assuming this position on the bed of the trampoline. The next step is to stand on the bed of the trampoline and hold an imaginary football at arms length in front of the body (1). One leg should be raised as if to kick this football and at the same time the performer should lean backward (2). Just as the balance is lost, the other leg should push slightly off the bed and be raised to the same position as the kicking leg. The arms continue to hold the imaginary football out in front of the body on the landing so that the elbows do not get in the way (3). The next step is to try the stunt with both legs being raised together from a stand, rather than a bounce.

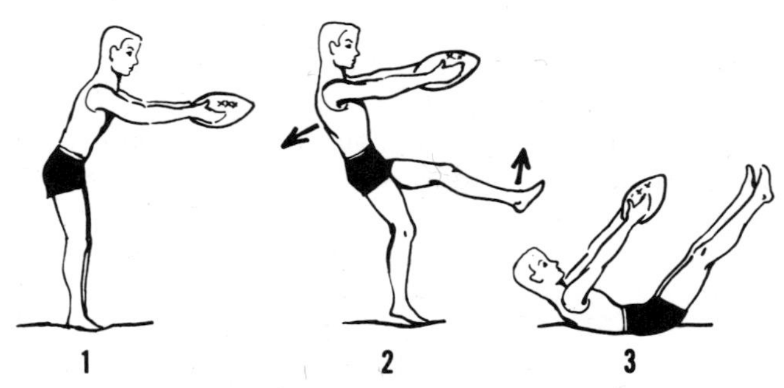

Fig. 5–7. Teaching Technique for Back Drop.

II. LOW INTERMEDIATE ROUTINE

1. Half-Twist to Back Drop (Fig. 5–8). This stunt starts as if the performer is going to do a front drop (1), but in the air the left hand is thrown across the chest and the head is turned to the right to look up at the ceiling (2). As the half-twist is completed, the legs are raised and the performer lands in a regular back drop position (3).

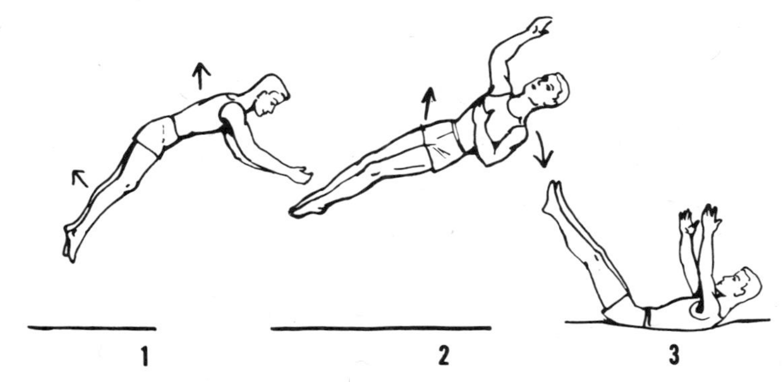

Fig. 5–8. Half-Twist to Back Drop.

TEACHING TECHNIQUES. Work into the stunt gradually. Start by standing on the bed, fall forward and twist on the way down while the feet are still in contact with the bed. Next do the stunt with a very low bounce.

2. Half-Twist to Feet (Fig. 5–9). As the performer rebounds from the bed after the back drop landing (1), the right arm is thrown across the chest and the left arm is pulled back and in close

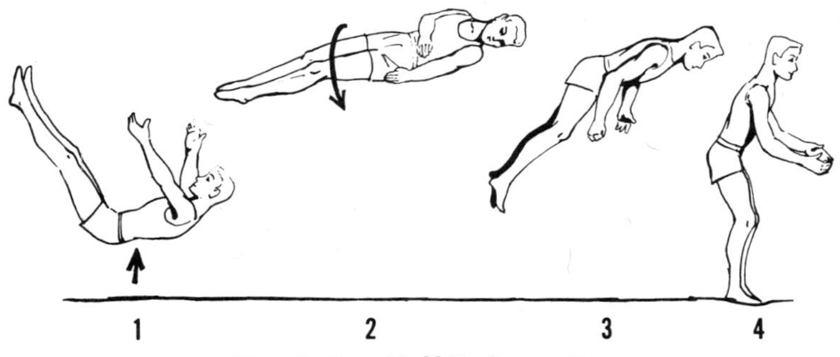

Fig. 5–9. Half-Twist to Feet.

to the left side of the body. The head turns to the left so that the face looks back toward the bed (2). The performer should get the feeling of lifting the hips and rolling them over (3). The landing is on the feet facing the opposite direction (4). A common mistake is to twist too soon before rebounding from the bed. The half-twist can be completed in this way, but the landing will be dead and it will be impossible to bounce out of it to accomplish the next stunt.

3. Straddle Touch Toes (Fig. 5–10). This is just a leap or pose in the air. It adds beauty and height to this routine that is composed largely of stunts that are done quite close to the bed. The performer should spring hard into the air following the back drop

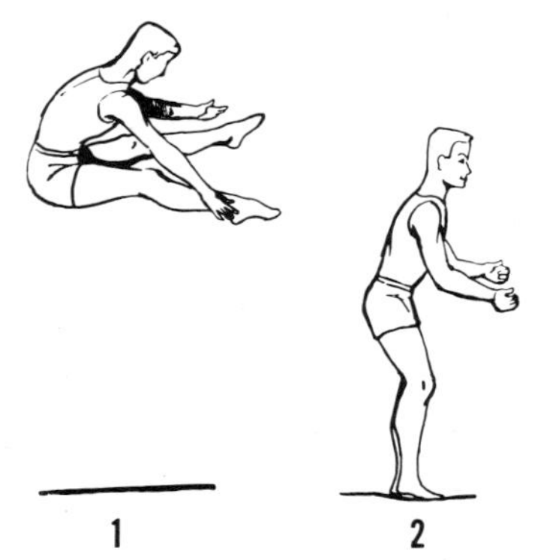

Fig. 5–10. Straddle Touch Toes.

half-twist to feet. At the height of the bounce, the legs are raised horizontally forward and spread wide apart. The trunk leans slightly forward and the arms reach for the toes (1). The legs are quickly lowered from this position to a regular vertical landing position (2).

4 & 5. Front Drop Half-Turntable to Front Drop (Fig. 5–11). The front drop has been described in Routine I. From the front drop landing the hands and forearms push to the right and the head moves vigorously to the left (1). The turntable is started with this push in the opposite direction from the intended movement while the body is straight. It is a common mistake to raise the head too high and look over the shoulder rather than to look at the upper arm. As the performer rebounds from the bed, the legs are tucked (or piked) thus shortening the body (2). This results in an increase in the speed of the turning motion. As the half-turntable is completed, the body is stretched for another regular front drop

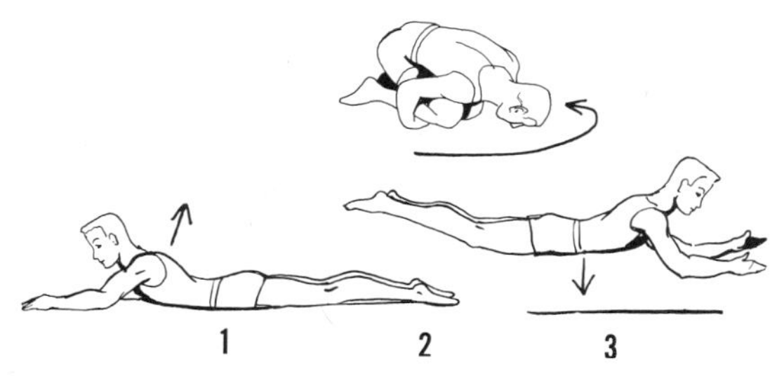

Fig. 5–11. Front Drop Half-Turntable to Front Drop.

landing (3). From the second front drop the performer should rebound back to the feet.

TEACHING TECHNIQUES. The turntable can first be tried from a hand-knee drop to another hand-knee drop. This lead-up is not necessary for most boys, however, as once a front drop is mastered the performer is ready to try the turntable without lead-up stunts.

6 & 7. Back Drop to Front Drop (Fig. 5–12). Both stunts have been described previously, but the movement between the two is new. From the back drop landing (1) the performer should get a kipping motion with the legs. This is done by extending them forcefully upward and forward at the time of rebound from the bed

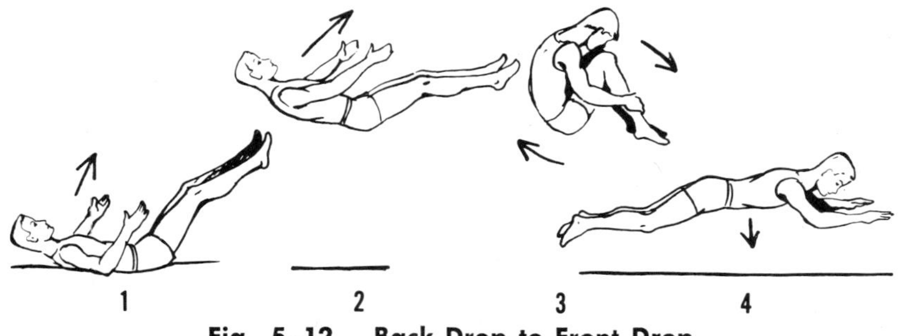

Fig. 5–12. Back Drop to Front Drop.

(2). The legs are drawn back under the body in the air (3). When the body reaches the horizontal position, the legs are stretched backward to a regular front drop landing (4). From this landing the performer rebounds to the feet.

TEACHING TECHNIQUES. This movement should be practiced from the back drop to a hand-knee drop at first.

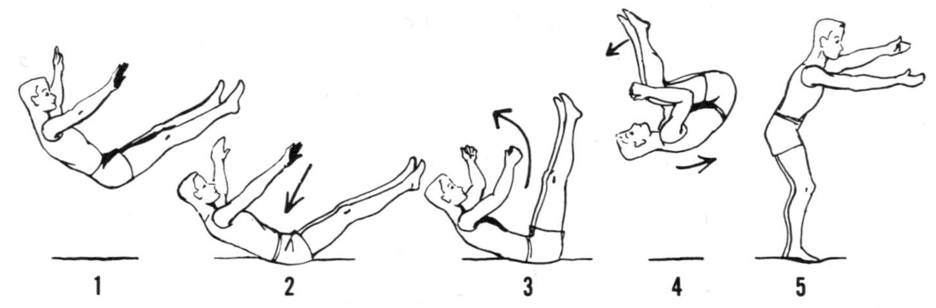

Fig. 5–13. Back Drop Pull-Over to Feet.

8 & 9. Back Drop Pull-Over to Feet (Fig. 5–13). The performer starts as if going into a regular back drop (1) but does not raise the feet as high. The landing is on the small of the back or the point of the buttocks with the legs at about a 30° angle with the bed. The upper back should be slightly off the bed and the head forward. The arms should be out to the side well off the bed (2). As the performer rebounds from the bed, there is a natural tendency to turn over backward as the center of gravity is located in the upper part of the body above the point of contact with the bed. This turning motion can be aided by starting to raise the legs and by pulling them over the head while still in contact with the bed (3). The legs can be tucked to shorten the radius and thus speed up the turning motion when in the air (4). The landing is on the feet in balance with the arms out to the side (5).

Teaching Techniques. This stunt can be approached very gradually by first doing a backward roll on the bed of the trampoline. The next step is to fall backward into the backward roll. By gradually increasing the height of the fall the backward roll eventually will become a backward pull-over. During this learning process the hands can be held in the regular position for a backward roll to protect the head and neck. If the landing is on the point of the buttocks rather than the small of the back during the initial steps, the turning motion will be facilitated.

Spotting. Remove about two springs from the side of the trampoline. Stand in this area between the frame and the bed of the trampoline. Lift under the shoulder with one hand and aid the turning motion with the other hand by pushing on the back of the thighs as the performer rebounds from the bed.

III. INTERMEDIATE ROUTINE

1. Back Somersault (Back Flip) (Fig. 5–14). The stunts taught up to this point have been reasonably safe to learn. Only one has involved a position in which the head is below the rest of the body. It must be impressed upon all students that the "back flip," or for that matter any stunt that involves the body being upside down in the air, is potentially very dangerous and unless safety rules are followed serious accidents might occur. Most of the really active students in a physical education class are overly anxious to learn a "flip." The instructor should not scare these students but rather caution them. Most boys in a physical education class are capable of learning a back somersault on the trampoline.

To start the back somersault, the arms reach in the normal way but possibly a little harder and a little higher so that they finish almost straight above the head. Before the feet leave the bed the rotation for the somersault is started by lifting the chest or arching the upper body slightly (1). At this point the hips must remain forward so that the center of gravity is almost above the feet or takeoff point. After the feet leave the bed, the body stretches momentarily with the head and upper body leaning backward (2). The knees are then pulled up toward the chest in a tuck position (3). The backward somersault—which was started by the chest lift

Fig. 5–14. Back Somersault (Back Flip).

that placed the head and upper body behind, and the hips slightly ahead of, the center of gravity—will speed up as the radius is shortened by pulling up the knees. As the legs reach the arms, the hands can grasp the shins, but this is not necessary (4). About halfway through the somersault, if the head is back, the performer should be able to see the bed of the trampoline. Shortly after the halfway point in the somersault the tuck is gradually opened up (5) ready for the landing (6).

TEACHING TECHNIQUES. Some instructors prefer to teach what is commonly called a "trampoline back" because it is easier for most students than the somersault described above. In the "trampoline back" the head and upper body lean back much more than in the tuck back somersault. This would result in a traveling back somersault if the hips were not kept well forward over the center of gravity. The hips thrust forward as well as upward during the first part of this type of somersault. After the takeoff the knees are drawn up a little, but this movement is not as pronounced as in the back tuck. Whatever method is taught first, the back somersault should certainly be learned completely before an attempt is made to put it in a routine. Several controlled preliminary bounces of medium height should be used before each practice trial.

The two most common mistakes made by those learning the back somersault are: 1) on the takeoff bounce the feet are thrust forward; 2) the upper body leans too far backward. Both of these mistakes result in a low traveling back somersault because the center of gravity is behind the feet on the takeoff. Traveling back somersaults can usually be corrected by moving the performer back on the bed and forcing him to start the somersault with only about three feet of bed behind him. Most performers soon learn to move forward or "gain" when presented with this situation. This technique should only be used with the learner in an overhead belt.

SPOTTING. There are two types of spotting that can be used. "On-the-bed" spotting can be used for all except the very heavy students if the spotter is strong. In "on-the-bed" spotting (Fig. 5–15) the instructor bounces with the performer. One hand grasps a rope, a towel, or the top of the performer's shorts and the other is free to help spin or support the performer in one way or another (1). The spotter usually counts 1, 2, 3 and on three kills his bounce so that his feet remain on the trampoline (2). The spotter should practice this preliminary technique before attempting to spot a somersault. The first step in teaching a back somersault by the "on-the-bed" spotting technique is to hold the towel around the

Fig. 5–15. "On-the-Bed" Spotting for Back Somersault.

waist with the left hand and use the right hand to support the upper back while the performer reaches with the arms and leans the head and upper body backward (3). The spotter momentarily supports the performer's weight in the air but tips him back to land on his feet. The next step is exactly the same except that the performer draws his knees up to his chest as he leans back on the spotter's hand (4). In the next step the spotter changes hands and grasps the towel that is wrapped around the waist with the right hand and uses the left hand under the hips of the performer to help spin him as he attempts the complete somersault (5). The last step in "on-the-bed" spotting is to stand on the frame of the trampoline and, as the performer leaves the bed to execute the somersault, step quickly onto the bed ready to give aid if necessary.

The only good method of spotting back somersaults on the trampoline, if the performers are large or if the teacher is small, is to use a belt suspended from the ceiling by ropes that run through pulleys (Fig. 5–16). The distance between the pulleys should be about the same as the height from the trampoline to the beam on which the pulleys are fastened. This overhead spotting rig can be easily installed by the teacher or maintenance man.

When using one of these overhead spotting belts, the spotter should keep the ropes taut as the performer bounces up and down. This involves considerable arm movement on the part of the spotter. The usual technique is to grasp the rope firmly with one hand and pull down as the performer bounces in the air and then relax and raise the arm as the performer descends. The other hand forms an

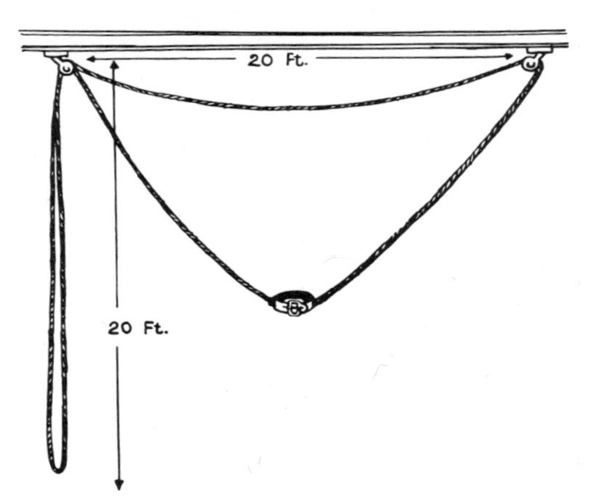

Fig. 5–16. Overhead Spotting Belt.

"eye" through which the rope can slide during the performer's preliminary bounces, but as the performer executes the somersault both hands grasp the rope ready to support the performer's weight if necessary.

2 & 3. Seat Drop Full-Twist to Seat Drop (Fig. 5–17). The back somersault is completed on the feet and then a seat drop is executed as described in Routine I. Before completely rebounding from the seat drop position, the performer starts the twist in the desired direction by pushing with the hands and turning the head and trunk slightly (1). The performer then leans backward from the waist so that the trunk and legs form a straight line almost parallel to the surface of the trampoline. One arm is thrown across the chest and the other backward and close to the side of the body. The head and upper body continue to twist in the direction started (2). In this position, with the body straight and the radius very short

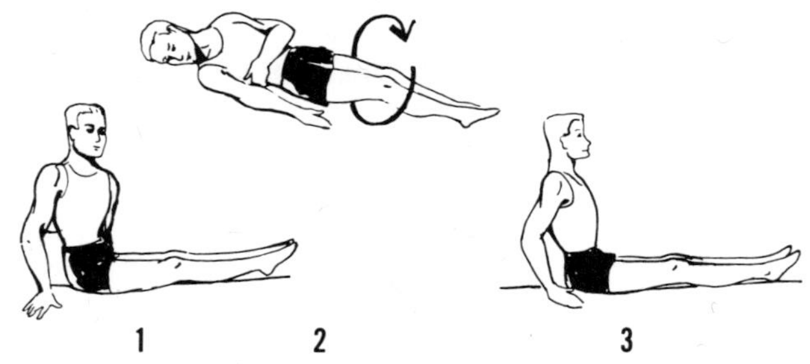

Fig. 5–17. Seat Drop Full-Twist to Seat Drop.

around the long axis, the twist is easy to complete. As it is completed the trunk is raised to an almost vertical position for the second seat drop landing (3). In this stunt the feet and legs point toward the same end of the trampoline, parallel to the side of the bed throughout the entire movement.

TEACHING TECHNIQUES. A lead-up stunt that can be used is a seat drop half-twist to stomach drop. This teaches the performer to lean the upper body backward during the twist.

4 & 5. Back Drop Half-Twist to Back Drop (Cradle) (Fig. 5–18). This stunt is a combination of two stunts that have already been explained in Routine II, the "back drop to front drop" and the "half-twist to back drop." Following the seat drop full-twist to seat drop the performer comes back to his feet. He must learn to "dig in" hard and use leg power to regain a reasonable amount of height after the seat full-twist to seat, which is a stunt that ends quite low.

Fig. 5–18. Back Drop Half-Twist to Back Drop (Cradle).

The cradle starts from a regular back drop landing (1). The motion is exactly the same as if the performer is going to go from the back drop to a front drop (2). When the bed can be seen, the twist starts in the air as described in the half-twist to back drop (3). The landing is in a regular back drop landing facing the opposite direction from the first back drop (4).

TEACHING TECHNIQUES. Learn the two lead-up stunts mentioned before attempting the cradle.

6. Half-Twist to Feet. In order to get back to the feet after the cradle a half-twist is executed. This move has already been explained in Routine II. Refer to Fig. 5–9.

7. Tuck Bounce. The performer will undoubtedly have lost most of his height at this point in the routine. The tuck bounce is designed to help regain height. It is necessary to "dig in" hard and use leg power to spring high in the air. The arms first stretch high above the head to add height to the bounce, and then they lower and grasp the lower legs as they are drawn up into a tuck position. This position is held momentarily and then the body is stretched again for the next landing on the feet.

8. Back Somersault. As this is the second back somersault used in this routine, it does not have to be described again. Refer to Fig. 5–14.

9. Seat Drop. This stunt was described in the first routine. It is used in this routine to enable the performer to regain control in case he is slightly off-balance after the back somersault.

10. Front Somersault (Fig. 5–19). Following the seat drop the performer returns to his feet. This landing is a very important one as the feet must be placed just right so as to obtain the correct position for the front somersault. The body should be slightly piked on the takeoff so that the hips are behind and the head in front of the center of gravity. The arms should be bent with the elbows close to the body and the hands about shoulder height (1). On the rebound the arms reach up, the hips lift backward, and the head starts forward (2). In the air the arms continue their motion forward, the head is tucked onto the chest, and the legs are drawn up into a tuck position. The hands usually grasp the shins in this tuck position (3). The performer must "time" the spin of the somer-

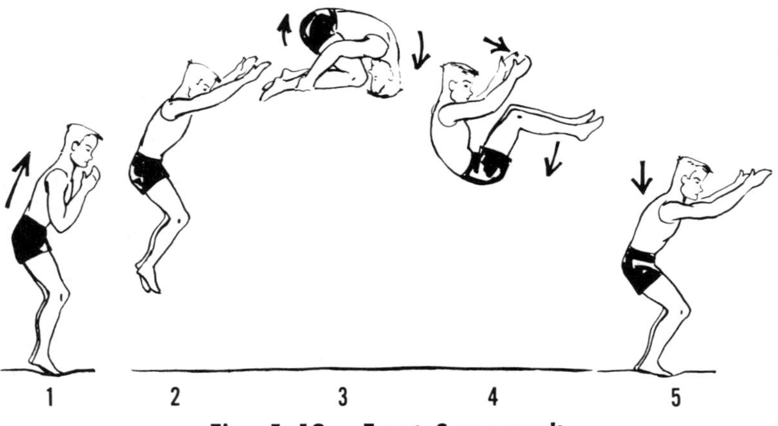

Fig. 5–19. Front Somersault.

sault and open out at the right time (4) in an upright position (5) as the bed can not be seen on the landing of the front somersault as in the back somersault. Although the front somersault seems easier at first for most performers, it is harder to get a balanced landing after the front somersault than after the back flip. As it is very difficult to land well enough to be able to do another stunt immediately following, the front somersault is seldom used in trampoline routines. Even though it is not used very much in routines, it is essential for a performer to learn the front somersault if he wants to continue with advanced trampoline work, as the same movement is used in several of the more advanced stunts.

Teaching Techniques. The first step is to do a hand-knee drop and on the rebound to tuck the head under and somersault over to the back. This should be tried several times until it can be ended in a seat landing. The next step is to do a knee drop and on the rebound tuck the head under in the same way and somersault to the back. After several trials this can be done to the seat and finally to the feet. Next the performer should start from the feet but at first should bend forward from the waist at right angles and somersault to a back landing and then a seat landing. The body can gradually be straightened on the takeoff and the height of the somersault increased so that the feet can be placed underneath on the landing. Performers should be cautioned to keep their knees apart and not to relax their legs on the landing. One of the most common accidents on the trampoline is to hit the chin against the knees on the landing of a front somersault. Most of these accidents can be prevented if the performers are warned ahead of time.

Spotting. The spotters standing around the trampoline, especially the one on the end the performer is facing, should watch

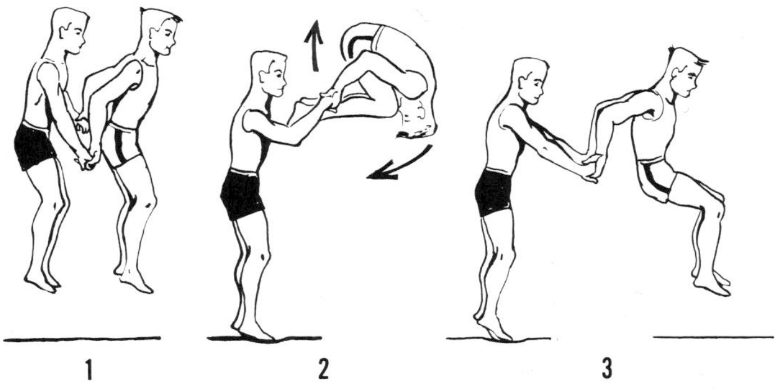

Fig. 5–20. On-the-Bed Spotting for Front Somersault.

carefully to prevent the performer from bouncing off the bed. Apart from this, spotting is not commonly used for the front somersault. If proper progression is followed, it is not necessary to help the performer. An overhead belt, recommended for use with the back somersault may also be used for the front somersault, however. A type of on-the-bed spotting may also be used (Fig. 5–20). In this method the spotter bounces directly behind the performer (1) and holds his hands throughout the entire stunt. Just as in any method of on-the-bed spotting the spotter must kill his bounce and remain in contact with the bed as the stunt is executed (2, 3).

IV. LOW ADVANCED ROUTINE

1. Layout Back Somersault (Fig. 5–21). A "layout" somersault is an arched body somersault. More backward spin has to be started off the bed than in a regular back somersault because the legs are not tucked to shorten the radius and thus speed up the spin. This means that the chest and upper body have to be leaned backward a little more than in the tuck back somersault. This in turn means the hips have to be carried further forward so that the center of gravity is not too far behind the feet. If the center of gravity does get too far behind the feet, the somersault will be low and the performer will travel backward. On the takeoff, therefore, the hips are forward, the upper body and head are back, and the arms are stretched vertically (1). In the air the arms move in a smooth pulling motion from a position above the head to one out to the side of the body, the head pulls hard backward, the chest and the stomach thrust well forward to give an arch to the body, and the legs

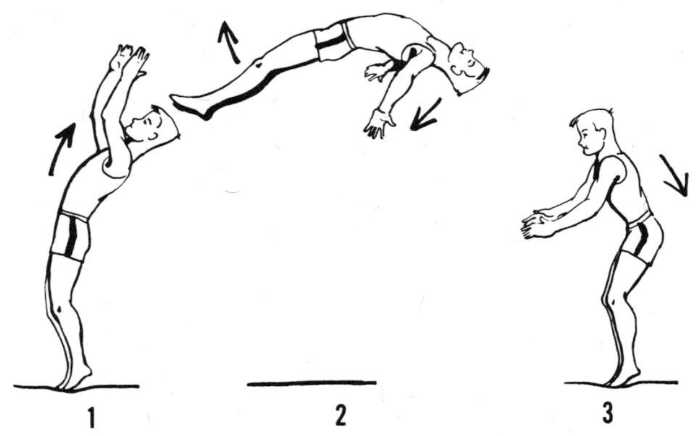

Fig. 5–21. Layout Back Somersault.

trail straight and together behind the upper body (2). As the somersault is completed, the head returns to an erect or maybe a slightly forward position and the body pikes slightly ready for the landing (3).

TEACHING TECHNIQUES. Even though the regular back somersault has been learned, the performer will probably have to get back into the belt to learn the layout back. The same teaching techniques and spotting techniques should be used in teaching this somersault.

2. Baroni (Fig. 5–22). The baroni is a half-twisting front somersault in a pike position. It is very similar to the roundoff in tumbling except that it is done without resting the weight on the hands. To present the baroni as described here it must be assumed that

Fig. 5–22. Baroni.

the teacher is acquainted with the roundoff and that the student has at least partially learned this stunt on the tumbling mats.

The takeoff position is the same as for the front somersault. The body should be slightly piked so that the hips are behind and the head and upper body in front of the center of gravity. The arms are bent so that the elbows are down and close to the side of the body and the hands are about shoulder height (1). The twisting motion is started before the performer leaves the bed by turning the head and upper body slightly to the side. During the upward flight the arms reach up and then forward and the hips lift directly up behind the body (2). As the performer reaches maximum height, the body is straightened and the legs pass directly over the head. A quarter-twist has been completed at this point (3). On the way down the body is piked again and the second quarter-twist is executed (4). The landing should be in approximately the same position as the takeoff (5).

TEACHING TECHNIQUES. The first step in learning the baroni is to do a roundoff from a knee landing to a knee landing with the hands touching the bed in between the two landings. The feet must go directly over the head and not around to the side. The eyes can be focused on the bed of the trampoline throughout this lead-up drill and, for that matter, while the baroni itself is executed. The next step is to do a two-foot roundoff from feet to hands to feet. The final step is to try the complete stunt but to work slowly from a low bounce to a higher one.

There is another method of teaching the baroni that is used very successfully by a few teachers. It is both a teaching technique and a method of spotting. Refer to Fig. 5–20—on-the-bed spotting for the front somersault. This technique is exactly the same for the baroni except that after the front somersault is half completed the spotter crosses his arms. This turns the performer 180° to land facing the spotter with his arms also crossed.

SPOTTING. This stunt can be spotted in an overhead belt. A twisting belt (see Fig. 5–26) makes it easier to spot the performer, but a regular belt can be used if the performer twists halfway round before attempting the stunt so that he unwinds the ropes as the stunt is done. Usually the stunt is learned without spotting by following the teaching techniques outlined above.

3. Back Somersault. The back somersault was taught in Routine III. Refer to Fig. 5–14.

4. Front One-and-One-Quarter Somersault to a Front Drop. This stunt does not need to be described in detail as it is much the same as the front somersault taught in the previous routine. The tuck position is held a little longer so that an extra quarter-somersault is executed. The performer straightens out and lands in a front drop position. This stunt is actually easier than a front somersault to the feet in which the performer does not see the bed until approximately the time of the landing. In this stunt the bed can be seen for some time before the front drop landing and therefore the landing position can be much more easily controlled.

Teaching Techniques. The stunt can first be done to a hand-knee landing.

5. Three-Quarter Back Somersault. Following the front one-and-one-quarter somersault to the front drop landing the performer returns to the feet. As the bounce will be quite low at this point in the routine, it is necessary to dig in hard and use leg power to obtain sufficient height for the next stunt. A three-quarter back somersault is a slow, lazy layout back somersault done to a stomach landing rather than to the feet. The same techniques that were used for the layout somersault apply to this stunt. The takeoff position and position in the air during the first part of the somersault are much the same but less chest lift and less head and arm pull are used so that only three-quarters of a somersault are executed. The landing is in a front drop position.

Teaching Techniques. Until the performer learns to adjust his position in the air and land in a good front drop, it is much safer to land in a hand-knee drop.

6. Front Drop to Back Drop (Fig. 5–23). The three-quarter back somersault ends in a front drop landing (1). As the performer rebounds from the bed, he pushes with the hands, lifts with the head,

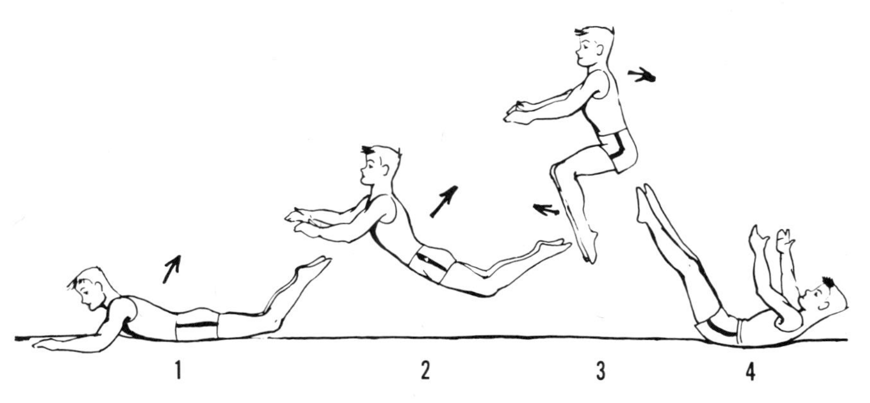

Fig. 5–23. Front Drop to Back Drop.

arches the upper body, and flexes the knees (2). In the air the knees are drawn up to the chest to shorten the radius around the axis of revolution (3). The movement ends in a regular back drop landing facing the same direction as the front drop (4).

Teaching Techniques. A front drop to seat drop can be tried first. However, it is unlikely that any lead-ups will be needed.

7. Half-Twist to Feet. This stunt was included in Routine II. Refer to Fig. 5–9.

8 & 9. Seat Drop, Half-Twist to Seat Drop (Swivel Hips). Refer to Fig. 5–5 in Routine I for this stunt.

10 & 11. Back One-and-One-Quarter Somersault Pull-Over to Feet (Fig. 5–24). Following the swivel hips the performer returns to the feet. It is necessary to dig in hard and use leg power to get enough height for this stunt, which is really a combination of two stunts—the back somersault (1) (2) and the back drop pull-over to feet. The back somersault is overspun so that the feet miss the bed (3). The tuck position in the somersault must be held longer than for a regular back somersault. The landing is on the small of the back (4). From this position the pull-over is executed exactly as described in Routine II, which was also finished with a pull-over (5) (6).

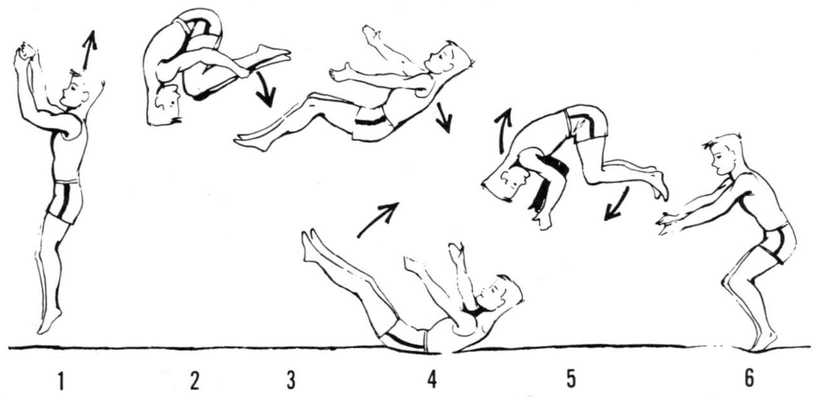

Fig. 5–24. Back One-and-One-Quarter Somersault Pull-Over to Feet.

Teaching Techniques. The tuck back somersault should be completely mastered before this stunt is attempted. The next step is to land in a seat drop landing. This requires very little extra spin but does give the idea of going slightly beyond a foot landing. The next step is to land on the back but to rebound back to the feet as in a regular back drop instead of pulling over to the feet.

V. ADVANCED ROUTINE

1. Front One-and-One-Half Twisting Somersault (Rudolph) (Fig. 5–25). The front somersault with a one-and-one-half twist is

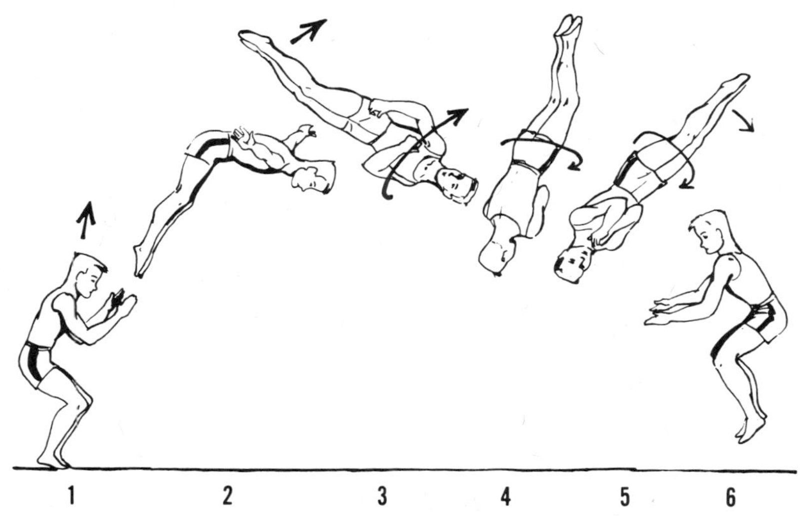

Fig. 5–25. Front One-and-One-Half Twisting Somersault.

started much the same as a baroni. On the takeoff the body is in a slight pike position with the hips behind and the head and upper body in front of the feet (1). The feet push up and back on the takeoff and the hips lift hard upward and backward. The arms also lift upward during this part of the stunt. About the time maximum height has been reached, the body should be upside down in a right angle pike position with the arms stretched out to the side of the body and the head back with the eyes focused on the bed (2). From this position the twist starts. If the twist is to the right, the left arm is thrown vigorously across the front of the body with the hand almost brushing the ankle and the right elbow is thrown backward (3). The head is also turned to the right and looks over the right shoulder. The body then straightens and both arms pull in close to the chest so that the radius around the longitudinal axis is as short as possible during the twist (4). The twist is completed with the body in a straight position (5). As the one-and-one-half twist is completed, the arms move out away from the body and the hips are slightly flexed so that the landing will be in a slight pike position (6).

Teaching Techniques. There are several stunts that can be considered lead-up stunts besides the baroni. Two of the best that help teach the twisting motion are the one-and-one-half twist to a back drop, which starts with a forward motion as if going for a front drop and the full twisting cradle. (The regular cradle goes from back to back with a half-twist; a full-twisting cradle goes from back to back with a one-and-one-half twist.)

SPOTTING. The only satisfactory way to spot this stunt is with a twisting belt suspended from an overhead spotting rig. There are two kinds of twisting belts available, both of which are very satisfactory. Both types use the same principle—an inner belt that spins within an outer belt. The performer is fastened into the inner belt and the supporting ropes are attached to the outer belt. The performer, with the inner belt fastened securely to him, can twist freely within the outer belt, which is prevented from twisting by the supporting ropes. Figure 5–26a shows a twisting belt with an

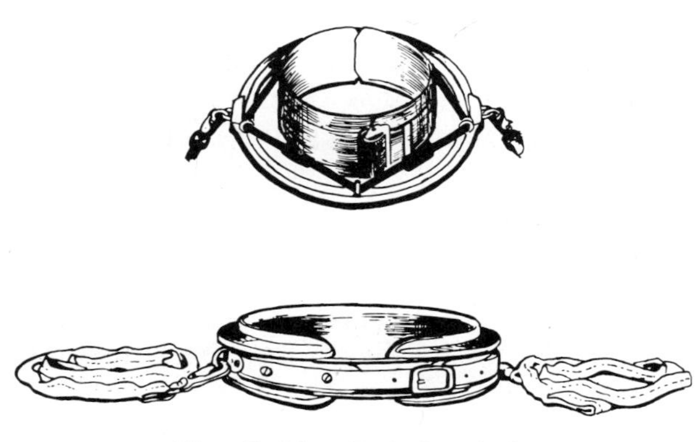

Fig. 5–26. Twisting Belts.

inner belt that spins within the outer belt on a roller bearing track. Figure 5–26b shows another type with an inner plastic belt that spins within an outer metal belt. Both inner and outer belts have very smooth surfaces that offer little resistance as they slide on one another.

2. Back Somersault. The back somersault is used a great deal in advanced trampoline work much as an extra bounce is used at the beginning level—as a method to regain control and equilibrium. In this routine there are five back somersaults used between stunts of greater difficulty. In competition the judges would deduct points for this, even though the somersaults were executed perfectly. Although it is considered poor combination to include a great number of ordinary back somersaults, most trampolinists, except the very advanced, will have to be satisfied with an exercise of this type. Refer to Fig. 5–14 in Routine III.

3. Baroni. Refer to Fig. 5–22 in Routine IV. The baroni is a very important stunt when a trampolinist reaches the advanced level. As well as learning twisting and double somersaults he must learn to combine somersaults into series and maintain control while doing so. This can best be accomplished by practicing series of alternating back somersaults and baronis. In this particular routine a series of "back-baroni-back" appears twice. If this combination can not be executed in perfect control, it will be very difficult to complete the routine.

4. Back Somersault. Refer to Fig. 5–14 in Routine III.

5. Full-Twisting Back Somersault (Fig. 5–27). The full-twisting back somersault starts much like a layout back somersault. The arms lift almost straight above the head with the hands a little wider apart than the shoulders. The upper body leans well back, but the hips are kept forward so that the center of gravity is approximately above the feet (1). Backward twists are usually started before the feet leave the bed, although this is not the only method that can be used. The twist is started with the upper body by turning the head, shoulders, and trunk slightly in the desired direction while the feet are still in contact with the bed. The feet can also help initiate the twist by pushing sideways on the bed on the takeoff. The twisting motion started on the bed will con-

Fig. 5–27. Full-Twisting Back Somersault.

tinue in the air especially if the body is kept straight to facilitate the twist (2). The arm motion is very important. Both arms lift above the head in a fairly wide position and then in the air are wrapped in close against the chest to shorten the radius around the twisting axis and thereby speed up the twist. In a twist to the left, the right arm is thrown across the front of the head in a straight position and then the elbow bends and the arm folds in close to the chest. The left arm throws backward with the elbow bending in close to the side and the hand against the chest (3). The straight body position with the arms wrapped in close to the chest is maintained until the twist and the somersault have almost been completed (4). The arms then extend out to the side to stop the twist and the body pikes slightly ready for the landing (5) (6).

TEACHING TECHNIQUES. The performer should be able to do a good layout back somersault and a full-pirouette before attempting a full-twisting back somersault. Most boys take far too many preliminary bounces before trying the twist. A good part of each practice session should be spent trying the twist after just one preliminary bounce at a very low height. It helps some performers to think about thrusting the right hip forward when trying to twist to the left.

SPOTTING. The only satisfactory way for most teachers to spot a full-twisting back somersault is with an overhead spotting rig and a twisting belt, as described for the front somersault with a one-and-one-half twist in this routine. Some very experienced spotters can spot a full-twist by hand by bouncing on the bed with the performer. This method is not recommended for most teachers. A regular belt can be used by turning 360° and wrapping the ropes around the waist before the stunt is started. The ropes unwind as the twist is executed.

6. Back Somersault. Refer to Fig. 5–14 in Routine III.

7. Three-Quarter Back Somersault. This stunt was included in the previous routine. It is a slow, lazy layout somersault that does not turn all the way to the feet but instead ends in a front drop landing. It was not illustrated in the previous routine because of the similarity between the three-quarter back and the regular layout somersault, which was illustrated in Fig. 5–21.

8. Cody (Fig. 5–28). The cody is a back somersault done from a stomach landing. It can be started from a regular front drop, but it is usually done after a three-quarter back somersault as in

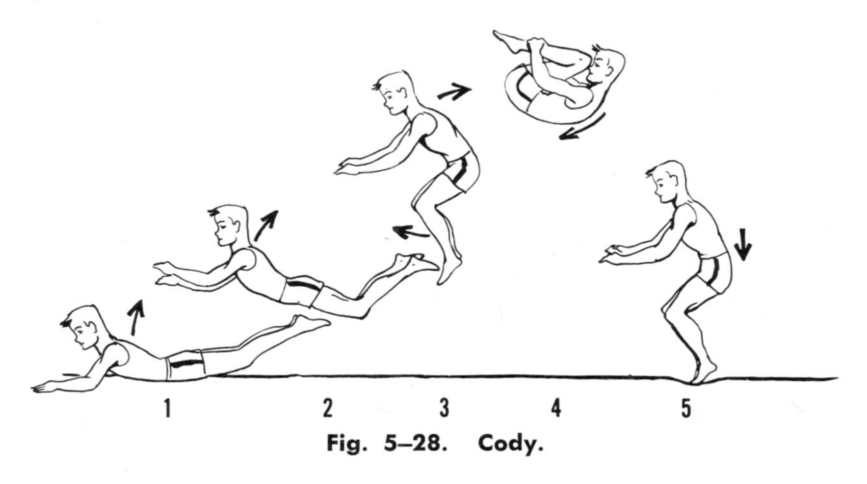

Fig. 5–28. Cody.

this routine. The landing at the start of the stunt is the same as a front drop except that the knees are flexed so that the feet are off the bed (1). The somersault is started by pushing from the bed with the hands and lifting with the head and upper body (2). As the performer rebounds off the bed, the upper body rebounds faster than the legs and lower body and thus starts the backward somersault (3). As the body leaves the bed, the knees are drawn up to the chest into a tight tuck (4). The radius is thus shortened and the rotation of the somersault speeded up. The performer opens out of the tuck for the landing (5).

TEACHING TECHNIQUES. The performer should master a front drop to a back drop before trying the cody. He should also be able to do a good tightly tucked back somersault.

SPOTTING. The cody can be spotted with an overhead spotting belt or with a hand spot. In the hand spotting method the spotter stands on the frame of the trampoline and, as the performer rebounds from the bed, quickly steps onto the bed and helps to turn him over to his feet. The spotter must be careful not to step onto the bed until the performer is completely clear of the bed.

9. Back Somersault. Refer to Fig. 5–14 in Routine III.

10. Baroni. Described in Routine IV, pages 173–74.

11. Back Somersault. Refer to Fig. 5–14 in Routine III.

12. Double Back Somersault. This stunt does not take a great deal of skill but does take considerable leg power. It is usually more difficult for a young boy to learn than for a more mature individual because of this. The double back somersault starts much like a layout back somersault. The arms lift hard straight up above the head. The head and upper body lean backward, but to compensate for this the hips stay well forward and must be forced in a forward and upward direction by the leg push at the time of takeoff. This type of takeoff results in a fast backward rotation being started without too much backward travel. The performer maintains this stretched position in the air momentarily and then the knees are drawn up into a tight tuck position. This position is maintained until the double somersault has been almost completed at which time the tuck is opened for the landing. The opening of the tuck and the timing of the landing must be done by "feel" as the rotation is too fast for the performer to "see" where he is until after the rotation has been slowed down by opening the tuck.

Teaching Techniques. Before starting on the double back somersault the performer should be able to do high tuck and high layout back somersaults in good control. As there is a natural tendency to start to open the tuck after the first revolution, the performer should be told to make a conscious effort to pull in the legs a little tighter at this time. Three things should be emphasized in a double back somersault:

1. A high bounce to give more time in the air.
2. A takeoff that gets lots of backward rotation started.
3. A tight tuck after the rotation has been started.

A boy who is not able to complete the double somersault must be lacking in one or more of these things.

Spotting. An overhead spotting rig should be used to teach this stunt.

6

Horizontal Bar

The horizontal bar, commonly called the high bar, was first used as a piece of gymnastic equipment by Jahn in Germany shortly after the start of the nineteenth century. The idea came from watching children play on the branches of trees. From this beginning the horizontal bar has developed into one of the most popular gymnastic events for both competitors and spectators.

One of the most important values of the horizontal bar is the development of courage, daring, and self-confidence. It also develops great finger, hand, and forearm strength, as a good grip is essential for performance in this event.

There is such a great variety of stunts and combinations that can be performed on the horizontal bar that it is impossible to include more than a sample of them in one chapter. An attempt has been made to include all of the basic skills as well as some of the more common and popular novelty moves. Ample material is contained for schools with even a very extensive instructional program in gymnastics. Readers wishing knowledge of very advanced work, however, will have to refer to other sources.

EQUIPMENT

A regulation bar is 94½ inches in length, 1⅛ inches in diameter, and 98½ inches above the mat. The bar should be made of spring steel. This material is expensive, but it is inadvisable to buy anything else because it will not have the proper performance quality. The width of a bar is important. Working between uprights that are close together is very disconcerting. The width also determines, in part, the amount of flex, or spring, the bar has. It is difficult for an inexperienced person to realize how important it is to have a springy bar. A bar should bend approximately four inches when being used by a person of average weight and spring back to a straight position when not in use. It is important that the bar be fastened to the uprights in such a way as to facilitate the flex or spring and not to limit it.

Most schools in the United States have only one bar. It is very desirable, however, to have more than one horizontal bar for classes or for team practice sessions and if possible three bars should be used. One of these should be adjusted to chest height, one to about head height, and one to regulation height. This makes it possible to practice all types of stunts and lead-ups without time-consuming adjustment of the bar. Needless to say the extra bars also permit three to work at a time rather than just one. If only one bar is available, it is best to plan one lesson so that only low bar stunts are practiced and the next lesson so that only a high bar is needed. This eliminates the need to adjust the bar during the class period. Certainly, if only one bar is to be purchased by a school it should be one that will adjust to all heights.

It can not be stressed too much how important it is to use a low bar for teaching stunts whenever possible. This is done primarily for safety but it also permits spotters to aid more effectively. Most performers will learn faster on a low bar because fear of height hinders learning.

HOMEMADE EQUIPMENT

The horizontal bar is one of the easiest pieces of equipment to make. Many gymnasts have made their own bar for backyard use. The steel pipe uprights, the wire cables used to support the uprights, the turn-buckles (or some other device for tightening the cables) and the floor plates (or stakes for fastening into the ground) are all common items readily available and relatively inexpensive. The bar itself is another matter, however. There is no inexpensive substitute for the high quality steel used by commercial manufacturers. This high quality steel can be purchased from any distributor of steel bars but it will be an expensive item wherever purchased.

The most important part of the actual construction or assembling of a homemade bar is the method of attaching the bar to the uprights. This must be a tight attachment so that the bar does not jerk back and forth as it is used and yet the attachment must not prevent the bar from bending or flexing during use. The usual method used is to cut a slot in the top of the uprights into which the bar will fit very snugly. The bar is held in place by a pin that goes through the upright and the bar.

Certainly making a homemade bar is a task that can be accomplished by an enterprising teacher or by students in a school shop. The best way to start is to examine a regulation bar owned by a nearby school to get ideas that can be used and then to install the bar according to the F.I.G. specifications given in the A.A.U. rule book.

CARE OF HANDS

The horizontal bar is the hardest event on the hands, especially when the gymnast reaches the giant swing stage. For most individuals that are doing considerable competitive work on the horizontal bar, it is best to work every other day and give the hands a day of rest in between. Not all gymnasts find this necessary, however; it might be something that can be decided on an individual basis. Certainly, with the amount of work usually accomplished in most class situations, students should be able to work on the high bar every day. A gymnast should use common sense and stop before the hands get too sore and start to blister or tear. Some tears occur suddenly but many have warning symptoms and can be prevented by stopping and resting the hands in time. Most inexperienced performers grip the bar too hard, which increases the hand problem. It is important to learn to cup the hand around the bar and not to squeeze hard as one swings. The bar should be cleaned with fine emory paper, sand paper, or steel wool to keep it free from caked chalk, which is particularly hard on the hands. Hand protectors are of special importance on the horizontal bar, and although other events can be worked without them they should always be worn for this event. For more information about the care of the hands refer to Chapter 1.

TYPES OF GRASPS

Illustrations of the various grasps used will aid the beginner to understand the description of the stunts that are included in this chapter. Several names are often commonly given the same grip.

TEACHING SUGGESTIONS

As was stated in Chapter 1, it is assumed that schools will not have enough horizontal bars to teach a "horizontal bar class" but will have to combine this piece of equipment with other gymnastic

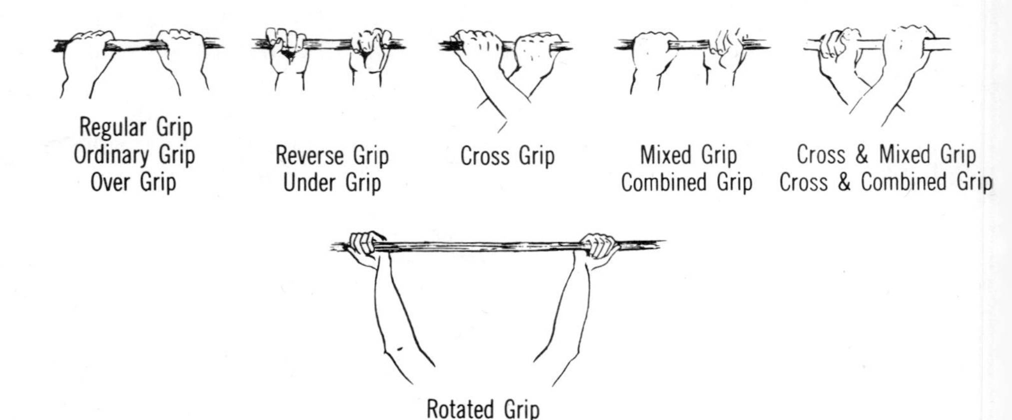

Fig. 6–1. Types of Grips.

events for a class situation. Many schools in foreign countries, especially Japan, have outdoor horizontal bar areas where there are many bars of different heights installed over sand or shavings. In a situation such as this a horizontal bar class can be taught.

Considerable time should be spent in developing a smooth swing by the beginner as a free swing facilitates the performance of both beginning and advanced stunts. A strong individual can often "muscle through" stunts, but this type of performance never looks so good as execution with a relaxed swing. The thumb and fingers should always be on opposite sides of the bar. From the hanging position the beginner starts his swing by raising the legs forward and then allowing them to drop downward and backward. The height is increased by pumping upward with the legs shortly after the body swings forward under the bar. This is a skill that must be learned as swing is developed for many stunts in this way. The arms and body should be in a straight line with the shoulders fully extended except during the leg pump. Immediately after the pump the hips move forward and upward so that the body is straight again. It is important to hold the shoulders in line with the body and not let them drop ahead of the legs as the back swing starts. On the back swing it is important to let the legs swing ahead of the shoulders and not to raise the shoulders so as to break the straight body line. The hands must be shifted over the bar a little on the back swing to prevent the grip from being pulled off the bar.

When dropping off the bar the performer should always do so at the dead spot on the back end of the swing. At this point the arms press down on the bar to lift the shoulders and the body pikes slightly. This will permit a safe landing in a vertical position without any forward or backward movement.

It is difficult to build a simple swing very high without having the grip torn loose from the bar on the backswing. When high swings are to be practiced, the performer must also execute a half-turn on the front end of the swing so as to swing down again in a forward direction. This is an excellent drill at all levels of ability. The swing can be pumped all the way to a handstand in this way without danger as long as the performer does not try to progress too fast. The technique for these "swinging half-turns" is included in Routine I, page 192–93, for the beginner and again in Routine V on page 294 for advanced performers.

SAFETY

Most of the safety precautions listed in Chapter 1 apply to the horizontal bar. Those that are particularly important are repeated here for emphasis, because the horizontal bar is potentially the most dangerous event in gymnastics.

1. Follow proper progression. Do not allow a new move to be tried until a performer has prepared for it and has the ability to accomplish it. A missed stunt on the horizontal bar is more dangerous than in other events.
2. Use magnesium on the hands to minimize slipping.
3. Use the low bar whenever possible to teach new stunts.
4. Use spotters if there is any doubt that the stunt might not be performed safely. Two spotters are much better than one in most cases.
5. Be sure to have the correct grip for the stunt being performed.

SPECIAL SPOTTING METHODS

Methods of hand spotting have been described throughout the chapter for most stunts. However, the teacher and coach should be familiar with several special devices also commonly used in spotting horizontal bar stunts. Because these devices can be used for many long circles, short circles, and changes from long to short or short to long circles, their use is described in this special section rather than with a particular stunt. Some gymnasts feel more secure with one of these methods than with hand spotting. Although the teacher should select the method of spotting that he believes is best, the performer's "feelings" can be given some consideration.

For extremely heavy gymnasts one of these methods might be definitely superior to hand spotting.

1. Wrist Strap. The wrist strap is a piece of belting sewn in the shape of a figure eight. The device should be about 12 to 14 inches long. Sometimes this is made out of leather, but it is best to be made out of a softer material such as nylon or cotton about two inches in width. The center part of this strap is placed over the bar so that the two loops hang below the bar. The hand goes through both loops and then grasps the bar beside the strap. One strap should be used for each hand. If the performer loses his grasp on

Fig. 6–2. Wrist Safety Strap.

the bar, he is prevented from flying away as he will hang by his wrists in the two straps. This is painful but better than flying away. Unfortunately, straps like this, because of improper use, have occasionally caused broken wrists by failing to circle the bar with the performer. Care should be taken to use the straps exactly as directed so that they will rotate around the bar with the gymnast's wrists. These straps are often used in conjunction with hand spotting or for the first few giant swings attempted alone after hand spotting has been used.

2. Overhead Safety Rig. A belt similar to the one described in Chapter 5, page 168, can be suspended from the ceiling above the horizontal bar by use of pulleys and ropes. One spotter can easily support the weight of the performer if he flies away by using an overhead safety device like this. Before a forward giant swing is attempted in this rig, a backward hip circle should be done so that the ropes are wound once around the bar. They will unwind during the forward giant. If two forward giants are to be done, two backward hip circles should be executed and so forth.

3. Bar Safety Swivel. A belt can also be suspended from the bar itself. Two ball-bearing swivels are needed, one on each side of the bar, with an outer sleeve that turns around an inner sleeve that is securely bolted to the bar. A belt is hung from ropes that are attached to the outer sleeve of these two swivels. The ropes should be just long enough to stretch from the swivel to the belt when it is fastened around a performer's waist as he hangs on the bar. The belt is often suspended by a combination of rope and rubber cable rather than just rope itself. If the performer loses his grip on the bar, he will be supported by the belt. A spotter must be placed under the bar and be alert to assist if the performer does lose his grip. The device will prevent him from falling to the ground but it does not prevent him from hitting parts of his body against the bar as he dangles helplessly in the belt. This rig can be used for movements that are very difficult to hand spot or that require many circles around the bar. If a twisting belt is suspended from the rig rather than from a regular safety belt, it permits pirouettes and various changes to be performed while securely fastened in the belt.

RULES

The horizontal bar rules as stated in the rule book are very brief and difficult to understand without elaboration or interpretation. The rules read as follows: "Exclusively swinging movements with no stops, offering a combination of giant swings with other variations or high value connecting movements."

From this statement we can learn that the routine should be continuous without any stops of holds. We can also learn that an exercise should not be composed entirely of giant or long swings as they are often called. Two terms that are sometimes used are "inner bar work" and "outer bar work." The first of these refers to short circles such as sole circles, hip circles, and seat circles and the second refers to all types of long swings or giant swings. In competition the performer should use a variety of both short and long circles and should change from one to the other throughout his exercise. The latest rules do not specifically call for vaulting movement, but nevertheless a vault is desirable in every exercise. There are many other "variations" and "connecting movements" besides the short circles and vaults that can be used to fulfill the requirements of the rules. Examples of these that are included in this chapter are: flank cut and catch, straddle cut and catch, shoot over bar to dislocate, and the kreis kehre.

ABBREVIATED ROUTINE DESCRIPTIONS

I. Jump to a hang with a regular grip, cast forward and swing backward, on the next forward swing make a half-turn to the left, swing forward and repeat with a half-turn to the right, on the first backward swing execute a knee uprise, forward knee circle, backward knee circle, disengage the leg and cast with a half-turn to a long underswing, hip swing up (pull over bar), short underswing dismount to a stand with the back to the bar.

II. Jump to a hang with a regular grip, cast forward with a half-turn left, swing forward and raise both legs between the arms on the next backswing, flank cut-away of one hand, kip, backward hip circle, drop kip, forward hip circle and cast backward away from the bar to a long underswing, on the first backswing raise the legs in a straddle position and execute a straddle rise, backward straddle seat circle, disengage legs and cast forward with a half-turn to a long underswing, kip, rear vault dismount over the bar to a stand with the side to the bar. (Alternate dismount—squat over the bar to a stand with the back to the bar.)

III. Jump to a hang with a regular grip, cast to a long underswing and back kip, backward seat circle, disengage the feet and drop kip, three-quarter backward giant swing, cast forward with a half-turn to a long underswing, raise the legs between the arms and on the back end of the swing shoot over the bar to a rear support, half-turn to front support, forward hip circle, cast backward to a long underswing with a half-turn to a back uprise, backward free hip circle, drop kip, straddle legs to a stand on the bar, one-and-three-quarters straddle sole circles backward, release the grip and push off the bar with the feet to a dismount with the back to the bar.

IV. Jump to a hang with an undergrip, cast to a long underswing, kip to handstand, giant swing forward, back uprise to front support, free hip circle backward, drop kip, cast to a handstand, backward giant swings to front support, cast forward with a half-turn to a long underswing, kip, squat the legs between the hands, forward seat circle, shoot to a dislocate, back uprise, backward hip circle, drop kip, cast backward to a long underswing, dismount with a backward flyway to a stand with the back to the bar.

V. Jump to a hang with a mixed grip, cast to a long underswing, "kreis kehre," kip, shoot (free hip circle) to handstand, backward giant swing, straddle-in to a sole circle and straddle-out to a handstand, backward giant swing, cross arm change, forward giant swing, stall out with a half-turn, rear vault to a catch, raise the legs between the arms and straddle cut-away to a catch, kip, forward hip circle, forward giant swing, pirouette, backward giant swing, pirouette, forward giant swing, dismount with a straddle over the bar to a stand with the back to the bar.

I. BEGINNING ROUTINE

1. Cast (Fig. 6–3). The starting position should be slightly to the right hand side of the bar because the first few movements will

Fig. 6–3. Cast.

result in a travel to the left. The performer stands behind the bar and jumps to a hang with a regular or overgrip (1). A small forward swing will result (2). As the body passes under the bar on the backswing, the head is tipped backward and the feet are extended backward so that the body is in an arched position for a fraction of a second (3). As the forward swing begins, the arms pull the chest up toward the bar and the legs are raised (4). As the forward swing progresses, the legs are brought close to the bar and the arms are allowed to straighten (5). The body is extended rapidly so that it forms almost a straight line from the hands to the feet (6). A smooth backswing should result. At the end of the backswing the hands are shifted over the bar a little for a more secure grip.

Teaching Techniques. Before attempting a cast a performer should learn how to develop a swing as explained in the introductory part of this chapter on pages 185–87. The next step is to practice the second half of the cast by jumping into position on a low bar. The performer grasps the bar at arms length and jumps into position with the legs close to the bar and the arms straight. He swings forward in a pike position and toward the end of the forward swing extends the body as in the regular cast. The bar can be released in this lead-up stunt in order to come to a stand in front of the bar as it is impossible to swing back under the bar when it is low. A third step that can be used in teaching the cast is to have the performer jump to a stationary hang on the high bar. From this position he raises his legs forward to a momentary "L" position and then drops them forcefully downward. As they whip backward under the bar, the head is tipped backward and the body is allowed to arch as a result of this rapid leg movement. The cast is then executed as described except the arms normally remain straight. This method is not as graceful, but the timing is easier to master.

SPOTTING. Two spotters should assist during the learning process on the low bar. They stand in front of the bar and help lift the performer's legs up to the bar with one hand and support under his back with the other hand during the body extension and release of the bar. When the cast is performed on the high bar, the spotter stands under the bar, to the side of the performer, with one hand on his abdomen and one hand on his lower back. By pushing and lifting with the hands at the right time the amount of initial swing can be controlled and the pull-up toward the bar can be aided. As the legs are raised to the bar, the hand shifts from the abdomen to a position under the legs to assist in the motion. The hand under the back aids in bringing about the body extension. After the cast is completed and the backswing starts, both hands shift to their original position to support the performer in case he loses his grip on the bar.

2. Swinging Half-Turn (Fig. 6–4). After the cast the body is extended during the entire backswing and as the forward swing starts (1). When the performer passes under the bar on the forward swing, a slight arch should develop (2). As the swing starts upward, the legs pump forward from the hips driving the entire body upward (3). Toward the height of the swing the body is extended again by raising the hips and at the same time the head and shoulders turn to the left. The right hand releases and reaches across the top of the left hand (4) and grasps the bar in an overgrip on the far side of the left hand. The forward swing is with a mixed grasp (5). During the turn there is a tendency for the legs to fly

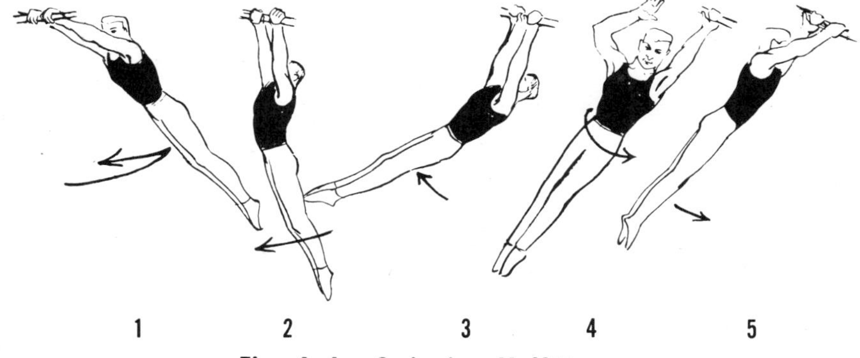

Fig. 6–4. Swinging Half-Turn.

apart. This must be controlled so that a bad habit is not formed that will carry over to more advanced stunts of a similar nature.

Teaching Techniques. The hand motions are practiced in a stationary hang on the bar and then from a very low swing. The start of the turn can be practiced without actually releasing the hand and completing the turn.

Spotting. The spotter stands on the right side of the performer as he makes the turn. The hip extension and turn can be aided by a lift under the right hip. As the performer's hand is released, his abdomen and back are grasped to ensure safety until the turn is completed.

3. Swinging Half-Turn (to the right). This is executed in the same way as the previous stunt but in the opposite direction.

4. Single Knee Swing-Up (Fig. 6–5). After the swinging turn to the right the performer swings forward in a combined grasp. On the front end of the swing the body is arched (1). This facilitates the next movement. Just as the backswing starts, the legs are raised toward the bar (2). One leg is placed between the arms and the knee is hooked over the bar (3). As the backward swing is completed, the arms press down hard to raise the body to the top of the bar (4). (After the uprise is accomplished with the aid of the knee, it should be attempted without hooking the leg. The legs are kept straight throughout and the hips are extended forward at the completion of the uprise with the bar close to the crotch.)

Teaching Techniques. In the routine this swing-up must be done with a mixed grip, but the stunt can best be learned from a stationary position on a low bar with a regular grip. Momentum

Fig. 6–5. Single-Knee Swing-Up.

can be gained from this stationary position by swinging the free leg downward several times before the swing-up is attempted. The first few times that the stunt is tried on the high bar a regular grip should be used.

SPOTTING. The spotter has more control of the learner on the low bar. He can help initiate the swing and can lift under the back and pull down on the free leg as the uprise is attempted. During the execution of this stunt on the high bar the spotter stands under the bar and aids the performer in raising the legs to the bar and in executing the uprise by pushing under the buttocks. The stunt can also be controlled at its completion by grasping the free leg to help the performer gain the top of the bar or to prevent him from going too far and falling forward over the bar.

5. Single Knee Circle Forward (Fig. 6–6). Upon the completion of the knee swing-up the left hand should be changed to a reverse grip so that both hands are in a reverse grip for the forward circle. This is very important as it is easy to lose the grip on the bar if a regular grasp is used. The hand change should be done very rapidly so that the forward movement does not have to be stopped. The hips are raised and the forward leg bent so that the bar is hooked in the bend of the knee. The fall starts with perfectly straight arms and the head stretched forward to keep the radius of the circle as long as possible (1). The two common mistakes are dropping the chin onto the chest and bending the arms during the fall forward. Near the bottom of the swing the body is piked rapidly and whipped under the bar (2). On the upward swing the arms may be bent slightly and the head leaned forward to shorten the radius, but this should not be done unless necessary to gain the top of the bar (3). (As soon as the forward circle has been accomplished with the knee hooked, it should be attempted as a crotch circle without the knee making contact. The hips should be kept forward at the start of this type of circle and the crotch should be pulled in close to the bar as the bottom of the swing is reached to prevent the hips from falling away from the bar.)

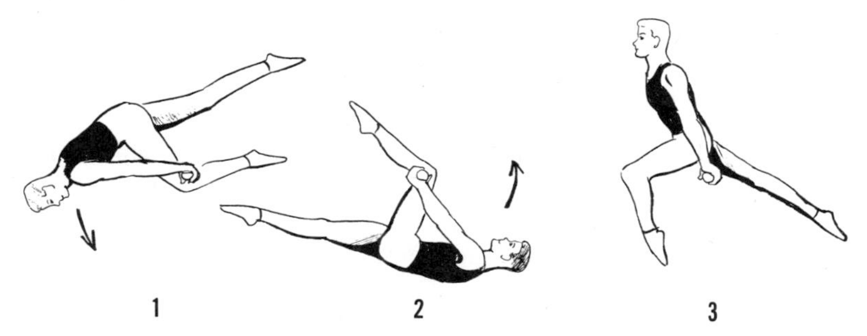

Fig. 6–6. Single-Knee Circle Forward.

TEACHING TECHNIQUES. Teach this stunt on a low bar where the performer is less apprehensive and where the spotter can assist better.

SPOTTING. The spotter stands behind the bar and reaches under the bar to grasp the wrist of the performer with the thumb in the direction of the circle. This hand can help in the downward swing, give confidence to the performer by helping him maintain his grip, and be used to keep the upper body from striking the ground if the grip is lost. The other hand is used to lift under the back if necessary to help the performer complete the circle. It can also be used to prevent the performer from going too far by grasping the free leg upon completion of the circle. Two spotters, one on each side of the performer, may be used for extra precaution.

6. Single Knee Circle Backward (Fig. 6–7). The forward knee circle is not quite completed to a position with the center of gravity directly above the bar. The backward knee circle is started from this off-balance position without a stop of movement that would result if the forward knee circle were completed to the top of the bar. The grip must be shifted from a reverse to a regular grip quickly as it is very dangerous to use a reverse grip for a backward

Fig. 6–7. Single-Knee Circle Backward.

circle. The back leg is swung vigorously forward and the head and shoulders are dropped backward with the arms straight so that the radius of the circle is as long as possible. The forward knee bends and hooks the bar (1). On the completion of the circle the arms may be bent slightly to shorten the radius and to facilitate the return to the top of the bar (2). (When the backward circle has been accomplished by hooking the knee, it should be attempted as a crotch circle. The principle is the same. There should be a good stretch away from the bar during the downward swing and a shortening of the radius by pulling the crotch in close to the bar during the upward part of the circle.)

TEACHING TECHNIQUES. Teach the backward knee circle on a low bar where the performer has more confidence and where the spotter can assist better.

SPOTTING. Spotting is much the same as for the forward knee circle. The spotter stands in front of the bar, beside the performer, and reaches under the bar with the near hand to grasp the performer's wrist in a regular grip. The back of the hand faces away from the performer with the thumb in the direction of the circle. This hand aids in initiating the downward swing and also provides assistance in case the grip is lost. The other hand is used to lift under the shoulder or chest of the performer to help him return to the top of the bar.

7. Disengage Leg to Underswing with Half-Turn (Fig. 6–8). Upon the completion of a backward knee circle the hips are usually kept forward in a position above the bar. In this routine, however, the hips must be allowed to move backward away from the bar as the circle is completed. They must also be raised upward somewhat to give room to disengage or unhook the leg (1). As the leg is disengaged, the foot is kept close to the bar. The foot of the free leg must also be brought close to the bar so that the body is in a pike position (2). As the shoulders fall back it is very difficult to hold this leg position since they have a tendency to drop away from the bar. During the forward movement the knees, or the thighs, should be brought close to the bar (3). When the swing has progressed well under the bar, the hips are extended and the body is pressed forward and away from the bar with the arms. During the extension the turn should start by turning the head, shoulders, and hips to the left (4). The right hand releases the bar, reaches over the left hand, and is placed in an overgrip on the far side of the left hand. The swing forward is with a mixed grip, the left hand under and the right hand over the bar (5). The two common mistakes are to let the legs drop away from the bar as the knee is disengaged and to start the turn too soon.

Fig. 6–8. Disengage Leg to Underswing with Half-Turn.

Teaching Techniques. The cast (Fig. 6–3) and the lead-ups for the cast are also lead-ups for this stunt. After these are learned, the next step is to practice the underswing from a regular front support, without a disengage of one leg preceding the movement, and without a turn being executed at the end of the movement. The underswing with a half-turn should also be practiced from a front support position on the low bar so that the feet will contact the ground about the same time that the hand has to regrasp the bar. The first few times that the stunt is tried on the high bar the bar can be released so that the performer drops to his feet just as the half-turn is completed.

SPOTTING. The spotting is a combination of the spotting used for the cast and for the swinging half-turns. As both of these have already been given, the method need not be repeated.

8. Hip Swing-Up (Fig. 6–9). This stunt is commonly called a pull-over. After the half-turn the body is stretched during the forward swing, but as the swing progresses the legs are raised upward toward the bar by using the arm, chest, and abdominal muscles (1). Actually they are pulled over the bar in a pike position so that the lower abdomen makes contact with the bar. The arms will probably have to be bent during this part of the swing-up (2). The stunt finishes in a front support position with a mixed grip, but the movement does not stop here (3).

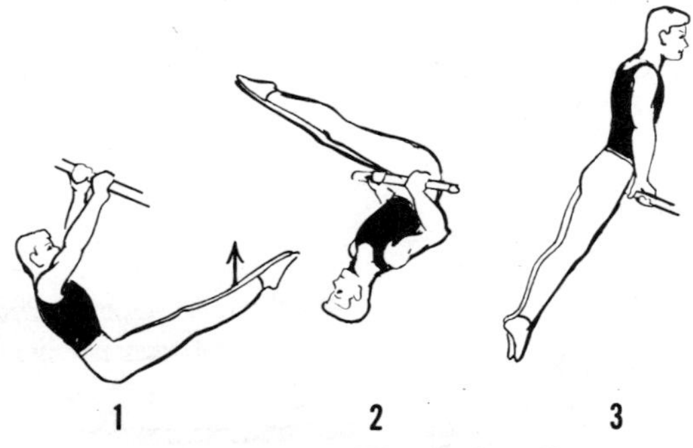

Fig. 6–9. Hip Swing-Up.

TEACHING TECHNIQUES. The stunt should first be tried on a low bar where it can be initiated from a jump and where a spotter can help more successfully. Next it should be tried from a stationary hang on a high bar. Although when done in this way it may be more difficult for some students, it is less dangerous. Familiarity with the movement is desirable before it is tried from a swing as inexperienced persons might allow the legs, abdomen, or hips to hit against the bar. In this routine the stunt is performed with a mixed grip. For some this is the easiest grip to use; others find it very awkward. During the learning process the student should be allowed to use the grip that is best for him. This might be a reverse grip for some and an overgrip foı others.

SPOTTING. The spotter stands beside the performer with one hand on the shoulder and the other under the lower back or buttocks. In this way he can aid in lifting and in the circling motion around the bar.

9. Underswing Dismount (Fig. 6–10). As the hip swing-up is

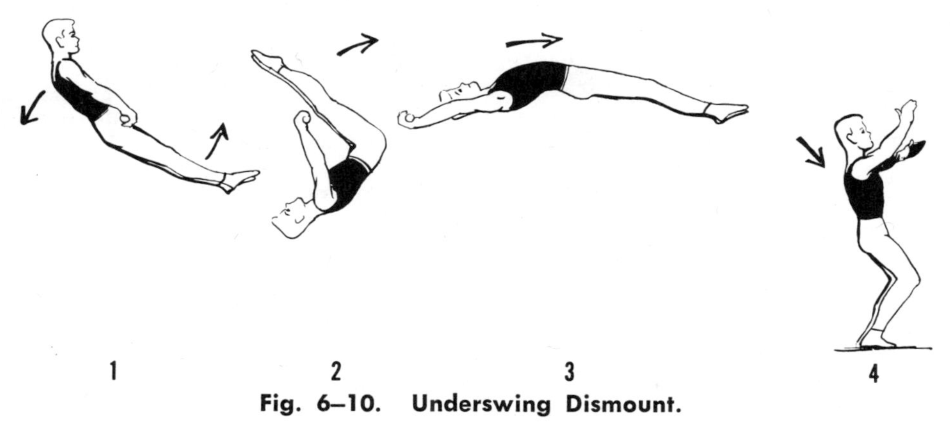

Fig. 6–10. Underswing Dismount.

completed, the hand with the reverse grip should be changed quickly to an overgrip. The movement of the hip swing-up continues with the head and shoulders falling backward and the legs moving forward under the bar (1). The start of this dismount is much the same as the start of the "underswing with a half-turn." The legs should be close to the bar and the body should be in a pike position as the upper body falls backward (2). As the forward swing is completed, the body is extended rapidly. When the arched position is reached (3), the hands thrust off the bar and the performer shoots upward and outward and drops to a landing with his back to the bar (side stand rearways) (4).

Teaching Techniques. The lead-ups for this dismount are: 1) the cast from a support to a long underswing; 2) the underswing dismount on the low bar starting from a stand on the floor; and 3) the underswing dismount on the low bar starting from a support.

Spotting. The spotter stands underneath the bar to the side of the performer. As the dismount begins, one hand is placed on the small of the back and the other on the shoulder. Both hands, especially the one under the back, can be used to bring about proper positioning during the stunt. The spotter must move forward with the performer and, as he approaches the ground, shift one hand across the chest and one hand across the back to be sure that the landing is completed on the feet.

II. LOW INTERMEDIATE ROUTINE

This second horizontal bar routine is more difficult than the second routines in most of the other events. It would be hard to compose an easier one, however, without repeating many of the stunts from the first routine. One way in which it can be reduced in difficulty is to omit stunts 8 and 9, the "straddle rise" and the "straddle seat circle backward," which are the two most difficult moves. The routine will flow smoothly without these stunts.

1. Cast Forward with a Half-Turn to a Long Underswing (Fig. 6–11). This mount starts exactly the same as the cast used as a mount in Routine I (1). The difference starts as the hips are extended toward the completion of the cast (2). At this time the turn is started by turning the head, shoulders, and hips to the left (or right) (3). The right hand is released and reaches over the left hand to an overgrip on the far side of the left hand. The forward swing is with a mixed grip (left under, right over) (4).

Fig. 6–11. Cast Forward with a Half-Turn to a Long Underswing.

TEACHING TECHNIQUES. Practice the following stunts as lead-ups: cast without a turn (Fig. 6–3), swinging half-turns, and cast from a support with a half-turn. This stunt is the same as shown in Fig. 6–8 except that the disengage of the leg is omitted. All of these lead-ups are included as stunts in Routine I.

SPOTTING. The spotting is a combination of the spotting described for the cast and the swinging half-turns in Routine I.

2. Flank Cut-Away (Fig. 6–12). On the end of the forward swing the back should be arched (1). On the backward swing the body is piked vigorously and the feet are passed between the arms and under the bar (2). The arch at the end of the forward swing

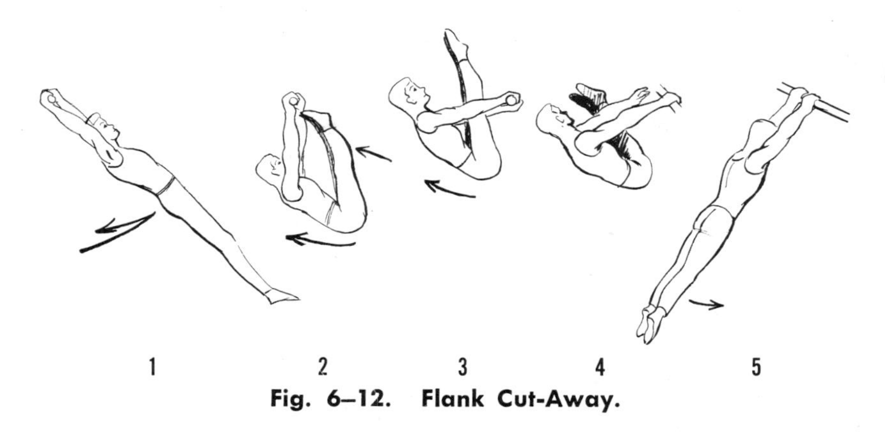

Fig. 6–12. Flank Cut-Away.

facilitates this movement. At first the knees will probably have to be bent to get the feet under the bar, but even a beginner should attempt this movement with a straight leg. Long hamstring muscles, which enable the body to flex fully and easily at the waist, enable this movement to be done with straight legs, especially if the legs are raised vigorously and quickly after forcing an arch at the end of the forward swing. This movement is very important to learn well as it is used so often in advanced horizontal bar work. The tight pike is held until almost the end of the back swing and then the legs are extended upward as the arms press down hard against the bar (3). At the extreme height of the swing, where there is little pull on the hands, the left hand, which is in an undergrip, is released. The hips are twisted to the left, without allowing the shoulders to twist too much, and the legs are dropped to the side (4). As soon as the legs pass the bar, the left hand should regrasp in an overgrip. The legs should be forced backward so that the body can be fully extended well before the vertical hang is reached (5). If this is not executed correctly, the performer will find that by the time the flank and regrasp have been completed he will be in a hang beneath the bar with no forward swing.

Teaching Techniques. The cut-away may be practiced by raising only one leg between the arms for the first few attempts. The double leg cut-away should be learned from an inverted pike hang on the low bar. The spotter pushes the performer back and forth to develop the necessary swing. This method enables the performer to concentrate on the cut-away without worrying about getting the feet between the arms and under the bar. The cut-away may also be tried by starting from a sitting position on top of the low bar. The performer falls back in a pike, swings forward under the bar in the inverted pike hang, and then on the backward swing executes the cut-away as described. The technique of arching on the front end of the swing and rapidly raising the legs between the arms can be practiced on a low bar by running forward instead of swinging forward under the bar.

SPOTTING. The spotter stands behind the bar on the right side of the performer with one hand on the back of the thigh and one hand under his lower back. The swing under the bar, raising the legs between the arms, and the upward and sideward leg thrust can be aided without changing position of the hands. The spotter should be ready at the time of the release and regrasp in case the performer loses his grip on the bar.

3. Kip (Fig. 6–13). If the flank cut-away is executed properly, there will be a reasonable amount of forward swing developed. At the end of the forward swing, the body should be arched slightly (1). On the start of the backward swing the body pikes rapidly and the ankles are raised to the bar (2). This position is held dur-

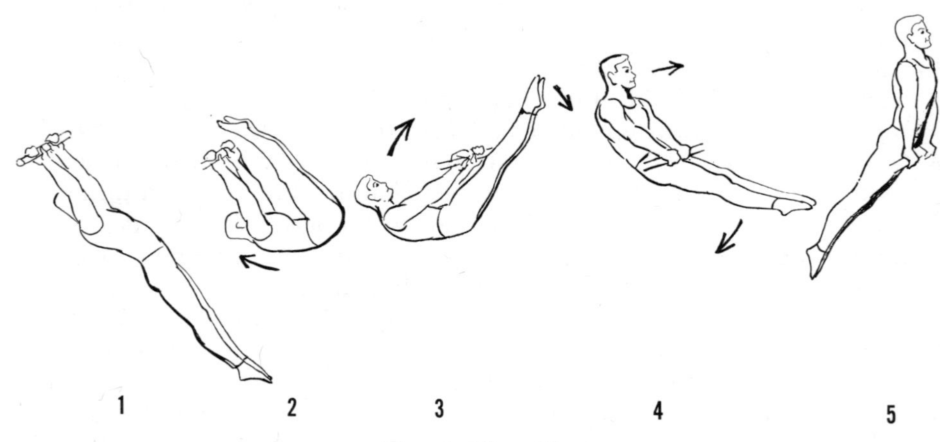

Fig. 6–13. Kip.

ing most of the backward swing, but toward the end of the swing there is a rapid extension of the body that raises the hips close to the bar (3). During this extension the legs are thrust upward and outward so that the bar slides up the front of the legs from the ankles to the hips (4). This motion can be likened to pulling a pair of sweat pants up from the ankles to the waist. After the kipping motion the legs swing downward and backward and the upper body swings upward and forward. During this part of the kip the arms press down hard and then the grip shifts up on top of the bar. The stunt finishes in a front support (5).

TEACHING TECHNIQUES. The snap-up, or kip-up, on the tumbling mat might be called the first step in the kip progression. The upper arm kip on the parallel bars and the kip on the end of the parallel bars are also good lead-up stunts. Before trying a kip on the high horizontal bar it should be practiced on a bar of about chest height. A good learning technique is to jump immediately into the pike position on the low bar. This enables the performer to concentrate on the kipping motion without worrying about the body extension and raising the legs to the bar prior to the kip. Actually the kip is no easier, and may be more difficult done in this way, but nevertheless it is a good technique to try. "Walk-out kips" are another good lead-up. The performer grasps a chest-height bar and runs forward with short fast steps under the bar until the body is extended in a straight line from the hand grasp to the feet. A push can be taken off the ground to get the angles to the bar. The kip is then performed as a regular kip.

SPOTTING. Spotting is difficult on the high bar, but some help can be given by lifting under the thighs and the lower back or buttocks. Spotting is of great help during the learning process on the low bar. Two spotters should be used one in front and one behind the bar. If they are on opposite sides of the performer they are less likely to get in each other's way. They both place one hand under the back of the thighs and the other under the back and aid in the same way. The spotter in front of the bar can aid primarily during the arch on the forward end of the swing and as the ankles are raised to the bar. The spotter in back can aid primarily during the rapid body extension and the completion of the kip.

4. Backward Hip Circle (Fig. 6–14). As the kip is completed, the legs will swing backward and upward. This will bring the per-

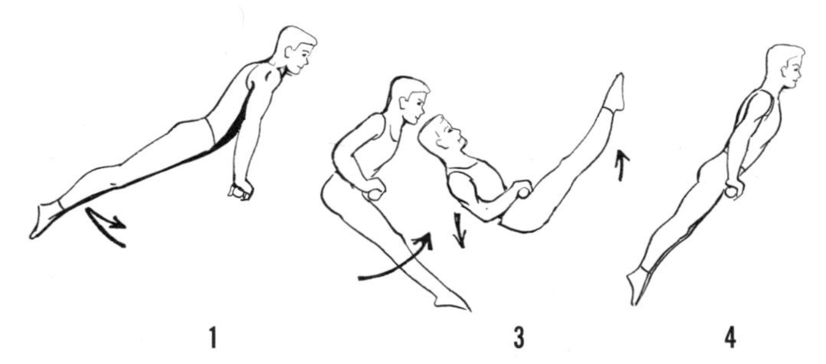

Fig. 6–14. Backward Hip Circle.

former to a free front support with the body some distance away from the bar. The arms should be perfectly straight (1). From this position he drops back toward the bar and as the lower abdomen makes contact with the bar the arms bend slightly and the body is piked (2). (The legs may also be bent during the learning process to shorten the radius and facilitate the circling motion.) The legs continue their forward motion under the bar and then circle upward around the bar as the upper body leans backward (3). The abdomen should maintain contact with the bar until the circle is completed in a front support position (4).

TEACHING TECHNIQUES. Teach on a bar of about chest height so that the spotters can work more effectively and so that the starting position can be reached by merely jumping into the support. This eliminates unnecessary preliminary effort. To start the circle from a stationary support position the legs are first swung forward under the bar and then whipped backward to the free front support.

SPOTTING. Two spotters should be used. The spotter in back of the bar lifts under the legs and abdomen to help the performer attain a good free front support and then quickly shifts one hand to the back of the thighs and the other to the performer's back to help keep him in close to the bar. The most important spotter stands in front of the bar and as the performer's legs come under the bar places one hand under the thigh and one under the shoulder to help in the completion of the circle. Good spotters do not do all the work for the performer but only assist as required.

5. Drop Kip or Cradle Kip (Fig. 6–15). Upon the completion of the backward hip circle the performer is in a front support position. The legs continue forward under the bar and the upper body falls

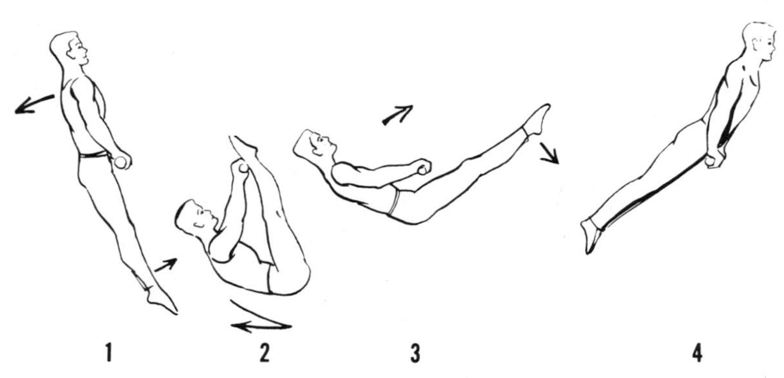

Fig. 6–15. Drop Kip or Cradle Kip.

backward with the arms straight (1). The ankles are brought to the bar and the hips are allowed to drop away from the bar so that the body ends in an inverted pike position. This position is maintained at the forward end of the swing (2) and during most of the backward swing. As the end of the backward swing is approached, the kip is executed in exactly the same manner as described earlier in this routine for a regular kip, pages 202–3 (3) (4).

TEACHING TECHNIQUES. This should be practiced on a low bar.

SPOTTING. Spotting is exactly the same as for a regular kip, page 203, except that the spotters have the additional duty of supporting under the performer's back as he falls backward from the support position.

6. Forward Hip Circle (Fig. 6–16). Following the drop-kip the gymnast is again in a front support position with an overgrip. Usually a reverse grip is used for a forward circle and a regular grip

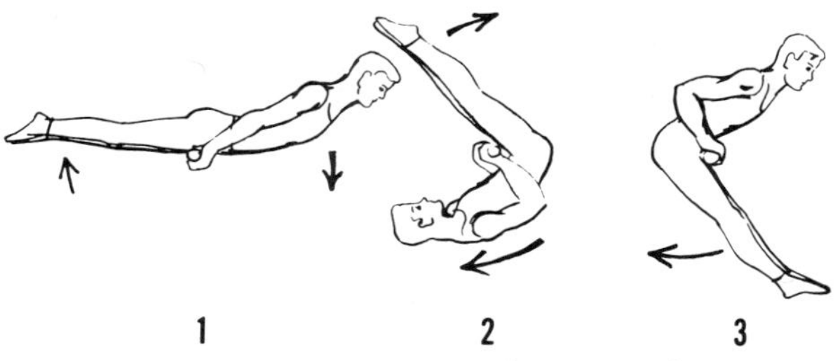

Fig. 6–16. Forward Hip Circle.

for a backward circle, but the forward hip circle is an exception to this rule. The first step is to stretch as tall as possible in the front support position and to start the fall forward with the body straight or even slightly arched (1). (It is a bad fault to try and increase the height at the start of the circle by raising the hips, placing the bar about the middle of the thighs, and thus developing a pike position.) This straight body position is held until well past the horizontal and then the head and upper body whip rapidly under the bar (2). The circling motion is increased by this piking action, which shortens the radius of the circle. The abdomen should maintain contact with the bar during the circle. This will not be a problem if the circling motion is continuous, but if it stops the hips will drop away from the bar. During the latter part of the circle the arms bend and the grip is shifted quickly up to the top of the bar to be ready to bear the weight in the front support position (3).

TEACHING TECHNIQUES. As with any short circle this stunt should first be learned on a low bar where the spotters can readily assist and where the performer will have more confidence. During the learning process the knees can be bent to shorten the radius during the second half of the circle.

SPOTTING. Use two spotters on opposite sides of the bar. The spotter on the back side reaches under the bar and grasps the performer's wrist in a regular grip. The other hand is used to lift under the performer's back as the circle is completed. The spotter on the front side of the bar helps the performer initiate the fast piking movement of the body by pushing on the upper back with one hand and holding the legs in close to the bar with the other.

7. Cast Backward from a Front Support to a Long Underswing (Fig. 6–17). This is not really a stunt in itself but a transition between the forward hip circle and the stunt that follows. If the forward hip circle is executed correctly, the legs will swing backward and upward and the upper body will lean forward over the bar as the circle is completed. As the upward leg movement lifts the body away from the bar, the performer pushes backward with the arms

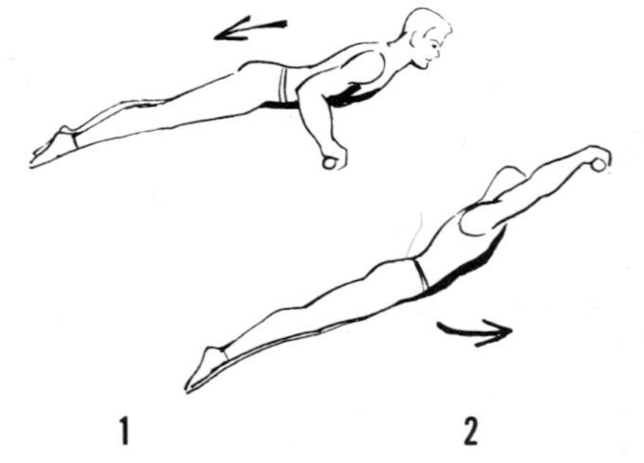

Fig. 6–17. Cast Backward from a Front Support to a Long Underswing.

(1) and straightens the arms to swing downward and forward in a hanging position (2). The amount of swing is controlled by the height of the cast. More swing can be gained if the legs whip hard upward off the bar and if the arm push is delayed until the legs are quite high. If the upward leg motion is not emphasized and if the backward push with the arms starts early, less swing will result. The stunt that follows determines the height of the cast. In this case a cast slightly below horizontal should provide ample swing. A cast much higher than this would be dangerous for inexperienced gymnasts as there is a danger of the hands peeling off the bar on

the forward swing. Gymnasts should learn very early to fully extend, or stretch, on the downward swing and make the body as long as possible from the hands to the feet. This means that the shoulders should be extended and that the body should not be arched. The position of the head is very important as it affects the position of the shoulders and body. It should be between the arms rather than raised high but it should be back enough so that the eyes can look at the bar.

TEACHING TECHNIQUES. The cast should be tried first on a low bar without a hip circle preceding. The gymnast must release and drop to a stand facing the bar when the stunt is executed on a low bar. The second step is to try the hip circle followed by the cast on the low bar. The next step is to try the cast on the high bar without the hip circle preceding it.

SPOTTING. During low bar practice of the cast the spotter stands beside the gymnast to be sure that he lands safely on his feet. For high bar practice the spotter stands on the side of the performer slightly behind the bar. As the gymnast swings down, he reaches up for the hips and places one hand in front of the hips. As the performer swings under the bar, the spotter quickly follows him and places the other hand behind his back. The hand in front controls the speed of the downswing and the amount of forward swing. The hand behind is ready to ensure a safe landing in case the gymnast's grip on the bar is lost. For the first few tries on the high bar the spotter can completely stop the swing under the bar by wrapping one arm around the front of the gymnast's legs.

8. Straddle Rise (Fig. 6–18). On the forward end of the long underswing the back is arched (1). As the back swing starts, the

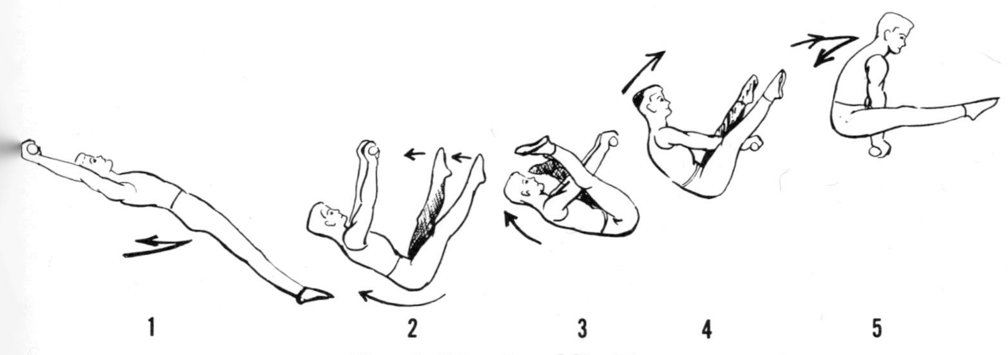

Fig. 6–18. Straddle Rise.

body is piked, the legs are straddled, and the feet are raised toward the bar (2). The feet pass under the bar and the legs fold in close to the chest (3). This movement of the legs causes a pull on the bar that in turn aids in the circling of the shoulders above the bar. As the shoulders rise, the pike is partially opened and the arms press down hard on the bar (4). At the completion of the rise, the arms pull the shoulders over the bar to a momentary straddle support position (5). This straddle rise does not have to be completed to a balanced position on top of the bar, as the seat circle that follows can be successfully executed from a straddle support that is off-balance backward.

TEACHING TECHNIQUES. The single knee uprise in Routine I is a good lead-up. At first this straddle rise should be performed with a very close hand grip, which makes the execution easier. Practice on a three-quarter height bar enables the spotter to aid the performer in obtaining the correct position and in timing the execution of the stunt.

SPOTTING. The spotter stands under the bar on the side of the performer. One hand is placed on the thighs and one hand under the lower back. Aid can be given in raising the legs and in correct positioning of the body in the pike position. As the rise is completed, the hand from the lower back can be shifted under the buttocks to give a boost or to control the downward movement if the rise is not completed. If the rise goes too far, the performer is in a dangerous position as the regular grip being used makes it difficult to retain a grasp on the bar. If the bar is released either purposely or unintentionally, the performer could very well fall on his face rather than drop off on his feet. The spotter should be ready to move quickly to ensure a balanced landing if the performer goes over the top of the bar. Possibly a second spotter should be stationed in readiness to guard against this.

9. Straddle Seat Circle Backward (Fig. 6–19). This circle starts from the momentary straddle support position reached in the straddle rise. The hips and legs are raised away from the bar as the head and upper body fall backward (1) and, as in the straddle rise, the legs fold in against the chest to a very tight pike position. In this inverted pike position the arms should remain well up in the crotch (2). The folding movement of the legs into the tight pike will produce a pulling action on the bar. The reaction helps to lift the body in the upward part of the circle (3). On the completion of the circle the pike is opened to almost a right angle (4).

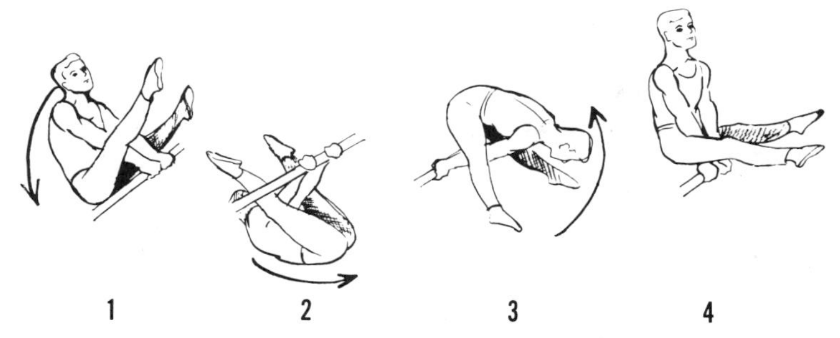

Fig. 6–19. Straddle Seat Circle Backward.

TEACHING TECHNIQUES. As with all short circles this one should be learned on a low bar. Placing the hands very close together makes the stunt easier. Some teachers suggest that as the backward straddle seat circle is learned, the knees should be bent and allowed to hook around the bar and that the arms should be bent and the back rounded during the upward part of the circle. Others say this technique develops bad habits that are difficult to change later. Whether to use them or not as a teaching technique might be decided on an individual basis. If a boy's goal is to become a competitive gymnast, he should not be taught bad habits that are hard to correct. However, if a boy is a slow learner and has no possibility of ever becoming an advanced gymnast, he might never accomplish this stunt unless he is allowed to simplify it during the learning process.

SPOTTING. During the learning process on the low bar, because of the straddle position of the legs, the spotter finds it difficult to position himself without interfering with the execution of the stunt. If the performer keeps the legs as narrow as possible in the straddle, the spotter will be able to assist better. He stands in front of the bar and reaches under the bar with the near arm to help position the legs in the tight pike position. With the other arm he lifts under the shoulders to help the performer complete the circle if necessary. If the circle is not completed, he must be ready to ensure a safe landing as the performer releases the bar and drops to the mat.

10. Disengage Legs to Underswing with a Half-Turn. This movement is not usually considered to be a stunt in itself but rather a connecting move between two stunts. Since it is almost identical to the disengage of one leg and underswing with a half-turn described in Routine I, Fig. 6–8, it will not be described again. The only difference is that the legs in this straddle disengage, disengage late rather than early. In order to develop the ability to turn in both directions it is recommended that this exercise be done to the right as the turn in the first routine was to the left. This turn, if done to the right, will end in a long underswing in a mixed grip with the right hand under and the left hand over the bar.

11. Kip. This stunt is the same as previously described in this routine, Fig. 6–13. However, the previous kip was done with an over grip and this one must be done with a mixed grip. (An alternative would be to change quickly from a mixed grip to a double over grip at the end of the forward swing just before the pike starts for the kip.)

12a. Rear Vault Dismount (Fig. 6–20). Following the kip the gymnast is in a front support position. The legs swing backward and upward as a natural movement of the kip. As they swing to about the height of the bar the gymnast turns to the right and pikes (1). The arms pull the center of gravity over the bar and then the right hand releases. The support is momentarily on the left arm (2). The left hand also releases as the body passes over the bar in approximately a right angle pike position. The performer completes a quarter-turn to the right (3) and drops to a stand with the right side of the body toward the bar (4). Just as the vault is completed, the right hand may momentarily regrasp the bar in an overgrip to give a steadying affect before the gymnast drops to the mat.

Fig. 6–20. Rear Vault Dismount.

Teaching Techniques. It is very dangerous to attempt this dismount on a high bar until it has been completely mastered on a low bar. In all the following lead-up stunts a double overgrip is used at first because the dismount is easier with this grip, but as it is done with a mixed grip in the routine the lead-up stunts must also be practiced with a mixed grip after they have been learned with the overgrip. Lead-up progression: 1) Jump from the ground and rear vault over a low bar; 2) start from a front support on a low bar, swing the legs forward under the bar, then swing them backward and upward and execute the dismount; 3) same as two but on the high bar; and 4) kip and rear vault dismount on the low bar.

Spotting. During the progression on the low bar the spotter stands in front of the bar and grasps the left upper arm. In this way he can control the body lean and insure a safe landing. Another spotter may be used, if necessary, on the back of the bar to aid the performer in raising the legs and hips at the start of the vault. When the dismount is tried on a high bar, the spotter waits on the left front side of the bar and reaches up to grasp the performer's waist as he drops to the mat. An extra precaution is sometimes taken in spotting this stunt. A horse or spotting table can be placed under the bar on the left-hand side. A spotter standing on such a raised surface can spot in the same way as he does on a low bar by grasping the performer's upper arm as he passes over the bar. This method of spotting is described in greater detail for more difficult stunts later in the chapter.

12b. Squat Vault Dismount (Fig. 6–21). This is an alternate dismount that may be used in place of the rear vault. Both move-

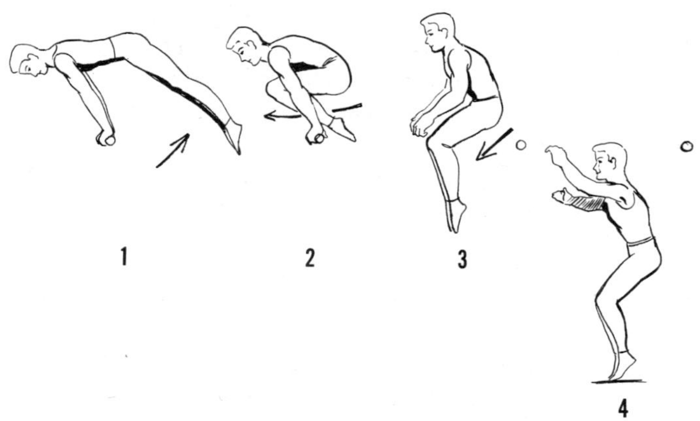

Fig. 6–21. Squat Vault Dismount.

ments are prerequisites for more advanced stunts and are important to learn at this time. Following the previous stunt in the routine, the kip, the legs swing backward and upward to a free front support. The arms pull the center of gravity forward over the bar and the hips are raised slightly (1). The knees are drawn forward toward the chest so that the legs can pass over the bar between the arms (2). As they pass over the bar, both hands thrust off the bar and the body straightens (3) prior to the landing with the back to the bars in a side stand rearways (4).

TEACHING TECHNIQUES. Use a low bar.

SPOTTING. During the learning process on the low bar two spotters are used. One stands on the back side of the bar, to the side of the performer, and helps him get a good cast away from the bar and, as the squat-over is started, helps him over the bar by lifting under his thigh. This spotter should be very careful not to get his arms caught between the learner and the bar. The second spotter stands on the dismount side of the bar and grasps the performer's upper arm. He helps the learned get the right amount of forward lean during the first part of the stunt and, as the bar is released, pulls the performer forward and supports on the landing. When the stunt is first tried on the high bar, two spotters stand in front of the bar and reach for the upper arm to assure a safe landing. The spotter may also stand on a table placed under the bar as described for the previous stunt.

III. INTERMEDIATE ROUTINE

1. Back Kip (Fig. 6–22). This exercise starts with a cast as described in Routine I, Fig. 6–3. An overgrip is used and a medium swing is necessary. On the end of the first forward swing the back is arched (1). On the backward swing the body is piked rapidly and the feet are brought between the hands and under the bar (2). Remember, those with tight hamstring muscles will have considerable difficulty getting the feet under the bar as the legs must be folded in close to the chest. At the top of the backswing in this inverted pike position the arms press down hard against the bar and the hips extend so that the legs are thrust vertically upward. The hips should be above the arms in this position and also above the height of the bar if a good back kip is to be executed (3). As the downswing starts, the hips drop between the arms again in a regular inverted pike position. At the bottom of the

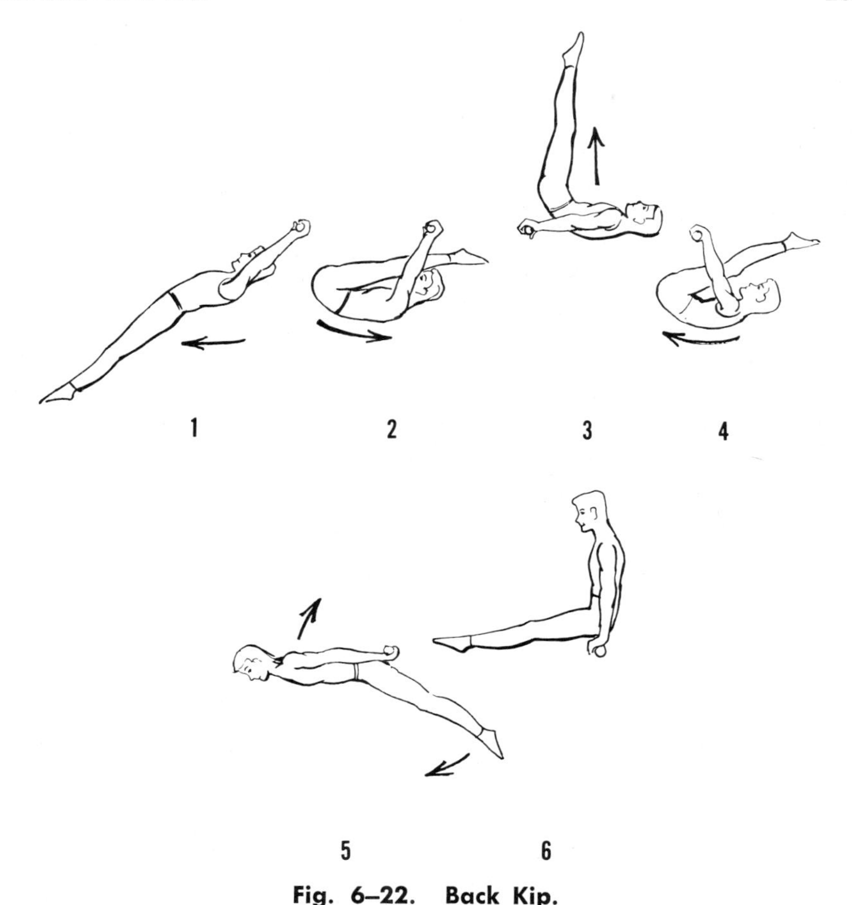

Fig. 6–22. Back Kip.

swing the legs should fold rapidly in toward the chest in a tight pike as described in the previous routine for the straddle rise and the straddle seat circle (4). This action will cause a hard pull against the bar and bring about a lifting reaction from the bar. As the upward swing starts, the body is extended. This brings the hips close to the bar, elevates the upper body, and causes the legs to slow down and trail (5). The arms can aid by pressing downward on the bar and pulling the shoulders back into a back support position with the bar resting just below the buttocks (6). The grip has to be shifted quickly up on top of the bar during the latter part of the kip.

Teaching Techniques. Both the straddle rise and the straddle seat circle that are included in the previous routine can be considered lead-ups for this stunt. The backward seat circle, which comes next in the routine, is also a lead-up. An important preliminary skill to learn is to develop swing in an inverted pike hang on the low bar. The spotter can initiate the swing with a small push. This small swing can then be increased by pressing down with the arms and extending the legs upward on the back end of the swing and by "beating" slightly with the legs on the front end of the swing. If the performer learns to swing back and forth in this way and gradually to increase the swing, he should have no trouble with the back kip.

SPOTTING. The spotter can lift under the hips as the body is extended on the back end of the swing. He can also lift under the shoulder with one hand and help delay the legs with the other hand at the time of the kipping motion. If the kip is not completed, the performer usually will drop to his feet in front of the bar. The spotter should be alert to see that the performer does land safely on his feet. Spotting is quite easy on the low bar, but on the high bar the spotter should stand on a bench placed under the bar to enable him to assist more effectively.

2. Backward Seat Circle (Fig. 6–23). The backward seat circle starts from the back support position with the bar resting just under the buttocks. From this position the shoulders fall backward and the legs are raised off the bar. The hips should drop between the arms so that the bar is about halfway between the heels and the buttocks (1). At the bottom of the circle the legs fold into the chest in a tight pike (2) and from this point the circle is exactly the same as a back kip (3) (4).

TEACHING TECHNIQUES. The backward seat circle should be learned on a low bar. The backward straddle seat circle described on pages 208–9 is a lead-up stunt.

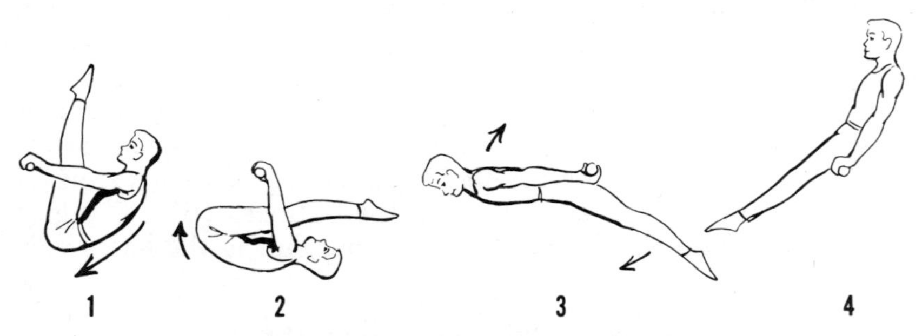

Fig. 6–23. Backward Seat Circle.

SPOTTING. During the learning process on the low bar the spotter stands on the front side of the bar and reaches under the bar with the near hand to catch the legs as the performer drops backward. This hand can help bring about the tight pike on the bottom of the swing and delay the legs at the time of the body extension. The other hand lifts under the shoulder if necessary to help the performer complete the circle. The spotter should be alert to watch for too much rotation brought about by not letting the hips lead during the circle. If this happens the performer will end up on his back unless the spotter is ready to catch him. When the stunt is first tried on the high bar, the spotter stands under the bar to aid if necessary but can not be of much assistance in the actual performance of the circle. He should be alert to ensure a safe landing in case the performer does not complete the stunt.

3. Disengage Legs and Drop Kip (Fig. 6–24). Upon completing the backward seat circle the performer drops backward as if to start another circle but the buttocks are allowed to drop farther

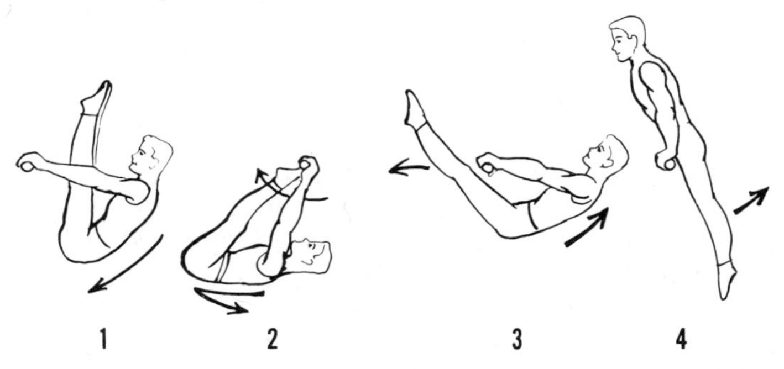

Fig. 6–24. Disengage Legs and Drop Kip.

from the bar (1). This will allow the feet to disengage, or pass under the bar. Considerable effort is required to hold the ankles close to the bar (2). From this point the drop kip is executed on the back end of the swing (3) (4) exactly as described for the regular kip, pages 202–5.

TEACHING TECHNIQUES. Practice should begin on a low bar. No special skills are necessary that have not already been learned.

SPOTTING. The spotter might have to assist the performer in holding the legs up to the bar at the time the feet are disengaged. Otherwise the spotting is the same as described for the kip, page 202–3, and the drop kip, pages 204–5.

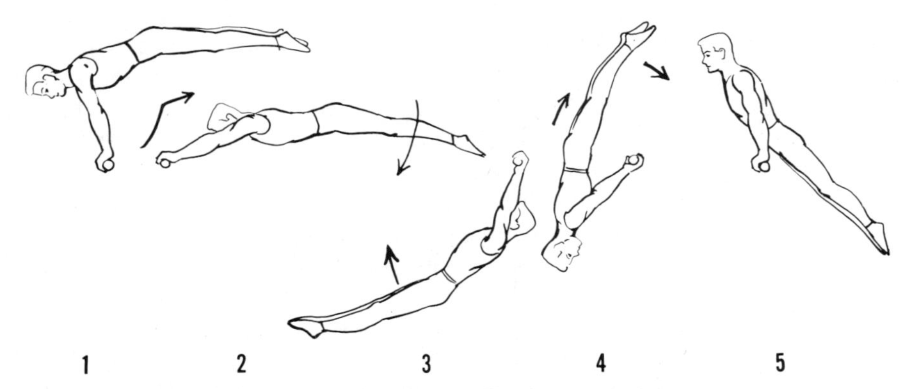

Fig. 6–25. Three-Quarter Giant Swing Backward.

4. Three-Quarter Giant Swing Backward (Fig. 6–25). As the drop kip is completed, the legs swing backward and upward from the front support position (1). The body is pushed backward from the bar at this time for the long underswing as described in Routine II, pages 206–7. For this stunt the cast should be about horizontal at first and then as the gymnast becomes more proficient the height can be increased (2). The entire body from hands to feet should be stretched and straight during the downswing with the grip relaxed and loose and the head very slightly behind the normal position so that the eyes can focus on the bar. An exaggerated backward position of the head is a bad fault. The swing progresses under the bar beyond the vertical hang in a stretched body position. The legs then pump upward from the hips bringing about a definite pike in the body (3). The grip should be tightened at this time as this is the danger point of the swing. The leg pump is very important as it gives the necessary momentum that enables the gymnast to complete a full giant swing. For the three-quarter giant, however, the pump does not have to be very vigorous. Following the leg pump the back arches and the head tips backward (4). The arms press hard against the bar to bring the hips into the bar. As the legs swing over the top, the grip shifts quickly to the top of the bar and the stunt finishes in a front support position (5).

Teaching Techniques. Actually the three-quarter giant swing is a progression of the hip swing-up described in Routine I, page 198. The performer can progress from a hip swing-up to a three-quarter giant by gradually increasing the amount of swing. Caution should be observed as the hips can drop down hard on top of the bar as the stunt is learned.

Spotting. The best way to spot this stunt is from horses or spotting tables placed under the bar. Two spotters should be used, one on each side of the performer. The bar should be at waist or chest height when the spotter is standing on the horse or table. This method of spotting is especially important as it is used for so many stunts on the horizontal bar. It is important to train students for more difficult spotting skills, needed in advanced work, so potential spotters should get considerable practice in assisting for three-quarter giant swings. The spotter's near hand reaches under the bar and grasps the wrist of the performer in a regular grip with the thumb in the direction of the down swing. This hand maintains its grip until the performer reaches the horizontal position on the upward swing. (There are other methods of grasping the wrist that are just as good. One of these will be described later for the forward giant swing and may be used at this time if desired.) The other hand lifts under the shoulder or upper back during the first part of the upswing. As the performer's hips are pulled toward the bar, the spotter should release the wrist and use this hand to prevent the performer from hitting his hips or abdomen against the bar by supporting under the thighs. The spotters should be very careful not to get their arms caught between the performer and the bar.

5. Cast Forward with Half-Turn to a Long Underswing. Following the three-quarter giant swing the performer passes through the front support position and then the upper body falls backward and the legs are raised up to the bar in a pike position. The cast to underswing with a half-turn is executed in much the same way as described in Routine I (Fig. 6–8) and Routine II (Fig. 6–11). The turn can be to either left or right.

6. Seat Rise to Rear Support with Half-Turn to Front Support (Fig. 6–26). The seat rise to rear support is very similar to the straddle rise in Routine II, pages 207–8. After the cast forward to an underswing with a half-turn, the gymnast swings forward with a mixed grip. We will assume that the turn was to the left so the left hand will be in a reverse grip and the right hand in an overgrip. On the forward end of the swing the back is arched (1). As the back swing starts the body is piked and the feet are raised toward the bar. The feet pass between the arms and under the bar in the same manner as described for the back kip in this routine, pages 212–13. The legs are folded in to the chest in a tight pike position (2). This movement, as has been described before, will cause a tug on the bar. The reaction of the bar will help lift the performer up over the bar.

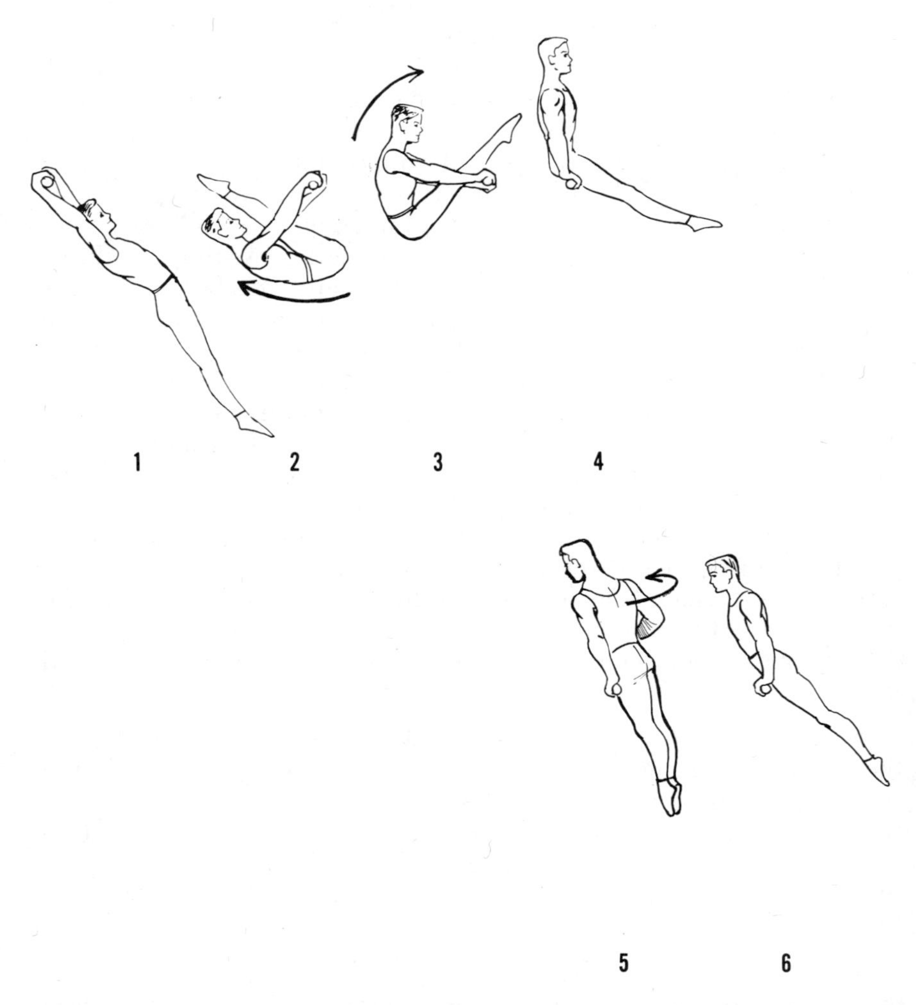

Fig. 6–26. Seat Rise to Rear Support with Half-Turn to Front Support.

As the shoulders rise on the back side of the bar, the pike is opened and the arms press down hard (3). The performer ends in a rear support position with the bar resting just under the buttocks (4). This seat rise is often described as a shoot over the bar. This describes the last part of the rise very well, as the pike is opened quite rapidly and the legs appear to shoot upward, forward, and then downward to a rear support. In this particular routine a half-turn to the left immediately follows the seat rise. During the turn the gymnast's hip rolls over his left hand, which is in an undergrip

(5). The right hand releases the bar and regrasps to the right of the left hand. Both hands are now in a regular grip and the performer is in a front support (6).

TEACHING TECHNIQUES. Increasing the swing in an inverted pike hang by pumping back and forth under the low bar is an important skill to learn so that a good seat rise can be executed. This technique was described for the back kip on pages 212–14. The seat rise should first be learned on the low bar with a double overgrip, which is somewhat easier than with the mixed grip used in this routine.

SPOTTING. A spotter standing on the back of the low bar or on a bench under the high bar can assist by lifting with one hand under the hips and one under the upper back. There are two danger points. If the seat rise is not completed, the performer sometimes somersaults backward. The spotter should be alert to ensure a safe landing on the feet if this happens. If the rise is executed too forcefully, the performer falls forward over the bar. Usually he can manage to land on his feet if this happens, but the spotter should be sure that he does not fall forward on his face. As this is a lot for one spotter to do alone, a second spotter should be stationed in front of the bar to be ready for an overshoot.

7. Forward Hip Circle. This stunt has been fully described in Routine II, Fig. 6–16. The combination of the previous stunt, the seat rise to a rear support with a half-turn to a front support, and the forward hip circle is a very unusual one. At first it might seem impossible as the natural tendency is to fall backward after the half-turn. With practice, however, it can be accomplished quite rhythmically. At first there will probably have to be a pause in the rear support, and again in the front support, before the forward hip circle.

8. Cast Backward to an Underswing with a Half-Turn to a Back Uprise (Fig. 6–27). The first part of this movement, the cast backward to underswing, has been described in Routine II, pages 206–7. In this stunt, however, to bring about a straight swing under the bar there must be a preliminary shift of the left hand so that it is centralized in front of the body. This hand shift is made just as the height of the cast is reached. The body then stretches for the downward swing (1), the right hand releases the bar, and the head and shoulders turn to the left under the left arm. The right hand reaches under the bar and also under the left hand to grasp the bar

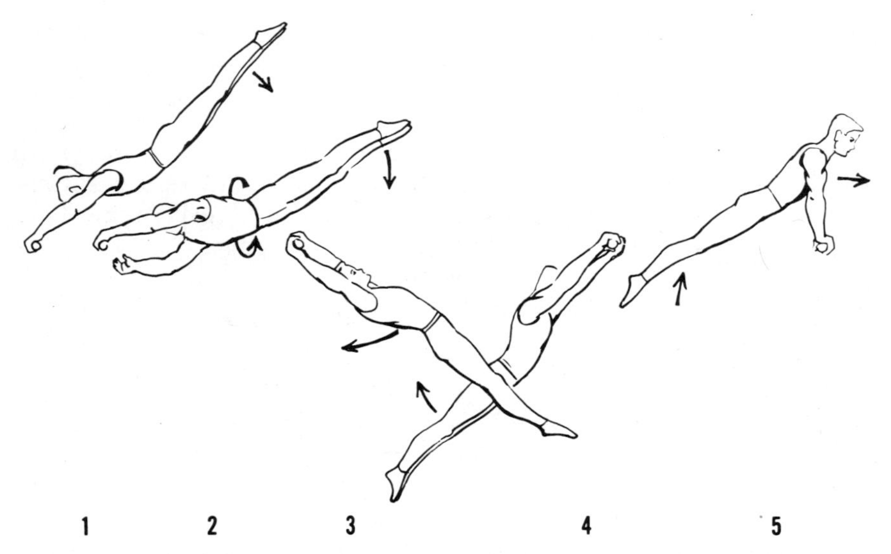

Fig. 6–27. Cast Backward to an Underswing with a Half-Turn to a Back Uprise.

again on the far side of the left hand (2). This movement brings about a half-turn so that about the time the right hand regrasps the bar it is in a regular grip with the left hand in an undergrip (3). The turn and regrasp should be completed quickly near the height of the cast so that a straight swing will result. A slow turn and a late grasp will result in a crooked underswing. An effort must be made to keep the body line straight from the hands to the feet. There is a tendency to bend at the waist, which will greatly reduce the amount of underswing and make the uprise very difficult. The downswing and swing under the bar are completed in this stretched body position (4). Immediately upon passing under the bar the arms press down very hard. This should cause the body to rise to the front support. In a good back uprise the arms are kept straight and the back is slightly arched from the time of the arm press to the front support. As the front support is reached, the left hand can be changed easily from a reverse to an overgrip (5).

TEACHING TECHNIQUES. An overgrip back uprise from a high under the bar cast should be completely mastered before the type of uprise used in this routine is attempted. If the grip is shifted well over the top of the bar during the arm press, the uprise will be easier. A quick lift of the hips so that the body assumes a slight pike position at the time of the arm press will also aid in completing the uprise. The secret of the back uprise is: 1) a high cast to bring about a big swing; and 2) enough strength to convert the swing to vertical movement by pressing down with the arms. As the height of the cast is increased, care must be taken that the hands do not peel off the bar on the back end of the swing. The back uprise should always be followed by a hip circle or similar movement. If the learner stops in the support, the abdomen will hit against the bar very hard.

SPOTTING. The spotter stands under and slightly behind the bar and, as the performer starts to press downward, he lifts upward under the thighs. He should be careful to lift vertically and not to push the legs away from the bar. When the cast with a half-turn is attempted, a spotter should stand under the bar to stop all swing as the gymnast reaches the vertical hang. This should be done until the performer is sure he is able to regrasp the bar, swing down in a straight line, and maintain his grasp on the bar during the uprise.

9. Free Backward Hip Circle (Fig. 6–28). As the back uprise is completed, the body drops toward the bar very rapidly in the front support position (1). Before contact is made, the hip circle can be

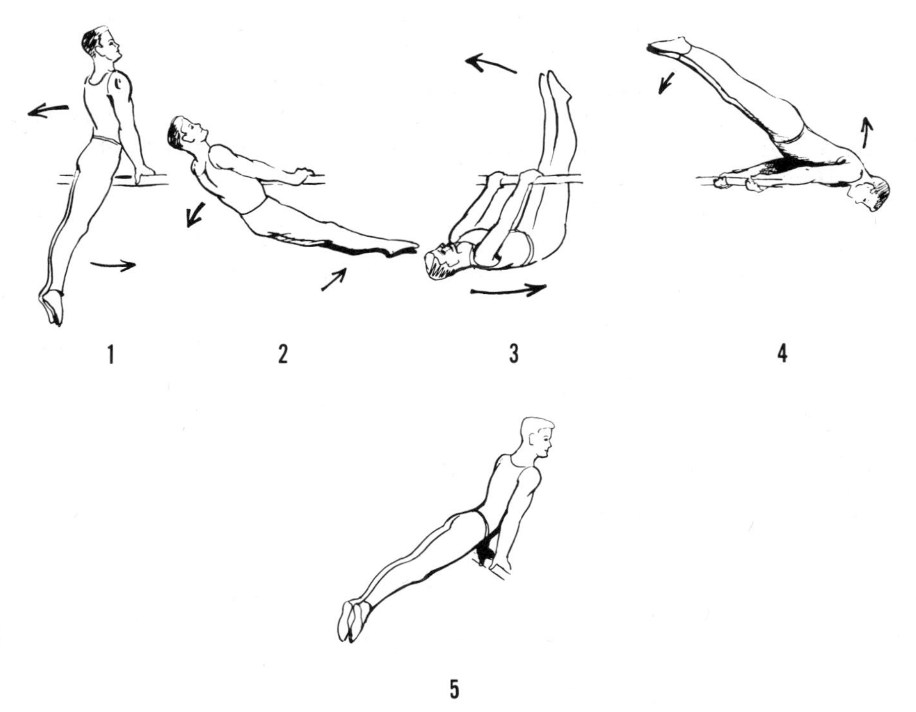

Fig. 6–28. Free Backward Hip Circle.

started by leaning the upper body backward and swinging the legs under the bar in a pike position (2) (3). As the shoulders start upward the body is extended and the head thrown backward (4). This causes a pull on the bar. The reaction results in lifting the body upward and over the bar. As the weight comes off the hands immediately after this pull, the grip is shifted up on top of the bar and the body returns to the same free front support position from which the circle was started (5). In a good free hip circle the arms are kept straight throughout.

TEACHING TECHNIQUES. The regular backward hip circle is, of course, an essential prerequisite. The free hip circle should be learned on a low bar. The performer starts in a front support and casts back to a high free support. From this position the stunt can be practiced exactly as it is in the routine.

SPOTTING. The stunt can be spotted from a horse placed under the bar, but this is usually not necessary if the free circle is completely learned on the low bar before it is attempted on the high bar. The spotter stands behind the low bar and reaches under with the near hand to lift underneath the performer's shoulder at the time of the body extension. At the same time the other hand supports under the front of the legs as they come over the top of the bar. With the two hands working together in this way the gymnast can be assisted in attaining the correct position during the critical part of the circle, which is as the hips are extended from the pike position. If the extension comes much too early, the performer will not circle over but will drop to the mat in front. If he grips securely, this is not dangerous. A second spotter should be placed in front of the bar to guard against this mistake by catching the performer under the back and lowering him to the mat.

10. Drop Kip. The drop kip in this routine is executed in exactly the same manner as described in Routine II, Fig. 6–15.

11. Straddle Sole Circle Backward (Fig. 6–29). As the drop kip is completed, the legs swing backward and upward away from the bar (1). At this time the hips are raised so that the body is in a pike position and the legs are straddled. The soles of the feet are placed on the bar on the outside of the hands with the legs no wider apart than is necessary (2). In this position the gymnast falls off-balance backward and makes the radius as long as possible by piking very tightly (3). On the upswing the radius is shortened by pulling on the arms and opening the pike somewhat (4). As the top of the upswing is reached, the hips can be pushed backward

Fig. 6–29. Straddle Sole Circle Backward.

over the bar by a forward push with the hands. A constant pressure should be kept on the feet throughout the circle to hold them against the bar.

TEACHING TECHNIQUES. It is difficult to get sufficient momentum from a front support position to execute this stunt well. In more advanced work it is executed following a giant swing and is actually easier to do in this way. It must first be learned, however, in the way it is presented in this routine in spite of the difficulty encountered. As with all short circles the stunt is practiced first on a low bar. Several techniques, all of which involve the principle of shortening the radius on the upswing, can be used to enable the circle to be completed even though it starts with very little momentum. The arms can be bent, the legs can be bent, or the width of straddle can be increased during the second half of the circle. None of these techniques is recommended unless the stunt can not be accomplished without them.

SPOTTING. The spotter stands on the front of the low bar and reaches under the bar and grasps the ankle with the near hand to assist in keeping the foot on the bar. The other hand is used to lift under the shoulder and aid in the completion of the circle. If the circle is not completed, the spotter can assist the performer as he drops off the front side of the bar to his feet.

12. Straddle Sole Circle Dismount (Fig. 6–30). As the straddle sole circle is completed in this routine, the gymnast stretches the radius as long as possible and falls backward as if he is going to do another circle (1). Just before the second circle is completed (2) the hands release the bar, the body is straightened, the head and chest are raised, and the feet push away from the bar (3). In this manner the gymnast drops to the mat with his back to the bar

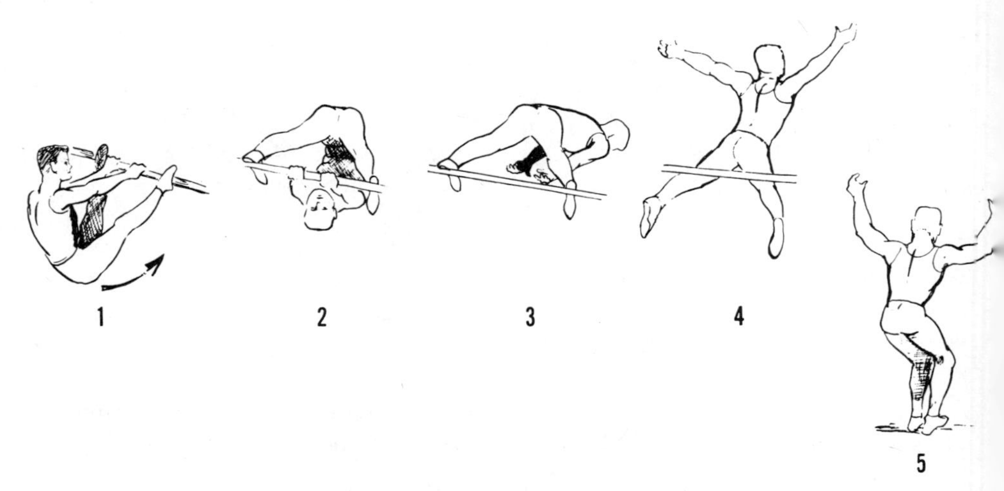

Fig. 6–30. Straddle Sole Circle Dismount.

(side stand rearways). As confidence is gained, a hard push can be given on the bar to give distance to the dismount and the body can be stretched to an arch in the air before the landing (4) (5).

TEACHING TECHNIQUES. Most beginners fail to complete the sole circle as they are learning the stunt. When this happens, they drop to the mat in front of the bar and thus have executed a sole circle dismount. The dismount should be learned in this way on the low bar.

SPOTTING. The spotter stands in front of the bar directly off the point of the performer's shoulder. During the learning process on the low bar the upper arm or shoulder can be grasped just before the hands release the bar. The spotter steps back and supports the performer as he pushes away and drops to the mat. The spotting is the same for the high bar except that contact cannot be made with the performer's upper arm until well after he has released the bar and is dropping toward the mat.

IV. LOW ADVANCED ROUTINE

1. Kip. Routine IV starts with a reverse grip cast of medium height. This movement is exactly the same as the start of the three previous routines. The kip, the first stunt in the routine, is not appreciably different from the kip as described in Routine II, Fig. 6–13, but is somewhat more difficult because of the reverse grip.

2. Forward, or Reverse Grip, Giant Swing (Fig. 6–31). As the kip is completed the shoulders are allowed to lean across the bar a little more than usual (1) and the legs are whipped hard backward and upward to a handstand (2). This involves pressing away from the bar very hard with the arms and then bringing the shoulders back over the bar. It is very important to attain an almost vertical handstand position to start the forward giant swing. Because of the arm strength needed to reach this position, a young boy with little strength might find the forward giant more difficult to learn than the backward giant. On the other hand a strong person usually finds the forward giant easier to learn than the backward one. It might be explained at this time that the terminology rule, which states a circle or roll is a forward movement when the face leads and a backward movement when the back of the head leads, is broken when speaking of giant swings. In this giant the back of the head leads but nevertheless it is called a forward giant swing. As soon as the handstand position is reached, the entire body should be stretched from the hands to the feet. This involves pushing out the shoulders, removing all arch from the back, and lowering the head between the arms (3). The entire downswing should be in a

Fig. 6–31. Forward, or Reverse Grip, Giant Swing.

straight line with a relaxed and loose grip (4). As the vertical hang is reached, the grip is tightened and the legs are extended so that the body starts the upswing with a slight arch. About 45° past the vertical the arms press down hard on the bar and pull the shoulders forward and above the bar. At the same time the head is raised and the hips are lifted rapidly upward so that the body assumes a pike position (5). This movement causes a hard pull on the hands and a reaction from the bar that helps lift the body upward for the completion of the giant swing. The pike position is held until the performer feels confident that he can swing over the top of the bar. The legs are then whipped up hard from the pike to an arched position (6). The head remains up until the body passes over the top of the bar. If another giant is to be done, the body is then stretched to a straight line and the head is lowered between the arms. The arms should be kept straight throughout the entire giant swing. A very bad habit is developed if the arms are bent in order to complete the stunt. This giant is considerably safer to learn than the back giant as the performer can easily drop off to his feet if the circle is not quite completed.

Teaching Techniques. The first step in learning forward giant swings is to learn the throw up to a handstand on the low bar. If the handstand is not quite reached, the performer can drop off the back of the bar to his feet. If the handstand is reached, he can twist off to the side and drop to his feet in front of the bar. During this learning process a spotter should stand in front of the bar and give assistance to attain the handstand by reaching across the bar to lift under the hips with one hand. He lifts under the shoulder with the other hand on the near side of the bar. He can also support the arm that retains hold of the bar as the twist-off is executed. There is no point in a gymnast trying the giant swing until he has learned to cast to a good vertical handstand on the low bar. The next step is to try the throw to handstand on the high bar and to concentrate on the straight body position during the swing down to the hang. A spotter stands under the bar and stops the performer by reaching around his hips with one arm. The third step is to do a three-quarter forward giant swing with two spotters assisting from horses placed under the bar. The three-quarter giant is much the same as the full-giant swing, but the hip lift on the upward part of the swing is less pronounced and the arms pull the shoulders over the bar sooner so that the performer ends in a front support. The spotters, during this step, help ease the performer in to the bar on the completion of the three-quarter swing rather than helping him over the top of the bar. When the complete giant is first attempted, it is a good technique to shorten the radius during the last part of the circle by pulling in the legs to a tuck position.

SPOTTING. Two spotters stand on horses placed underneath the bar so that the bar is about their waist height. They stand on the back side of the bar and reach over the bar with the near hand to grasp the wrist of the performer in a regular grip with the thumb in the same direction as the circle. This hand maintains its grip until about the horizontal position on the back end of the swing. This grip is used to help the performer hold onto the bar or to prevent him from flying away if his grip is lost. After the horizontal position has been reached on the upswing, there is no need to retain this grip; the hand can be shifted to help position the shoulders in the handstand or to regrasp the wrist if another giant swing is to follow. The other hand lifts under the performer's upper arm, chest, or abdomen on the upswing to assist him in reaching the handstand position. Two spotters can easily push the performer over the top. There are other methods of hand spotting used that are equally as good as this one. One of these that can be used is described for the three-quarter backward giant swing on pages 216–17. The spotters should gradually allow the performer to do more and more on his own until he needs no assistance. The horses are then removed and the spotters stand to the side of the performer behind the bar to catch him in case the grip is lost when he first tries the giant on his own.

3. Back Uprise from a Forward Giant Swing (Fig. 6–32). Several complete giant swings can be performed before this stunt is executed; however, in advanced competition usually only one, and

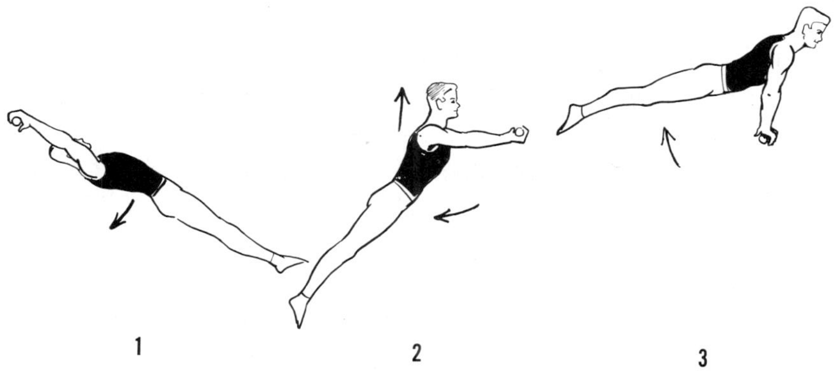

Fig. 6–32. Back Uprise from a Forward Giant Swing.

never more than two, are used before another stunt is performed. When giants are first being inserted into a routine, two, or possibly three, may be used to good advantage. Any more than this are superfluous and would use up energy that might be needed later to complete the routine. As the performer passes over the top of the bar in the giant swing just preceding the back uprise, he stretches the same as usual and swings down as for another giant (1). Everything is the same until the upswing is started. The arm pull starts as soon as the body passes under the bar and the shoulders are pulled forward toward the bar (2). The body can hold a slightly arched position with the head up during the entire uprise. Because of the great momentum resulting from the giant it is unnecessary to pike. Although this uprise is done with a reverse grip, it is much the same as the one described in Routine III, pages 219–20. As the body rises to the free front support position, there is a point when there is no weight on the hands. At this time the grip is released and both hands are quickly changed to an overgrip (3). Actually a little extra thrust downward with the hands usually precedes the hand change just as the body reaches the weightless position.

TEACHING TECHNIQUES. The first step is to learn a regular grip back uprise from an under bar cast. Next in the progression is a reverse grip uprise from a cast but without any grip change. The grip change, first with one hand at a time and later with both hands together, can also be practiced from a cast. When the uprise is first tried from the forward giant, the hand change can be made one at a time until confidence is gained.

SPOTTING. Spotting should be the same during the downswing as for the giant. The spotters stand on a horse and reach across the bar with the near hand to grasp the performer's wrist. The other hand supports under the performer's chest or abdomen at the time of the hand change and as the body drops to the bar on the completion of the uprise. Another technique for spotting the back uprise is described in Routine III, pages 219–20.

4 and 5. Backward Free Hip Circle and Drop Kip. These stunts are executed as described in Routine III, Fig. 6–28, and Routine II, Fig. 6–15.

6. Backward, or Overgrip, Giant Swing (Fig. 6–33). Following the drop kip the legs are cast backward and upward to almost a handstand position (1). This cast backward from the front support to a long underswing was described in Routine II, pages 206–7.

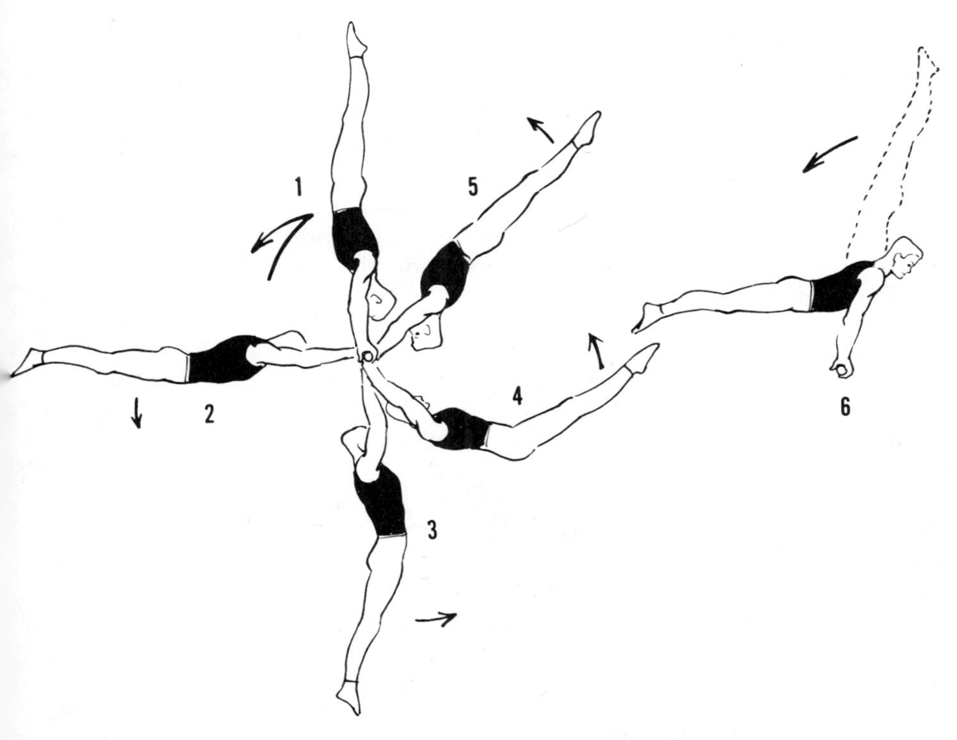

Fig. 6–33. Backward, or Over Grip, Giant Swing.

The entire body from the hands to the feet should be stretched and straight during the downswing with the grip relaxed and loose (2). The head is held very slightly back during the downswing so that the eyes can focus on the bar. An exaggerated backward position of the head is a bad fault, however. The stretched position changes to a slight arch during the swing under the bar (3). The legs then pump upward from the hips bringing about a definite pike in the body and the grip is tightened as this is the danger point of the swing (4). The pull against the bar resulting from the leg pump brings about a reaction from the bar that helps lift the weight of the body upward. As the bar reacts in this way, the hips are thrust upward into an arched body position, the head is dropped backward, and the hands are shifted up on top of the bar (5). The gymnast passes over the top of the bar in this arched position with the head up. If another giant swing is to follow, the body should be quickly stretched to a straight line and the head lowered to almost a normal position. One, two, or even three complete backward giant swings may be done in this routine. As was stated earlier, in advanced work, a gymnast seldòm does more than one giant swing before moving to another stunt, but at this level an extra one or two giant swings is not a serious mistake and actually good training. To get out of the last giant swing the performer lowers his body to a front support from the handstand position (6). It is very difficult to lower in this way if the circling movement is too fast over the top of the bar. The lift should not be too vigorous on the last giant so that there is a pause on the top before the legs are lowered.

Teaching Techniques. First, the gymnast must learn to cast up to a handstand position on a low bar and drop off to the feet on the back side of the bar. If the cast is too high, he can twist off and drop to the mat in front of the bar. Another lead-up is the three-quarter backward giant, which has been described in Routine III, page 216. The completion of the giant swing is made easier by drawing up the legs into a tuck to shorten the radius. This is a good technique to use to enable a beginner to make a complete circle on his own and gain confidence by so doing. It is much better than bending the arms, which will also make the giant swing easier to complete. Bent legs can easily be corrected later but bending the arms becomes a bad habit that is hard to correct.

Spotting. Two spotters stand on the front side of the bar on horses or tables so that the bar is between waist and chest height. The spotter's near hand reaches under the bar and grasps the wrist in a regular grip so that the thumb will lead on the downswing. The spotters might have to bend their knees to enable them to reach under and get this grip. This hand helps the performer maintain his grasp on the bar or, if he does lose his grip, keeps him from falling. It is released after the horizontal position on the upswing has been reached, as the danger point is then passed. If another giant swing is to be done, this hand reaches quickly under the bar to catch the wrist again. The other hand lifts under the shoulder or upper back during the latter part of the upswing and the performer is thus pushed over the top of the bar. If the arch following the leg pump on the upswing is started much too early, it will be impossible for the spotters to push the performer over the top. In this case the spotters must be ready to support under the body or shoulder with one hand and retain the grasp on the wrist with the other hand as the performer drops back down. The gymnast should also be ready to shift his grip under the bar and bend the arms and hips so that his hands will not be pulled loose if he fails to complete the giant. It is much better for the arch to come too late rather than too early when a back giant is being learned because of this danger. When the giant swing is first tried completely alone, the spotter should stand under the bar ready to stop the downward swing if the giant is not completed. There are several other types of spotting in common use. Refer also to pages 187–89 for other methods of spotting giant swings.

7. Cast Forward with a Half-Turn to a Long Underswing. This stunt has been included several times in previous routines.

8. Kip (Preceded by Grip Change) (Fig. 6–34). Following the cast forward with a half-turn the gymnast swings forward with a mixed grip (1). Toward the end of the forward swing the legs start to raise in a pike position and the arms bend and pull the shoulders toward the bar (2). Just after the pull is given, the hand with the

Fig. 6–34. Kip (Preceded by Grip Change).

overgrip can release the bar and quickly grasp in an undergrip. When a grip change like this is done before a kip, there can be no arch on the front end of the swing. After the grip change is made, the legs continue up to the bar, the arms are straightened, and the kip is executed in the normal way described in Routine II (3) (4).

Teaching Techniques. The lead-ups for this stunt are the kip with a regular grip, reverse grip, and mixed grip, all of which have been previously included.

Spotting. The spotter stands on the front of the bar beside the performer as the grip change is made ready to catch him if the regrasp is missed.

Fig. 6–35. Forward Seat Circle Shoot to Dislocate.

9. Forward Seat Circle Shoot to Dislocate (Fig. 6–35). As the kip is completed, the legs are swung backward and upward away from the bar. When they reach the horizontal position the hips are raised, the body is piked (1), and the feet are brought forward over the bar between the hands (2). At first the knees will probably have to be bent but later this movement can be done with straight legs. As the feet are brought over the bar, the shoulders should lean well forward. The circle is not a smooth circular motion but starts as a drop straight downward toward the mat from a tight pike position with the hips high (3). At the bottom of the drop the legs fold into an even tighter pike (4). Loose hamstring muscles are essential to attain this position. At this point in the circle there will be a hard pull on the hands so the grip needs to be very tight. The bar will react to this downward tug by lifting the body upward for the completion of the circle. The extension of the body commences soon after the upward movement starts. The legs are thrust upward and slightly forward and the arms press down on the bar (5). As the hips pass over the bar, the legs should be almost vertically above them (6). From this position the arms push the body forward and the hips are fully extended. During this extension the legs should remain high if possible so that the extension can be completed above the horizontal position (7). Just after the thrust forward, but before the extension is completed, the hands will probably have to be moved wider than shoulder width apart to facilitate the complete rotation of the shoulders. The gymnast swings downward in this position with the hands slightly wider than shoulder width apart and in a rotated grip (8). This rotation of the shoulders as the body is extended forward is commonly called a dislocate in horizontal bar terminology.

Teaching Techniques. Many steps are necessary in the progression before this type of forward seat circle is tried, and as usual, they are tried on the low bar. The first step is to learn an elementary seat circle starting from a rear support. The hips are raised high from this position and the heels are brought in contact with the bar. The shoulders are then allowed to fall forward. As the heels are kept in contact with the bar during the entire circle, this is a true circle rather than a drop down and rebound back up over the bar as is used for the circle in this routine. As the upward swing slows down, the legs are thrust forward over the bar and the arms press downward. If the hips were raised high at the start, there should be enough momentum developed to bring the gymnast back to a rear support on the bar. The second step is to try a seat circle with the legs free of the bar. This also starts from a rear support. The hips are raised high and the legs brought forward to the chest in a tight pike position. Underneath the bar the pike compresses still tighter. The reaction from the tug on the bar will lift the gymnast up over the bar to complete the circle. If the pike is opened to approximately a right angle as the arms press downward, the gymnast will return to the top of the bar in a sitting position. The third step is to perform the forward circle exactly as described in the routine except that the grasp is released and the gymnast shoots over the top of the bar to land on his feet on the far side. The fourth step in the learning process is to learn the dislocate from a sitting position on the low bar. From this position the gymnast swings his legs upward in front of the face to a pike. The hips should be raised well off the bar during this movement to resemble (6) in Fig. 6–35. From this position the gymnast thrusts backward with the arms in order to shoot forward away from the bar. The shoulder rotation, or dislocate, can be practiced in this way without using a seat circle to precede it. Before this step is tried, the gymnast should practice obtaining a rotated grasp on the low horizontal bar or on one of the parallel bars until all the body weight can be borne on the hands. He should also stand on a chair under the high bar, obtain a rotated grasp, and then step off the chair and swing back and forth to become thoroughly accustomed to this unusual type of grip. The final step is to raise the bar to three-quarter height so that a swing through can be completed. The dislocate from a sit on the bar can thus be tried at a height where the spotter can aid effectively. The complete stunt, combining the seat circle and the dislocate, should also be tried on a low bar where spotters can assist before it is tried on the high one.

SPOTTING. To assist for the seat circle the spotter stands on the back side of the low bar and reaches under the bar with the near hand to grasp the wrist of the performer in a regular grip. The other hand also reaches under the bar and grasps the lower leg to position the legs during the circle. This hand releases shortly after the hip extension starts and shifts under the upper back to lift the performer up over the bar to complete the circle. When the shoot out with a release of the bar is first tried, it is advisable to use two spotters, one on each side of the bar. The spotter on the back of the bar does not make any preliminary contact but waits in readiness and places one hand under the hips and one under the shoulder of the performer as he swings under the bar. The hand under the hip is used to lift the performer over the bar and the hand on the shoulder to thrust him forward. The spotter in front of the bar also lifts under the hips as the performer shoots over the top of the bar and then grasps him with one arm across his chest and one arm across his back to make sure that he lands on his feet as the bar is released. When the dislocate is first tried on a low bar, two spotters on the front side actually support with both hands under the body as the extension occurs to enable the performer to complete the shoulder rotation with ease and to slow down the movement as he swings back under the bar in a rotated grasp.

10. Back Uprise in Rotated Grasp (Fig. 6–36). After the dislocate and shoot forward to a rotated grasp the gymnast swings downward and backward under the bar. The entire body should be stretched in a straight line from the hands to the feet (1). If a good down swing is obtained, the performer should have no difficulty in completing a back uprise to a front support on the back swing. This

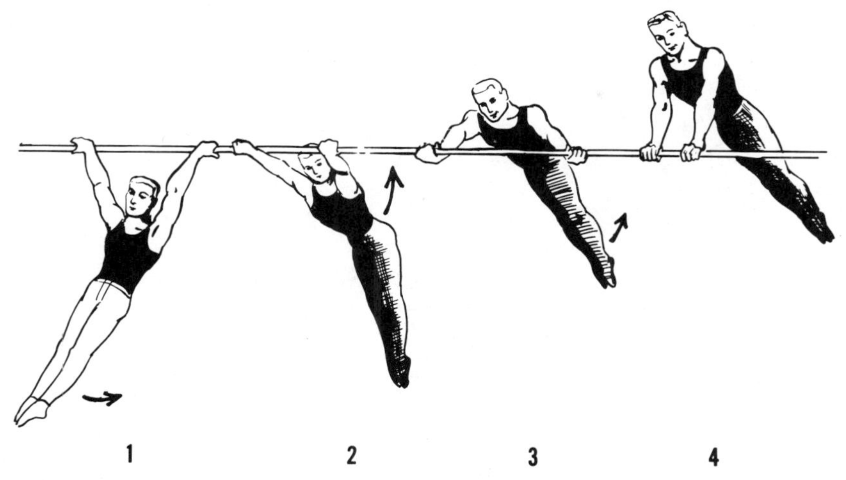

Fig. 6–36. Back Uprise in Rotated Grasp.

uprise is executed in the same way as described in Routine III, pages 219–21. Because the hands are in a rotated grasp some gymnasts might not be able to get as powerful an arm press as is possible with a regular or reverse grip, therefore, the hips might have to be piked to facilitate the completion of the stunt (2). Just as the body reaches the weightless position toward the top of the uprise, the hands are quickly changed from a rotated to a regular grip (3) (4).

SPOTTING. The spotter stands on a bench to the side of the gymnast and slightly behind the bar. As the gymnast swings under the bar the spotter lifts under the thighs, being careful to lift vertically rather than to push him away from the bar. The spotter must be alert to catch the performer if he loses his grip or misses the recatch.

11 and 12. Backward Hip Circle and Drop Kip. These stunts have been described in Routine II, Figs. 6–14 and 6–15.

13. Backward Flyaway Dismount (Fig. 6–37). The drop kip is followed by a cast backward away from the bar as described in Routine II, pages 206–7 (1). The height of the cast depends on the skill of the gymnast. Eventually this cast should go to a handstand to precede the flyaway dismount. (When the flyaway has been perfected from a cast, it can be made much more spectacular by performing it after a backward giant swing. One or two backward giants could easily be inserted into this routine preceding the dismount.) To start the downswing after the cast the body should first stretch in a straight line from the hands to the feet (2). The

Fig. 6–37. Backward Flyaway Dismount.

shoulder extension is especially important. Almost immediately after the stretch the body should pike very slightly so the toes lead in the downswing. This is not essential but it does aid in the timing of the rest of the flyaway. Under the bar the hips are relaxed. This allows the body position to change from a slight pike to a slight arch as the gymnast swings directly under the bar. The most important part of the flyaway now starts. This is a rapid whip forward and upward of the legs, starting immediately after the vertical position (3). The body starts to extend again with a forceful upward lift of the hips as the swing approaches the horizontal position. The head starts backward during this extension. If the timing is correct the hands will be pulled off the bar. At the time of the release the chest should lift high so that the body and arms form a straight line (4). It is a common and very bad mistake to give a pull with the hands on the bar just before the release. This type of a release results in the body and arms forming an angle rather than a straight line. After the release the hips continue upward so the body is in a hollow arch with the head well back (5). The arms usually go straight out to the side during the flight in the air. The flight should carry up above the bar and the arched position should be held throughout the rotation (6) until just before the landing when a pike position is assumed again. Adjustments can be made for the landing by piking early or late, depending on whether too little or too much rotation has been obtained from the release. The landing is with the back to the bar in a side stand rearways (7).

TEACHING TECHNIQUES. The backward flyaway involves almost the same movements as the backward giant swing except the timing is different. The leg pump comes a little earlier as does the hip extension. This brings about a lift upward and away from the bar instead of one that carries upward and then backward over the bar. If this similarity is explained to the student, it might speed up the learning process. The student starts to learn a flyaway by swinging back and forth under the bar. He should pump up his own swing by whipping the legs forward and extending the hips upward so that he learns the timing for the release as he builds the swing higher. The chest lift and straight line through the body and arms at the time of the release should be emphasized at this stage. It will be difficult to get enough rotation from a low swing under the bar so, if necessary, the legs can be tucked to shorten the radius. The next step is to try the flyaway from a support with a low cast and gradually build up to the high cast (and eventually to a flyaway from a giant swing).

SPOTTING. When the flyaway is done from a swing under the bar, a hand belt can be used. Spotters stand on each side of the performer about three or four feet in front of the bar. One hand holds the end of the belt rope and keeps the rope taut as the performer swings back and forth. The second hand slides on the rope and on the end of the forward swing, where the release occurs, slides in very close to the waist so that it is in a good position to lift the performer as he releases the bar. Some teachers use this method to spot a flyaway that is started from a support, but a hand belt is not as satisfactory as a belt suspended from overhead. For best results the belt should be suspended from a point six to eight feet in front of the bar for spotting horizontal bar dismounts. When hazardous dismounts such as this are first tried without a safety belt, it is advisable to provide an extremely soft landing surface in case of a mishap. A safety canvas or net held about a foot or two off the ground by six to eight men provides a relatively soft landing surface. Sometimes a tumbling mat is held in the same way. In some gyms they have a piece of foam rubber about ten feet long, six feet wide, and a foot thick. It is covered, as a regular tumbling mat, with canvas or plastic. This can be positioned where needed for extra safety on dismounts. Small pieces of foam rubber stacked up as for the pole vault or high jump are now being used in some gyms for horizontal bar dismounts.

V. ADVANCED ROUTINE

1. Kreis Kehre (Fig. 6–38). This is a German term that has been adopted by American gymnasts. In English terminology a kreis kehre is a back uprise with a half-turn over the bar to a straddle support. This routine starts with a mixed grip and cast to a long underswing. The cast should be very high so as to get a good backward swing (1). As the gymnast passes under the bar (2), the arms press down hard as in a regular back uprise and the shoulders are drawn upward and forward toward the bar. During this movement the body pikes, the legs start to straddle, and the weight is shifted over the arm with the reverse grip, which we will assume is the right hand in this routine (3). As the shoulders come over the bar, the head and shoulders start to turn to the right, the left hand is released, and the left leg passes over the top of the bar (4). The half-turn is completed with the left hand regrasping the bar in an overgrip on the far side of the right hand. At this time the left leg passes over the top of the bar again so that the performer is in a support with the legs straddling the arms (5). The right hand, which was in an undergrip before the turn, is also in an overgrip when the turn has been completed. If the stunt is well performed, the hips should be very high over the bar as the turn is made and the straddle support position should be reached just as the gymnast falls off-balance backward. A common mistake is to pull the shoulders too far over the bar during the uprise. If this is done, the turn and regrasp can not be completed until about halfway through the downswing. The beauty of the stunt is lost if it is performed in this way. When the straddle support position has been reached, the gymnast falls backward as if to start a straddle seat circle (6), but instead of completing the circle the legs are disengaged under the bar with a cast forward with a half-turn to

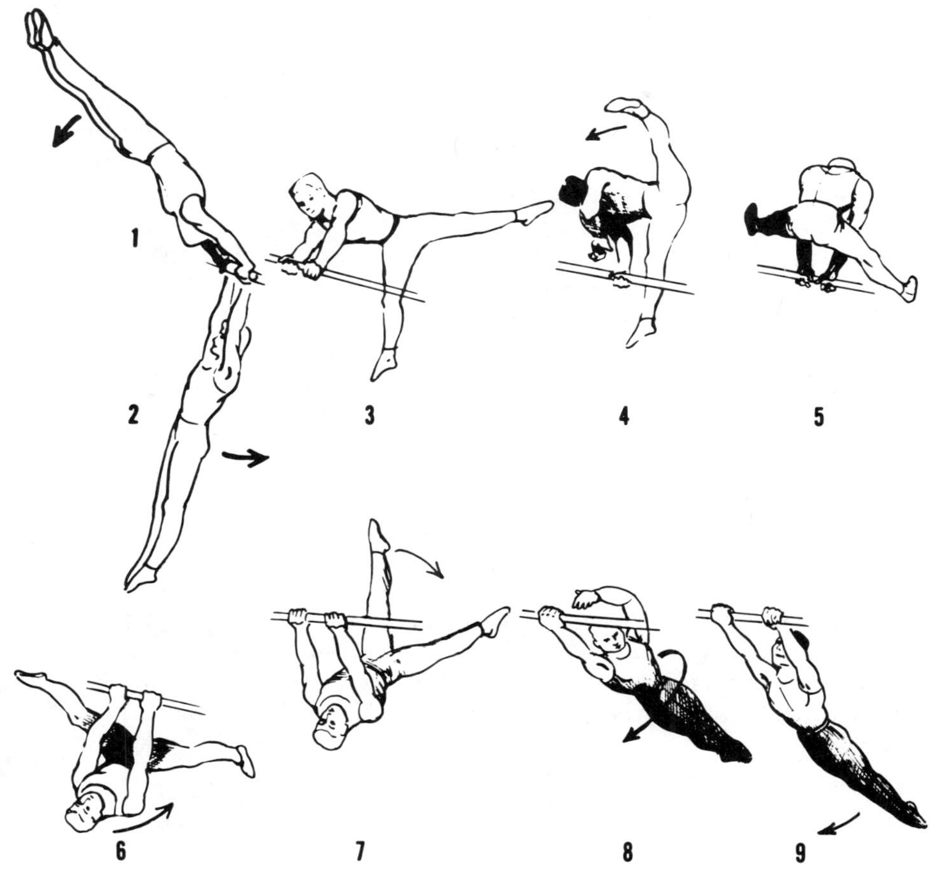

Fig. 6–38. Kreis Kehre.

the right (7). The left hand releases the bar and reaches around to regrasp again on the other side of the right hand (8). The gymnast swings forward with a mixed grip, right hand under, left hand over (9).

TEACHING TECHNIQUES. The gymnast should try the kreis kehre first on the low bar without a back uprise preceding it. This lead-up starts in a front support by swinging the legs under the bar and then backward and upward to a free front support. The hips are raised immediately, the weight is shifted onto the right hand, the legs are straddled, and the turn is started just as in the regular stunt. The next step is to try the first part of the stunt on the high bar. The shift of weight to the support arm, the hip lift, and the straddling of the legs can all be practiced without passing over the bar and without releasing the grip. Sometimes when this is done the performer swings back downward on the same side of the bar and sometimes he falls forward over the bar. In either case there is not much danger as there is little possibility of losing the grip. The third step is to try the stunt in its entirety except for the completion of the movement of the left leg. In this modified version of the kreis kehre the left leg passes over the bar only once as the turn is made. Instead of going over the top of the bar the second time it goes underneath as the left hand regrasps. As the performer falls backward it is therefore only necessary to disengage the right leg. Following the kreis kehre there is another half-turn in this routine, but during the learning process there is no need to practice this half-turn until the kreis kehre itself has been completely learned.

SPOTTING. This is a very difficult stunt to spot because of the wide straddle of the legs, which makes it difficult for a spotter to position himself without interfering with the movement. During practice on the low bar a spotter can stand on the back side of the bar very close to the right hand, which is in the undergrip, and grasp the support arm to keep the performer on balance as he turns. When the stunt is practiced on the high bar, the spotter stands almost directly under the bar and is alert to catch the performer if he falls. He must be quick to move out of the way of the legs and also quick to assist if necessary.

2. Kip. As the previous stunt is completed the gymnast swings forward with a mixed grip (right hand under, left hand over). On the forward end of the swing the body is arched and then on the backswing the kip is executed as previously explained in Routine II, Fig. 6–13.

3. Shoot to Handstand (Fig. 6–39). This is also called a free hip circle to handstand or a flange to handstand. As the kip is completed the legs swing backward and upward to a high free front support (1). As the upward motion ends, the right hand is quickly shifted from the reverse to a regular grip. The shoot to a handstand starts from this high free front support position with a regular grip. As the body drops back toward the bar and the hips get to within about one foot of the bar, the shoulders are allowed to drop backward and the body pikes to form an angle of approximately 135° (2). The gymnast swings under the bar in this position. Actually, if done correctly, it is as much of a drop as a circle so that at the

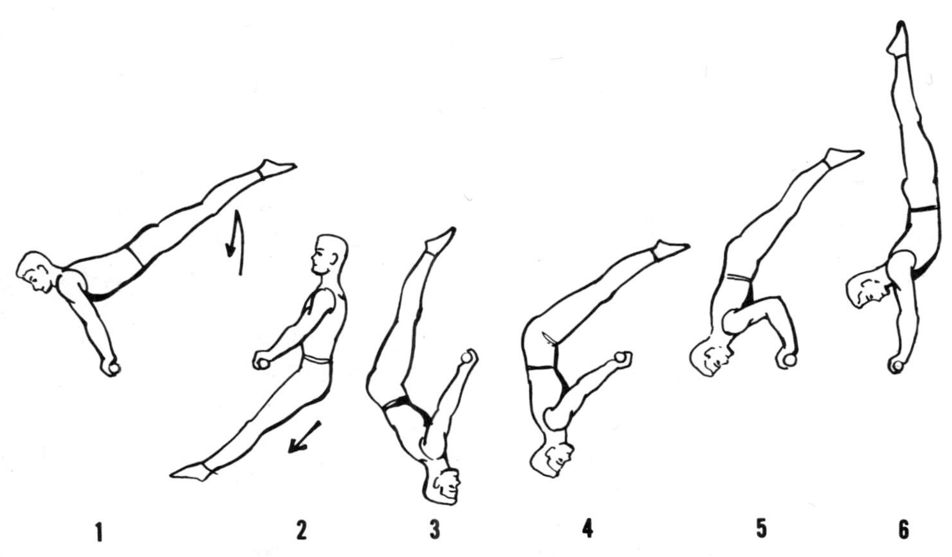

Fig. 6–39. Shoot to Handstand.

bottom of the downward movement there is a sharp pull on the bar (3). The bar reacts with a lift that drives the gymnast upward on the other side of the bar. By the time that this lifting effect is felt, the legs have circled around the bar so that the thighs are directly above the bar. The shoulders have also passed slightly under the bar and are on the upward part of the circle (4). From this position the body is extended and the head is lifted backward. If this movement is executed skillfully, the gymnast will be able to shoot all the way to the handstand with straight arms. Usually, however, after the lifting action of the bar has been completely transmitted to the body, the arms have to be bent, the grip has to be shifted over on top of the bar, and the last part of the movement to the handstand aided by a strong push with the arms (5). This stunt looks very pretty if done to a vertical position, but this is very risky in a routine as a slight miscalculation could cause a complete miss. Usually a performer will shoot for a position 10° to 20° behind the vertical position (6).

Teaching Techniques. This stunt is learned on a low bar. There are two different teaching methods used. In one the performer is told to think of the stunt as a high cast forward under the bar. The cast can gradually be increased in height until the shoot to handstand is performed. This teaching technique is simple but depends on careful spotting or it can be dangerous. The second technique is to start with a free hip circle that is completed by pushing away from the bar to drop to the feet on the back side. The circle can gradually be done higher and higher with a harder and harder arm push until the shoot to handstand is accomplished.

SPOTTING. For the first method explained above two spotters should be used on the front side of the bar. As the cast forward under the bar is performed, the near hand reaches under the bar and is placed on the performer's shoulder. This hand can be used to lift upward. The other hand is placed under the performer's lower back to support weight as the cast is completed and he drops back to the mat. As the cast gets higher and higher this hand can be used to push the performer over the top of the bar so that he drops to his feet on the back side. For the second teaching technique explained above the spotters should stand behind the bar and reach under the bar with the near hand to lift under the performer's shoulder. The other hand supports under the legs as they shoot over the bar to help direct them to the handstand position. When the shoot to handstand is first tried on the high bar, the spotter stands under the bar to stop all backward swing under the bar if the shoot is not completed and the performer swings back down on the front side.

4. Backward Giant, Straddle-On and -Off the Bar to a Backward Giant (Fig. 6–40). This giant swing has already been described in Routine IV, pages 228–31. Either one or two giants can be done but more than two would be considered poor routine composition. The downward swing for a backward giant is always done in a stretched body position (1). The straddle onto the bar is started on the upswing. The legs are pumped forward at the same time as for a regular backward giant swing—that is 30° to 45° beyond the vertical (2). The hip lift does not occur as in a regular giant swing, but the body continues to pike, the legs are straddled (3), and the soles of the feet are brought to the bar, one on each side of the hands. The feet, which should not be straddled too wide apart, make contact after the hips have passed over the bar and about the time the shoulders are directly above the bar (4). It requires strong abdominal muscles to bring about the pike and to place the feet on the bar. (It might be noted that advanced performers start their straddle much later than is recommended here. Japanese gymnasts swing almost to a handstand before dropping their feet to the bar, but even Japanese coaches do not recommend this method during the learning process.) The sole circle is executed as described in an earlier routine on pages 222–23 (5). As the

Fig. 6–40. Backward Giant, Straddle On and Off the Bar to a Backward Giant.

radius of the circle is reduced greatly from the giant swing to the sole circle, the speed of rotation should speed up. It depends on the speed of the circle when the feet can be removed from the bar for the straddle off. They are removed usually about the time that the arms reach the horizontal position on the upward part of the circle (6) and thrust up in the air as the arms press downward to bring the shoulders back over the bar (7) (8). It is safer to straddle off a little late rather than too early. Straddling off late will not look very good and might make it more difficult to perform the next stunt, but straddling off too early will bring about a complete break in the routine. If this stunt is performed well, the arms should stay straight during the whole movement; however, beginners often have to bend their arms to press back to the handstand position during the straddle off.

Teaching Techniques. The prerequisites are a backward sole circle and a well-controlled backward giant swing. Before the gymnast tries the combination of the two stunts on the high bar, the straddle-off should be practiced on the low bar with the aid of a spotter. The straddle-on to a sole circle can be practiced on the high bar without making any attempt to execute the straddle-off. This enables the gymnast to concentrate on the first part of the stunt.

SPOTTING. During the learning process on the low bar two spotters stand on the front side and lift under the shoulders of the learner as he completes the sole circle and starts the body extension. They help push him over the bar so that he can drop to his feet on the far side or, if he does fail to go over the top, they catch him as he falls backward on the near side of the bar. When the stunt is tried on the high bar, the spotters stand under the bar to stop the swing downward and backward in case the performer extends too soon and does not get over the top as he straddles off.

5. Backward Giant, Cross Arm Change to Forward Giant (Fig. 6–41). One or two backward giant swings are performed after the straddle on and off the bar. Immediately after passing through the handstand position just as the downswing is started one hand releases and crosses over the other to grasp again in a regular grip (1). In this routine the stunt is described with the left hand reaching across the right to the cross grip. The body is stretched as long as possible from the hands to the feet. The gymnast must resist the natural tendency to twist during the downswing and approximately the

Fig. 6–41. Backward Giant, Cross Arm Change to Forward Giant.

first 30° of the upswing, but it will be impossible to stop all the twisting motion (2). The pump of the legs starts as for a regular backward giant about 30° beyond the vertical. More twist will develop at this time, but the tendency should still be resisted. The body straightens at about the horizontal position or slightly beyond and the twist is no longer resisted (3). The grip is retained until slightly before the handstand position is reached. The right hand then releases and regrasps in approximately the same position on the bar but in a reverse grip. After the half-turn the left hand is also in a reverse grip (4). After passing over the top of the bar the body is stretched and the head dropped between the arms for a forward giant swing (5).

TEACHING TECHNIQUES. The first step is to cast up to a handstand on a low bar and practice crossing one hand over the other. The first step on the high bar is merely to swing back and forth under the bar with a cross grip to practice the leg pump and feel how the twist has to be resisted. The next step is to cast backward from a front support on the high bar, shift the right hand over the left, and practice swinging underneath and up to about the horizontal position before turning quickly and dropping off to the feet. This gives a good opportunity to practice all the techniques of the complete cross-over change but without actually doing a giant swing before or after the turn.

SPOTTING. The safety man spots from a horse placed under the bar in much the same way as described for the forward giant or backward giant. The performer's wrist cannot be grasped, however, until after the hand has reached across the top of the other. It is easier for the spotters to reach under the bar to grasp the performer rather than over the bar, and to grasp higher on the arm than when spotting regular giant swings. This stunt can also be spotted by placing the performer in a twisting belt attached to the swivel safety rig described on pages 188–89.

6. Forward Giant, Stall Out, to a Rear Vault Catch (Fig. 6–42). After the cross arm change the gymnast executes one, or at the most two, complete forward giant swings. On either the second or third one he does not quite complete it but "stalls out" and reverses direction for the swing-down. Instead of piking on the upward swing just before the stall out, the body remains in a slight arch and swings up purely from the momentum gained on the previous downswing (1). After passing the horizontal position on the upswing the arms pull the shoulders forward slightly toward the

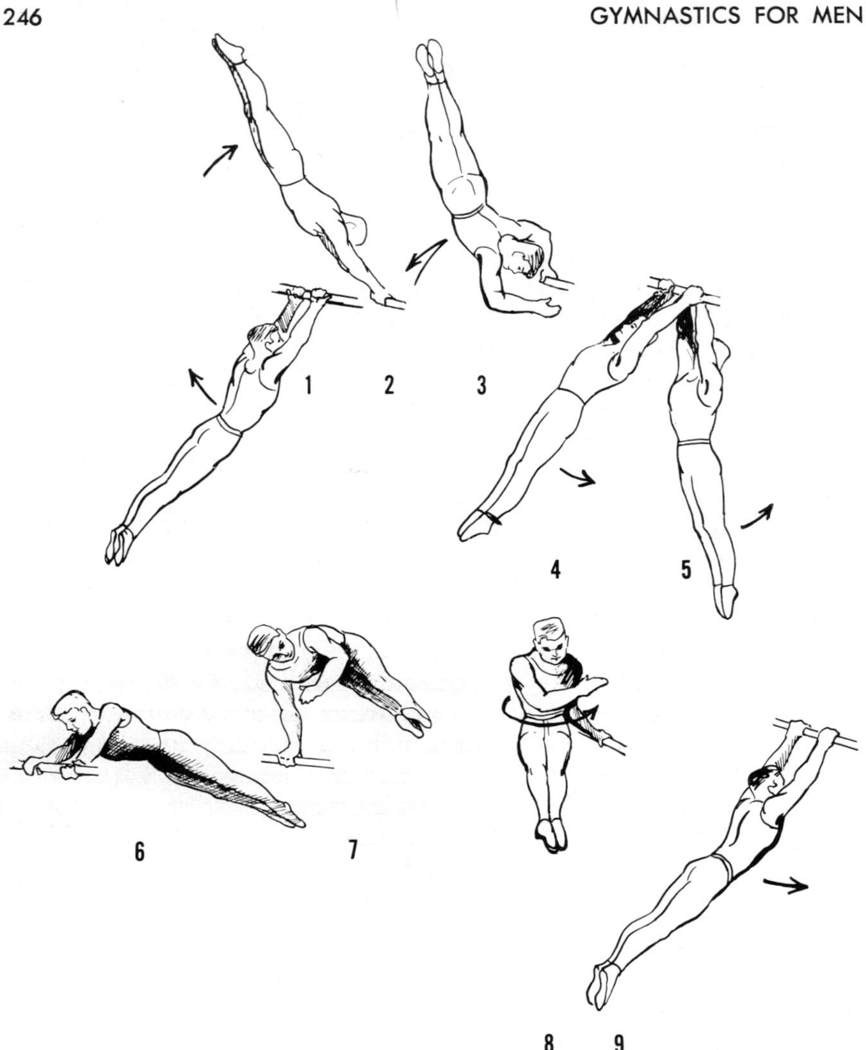

Fig. 6–42. Forward Giant, Stall Out to Rear Vault Catch.

bar and the left hand is released and placed in an overgrip directly in front of the face. This centralization of the hand is very important for a straight downswing. The upswing should continue in a mixed grasp to at least 45° above the horizontal after the left hand change (2). At the dead point on the top of the upswing the right hand reaches under the left hand to grasp the bar on the far side of the left hand. This hand reaches as if for a reverse grip, but during the reach the head and shoulders are turned so that by the time the gasp is made the right hand is actually in an overgrip and the left hand has become an undergrip. The eyes should look at the point on the bar where the grasp is to be made. The grip should be a secure one with the hand wrapped well around the bar (3). At the time the right hand is changed and the turn executed there is a great tendency to pike. This must be resisted or the downswing will be poor. During the release and turn both arms might have to be bent slightly, but as soon as possible they should be fully extended and the entire body stretched in a straight line for the downswing (4). This stretched position is held throughout the downswing and under the bar (5). On the upswing the arms start pressing down and the body pikes and turns to the left, in the direction of the hand with the undergrip (6). The press down and turn continues during the upswing and most of the weight is shifted to the right arm. The left hand gives a final vigorous pull and then releases just before the top of the bar is reached (7). The gymnast should pass over the bar in a right angle pike position having completed a quarter-turn. The right hand also thrusts off the bar just as the buttocks pass over the top. This position is clearly illustrated in the photo on page 248. At this time the head and shoulders turn back toward the bar to complete the half turn. If the vault is done well, both hands will regrasp at almost the same time but if this is not possible the left hand should grasp immediately and the right hand later (8). As soon as the catch is made with both hands in an overgrip the legs should be extended backward and the shoulders thrust away from the bar to stretch the body as early as possible so that a reasonable amount of downswing can be obtained (9). It will be difficult to get enough swing for the following stunt unless the vault is executed skillfully.

Teaching Techniques. The teaching method for the stall out is to practice it from a support position with one hand already in an overgrip and centralized. From this position the performer casts up and reaches under as in the regular stunt. The spotter stands under the bar ready to catch in case the grip is missed and to stop the swing under the bar as the performer swings down. The next step is the same except that the first hand is placed in an overgrip and centralized during the cast back from support. The teaching method for the vault is more complicated. The first step is to start on a low bar by jumping from a stand. The turn and regrasp also can be practiced partially in this way. Next, some teachers have their students cast from a support to the vault over the low bar, but this step may be omitted as it sometimes teaches bad habits. The

University of Washington News Service photo

Mike Flansaas Performing a Rear Vault to a Catch on the Horizontal Bar. Mike is an all-round performer who is expected to develop into one of the best in the nation. As only a sophomore he placed sixth in the nation in the long horse vault.

next step is to start from a high under-bar cast and practice the first part of the vault without actually releasing and passing over the top of the bar. The final lead-up stunt is to start from a high under-bar cast and vault over the bar to a dismount without attempting to catch. As this step is practiced, one hand, and later both hands, can be placed on the bar as if a regrasp is going to be executed. When the hands can be placed consistently on the bar, the performer is ready to attempt the vault to the catch. It can be practiced from the under-bar cast before it is tried from the stall out.

SPOTTING. One spotter stands on the back side of the bar to catch the performer in case his grip is pulled loose on the upswing. Another spotter stands on the recatch side of the bar and reaches up to grasp the hips of the performer as soon as possible after he passes over the bar and supports some of his weight as he drops to the ground, or as he recatches and swings under the bar. The spotter must be behind the performer to do this.

7. Straddle Cut and Catch from an Inverted Pike Hang (Fig. 6–43). The gymnast swings forward under the bar after the rear vault catch and at the front end of the swing arches (1) and then raises the legs to pass under the bar and between the hands (2). The legs fold in close to the chest so that there is a hard pull on the hands and then, as the bar reacts with the usual lift, the pike is opened somewhat, but not very much, and the arms press down hard on the bar to raise the shoulders as high as possible (3). At the time of the release the legs are thrust upward and then straddled wide apart as they pass between the hands and the bar before the recatch (4). Holding on too long will cause the legs to hit against the bar, releasing too soon will make a recatch impossible as the performer will fly backward and drop to his feet on the mat. The recatch is made in an overgrip and the gymnast then swings forward under the bar (5) (6).

TEACHING TECHNIQUES. The straddle cut and catch should be practiced on a low bar. If the gymnast has not learned to pump up a swing in the inverted pike hang, a spotter will have to push the performer back and forth to develop the necessary swing. At first the straddle cut is practiced to a standing position on the mat rather than to a recatch. The next step is to try the recatch on a low bar so that the feet will contact the ground before the hands have to bear any weight. The height of the bar is then increased somewhat so that the recatch can be made before the feet hit the mat.

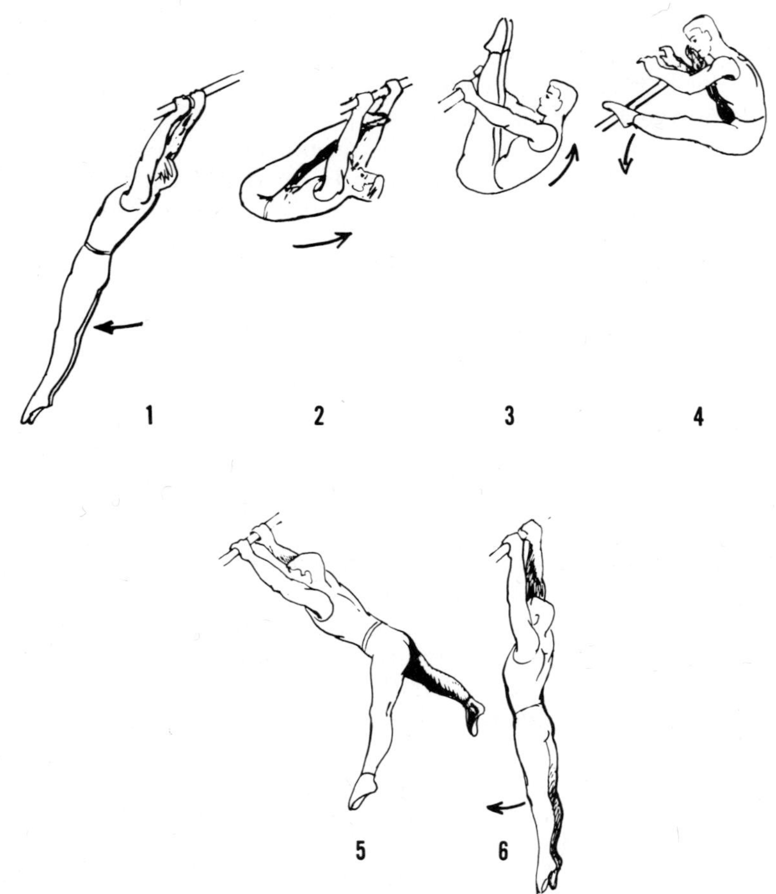

Fig. 6–43. Straddle Cut and Catch from an Inverted Pike Hang.

SPOTTING. The spotter stations himself almost directly behind the performer and reaches up to grasp his back with both hands at the time of the release to prevent a fall and also to aid in the forward rotation. When the bar is raised, the spotter will not be able to make contact at the time of release but positions himself in the same location ready to catch if the bar is missed.

8. Kip. This kip is performed as described in Routine II, Fig. 6–13.

9. Forward Hip Circle Cast to Handstand (Fig. 6–44). As the kip is completed the body is allowed to remain in contact with the bar

(1). The hip circle forward is started from this front support position and is executed as described in Routine II, pages 205–6 (2) (3). As the hip circle is completed with the upper body having passed just beyond the vertical position but with the legs still trailing under the bar, the hands are changed quickly from an over- to an undergrip. The cast up to handstand is executed from this position with a rapid forward lean of the upper body and a hard whip of the legs backward and upward (4) (5) (6) as described for the forward giant swing in Routine IV, pages 225–27. The kip, forward hip circle, grip change, and cast to the handstand should all be combined smoothly without any break in rhythm. There are no special teaching techniques for this movement. As both the forward hip circle and cast to handstand have been included in previous routines, it is just a matter of practicing the grip change between the two.

Fig. 6–44. Forward Hip Circle Cast to Handstand.

SPOTTING. Spotters can assist from horses placed under the bar but this is probably not necessary. If the parts incorporated have been learned well, the performer should have little trouble in accomplishing this move on his own. Spotters should stand in readiness under the bar to catch if necessary.

10. Forward Giant, Half-Pirouette to Backward Giant (Fig. 6–45). Either one or two forward giant swings can be done at this point. These were thoroughly described in Routine IV, pages 225–27. The half-pirouette starts during the last part of the upswing (1). As the shoulders are pulled forward toward the bar, the weight shifts

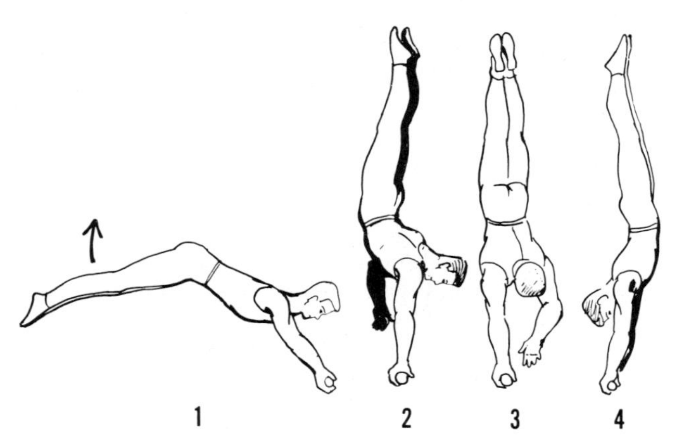

Fig. 6–45. Forward Giant, Half-Pirouette to Backward Giant.

over one arm and then as the legs whip upward out of the pike position the head looks in the direction of the turn and the shoulders start to twist. About ten degrees before the top of the swing one hand releases the bar (2) and reaches around the support arm ready for the regrasp (3). At the top of the swing the free hand should regrasp in a regular grip on the other side of the support arm (4). The gymnast is now ready to swing down on the other side of the bar in a double overgrip. The body is stretched as long as possible and the backward giant is performed as described in Routine IV, pages 228–31.

TEACHING TECHNIQUES. Before attempting this stunt the gymnast ought to be able to do reverse grip giant swings in fast tempo so that he swings quickly over the top of the bar. The hands should be close together on the bar when pirouette movements are attempted, as this makes the turn much easier and helps to bring about a straight downswing. The pirouette motion can be practiced first on the floor parallel bars by kicking up to a reverse grip handstand from one side and turning to a regular grip before dropping off to the feet on the other side. Next the gymnast should practice casting from a support to a reverse grip handstand on the low horizontal bar and pirouetting to a regular grip before dropping off to the feet on the other side.

SPOTTING. On the floor parallels and the low horizontal bar a spotter can stand close to the performer on the back side of the bar, near the support arm, to aid him in making the turn and prevent him from dropping back down on top of the bar. When the pirouette is attempted on the high bar, the spotter stands under the bar to grasp the performer around the hips and to stop all swing under the bar if it becomes crooked.

11. Backward Giant, Half-Pirouette to Forward Giant (Fig. 6–46). This is a much different type of movement from the one just described and is somewhat harder. It is often called a "blind-change." At the handstand position of the first backward giant the hands should be shifted quite close together. On the upward swing of the second giant the legs pump forward as usual (1) and then the hips lift upward as for the completion of a regular giant swing (2).

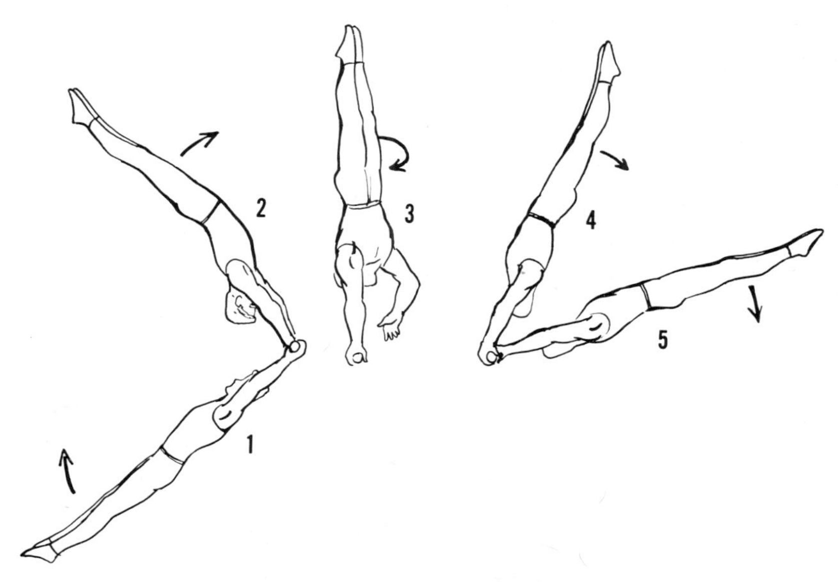

Fig. 6–46. Backward Giant, Half-Pirouette to Forward Giant.

As the back is arched the pirouette is initiated by a turn of the head and the hips with the shoulders following. The hand grip is held as long as possible, but one hand finally releases close to the top of the circle (3). The pirouette is completed on top of the bar with the free hand reaching around the support arm to regrasp the bar on the other side in a reverse grip (4). It is very important to keep fully extended in a straight line during the turn and not to allow the shoulders to get ahead of the motion. As soon as the downswing starts, both arms must continue to press away from the bar in a fully extended position to ensure a straight downswing. The head is lowered between the arms as usual for the forward giant swings (5).

Teaching Techniques. High swinging half-turns are an excellent lead-up for this stunt as well as being a good warm-up for advanced performers to use every day. These start with a medium height swing under the bar. At the top of the forward swing the gymnast turns to swing down in the other direction. One hand reaches across the top of the other hand to regrasp in an overgrip and then the second hand is also quickly changed to an overgrip. The height of the swing can be gradually increased with a leg pump and hip lift just as in a backward giant swing. If these half-turns were carried high enough, the gymnast would eventually go over the top of the bar instead of reversing direction and swinging back down again. When this happens, the first hand, as it is changed, is placed in a reverse grasp instead of a regular grip and the second hand does not have to change at all as the direction of the swing has not changed. In this way the gymnast can learn this pirouette as a progression of the swinging half-turns.

Spotting. As the pirouette is learned a spotter can assist from a horse placed under the bar. The next step is to have the spotter stand under the bar ready to catch the gymnast if the grip is missed or to stop all backward swing under the bar if the swing is crooked.

12. Forward Giant to Straddle over Dismount (Fig. 6–47). Two or three circles should be done after the blind change. Halfway through the second or third giant as the upswing starts the back is arched (1). The hips are not raised as in a normal forward giant but the arch is held and the feet are allowed to swing high. During the upswing the shoulders are drawn forward and upward over the bar as in a back uprise (2). As the upswing slows down, the hips are raised, the legs start to straddle, and the shoulders are drawn forward over the bar vigorously (3). Just as the weight

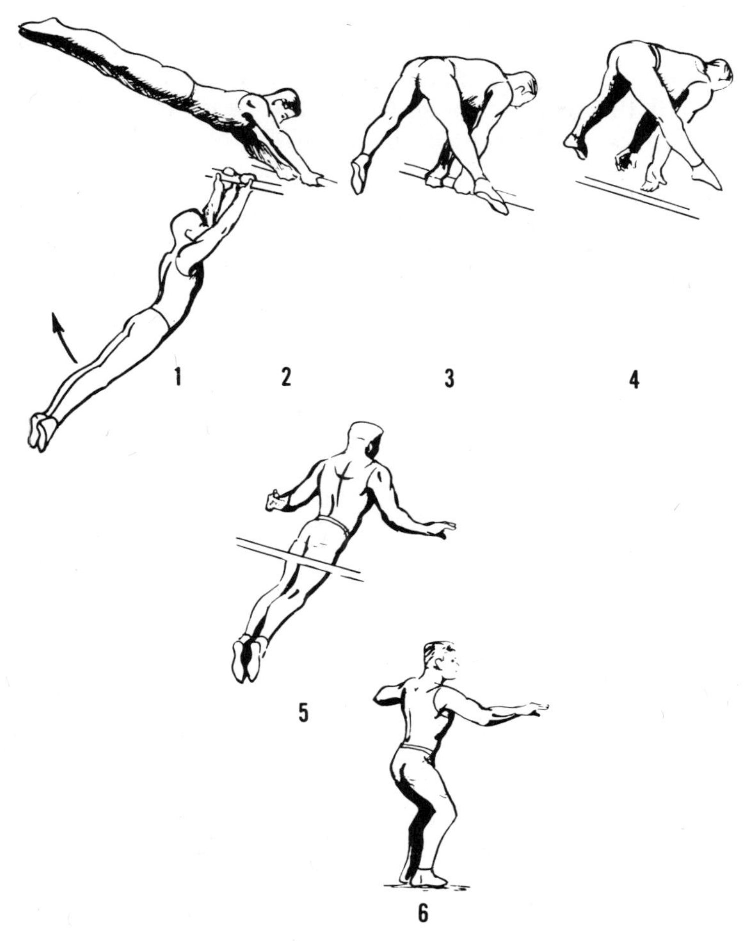

Fig. 6–47. Forward Giant to Straddle over Dismount.

passes over the bar the arms push off hard (4). When the feet have cleared the bar, the head and chest are raised, the body is arched, and the legs are brought together (5). The legs pike again, of course, for the landing with the back to the bar in a side stand rearways (6). If this dismount is performed well, the body should swing up to a position at least 45° above the horizontal in an arched position before the hips are lifted and the legs straddled.

Teaching Techniques. The "feeling" of straddling over the bar can be experienced by performing the stunt from a front support position. This can first be done on a low bar and then on the high bar. The next step is to practice from a high under-bar cast.

Spotting. One or two spotters stand in front of the bar directly in front of the performer's shoulders. They reach for the upper arm to grasp it if the feet are caught or if the head and chest are not raised high enough during the dismount.

7

Rings

As well as being a competitive event, the rings, in one form or another, are a piece of play equipment. A long row of rings is sometimes found in parks and schools. These are called traveling rings. Children swing from one to the other and progress down the row. A set of two rings, similar to competitive rings, is a common item found suspended from children's backyard play equipment. They are also found in many parks. Because there is opportunity to use rings during play and recreational hours it is an excellent activity to include in the instructional program of the school.

Probably the main contribution of the rings to the physical education program is development of arm, shoulder, and upper body strength. The event, as performed in competition, requires greater strength than any of the others. The rings also contribute to shoulder flexibility because a great number of stunts require twisting and turning of the shoulder girdle. As rings can be used by handicapped individuals who have little use of their legs, they have special value in our school program.

Young children may be taught skills on the rings that involve hanging positions but should not be required to do support work. Routine I, in this chapter, includes only hanging skills and thus may be used for the upper elementary age. Starting with Routine II, considerable strength is required. It is not recommended that this, or later routines, be presented before junior high school.

EQUIPMENT

There have been a number of changes in the competitive ring event in recent years. In fact, until 1962, there were two ring events—the still rings and the flying rings—included in competition in the United States. The flying rings were dropped from most competition because of their danger and because many coaches believed that we should include only the international events in our gymnastic program. During the mid-1950's the ring itself was changed from a leather covered metal ring to a laminated wooden one. Swivels were introduced in the 1950's and made an official part of the ring suspension mechanism. These prevent the ropes from winding up as the gymnast circles in one direction or the other. The suspension rope has changed from fiber to wire cable and the belting used to fasten the ring to the rope is now usually made of nylon or cotton rather than leather.

The rings are the least expensive piece of gymnast equipment to buy. Even floor exercise, if a number of mats are used, costs more. Once purchased the equipment will last indefinitely if it is properly cared for. The rings are suspended from a height of 18 feet and are 19⅝ inches apart. The bottom of the ring should be 8 feet 2½ inches from the floor. The belting with which the ring is held is 27½ inches long. (It is actually twice this length because it passes through the ring and is in the form of a loop.) This belting is attached to a wire cable that in turn is attached to ball-bearing swivels. The swivels are hung from the bracket that is fastened onto the beam or the ceiling. This bracket should permit the rings to swing freely forward and backward. The ring itself is made of laminated wood 1⅛ inches in diameter. The inside diameter of the ring is 7 inches.

For teaching purposes rings of different height must be available. Even advanced performers have occasion to use rings only three or four feet off the floor as they learn new skills. Rings that can be raised up and down and are adjustable to any height are available through most manufacturers. These are very desirable for teaching purposes but are not satisfactory for top level performance as they do not have swivels and they have considerable "give" or "sag" because the suspension ropes run through pulleys across the ceiling and down the wall to their attachment rather than being securely fastened directly above the rings. Two sets of rings are actually needed—a regulation set and an adjustable set. Two sets of nonadjustable rings may be substituted for the adjustable set. One of these should be approximately 4 feet off the floor, the other about 5½ feet or 6 feet. These do not provide quite the range of height that is needed for all teaching purposes but it is better than not having any height range. The cost of two sets of rings like this is no more than one set of adjustable rings, and two pieces of equipment do enable an extra student to participate. It is a simple matter to run a light line through a pulley on the ceiling at the side of the gym so that rings may be pulled up to the ceiling when not in use so as to be out of the way for other activities.

HOMEMADE EQUIPMENT

Rings are very simple and inexpensive to make and install. All necessary parts can either be made in the school shop or be purchased from an ordinary hardwood store. Swivels are not necessary for teaching purposes and may be omitted until funds are available to purchase them.

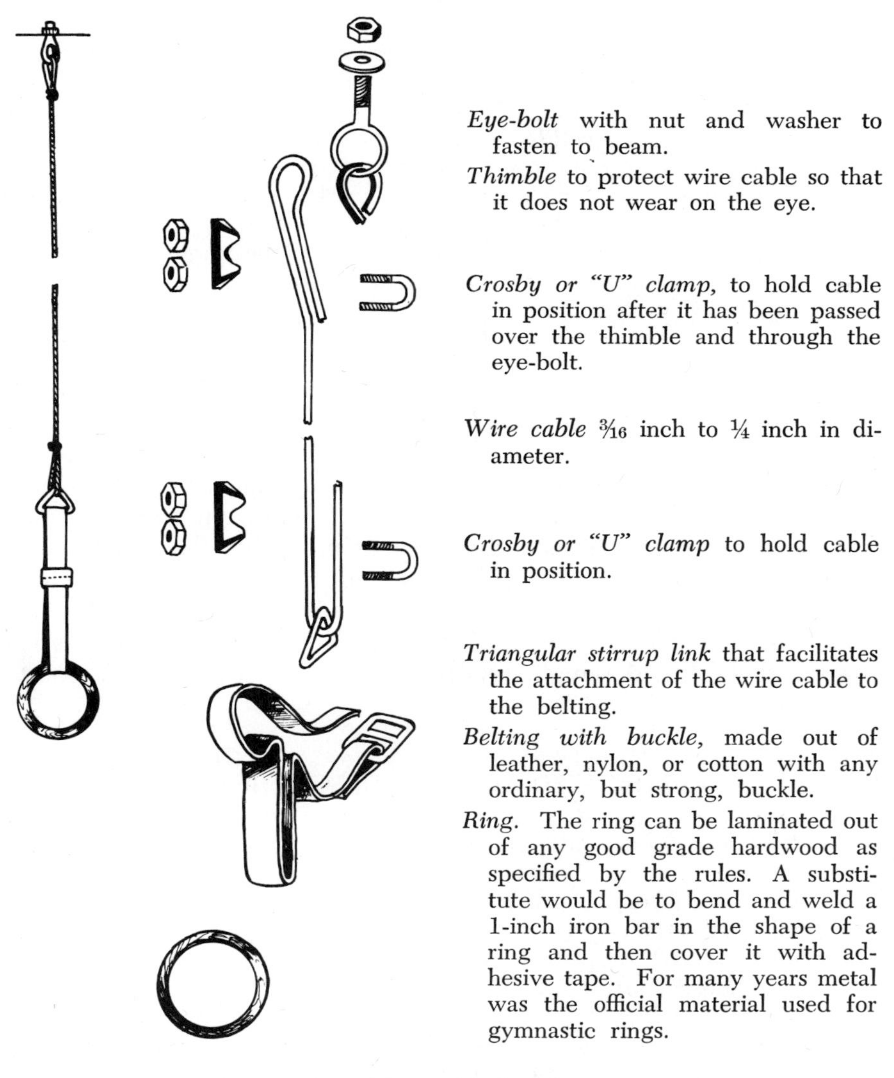

Fig. 7–1. Inexpensive Method of Ring Installation.

SAFETY

Some of the safety precautions presented in Chapter 1 need to be emphasized for the ring event.

1. The equipment should be checked periodically for weaknesses and loose bolts.
2. Low rings should be used for many stunts during the learning stages.
3. Spotting is very important for two reasons: Part of the performer's weight must be supported as some stunts are learned to prevent injury to his shoulders. When certain skills are executed incorrectly, it places a sudden strain or jerk on the hands, which tends to pull the grip loose from the rings.
4. Magnesium should be available to keep the hands dry and thus minimize slipping.
5. Adequate padding must be provided below the rings.

RULES

A ring exercise must combine movements of swing and strength with a number of held positions. There must be at least two handstands, one of which is reached by using a great amount of strength, one of which is accomplished by using swing that originates from a hanging position. In addition to the two handstands there must be one hold of pronounced difficulty. Holds must be of at least three seconds duration on the rings (only two seconds in other events). Although the performer swings back and forth on the rings, the rings themselves should not swing during the exercise, that is, they should remain relatively stationary under their point of support.

ABBREVIATED ROUTINE DESCRIPTIONS

I. Pendulum swing, raise the legs to a straight body inverted hang (HOLD), pike to a bent body inverted hang, single leg cut and catch, swing downward to a hang and upward to a bent inverted hang, skin-the-cat, bent inverted hang, lower to a hanging half-lever (HOLD), drop the legs to a hang and swing up to a bird's-nest, swing downward to a hang and then upward to a low straddle cut-off backward.

II. Muscle up, support half-lever (HOLD), press to a shoulder balance with bent knees (HOLD), lower to an inverted hang, dislocate, kip, slow forward roll, roll forward to a bent inverted hang, inlocate, straddle cut-off forward.

III. Pendulum swing, front uprise, roll forward to a bent inverted hang, inlocate, kip, cast backward to a hang, back kip, slow backward roll, support half-lever (HOLD), press to a shoulder balance (HOLD), fall forward out of the shoulder stand to a back uprise, roll backward to a bent inverted hang, dislocate, fly away backward.

IV. Raise straight body to an inverted hang, dislocate, shoot to a shoulder balance (HOLD), lower slowly to a horizontal lever between the rings (French lever), lower to a back lever below the rings (HOLD), dislocate from the back lever, back kip, support half-lever (HOLD), press a handstand with bent body (HOLD), lower slowly to a support, roll backward to a bent inverted hang, dislocate, high straddle cut-off backward.

V. Slowly raise with straight body to an inverted hang, dislocate, shoot to a handstand (HOLD), lower slowly to a support, stretch the arms sideways to a cross (HOLD), bend the arms and raise the legs to a bent inverted hang, dislocate, fast backward roll below the rings, front lever (HOLD), bend body to a bent inverted hang, kip to a support half-lever (HOLD), straight body press to a handstand (HOLD), lower to a support, cast forward to a hang, back uprise, fall backward to a straddle cut-off.

I. BEGINNING ROUTINE

1. Pendulum Swing (Fig. 7–2). The swing is started by bending at the waist and raising the legs forward (1). The legs are then dropped and allowed to swing freely backward into an arch (2).

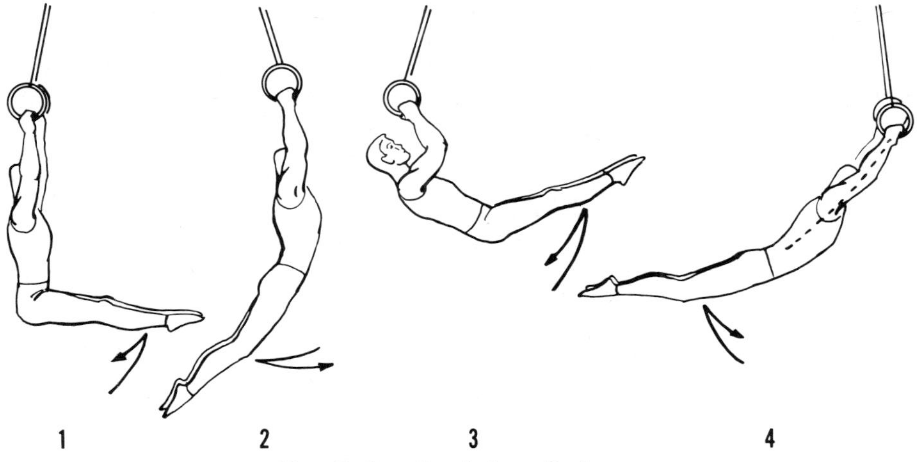

Fig. 7–2. Pendulum Swing.

As they swing forward, the body is slightly piked again just after it passes the vertical hang. Once this swing is started it may be increased in height by pumping with the legs as they swing forward and upward and by bending the arms slightly and raising the entire body at the top of the forward swing (3). At the top of the backward swing the shoulders must be relaxed so that the entire body may swing high at this end of the pendulum (4). [Note the shoulder position indicated by the dotted line in (4).]

Spotting. A spotter stands by the side of the performer and pushes under the lower back on the forward swing and under the abdomen during the backward swing. He can aid in developing a good pendulum swing in this way and also be ready to support with either hand if the learner loses his grip.

2. Straight Body Inverted Hang (Fig. 7–3). On the forward end of the pendulum swing the body bends to almost a right angle pike. The arms are kept straight and press forward and downward to help raise the body (1). As the center of gravity reaches the plane between the arms (2), the body is slowly extended upward until it is straight and held vertically between the ropes (3). The head should remain forward during the body extension. It is then placed backward and the body assumes a slight arch (4). This position is Held for at least three seconds.

Teaching Techniques. The legs may be straddled and kept in contact with the rings and ropes as the body is extended. The feet are slowly removed from the ropes when the straight body position has been reached. The head should not be tipped backward nor the body arched until the student is familiar with the head forward position. The arms should be squeezed in tightly against the side to help stabilize the body.

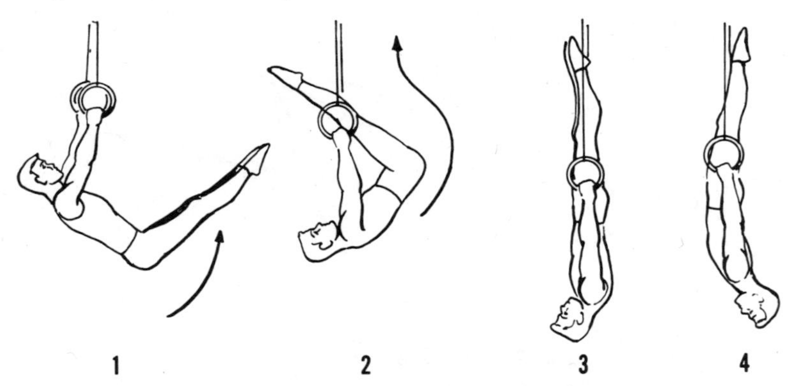

Fig. 7–3. Straight Body Inverted Hang.

SPOTTING. This position should be practiced on low rings where a spotter can help by placing one hand in front and one hand behind the thighs to keep the performer in balance. When it is tried on high rings the spotter stands in readiness to catch in case the balance is lost.

3. Bent Body Inverted Hang (Fig. 7–4). From the straight inverted hang the head is returned to a normal position and the body piked so that the knees are directly above the face. The eyes should look at the knees in this position.

Fig. 7–4. Bent Body Inverted Hang.

4. Single Leg Cut and Catch (Fig. 7–5). Either leg can be cut but in this routine it will be described with the right leg. The first step is to rotate backward by raising the hips and lowering the feet in the bent inverted hang (1). From this position the stunt is started by rotating forward in the pike position. The right leg straddles out to the side and both arms are bent to raise the shoulders up toward the rings (2). As the right leg touches the right arm, the right hand releases momentarily so that the leg can pass on the outside of the ring between the ring and the hand. The left

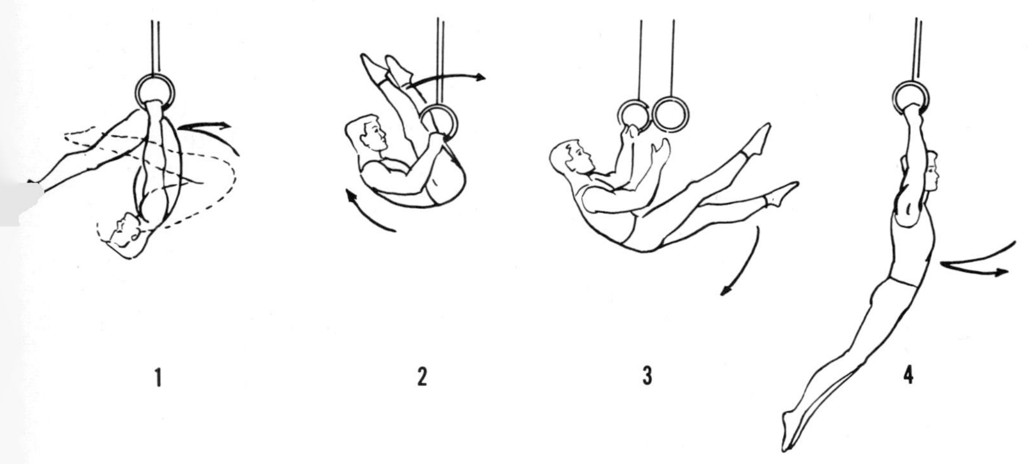

Fig. 7–5. Single Leg Cut and Catch.

leg swings between the two rings (3). The right hand grasps the ring again as quickly as possible and the legs are joined together to swing downward to the hanging position (4). The head should be forward on the chest and the eyes looking at the right ring during the rock forward, release, and recatch.

TEACHING TECHNIQUES. The stunt is learned on three-quarter height rings so that the feet will hit the ground about the same time the ring has to be regrasped. If the ring is missed, there is no danger of having the left hand torn loose from the other ring. The cut and catch should also be learned from a rocking motion forward and backward in the bent inverted hang. On each forward rotation the leg is straddled, the arms are bent, and the eyes focus on the ring to be released. After momentum is built up in this way, the ring is released on about the third or fourth movement forward.

SPOTTING. If the right ring is to be released, the spotter stands on the left side. During the rock forward he lifts with one hand under the upper back and during the release and recatch he supports weight under the lower back. When the performer first tries the stunt on his own, the spotter should stand close, ready to reach in across the chest and catch the upper body if the ring is not recaught as the left hand will probably be pulled loose from the other ring.

5. Bent Body Inverted Hang. After the single leg cut and catch, which ends in a hanging position, the gymnast swings upward to another bent body inverted hang, Fig. 7–4.

6. Skin-the-Cat (Fig. 7–6). From the bent body inverted hang (1) the body is rotated backward as far as possible (2). The hips are then extended and the legs stretched down toward the floor (3). From this position the hips are pulled back up between the arms (4), using the muscles of the shoulder girdle, and the body returns to the bent inverted hang. The legs should remain straight throughout the entire movement.

TEACHING TECHNIQUES. Teach on low rings so that the feet can touch the mat in the skin-the-cat position. A jump can be taken to aid in the return to the bent inverted hang. The rings are gradually raised so that the body has to stretch more and more to touch the floor. To shorten the radius, and thus make the skin-the-cat easier, the knees may be bent during the entire movement as it is being learned.

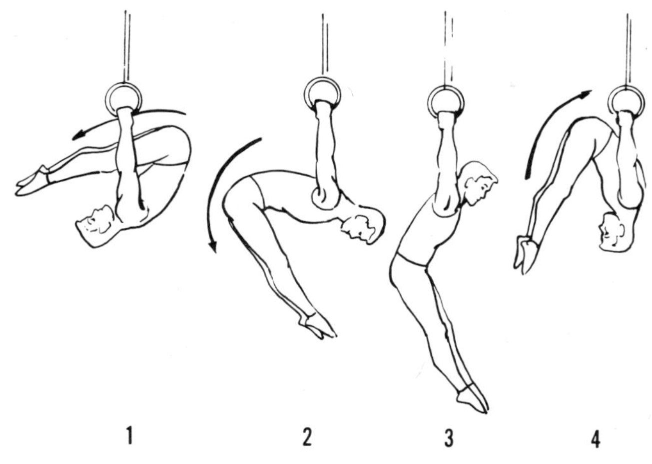

Fig. 7–6. Skin-the-Cat.

SPOTTING. The spotter stands on the side and grasps the thigh to aid as needed. If the grip on the rings is released, the spotter catches the performer's upper body and makes sure he lands on his feet.

7. Hanging Half-Lever (Fig. 7–7). From the bent inverted hang the body is rotated forward slowly until the legs are horizontal and the arms and trunk are in approximately a straight line. The first part of this movement is controlled by the muscles of the shoulder girdle, but the last part involves primarily abdominal strength to hold the legs in the half-lever. This position is HELD for at least three seconds.

Fig. 7–7. Hanging Half-Lever.

TEACHING TECHNIQUES. This skill may be practiced by lowering and holding the position with both legs bent, or with one leg straight and the other bent. Lowering slowly should be emphasized as it is much harder to stop if the movement is fast. A sharp pike keeps the lever short and therefore makes the stunt easier.

SPOTTING. A spotter may place a hand under the back of the legs to support some weight as the legs are lowered and during the half-lever.

8. Bird's Nest (Fig. 7–8). After holding the half-lever the legs are dropped to a hang and then swung upward toward the rings again. As the feet approach the rings, the knees are bent and the hands are turned forward so that the toes can be placed into the

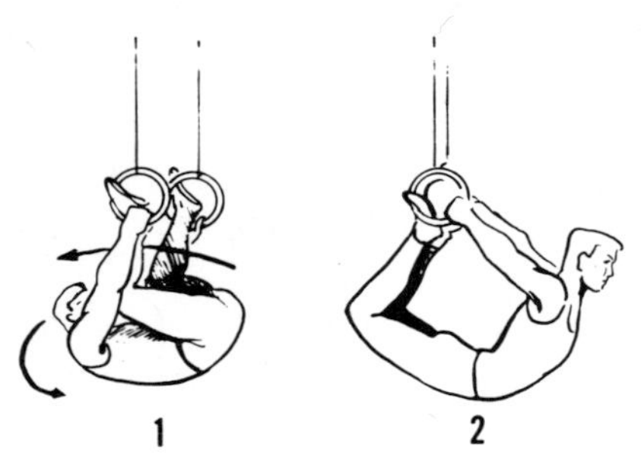

Fig. 7–8. Bird's Nest.

center of the rings (1). The insteps are rested on the rings as the knees and hips pass between the arms. The body is arched with the abdomen toward the mat (2). This position is shown momentarily and then the hips return to the bent body inverted hang position and the feet are removed from the rings.

SPOTTING. The spotter should stand in readiness to catch the performer in case the feet slip out of the rings.

9. Straddle Cut-Off Backward (Fig. 7–9). As the performer comes out of the bird's nest, the legs are swung downward to a hang as forcefully as possible and pumped backward beyond the vertical as in a pendulum swing (1). As they swing forward past the vertical again, the body is piked and the legs are straddled (2). This should permit them to swing upward quickly toward the arms because both the pike and the straddle shorten the radius. The arms should press forward and downward on the rings to increase the momentum. As the legs approach the arms, a hard pull is given, the head is thrown back, and then the rings are released (3). The rotation continues after the release (4) and the feet circle around to the mat (5).

TEACHING TECHNIQUES. Students may get the "feel" of swinging the legs up and releasing the rings with the legs together between the arms rather than straddled. When the straddle is first

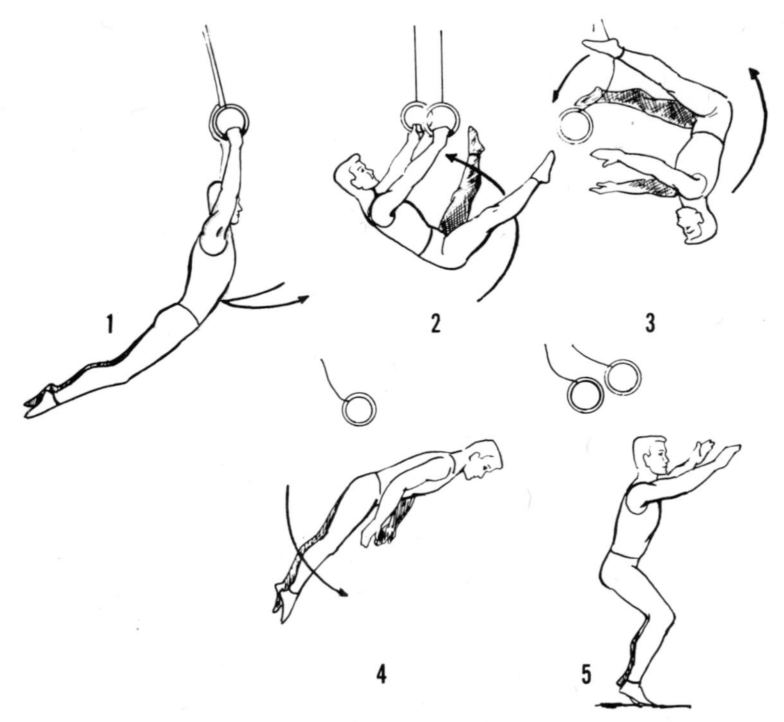

Fig. 7–9. Straddle Cut-Off Backward.

tried, several good pendulum swings should precede the attempt and a couple of "dry runs" should be taken before the rings are actually released. Students might be informed that the way that the cut-off is executed in this routine is not considered good technique for advanced performers. Good gymnasts pull much harder and sooner with the arms and are actually above the rings during the cut-off. Even beginners can gradually work toward a higher dismount.

SPOTTING. This dismount is not difficult but it can be dangerous if not spotted carefully. Two spotters are used, one on each side of the performer. The technique is illustrated in the first photo on page 268. They place one hand over the top of the shoulder between the arm and neck to rest on the chest before the pendulum swing is started. This hand is used to support weight as the rings are released. The other hand lifts under the lower back and pushes the performer over to his feet if necessary. Spotters should not push too hard as it is possible to overspin this dismount. A third spotter can be used behind the performer to guard against this.

The first photo illustrates the method of spotting a backward straddle cut-off. Photo 2 shows how a beginner might use his legs against the straps while learning a shoulder stand. Photos 3 and 4 illustrate the spotting techniques for an inlocate and dislocate, respectively.

II. LOW INTERMEDIATE ROUTINE

1. Muscle-Up (Fig. 7–10). The muscle-up starts from a hang with a high or false grip (1). In a high grip the little finger side of the hand is shifted from the regular position over the top of the ring so that the ring actually runs across the heel of the hand and the wrist. The arms have to be bent to assume a false grip but after it has been attained they should be straightened again (2). In competition it is considered good technique to straighten the

Fig. 7–10. Muscle-Up.

arms before the routine is started. The body is pulled up toward the rings and the legs are raised forward in a pike. The rings should be kept close together and pulled to the chest, rather than to a point beside the shoulders as is often done (3). The critical part of the muscle-up is the change from a hang to a support. It is accomplished by dropping the legs downward from the pike and quickly leaning the head and shoulders forward over the rings. The rings have to be turned 180° as the hands shift up on top (4). From this bent arm support the gymnast pushes to a straight arm support (5). There is no substitute for a good strong set of triceps muscles for this last movement.

Teaching Techniques. The high grip must be learned first. This is done with the rings about head height and the feet on the floor. Once the grip is obtained the legs are bent until the hands bear the weight. The straight arm position can be practiced at this time with care being taken not to lose the high grip as the arms are straightened. The muscle-up also can be practiced with the feet on the floor. The arms should do most of the work but the legs can aid as they straighten. A jump can be given, if necessary, at the critical point. This jump also provides a little momentum for the press from the bent arm to the straight arm support. Emphasize in teaching that the rings must be kept close together and pulled to the chest and not to the outside of the shoulders. Dips should be practiced on the parallel bars to develop strength for the last part of this stunt.

SPOTTING. The spotter stands to the side and lifts upward on the thigh to assist. Remember that spotters should assist only as much as is necessary and should leave most of the work to the performer.

2. Support Half-Lever (Fig. 7–11). This is a common position in gymnastic routines of all levels of difficulty and is usually called an "L." From the support position at the end of the muscle-up the legs are raised forward to a horizontal position and are HELD there for at least three seconds.

Fig. 7–11. Support Half-Lever.

TEACHING TECHNIQUES. This should be practiced on low rings. One leg can be bent at first to make it easier or a partner can assist by supporting a little of the weight. A good drill is to raise the legs to the "L," hold momentarily, and then lower and repeat several times.

3. Press to a Shoulder Balance (Fig. 7–12). The shoulder balance is started from the "L" lever by raising the hips backward, increasing the pike, and bending the arms so that the shoulders are just above the front edge of the rings. The head must be back at this time and throughout the whole movement (1). In this routine, to make the remainder of the press easier, the legs are bent (2) and gradually uncurled to a slight arch (3). The shoulders are lowered

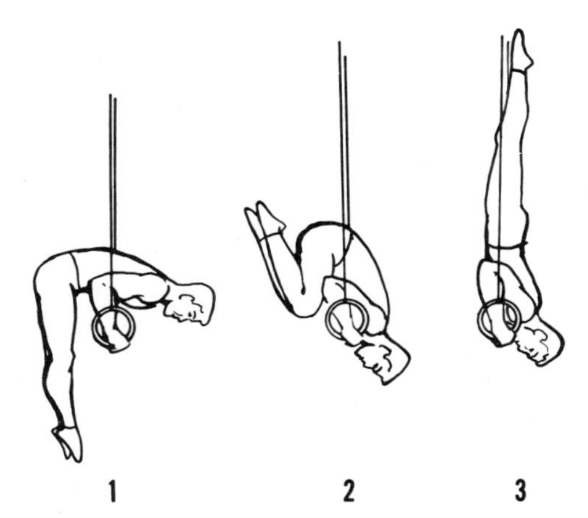

Fig. 7–12. Press to a Shoulder Balance.

to a position slightly above and in front of the hands. The balance is HELD for at least three seconds.

TEACHING TECHNIQUES. The shoulder balance is learned on low rings. As the legs are straightened above the head, they are straddled and hooked around the ropes. Refer to the second photo on page 268. The arms can also be rested against the straps during the first part of the press for extra stability. The rings should not be kept stationary but be moved as needed. The elbows turn out and the rings are moved toward the head to correct an overbalance. The elbows turn in and the rings are moved away from the head to correct an underbalance.

SPOTTING. A spotter can assist in getting the buttocks up to the proper position by lifting under the hips. As the legs are uncurled, he helps maintain the balance with one hand on the abdomen and one on the back.

4. Lower from a Shoulder Stand to an Inverted Hang (Fig. 7–13). From the shoulder stand the hands are pushed out to the side a short distance. The shoulders are then lowered between the rings (1). The pull of gravity is resisted with the arm flexor muscles to keep the movement slow and under control. The stunt ends in a straight body inverted hang (2).

TEACHING TECHNIQUES. The first few times that this stunt is tried the legs may be spread and actually wrapped around the ropes. The legs can control both the speed of the movement and the balance in this way. After confidence is gained, the feet are just rested on the inside of the ropes. This does not control the

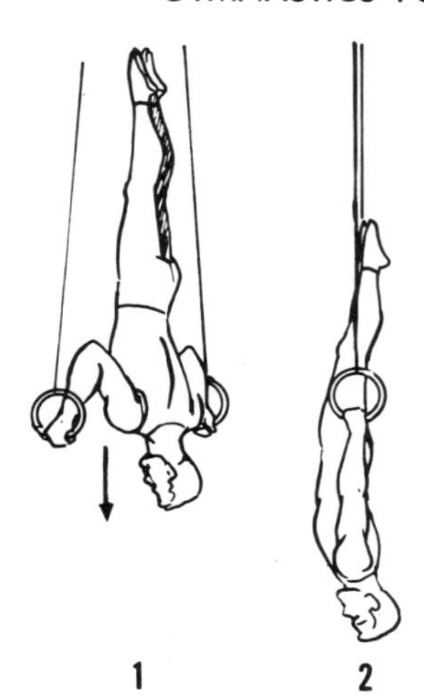

Fig. 7–13. Lower from a Shoulder Stand to an Inverted Hang.

speed of descent very much but it can help maintain the balance.

SPOTTING. A spotter stands on each side and supports weight under the shoulder just in case the performer loses control. The first time that the stunt is tried with the legs free of the ropes the spotters should be especially alert.

5. Dislocate (Fig. 7–14). This is probably the most common ring stunt at all levels of competition. From the straight body inverted hang the legs are piked rather rapidly to a bent body inverted hang (1). They drop to a rather tight pike and then rebound out of it. This compression and rebound facilitates the start of the dislocate. The body extends rapidly to an arch position about 45° above the horizontal. This extension will raise the shoulders somewhat between the rings. At the same time the head is lifted backward and the arms are thrust straight out to the side as wide as possible with the palms outward. As the arms are pushed sideways they should also press downward on the rings. This will also help raise the shoulders between the rings (2). In this position the shoulders rotate, or dislocate as it is called, and then the rings are smoothly pushed forward in front of the face (3) for the downswing to a hang (4).

TEACHING TECHNIQUES. A good exercise that prepares the shoulders for a dislocate is to hold a towel above the head with a hand on each end and then with the towel stretched and the arms straight lower it down behind the head to the buttocks. The towel is then raised in the same way and the movement repeated over and over.

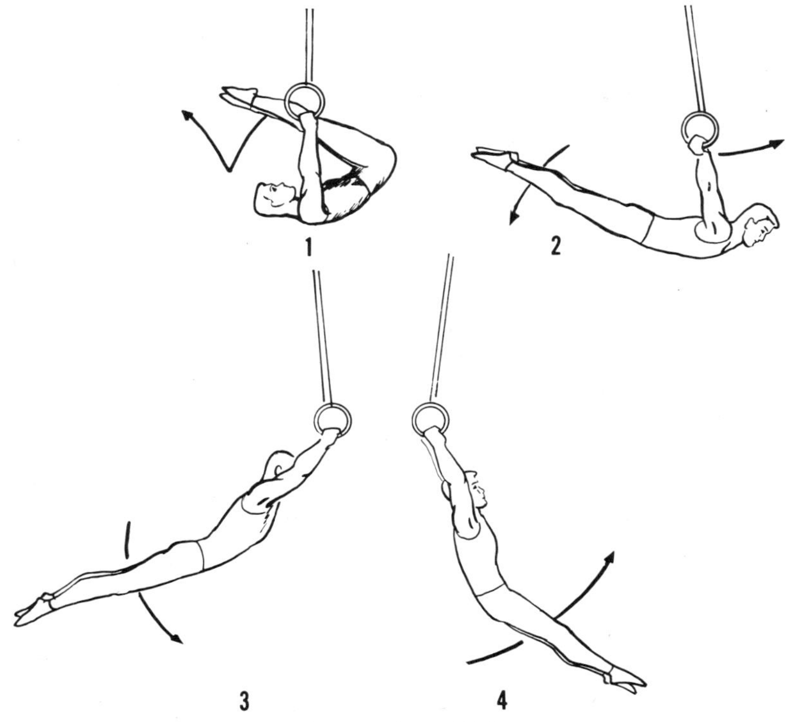

Fig. 7–14. Dislocate.

A lead-up is to do a skin-the-cat on low rings until the feet are on the floor and then practice the arm motion of the dislocate. The next step is to shoot backward from a bent inverted hang on low rings to a stand and at the same time practice the arm motion. The rings can gradually be raised until almost the whole stunt is completed before the feet contact the mat. Another technique is to practice the dislocate on high rings but to release the rings and drop to the mat before the hands have to bear any appreciable amount of weight. These suggestions are all very worthwhile but they are not a complete substitute for careful spotting. Spotting is a vital part of the teaching method for the dislocate as well as being a safety precaution.

Points to emphasize for the dislocate are:

1. Keep the arms straight throughout. Bending the arms is a bad habit that is difficult to correct later. Even though it does prevent a jerk as the dislocate is completed it should not be encouraged.
2. The higher the shoulders can be raised between the rings the easier the dislocate will be. The shoulder lift is brought about partially

by the backward and upward motion of the legs. (The movement of the part, the legs, is transferred to the whole, the body.) A press downward with the arms as they are pushed sideways also raises the shoulders.

3. The rings should be moved rapidly but smoothly forward after the shoulder rotation has occurred.
4. Do not stress the turning of the rings. They will turn 360° during the dislocate, but this occurs naturally if the stunt is executed as described.

SPOTTING. The spotters (two) do most of their work during the learning process with the rings about head height. One hand is placed under the shoulder, the other on the leg at about the knee. The hand under the shoulder lifts during the body extension to help raise the shoulders between the rings and to support weight as the shoulders are rotated. This hand might have to shift quickly to the chest during the shoulder rotation. The other hand directs the extension of the legs and then delays their downswing until the shoulders have been rotated and the rings pushed forward in front of the face. Refer to the fourth photo on page 268. Students must spot conscientiously as shoulders may be injured while learning the dislocate. When the student first attempts the dislocate on his own, the spotter must stand really close and reach in with one arm behind the performer's back to catch him if his grip is pulled loose.

6. Kip (Fig. 7–15). As the legs swing upward from the hanging position to the bent inverted hang, the feet should be raised somewhat between the ropes, that is, in an open pike position. From this open pike the legs are dropped to a closed, or tight pike, in the bent inverted hang (1). This movement facilitates the one to follow, which is a forceful and explosive extension of the body in a

Fig. 7–15. Kip.

direction 45° above horizontal or higher. The extension is not quite completed but stops a little short of a straight body position (2). This extension (plus the arm pull) should elevate the hips to a position almost between the rings. The arms bend and pull the head and shoulders upward and then forward over the rings (3). As the position changes from a hang to a support the rings have to be turned 180°. This comes naturally for most students but some have to be instructed to turn them. When the kip is being practiced as an individual stunt, the arms should press quickly from the bent arm support to a straight arm position as the legs swing downward (4a). In this routine, before the kip is completely finished, the head and shoulders are leaned well forward over the rings and the hips are raised backward to start the next stunt, which is a slow forward roll (4b). Because of this, the kip is not so difficult a stunt in this exercise as it would be in most routines that require it to be finished in a straight arm support.

TEACHING TECHNIQUES. The kip on the rings is more difficult than on any other piece of equipment because it must be done from a position with the center of gravity stationary and directly below the point of support. In most kips on other equipment the center of gravity swings under the point of support and is much higher at the time of the kipping action. This means that the kip should be presented first on some other piece of equipment. As a false grip makes the kip much easier for most students, it is usually taught in this way on the rings, even though it must be done with a regular grip in most routines. Younger students who lack strength might find a false grip kip harder. Since there will undoubtedly be many unsuccessful attempts before the kip is learned, it should be practiced on three-quarter height rings where the feet can drop to the mat after each attempt.

SPOTTING. The kip is not a dangerous stunt but a spotter is usually used to aid in the learning process to lift under the back with one hand and the buttocks with the other.

7. Forward Roll (Fig. 7–16). The forward roll usually starts from a straight arm support, but in this routine it starts from a bent arm position by lowering the head and shoulders forward and raising the hips before the preceding kip is completed. See (4b) in Fig. 7–15. This slow forward rotation continues and the head and shoulders are lowered below the rings (1). The pull of gravity is resisted by the arm flexor muscles so that it is a smooth movement from the support to the hang rather than a fast drop. As the change

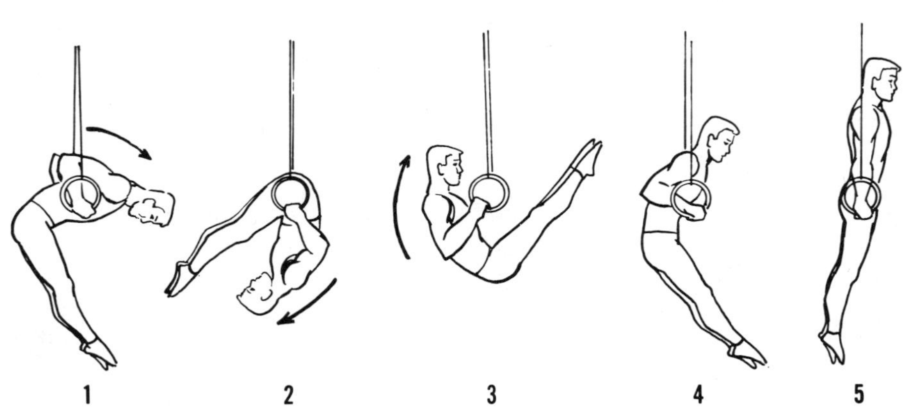

Fig. 7–16. Forward Roll.

in position is made, the rings turn 180° and the hands shift into a false grip. The arms never completely straighten in the hanging position (2). The last part of the slow forward roll is much the same as a muscle-up. As the rotation continues, the arms increase the amount of bend and pull the head and shoulders up and above the rings (3). The rings are kept close together and are pulled to the chest. At this point the legs are dropped downward and backward and the head and shoulders are leaned forward over the rings. The rings turn 180° and the grip shifts up on top to the support position (4). In most routines the gymnast would press from this point to a straight arm support (5), but in this routine the performer continues into the next stunt from the bent arm position.

Teaching Techniques. There is no substitute for strength in the execution of this stunt. The practice of the stunt itself will develop strength, but other muscle-developing exercises must also be used. The roll should be learned on three-quarter height rings where the spotter can aid effectively.

Spotting. The spotter stands to the side of the rings and grasps the lower leg with one hand. He helps raise the hips upward by lifting on the leg. As the head and shoulders are tucked forward, he places the other hand on the upper back and supports weight as the body is lowered below the rings. At this time the hand on the leg delays the forward rotation of the legs. Too much forward rotation is the most common mistake in this stunt and the spotter can aid considerably in correcting it. Halfway through the roll the spotter's hands are quickly shifted so that one can lift under the back and one under the buttocks.

8. Roll Forward from a Support to a Bent Body Inverted Hang. Since this is exactly the same movement as the first half of the forward roll, it will not be explained or illustrated again. As the bent inverted hang is reached the false grip is changed to a regular one.

9. Inlocate (Fig. 7–17). From the bent inverted hang the body is extended upward and forward (1) to start a good backward swing through the hanging position. The hips lead during the downswing with the body in a slight pike (2). After passing the vertical position in a slight pike, the legs are pumped vigorously backward so that the heels lead with the body in an arch. The arms press downward hard and are pushed to the side with the palms outward. They must stay perfectly straight. The heel lift plus the downward press of the arms raises the shoulders a little between the rings (3). The hips are then raised quickly and the head and upper body tucked under so that the eyes can look at the feet (4). The palms of the hands turn inward at this time and the rings complete a 360° turn as the inlocate is finished in a bent body inverted hang (5).

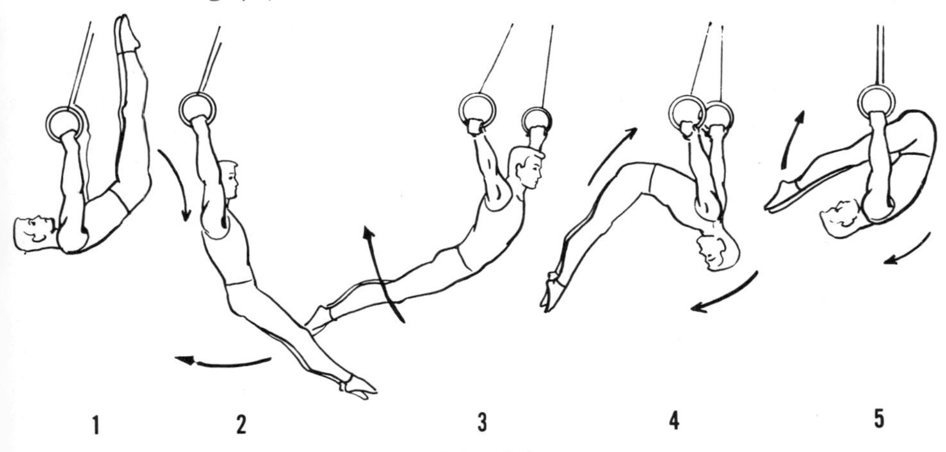

Fig. 7–17. Inlocate.

Teaching Techniques. Use the same shoulder flexibility exercise with a towel explained for the dislocate. Other shoulder-stretching exercises should also be done. The arm movement and the head and shoulder tuck can be practiced on low rings with the feet on the ground bearing all of the weight. A progression from this is to raise the rings to about face height and practice the arm, head, and shoulder movements by jumping off the mat and circling to the bent body inverted hang. A good method of teaching the inlocate is from a pendulum swing. On each backward swing the arms press downward a little harder and the heels are lifted a little higher until the performer can "feel" the point where the hips should be raised and the head and shoulders tucked under. Spotting is a vital part of the teaching techniques for the inlocate.

SPOTTING. Two spotters stand, one on each side of the rings, and lift upward with one hand under the performer's hips and one under his knees. Weight should be supported under the hip even after the inlocate has been completed as often there is a sudden jerk as the performer drops into the inverted hang position. Spotting should be done very conscientiously as shoulders can be injured while learning the inlocate. Refer to the third photo on page 268.

10. Straddle Cut-Off Forward (Fig. 7–18). This dismount starts from the bent body inverted hang, or actually a little before the bent inverted hang is reached, as the inlocate is completed. The forward rotation continues from this position and should be as fast as possible. The legs straddle and rotate forward until they hit the arms (1), which bend and pull the upper body up toward the rings. The head, shoulders, and chest are whipped forward just as the legs hit the arms. The rings are released at this time with the body in a tight straddle-pike position and the head forward between the legs (2). This compressed pike should be maintained until enough forward rotation has occurred to permit the performer to open up to land on his feet (3) (4). It is very difficult to keep the legs straight on this stunt but an effort should be made to do so.

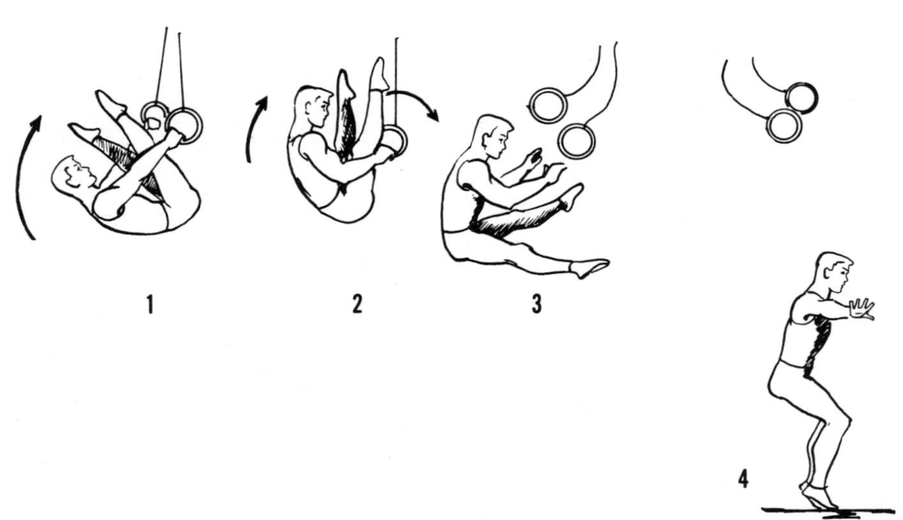

Fig. 7–18. Straddle Cut-Off Forward.

TEACHING TECHNIQUES. The single leg cut and catch in Routine I is a lead-up. Single leg cuts, with both legs, may also be practiced as a dismount before the straddle cut-off is attempted. The straddle dismount is first tried from a rocking motion back and forth in the bent inverted hang. The forward end of this rocking motion ends in the position illustrated by (2) in Fig. 7–18. The legs may be bent during the learning process. This permits the learner to rock farther forward before the rings are released. One of the most common faults is to open out of the straddle-pike too soon. This point should be stressed.

SPOTTING. Spotting is easier if the forward cut-off is learned on rings at three-quarter height. The spotter stands behind and slightly to one side. One hand is placed on the neck to give a forward push, if needed, as the rings are released; the other is placed on the front of the upper arm to prevent a possible overspin. Remember that a spotter should assist only as much as needed. Spotting for this stunt is very simple but also very important as the dismount is somewhat dangerous. Refer to the photo on page 299.

III. INTERMEDIATE ROUTINE

1. Front Uprise (Fig. 7–19). This routine also starts with a pendulum swing, which was described in Routine I, pages 261–62. One swing should be enough prior to the front uprise. As the body swings forward beyond the vertical hang, the legs pump vigorously

Fig. 7–19. Front Uprise.

forward and upward into a slight pike (1). At the same time the arms press downward on the rings. As the height of the swing is reached (2), the hips are thrust upward between the rings so that momentarily the body is almost straight (3). The arms then quickly pull the rings backward under the shoulders and the head and trunk are leaned forward (4). The rings are turned 180° during the last fast piking movement and the hands change from a hanging to a supporting grip. To finish most front uprises there should be a quick press to a straight arm support (5), but in this routine the performer does not straighten the arms. Instead he proceeds immediately into the next stunt from the bent arm position.

TEACHING TECHNIQUES. It helps some students to think of this stunt as a fast muscle-up from a swing. The timing can be learned by swinging back and forth in the pendulum swing to practice the leg movement and arm pull on the front end of the swing.

SPOTTING. A spotter stands on the side and assists by pushing forward and upward on the buttocks.

2. Roll Forward from a Support to a Bent Body Inverted Hang. This movement is the first half of a forward roll, which was described in Routine II, pages 275–76.

3. Inlocate. Refer to Routine II, pages 277–78.

4. Kip. Refer to Routine II, pages 274–75. In this intermediate exercise the students should attempt to keep their arms straighter than illustrated in the second routine. As the kip is completed the arms should be pressed out quickly to a straight arm support. It will depend on how well the kip is executed whether the arms will actually reach a straight position in this routine. If the kip is not well executed, the cast backward to hang, which follows, will have to be started from a bent arm support.

5. Cast Backward from a Support to a Hang (Fig. 7–20). The legs will swing backward in the support position following the kip (1). As they reach the end of the back swing, the arms are bent and the body is extended backward into an arch (2). The rings are pushed obliquely forward (3) and the arms straightened so that the change from the support to the hang is done smoothly without a jerk. The arms should be completely straightened while the feet are still quite high so that a good forward swing will result (4). This stunt may be done with straight arms after it has been thoroughly learned with them bent.

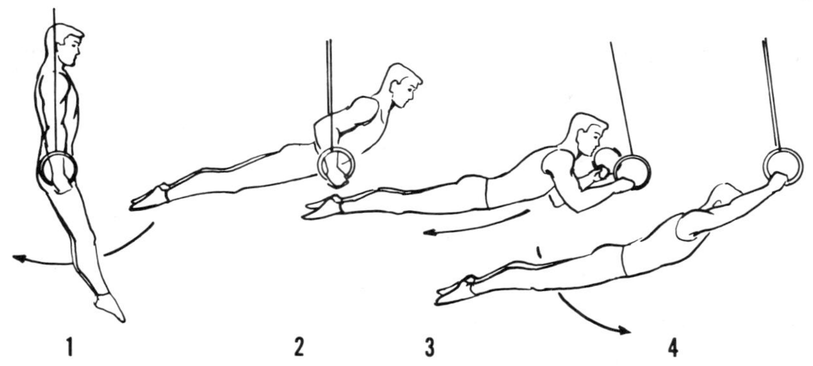

Fig. 7–20. Cast Backward from a Support to a Hang.

TEACHING TECHNIQUES. This stunt should be tried first on rings of three-quarter height so that the feet will contact the mat before there is any possibility of the hands being pulled loose from the rings. When it is first attempted on rings of regulation height it may start from a support in which the arms are fully bent.

SPOTTING. The spotter stands beside the rings and places one hand on the thighs as the body is extended backward and the other hand on the abdomen. Both hands support weight as the arms are pushed forward and during the downward swing.

6. Back Kip (Fig. 7–21). As the legs swing forward past the vertical hang, they are pumped upward vigorously into a pike. The arms bend and start to pull the hips up toward the rings (1). As the feet swing up between the ropes, the body pikes a little more and the arms pull the rings to a position just in front of the hips (2).

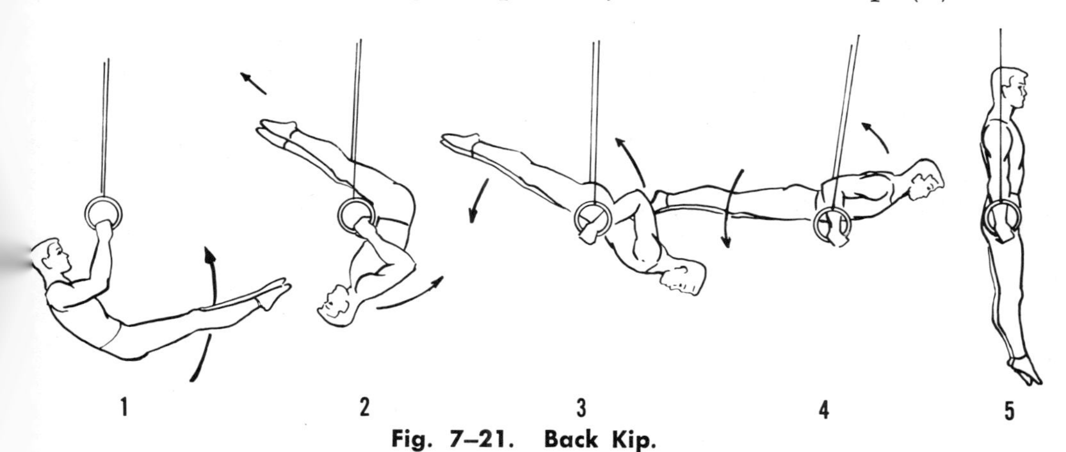

Fig. 7–21. Back Kip.

The rings are held in this position with muscle power as the body is quickly extended with the legs shooting about 30° above horizontal (3). The extension is completed all the way to an arch with the head back (4). The legs swing downward and the head upward, as the rotation continues, to finish in a straight arm support (5).

TEACHING TECHNIQUES. A prerequisite is a pull-over on the horizontal bar. A pull-over should also be practiced on low rings. If the rings are placed in front of the hips after the jump off the floor, the stunt is almost the same. The next step is to try the back kip on low rings from a bent body inverted hang with a false grip. This enables the learner to concentrate on getting the rings in the correct position in front of the hips and on the body extension. It would be very difficult to perform a back kip without a swing if a false grip were not used. The final lead-up is to learn the stunt from a pendulum swing.

SPOTTING. This is a difficult stunt to spot when it is done from a swing. A spotter can try to assist by lifting under the shoulder or chest, but the performer is too high above the spotter's head for him to be of much assistance. He should be alert to aid if the stunt is missed. During the learning process on low rings the spotter can be of great assistance. One arm reaches between the performer's arm and head so that the hand can be placed on the abdomen. During the backward rotation this hand will be directly under the center of gravity and can be used to lift the performer upward between the rings.

7. Backward Roll (Fig. 7–22). The backward roll starts from a support position by raising the legs forward and allowing the upper body to lean backward (1). As the backward rotation continues the arms are bent, the upper body is lowered below the rings, and the legs are raised upward between the ropes. The hands change into a high grip as the position changes from a support to a hang (2). The pull of gravity is resisted by the arm flexor muscles so that the rotation is slow and even rather than a fast drop below the rings. The arms are never completely straightened in the hanging position. From this point the stunt becomes a slow back kip with a high grip. The pike is increased and the arms pull the hips up to the rings (3). The rings are kept in front of the hips and the body is extended (4). As the body is arched with the head back (5), the rotation continues to the support position (6).

TEACHING TECHNIQUES. The stunt should be learned on low rings so that spotting can be more effective. The pull-over on the

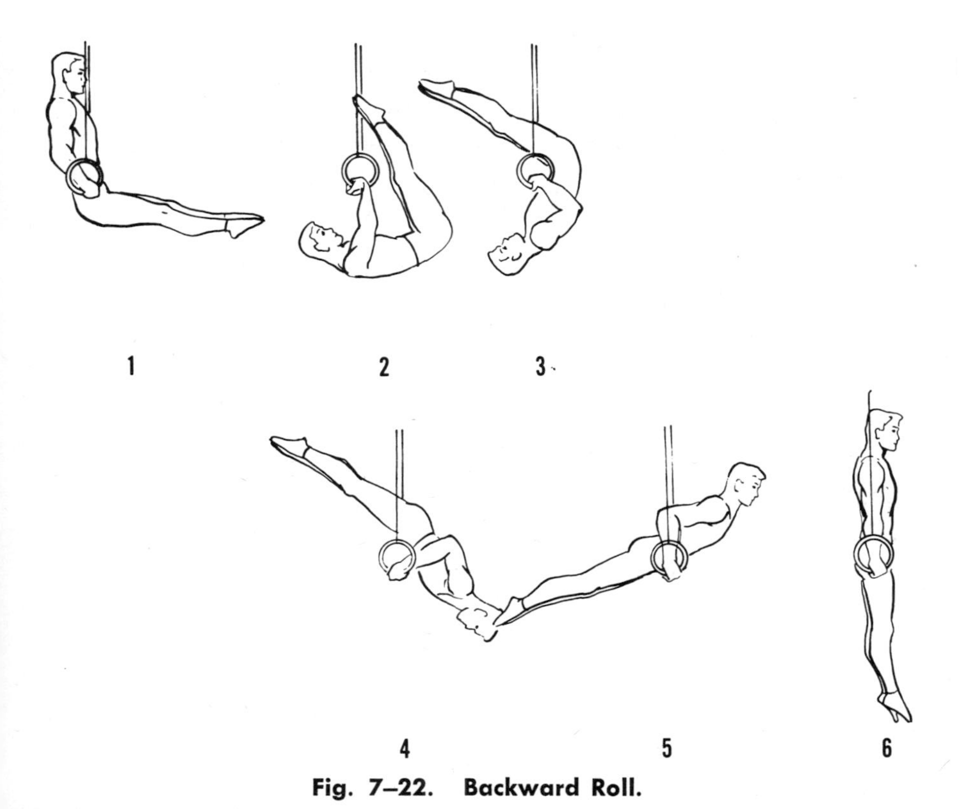

Fig. 7–22. Backward Roll.

horizontal bar and jumping into the second part of the roll on low rings are the two lead-ups.

SPOTTING. The first part of the roll is spotted by supporting weight with one hand under the back of the thigh and one hand under the back. The second part is spotted as described for the stationary back kip on the low rings (a teaching technique for the back kip).

8. Support Half-Lever. As the backward roll is finished, the legs are raised forward to a half-lever or "L" support. This position was included in Routine II, Fig. 7–11. It should be HELD for at least three seconds.

9. Press to a Shoulder Balance. The press to shoulder stand was described in Routine II, pages 270–71. In this exercise the legs should remain straight during the entire press. In the previous routine the legs were permitted to bend to make the stunt easier. The balance should be HELD for at least three seconds. Teaching techniques and spotting methods are the same as previously given.

10. Fall Forward from a Shoulder Balance to a Back Uprise (Fig. 7–23). From the shoulder balance (1) the fall is started by tucking the head on the chest and piking slightly. The shoulders are dropped below the rings and as the hands change from a supporting

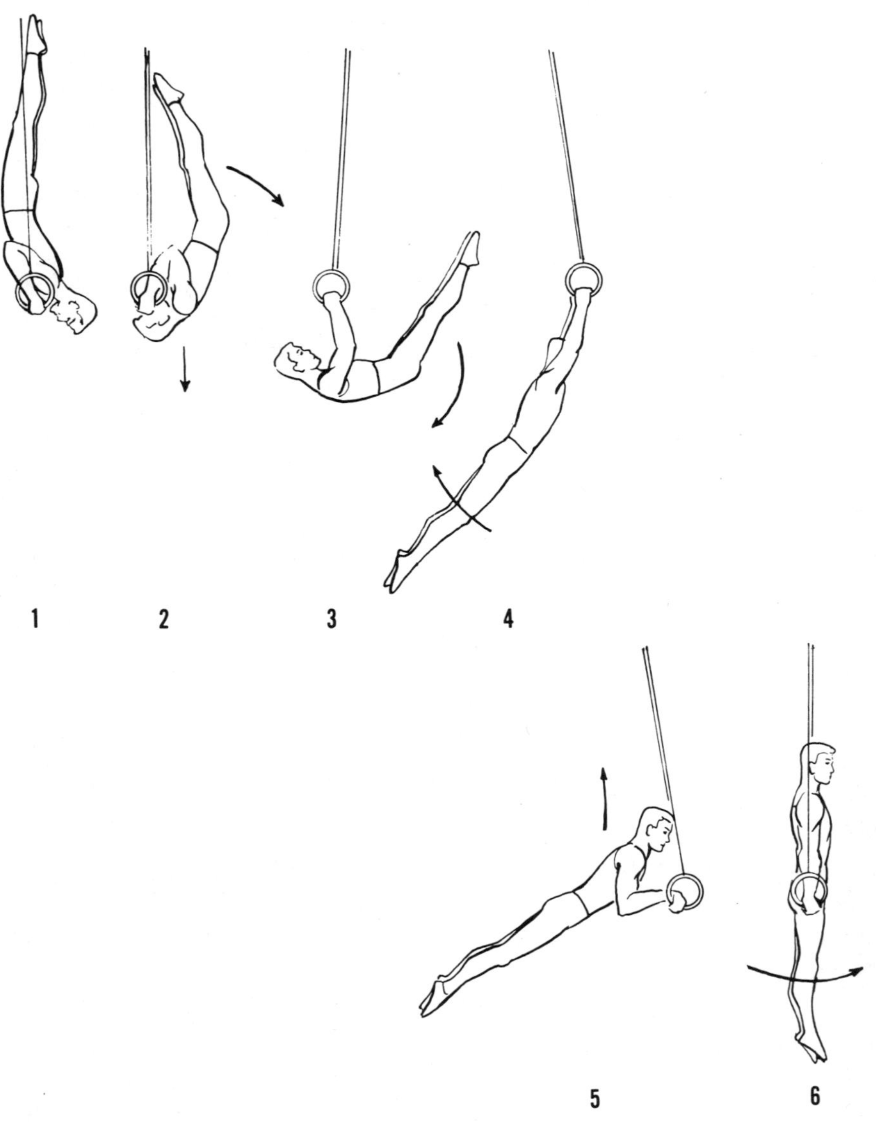

Fig. 7–23. Fall Forward from a Shoulder Balance to a Back Uprise.

to a hanging grip the rings are turned 180° (2). The shoulders lead the fall with the hips and feet trailing behind. When the arms are almost straightened the shoulders come to a stop. This increases the speed of the hips on the downswing (3). As they reach the vertical position the legs are pumped backward in an arch and the arms and shoulders are rapidly, and fully, extended (4). This brings about a rebound that aids in converting the backward swing to vertical movement. As the feet raise backward the rings are pulled down past the shoulders (5) in one fast continuous movement to the hips. The rings must be turned 180° and the hands changed from a hanging to a supporting grip during the uprise. The back uprise finishes in a straight arm support position (6).

TEACHING TECHNIQUES. As a student learns the shoulder balance he probably falls forward out of it many times; thus this movement is not a new one. It is difficult, however, to time the back uprise from the fall. The fall and the back uprise should be practiced separately. The fall is practiced at first on three-quarter height rings so that the feet will contact the ground. The back uprise is practiced from either a pendulum swing or a cast from a bent body inverted hang. The timing can be practiced by swinging back and forth in the pendulum swing without making any attempt to complete the uprise. The following factors contribute to the back uprise:

1. A good downswing.
2. A sudden straightening of the arms from a slightly bent to a fully extended position directly below the rings. This gives a rebound effect.
3. A pump backward of the legs from a pike to an arch.
4. A hard pull with the arms.

The back uprise can be made a little easier by piking again as the rings are pulled toward the hips. Most beginners will not be able to pull all the way to a support with the back arched but will have to pike like this as the stunt is finished.

SPOTTING. As the fall is practiced the spotter catches some of the weight until the performer is confident that he can maintain his grip on the rings. The spotter can assist in the execution of the uprise by lifting upward on the front part of the performer's thigh as the pull with the arms starts.

11. Roll Backward from a Support to a Bent Body Inverted Hang (Fig. 7–24). As the legs swing forward in the support position upon the completion of the back uprise, they are allowed to continue upward into a pike. At the same time the trunk leans back-

Fig. 7–24. Roll Backward from a Support to a Bent Body Inverted Hang.

ward (1). As the backward rotation continues, the arms bend and the hands shift into a high grip so that the body can be lowered slowly below the rings (2). The arms are straightened as the bent inverted hang is reached and the grip returns to a normal one (3).

SPOTTING. The spotter supports weight with one hand under the buttocks and one under the upper back during the movement.

12. Dislocate. This stunt was included in Routine II, pages 272–73.

13. Flyaway Backward (Fig. 7–25). The dislocate preceding should finish with a good downward and forward swing (1). As the vertical hang is reached, the legs whip forward hard into a pike and the arms start to pull the shoulders upward (2). About horizontal, or slightly above, the hips thrust forward into an arch, the head drops backward, and the arms give a final vigorous pull and then release the rings (3). This arched position is maintained (4), if possible, until the landing (5), but usually the body will have to be piked again to bring about enough rotation.

TEACHING TECHNIQUES. The stunt may be practiced from a pendulum swing. The timing of the pull and hip lift is practiced without releasing the rings. It is possible to work into this dismount gradually from an easy turnover with the grip maintained very late.

SPOTTING. The spotter stands on the side and lifts with one hand under the back during the upswing. As the rings are released, this hand reaches under the shoulder or chest to support weight and to make sure there is sufficient rotation to land on the feet. The other hand reaches in behind the back just prior to the landing to control a possible overspin. If an overhead spotting rig is sus-

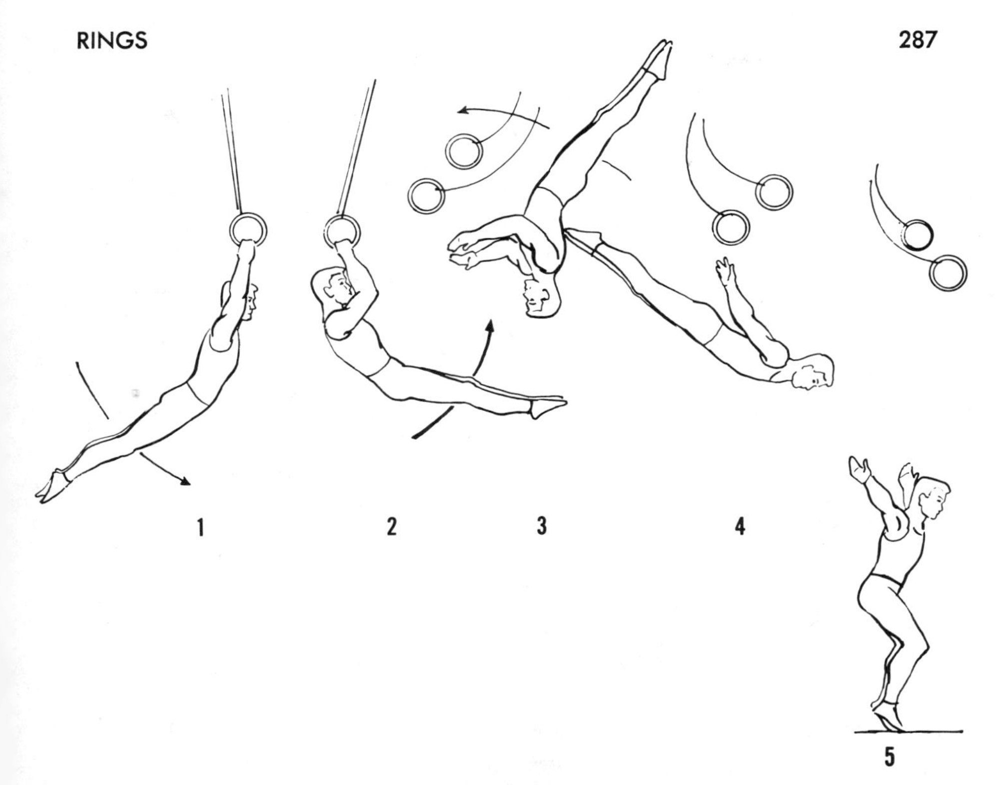

Fig. 7–25. Flyaway Backward.

pended above the rings, this may be used to spot the flyaway. A hand belt held by two spotters will serve the same purpose.

IV. LOW ADVANCED ROUTINE

1. Raise Straight Body to Inverted Hang (Fig. 7–26). This movement is used to start a great number of competitive routines. It is started just as a pendulum swing by raising the legs forward (1), then dropping them downward so that the body swings backward in an arch (2). On the forward and upward swing the arch is maintained with the head back. The arms stay straight and press downward on the rings throughout the whole upward movement (3). The hands should be kept close together so as to keep the center of gravity as close to the point of support as possible until the straight body inverted hang is reached (4).

TEACHING TECHNIQUES. Start with a fairly large pendulum swing and gradually reduce it so that the movement eventually becomes a slow raise rather than a fast swing up to the inverted hang.

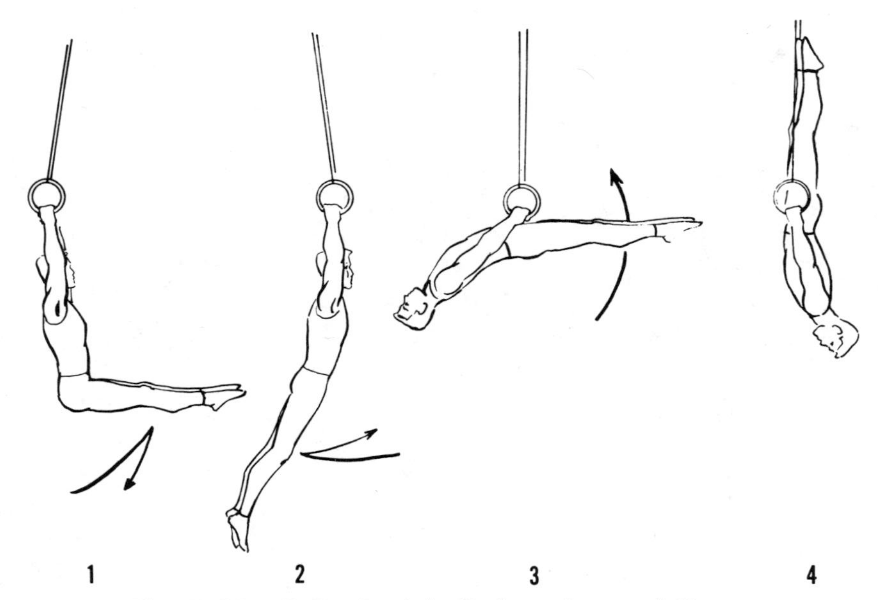

Fig. 7–26. Raise Straight Body to Inverted Hang.

2. Dislocate. Before starting the dislocate the legs are dropped from the straight body position to the bend body inverted hang with the eyes looking at the knees. The extension to start the dislocate should follow rhythmically from this movement. Refer to pages 272–73 for a complete description of the dislocate.

3. Shoot to Shoulder Stand (Fig. 7–27). This is also called a "bird-up" or a "flange." The downward and forward swing from the dislocate provides the momentum necessary for a good start (1). As the legs pass under the rings, they pump forward and upward into a pike and the arms start to bend (2). The upward motion continues in a pike until the feet are between the ropes. By this time the arms have pulled the shoulders almost up to the rings (3). The body is extended rapidly into an arch with the head back (4). The legs shoot upward almost directly between the ropes and the hands change to a supporting grip. The rings turn 180° during the change from a hang to a support. The shoulder stand is HELD for at least three seconds (5).

TEACHING TECHNIQUES. The back kip is an important lead-up. The peach basket on the parallel bars and the flange to handstand on the horizontal bar are similar movements that provide background. During the latter part of the movement the legs may be

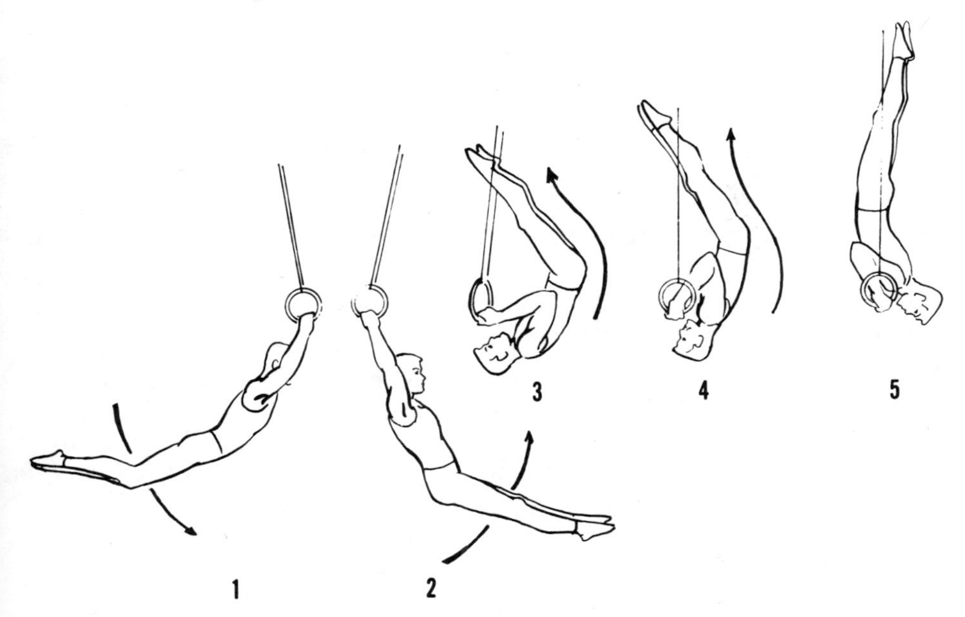

Fig. 7–27. Shoot to Shoulder Stand.

spread apart to rest against the ropes to help maintain balance. The flange can be practiced from a pendulum swing as well as a dislocate.

SPOTTING. A spotter aids in the shoot by pushing upward under the upper back as the extension is started. If a horse is placed beside the rings, the spotter can be of much more assistance from a position on top of it. He can lift the performer's legs during the extension and can also support the legs as the balance is reached.

4. Lever Between the Rings (Fig. 7–28). This is often called a French lever. The movement is started from the shoulder stand by straightening the arms gradually and pushing the head and shoulders slowly forward and slightly upward away from the rings. The body is lowered as this is done to keep the center of gravity approximately over the hands (1). As the arms straighten the rings are turned a quarter-turn outward so that the palms of the hands are forward. This position enables the muscles to work more effectively. The arch is maintained during the entire movement, which ends in a horizontal position between the rings (2). The French lever is sometimes held for the full three seconds, but in this routine

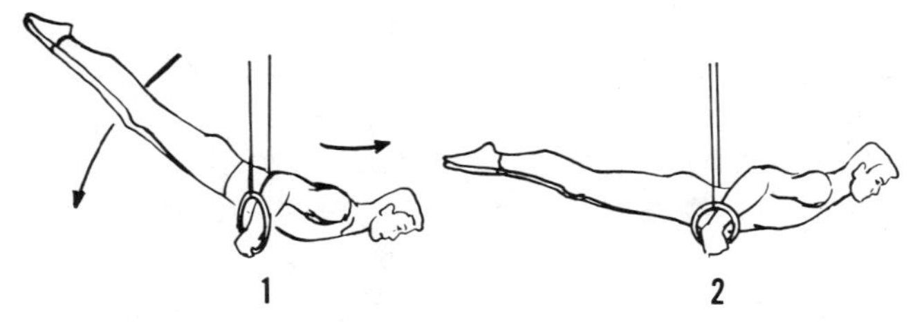

Fig. 7–28. Lever Between the Rings (French Lever).

it is used only as a momentary position because it is preceded and followed by held positions.

Teaching Techniques. The French lever can be practiced on low rings where a partner is able to support weight with one hand under the legs and one under the chest. One leg can be bent to make the lever easier as it is learned. Some students find it easier to practice this stunt from a support position rather than a balance. From the support the legs are raised backward and upward and the upper body is lowered forward and downward. Probably the easiest way of all to practice the French lever is to start from a stand on the floor between rings lowered to about hip height. The upper body is leaned forward and one leg raised backward so that the student is in a horizontal stand on one leg (scale position). From this one-leg stand the weight can be gradually transferred from the support leg to the rings.

5. Back Lever (Fig. 7–29). From the French lever the body is lowered slowly below the rings in the horizontal position. The arms are gradually straightened until they are fully extended. Some gymnasts prefer the hand position used for the French lever but

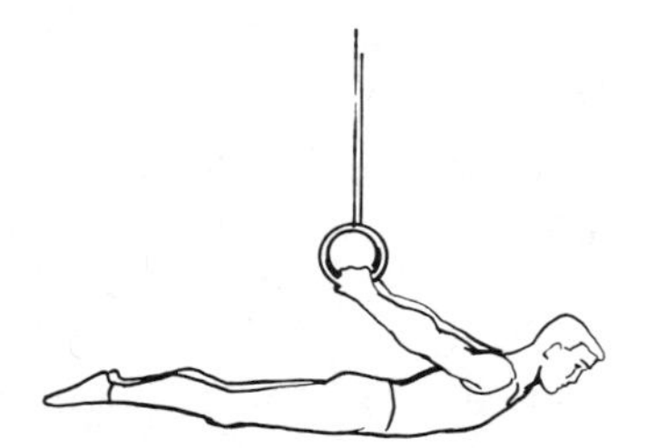

Fig. 7–29. Back Lever.

others prefer to turn the rings a quarter-turn so that the palms face inward. Hold the back lever for at least three seconds.

Teaching Techniques. The easiest way to practice the back lever is from a skin-the-cat position on low rings with the feet on the floor. The feet are raised off the floor and held in a tuck position and then slowly extended. Another method is to lower from a straight body inverted hang. If the rings are held in close together so that the upper arms press against the side of the rib cage, the back lever will be somewhat easier. As with most levers, it may also be practiced with one leg bent to make it easier. A partner can be used to support weight under the legs.

6. Dislocate from a Back Lever (Fig. 7–30). Some students who have loose and flexible shoulders can accomplish this stunt by simply relaxing in the shoulders and swinging downward to a hang. For those with tight shoulders it might be a very difficult stunt. These individuals will have to give a sudden quick and vigorous press downward on the rings to lift the weight off the shoulders momentarily. At this instant the shoulders are rotated (1), that is,

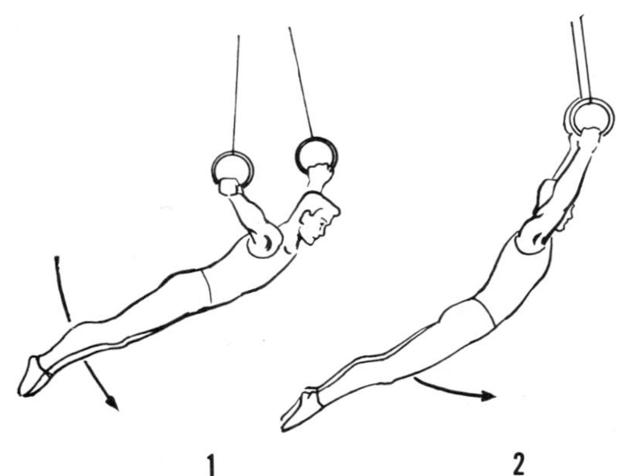

Fig. 7–30. Dislocate from a Back Lever.

the arms are pushed out to the side and then quickly forward so that the body can swing forward in a hanging position (2).

TEACHING TECHNIQUES. The disengaging, or dislocating, of the shoulders can be practiced on low rings with most of the weight supported by the feet on the mat. The next step is to try it from the lever with the assistance of a spotter who lifts under the thighs and chest as the shoulders are rotated.

7. Back Kip. Refer to Routine III, pages 281–82. Because there will be very little swing following the dislocate from a back lever the back kip will be more difficult than in the previous exercise.

8. Support Half-Lever. Refer to Routine II, page 270. This position is HELD for at least three seconds.

9. Bent Body Press to a Handstand (Fig. 7–31). From the support half-lever (1) the arms are bent to about a right angle (not any more than this) and the hips raised backward. The head tips backward and stays this way throughout the whole press. The hips are raised until they are approximately between the ropes (2). At this time the center of gravity will be over the points of support. The legs are slowly raised toward the handstand position (3) and as they approach the vertical the arms start to extend (4). The press is finished with the arms locked out and the line through the arms and trunk almost straight (5). It is considered good form in a handstand on the rings to turn the front edge of the rings slightly outward. This handstand is HELD for at least three seconds.

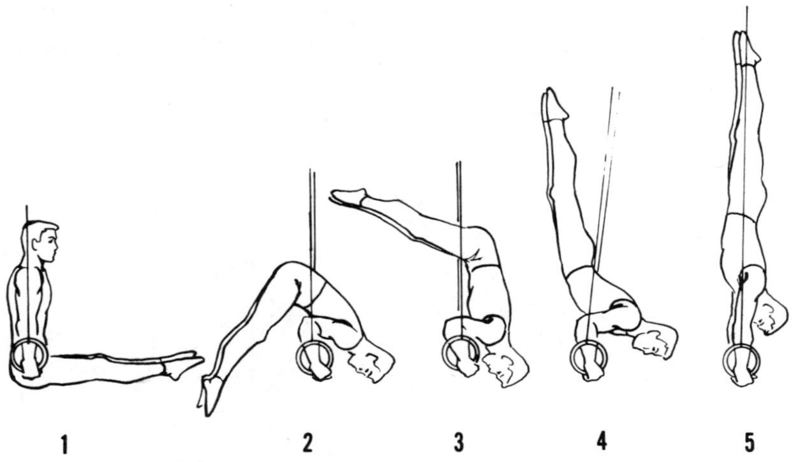

Fig. 7–31. Bent Body Press to a Handstand.

TEACHING TECHNIQUES. The handstand press is more difficult on the rings than on the floor or parallel bars. Teach it first on the floor, then the parallels, then the rings. It is usually learned on low rings where it can be started from a jump off the floor. If the balance is lost, the body is tucked somewhat and the arms bent. If on low rings the feet will contact the floor. The same technique is used for falling out of a balance on the high rings. The ropes are very important in learning the handstand. As the press is finished the legs are spread to contact the ropes. At first they are wrapped around them but later they are just rested against them. As the press is learned the legs can be tucked up tight and the forearms and upper arms can be rested against the straps. The rings are held quite close together with the forward edge turned inward during the press. When the handstand is reached, the gymnast should practice taking the arms off the straps and turning the front edge of the rings out a little while he still has his legs wrapped around the ropes. Many gymnasts never learn to move the rings to control a balance but think of them as a stationary piece of equipment. They should be moved forward to control an overbalance and backward to control an underbalance.

SPOTTING. There is not much a spotter can do to assist for this stunt and, if the proper progression has been followed, it is not dangerous for the gymnast to try it on his own.

10. Lower from a Handstand to a Support (Fig. 7–32). Gravity will take care of this movement. The job of the gymnast is to make it look good by keeping the back arched and lowering slowly. The head and shoulders are shifted forward from the handstand as the body starts downward (1). As the horizontal position is approached, the shoulders will be well forward of the hands and the body will pass through a planche position (2). Most gymnasts turn the front edge of the rings out at this time so that the palms face forward but before reaching the support position they must be turned back again (3).

Fig. 7–32. Lower from a Handstand to a Support.

TEACHING TECHNIQUES. This movement can be practiced at the same time as the handstand on the low rings. At first it is done with a bent body or with one leg bent in the same manner as a lever is practiced.

11. Roll Backward from a Support to a Bent Inverted Hang. This movement continues rhythmically from the previous stunt without a pause in the support position. Refer to Routine III, pages 285–86, for a description and illustration.

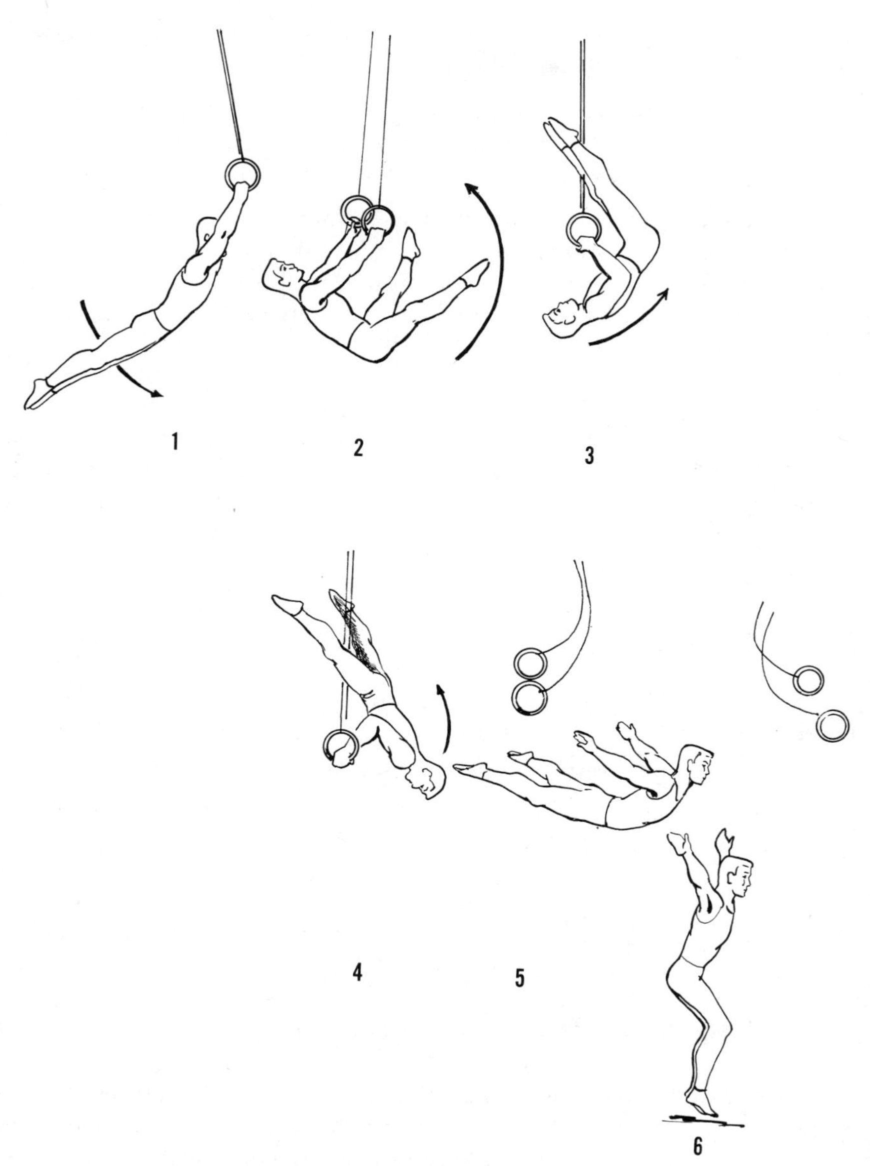

Fig. 7–33. High Straddle Cut-Off Backward.

12. Dislocate. Refer to Routine II, pages 272–74.

13. High Straddle Cut-Off Backward (Fig. 7–33). The straddle cut-off backward was used also as the dismount in Routine I. In the previous routine it was done as an elementary stunt below the rings. As done in this routine, above the rings, the high straddle cut-off backward is considered an advanced skill. The dislocate should be done quite high so that a good downswing results (1). On the upward swing the legs pump forward into a straddle pike (2) and as they continue upward the arms bend and pull the shoulders toward the rings (3). As the legs approach the ropes, the body extends rapidly, the head whips backward, the arms give a final vigorous pull, and then the rings are released (4). If everything to this point has been executed properly, the body should be in an arch above the rings. If considerable backward rotation has been obtained, the arch can be held almost to the landing (5) but sometimes the body will have to be piked again in order to get the feet down to the floor (6).

TEACHING TECHNIQUES. It helps some students to think of this as a straddle leg shoot to shoulder stand with a release of the rings. Most gymnasts are too anxious to get the feet around to the mat and because of this do not ride the swing high enough. Almost the entire movement can be practiced without a release of the rings. In this learning technique the performer ends in a position similar to the one in (4) with the legs resting on the straps. He then drops back down to a hang.

SPOTTING. The spotter stands beside the rings, in readiness, and reaches in quickly to catch the chest with one hand if the dismount is underturned or to catch the back with the other hand if it is overturned.

V. ADVANCED ROUTINE

1. Straight Body Raise to an Inverted Hang (Fig. 7–34). The straight body raise to an inverted hang is easier if done with a high grip and if started in an arched position (1). From the hang the arms are bent slightly as the legs start upward (2). The body is raised in an arch, with the head back, by pressing down on the rings very hard. After the horizontal position the arms are straightened (3). The grip is changed to a regular grip as the inverted hang is reached (4). This position is not held but there is a momentary pause.

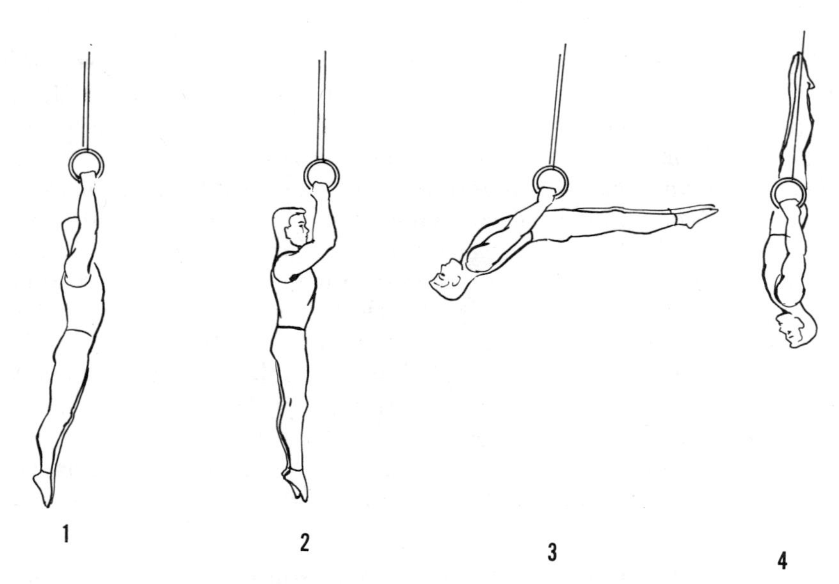

Fig. 7–34. Straight Body Raise to an Inverted Hang.

TEACHING TECHNIQUES. A very slight pendulum swing can be used to get the movement started and also one leg can be bent to make it easier.

2. Dislocate. From the straight body inverted hang the legs are dropped rather quickly to the bent inverted hang. They rebound upward out of this position and immediately extend backward for the dislocate. Refer to Routine II, pages 272–74, for a description of the dislocate.

3. Shoot to a Handstand (Fig. 7–35). This is sometimes called a flange to a handstand or a bird-up to handstand and is very similar to the shoot to shoulder stand. The dislocate should be high so that the downswing is as fast as possible (1). On the upswing the legs pump forward hard into a pike (2). As the hips swing above horizontal, the arms start to bend and pull the shoulders toward the rings (3). The hands are quickly changed from a hanging to a supporting grip and before the upward momentum stops they start to press to the handstand. The feet probably pass between the ropes as the change of grip occurs with the body still in a slight pike (4), but as the arms press quickly to a handstand the feet shoot straight up between the ropes (5). The handstand position with arms locked and the front edge of the rings turned out slightly should be HELD for at least three seconds (6).

Teaching Techniques. The gymnast progresses from a shoot to shoulder stand into this stunt. It may be practiced from a high pendulum swing rather than a dislocate and the legs can be used against the ropes as the shoot is completed.

Spotting. A quick hard push on the upper back just as the shoulders are pulled toward the rings will assist in the execution of this stunt.

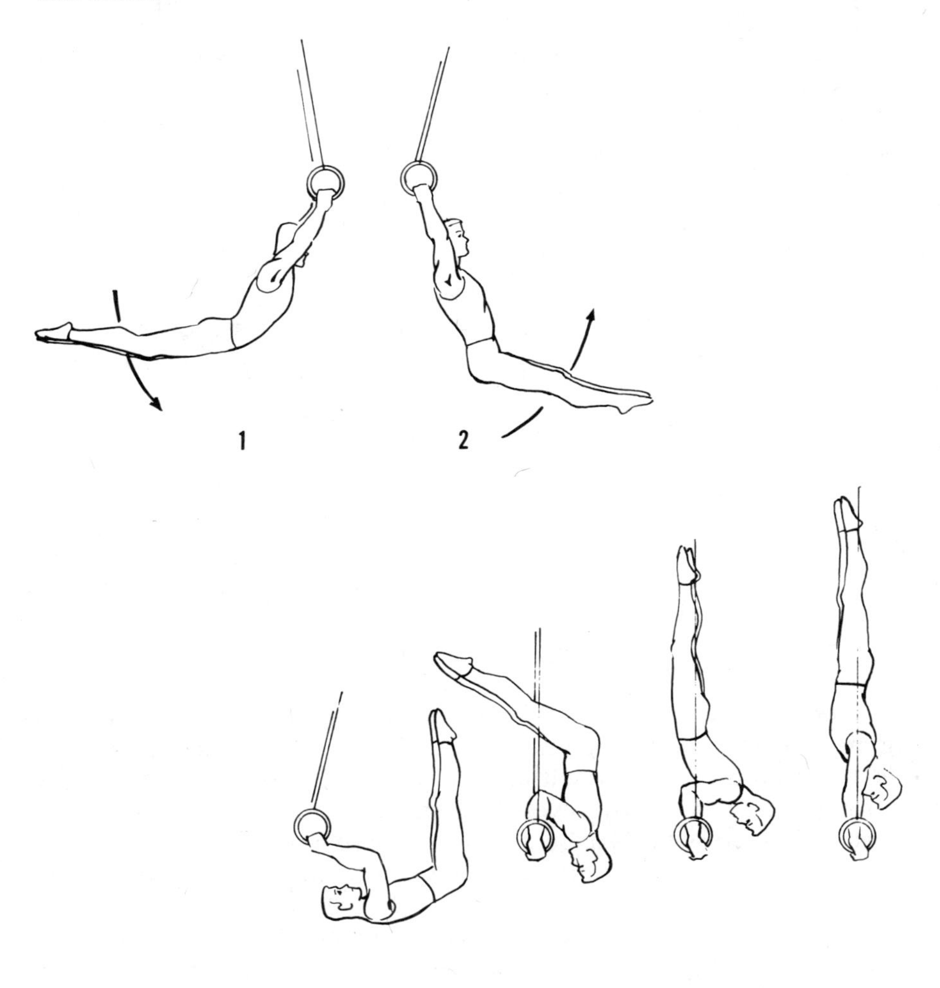

Fig. 7–35. Shoot to a Handstand.

4. Lower from a Handstand to a Support. Refer to Routine IV, page 293. This movement must be controlled even more than the similar one in the previous routine as the legs should stop in a vertical support position. In Routine IV they swung through a support position and continued forward and upward.

5. Cross (Fig. 7–36). This stunt was formerly known as the "iron cross" but in recent years the "iron" has been dropped and it is simply called the "cross." After a momentary pause in the straight arm support position with the body absolutely vertical (1), the arms are pushed slowly out to the side (2) and the shoulders lowered between the rings until the arms are horizontal (3). The cross is HELD for at least three seconds.

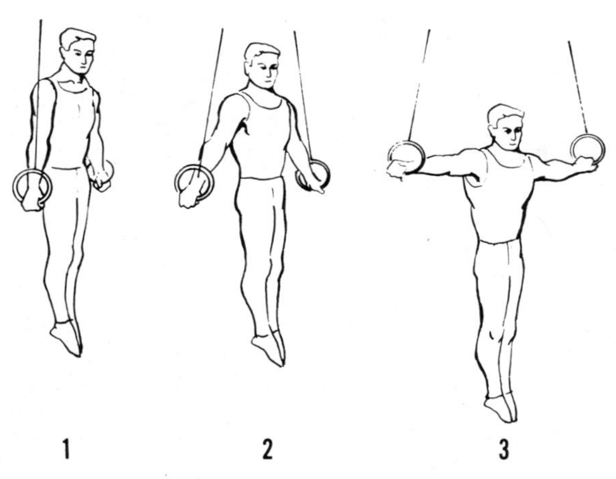

Fig. 7–36. Cross.

TEACHING TECHNIQUES. This stunt is a real challenge for most gymnasts and one that gives a great amount of satisfaction when it is accomplished. It is within the possibility of many naturally strong high school boys even though they are not advanced gymnasts. The cross takes as much mental preparation as it does physical preparation. One must possess determination and have a positive attitude.

There are several techniques used by gymnasts to make the cross easier. One might work for one individual while another will help another person. They are not considered good form but might be used until sufficient strength is developed to do the cross properly.

1. Use a false grip with the hand curled up over the top of the ring. This shortens the length of the arm.

The first photo illustrates the method of spotting for a forward straddle cut-off. The other three show three techniques used in learning the cross.

2. Turn the front edge of the ring out to the side so that the heel of the hand or even the wrist can also rest on the ring. This also tends to shorten the distance from the shoulder to the point of support.
3. Roll the shoulders forward by twisting the arm forward. This is the most approved method of making the cross easier.

Whatever techniques are used, there is no substitute for good strong arm depressor muscles.

Some of the techniques used for developing the necessary strength for the cross are as follows:

1. Put the arms through the straps and then grasp the rings. The points of support are then the forearms instead of the hands. Practice holding the cross this way or practice lowering to the cross and then pulling back to the support (second photo, page 299).
2. Use a bicycle inner tube that has been cut so that it is in one long piece. A number of old trampoline cords tied together will serve the same purpose. Place one end of the tube over each ring and grasp it and the ring at the same time. The loop of tube that hangs between the rings should be just long enough for the feet to touch when in a support position. As the shoulders are lowered between the rings for the cross, the feet stand on the inner tube and stretch it. The tube will thus support some of the body weight (third photo, page 299).
3. A spotter can reach up and grasp the feet of the gymnast while he is in the support position. He holds some of the body weight as the performer lowers to the cross (fourth photo, page 299).

6. Lower from a Cross to a Bent Inverted Hang (Fig. 7–37). From the cross the arms are pulled forward in front of the body and the legs raised forward in a pike (1). This is a difficult move especially after holding the cross for three seconds. The hands usually shift into a high grip as the rings are pushed forward so as to have

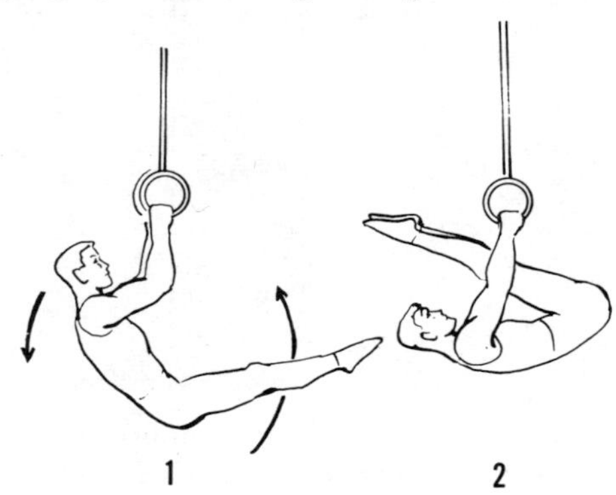

Fig. 7–37. Lower from a Cross to a Bent Inverted Hang.

more power to press down on the rings and raise the legs to the bent inverted hang (2).

TEACHING TECHNIQUES. Use a spotter to lift under the back of the thighs and the lower back as the movement is practiced.

7. Dislocate. It is difficult to do a ring routine without using a dislocate at least a couple of times. If a reference is still needed for a dislocate turn to pages 272–74 in Routine II.

8. Backward Roll Below the Rings (Fig. 7–38). This stunt moves very fast and is nothing more than a bent arm, bent body dislocate. It is very effective in a routine because of the change of pace. The

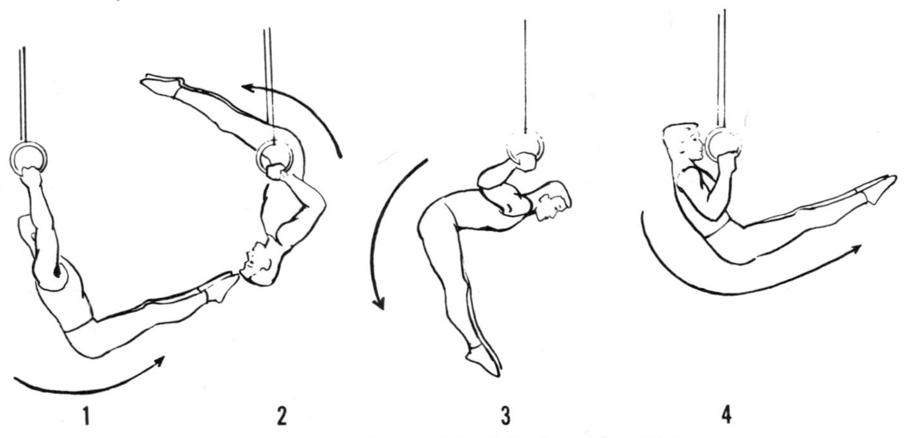

Fig. 7–38. Backward Roll Below the Rings.

Hickman roll, as it is often called, was a very common movement in the old flying ring event. As the legs swing forward beyond the vertical hang they are pumped upward, as for so many stunts, but in this case they pump into a little tighter pike (1). As they swing between the rings the pike is maintained and the arms are bent (2). About halfway through the circle the arms are pushed out to the side but are never completely straightened and the rings are turned very quickly 360° (3). The body makes a complete backward circle in a right angle pike position (4).

TEACHING TECHNIQUES. This is a very easy stunt and really needs no special teaching methods or lead-ups. The knees may be bent into a tuck throughout the role to shorten the radius of the circle and thus make it easier. Some advanced gymnasts prefer to do the stunt this way. It does not look quite as good because of the bent legs but the roll moves faster and in this respect it looks better.

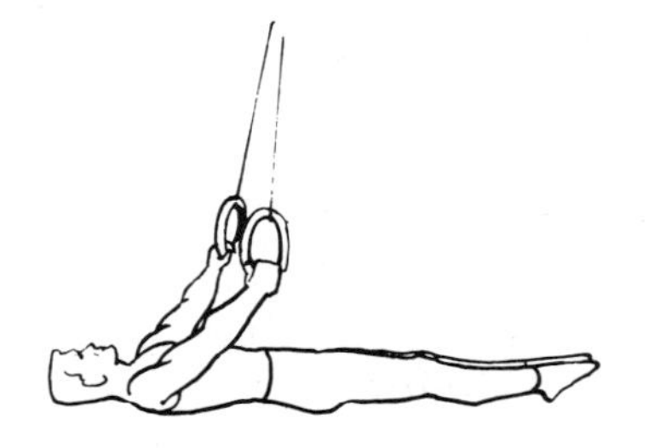

Fig. 7–39. Front Lever.

9. Front Lever (Fig. 7–39). As the backward roll is finished the hands roll up over the rings into a high grip and the body extends forward to a horizontal position. It might be difficult to get the high grip as the roll is finished because it has to be done very quickly. The front lever can be held without it but it is harder. (And also more difficult to get into the next stunt if the lever is done with a regular grip.) The beauty of this combination comes from a fast roll followed by a rapid extension forward into a motionless front lever. This position should be HELD for at least three seconds.

TEACHING TECHNIQUES. You seldom see a well-executed front lever. It is either too low, too high, or executed with the buttocks sagging in a slight pike. A good front lever should be horizontal with the body perfectly straight or in a very slight arch with the head back. If a regular grip is used, the rings should be turned so that the palms of the hand face the feet and they should be pushed toward the feet as far as possible by depressing the shoulders. The front lever is usually learned on low rings by pushing up off the floor into the horizontal position. One leg can be bent to make the lever easier. The next step is to lower down into the horizontal position from a straight body inverted hang. One leg can also be bent as this is practiced. A partner can be used to support some of the weight as the stunt is learned.

10. Front Lever to a Bent Inverted Hang (Fig. 7–40). The best way to perform this movement is to press down hard with the arms and raise the legs and then the hips (1a) to the bent inverted hang. This is very difficult to do especially in this routine in which a cross, as well as the front lever, has been held. An alternate method is to quickly flex at the waist. In this technique the legs are raised rapidly in a pike and the hips are allowed to drop somewhat below the horizontal position (1b). From this shortened body position the hips can be raised much easier to the bent body inverted hang (2).

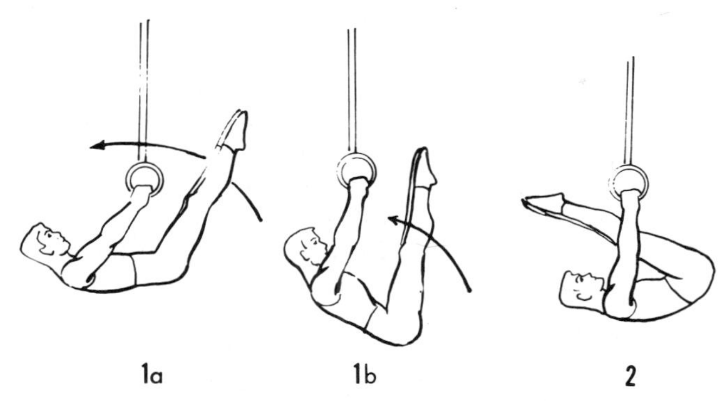

Fig. 7–40. Front Lever to a Bent Inverted Hang.

TEACHING TECHNIQUES. The legs can be drawn up into a tuck to make this movement easier for practice purposes.

11. Kip to an "L" (Fig. 7–41). This is a difficult movement with a regular grip. Fortunately, in this routinc, the gymnast will probably have a high grip. The body extension has to be almost vertical and it is not as complete as for most kips—that is, it is only a partial extension. The arms bend and pull very hard on the rings during the extension (1). It is possible to do the kip with straight arms

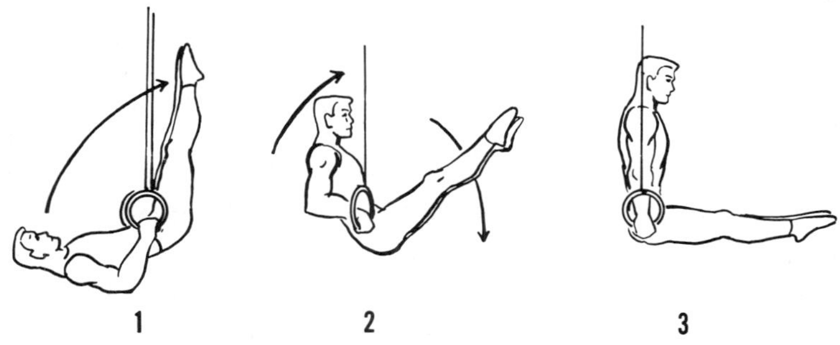

Fig. 7–41. Kip to an "L."

but it is quite difficult. The hands change from a hanging to a supporting grip and then the arms press downward (2). The legs lower to a horizontal position as the trunk rotates forward to a vertical one (3). The half-lever is HELD for at least three seconds. Refer to Routine II, page 275, for teaching techniques and spotting methods.

12. Straight Body Press to a Handstand (Fig. 7–42). The press starts by lowering the legs from the support half-lever to a vertical position. This motion continues backward and upward and the trunk is leaned forward (1). The arms should stay straight during this first part of the press; it is a common mistake to bend them too soon. During the press the legs are lifted backward in an arch by pulling with the hip extensor muscles, the arms bend, and the rings are turned so that the palms are forward (2). As the press progresses and the legs approach the ropes, the arms bend more to bring the shoulders closer to the points of support and the rings are turned back again so the palms face inward (3). The press is finished by straightening the arms to a handstand (4), which is HELD for at least three seconds.

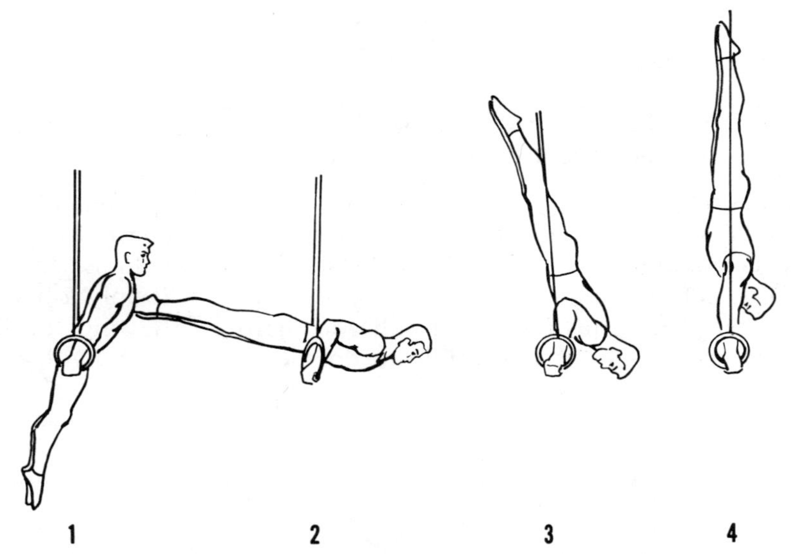

Fig. 7–42. Straight Body Press to a Handstand.

TEACHING TECHNIQUES. The straight body press to a shoulder stand is a lead-up. A slight swing in the support position can be used to get the press started and to make it easier as it is learned. There are two techniques that can be used to develop momentum for the press without actually taking a swing. One is to drop the legs quite quickly from the "L" to the straight body position. Another is to thrust the hips slightly forward in front of the hands as the legs are lowered from the "L." Using an exaggerated arch or allowing the knees to bend will shorten the body and facilitate the press.

SPOTTING. If this stunt is learned on low rings, a spotter can assist by lifting under the thigh with one hand and the shoulder with the other.

13. Lower from a Handstand to a Support. Refer to Routine IV, page 293. The motion can be much faster than in the previous routine as the body must swing forward as the support position is reached.

14. Cast Forward from a Support to a Hang (Fig. 7–43). The gymnast swings forward in a support position (1). As the feet swing to about the height of the rings (2) the hands are pushed sideward (3) and then backward (4). The shoulders drop between the rings and the body swings downward and backward in a hang (5).

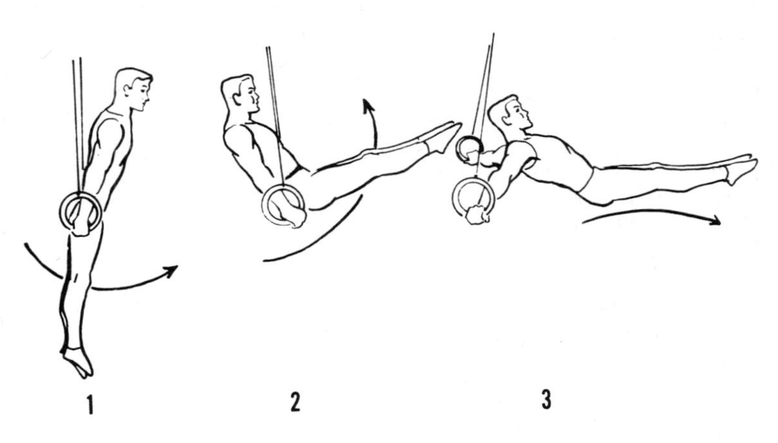

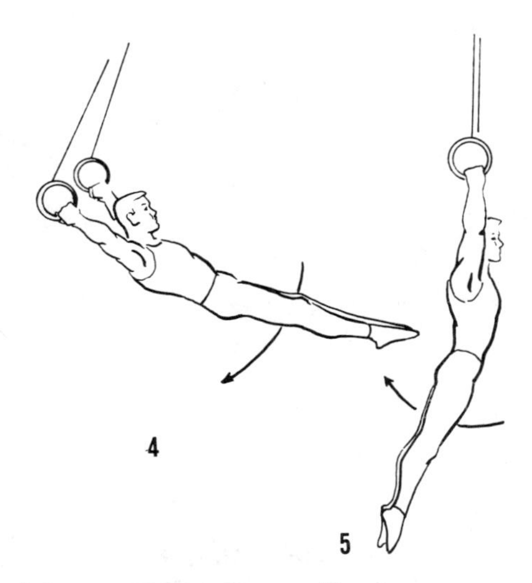

Fig. 7–43. Cast Forward from a Support to a Hang.

15. Back Uprise. Refer to Routine III, pages 284–85.

16. Straddle Cut-Off Backward from a Support (Fig. 7–44). The back uprise is finished with the arms straight in a support and with the body behind the vertical position (1). As the hips swing forward toward the rings, the hands are moved in close together and the arms bend a little so that the rings rest against the lower abdomen. The movement continues smoothly through this position. The legs straddle and swing forward and upward in a pike. At this time the upper body also leans backward (2). Backward rotation continues in a pike through the inverted position (3) and until the head and shoulders swing upward to above horizontal. The arms remain bent during the whole circle and hold the rings in close to

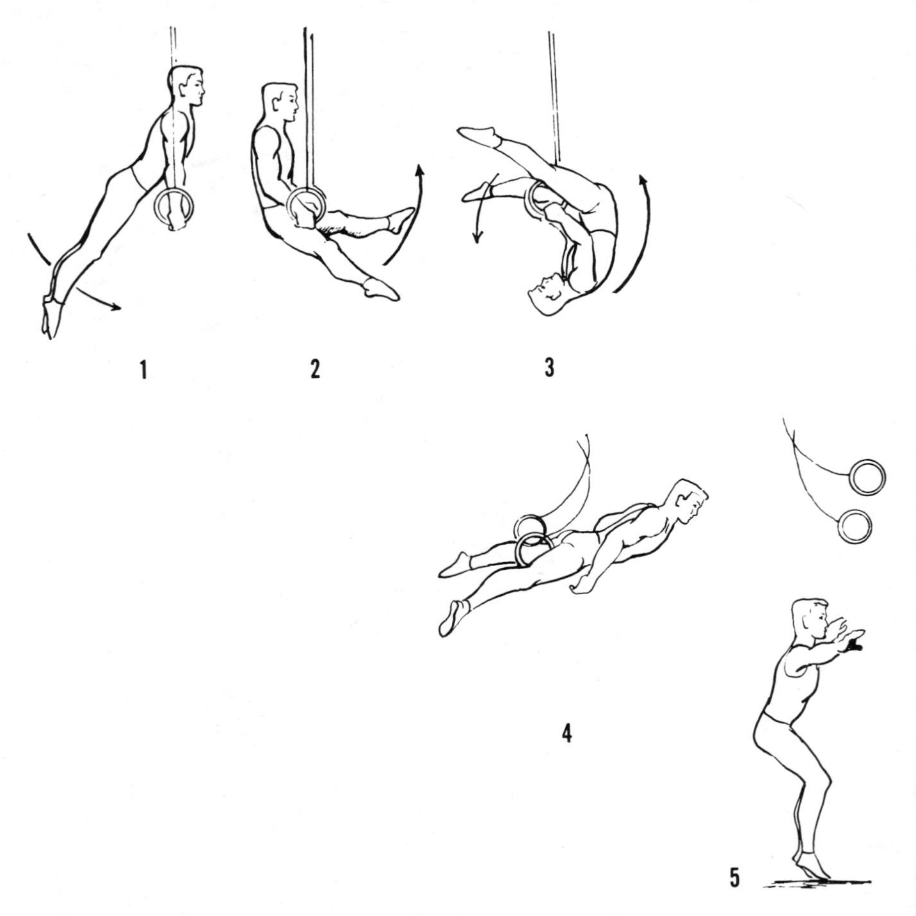

Fig. 7–44. Straddle Cut-Off Backward from a Support.

the lower abdomen or in the crotch. The body is extended rapidly into an arch and then the rings are released (4). If sufficient backward rotation has been developed, the arch can be maintained as the gymnast drops to the floor for the landing; but usually the body will have to pike to get the feet to the mat (5).

Teaching Techniques. The movement is practiced without releasing the rings.

Spotting. Spotting is very important as often, when this dismount is being learned, there is not sufficient rotation developed to circle to the feet. The gymnast might fall forward on his face if the spotter did not reach in with one arm across the chest and support the upper body long enough so that the feet can drop to the mat for the landing.

8

Parallel Bars

The parallel bars are one of several gymnastic events that were introduced into the gymnastic program early in the nineteenth century by the father of modern gymnastics, Jahn, a German. It is an especially good event for all levels of ability as there are a variety of stunts that can be learned by beginners, intermediates, and advanced performers. Probably the particular contribution or value of this event is the development of upper body strength. This statement should not be misunderstood, however, because even though an advanced routine takes considerable strength, by using skills in which the students sit on the bars and that only require a momentary support even boys who are quite weak can be taught to perform on the parallel bars.

EQUIPMENT

The parallel bars are one of the most expensive pieces of gymnastic equipment but once purchased they will last for a long while. Occasionally the wooden top rails will be broken but these can be replaced quite easily although the cost of even one rail is high. Official bars are 11½ feet long with the points of support 8½ feet apart. This means 1½ feet of bar will protrude beyond the supports. The height should be adjustable in two-inch steps from approximately 3′ 9″ up to 5′ 7″. Most bars will adjust higher than 5′ 7″ but according to the rules they do not need to go higher than this and there is no particular reason for them to go higher. For competitive purposes the bars may be adjusted from 5′ 3″ to 5′ 7″. For teaching purposes it is real essential that they go as low as 3′ 9″. The width must be adjustable from 16½″ to almost 19″ for competition. Most regulation bars will go wider than this but few will go narrower than 16½″. In this respect some bars are not entirely suit-

University of Washington News Service photo

Bob Hall Holding a One-Arm Handstand on the Parallel Bars. Bob was Athletic Association of Western Universities Conference Champion on the side horse, horizontal bar, and all-round in 1965. He placed second on the side horse and fourth in the all-round in the N.C.A.A. meet in the same year. Bob also earned a berth on the U.S. National Team that participated in Austria in the summer of 1965.

able for younger gymnasts as children often need bars closer together than this. The solution is to have another set of bars that will go narrower than 16½″ but might not meet specifications in other respects. If only one set of bars can be purchased, it would be best to get official bars for high school age and above and to be satisfied with nonregulation bars that will adjust to a narrow width for junior high school age and below.

The top rails should be "springy." There should be about 2½ inches of bend or dip in the center of the bars when a man's weight is put on them and they should spring back to a straight position when the weight is removed.

Features that should be looked for when selecting parallel bars besides those concerning specifications mentioned above are stability, movability, ease of adjustment, and weight.

1. Stability. Bars must be stable. Check to see that they do not tip easily or shake excessively when a heavy person works on them.

2. Movability. The old style parallel bars that have small metal wheels under each corner that are lowered by a foot pedal when the bars have to be moved are not satisfactory. These wheels break easily and scratch the gym floor, and because of their small size the bars are difficult to roll. New style bars usually have a removable transporter cart that attaches to the frame of the bars when they have to be moved. This type of device is very satisfactory if it attaches easily and if it is sturdily constructed. The wheels should be rubber-covered and reasonably large.

3. Adjustment. Adjustments for height and width should be able to be made quickly. Bars that adjust by hand are better than those that require a wrench or special removable gadget that can be easily misplaced.

4. Weight. If bars are quite light, check their stability very carefully. If bars are quite heavy be sure that they have a sturdy transporter cart that enables them to be moved easily.

HOMEMADE EQUIPMENT

It would be very difficult and expensive to make a set of adjustable bars, but bars of a single height and width are easy to make and relatively inexpensive. With bars that can not be adjusted it might be necessary to have several bars of different heights and widths to accommodate all body sizes in the school. In one outdoor

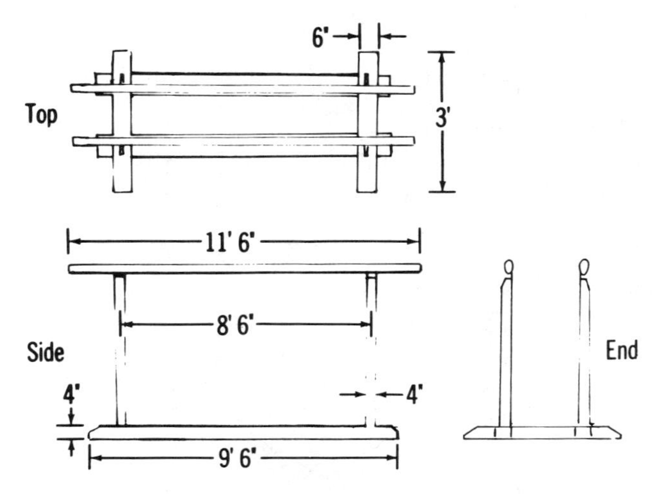

Fig. 8–1. **Homemade Parallel Bars.**

gymnastic area the author has observed nine parallel bars of three different heights and three different widths for each height. These nine bars were constructed for less than the cost of a factory-made set of bars and were actually better for a class situation because so many boys could be kept active. Even if factory-made bars of official specifications are available, extra homemade bars of different heights and widths are advantageous for use in classes.

Homemade bars can be made according to the following specifications for an approximate cost of seventy-five dollars. Height and width measurements are omitted purposely. These can be established according to the needs of the group for which the bars are constructed.

1. Base. The base is made of two pieces of lumber 9′ 6″ x 6″ x 4″ and two 3′ x 6″ x 4″ tapered down on the ends beyond the uprights as indicated. The top of the base should be rounded so that there

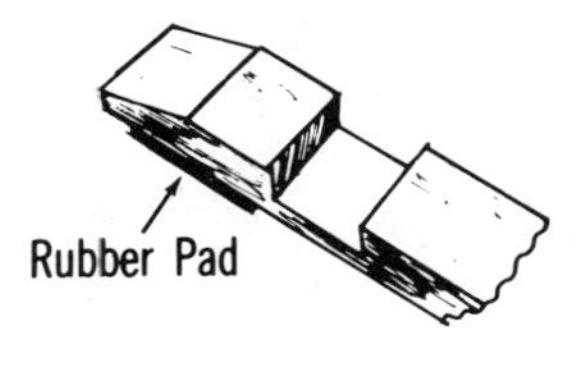

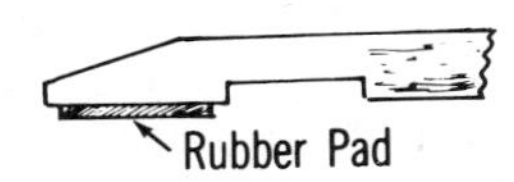

Fig. 8–2. **Base Construction.**

will be no sharp edges. The cross pieces are jointed into the long pieces so that the top and bottom will be flush. Hard rubber pads are fastened under the ends of both the length and cross pieces.

2. Uprights. Uprights are made of pieces of 4" x 4" of the desired height. The edges are rounded slightly and the top is tapered on the outside edge so that it is about 1½ inches across the top.

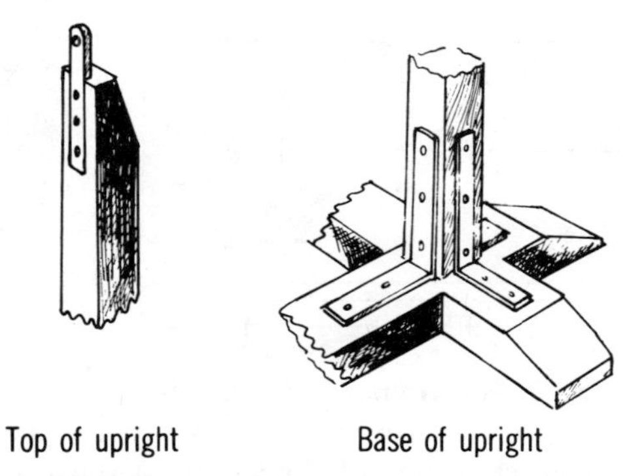

Fig. 8–3. Construction of Uprights.

Each upright is fastened to the base by means of two large and strong angle irons that are bolted in place. On the top inside side of the upright is bolted a flat metal bar that extends about 1 inch above the wooden upright and has a hole on the top to which the top rail is bolted.

3. Top Rail. The top rail is made out of a piece of wood 11½' x 2" x 1⅝". It is shaped in the form of an egg with the large end of the egg to the top. This bar rests on a metal cradle and is fastened to the cradle with four wood screws. On the bottom of the cradle is welded a small piece of metal bar in which there is a hole for the bolt that fastens the cradle to the upright.

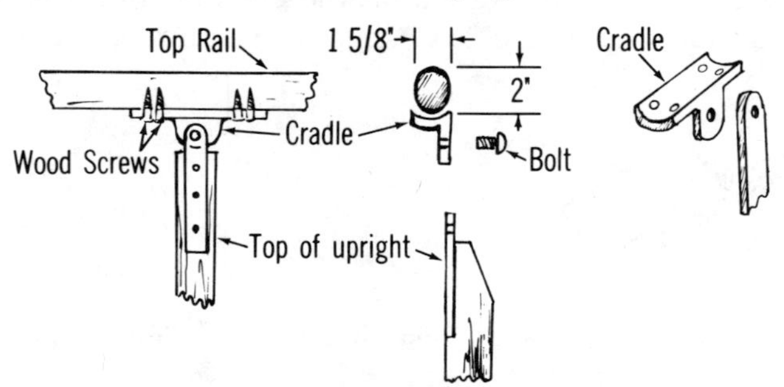

Fig. 8–4. Top Rail Attachment.

4. All bolts, angle irons, and metal bars should be sunk flush with the wooden surface.

TEACHING SUGGESTIONS

It has already been suggested in several other places in this book that bars of different heights should be provided. If there can be two sets so that one can be left at regulation height and one left at a low height, it will facilitate class work. A set of floor parallels (a very low set of unadjustable parallel bars that are usually about 1 foot high) will also be very helpful for class use. If only one set of bars is available, lesson plans should be made so that time will not have to be wasted adjusting the height of bars during a class period. Teach stunts that require practice on low bars one class period and those that require the bars to be set at normal height in another period.

Students in the same squad should be able to use the same width bars so that bars do not have to be continually adjusted for width. When squads are rotated, the bars can be quickly adjusted for the new squad if necessary.

So that more individuals are kept active many stunts can be practiced by two students at a time, one on each end of the bar. Sometimes a series of stunts can be assigned that start at one end of the bar, progress down the bar, and end with a dismount from the other end. The next performer can start before the one ahead of him is off the bars.

Much time should be spent practicing a support swing. In the support position the arms should be straight and the swing should be a free one from the shoulders. Although the shoulders do shift forward and backward during the swing, the center of gravity is not kept over the hands. Especially when the body is forward, the shoulders should not be allowed to lean too far backward. At this time the gymnast should press backward with his hands on the bar to keep his shoulders forward. A support swing should be practiced with the body almost straight on the front end of the swing. On the back end the hands push off the bar so that there is a slight jump off the hands.

There are several good exercises that might be used on the parallel bars to develop strength. Examples are:

1. Support Dips. This exercise starts in a straight arm support. The gymnast bends the arms and lowers down until the shoulders are just a few inches above the hands and then pushes back up to the straight arm support.

2. Swinging Support Dips. This exercise is the same as No. 1 except that it is done while swinging. The arms are bent on the back end of the swing, remain bent during the forward swing, and straighten on the front end of the swing. The backward swing is with straight arms. Variations of this exercise are to dip on the back swing rather than the forward swing or to dip on both the forward and backward swings.

3. Holding a Half-Lever. In this exercise the gymnast is timed to see how long the legs can be held forward at right angles to the body.

4. Handstand Dips. From the handstand position on the floor-parallels the arms are bent until the shoulders touch the bars. From this position the gymnast presses back to a handstand. This exercise may be done with the feet leaning against the wall, or with someone assisting the balance, or entirely alone.

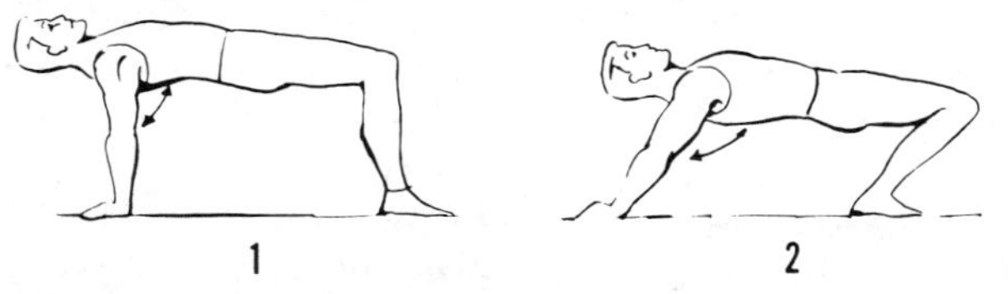

Fig. 8–5. Shoulder-Stretching Exercise. Increase the Size of This Angle to a Maximum.

Another exercise that is important in preparing students for parallel bar work, although it is not actually performed on the bars, is illustrated in Fig. 8–5. Gymnasts who do this exercise regularly will develop the flexibility that is necessary for a high forward swing in the support position, which is essential for good parallel bar execution.

SAFETY

If the general safety rules given in Chapter 1 are observed, this will be a very safe event. The following safety points might be emphasized for the parallel bars.

1. Place mats in the position that will provide maximum safety. Special mats that fit around the uprights and cover the area under the bar should be used. A regular mat can be cut and shaped in

the school shop if a commercial mat is not available. Other mats should be placed along the side of this mat so that there are no dangerous ridges on which the performer can land. The ends of the bars are seldom used, but when they are, place mats there.

2. Use low bars whenever possible to teach and practice new stunts.

3. Spotters should be careful when spotting with their arms above the bars that they do not get them caught between the performer and the bars. To avoid injury to the spotter, assistance should be given with the arms below the bar, if possible.

4. Use the free-support position with caution for younger and weaker students. They can easily lose control in a support and fall between the bars causing injury to the shoulders. Until it is obvious that a student has strength to control a support position, he should work on low bars so that his feet will contact the ground, if he loses control, before the shoulders are stretched beyond their limits of movement.

RULES

A parallel bar exercise should be composed primarily of swinging and vaulting movements, but there must be at least one and not more than three held positions. There must be at least one part requiring a great amount of strength. There must also be one difficult stunt, above or below the bars in which the grip of both hands is momentarily released. The held positions usually used are half-levers or handstands. The strength move is usually a press to a handstand. Other holds and strength moves may be used, however. An under-bar somersault, or peach basket, as it is often called, is the under-bar release commonly used by advanced gymnasts. A backward over-bar somersault and a stutz are the two common over-bar releases used in advanced work.

ABBREVIATED ROUTINE DESCRIPTIONS

I. Single leg cut on mount, straddle seat, press to upper arm balance (HOLD), roll forward to straddle seat, straddle travel to outer side seat on right bar, right leg circle over both bars to straddle seat facing the opposite direction, straddle travel, forward roll to upper arm hang, back uprise, rear dismount (or front dismount).

II. Run, jump to upper arm hang and backward roll to half lever (HOLD), press upper arm stand (HOLD), roll forward to upper arm hang, back uprise, dip turn to upper arm hang, swing legs forward to kip position and upper arm kip, support half-turn with single leg swing over one bar, layback to front uprise, swing to upper arm balance (HOLD), side tip off dismount.

III. Glide kip on end of bars, forward roll, back uprise, swing legs forward to a half-lever (HOLD), press a handstand bent arms straight legs (HOLD), lower to upper arm balance, lower legs to pike position and upper arm kip, stutz and layback to upper arm hang, backward shoulder roll to support, swing legs forward then backward to handstand (HOLD), under-bar cast, back uprise to double rear dismount.

IV. Double rear mount, moore to half-lever (HOLD), press handstand straight arms, straight legs (HOLD), forward pirouette, stutz, under-bar cast, back uprise straddle cut and catch, layback, backward shoulder roll to support, rear vault over side of bar, glide kip, front vault over the bar to a layback, front uprise, swing to handstand, quarter-pirouette to straddle cut-off dismount.

V. Peach basket to half-lever (HOLD), straight body bent arm press to handstand (HOLD), back over bar somersault, stutz to layback, front uprise, swinging pirouette, under-bar cast, back uprise straddle cut and catch swing to handstand (HOLD), stutz to layback, front uprise, front somersault dismount.

I. BEGINNING ROUTINE

1. Single Leg Cut on Mount (Fig. 8–6). The starting position is a stand facing the end of the bars (cross stand frontways). The performer should be fairly close to the end so that both hands can be placed on top of the bars with the arms slightly bent rather than

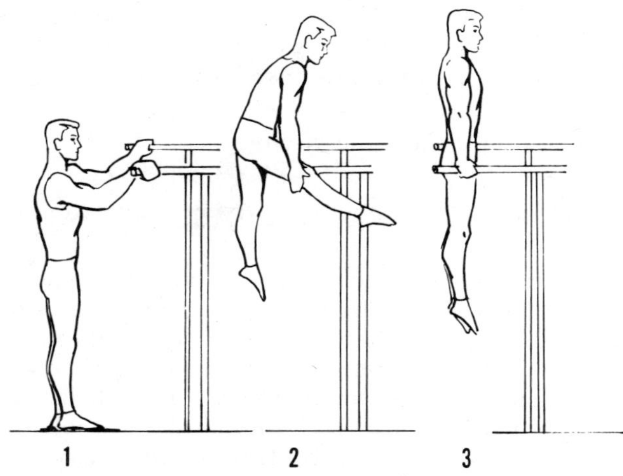

Fig. 8–6. Single Leg Cut on Mount.

straight (1). From this position he jumps in the air and presses down hard with both arms so that the arms do as much of the work as the legs in propelling the body upward. The right leg raises forward and to the side during the jump and passes from the outside to the inside of the right bar. The right hand has to release and regrasp the bar as the right leg passes over. Most of the weight should be quickly shifted to the left hand at the time of the release (2). The performer ends in a straight arm support position on the end of the bars (3).

TEACHING TECHNIQUES. The hands should always be placed on the extreme end of the bars. The stunt should be learned on low bars without attempting to regrasp at first. As the leg comes over and between the bars, the performer can drop to a standing position. The regrasp also should be tried first on the low bars. The bars can be gradually raised to official height. The rules permit the use of the reuther board when mounting the parallel bars. It is not necessary to use the board during practice on the low bars, but when the bars are raised to regulation height the aid of the reuther board will greatly facilitate the execution of this mount.

SPOTTING. A spotter should be used behind and slightly to the side of the performer. He grasps the waist of the performer and helps lift during the jump. He also supports some of the weight at the time of the hand release and recatch to give the performer confidence and to support him in case the bar is missed. As the bar is caught, the spotter must be careful to stay out of the way of the legs as they swing backward.

2. Swing Forward to Straddle Seat. As the single leg cut on mount is completed, there is a natural swing backward of both legs in the support position. The legs then swing forward and are placed on the bars in front of the hands in a straddle or cross seat.

3. Press to Upper Arm Stand (Shoulder Stand) (Fig. 8–7). In the cross seat position the hands release the bars behind the legs and are shifted to the front of the legs close to the thighs (1). From this position the performer rocks forward raising the hips in the air so that the hands support the weight momentarily. The legs will leave the bars at this time (2). As soon as the weight is on the hands and the hips are in the air, the elbows should be dropped out to the side so that the upper arms rest on the bars (3). The legs are then gradually brought together and raised to the balance position. The head should be kept back during the entire movement. The balance is HELD for at least two seconds with the back slightly

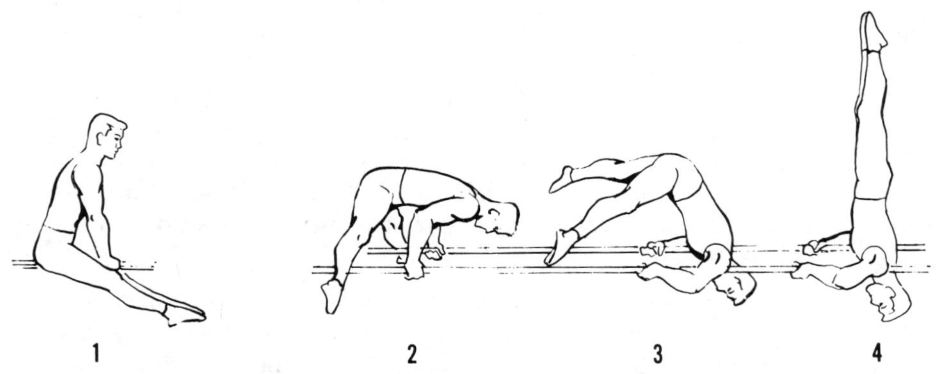

Fig. 8–7. Press to Upper Arm Stand (Shoulder Stand).

arched and the toes pointed (4). Overarching is a bad habit that is hard to break and one that causes many problems when learning more advanced stunts.

TEACHING TECHNIQUES. Practice first on floor parallel bars and then on low parallel bars before trying on bars of regulation height.

SPOTTING. The spotter stands on the side of the bars and reaches under the bar with the near arm to support the lower back of the performer in case he overbalances. With the other hand he holds the performer's elbow down in position so that he can not possibly slip between the bars. When this stunt is learned on lowered bars, it is almost impossible to reach under the bar. In this case the spotting is done above the bars with the spotter being very careful not to get his arm caught if the performer falls off-balance. This could result in serious injury to the spotter.

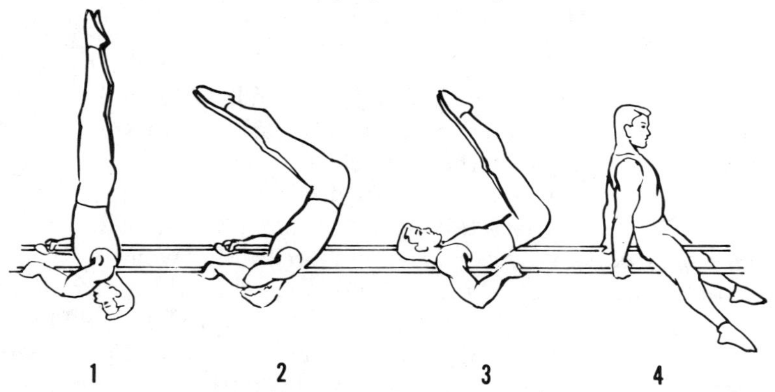

Fig. 8–8. Roll Forward to Straddle Seat.

4. Roll Forward to Straddle Seat (Fig. 8–8). The first motion from the upper arm balance (1) is to lower the legs to a pike position. The hips must move forward as the legs are lowered so that the center of gravity is kept over the point of support (2). As soon as this pike position is reached, the performer moves his head forward so that the chin is almost on the chest and allows himself to fall forward (back leading) off-balance. At this time the legs are straddled and the hands release the bars and are quickly placed under the lower back (3). This allows the roll to be completed by rolling on the upper arm then forearm until the straddle seat position is reached (4).

Teaching Techniques. Practice first on low parallel bars from a straddle seat instead of the upper arm balance. In this position the performer is already in the pike position and already has his legs straddled so the roll is much easier.

Spotting. This stunt is spotted in the same way as the upper arm balance with one hand under the bar supporting the performer's lower back and the other hand holding his elbow down so that he will not slip between the bars. On the low bars the spotter should get down on his knees so that he can spot in the same way.

5. Straddle Travel to Outer Side Seat on the Right Bar (Fig. 8–9). Following the forward roll the hands must be shifted from behind the body to the bars in front of the legs (1). The performer quickly swings the legs backward and leans the upper body forward to support the weight on the hands. If this motion is performed smoothly, the arms should remain straight and the legs should swing backward and upward over the bars without bending (2). The legs are closed together as the performer swings forward in a support posi-

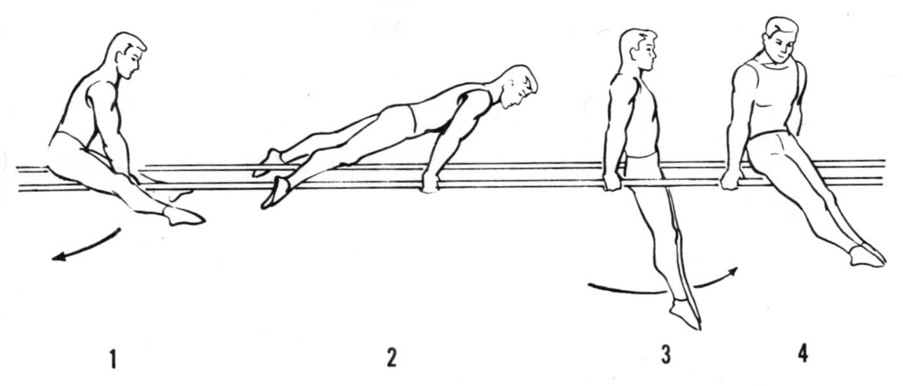

Fig. 8–9. Straddle Travel to Outer Side Seat on the Right Bar.

tion (3). On the front end of the swing the body is piked and the legs are raised upward and placed on the right bar. The knees should remain straight (4).

TEACHING TECHNIQUES. Practice first on the low parallel bars.

SPOTTING. Weak individuals should be spotted to make sure they do not loose balance in the support position. The spotter aids by grasping their upper arms.

6. Outer Side Seat, Half-Turn to Straddle Seat (Fig. 8–10). From the outer seat on the right bar (1) the right leg is raised and swung over the right bar and then the left bar. The right hand releases the right bar and also reaches for the left bar. During this move-

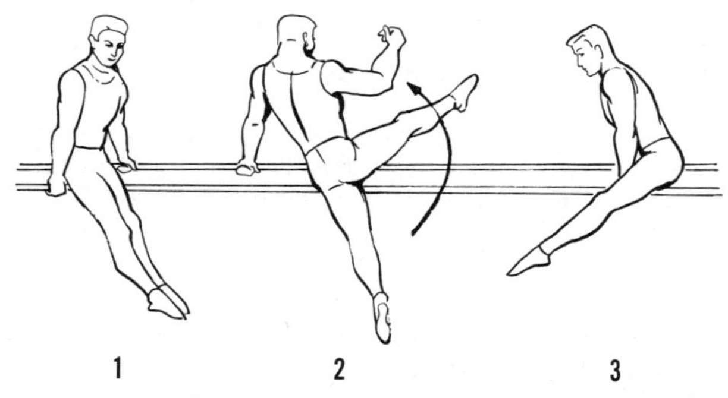

Fig. 8–10. Outer Side Seat, Half-Turn to Straddle Seat.

ment the weight is borne by the left hand and the left thigh (2). When the right hand contacts the left bar the left hand is shifted to the right bar. The performer is now in a straddle seat facing the opposite direction (3).

7. Straddle Travel to Straddle Seat. From the straddle seat position the performer rocks forward as in the previous straddle travel in this routine, swings the legs backward and upward over the bars, and swings forward in a support position. On the front end of the swing the legs are raised and straddled over the bars to another straddle seat.

8. Forward Roll to Upper Arm Hang (Fig. 8–11). From the straddle seat position the hands are shifted from behind the body and placed on the bars in front of, and close to, the thighs (1). The weight is then rocked forward onto the hands and the hips are raised as for the upper arm balance. The elbows are dropped out to the side so that the weight rests primarily on the upper arms

Fig. 8–11. Forward Roll to Upper Arm Hang.

(2). As the hips continue forward the chin is moved toward the chest, the legs are closed together, and the hands release the bar and are moved quickly to grasp again in front (3). As the point of support is the upper arms, the elbows must be kept out to the side during the entire movement. The performer ends in an upper arm hang (4).

SPOTTING. Spot in the same way as for the upper arm stand by reaching below the bar to support weight under the lower back with one hand as the performer rolls forward and swings down between the bars. The other hand holds the elbow out to the side.

9. Back Uprise (Fig. 8–12). As the performer swings down between the bars in the previous stunt, the hands must grasp the bars

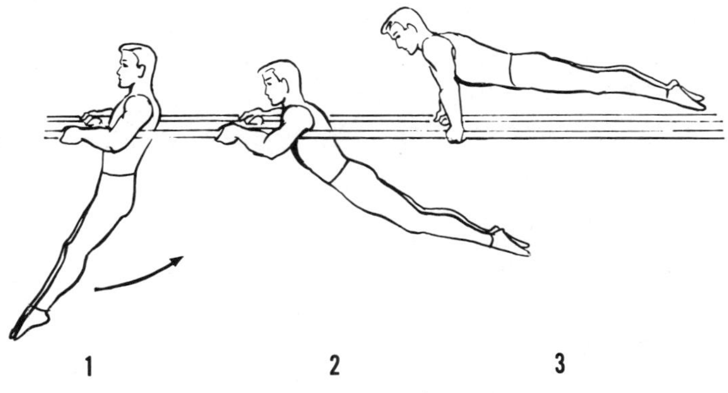

Fig. 8–12. Back Uprise.

as soon as possible with the arms bent to about a right angle. The body is extended, but not completely, so that there is still a slight pike at the hips (1). The swing in the upper arm hang will continue backward and upward as a result of the momentum from the roll. At the start of the upswing the feet are pumped backward so that the body is in an arch (2). This leg motion increases the speed of the swing and helps lift the arms off the bars for the uprise. The arms press downward and pull forward and lift the shoulders forward and upward so that the performer finishes in a free front support (3).

Teaching Techniques. Practice the back uprise first from a forearm support on the bars (Fig. 8–13). The motion of the uprise can be learned from this position, which does not involve as great a vertical change as from the upper arm hang to the support. Next, eliminate the forward roll and try the uprise from an upper arm hang. Pump the legs back and forth a few times in the upper arm hang before attempting the uprise.

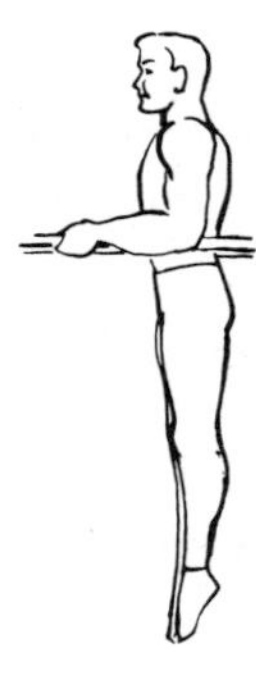

Fig. 8–13. Forearm Support.

Spotting. The spotter stands beside the bars and pushes on the front of the thighs to accentuate the backward leg motion and then lifts under the thighs or abdomen to aid in raising the performer from the hang to the support.

10a. Rear Dismount (Fig. 8–14). In this routine a choice of dismounts is given. As the rear dismount fits best into the exercise, it is given first. Following the back uprise the performer is in a front support position with the legs back well behind the point of support. From this position the body swings downward and forward through a vertical front support (1). On the upswing the body is piked and the legs are swung forward and over the left bar (2). The right hand thrusts off the right bar to push the entire body to the left. The left hand releases the left bar and then the

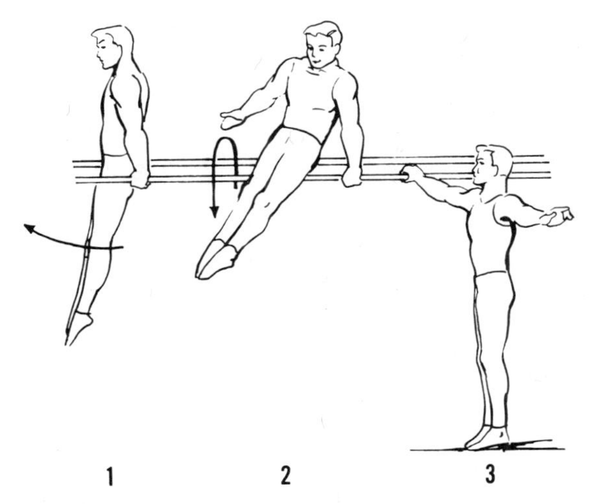

Fig. 8–14. Rear Dismount.

right hand grasps it as the performer drops to the mat with his right side to the bars. The right hand helps the performer maintain control on the landing (3).

TEACHING TECHNIQUES. This stunt should first be tried on the low bars. The performer can swing back and forth a few times and then execute the dismount as described. Another good lead-up is to run and jump to a support on the low parallels and to dismount as the legs swing forward as a result of the momentum from the run.

SPOTTING. The spotter stands beside the performer and grasps his upper arm when on the low parallels or the forearm when on the high parallels. He can help maintain balance in the support position, pull the performer sideways as he comes over the bar, and aid in the landing.

10b. Front Dismount (Fig. 8–15). For variation this stunt can be used in place of the rear dismount but it does not fit into the routine quite as well because it is necessary to include an extra, or intermediate, swing in the support position. The forward swing should be as high as possible in order that a good backward swing be obtained (1). The backward swing should be accentuated so as to get a high front dismount. At the height of the backward swing the left hand pushes vigorously off the left bar and pushes the entire body over the right bar (2). The left hand shifts to the right bar and the right hand releases (3) as the performer drops to the mat with his left hand grasping the bar (4).

Fig. 8–15. Front Dismount.

TEACHING TECHNIQUES. The front dismount should be learned first on the low bars. The performer swings back and forth a few times in a support position and then dismounts as described.

SPOTTING. The spotter stands beside the performer and grasps his arm to pull him sideways over the bar and to help him maintain balance on the landing. A mat may be draped over the right bar behind the hand. If the legs are not pushed far enough to the side, this will prevent painful contact with the bar.

II. LOW INTERMEDIATE ROUTINE

1. Jump to Upper Arm Hang, Backward Shoulder Roll to Half-Lever (Fig. 8–16). Stand facing the end of the bars (cross stand frontways) about 15 feet away. Run and jump to an upper arm hang landing about one-third of the distance down the bars. A reuther board may be used for the mount if the performer wishes. On the takeoff the legs should be lifted backward so that the body is in almost a horizontal position at the time the arms contact the bars. The hands should reach well forward so that the arms are almost straight and grasp very securely to prevent sliding on the bars during the forward swing (1). A jump into this position will produce a good swing in the upper arm hang, whereas a jump to a more vertical body position will develop very little swing. During the

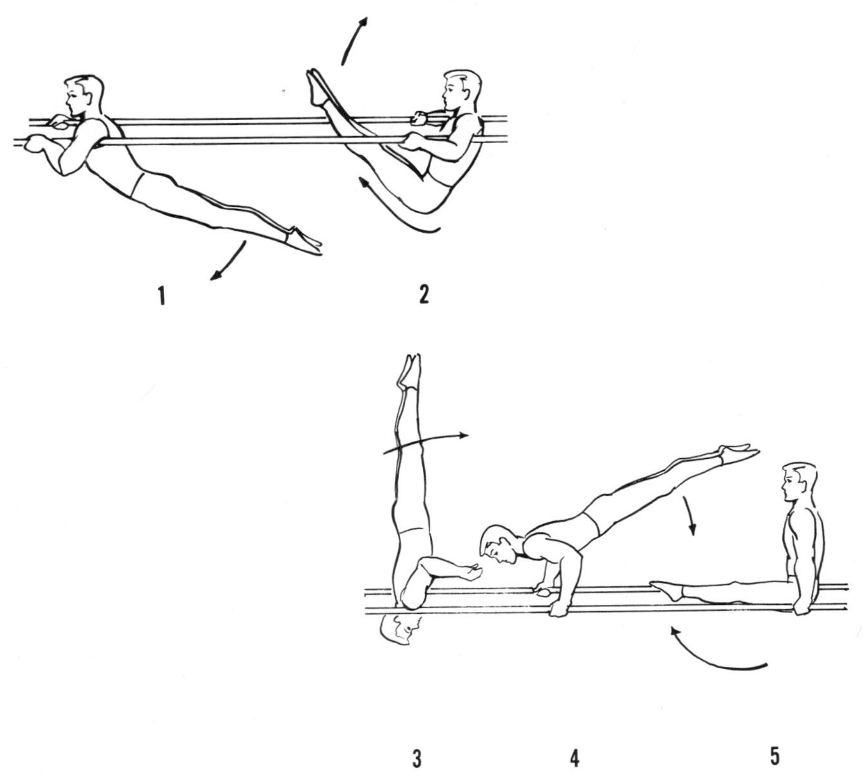

Fig. 8–16. Jump to Upper Arm Hang, Backward Shoulder Roll to Half-Lever.

downward part of the swing and through the vertical position the body should be stretched as long as possible. On the upward swing the legs pump forward, the body is thus piked, and the arms press down vigorously (2). This press with the arms should continue during the upswing until the body is about 45° above the horizontal. Toward the top of the upswing the body is extended, the head is lifted, and the hands release and reach over the shoulders to regrasp the bars (3). The elbows, of course, should remain out to the side during the entire stunt to prevent slipping between the bars. As soon as the hands regrasp the arms press away from the bars lifting the shoulders forward and upward as the body swings downward to the support position (4). As the vertical support is reached, the legs are raised forward to a right angle pike. This is called a half-lever or an "L" support and it should be HELD for at least two seconds (5).

TEACHING TECHNIQUES. There are many lead-up stunts that can be used in preparation for this mount. A preliminary stunt that is sometimes used is a backward roll from a straddle seat on the bars to another straddle seat. In this stunt the body stays piked and the legs stay straddled throughout. The elbows stay out, of course, and the hands press down on the bars until the legs are well over the head and approaching the bars again. A very useful lead-up is to swing back and forth in the upper arm hang and then execute a backward roll to a straddle seat on the bars. In this stunt the body is piked considerably and the feet reach well over the face as they are raised. As soon as the legs get above the bars they can be straddled ready for the landing in the cross seat position. The next step is to start from a swing in the upper arm hang and roll backward to a support position. At first the body should remain in a pike and not be extended as is done by a more proficient performer. Another good preliminary exercise is to practice the half-lever on the floor parallel bars. Contests between two students to see who can hold the lever the longest create much interest. Timing each individual to get a class champion is also a good technique. This drill strengthens the abdominal as well as the arm and shoulder muscles, all of which are used to hold this position.

SPOTTING. Two spotters should be used, one on each side of the bars. They hold the elbow down with one hand and lift under the lower back with the other hand. Refer to photo, page 345.

2. Press to Upper Arm Stand (Fig. 8–17). This is approximately the same stunt as described in Routine I (Fig. 8–7), but it takes more strength as it starts from a half-lever instead of a cross seat. From the half-lever the hips are raised backward and the shoulders are lowered toward the bars. The body remains in approximately

Fig. 8–17. Press to Upper Arm Stand.

the right angle pike with the head slightly back (1). This movement requires reasonably strong arm, shoulder, and back muscles. As the shoulders approach the bars, the elbows are dropped out to the side and the legs are raised slowly upward. The performer should finish in a balance with the head back and the body slightly arched (2). The balance is HELD for at least two seconds.

TEACHING TECHNIQUES. Teachers should remind students whenever a balance is taught that an excessive arch is considered poor form so that they will learn to control their arch right from the beginning. The forward roll and the previous upper arm balance executed from a cross seat are lead-ups for this stunt and might be reviewed at this time on the low parallel bars or floor parallels.

SPOTTING. A spotter on each side of the bar holds the elbow down with one hand and reaches under the bar to the lower back with the other hand to prevent overbalancing.

3. Roll Forward to Back Uprise (Fig. 8–18). From the upper arm balance the roll is started by pressing with the hands and moving the chin toward the chest (1). The body is piked very slightly on

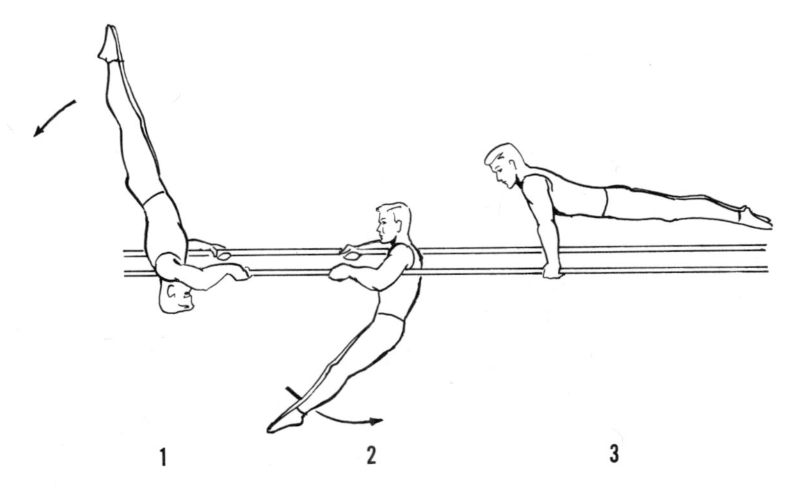

Fig. 8–18. Roll Forward to Back Uprise.

the downswing and the hands are released and shifted to the bars in front of the face (2). The elbows, as in all upper arm hang positions, are kept out to the side. From this point the back uprise is executed in exactly the same way as described in Routine I (Fig. 8–12) and ends in a free front support (3).

TEACHING TECHNIQUES. The forward roll from the cross seat to upper arm hang should be reviewed as a lead-up for this stunt. When the roll is first tried from the balance, the body can be piked considerably on the way down to reduce the speed of the downswing. This will make the uprise harder but will make the roll-down safer.

SPOTTING. At first the spotter assists with one hand on the elbow to keep it in position and one hand under the lower back (reaching under the bar) to slow down the downswing. When the roll-down can be performed safely, the spotter then pushes under the front of the thigh to aid in the back uprise after the performer passes through the vertical position and starts the upswing.

4. Half-Turn from Support to Upper Arm Hang (Elementary Stutz) (Fig. 8–19). It is very important to do a good back uprise in order to execute this half-turn immediately after the uprise. Unless the

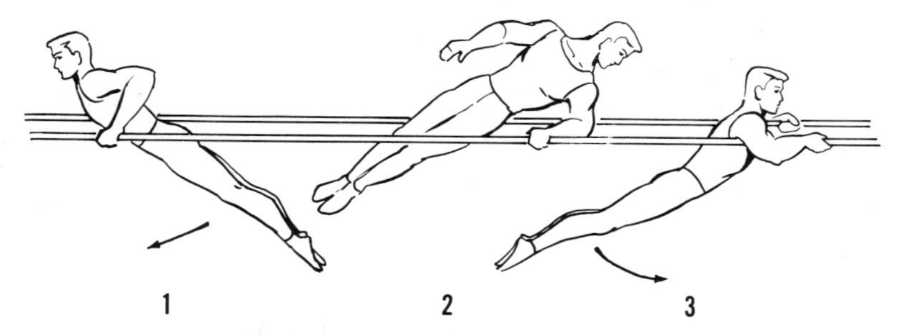

Fig. 8–19. Half-Turn from Support to Upper Arm Hang (Elementary Stutz).

arms can be fully straightened by the time the backward and upward motion of the uprise has been completed, it will be difficult to continue with the routine without taking an extra swing. This stunt starts from the free front support position. The arms are bent as the body starts to swing downward and forward (1), and then on the upswing the legs are pumped forward in a pike. As the upswing is completed the hips are thrust upward so that the body straightens and the turn is started by thrusting off the bars with the hands and turning the shoulders and hips in the desired direction. If the turn is to the left, the right hand thrusts harder than the left so that the right shoulder is raised (2). Care must be taken not to raise either shoulder too high from the bars as this will tend to lower the legs. The hands release the bars and the performer drops to an upper arm hang after completing the 180° turn and grasps the bars securely with the hands while the legs are still at the height of the swing (3). The legs and hips must remain high until after the turn has been completed so that a forward swing will result in the upper arm hang.

TEACHING TECHNIQUES. Dip swings should be mastered completely before the "dip turn," as it is often called, is tried. In dip swings the performer dips at the height of the backswing, holds the bent arm support during the forward swing, and then pushes out to a straight arm support at the height of the forward swing. He then swings backward in the straight arm support and repeats the movement again. The turn should first be practiced on low bars so that the feet will drop to the mat between the bars before the arms make contact. The hands can regrasp after the turn even though the arms do not land on the bars. This will prevent many painful landings during the learning process. A common mistake is to kill the swing and make the 180° turn in almost a vertical position. This results in a hard and painful landing on the upper arms.

SPOTTING. The spotter stands beside the bars and lifts under the buttocks on the upswing. He should be on the right if the turn is to the left. A skillful spotter can help hold the body up in position as the turn is made and can even assist in the turn by applying the right pressure. After the turn he quickly reaches under the performer with both arms to support weight under the stomach and thighs. In this way he can make the landing on the bars much softer.

5. Upper Arm Kip (Fig. 8–20). Following the "dip turn" the performer swings downward and forward in an upper arm hang (1). On the upswing the legs are piked and raised over the head to an inverted pike position. In this position the weight rests on

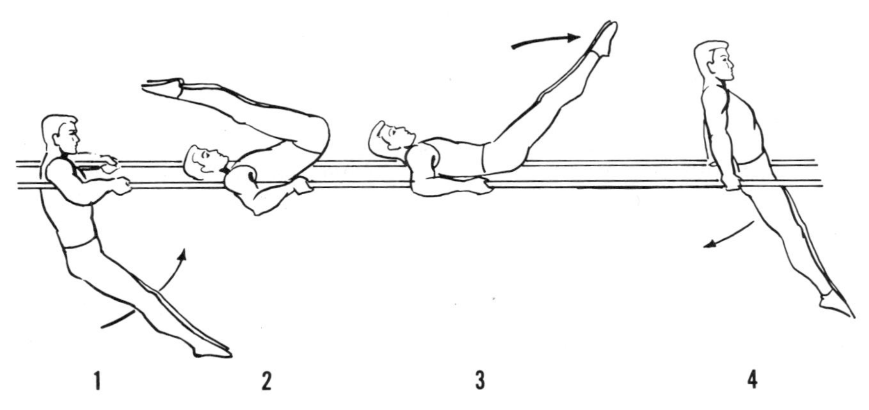

Fig. 8–20. Upper Arm Kip.

the upper arms, the hips are well above the bars, the head is forward, and the legs are in a sharp pike so that the knees are over the face (2). The hands must press downward hard on the bars during the upswing and continue the downward pressure so that this position can be held momentarily. The kipping motion, which is really just a rapid extension of the body, starts from this position. The legs thrust hard upward, forward, and downward to accomplish this extension and the arms press down hard on the bars (3). The leg motion and the arm press will raise the upper body to a straight arm support position (4).

TEACHING TECHNIQUES. The first step is to sit between the floor parallel bars and then lean back until the upper arms are resting on the bars. From this position the feet are kicked up off the floor to the inverted pike position. The kip is executed in the same way but the legs are spread so that the performer ends in a straddle seat on the bar. This method can also be tried on the low parallel bars. When the kip is first tried with the legs together, rather than to a straddle seat, the beginner sometimes goes too far and falls forward between the bars. This is dangerous not only because of the fall but because it is possible to wrench the shoulders. Beginners should be spotted carefully, therefore, on the low bars.

SPOTTING. The spotter stands on the side, reaches under the bar, and aids in getting the hips up high above the bars in the inverted pike position. He can also support under the lower back to keep the hips high during the start of the body extension. He should also be alert to lift under the chest upon the completion of the kip in case the performer goes too far forward. During the learning process on the low parallels the spotter can grasp the performer's upper arm and prevent him from going too far forward upon completion of the kip.

6. Support Half-Turn with Single Leg Swing over One Bar (Fig. 8–21). After the upper arm kip the performer will swing backward in a support position. He then swings forward again before starting the single leg swing overturn (1). This might be considered an extra, or intermediate, swing but as the backward swing is the natural completion of the previous stunt and the turn is started on the forward swing, this is not a major fault especially at the low intermediate level. During the forward swing the amount of swing should be reduced by gripping hard with the hands to slow the motion down. As the upward swing starts, the right leg is raised and swung over the left bar to start the turn (2). The left leg swings only slightly beyond a vertical position. The right hand

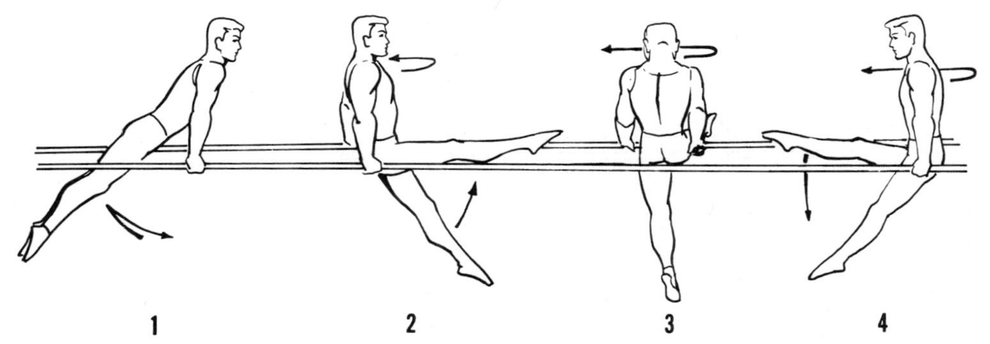

Fig. 8–21. Support Half-Turn with Single Leg Swing over One Bar.

pushes off the right bar and shifts to the left bar. In this support on the left bar the right leg should be close to the left hand and held forward in a right angle pike position and the right hand should be close to the leg (3). If the performer stretches too far forward with the leg or places the right hand too far from the leg it is very difficult to complete the turn. The turn should continue smoothly without a hesitation with the weight supported by the hands and with both legs clear of the bar. The left hand shifts backward to the other bar as the 180° turn is completed with the right leg swinging over the bar again to the support position (4).

Teaching Techniques. This stunt should be practiced first on the low parallels from a very small swing. It can be practiced in two parts with the circling leg resting on the bar after the first quarter-turn.

Spotting. If the stunt is learned on the low parallels, a spotter can spot behind the performer by reaching over the top of the bars to grasp the back and prevent a backward fall. Another spotter can spot on the other side and be quick to step forward to catch the performer if he loses his balance forward. This spotter must stand out of the way of the circling leg and move in if needed.

7. Layback (Fig. 8–22). This is not usually considered to be a stunt but rather a connecting move between stunts. It is such an important parallel bar movement, however, that it is described here as a separate part of this routine. After the single leg swing-over has been completed the circling leg will swing backward. This motion should be accentuated by pumping backward hard with the leg so that a reasonably high backswing can be attained (1). At the end of the backswing the arms push backward and the performer lowers the upper arms to the bar with the arms only very

Fig. 8–22. Layback.

slightly bent (2). This motion should be performed quickly yet smoothly while the legs are still at the height of the backswing. From this position the performer starts a forward swing in an upper arm hang (3).

SPOTTING. Although there are no real lead-up techniques for this stunt, the spotter can aid in the learning process and is a definite part of the teaching procedure. The spotter stands beside the high parallels and as the performer starts the upswing, he reaches under the bars and places one hand on the abdomen and one on the thighs. At the end of the backswing he pushes backward and helps lower the performer to the bars. As well as providing support the spotter can bring about proper timing by applying pressure and directing movement at the right instant.

8. Front Uprise (Fig. 8–23). This is one of the most important parallel bar stunts, even in advanced work, as so many stunts that follow depend on correct execution of the front uprise. If the backswing after the single leg swing over is high the layback can be executed with the feet as high as the bars. This will result in a good swing forward in an upper arm hang and will facilitate the performance of the front uprise. The arms should be almost straight in the upper arm hang for the execution of the front uprise. (It might be remembered that the arms were bent about right angles for the back uprise.) The body is stretched on the downswing and then on the upswing the legs pump forward in a pike position (1). The arms press downward and also pull the body forward. During the last part of the upward and forward movement the hips are thrust forward so that the body is reasonably straight after the completion of the uprise (2).

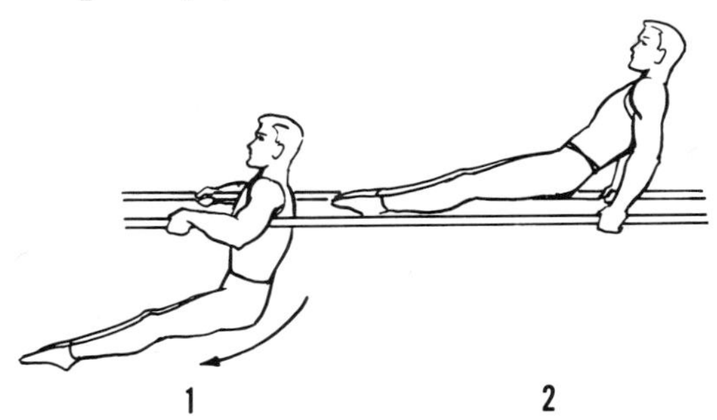

Fig. 8–23. Front Uprise.

Teaching Techniques. The front uprise can be tried first from a forearm support on the low parallels just as was the back uprise. Less vertical movement is involved from the forearm support to the straight arm support than from the upper arm hang to the straight arm support and therefore this lead-up is much easier. The next step is to take several extra swings in an upper arm hang before trying the uprise. At this stage in the learning process the uprise can also be tried from a run and jump to an upper arm hang with an immediate uprise on the forward swing. The body should be in an almost horizontal position after the jump to the upper arm hang or little forward swing will result. The layback and uprise can be practiced together as a drill for gymnasts of all levels of ability. This drill consists of a layback, a front uprise, a backward swing in a straight arm support followed by another layback to start the cycle over again. It may be repeated over and over and can be used as a contest between class members to see who can do the most. It might be mentioned at this time that some advanced gymnasts finish their front uprise in quite a pike position rather than with a fairly straight body. This method is not recommended for beginners even though advanced performers might be successful with it.

Spotting. The spotter stands beside the bars and aids in the forward swing and the vertical lift by pushing and lifting under the buttocks.

9. Swing to Upper Arm Balance (Fig. 8–24). Following the front uprise there will be a natural swing backward in a support position (1). As the feet swing well above the bars the arms start to bend (2). The legs continue to raise backward and the upper arms are lowered to the bars with the elbows to the side so that the performer finishes in a vertical balance with the back slightly arched and the weight supported on the upper arms (3). The back is arched and the head remains slightly back during the entire movement. As with all holds on the parallel bars this balance should be HELD for at least two seconds.

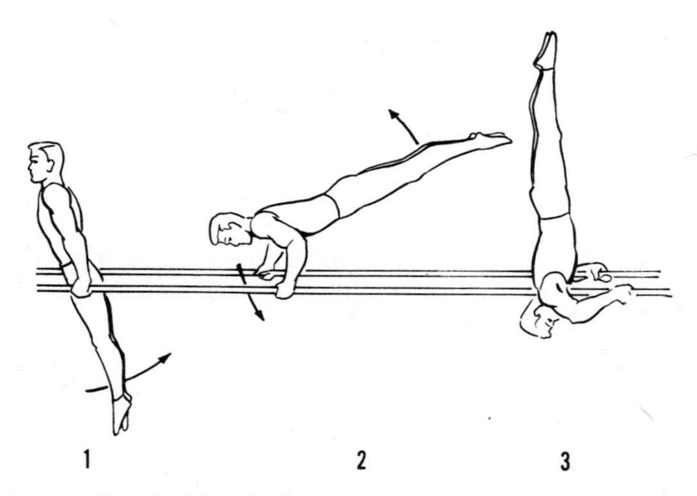

Fig. 8–24. Swing to Upper Arm Balance.

TEACHING TECHNIQUES. The lead-up techniques given for the press to an upper arm balance described in the first routine are all lead-ups for this stunt as well. The swing to the balance should first be tried on low bars using several extra preliminary swings. In the learning process the hips can be piked to make the movement much easier. The body can be gradually straightened as the stunt is practiced so that it can be done with an arched position being held throughout.

SPOTTING. The spotter holds the elbow out with one hand and prevents an overbalance with the other hand by supporting behind the lower back. On the low bars this second hand will have to reach above the bars but on the high parallels it should reach under the bar.

Fig. 8–25. Sideward Tip-Off Dismount.

10. Sideward Tip-Off Dismount (Fig. 8–25). This is a cartwheel-like motion from the upper arm stand to the mat. The motion is started by pushing up with the right hand (or left hand if executed to the other side) and lifting the right shoulder away from the bar (1). Once the motion is started the stunt is nothing more than a fall to the mat maintaining the slight arched position until the landing. During the fall the right hand releases the bar (2) but the left hand retains its grip to help maintain balance as the performer lands with his left side toward the bars (3).

Teaching Techniques. Learn on low parallel bars where the spotter can help more effectively than on high bars. Emphasize that the head must remain back during the first half of the tip-off.

Spotting. The spotter should be on the dismount side of the bars behind the performer. He reaches up with both hands and grasps the hips and supports very carefully during the first part of the sideward tip-off to be sure that the motion is perpendicular to the bars. This is an easy assist if the stunt is practiced on low bars. A beginner often loses his sense of direction and might fall forward or backward onto the bars. The spotter maintains contact to ensure a balanced landing. Refer to the photo on page 345.

III. INTERMEDIATE ROUTINE

1. Glide Kip (Fig. 8–26). This routine starts in a stand facing the end of the bars (cross stand frontways). The arms are straight and the hands are on the end of the bars with the thumbs along the inside surface of the bar (1). The gymnast jumps upward and raises his hips backward so that the body assumes a slight pike position (2). From this position the swing is forward under the bars.

Fig. 8–26. Glide Kip.

The arms stay straight and the feet glide forward a few inches off the ground. On the front end of the swing the body is stretched from the hands to the feet and may be slightly arched (3). As the backswing starts the legs are raised rapidly to (4) a pike position with the knees over the face. The head should stay forward in this position. On the back end of the swing in this inverted pike-hang (5) the body is extended rapidly so that the hips are raised to a position between the hands (6). The legs shoot upward, forward, and downward, the hands press downward on the bars, and the head and shoulders circle upward to a front support position (7). A good performer can complete the kip with straight arms but a beginner might have to bend his arms to get above the bars.

Teaching Techniques. The kip on the low or high horizontal bar is almost identical to this stunt; if these have been accomplished, the kip on the parallel bars will be easy. The upper arm kip is an excellent lead-up for the glide kip. Another step is to practice the kip without a glide and to spread the legs as it is completed so as to finish in a straddle seat on the bars. This lead-up starts in the same starting position as the glide kip but the legs are raised immediately, either one or two at a time, to the pike position. The performer swings forward, or beats forward as it is usually called, in the inverted pike hang and then beats backward in the same position. The head should be forward with the eyes looking at the knees. On the back end of the swing the body is extended rapidly as in the glide kip, but as the legs come above the bars they are straddled so that the kip is finished in a straddle seat. The next step starts in the same manner but is completed with the legs together to a support rather than to a straddle seat.

Spotting. A spotter can facilitate the learning of this stunt considerably by assisting in the correct way. He stands beside the performer and places one hand under the back and the other hand on the back of the thighs. The performer can be guided and assisted into the inverted pike and then during the kipping motion assisted by a lift with both hands. Beginners often raise their hips too high and drop their head backward in the inverted pike. This might result in a complete backward circle and a dangerous fall between the bars unless the spotter is alert to guard against this.

2. Straight Body Forward Roll (Fig. 8–27). This is not a new stunt but a combination of two that have been included in previous routines. As the kip is completed the legs swing backward and upward and the shoulders are lowered toward the bars (1). This first

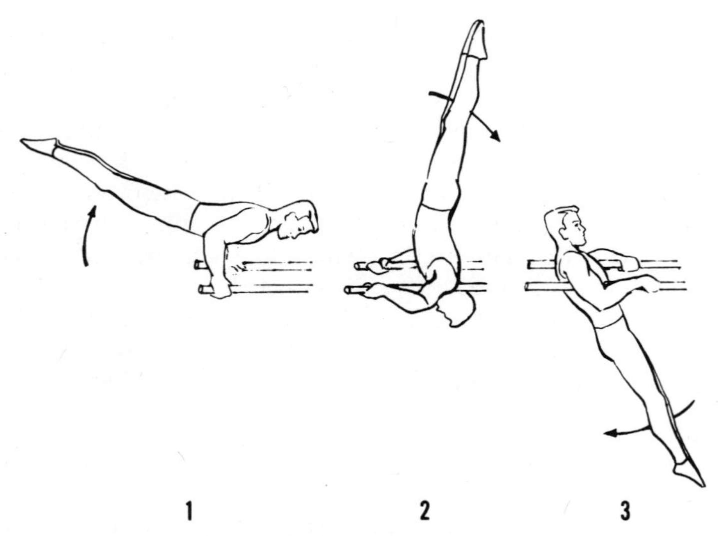

Fig. 8–27. Straight Body Forward Roll.

part of the roll is the same movement as the swing to upper arm balance in Routine II (Fig. 8–24) except that the movement does not stop in the upper arm balance but continues forward (2). The last part of the roll is the same movement as the roll forward to upper arm hang (Fig. 8–11) included in Routine I (3). The teaching techniques, lead-up skills, and spotting methods are the same as previously given.

3. Back Uprise (Fig. 8–28). This is a very common stunt on the parallel bars and an essential one for both beginners and advanced

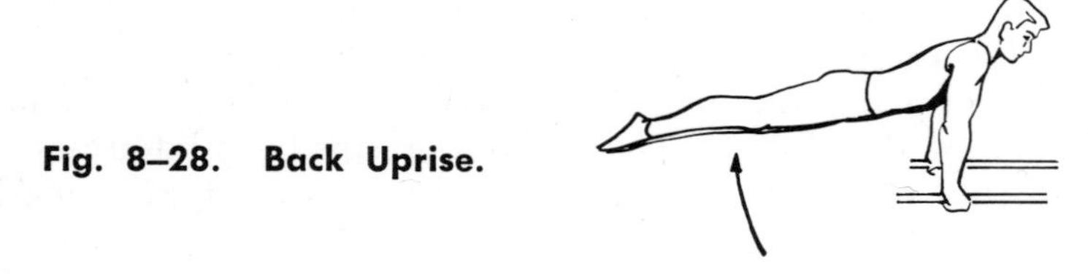

Fig. 8–28. Back Uprise.

performers. It has been included once in each of the previous routines, appears twice in this routine, and is also included once in the following two routines. Refer to the description for the back uprise given in Routine I, pages 321–22.

4. Half-Lever (Fig. 8–29). This stunt also was included in Routine II and is executed in the same way in this routine. The lever should be HELD at least two seconds.

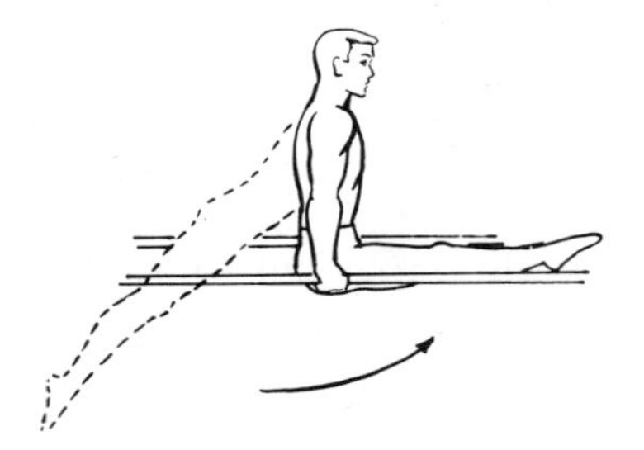

Fig. 8–29. Half-Lever.

5. Press a Handstand, Bent Arms, Straight Legs (Fig. 8–30). From the half-lever the hips raise backward, the shoulders lean forward, and the arms bend to about a right angle (1). The head should be tipped backward at this time and remain back during the entire stunt. The hips are raised until the center of gravity is over the point of support (2). The legs are then gradually raised upward and the arms are straightened to the handstand position (3). In a handstand the body should be stretched so that the line through the arms and upper body is almost straight. This means that there will be very little arch in the back. The head should be slightly back but this position should not be exaggerated. The balance is HELD for at least two seconds.

TEACHING TECHNIQUES. The handstand should be learned on the floor, then the floor parallels, and then the low parallels before it is tried on the regulation bars. At first it is safer, on bars of any height, to try the handstand on the end facing away from the bars. If the handstand is overbalanced it is then quite easy to release one

Fig. 8–30. Press a Handstand, Bent Arms, Straight Legs.

hand and twist off to the side to land on the feet without much danger of landing on the bars. When handstand presses are learned, the easiest way to accomplish them is to start from a frog balance with the knees resting on the elbows. From this position the hips are raised and then the legs are straightened. The next step is to try the press with the legs between the arms but with the knees bent until the center of gravity is over the point of support. Still another step is to keep the legs straight but to straddle them wide apart. This makes the press somewhat easier than when the legs are kept together. Certainly a prerequisite for the press is sufficient arm and shoulder girdle strength. A handstand press is considered to be a strength move even for advanced gymnasts in competitive gymnastics. Practicing the lead-up presses is the best way to develop the desired strength but other strength exercises should be done as well. After a bent arm press has been learned, the next step is to keep the arms straight as well as the legs. This is considered a harder press but for some individuals who possess considerable flexibility it is easier. In the straight arm press the shoulders are leaned well forward of the hands as the press starts and then shift gradually back into position over the hands as the handstand is completed.

SPOTTING. If the performer learns the technique of twisting off to the side if the balance is lost and dropping to the feet while still maintaining a grasp on the bars with one hand, a spotter is not absolutely essential. One is usually placed, however, beside the performer on the side of the hand that is to maintain its grasp. He stands in readiness to aid if necessary.

6. Lower to Upper Arm Balance (Fig. 8–31). Maintaining the center of gravity directly over the point of the support, the arms

Fig. 8–31. Lower to Upper Arm Balance.

are bent and the shoulders lowered toward the bar (1). As they approach the bar the elbows are dropped out to the side so that the upper arms make contact with the bar (2). The body maintains a slight arch with the head back during the whole movement. As the previous stunt was a two-second hold this stunt should only be a momentary pause to demonstrate control of movement before preceding to the next part.

TEACHING TECHNIQUES. Pushing up and lowering down from a headstand to a handstand on the floor is a good lead-up. The same drill should also be used on the floor parallels.

SPOTTING. A spotter should stand beside the performer to aid him in maintaining his balance and to support some of his weight when the stunt is tried on the floor or floor parallels. If the stunt is learned on the floor parallels, a spotter should not be needed when it is tried on the regulation bars.

7. Upper Arm Kip (Fig. 8–32). After the performer pauses momentarily in the upper arm stand, the hips flex and the chin is placed on the chest (1). As the pike increases the hands transfer

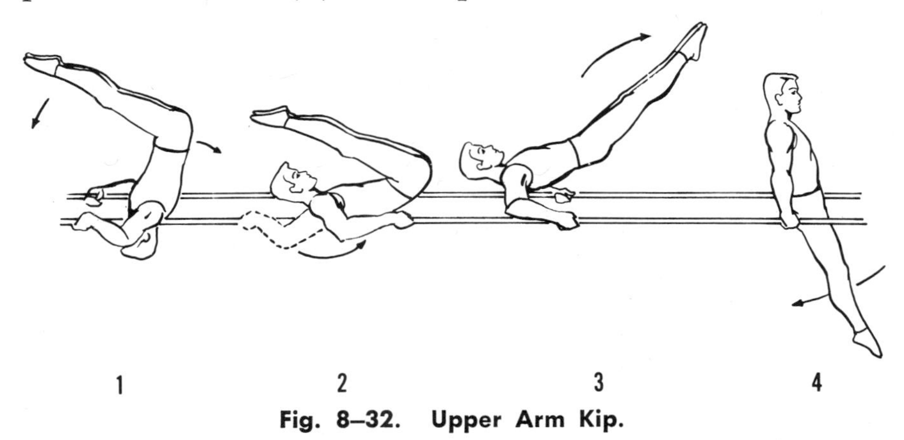

Fig. 8–32. Upper Arm Kip.

to a grip on the bars under the hips. The balance should be maintained momentarily in this inverted pike position with the point of support being the upper arms (2). The gymnast is now in position to execute the upper arm kip as described in Routine II, pages 329–30 (3) (4).

TEACHING TECHNIQUES. Lead-ups have already been given for the upper arm kip in Routine II, but one more point might be mentioned at this time regarding getting into position for the kip. The hips should stay high as the legs are lowered from the upper arm balance to the kip position to prevent loss of balance prior to the kipping motion.

SPOTTING. A spotter can be utilized to reach under the bar and support under the lower back to insure that the hips stay well above the bars in the inverted pike position.

8. Stutz and Layback (Fig. 8–33). "Stutz" is a German term that is commonly used in American gymnastics to refer to a swinging half-turn in a support position. Although it is a very difficult stunt to do well it is one that can be started at the intermediate level. After the upper arm kip the performer swings backward in a support position. The turn is not executed until the end of the first forward swing. The backward swing therefore is an intermediate swing and must be considered a fault. In advanced gymnastics it is a major error but at the intermediate level it is sometimes neces-

Fig. 8–33. Stutz and Layback.

sary to have an extra swing preceding a difficult stunt like the stutz. Students should be informed that it is contrary to the rules but that there is a reason for including it. Let us consider that the stutz begins at the height of the back swing (1). During the downward portion of the swing the body is slightly arched. After passing the vertical position it starts to pike slightly and as it continues higher the pike increases a little (2). During this part of the stutz the arms push backward on the bars, thus keeping the weight well forward. It is a common mistake to let the shoulders lean back too far at this point. As the toes get to about shoulder height, the hips are thrust upward, the right hand releases the bar and reaches over the chest, and the head turns to the left so that the eyes can look down the left or support arm (3). If there has been a relaxed swing and a good hip lift the height of the swing will actually increase as the turn is completed with a quick movement of the left hand over to the right bar as the right hand grasps the left bar (4). In many routines the stutz is completed with a forward swing in a support position, but in this exercise it is followed by a layback which is described in Routine II, pages 331–32 (5) (6).

Teaching Techniques. There are many teaching techniques used for the stutz. These are listed in the approximate order in which they would be used. The dip turn to upper arm hang, which was included in Routine II, is an excellent lead-up for the stutz. A dip turn to a support can also be used before a straight arm stutz is attempted. The high forward swing can be practiced with only one arm releasing the bar. In this lead-up the performer turns over the bar and dismounts to the floor. Practice for the stutz should always be on low bars with the bars padded or on the extreme end of the bars facing away from the equipment. The low bars permit the gymnast to drop to his feet without much danger of injury or painful contact with the bars. Padding the bars or eliminating the danger of the bars by performing on the end also prevents many painful bumps and bruises. It might be noted that this stutz is described as an intermediate gymnast would execute the stunt. An advanced gymnast would carry the forward swing much higher and would complete the turn at almost a vertical position. Even an intermediate gymnast should work toward as high a stutz as possible.

Spotting. Spotting is not essential if the techniques outlined are followed, but there are two methods that are often used. Both of these are good teaching methods as well as spotting methods as they aid in developing correct techniques. One is to use a single rope from an overhead spotting rig fastened to the belt in the center of the performer's back rather than on the side of his body. By pulling on this single rope the spotter can contribute to the height of the stutz, help bring about the twist, and support the performer's weight as the half-turn is completed. The other method is to have a strong spotter stand on a horse or table beside the parallel bars and reach over the bars to catch the performer under the abdomen and legs as he turns. It is dangerous to spot above the bars in this way, but a strong spotter seldom has any trouble. Using this method, a skillful spotter can aid the gymnast to get a high swing and a good lift so that a high stutz will result. Refer to the last two photos on page 345.

9. Backward Shoulder Roll to Support (Fig. 8–34). After the stutz and layback the gymnast swings forward in an upper arm hang (1). From this point the stunt is exactly the same as the mount in

Fig. 8–34. Backward Shoulder Roll to Support.

Routine II, pages 324–26 (2) (3), except that it is completed with a forward swing instead of ending in a half-lever (4).

10. Swing to Handstand (Fig. 8–35). The forward swing following the previous stunt is an intermediate swing and must be considered a fault in a gymnastic routine. It is included purposely here to make the swing to handstand easier for the gymnast who is just learning the stunt. During the first part of the backward swing the body is piked slightly (1) and as the vertical position is reached the feet are pumped backward and the body is arched (2). As the feet continue upward, the shoulders lean well in front of the hands (3). This is an important part of the stunt that beginners often omit because the position feels awkward at first. As the

The first photo illustrates the spotting for a backward roll. The performer has just released the bars below the hips and is reaching for them again in front of the body. The release was a little too soon in this photo. Photo 2 shows the method of spotting for a tip-off dismount from an upper arm stand. The two photos at bottom illustrate two similar methods of spotting a stutz. The first performer has just completed the stutz to a horizontal position. The second gymnast is in the process of learning a stutz to a handstand. The spotter has just caught him a few degrees short of the hand balance. Notice that the spotter is standing on a specially constructed table. This table can be raised by adding sections.

Fig. 8–35. Swing to Handstand.

legs approach the vertical position, the shoulders move back over the point of support. A strong forward pushing action with the hands will aid in the completion of the handstand (4). Remember that all balances should be done with a stretched body without too much arch. The line through the arms and upper body should be almost straight. This balance is HELD for at least two seconds.

TEACHING TECHNIQUES. A swing to handstand should not be attempted until the learner is reasonably proficient at kicking to, and holding, a handstand on the floor or floor parallels. The stunt is learned at the end of the low bars, facing away from the equipment, by swinging back and forth several times in a support position before attempting the handstand. If the performer swings beyond the balance, he can release one hand and twist off to a safe landing on his feet. At this stage straight arms should be emphasized. Bending the arms makes the stunt easier but it is a bad habit and difficult to break once started.

SPOTTING. The spotter stands beside the end of the low bars during the learning process and lifts under the abdomen with one hand and supports the performer's upper arm with his other hand. The shift of the shoulders forward and then backward over the hands can be partially controlled with this second hand. If the performer swings back down, the spotter aids him in maintaining balance in the support position or, if he twists off, the spotter aids him in landing safely on his feet. Another method of spotting, when the swing to a handstand is tried in the center of the bars, is to have a spotter stand in a straddle position with one foot on each bar in front of the performer. The spotter grasps the back of the performer's legs as he approaches the balance.

11. Under-Bar Cast (Fig. 8–36). To get into position for the under-bar cast the gymnast lowers down from the handstand to the support in much the same manner as he swung to the handstand. The shoulders are allowed to shift well forward as the legs start downward (1) to the support position. The under-bar cast starts just after the vertical support is reached (2) by falling backward between the bars. The arms stay straight and the legs are raised to a pike position (3). At the bottom of the swing the legs fold in to the chest in a tight inverted pike (4). As the upswing starts the body is extended rapidly with the legs being thrust upward and forward (5). At this time the hands pull hard on the bars, then release so that the arms can be shifted through the bars

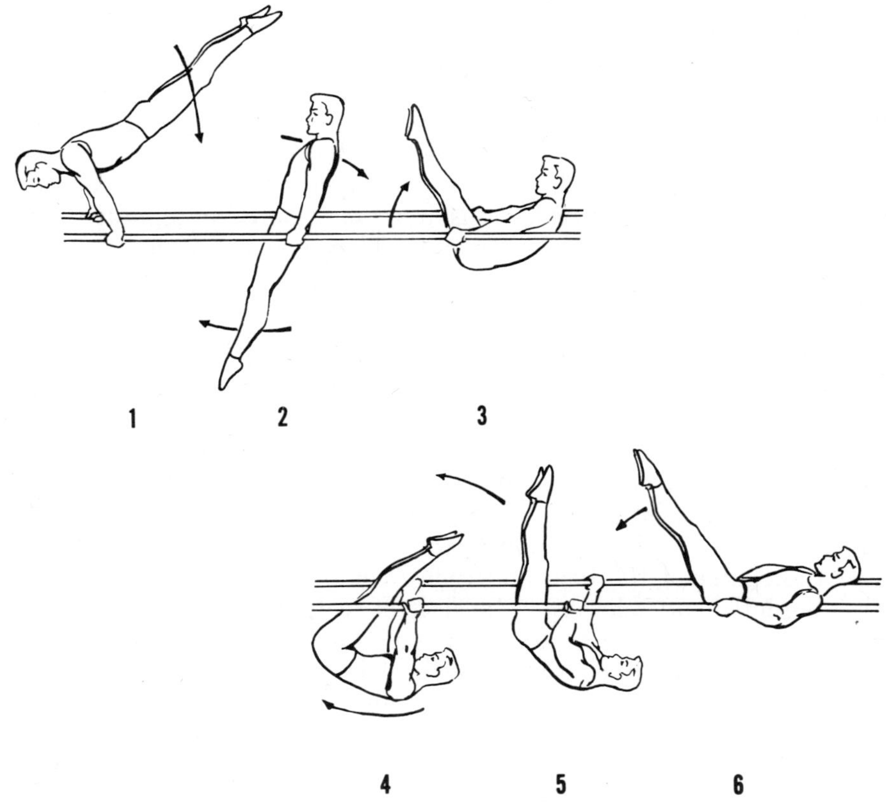

Fig. 8–36. Under-Bar Cast.

to the upper arm hang position. The hips and legs should still be above the bars as the gymnast attains this arm position (6). If the cast is well executed, there will be a good backward swing in the upper arm hang.

TEACHING TECHNIQUES. The cast is learned from a stand between the bars by jumping upward and raising the legs from the standing position to the inverted pike. Except for this start the cast is executed in the same way as described in the routine.

SPOTTING. During the learning process while the stunt is being learned from a stand the spotter stands beside the gymnast and, as he swings forward in the inverted pike, lifts under the lower back with one hand and the upper back with the other. When the stunt is first tried from a support position above the bars, the spotter should reach up between the bars and support weight as soon as possible because there is danger that the hands will peel off the bars as the performer falls backward into the pike position.

12. Back Uprise. After an under-bar cast the gymnast should get a good backward swing in the upper arm hang position. A good swing will enable a high back uprise to be executed as described in Routine I, pages 321–22. In a back uprise that precedes a double rear dismount it is necessary to pull hard with the arms as well as to press down on the bars so as to develop forward as well as upward movement. Because of this it is very hard to separate the uprise and the double rear dismount. They become a single stunt rather than two stunts that are combined. Refer to Fig. 8–37, page 349.

13. Double Rear Dismount (Fig. 8–37). As the legs swing above the height of the bars in the back uprise, the weight starts to shift over the left arm (or right), the body starts to pike, and the legs start to point out toward the right so that they can swing over the right bar (1). As the legs swing forward over the right bar the right arm thrusts off and the weight is shifted still farther over the left arm (2). The legs remain in the pike position and swing back over the center of the bars and then over the left bar. About this time the left hand releases. The shift of weight to the left and the thrust with the right arm, together with the momentum developed by the leg swing, will cause the performer to carry over the left bar (3) and drop to a landing with the right side of the body toward the bars in a cross stand right (4). The right hand grasps the left bar shortly after the legs have passed over and can be used to aid in attaining a balanced landing.

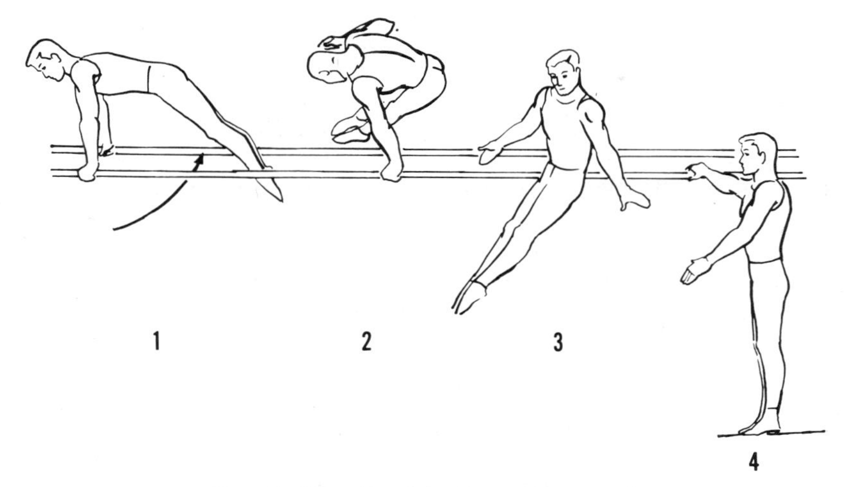

Fig. 8–37. Double Rear Dismount.

Teaching Techniques. This stunt is learned on low bars from a support swing rather than following a back uprise. The single rear vault, of course, is a prerequisite. The next step is to swing the legs over the right bar at the back end of the support swing and then back in between the bars as they swing forward. The right hand releases and then recatches the right bar as the legs swing back to the center of the bars so that the stunt is completed in a support. The next step is to move to the end of the bars facing out. The gymnast can progress gradually toward a double rear dismount first from a support position and later from a back uprise without danger of hitting against the bars during the learning process. When it appears that he could clear the bar, if there were one there, a test can be made by holding a broom handle where the bar should be. If the legs or buttocks do hit the broom handle, it can be dropped quickly so that it does not interfere with the completion of the stunt to the feet. When the broom handle can be cleared consistently, the double rear vault can be tried in the center of the bars with the left bar padded in case it is not cleared.

Spotting. As the stunt is learned on low bars, the spotter stands on the left side of the bars slightly behind the performer's left arm with his left hand on the performer's upper arm. This hand is used to control the lean to the left and to pull the performer over the bar as it is released. The right hand reaches across the top of the bar and is placed under the buttocks as the legs start to swing over the right bar. This hand can actually help lift the legs and buttocks over the bars. The spotter must be very careful not to get his arm caught between the performer and the bar.

IV. LOW ADVANCED ROUTINE

1. Double Rear Mount (Fig. 8–38). This routine starts with a stand facing the side of the bars with one hand in an undergrip and the other in an overgrip (side stand frontways). The reuther board is usually used for this mount (1). The first part of the stunt is a jump to a straight arm support, although the movement does not

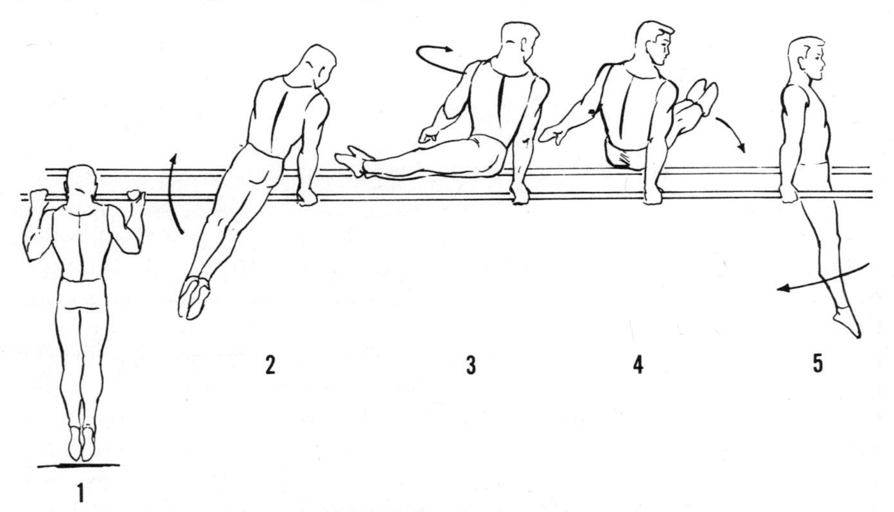

Fig. 8–38. Double Rear Mount.

stop here. The arms help by first pulling, then pressing down. Immediately after the jump the weight shifts toward the hand with an undergrip, the hips start raising backward, the legs are lifted in a pike in the opposite direction of the weight shift, and the head and upper body start to turn toward the hand with the undergrip (2). In this explanation the turn will be to the right. As the straight arm support is reached, the legs should be in almost a right angle pike position. The left hand then pulls the legs toward the bars, thrusts downward, and then releases (3). The head and shoulders continue to look and twist to the right and the movement is completed by pivoting on the right arm with the legs passing over first the near bar and then the far bar (4) until they can be swung down between the bars. The mount finishes in a straight arm support (5) with the left hand grasping the far bar after the legs have passed over it. During the pivot on the right arm the hips should be kept close to the arm giving the appearance that the performer is sitting on his right hand.

TEACHING TECHNIQUES. This mount is taught on low bars and then the bars are gradually raised until it can be performed at regulation height. The stunt can be practiced, except for the regrasp, with the far bar removed so that there is no danger of hitting the legs against it. The far bar, if left in position, can be padded to eliminate painful contact with it. The same mount can be practiced on the side horse as the techniques involved are the same.

SPOTTING. During the learning process on lowered bars the spotter stands behind and slightly to the right of the performer. He grasps high on the support arm with his right hand and the back of the shorts, or belt, of the performer with his left hand. The right hand controls the shift of weight and the balance during the mount while the left hand lifts and aids in the pivot by pushing in the right direction. The left hand can be used in a slightly different way by grasping under the back of the performer's left thigh. In this position it can lift, aid in the pivot, and also aid in keeping the legs in the pike position. As it reaches across the top of the bars, however, there is danger of getting it caught between the bars and the performer. The first photo on page 352 illustrates this spotting technique.

2. Moore to Half-Lever (Fig. 8–39). The double rear mount is completed with the body swinging backward in a support. It will take considerable practice to complete the double rear mount with enough swing to be able to proceed into the moore. As the legs pass the vertical position, the hips start to raise (1). As the feet reach the height of the bar on the back swing, the hips are high in the air with the body in a definite pike. The head and shoulders twist to the left (2). (Because the mount was executed with a

Fig. 8–39. Moore to Half-Lever.

The first photo illustrates spotting for a double rear mount. Photo 2 shows two spotters assisting during a front somersault dismount. One is pulling and one has just pushed on the shoulder. Both are using only one hand. It is recommended that spotters use two hands, as explained in the text, until they gain experience. The last two photos illustrate spotting for a peach basket. One demonstrates the starting position, the other the completion of the assist. The speed of the upper body upward between the bars is made apparent in the last photo by the blurred condition of the head and trunk. The performer's feet should not be apart. This is an example of poor leg form.

HUS
HUSKI

right turn, many performers will also want to use a right turn for the moore.) The left hand thrusts off the left bar pushing the hips and feet over the right bar and then grasps the right bar in an undergrip close to the right hand (3). At this point the body is in approximately a right angle pike with the weight partially shifted over the bar, but the center of gravity should still remain between the bars so that the performer feels he is going to fall forward. The turning movement should continue smoothly as the right hand releases and reaches for the far bar. As the feet pass over the right bar for the second time, the pike is opened (4) and the right hand grasps the far bar so that the gymnast has completed a half-turn and is in a support position swinging forward (5). As the vertical position is reached, the legs are raised forward to a half-lever (6). This "L" position is HELD for at least two seconds.

TEACHING TECHNIQUES. The moore is learned on low parallel bars. At first it can be practiced at the end of the bars facing out so that the legs do not have to clear the bar as they come back between the bars. Next it is practiced about a foot from the end of the bars facing in. In this lead-up the legs do not have to clear the bar during the first quarter-turn but must clear during the second half of the moore. The third step is to practice in the center of the bars with the bar that is used during the turn padded in front of the hand.

SPOTTING. One method of spotting is to use a single rope from an overhead spotting rig attached to a belt at the center of the performer's back. On the low bars a spotter can hand spot from a position close to the left bar, if the moore is to be executed over the right bar, by reaching across the top of the bar to grasp the upper arms of the performer. The spotter can control the shift of weight in this way and aid by supporting weight as the legs return to the center of the bars. The main task of the spotter, and this is easy to accomplish, is to prevent the performer from falling forward and hitting his face against the far bar as the moore is executed. If the performer falls backward, there is little danger, as he will drop to the mat on his feet.

3. Press a Handstand with Straight Arms and Straight Legs (Fig. 8–40). This straight arm press is so similar to the bent arm press included in Routine III, page 339, that little explanation will be given here. The shoulders must lean well forward over the hands as the press starts (1) (2) and then gradually shift back over the point of support as the handstand is completed (3). The balance should be HELD for at least two seconds.

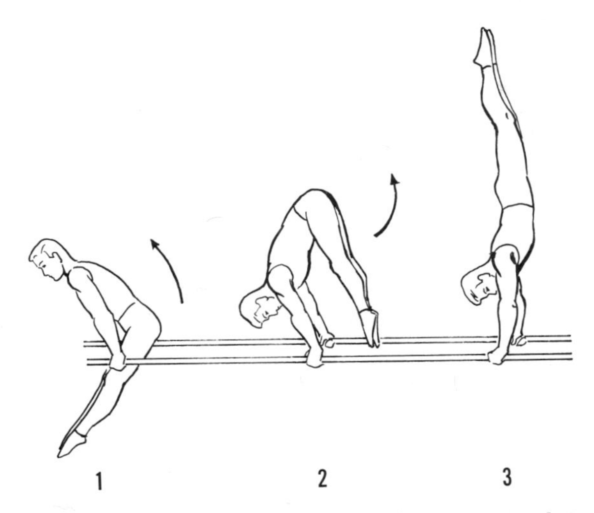

Fig. 8–40. Press a Handstand With Straight Arms and Straight Legs.

TEACHING TECHNIQUES. Teaching techniques are the same as were listed for the bent arm press. Although this is classified as a strength move, flexibility will certainly aid in the execution. A flexible person will be able to shift the shoulders farther forward before the arms are forced to bend. A flexible person will also be able to pike tighter during the first part of the press and thus make it much easier to raise the center of gravity over the point of support. An important technique, therefore, is to work on flexibility because as flexibility increases the difficulty of the stunt decreases.

4. Forward Half-Pirouette (Fig. 8–41). In the handstand position the weight is shifted largely, but not completely, to one arm (in

Fig. 8–41. Forward Half-Pirouette.

this routine it will be the left arm) and the body is turned to the left (1). The turning movement continues with a quick but slight thrust off the right hand as it shifts to the left bar close to the left hand. At this time a quarter-turn has been completed, but the performer is not in a handstand position on one bar as the center of gravity was not completely shifted over the bar (2). The turning movement continues with the left hand shifting quickly to the far bar to complete the 180° turn to a handstand facing the other direction (3). As the handstand was held prior to the start of the pirouette, it should be held only momentarily after the turn before swinging down between the bars for the next stunt.

TEACHING TECHNIQUES. The prerequisite for the handstand pirouette is a well-controlled handstand in a stretched position with little arch. Performers who hold a handstand with considerable arch will find a pirouette quite difficult. The stunt is first practiced on the floor parallels, then the low parallels, before being tried on the bars of regulation height. There are no real teaching techniques other than this progression from low to high bars. Three common mistakes are: The weight is shifted completely over one bar, the right hand is placed too far from the left hand, and the pirouette is done slowly in parts rather than as one continuous movement. The first two mistakes help to bring about the third one.

SPOTTING. Spotting is not necessary if the progression from floor bars to low bars to high bars is followed. A gymnast who has a well-controlled handstand will find it easy to twist off and land on his feet if the pirouette is missed as it is learned on the floor bars.

5. Stutz (Fig. 8–42). Immediately following the pirouette the body is allowed to swing downward from the handstand to the support position. The first part of this movement should be slowed down so that the stutz can be more readily controlled. The shoulders are shifted forward and the bars are gripped tightly to control the speed of the downswing (1). During the last half of the downswing the speed is allowed to increase so that it will aid in the execution of a high stutz. This stutz is executed in the same manner as described in Routine III, pages 342–43, except that the forward swing should be allowed to progress higher before the hip lift and turn (2) (3) (4) (5).

TEACHING TECHNIQUES. The execution of a high stutz requires considerable freedom of movement in the shoulder girdle. The flexibility exercise described on page 314 is important to practice as

Fig. 8–42. Stutz.

the high stutz is being learned. The other teaching techniques are the same as previously presented on page 343.

SPOTTING. As the performer tries to go higher and higher in the stutz a spotter can aid in the learning process by standing on a table beside the bars and lifting under the hips or thighs to bring about a high turn. Refer to the last photo on page 345.

6. Under-Bar Cast. After the stutz the gymnast swings forward in a support position and executes the under-bar cast as described in Routine III. Refer to Fig. 8–36.

7. Back Uprise, Straddle Cut and Catch to Layback (Fig. 8–43). Although these are three different stunts, they are impossible to separate in this routine as they are all part of the same movement. The back uprise is much like the one that preceded the double rear dismount in Routine III. As the previous stunt, the under-bar cast, is completed, the gymnast swings backward in an upper arm hang (1). A slight pike is maintained during much of the back swing and then from this position the heels whip upward as the arms press down on the bars (2) (3). This technique will result in a high

Fig. 8–43. Back Uprise, Straddle Cut and Catch to Layback.

uprise. After the feet have swung above the height of the bars the hips life upward, the legs start to straddle, the arms give a vigorous thrust upward, and the legs straddle forward above the bars (4). The hands release the bars (5) and then recatch behind the legs as the legs complete their forward movement and are joined together in front of the body. As the bars are caught the legs should be stretched forward and even the hips should be in front of the hands. During the backward swing the arms are allowed to bend so that the swing is in a bent arm support (6). Toward the back end of the swing the arms are partially straightened as they push backward for the layback as described in Routine II, pages 331–32 (7) (8).

Teaching Techniques. During the learning process of this stunt the gymnast should wear long pants and/or the bars should be padded to minimize bar burns and bruises. As most of the lead-ups are done from a support position rather than a back uprise the low bars can be used a great deal. There are many lead-ups that can be used. The number selected from the following list depends on the skill of the learner.

1. Single leg cut and catch from a support swing using first the right leg then the left leg.
2. Straddle cut-off dismount from a support swing on the end of the bars facing away from the equipment.
3. Straddle cut-on mount from a jump facing the end of the bars to a support.
4. Straddle cut and catch from a support swing on the end of the bars facing the equipment.
5. Straddle cut from a support swing to a straddle seat in the center of the bars. Gradually progress from this to the complete cut and catch.

Although it is just as hard to do the straddle cut and catch from a support as from a back uprise, this method enables the learner to concentrate on the cut and catch during the learning process. All of the above steps, except the straddle cut-on mount, can be used following a back uprise.

SPOTTING. This is a difficult stunt to spot and fortunately one that is not really necessary to spot when it is tried in its entirety. The lead-ups on the end of the bar facing away from the equipment should be spotted in front in case the performer catches his legs and falls forward. The lead-ups on the end of the bar facing toward the equipment should be spotted behind in case the gymnast falls backward. Some teachers use a single rope from an overhead spotting rig attached to a belt in the center of the performer's back to support weight as this stunt is learned. This method aids at the start of the stunt but interferes with its proper completion.

8. Backward Shoulder Roll to Support. The previous stunt, the straddle cut and catch, is completed with a layback to an upper arm hang. The gymnast swings forward in the upper arm hang and executes a backward shoulder roll to support as described in Routine II, pages 324–26. This backward roll, however, is completed in the same way as the one in Routine III, Fig. 8–34, with a forward swing in a support.

9. Rear Vault over One Bar to Catch, Glide Kip, Front Vault to Layback (Fig. 8–44). In the United States one seldom sees stunts that are performed over the side of the bars but in some foreign countries this type of work is done more often. Gymnasts could very well use more of these unusual moves when they compose their own

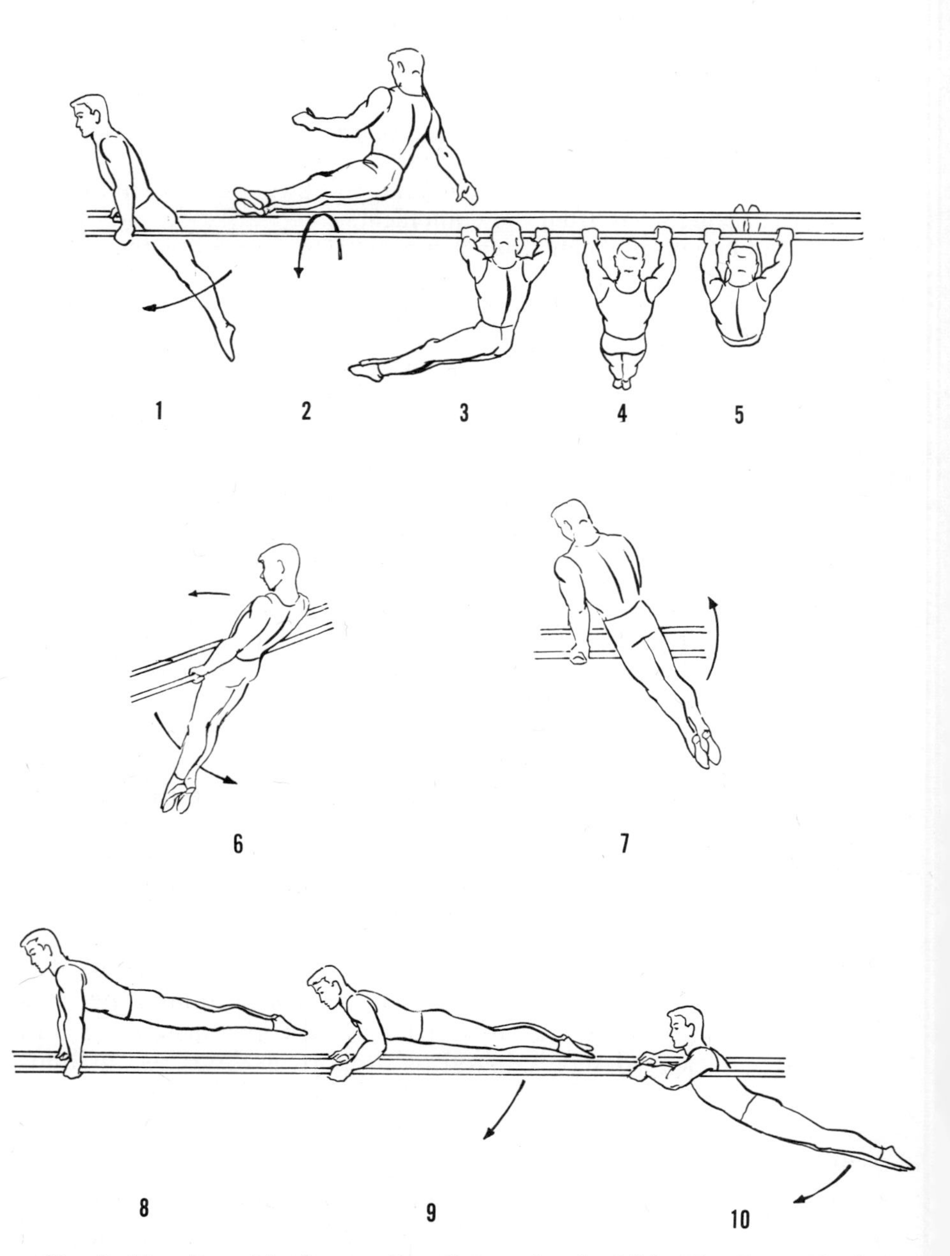

Fig. 8–44. Rear Vault over One Bar to Catch, Glide Kip, Front Vault to Layback.

optional exercises. As the backward roll is completed, the gymnast swings forward in a support position (1). On the front end of the swing the legs are raised in a pike and swung over the left bar (or right). Both arms thrust off the bars and release. The gymnast passes over the bar as in a simple rear vault dismount (2) but, as the bar is cleared, the head and upper body turn back toward the bar and the bar is grasped in an overgrip with the arms straight (3). From this position the feet glide forward close to the floor and the body is extended (4) just as in a regular glide kip, which was used as the mount in Routine III, pages 336–37. As the backward swing starts, the legs are raised in a pike so that the ankles almost touch the far bar (5). This is not a good position for the start of the kipping motion as the far bar prevents the gymnast from raising the legs to the correct position. Because of this the kip is a difficult one to execute. Toward the back end of the swing the body is rapidly extended from the pike position, the hips are raised close to the bar, and the arms press down hard on the bar (6) just as in a kip on the horizontal bar. Considerable strength is required to hold the body close to the bar and complete this kip to a front support. As the kip is completed, the upper body leans forward over the bar and to the left. The legs are swung backward, upward, and to the right so that a quarter-turn is executed as the body swings up to a free front support (7). Both hands thrust downward on the bar and release. The left hand is replaced in the same spot but with the fingers on the outside instead of the inside of the bar. The right hand is shifted to the far bar (8). Immediately upon catching in the support, while the legs are still above the bar, the hands push forward on the bars so that the shoulders are moved backward behind the point of support (9). The gymnast drops to his upper arms on the bars with the arms almost straight and swings forward in an upper arm hang (10). This movement from the support position to the upper arm hang is nothing more than a layback, which was first described in Routine II.

Teaching Techniques. Each of the three stunts in this series should be practiced separately. The rear vault to catch is practiced at first with the feet dropping to the floor as the bar is recaught. The glide kip is practiced from a stand with the hands already grasping the bar, as was done in the mount in Routine III. The front vault is practiced from an outer front support by whipping the legs under the bar, then backward and upward for the vault.

SPOTTING. The spotter stands slightly behind the performer as he rear vaults over the bar and reaches under his upper back with the left arm as the bar is recaught. As the kip is executed, this hand stays in the same position and the right hand assists under the thighs. For the front vault the spotter must shift to the performer's left side. The left hand grasps the performer's left upper arm and the right hand lifts under his left hip.

10. Front Uprise. On the front end of the forward swing that follows the layback a front uprise is executed as described in Routine II, pages 332–33. This front uprise must be a high one so that the swing to handstand can be accomplished.

11. Swing to Handstand, Quarter-Pirouette to Straddle Cut-Off Dismount (Fig. 8–45). The best way to finish this routine is to make the swing to handstand, pirouette, and cut-off all one continuous movement; however, they may be done as three separate stunts. The swing to handstand is the same as in Routine III, page 344 (1) (2) except that the pirouette starts slightly before the handstand is reached by shifting the weight to the left arm (or right) and turning the head and shoulders to the left (3). The right arm thrusts off the right bar and regrasps the left bar about 1 foot from the left hand (4). Without pausing in the handstand on one bar the shoulders are allowed to shift forward of the point of support. At this time there is a thrust upward and outward off the bar with a rapid shoulder extension as the legs straddle and pike (5). In the air the head and chest are raised and the body stretched in an arch if possible (6) before the landing with the back to the bars in a side stand rearways (7).

TEACHING TECHNIQUES. As teaching techniques for the swing to handstand and pirouette have already been given, only those for the straddle cut-off will be included here. Two lead-up stunts, the straddle cut-off on the end of the bars, where the feet are less likely to get caught, and the squat dismount off the side of the bars should be tried first. Both of these lead-ups and the straddle cut-off itself should be tried on the low parallels where the spotter can assist more effectively during the learning process.

SPOTTING. As this stunt is learned on the low bars, the spotter stands directly in front of one of the performer's shoulders and grasps his upper arm with both hands. The spotter assists in attaining the initial shoulder lean and then steps back quickly and pulls the performer clear of the bar. The spotter also helps lift the

1 2 3 4

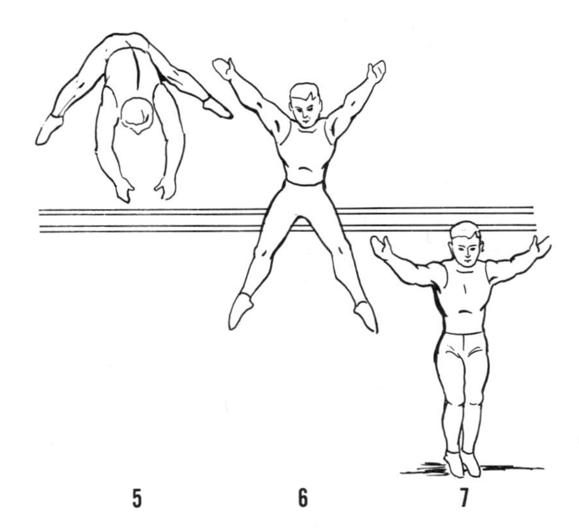

Fig. 8–45. Swing to Handstand, Quarter-Pirouette to Straddle Cut-Off Dismount.

upper body so that the performer can get his feet down in time for the landing. The grasp is maintained on the upper arm to ensure a safe landing.

V. ADVANCED ROUTINE

1. Peach Basket to Half-Lever (Fig. 8–46). The peach basket is also called an under-bar somersault. In this routine it is used as a mount, starting from a stand between the bars with the arms straight and the hands on the inside of the bars (1). It is possible to use an outer grip when the peach basket is used as a mount but not when it is used during a routine. The first movement is a jump straight upward so that the shoulders are above the bars. The legs start to raise forward in a pike at this time (2). As the shoulders drop downward between the bars, the legs are raised above the face and the pike is increased. The gymnast swings forward under the bar in an inverted pike (3). As the arms pass the vertical position and the upswing starts, the body is extended rapidly. The hips should be kept high and the feet should not be permitted to drop below the bars (4). The arms pull hard during the body extension (5) and then as the straight body position is reached the head and chest lift upward between the bars and the hands release and move rapidly forward and upward between the bars to grasp in a straight arm support (6) (7). The legs swing forward and are then raised to a half-lever position, which is HELD for at least two seconds (8) (9).

TEACHING TECHNIQUES. The first step is to get the "feel" of the basket by circling through the inverted pike and dropping to the feet between the bars. The back kip as done on the rings, horizontal bar, or end of the parallel bars should be learned before the peach basket. The techniques for these stunts are the same except that the hands do not have to release the equipment. On the parallel bars the performer stands between the end of the bars facing away from the equipment with the grip on the outside. The grip rolls around the end of the bars as the kip is executed. Except for this the techniques are identical to the peach basket. The next step is to try the basket to an upper arm hang rather than a support. This is the same stunt except that not as much height is needed to complete it. Two common mistakes are: an overcircling in the inverted pike resulting in the feet being below the bars, and releasing the bars too soon, which results in a low-traveling basket. This second mistake makes it almost impossible to get enough height to catch in a support position.

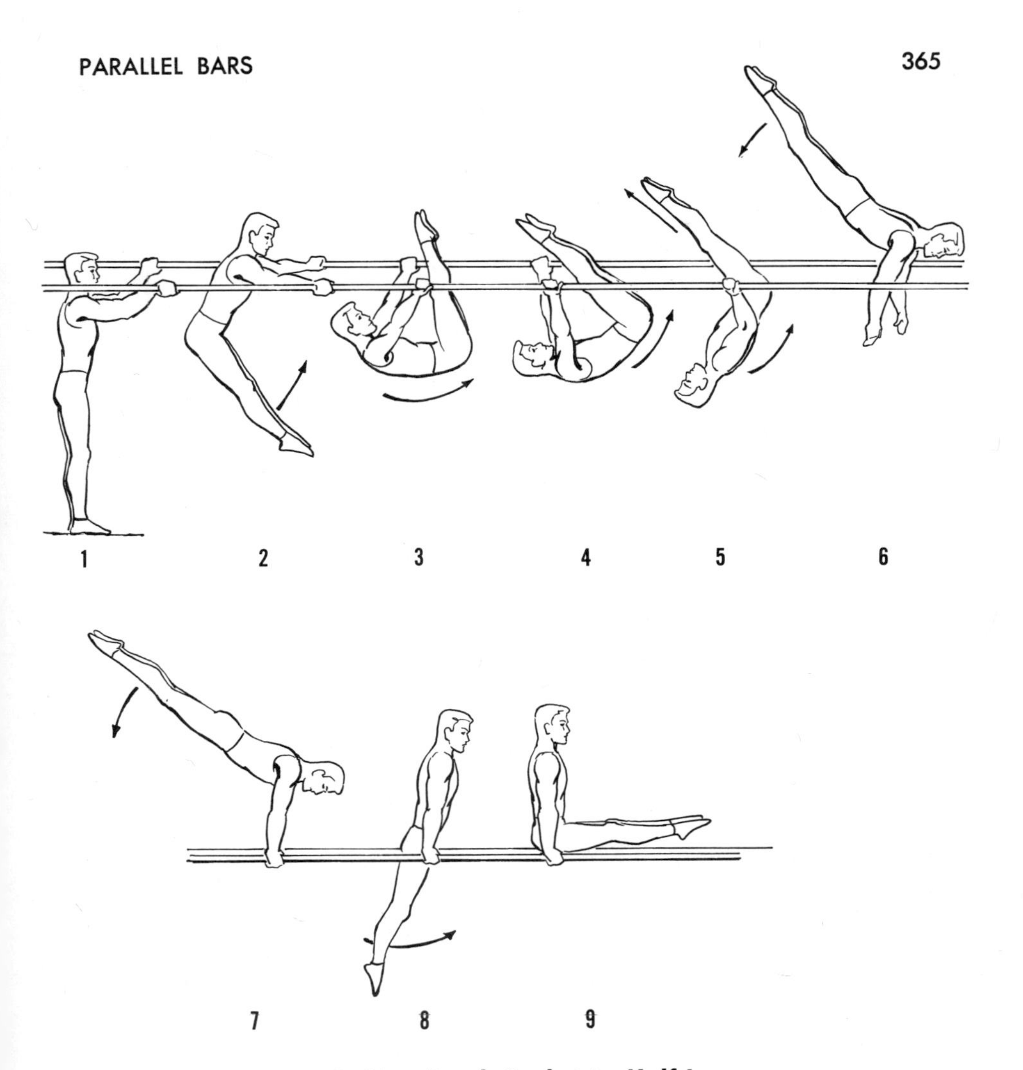

Fig. 8–46. Peach Basket to Half-Lever.

SPOTTING. The spotter stands on the performer's left side and reaches under the bar and over the performer's shoulder with his right hand. The hand reaches down as far as possible so that it is on the chest or even the upper abdomen. As the performer circles in the inverted pike, the spotter's hand should be under his abdomen to lift him up between the bars. The two photos on page 353 illustrate the spotting for a peach basket. The spotter's left hand is free to reach quickly under the gymnast's chest in case the bars are released too soon. The basket can also be spotted by using a belt suspended from an overhead safety rig. The ropes come down between the bars in front of the performer.

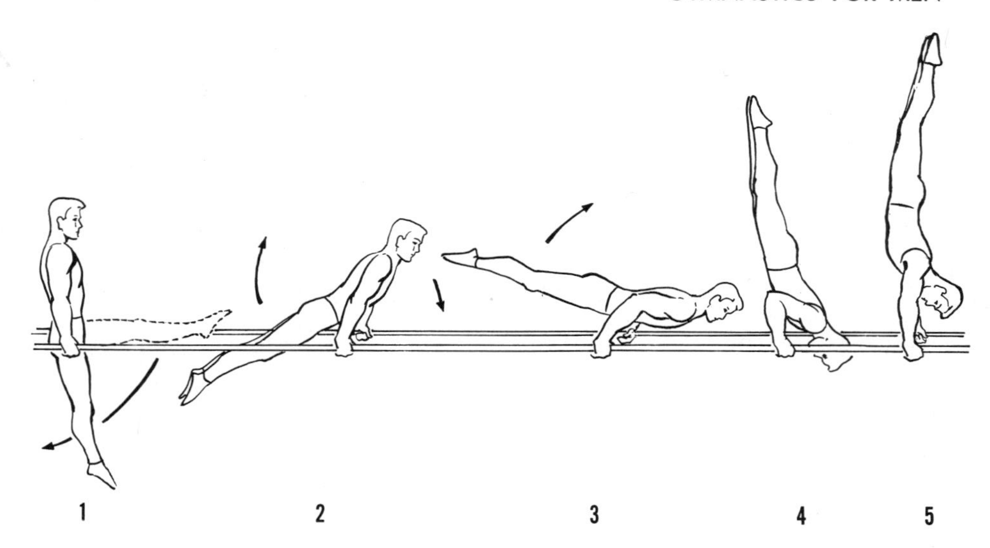

Fig. 8–47. Straight Body Bent Arm Press to Handstand.

2. Straight Body Bent Arm Press to Handstand (Fig. 8–47). The press is started from a half-lever by lowering the legs to the vertical support (1). As they continue backward and upward the head and upper body are leaned forward, the arms are bent, and the back is arched (2) (3). If the head and upper body are moved well in front of the point of support, the center of gravity will be only slightly behind the hands and the press will be easier. This is a strength stunt, however, in which skill can never be completely substituted for strength. As the legs approach the vertical position, the bend in the arms has to be first increased and then gradually straightened (4) until the handstand is reached (5). This balance is HELD for at least two seconds.

TEACHING TECHNIQUES. This press can be practiced from a chest rock on the floor. The rocking motion helps in getting the press started and makes it somewhat easier. Several techniques can be used on the bars to make the press easier as it is learned. Lowering the legs rapidly from the half-lever or moving the hips slightly in front of the hands as the legs are lowered will also create a slight backward swing that will facilitate the press. Neither of these two techniques of "cheating" in the press should be used in competition but might be used as learning techniques.

SPOTTING. Spotting is not necessary from a safety standpoint if proper progression has been followed. If the press is practiced on low bars, a spotter can aid by lifting under the abdomen with one hand and the shoulder with the other. This type of assist may speed up the learning process.

3. Back Over-Bar Somersault (Fig. 8–48). This stunt is also called a back toss and is a very spectacular stunt if executed well. It starts with a good stretch upward in a handstand. The first part of the downswing should be slowed down somewhat (1) but the later part should be free and relaxed (2). As the upswing starts, the toes are allowed to get ahead of the hips so that the body is in a definite pike. The head should be in a normal position. The arms

Fig. 8–48. Back Over-Bar Somersault.

push the weight forward to make sure that the shoulders stay approximately over the hands (3). A common mistake is to allow the shoulders to lean too far backward at this time. The swing should carry above the horizontal in the pike (4) and then the hips are thrust upward, the head drops backward, and the back is arched (5). Rather than thinking about releasing the bars, the gymnast should wait until the hip thrust lifts the hands off the bars. As the hands are lifted off the bars, they circle quickly (6) and recatch as soon as possible while the body is still in almost a handstand position (7). Following the recatch the legs swing downward and forward in the support position.

TEACHING TECHNIQUES. The back over-bar somersault should be learned on low parallels so that the feet will land on the mat between the bars before the upper arms can contact the rails if the recatch is missed. If the bars will not adjust to a low height, place several folded mats between them. This will give the same effect as lowering the bars several more inches. During practice the gymnast should not attempt to swing or press to a handstand each time but should stand on the bars and kick to the balance. This conserves energy for the practice of the stunt itself. Another good technique is to practice occasionally from a support swing rather than from a handstand. This reduces the speed of the swing and makes it easier to keep the shoulders in the correct position. It also enables the gymnast to concentrate on the lift and forces him to lift hard because there is less speed.

SPOTTING. Two common methods of spotting are used. Some coaches insist on hand spotting, some on belt spotting. If hand spotting is used there should be a spotter on both sides of the bar. They stand beside the performer and grasp his upper arm in a mixed grip with the top hand in a regular hold and the bottom hand in a reverse hold. As the stunt is executed, the spotters maintain their grasp from start to finish. Hand spotting interferes with the performer's arm movement, but in spite of this it is a good method to use. An overhead spotting rig is also used very successfully to spot this stunt. In the support position the ropes are in front of the performer. In the handstand position they run from the belt downward over the chest and then under the shoulders and up to the ceiling behind the performer. The spotter should be careful not to pull while the performer is in the handstand or during the downward swing.

4. Stutz to Layback. As the back somersault is completed the performer swings forward in a support position and executes the

University of Washington News Service photo

Mike Lovell Just Completing a Front Somersault Dismount off the Parallel Bars. Notice his hand is just ready to regrasp the bar as he drops to the mat. Mike has placed in N.C.A.A. competition in several events and is rapidly developing into one of the best all-round men in the country.

stutz to layback as described in Routine III (Fig. 8–33), except that the stutz for an advanced performer should be much higher.

5. Front Uprise. The gymnast swings forward in an upper arm hang after the layback. The uprise is performed as explained in Routine II (Fig. 8–23). This uprise should be an extremely high one as the next stunt requires considerable swing that can be obtained only from a high uprise.

Fig. 8–49. Swinging Half-Pirouette.

6. Swinging Half-Pirouette (Fig. 8–49). This stunt is very similar to the handstand pirouette in Routine IV except that the turn starts slightly before the balance position has been attained. Following the front uprise the performer swings backward in a support (1). The upward swing is the same as for a handstand (2) except that it should be harder and faster. About 30° before the vertical is reached the shift of weight and turn toward the left (or right) are started (3). About 10° before the vertical the right hand pushes off the right bar (4) and shifts to the left bar (5). Although most of the weight was shifted to the left hand before the right hand was changed, the center of gravity should remain between the bars during the whole stunt. The swinging pirouette should be a continuous stunt that goes "through" the handstand not "to" the vertical position. Immediately as the right hand contacts the left bar, the left hand thrusts off and reaches for the right bar (6). During the shift of the left hand the 180° turn is completed and the legs pass beyond the vertical position to start their downward swing (7).

TEACHING TECHNIQUES. Be sure that this stunt comes after the regular handstand pirouette in the stunt progression. The second step in learning the swinging pirouette is to kick to a handstand toward the end of the floor parallel bars, execute the pirouette, and then drop to the feet off the end of the bars. The next step is to try the pirouette on the end of the low bars facing out. If it is missed it is relatively easy to drop to the feet off the end of the bars without danger of hitting them. The final step is to practice in the center of the low bars with the bars padded for protection.

7. Under-Bar Cast. As the swinging half pirouette is completed, the gymnast swings down to a support position and performs the under-bar cast as described in Routine III (Fig. 8–36).

8. Back Uprise, Straddle Cut and Catch, and Swing to a Handstand. Most of this stunt is the same as one included in Routine IV (Fig. 8–43). In Routine IV the straddle cut and catch is followed by a layback, but in this routine the legs are swung higher and instead of pushing backward to an upper arm hang the arms are straightened to a handstand.

9. Stutz to Layback. This stunt was first included in Routine III (Fig. 8–33), and has been included several times since. The stutz, along with the front and back uprise, and the under-bar cast are stunts that are often repeated in parallel bar work.

10. Front Uprise. Refer to Routine II (Fig. 8–23) for the front uprise.

Fig. 8–50. Front Somersault Dismount.

11. Front Somersault Dismount (Fig. 8–50). The gymnast should raise as high as possible on the front uprise to bring about a good back swing. As the body swings backward past the vertical, the hips are allowed to lead in a slight pike (1). As the upswing starts, the legs whip backward into an arch (2). This motion is important in giving "lift" or height to the dismount. The hips are then raised quickly upward in a pike (3). As the hips get almost over the shoulders, the hands thrust off hard, upward and to the side, and the head and shoulders tuck under the hips (4). After the release the body is in a tight pike position in the air (5). As the gymnast drops to the mat, the pike is opened and the hand toward the bar grasps (6) to give stability to the landing in a cross stand (7). A photo of the completion of a front somersault dismount can be found on page 369.

TEACHING TECHNIQUES. The front somersault from a support swing to an upper arm hang between the bars is often used as the first step in the teaching progression. This step is tried on bars of regular height. Usually the bars are lowered, however, and the first step used is a somersault from a support swing to a stand between the bars (with spotters assisting). The feet will contact the floor before the upper arms can contact the top rails if the bars are low enough. This technique can be practiced until the bars can be caught in a support so that the somersault not only starts in a support but also finishes in one. When the somersault is first tried as a dismount, the bar should be padded with a mat. Some teachers have the learner bend his arms, place his shoulder on this mat, and roll over the bar on the first few attempts to gain confidence in moving to the side. As this step is not necessary and may teach bad habits, it should be used sparingly. The front somersault is never tried following a front uprise until it can be performed well from a support swing.

SPOTTING. Spotting is a vital part of the teaching techniques for this stunt as it is for so many gymnastic skills. Except for the somersault to the upper arm hang the spotters work with the gymnast in all phases of the learning process. A spotter on both sides of the bar grasp the upper arm in a "turning grip." This turning grip is a combined and crossed grasp with the upper hand in the reverse grip and the lower hand in a regular grip. During practice to a stand between the bars or to a recatch both spotters help the gymnast during the entire stunt and retain their grip at the finish to make sure balance is maintained. When the somersault is used as a dismount, the spotter on the dismount side pulls as well as turning. The spotter on the other side pushes the performer sideways and then releases his grasp as the stunt is completed. This technique is shown in the photo on page 352.

9

Side Horse

The side horse is usually referred to as the pommel horse in most foreign countries. It is a difficult event, probably the most difficult, although it is very hard to compare gymnastic events because they are so different in nature. Gymnasts generally agree that it takes longer and more dedicated practice to become proficient on the side horse than in the other events. Many beginners dislike the event, but it has a definite attraction for others, probably because it is such a challenge. It develops into the favorite event for a great many experienced gymnasts and is one in which many individuals decide to specialize.

Side horse work tends to develop wiry muscles and muscular endurance rather than large muscles with explosive power. Because the event does not take great strength, boys with long, thin body builds who find it difficult to succeed in some of the other events do quite well on the side horse. Also, because it does not call for movements of maximum effort and is not particularly hard on the hands, gymnasts can work longer on the side horse than in most of the other events. The side horse develops strong wrists and forearms and in this respect has special value. It also develops the qualities of perseverance and determination. Students who learn these things in the gymnasium are likely to carry them over into other activities of life.

Even though the side horse does not take a great amount of strength it is too difficult an event for children. In some of the other gymnastic activities the skills can be modified and adapted to the needs and abilities of individuals who are not yet developed physically. It is difficult to do this on the side horse as all stunts involve a support with very little opportunity to rest weight on the legs or buttocks. Because of this, it is recommended that the side horse not be included in the program until at least junior high school and possibly not until high school. It should be the last event to be presented, after students have had experience on some of the other equipment.

The side horse is a very safe event. The only injuries that are likely to occur are bruises and abrasions on the legs, especially the knees and ankles. These can be painful and are one of the main reasons why some beginners dislike the event. Wearing long pants for side horse practice will prevent some of these minor wounds. Long pants have one other advantage but also a disadvantage. They permit the legs to slide better against the leather of the horse for beginning work but they are often grasped with the pommel as the leg is cut across the top of the pommel. Spotting is not necessary for most side horse work. The reader will notice that it has been omitted for most of the stunts in this chapter.

Many instructors are not able to demonstrate for their classes. This is a handicap but not a serious one as far as the side horse is concerned. There are two common methods of demonstrating leg movements that do not involve performance. One is to use the first and second fingers of one hand to represent the legs and the thumb edge of the other hand to represent the horse. The other technique is to stand by the horse and use the arms to represent the legs. Almost all leg motions can be demonstrated in one of these ways. It is easy, of course, to also show the hand positions and changes while standing on the floor by the horse.

The illustrations in this chapter are shown on the section of the horse on which they are executed and in the direction they actually face during the routine. Wherever possible back views are illustrated. This makes it much easier to actually follow the directions of the leg circles as the right leg appears on the right and the left leg on the left when observed from the back. Unfortunately it is not possible to show all back views because when a 180° turn occurs the performer will change the direction that he faces. In order to keep continuity in the routine, therefore, some illustration must be shown from the front.

All students seem to develop one direction of performing circles that is easier than the other direction. Because of this, some individuals will have to perform the exercises in this chapter in the reverse direction from that described. When it says to start facing the right end, they will start facing the left end. Once started the direction can not be changed without causing a break in continuity. The exercises, therefore, will have to be reversed in their entirety.

EQUIPMENT

The side horse is the same piece of equipment as the long horse but it is not as high and it has pommels added. The official horse used in most countries, as specified by the F. I. G. rules, has four legs. For stability it must be fastened to a floor plate with a chain and turn-buckle that attaches to the center section of the horse. Most of the side horses used in this country have a heavy base with two vertical uprights supporting the top section. This style is more stable and is recommended for school use.

The top section of a side horse is made of wood, padded with felt, and covered with leather. It is important that the top meets official specifications. It should be 63 to 64 inches long and approximately 14 inches across the top. Wooden pommels are used 4¾ inches high. The width between them should be adjustable between 15¾ and 17¾ inches. The height from the top of the pommels to the floor is 48 inches. Other specifications can be obtained from the rule book if needed.

The leather on the side horse should be cleaned and lubricated three or four times a year, or more often if it is used a great deal. Saddle soap can be used to clean it, but a solution of two tablespoons of oxalic acid to one gallon of water does a better job. Neat's-foot oil is the best lubricating substance.

In several chapters directions have been given for constructing the piece of equipment or a substitute for it. A side horse can be made by a reasonably skilled coach or student, but it is a difficult job. Because it is quite unlikely that anyone will want to construct one, space is not devoted to this topic. It is recommended that the side horse be purchased from a regular manufacturer, as it is questionable whether a homemade one will prove satisfactory.

RULES

A side horse exercise should be composed of exclusively swinging movements with no stops. Double leg circles must predominate, but there must be single leg circles and scissors both forward and rearward. One type of scissors must be executed at least twice in succession. All three sections of the horse must be utilized in the performance of the routine.

On the side horse, as with most events, certain requirements of the rules must be omitted for the beginner and intermediate.

PRINCIPLES OF GOOD SIDE HORSE PERFORMANCE

1. The body is kept almost straight in all support positions.
2. The shoulders are depressed in support positions. Another way of expressing this is to say "stay tall" in support positions.
3. The arms are kept rigidly straight in the performance of almost all skills on the side horse.
4. The pommels are gripped tightly.
5. The center of gravity is usually kept between the hands. This means that the weight is not shifted completely to one arm as the other arm releases the pommel or is lifted off the end of the horse.
6. The hands thrust hard off the horse before releasing to let a leg, or both legs, pass between the hand and the horse. This is true of almost all side horse skills.
7. The hips, as well as the legs, should swing in most side horse skills. In single leg work, the noncircling leg should swing as well as the circling leg.
8. Single leg circles and scissors are pendulum-type movements. The legs stay close to the horse in a vertical plane. Double leg circles are true circles with the legs and the hips swinging away from the horse in a horizontal plane.

TERMINOLOGY

Most of the terms listed here are also included in the Glossary on page 461. Terminology is so essential for understanding of side horse work, however, that the more important ones are also presented here so that the reader does not have to search through a long alphabetical list.

Some of the old terms, such as neck, saddle, and croup, have not been used but instead left end, center section, and right end have replaced them. When a 180° turn occurs, the ends are changed so that the left end becomes the right end and vice versa. Clockwise has been used for a circle in which the legs move in the same direction as the hands of a clock. Counterclockwise refers to a leg circle in the other direction. These two terms have replaced the very confusing terms of "left" and "right." Many of the old competitive terms that have been standard throughout the United States for years have been retained in preference to the new ones that were introduced in 1965 from international terminology. At the time of writing there is considerable confusion regarding many of these new terms. Until they are completely accepted, and understood, it seems wise to continue to use the old ones.

1. Supports:
   Front support—A position facing the horse with the weight supported by the hands and with the front of the thighs touching the horse.
   Rear or back support—A position facing away from the horse with the weight supported by the hands and with the back of the thighs touching the horse.
   Straddle support—A position in which the weight is supported by the hands with one leg in front and one leg behind the horse.
2. Types of circles:
   Single leg circle—a circle in which one leg circles around the point of support.
   Double leg circle—a circle in which both legs circle around the point of support.
   Undercut—refers to a single leg circle, either half or full, that starts with one leg going underneath the other leg before passing over the horse.
3. Amount of circle:
   Half—refers to a single or double leg circle that moves only halfway around the point of support.
   Full—refers to a single or double leg circle that moves completely around the point of support.
4. Feints:
   Single feint—refers to a half leg circle that is started but not completed. One leg is swung over the horse, but the hand does not release the pommel as for a regular leg circle.
   Double feint—occurs when the back leg in a straddle support is swung forward over the horse to a feint. Both legs end up straddling one arm in the feint position.

ABBREVIATED ROUTINE DESCRIPTIONS

I. Stand facing the right end of the horse with the right hand on the end and the left hand on the right pommel, jump into a right leg half-circle counterclockwise to a straddle support on the end, simple half leg circle travel to a front support in the center, right leg half-circle counterclockwise, right leg half-circle clockwise, left leg half-circle clockwise, left leg half-circle counterclockwise, right leg half-circle counterclockwise to a straddle support, swing the left leg forward over the horse to a double feint on the left arm, swing the left leg backward over the horse and turn left on the left arm, swing the left leg over the center of the horse and continue to turn left to a front support on the end (the right hand releases the right pommel and shifts to the end of the horse during this movement), thrust off the pommel with the left hand and turn a quarter-turn left to a dismount with the right side of the body to the horse.

II. Stand facing the left end of the horse with the left hand on the end and the right hand on the left pommel, jump into a right leg full-circle clockwise (undercut) to a front support on the end, simple half leg circle travel to a front support in the center, left leg half-circle clockwise, left leg half-circle counterclockwise, right leg full-circle counterclockwise, double leg half-circle counterclockwise, right leg full-circle counterclockwise (undercut), left leg half-circle counterclockwise, left leg half-circle clockwise and turn to the right on the right arm to a front support with the left hand on the end of the horse, left leg full-circle clockwise with a quarter-turn right to a dismount with the left side of the body to the horse.

III. Stand facing the right end of the horse with both hands on the end section, jump into a simple loop mount around the end to a rear support on the end of the horse (after the 180° turn the performer will be on the left end of the horse), left leg half-circle counterclockwise, right leg half-circle clockwise, left leg half-circle clockwise, swing the right leg forward to a double feint on the right arm, travel with a full-circle of the left leg counterclockwise to a rear support in the center, left leg half-circle counterclockwise, backward scissor to the right, left leg half-circle counterclockwise, right leg half-circle counterclockwise, forward scissor to the left, forward scissor to the right, simple half leg circle travel to a front support on the left end of the horse, double leg half-circle counterclockwise, right leg half-circle counterclockwise (undercut), right leg swing forward to a double feint on the right arm, swing the left leg backward over the horse to a traveling backward scissor to a straddle support in the center of the horse, left leg half-circle counterclockwise, rear dismount to the right to a stand with the right side of the body to the horse.

IV. Stand facing the right end of the horse with the right hand on the end and the left hand on the right pommel, jump to a double rear mount to a rear support in the center, left leg half-circle counterclockwise, backward scissor to the right, backward scissor to the left, right leg half-circle clockwise, left leg half-circle clockwise, simple moore around the right pommel to a rear support in the center, right leg full-circle counterclockwise (undercut), double leg half-circle counterclockwise, kehre-out to a rear support on the left end of the horse (it will be the right end after the 180° turn has been completed), left leg half-circle counterclockwise, continue swinging the left leg over the end of the horse and turn left to a front support in the center (the right hand is shifted from the end of the horse to the far pommel), right leg half-circle counterclockwise, forward scissor to the left, right leg half-circle counterclockwise, two-and-a-half double leg circles counterclockwise, triple rear dismount on the left end of the horse to a stand with the right side of the body to the horse.

V. Stand facing the right end of the horse with the right hand on the end and the left hand on the right pommel, jump to a double leg circle counterclockwise, loop around the end of the horse to a rear support (the right end now becomes the left end of the horse as these movements involve a 180° turn), double leg circle counterclockwise, right leg half-circle counterclockwise (undercut), swing the right leg forward to a double feint on the right arm, traveling backward scissors to the center section, left leg half-circle counterclockwise to front support, two double leg circles counterclockwise, tromlet to a rear support on the right end, double half leg circle counterclockwise, kehre in to a rear support in the center, two-and-a-half double leg circles counterclockwise, moore on the right pommel to a rear support, double leg half-circle counterclockwise, right leg half-circle counterclockwise, forward scissors to the left, forward scissors to the right, forward scissor to the left, right leg half-circle counterclockwise, one-and-one-half double leg circles counterclockwise, kehre out, double leg half-circle counterclockwise, loop around the end of the horse and rear dismount to a stand with the right side of the body to the horse.

I. BEGINNING ROUTINE

1. Half Leg Circle Mount (Right Leg Half-Circle Counterclockwise) (Fig. 9–1). The mount in this routine starts facing the right end of the horse with the left hand on the right pommel and the right hand on the end (1). The student jumps off both feet and raises the legs and hips to the right. The shoulders lean slightly over the

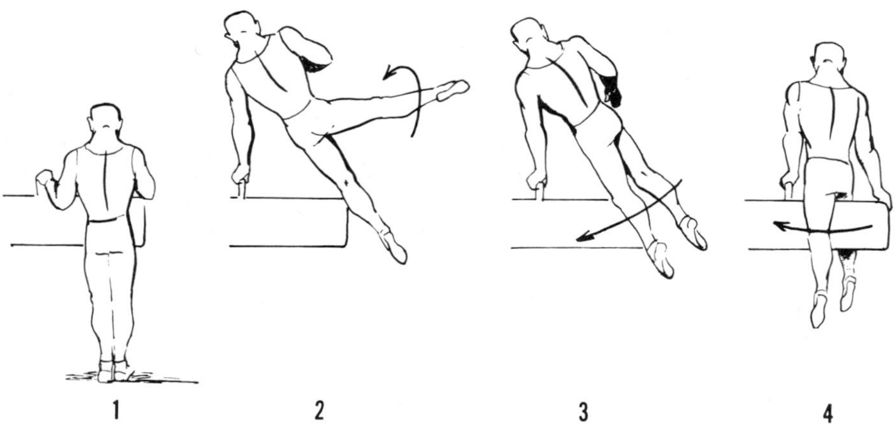

Fig. 9–1. Half Leg Circle Mount.

left arm as it straightens, but the center of gravity must not be shifted too far to the left. The right arm thrusts off the end as the right leg is raised above the horse (2). The right hip is then rotated forward. This has the effect of swinging the right leg over the top of the horse but also keeps the body line straight for a good pendulum downward swing (3). If the right leg were raised forward over the horse and held in a horizontal position, little swing would result. As the body swings to the left with the legs close to the sides of the horse, the right arm is replaced on the end with the fingers facing outward or even slightly backward. It is important to get accustomed to this hand position at the beginning as it is very important in advanced work. It makes it much easier to keep the arm straight. The mount ends in a straddle support on the right end of the horse (4).

Teaching Techniques. On the jump it is important that the left leg and hips also be raised to the right as well as the leg that is to circle over the horse. At the height of the jump the right hip is rotated forward to bring the right leg over the horse rather than the right leg being raised horizontally forward. As the right hand is replaced on the end of the horse, the fingers should be turned toward the end of the horse or even slightly backward.

2. Half Leg Circle Travel (Fig. 9–2). As the hips swing to the left after the mount, the left leg is raised over the center section (1) to a feint on the left arm. This will result in a double feint as the right leg is also on the front side of the horse. The right arm shifts from the end of the horse to the pommel in front of the left hand during this leg movement (2). The pommel must be gripped very tightly. The right leg then swings backward over the horse (3) followed by the left leg (4). As soon as the left leg passes over

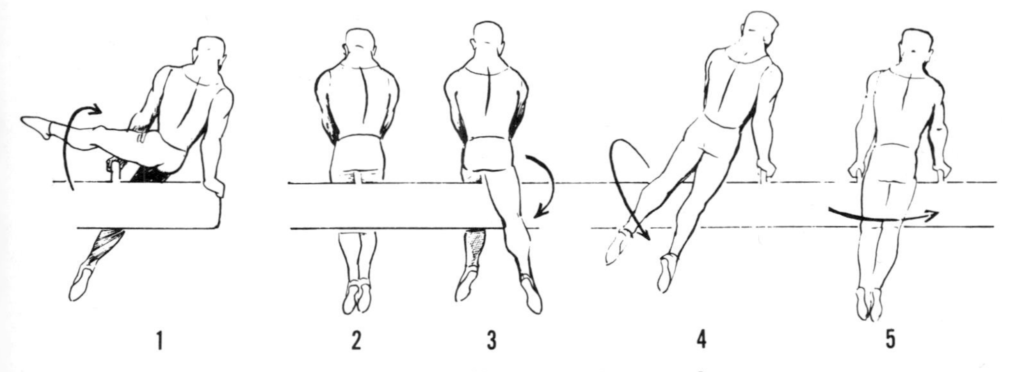

Fig. 9–2. Half Leg Circle Travel.

the top of the horse, the left hand shifts to the left pommel so that the travel ends in a front support in the center (5).

TEACHING TECHNIQUES. Rhythm must be emphasized. Both legs and the hips should swing during this travel. Because both hands must be on the same pommel during the travel, the left hand should be placed well back on the pommel at the start of the routine to leave plenty of room for the right hand to go in front. This travel can be made much easier by shifting the left hand to the left pommel much earlier than described above—usually as the right leg swings backward over the horse. This alternate method looks almost as good and may be used by those who have trouble with the usual method.

3. Half Leg Circle Forward from Front Support (Right Leg Half-Circle Counterclockwise) (Fig. 9–3). This stunt enables a beginner to get the "feel" of a good pendulum swing. It is almost identical to the half leg circle mount. As the body swings to the right in the front

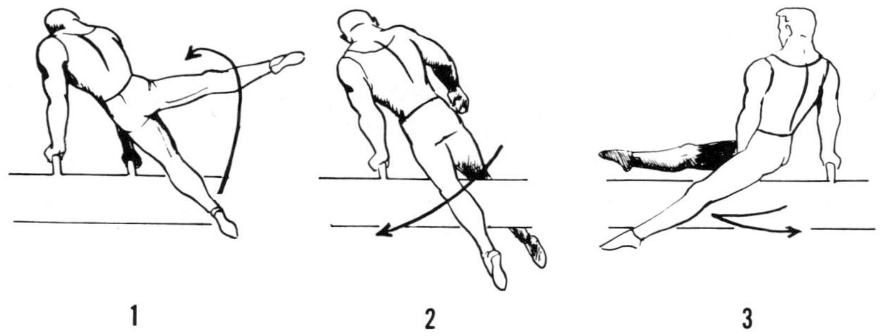

Fig. 9–3. Half Leg Circle Forward from Front Support.

support position upon completion of the travel, the right leg is swung high above the horse. The hips and left leg should also be raised to the right. To compensate for this, the weight is shifted somewhat over the left arm, but the center of gravity should not be moved too far to the left (1). At the top of the swing the right arm thrusts off the pommel and the right hip is rotated forward so that the right leg can swing down close to the front side of the horse (2). This leg should not be circled in a horizontal plane. As the legs and hips swing downward to the left, the right hand regrasps the pommel and the body swings through the straddle support position. The hip movement stops when the crotch comes in contact with the left arm, but the legs continue to swing upward to the left (3).

TEACHING TECHNIQUES. Both arms should be kept rigidly straight, especially as the weight drops back down on the right arm after the circle. The lead-ups are to practice the hand thrust off the pommel from a stationary front support position and then to practice it from a swing in the front support.

4. Half Leg Circle Backward from Straddle Support (Right Leg Half-Circle Clockwise) (Fig. 9–4). In advanced side horse work this movement would be considered a break in the exercise as there is a

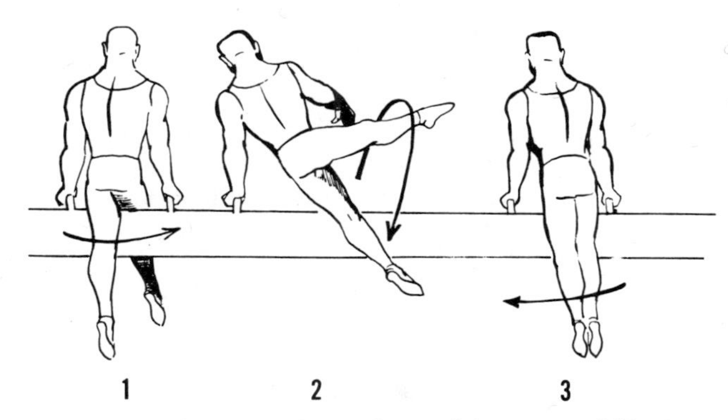

Fig. 9–4. Half Leg Circle Backward from Straddle Support.

reversal of direction. In beginning work, the combination of a half leg circle forward followed immediately by the same leg circling backward is excellent practice for developing a good pendulum swing. From the straddle support with both legs raised high to the left, the position in which the previous half leg circle finished, the legs drop downward, the hips swing to the right and the shoulders are shifted to the left (but not too far) (1). As the legs and hips swing upward to the right, the right hand thrusts off the pommel, the right hip is rotated backward so that the right leg swings over the top, and the shoulders are leaned forward over the horse (2). The legs then swing downward to the left in a front support (3).

TEACHING TECHNIQUES. A good lead-up is to practice swinging back and forth in the straddle support position raising the legs as high as possible in each direction. The hips should swing as much as they can between the arms. The thrust off the pommel can be added to this practice without circling the leg but instead dropping back down in the straddle swing. The right leg must swing like a pendulum, vertically, not be raised forward in a horizontal plane.

5 and 6. Left Leg Half-Circle Clockwise and Left Leg Half-Circle Counterclockwise. These are the same two movements just described in Stunts 3 and 4 except the left leg is the circling leg.

7. Right Leg Half-Circle Counterclockwise. This is another half leg circle forward exactly the same as described in Stunt 3.

8. Double Feint on the Left Arm (Fig. 9–5). Upon the conclusion of the series of half leg circles preceding this stunt the student is in a straddle support in the center of the horse with the right leg forward (1). The motion of the hips and the legs is to the left as

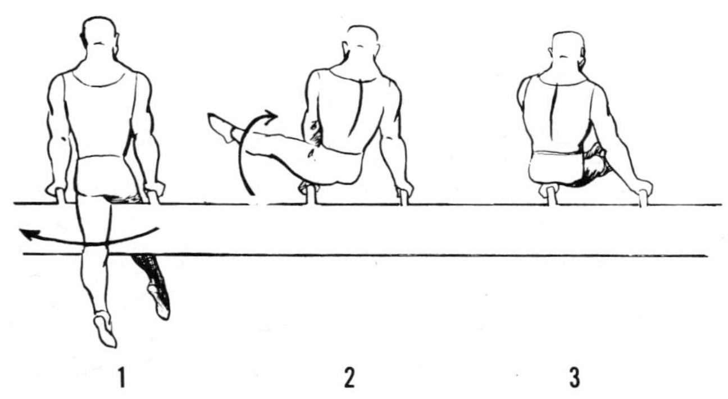

Fig. 9–5. Double Feint on the Left Arm.

the last half leg circle is completed. The weight is shifted primarily to the left pommel and the left leg swings upward and forward to straddle the left arm (2). The left hand is high in the crotch in this double feint, or straddle feint, as it is sometimes called (3).

TEACHING TECHNIQUES. Swinging into a single leg feint from a front support is a lead-up. This drill should be practiced first to the left and then to the right rhythmically so that the students learn to work both sides at the elementary level. Swinging in and out of a double feint from the straddle support is also good practice to develop rhythm.

9. Double Feint Pivot-Travel Dismount (Fig. 9–6). This is a complicated name for a very simple skill. Unfortunately, side horse terminology and descriptions are sometimes far more difficult than the execution of the stunts. In this routine the pivot from the double feint is not completed as a travel to a support on the end of the horse, as is usually done, but rather finished as a dismount. From

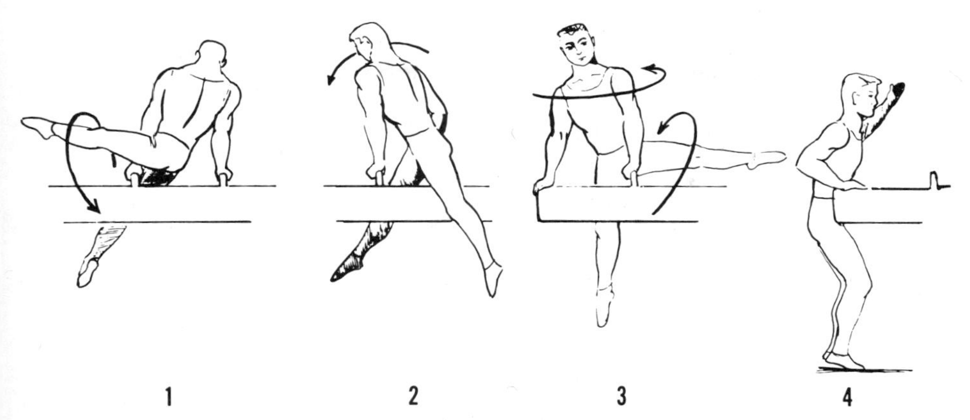

Fig. 9–6. Double Feint Pivot-Travel Dismount.

the double feint position the left leg is swung backward over the end of the horse (1). The movement of this leg continues up and over the right pommel. The right hand thrusts off the right pommel and the trunk turns and leans to the left over the left arm (2). The turn continues to the left around the right leg, which remains almost perpendicular and rests against the horse. The right hand is placed on the end of the horse (3). The left leg continues circling in the same direction and the left arm thrusts off the pommel as the student drops to the mat with another quarter-turn left to end with his right side toward the horse (4).

II. LOW INTERMEDIATE ROUTINE

1. Undercut Full Leg Circle Mount (Right Leg Full-Circle Clockwise) (Fig. 9–7). From a stand facing the left end of the horse with the right hand on the left pommel and the left hand on the end (1) the gymnast jumps upward and forward and raises the legs and the hips to the left. As the legs and hips get above the top of the horse (2), the left hand thrusts hard off the end of the horse to raise them still higher. The left hip is rotated backward so that the right leg can pass under the left leg and over the top of the horse (3). The hips and legs swing downward to the right and the left hand is placed back on the end of the horse with the fingers to the side, or even slightly backward, so that the arm will not collapse (4). The hips and both legs swing high to the right, the right hand thrusts off the pommel so that the right leg can swing over the top of the

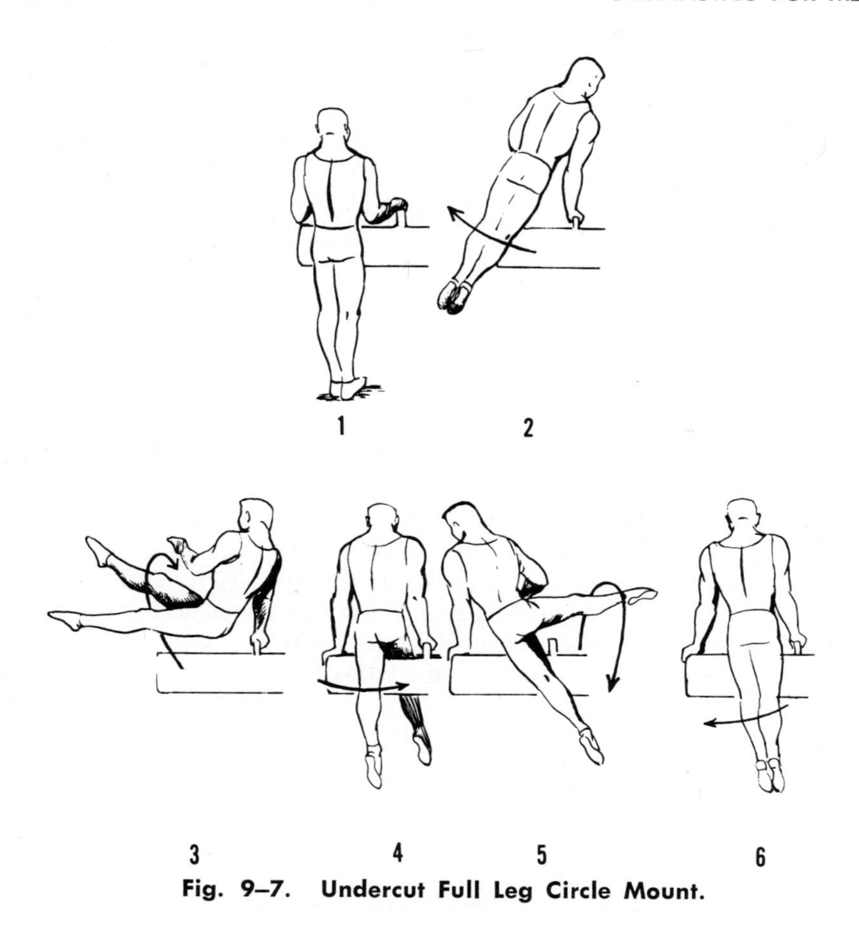

Fig. 9–7. Undercut Full Leg Circle Mount.

horse, and the shoulders lean forward (5). The mount finishes in a front support position (6).

TEACHING TECHNIQUES. This circle can be practiced as two half leg circles. The first part might be easier from a front support on the horse rather than from the floor and in the center section of the horse rather than at the end. When the first half of the circle is tried as a mount, it is very important to raise the legs and hips high to the left before the hips are rotated to allow the right leg to undercut. It is a bad mistake to try undercutting the leg immediately after the jump from the floor. As the second half of this circle is exactly the same as the half leg circle backward from a straddle support that was included in Routine I, this part of the circle has already been accomplished.

2, 3, and 4. Half Leg Circle Travel (to a Front Support in the Center), Half Leg Circle Forward from Front Support (Left Leg Half-Circle Clockwise), Half Leg Circle Backward from Straddle Support (Left Leg Half-Circle Counterclockwise). These skills were all included in Routine I, pages 381–83. The half leg circle travel moves to the right in this exercise whereas it moved to the left in the first one. There is actually a break after the half leg circle forward with the left leg as the direction is reversed for the half leg circle backward with the same leg. Since at this ability level the combination of these two stunts enables a student to practice a good pendulum swing, it has been included in spite of the fact that it would be considered a fault in competition.

5. Full Leg Circle from Front Support (Right Leg Full-Circle Counterclockwise) (Fig. 9–8). After the preceding half leg circle the body swings to the right in a front support (1). The first half of the circle is exactly the same as a half leg circle forward from front support. Refer to page 382 in Routine I. The right leg is swung high to the right. The hips and noncircling left leg should also be swung to the right. To compensate for this the weight is shifted somewhat to the left arm, but the center of gravity should not be moved too far to the left or there will not be a good downswing in the straddle support. At the top of the swing the right arm thrusts off the pommel and the right hip is rotated forward (2) so that the right leg can swing down close to the front side of the horse. As the legs and hips swing downward to the left, the right hand regrasps the pommel and the body swings to the left through the straddle support position (3). The hips and both legs are swung upward to the left very forcefully and the left arm thrusts off the pommel. To compensate for the legs being swung to the left, the weight must be shifted partially, but not completely, over the right

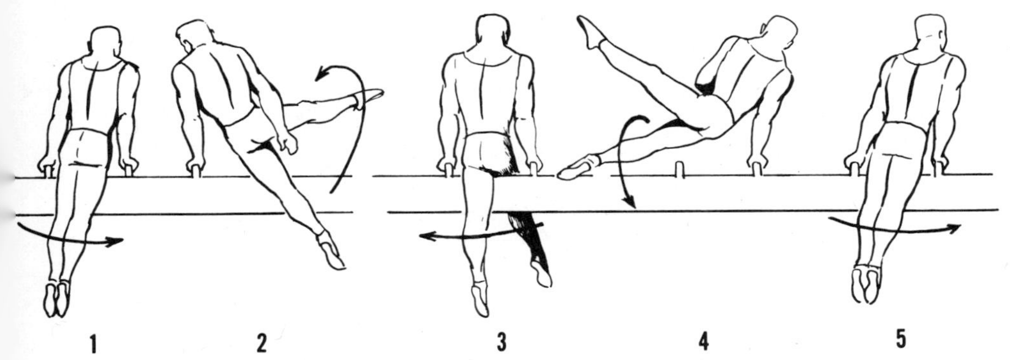

Fig. 9–8. Full Leg Circle from a Front Support.

arm. The left, or noncircling, leg should actually be raised much higher than the right leg so that the right leg can pass underneath. At the top of the swing the left hip is rotated forward. This has the effect of drawing the right hip and right leg backward over the horse (4). It is a common mistake to try and lift the right leg backward over the horse without raising the left leg very high and by rotating the left hip backward instead of forward. The body swings downward to the right in the front support position upon completion of this stunt and the left hand regrasps the pommel (5).

TEACHING TECHNIQUES. Refer to the half leg circle forward from a front support for teaching techniques for the first half of this circle. The second half of the circle can be practiced alone from a straddle support. The noncircling leg can be placed on the end of the horse during the learning procedure while the circling leg passes underneath. Considerable time should be spent just practicing the thrust with the left arm and the high swing of the left leg while swinging back and forth in the straddle support. A good technique used to develop a high left leg swing is to have a partner stand at the end of the horse and hold his hand about head high so that the performer can attempt to kick this hand with the left leg during the second part of the circle. This circle can be practiced from a jump from the floor and completed to a stand on the floor. This provides an excellent opportunity to practice the thrust on both the first and second half of the circle.

6. Double Leg Half-Circle Forward (Counterclockwise) (Fig. 9–9). The legs swing to the right in a front support as the single leg circle is completed. The right arm thrusts off the pommel, both legs are raised over the horse, and the right hip is rotated backward so that the hips face somewhat upward (1). The weight must be shifted slightly toward the left arm but not too much in this direction. As the legs pass over the horse the hips are fully extended, the head

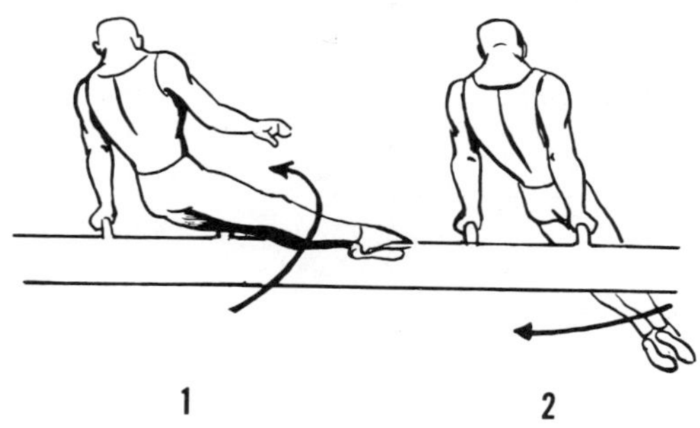

Fig. 9–9. Double Leg Half-Circle Forward.

and shoulders are leaned backward over the horse so balance can be maintained, and the right hand regrasps as quickly as possible with the arm rigidly straight so that it does not collapse (2). The gymnast finishes in a rear support position swinging to the left.

Teaching Techniques. There are several lead-ups that can be used for this stunt. Flank vaults over the horse from a slight run and then from a stand are the first two. A flank from a front support to a dismount rather than to a rear support is the next step. Actually, during this stage of learning, the rhythm for the flank is best developed from a feint; thus it should be practiced in this way. The most common mistake in learning the double leg half-circle is to lean the head and shoulders too far forward at the start. The shoulders lean only slightly forward and then, as the legs pass over the horse, they must lean quickly backward.

Spotting. If the feet hit the top of the horse, the student might fall forward on his face. A spotter can position himself in front to catch the shoulders if necessary.

7. Full Leg Undercut Circle from a Rear Support (Right Leg Counter-clockwise) (Fig. 9–10). Following the previous stunt the body swings toward the left in a rear support. Both legs and the hips

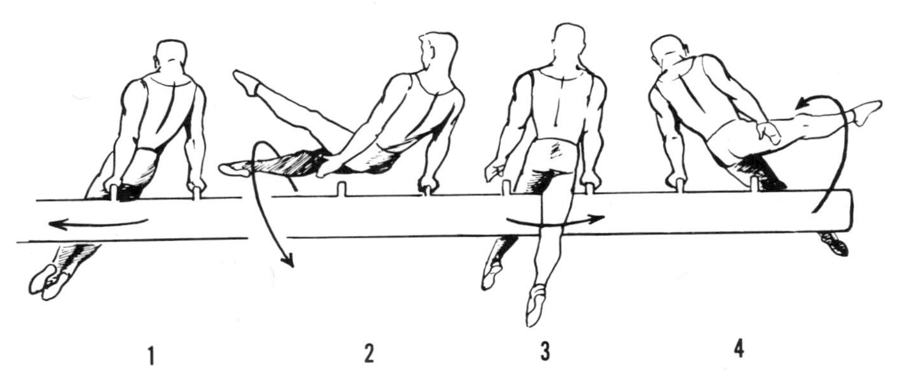

Fig. 9–10. Full Leg Undercut Circle from Rear Support.

are swung forcefully upward and the weight is shifted somewhat toward the right arm. The body should be piked a little with the hips facing slightly upward (1). The left hand thrusts hard off the pommel just as the last lift is given with the legs. A forward rotation of the left hip at the height of the upswing causes the hips to face downward and the right leg to pass under the left leg and over the horse (2). The body is extended to bring about a good downswing and the left hand grasps the pommel as soon as possible (3). The body swings to the right through the straddle support and then both legs and the hips are swung upward to the right with some of the weight being shifted to the left arm. The shoulders lean backward and the right leg passes over the top of the horse to swing downward to the left in a rear support (4).

TEACHING TECHNIQUES. This is a very valuable skill as the same principles apply to many advanced stunts. The common fault is to start to undercut the right leg too soon before swinging both legs up to left. As a lead-up, the legs may be placed on top of the horse during the undercut.

8. Half Leg Circle Backward from a Rear Support (Left Leg Counterclockwise) (Fig. 9–11). This is a little different type of half leg circle than those already included because it starts from a back

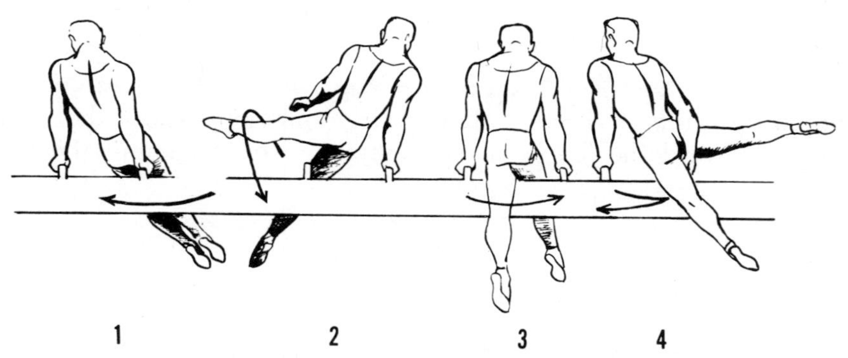

Fig. 9–11. Half Leg Circle Backward from a Rear Support.

support. The body swings to the left in a rear support upon completion of the previous circle (1). Both legs and the hips are swung upward and the weight is shifted toward the right arm. The left arm thrusts off the pommel, the left hip is rotated backward, and the left leg circles backward over the top of the horse (2). The body is extended as the legs swing downward in a straddle support and the left arm regrasps the pommel (3). The shoulders lean to the left and both legs are swung as high as possible to the right until stopped by the right arm (4). This is a break, or dead spot, in the exercise as the direction of movement is reversed for the next stunt. It is included, even though it would be considered a fault in competition, because it is a very important lead-up movement for the backward scissor, which is a part of the next routine.

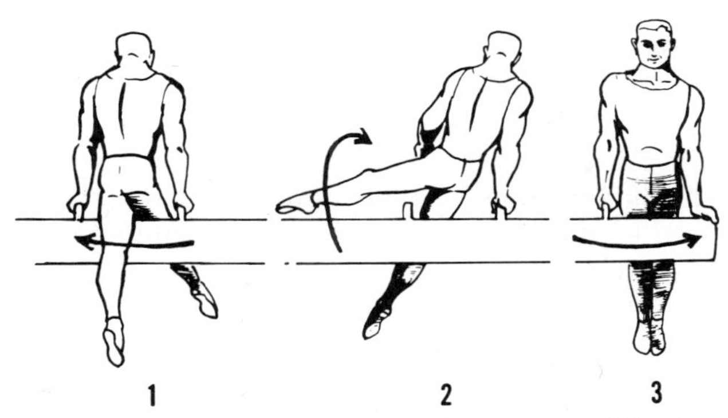

Fig. 9–12. Travel with a Half-Turn from a Straddle Support in the Center to a Front Support on the End.

9. Travel with a Half-Turn from a Straddle Support in the Center to a Front Support on the End (Fig. 9–12). This is another skill that is far harder to describe than it is to execute. It is an easy move that is very similar to the "pivot-travel dismount" in Routine I, but it is done in the opposite direction. As the performer swings to the left in the straddle support (1), the right leg is stopped in front of the horse just beyond the vertical position. The head and trunk turn to the right and the weight is leaned completely over onto the right arm. The left hand releases the pommel and the left leg, which is in back of the horse, starts to swing forward over the top (2). The body turns 180° from its starting position to a front support with the left hand on the end of the horse (3). The fingers should be turned out to the side or even slightly backward so that the arm will not collapse. As the front support is reached, the weight must be leaned well forward over the horse. If this is not done quickly, the performer will lose his balance backward.

10. Left Leg Full-Circle (Clockwise) to a Dismount with a Quarter-Turn (Fig. 9–13). This left leg full-circle is similar to the right leg full-circle described on pages 387–88 in this routine but, because it is on the end of the horse and because it follows a stunt that provides very little momentum, it is more difficult. Following the previous stunt the swing will be to the left in a front support. Both legs and the hips swing high to the left, the shoulders shift somewhat to the right, the left hand thrusts off the end, and the left hip rotates forward so that the left leg circles over the horse (1). Because the circle is done on the end of the horse, the left leg does not have to be raised so high as usual as it can go around the end instead of over the top. The left hand is replaced on the end of the horse as soon as possible with the fingers pointing slightly backward. The swing is to the right in the straddle support (2). In this single leg circle, unlike a normal one, only the circling leg is swung high during the second part. The hips and the noncircling right leg swing a little beyond the vertical and then stop. The left leg continues upward over the horse and most of the weight is shifted to the left arm. The right hand pushes away from the pommel to bring about the quarter-turn to the right. This swings the left leg over the top (3) and the performer drops to the mat with his left side toward the horse (4).

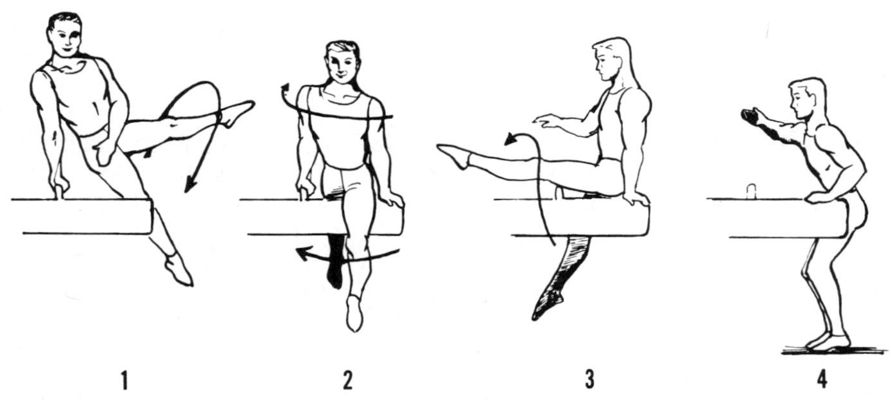

Fig. 9–13. Left Leg Full-Circle to a Dismount with a Quarter-Turn.

Teaching Techniques. Refer to the thrusting exercises suggested previously for the half leg circles and single leg circles. These should be practiced on the end of the horse at this time. The second half of this circle should be practiced alone from a straddle support as it is quite different from a regular single leg circle.

Spotting. There is a possibility that the performer might fall off backward during the second part of the circle. A spotter can be positioned near the end of the horse to guard against this.

III. INTERMEDIATE ROUTINE

Note: The rules state that a side horse exercise must use all three sections of the horse. All routines in the chapter, except this one, satisfy the requirement. This exercise could not be used in competition without a penalty being imposed.

1. Elementary Loop Mount (Fig. 9–14). This exercise starts from a side stand frontways (see definitions) close to the right end of the horse. The right hand is placed on the end toward the far side with the fingers over the edge. The left arm should be held out to the side about shoulder height (1). The performer jumps to a support on the right arm, turns 90° to the left, and places the left hand on the end of the horse with the fingers over the near side. The hips are raised slightly in a pike and the weight is leaned forward over the end of the horse (2). It is a common mistake to lean too far forward, however. The legs swing around the end of the horse but not too close to the end. The turn continues with the shoulders leading and the weight is shifted almost entirely to the left arm (3). As the turn progresses the legs are raised in more of a pike and the right arm thrusts off the horse (4). The left arm must be kept rigidly straight at this time. The legs swing over the top of the horse, the body is extended, the shoulders lean backward, and the right hand grasps the pommel as soon as possible (5). A 180° turn has now been completed to a rear support. After the turn the performer will be on the left end of the horse.

TEACHING TECHNIQUES. There are many lead-ups for this stunt. The first step is to jump to a stationary support on the end of the horse to get the "feeling" of the balance. The next few steps can best be learned on a buck horse, if one is available, or on the regular horse with the near pommel removed. Before trying to finish in a rear support the loop can be tried as a vault. The learner starts by walking around the end of the horse to the right and executing a simple rear vault. He then gradually moves around the end of

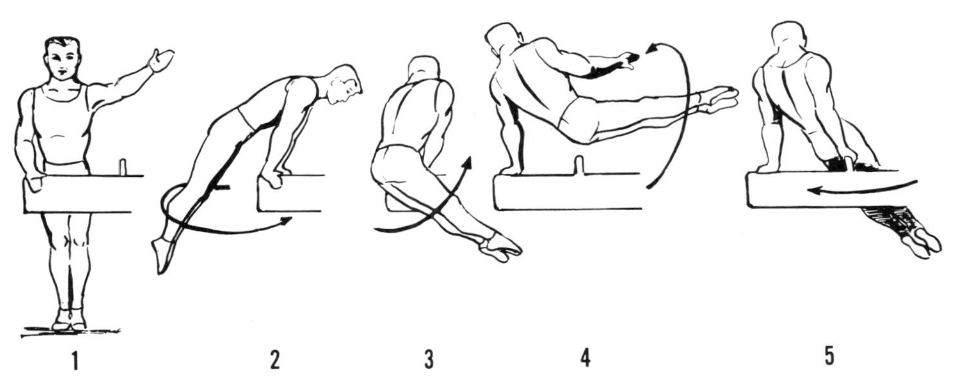

Fig. 9–14. Elementary Loop Mount.

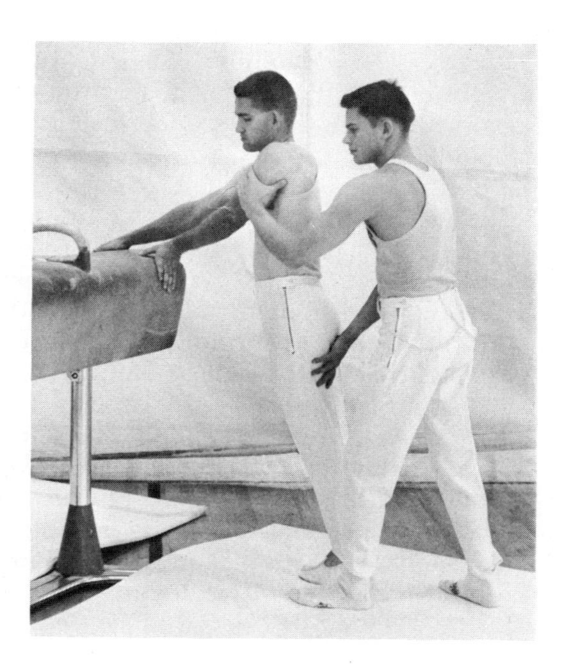

The first photo shows the starting position for spotting a simple loop mount. The second one demonstrates how the spotter has stepped in and is following the performer around during the mount. This is the same general spotting technique that is used for "double rears" on the side horse.

the horse to the left, in successive attempts, so that a little more loop, or turn around the end of the horse, is added each time. He finally works all the way around so that the vault is started as in the regular mount but still finishes with a dismount over the end of the horse. The final step is to try the loop as a mount but to end up sitting on the end of the horse instead of in a support position.

SPOTTING. A spotter can assist during this stunt by standing behind the performer. The right hand is placed on the buttocks and lifts and pushes throughout the mount. The left hand is placed on the left upper arm to control the balance and the shift of weight. The spotter must step in toward the horse and stay close to the performer as he jumps forward. This technique is illustrated in the photo on page 394.

2, 3, 4, and 5. Left Leg Half-Circle Counterclockwise, Right Leg Half-Circle Clockwise, Left Leg Half-Circle Clockwise, Swing the Right Leg Forward to a Double Feint on the Right Arm. These skills, or ones very similar, have been included previously in Routine I or II. Most of the previous half leg circles were done in the center section of the horse. A certain amount of drill will be needed, especially with the thrust off the end of the horse, before this series of half leg circles can be done rhythmically.

6. Full Leg Circle Travel from a Double Feint to a Rear Support (Left Leg Full-Circle Counterclockwise) (Fig. 9–15). This stunt begins from a double feint on the right arm, which is on the left pommel (1). The left leg circles backward over the horse to start the travel. The left arm thrusts off the end of the horse to shift the weight completely to the right arm (2). Instead of the left hand being placed back on the end it is transferred to a position on the left pommel behind the right hand. In the previous series of stunts the

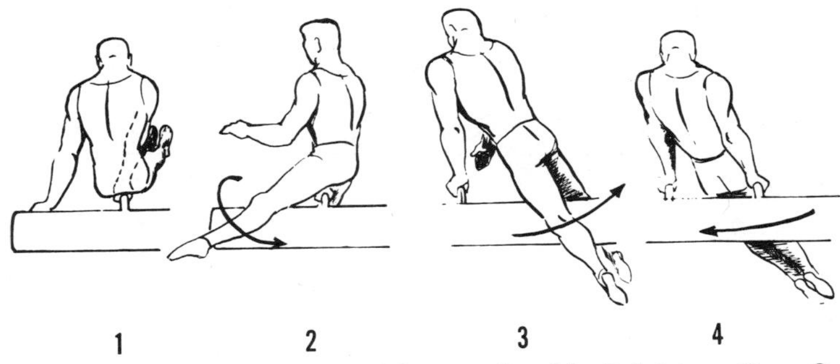

Fig. 9–15. Full Leg Circle Travel from a Double Feint to a Rear Support.

right hand should be placed well forward on the pommel so that there is room for the left hand behind it. In most travels the hand is placed in front, but in this travel it is better to place it in back. It may be a little more difficult to get it into position but it makes the completion of the stunt considerably easier. After the left leg passes over the left end of the horse, it must be dropped downward forcefully to develop a good pendulum swing to the right. Both legs are swung upward to the right very vigorously in the straddle support position. The right hip is rotated backward so that the left leg can circle over the center section of the horse (3). As soon as it does so the hips are extended, the shoulders are leaned backward, and the right hand shifts from the left to the right pommel (4). During this second part of the circle the hands must grasp the left pommel very tightly with the arms perfectly straight and the shoulders must be extended so as to make the position as tall as possible.

TEACHING TECHNIQUES. The second part of the circle is the difficult part. It can be practiced alone from a straddle support with the right hand already shifted to the right pommel, and then later with both hands on the left pommel. During the learning stages the foot may be placed on top of the horse as it passes over.

7. Left Leg Half-Circle Counterclockwise. Half leg circles have already been explained in previous routines. This one starts from a rear support and ends in a straddle support.

8. Backward Scissor (Fig. 9–16). In this exercise the backward scissor starts from a swing to the right in a straddle support with the right leg on the front and the left leg on the back side of the horse (1). Both legs are swung hard to the right and upward as high as

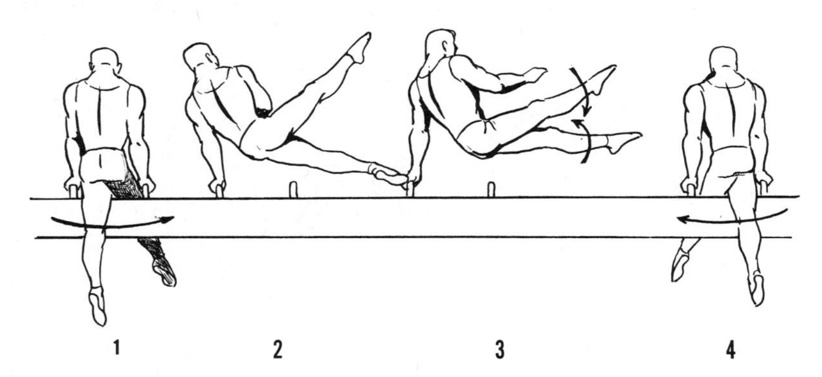

Fig. 9–16. Backward Scissor.

possible. The shoulders are leaned over the left pommel, but the center of gravity should remain over the center of the horse or the rhythm of the scissor will be lost. If there is a very slight flex at the hips during this swing, it will facilitate a high leg movement. The feet are whipped upward from the slight pike just prior to the thrust off the pommel with the right hand (2). The lift of the left leg should be emphasized as this is the one that must pass underneath during the scissor. At the height of the lift the hips are rotated to face upward. This will cause the legs to "scissor" with the left leg moving forward and the right leg passing backward over the horse (3). On the downswing the body should be extended for maximum swing and the right hand grasps the pommel as soon as possible. The legs should be kept reasonably close together so that they drop down close to the horse in a pendulum-type swing to generate enough momentum for the stunt to follow (4).

TEACHING TECHNIQUES. Half leg circles are the first lead-up. The best one to prepare the student for a backward scissor to the right is a left leg half-circle counterclockwise from the rear support position. Swinging back and forth in the straddle support and attempting to swing the legs high is another lead-up. The thrust of the right hand can be practiced in this way too, without scissoring. When the scissors are attempted, the feet can be rested on top of the horse during the first few trials. Probably one of the best lead-ups is the traveling backward scissor, which is done from a feint rather than from a straddle support. Refer to pages 399–400 in this chapter for the traveling backward scissor.

9 and 10. Left Leg Half-Circle Counterclockwise, Right Leg Half-Circle Counterclockwise. These two half leg circles are used to get the legs in position for the next stunt. The second one should be done as high as possible so as to develop lots of downward swing in the straddle support.

11. Forward Scissor (Fig. 9–17). As the previous half leg circle is completed, the student swings to the left in a straddle support with the right leg in front and the left leg in back of the horse (1). Both legs and the hips are lifted high to the left (the left leg especially high) (2). The left hand thrusts off the pommel and the shoulders are shifted slightly to the right, but not too far, as the center of gravity must remain over the center section of the horse for a good downswing following the scissor. The right hand must grip the pommel very tightly as the left hand thrusts off (3). At the height of the leg swing the hips are rotated so that they face

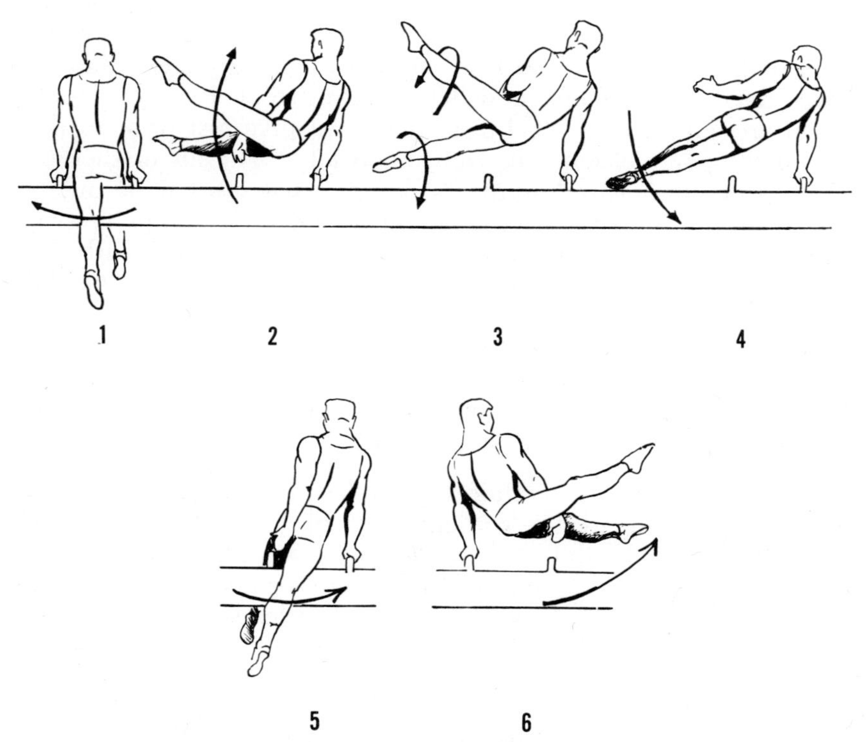

Fig. 9–17. Forward Scissor.

downward. This will cause the legs to scissor with the left passing over the top of the right (4). The body is extended and the left hand regrasps the pommel as soon as possible after the legs swing downward in a narrow straddle with the left leg in front and the right leg in back of the horse (5). If the legs are kept close to the sides of the horse, a good pendulum swing results. The left arm must be ready to bear the weight as it regrasps the pommel after the scissor. A straight arm and a tight grip is necessary in order to be ready for the next scissor to the right (6).

Teaching Techniques. Half leg and single leg circles are lead-ups for forward scissors. Refer in the previous two exercises to the following stunts or to the lead-ups for them:

1. Half leg circle forward from a front support.
2. Full leg circle from a front support.
3. Swing back and forth in a straddle support practicing the thrust off the pommel.

4. Full leg circle from a front support dropping to a stand instead of finishing in a support.
5. Another lead-up is to practice the complete scissor but to place one foot on the top of the horse as they are executed.

Scissors must be learned to both sides and in this exercise one to the right immediately follows. These lead-ups should be practiced in both directions, especially to the weak side, whichever it is, so that the scissors will be of equal height. Scissors should be practiced until about ten can be done consecutively. One important factor that must be mentioned to students when they are learning scissors is to keep the shoulders approximately in line with the horse. The hips twist, but the shoulders should not.

12. Forward Scissor to the Right. Repeat the scissor exactly as described but in the opposite direction.

13, 14, 15, and 16. Half Leg Circle Travel to a Front Support on the Left End of the Horse, Double Leg Half-Circle Counterclockwise, Right Leg Half-Circle Counterclockwise (Undercut), Right Leg Swing Forward to a Double Feint on the Right Arm. These skills, or ones very similar to them, have been included in previous routines. They will probably be more difficult in this routine because they are done on the end of the horse instead of in the center. The double leg half-circle is also more difficult because the legs must pass over the top of the pommel. The undercut half leg circle has not been given previously, but it is exactly the same as the first half of the right leg full undercut circle on pages 389–90.

17. Traveling Backward Scissor (Fig. 9–18). This skill starts from a double feint on the right arm, which is on the left pommel. The left hand is on the left end of the horse (1). The left leg swings

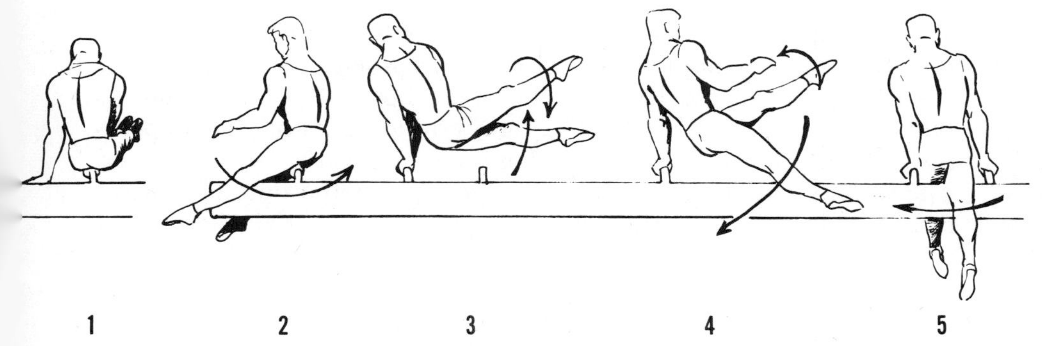

Fig. 9–18. Traveling Backward Scissor.

backward over the horse, the left hand pushes off the end to shift the weight entirely over the pommel, and the left hand is placed on the pommel behind the right hand (2). In the execution of the previous series of stunts the right hand must be placed well forward on the pommel to leave enough room for the left hand. The left leg swings downward hard to develop momentum for the upswing, but actually most of the lift comes from a backward and upward whip of both legs using a tight grip with both hands on the pommel to resist against the tendency for this leg whip to force the shoulders to the left over the pommel (3). When the legs are well above the horse the hips are rotated to face upward, which cause the legs to scissor (4). The right hand is quickly shifted from the left pommel to the right pommel as the legs swing downward close to the sides of the horse in a pendulum swing with the left leg in front and the right leg behind the horse (5).

TEACHING TECHNIQUES. Single half leg and full leg circle travels provide the background for traveling backward scissor. Refer also to the lead-ups given for the regular backward scissor. The traveling scissor should probably appear before the regular backward scissor in the teaching progression. At least the backward scissor from a feint without a travel should come first. Considerable time should be spent practicing the leg swing for a backward scissor from a feint without actually executing the scissors. This can be practiced in the center section at first rather than on the end of the horse as in this routine.

18. Left Leg Half-Circle Counterclockwise. As this half leg circle is used to develop swing for the dismount, special emphasis should be placed on making it as high as possible.

19. Single Rear Dismount (Fig. 9–19). The previous half leg circle is finished with both legs swinging downward to the right in a front support (1). As they swing upward to the right, the weight is shifted almost completely to the left arm and a little forward over the horse. When the legs are above the horse, the hips rotate so that they face upward (2). The right arm gives a pull on the pommel and then it thrusts downward and releases as the legs pass over. The feet should be raised as high as possible as the buttocks passes over the horse (3). To complete the dismount the right hand reaches back for the horse, the left hand releases the left pommel and the legs are dropped quickly from the pike to a landing with the right side of the body toward the horse (4).

TEACHING TECHNIQUES. The student should have had the experience of doing the rear vault over the vaulting horse before trying

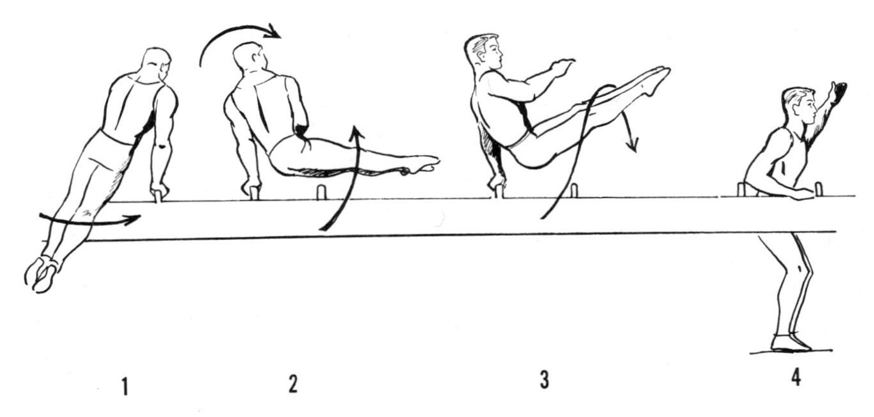

Fig. 9–19. Single Rear Dismount.

this dismount. The vault should be reviewed over the side horse, first from a run and then from a stand. The double half leg circles that have been included in previous routines are also a lead-up. Probably the easiest way to do this dismount is from a feint on the left arm for a dismount to the right. Considerably more swing can be developed from the feint than from a half leg circle. Some students find it easier to practice on the end of the horse where the legs do not have to be raised over the pommel. (There is an alternate method of doing the rear dismount. As the left leg swings backward over the horse from the previous half leg circle, the hips are raised in the air away from the horse, the shoulders are leaned well forward, and the body circles in more of a horizontal plane than a vertical plane. This method takes more arm and shoulder strength and is a similar motion to one used in advanced work to start double leg circles.)

SPOTTING. A spotter can step in quickly on the back side of the horse and assist in this dismount by supporting the left upper arm with his left hand and by lifting under the back of the thighs with his right hand. A safety spotter can be positioned on the other side to catch the upper body in case the performer pitches forward over the horse.

IV. LOW ADVANCED ROUTINE

By the time that gymnasts have reached this level they should know in which direction they prefer to circle. They should not be forced to try the more advanced stunts in both directions but allowed to select the direction that is easiest for them. Many gymnasts will want to start this routine facing the left end of the horse, instead of the right, and circle clockwise throughout.

1. Double Rear Mount (Fig. 9–20). This exercise starts from a stand facing the right end of the horse at arms length with the right hand on the end and the left hand to the back side of the right pommel (1). From this position the gymnast jumps and raises the legs to the right (2). He should lean over the left hand and keep the side of the body close to the arm and the center of gravity directly over the pommel. The right arm presses downward and backward on the end of the horse so as to pull the legs forward over the end.

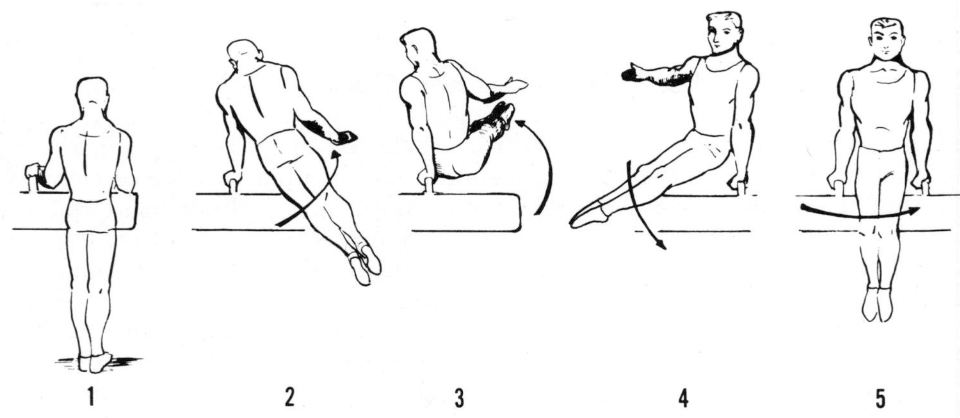

Fig. 9–20. Double Rear Mount.

Most good gymnasts then raise this arm out to the side during the turn. The pivot arm stays rigidly straight and the head turns to look over the left shoulder shortly after the jump and stays in this position throughout the turn (3). The buttocks almost rest on the left hand as the legs continue to circle and pass over the center section (4). During the turn the body maintains a pike of slightly more than a right angle, but as the legs pass over the far pommel it is extended, the shoulders lean backward, the right arm grasps the pommel, and the center of gravity moves between the pommels. The mount ends in a rear support with the legs swinging to the left (5). The gymnast must be careful to lock out the right arm or it will collapse as the weight is shifted to it.

Teaching Techniques. Instead of finishing in a rear support the learner can drop off the front of the horse to a stand as he completes the turn. Next he should end sitting on the horse. Refer to spotting as this is the most important factor in teaching the double rear mount.

SPOTTING. The spotter is important both for safety and to facilitate the learning of this stunt. The spotter stands behind but slightly to the left of the gymnast. He grasps the left upper arm with his left hand to control the shift of weight and the balance. The right hand is placed under the right buttock and is used to lift and push during the mount. The spotter must step in toward the horse and slightly to the right very quickly as the performer jumps into the mount.

2, 3, 4, 5, and 6. Left Leg Half-Circle Counterclockwise, Backward Scissor to the Right, Backward Scissor to the Left, Right Leg Half-Circle Clockwise, Left Leg Half-Circle Clockwise. These movements have all been included in previous routines. The backward scissors are done in succession in this exercise but are the same as described in Routine III. As the right leg half-circles after the scissors, the right hand should be placed on the front part of the pommel in preparation for the simple moore.

7. Simple (or Baby) Moore (Fig. 9–21). Many side horse performers say this stunt is harder than a regular moore, but it is usually used as a lead-up for the moore. The starting position is a

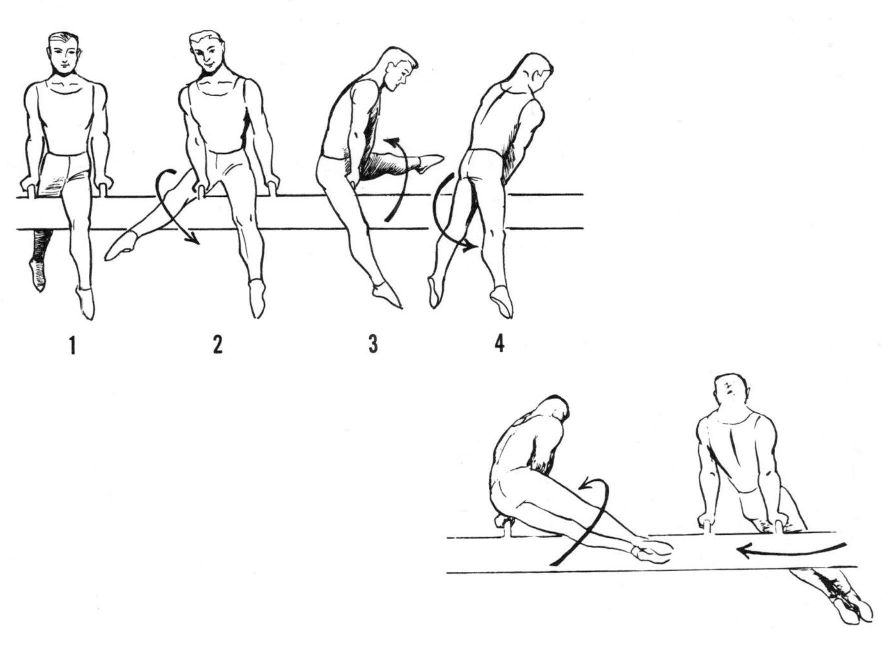

Fig. 9–21. Simple (or Baby) Moore.

straddle support with the left leg in front and the right leg in back of the horse (1). In the previous series of half leg circles the right hand should have been placed well forward on the pommel so as to leave room for the left hand. The right leg swings over the horse as if going into a double feint on the right arm and the weight is shifted onto this arm (2). The right leg continues beyond the feint position until it is almost vertical and rests against the side of the horse. The left leg circles backward over the center of the horse, the shoulders turn 90° to the left and the left hand shifts to an undergrip on the right pommel beside the right hand. As the hand shift is made the arms may be very slightly bent and the upper thighs may rest against the back of the forearms momentarily (3). It is very important to grip the pommel tightly with both hands, and then to extend the arms and shoulders fully to make the position as tall as possible. The left leg continues to circle in approximately a horizontal plane over the end and then the right leg pushes off the side of the horse to swing the hips backward away from the side (4). The left leg catches up with the right leg about this time, the shoulders complete another 90° turn to the left, and both legs are swung over the center of the horse as in a flank vault (5). Just before the legs pass over the top the right hand releases the pommel. As soon as the legs clear the horse, the hand is placed quickly on the other pommel and the body extends to the rear support position (6).

TEACHING TECHNIQUES. The following steps should be followed in learning the baby moore:

1. Turn 90° from the straddle support to the position with both hands in an undergrip on one pommel. Extend the arms and practice holding the balance in this position.
2. Circle from the starting position to a front support on the far side of the horse.
3. Execute the first half of the stunt as it is supposed to be done but conclude it by swinging only the right leg over the far pommel to finish in a straddle support facing the opposite direction from the starting straddle support.
4. Execute the entire leg movement as it is supposed to be done but shift the right hand to the far pommel before both legs pass over the center of the horse to complete the stunt. This hand can be used to aid the balance and can give a thrust before the legs pass over.
5. Remove the far pommel and execute the complete stunt to a sit on the horse or as a dismount to a stand with the back to the horse. These same two techniques may be used without removing the pommel but hitting the pommel with the knees can be quite painful and can cause the performer to hold back.

SPOTTING. A spotter can stand behind the performer in the starting position and step in quickly to grasp the left upper arm with his left hand to control the shift of weight and balance. His other hand is used under the buttocks to guide the performer around. It requires a very agile spotter to be able to move in and help in this way. Even if he is not quick enough to give assistance, he will be in position to catch the performer in case the legs hit the horse as the moore is completed.

8 and 9. Undercut Circle from a Rear Support (Right Leg Counterclockwise), Double Leg Half-Circle Forward (Counterclockwise). This is a common combination in advanced side horse work that is used to get into double leg circles as well as into a kehre-out, which follows in this exercise. The right leg full undercut circle has been included in Routine II, pages 389–90. Refer to page 407 in this routine for an explanation of the double leg half-circle, which is given as part of the double leg full-circle.

10. Kehre-Out or Double Rear Out (Fig. 9–22). This stunt is not much different from the double rear mount, which is a "double rear in." It is difficult to separate the kehre-out from the previous double leg half-circle because they flow together. As the double leg half-circle is completed in a front support, the hips are moved backward away from the horse, but they should not be raised upward to any extent. The kehre-out starts from this position (1). The legs continue their counterclockwise circle and raise upward to the right. The right hand pushes backward on the pommel and then releases as the legs pass over the horse with the body in a pike somewhat greater than a right angle (2). The center of gravity is shifted over the left hand, the shoulders are turned to the left with the head looking over the left shoulder, the upper body is leaned backward, which tends to lift the feet a little without increasing

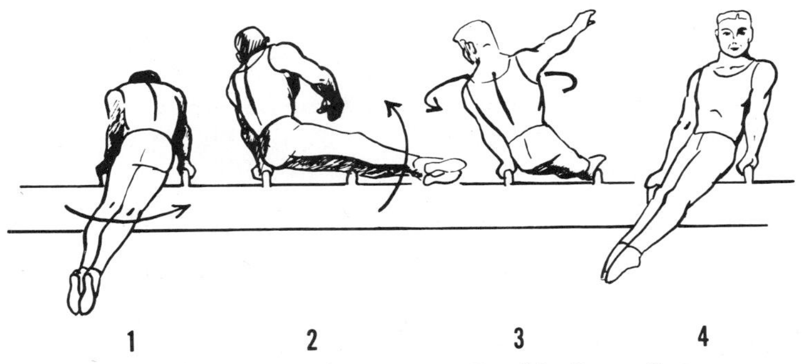

Fig. 9–22. Kehre-Out or Double Rear Out.

the pike, and probably most important of all, the side of the body is brought in close to the left arm so that the buttock is almost resting on the hand (3). Most good side horse performers will raise the right arm upward at this time, but this is not necessary. This position with the body in a pike of 15° to 20° greater than a right angle is maintained on the pivot arm until the legs have almost completed the 180° turn. As the legs pass over the end of the horse, the body is extended, the shoulders are leaned backward, and the right hand is placed on the end of the horse (4). It is necessary to remind the gymnast at this time about the importance of the hand position on the end of the horse with the fingers facing out to the side or even backward. This position feels awkward at first, but it prevents the arm from collapsing.

TEACHING TECHNIQUES. A modified kehre-out, with the left leg forward in a straddle support and the buttock resting on the left hand at the start, can be used as a lead-up. It is difficult to get much turn from this position but the performer can get the "feel" of the stunt. The kehre-out is usually practiced from a feint as it is easier for most individuals when started in this way. The double rear mount, which started this routine, is easier for some gymnasts and can be used as a lead-up. Another lead-up is to practice the kehre-out as a dismount, or to a sitting position on the end of the horse, rather than to a rear support.

SPOTTING. Spotting is the same as for the double rear mount or for the baby moore. Contact cannot be made with the performer before the kehre starts as the spotter would be in the way of the legs at this time. The spotter must be very alert, therefore, and step in quickly to grasp the pivot arm with one hand and to push under the buttocks with the other hand.

11. Left Leg Half-Circle Counterclockwise. After the kehre the left hand is in a rotated grip on the pommel. During this half leg circle it must thrust off in this grip, but after the circle it is placed back on the pommel in a regular grip.

12. Travel with a Half-Turn from a Straddle Support on the End to a Front Support in the Center (Fig. 9–23). This is another stunt that is more difficult to name than it is to execute. It is very similar to the dismount in Routine I and also similar to another travel-turn in Routine II, page 391. When the preceding half leg circle is completed, the gymnast will be in a straddle support with the right leg in front and the left leg behind the horse (1). The left leg continues as if to complete a full leg circle over the end of the

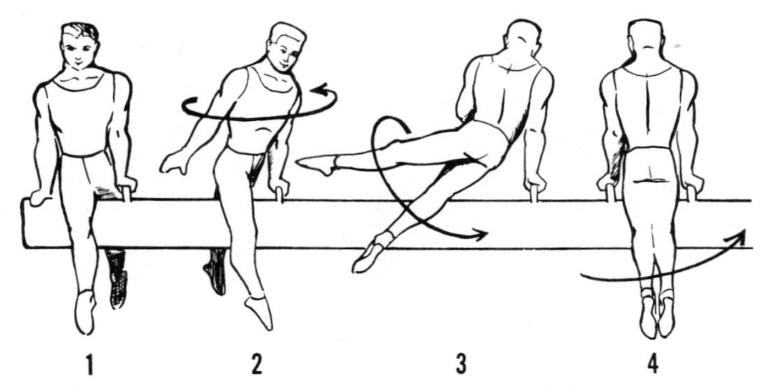

Fig. 9–23. Travel with Half-Turn from Straddle Support on End to Front Support in Center.

horse, but before it does so the right arm thrusts off the end and the body turns to the left (2). The 180° turn is completed as the left leg passes over the end of the horse and the right arm is placed on the far pommel (3). The body swings to the right in the front support position in the center of the horse as the travel is completed (4).

TEACHING TECHNIQUES. As this turn is completed, the left hand will be in a rotated grip on the pommel. This is a very poor grip for the next two stunts—the right leg half-circle and the forward scissor. Both the half leg circle and the scissor can be accomplished with the rotated grip, but there is a technique that can be used that will solve this problem. This turn is such a simple one that the gymnast does not really need a tight grip with the pivot hand. Momentarily during the turn the hand can be opened so that the weight is supported on the palm with the fingers and thumb extended. While the hand is in this position, it pivots on top of the pommel and then grasps again with the fingers on the other side. Another technique that can be used is quickly to change the left hand from the rotated to a regular grip as the half leg circle is executed so that it is in a position to give a good thrust for the scissor.

13, 14, and 15. Right Leg Half-Circle Counterclockwise, Forward Scissor to the Left, Right Leg Half-Circle Counterclockwise. These stunts have all been included in previous routines.

16. Double Leg Circles (Two-and-a-Half Counterclockwise) (Fig. 9–24). The double leg circle is the backbone of advanced side horse performance. Unless they are learned well, other advanced skills will be difficult or impossible. In this routine the double leg

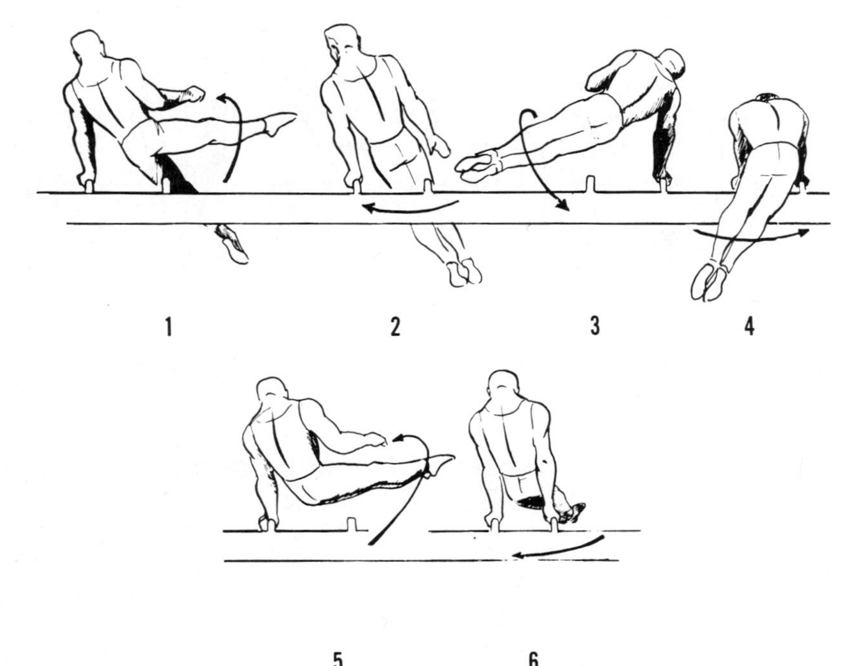

Fig. 9–24. Double Leg Circle.

circles are started as the right leg swings forward over the right end of the horse in the previous half leg circle. At this time the left leg should also be swung upward to the right on the front side of the horse (1). Just as the right leg passes over, the hips are extended and the left leg pushes backward against the horse. These two movements propel the legs and hips forward away from the horse, a position that is necessary in order to get the double leg circles started. The right hand, of course, grasps the pommel as soon as possible after the half leg circle is completed, the legs are placed together immediately, and the shoulders lean backward over the horse to compensate for the forward and extended position of the body (2). As the legs circle counterclockwise, the weight is shifted somewhat from the left to the right hand, but the center of gravity must remain between the pommels. As the legs approach the left end for the flank backward over the horse, the hips are lifted quickly into a pike. If a good swing has been developed, the pike will be very slight, but it must be instituted quickly and sharply even though it is slight. At the same time the hips are rotated downward (3). This forward and downward rotation of the left hip should start early, before the legs actually pass over the horse. If this rotation does not occur, the hips and legs will cause the shoulders to twist and make the continuation of the circle very difficult. The left hand thrusts off the pommel and then is quickly replaced as the legs pass over the end (4). The shoulders are shifted forward over the horse and the weight is shifted somewhat from the right to the left arm, but the center of gravity must still remain between the pommels. As the legs approach the right end for the flank forward over the horse, the right hand thrusts off hard and the hips start to rotate upward (5). The body is quickly extended and the right hand grasps the pommel again as soon as possible. During the extension the hips remain rotated upward and the chest is thrust forward (6). This hip rotation helps the feet to clear the end of the horse.

TEACHING TECHNIQUES. The two necessary prerequisites are a flank vault from a front to a rear support and a single leg undercut circle from a rear support. There is considerable difference of opinion among coaches as to how a double leg circle should be taught. Some say to start from a feint so that a good swing can be obtained. This enables the beginner to flank back over the horse without exaggerating the hip lift. Others say to learn it from a single leg circle, as this is the way it is usually started in an exercise. Others say to start it from a jump from the floor facing the horse. Possibly every student should experiment and decide which method seems to be best for him. Whatever method is used, the learner can drop to a stand on the floor after the completion of one circle and later after one-and-one-half circles.

Some points to stress throughout the learning process are:

1. Grip the pommels very tightly.
2. Thrust off the pommels hard but replace the hands as quickly as possible.
3. Keep the arms rigidly straight and the shoulders extended.
4. Hold the head in a normal position.
5. Keep the shoulders in line with the horse and do not hunch them.
6. Keep the center of gravity between the pommels and try not to raise it too much (or at all) as the hips are piked in back.
7. Describe a circle with the hips as well as the feet, that is, swing from the shoulders.
8. A perfect circle will be smooth and even, but for most side horse performers, even good ones, there will be an uneven 1-2 rhythm which comes from a flank over (one) and a flank back (two) with a pause while the legs swing in back. As the swing gets bigger the count will become more even.

There is a tendency for the legs to spread apart on the flank over and to bend on the flank back. This should be corrected early before it becomes a habit. Have the performer hold a gym slipper between his feet or knees during practice so that he has to squeeze them together as he circles to keep it there. A piece of chalk wrapping paper is often used as a substitute for the slipper.

The best teaching technique for the double leg circle is to encourage the student to practice for hours and hours.

17. Triple Rear Dismount (Fig. 9–25). The first two-thirds of this dismount needs no explanation as it is the same as the kehre-out. Another name for the kehre is a "double rear," meaning that the rear of the body passes over the horse twice. In a triple rear it passes over the horse three times. Adding the extra one-third does not make the stunt any more difficult, and might actually make it easier for some, because there does not have to be a stop in the

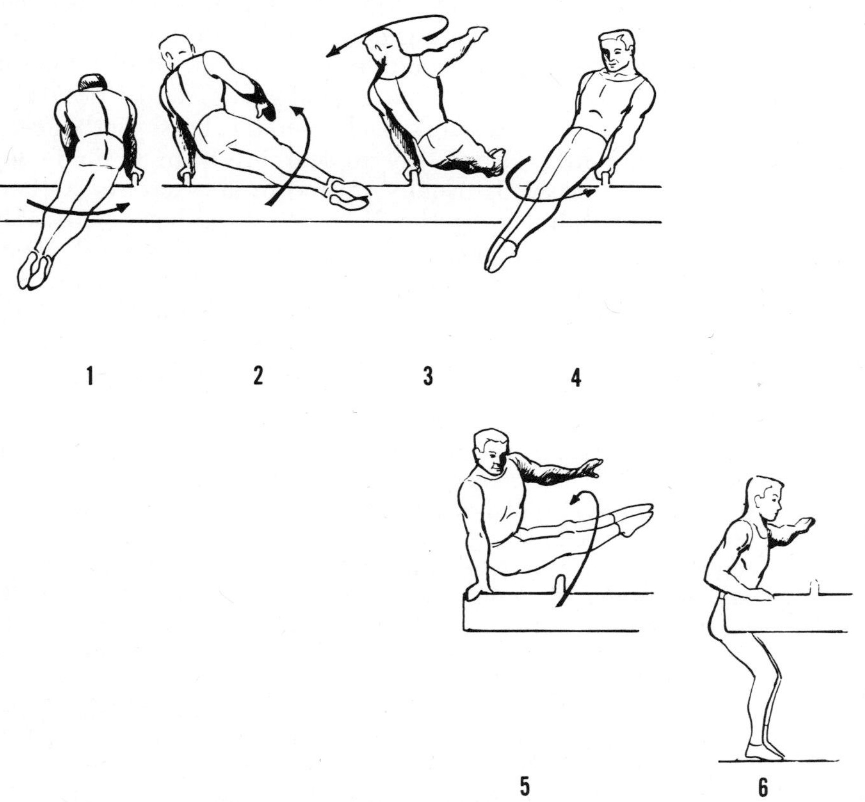

Fig. 9–25. Triple Rear Dismount.

natural movement. The triple rear starts with the legs on the back side of the horse after the completion of two-and-one-half double leg circles (1). There is no break in rhythm as the dismount starts. The left buttock is moved over toward the left arm so it almost sits on the hand (2) (3). As the legs pass over the end of the horse, the body is extended and the hand is placed on the end with the fingers facing outward or even slightly backward (4). This hand position is important to prevent the arm from collapsing as the weight is shifted almost entirely to it. The legs continue to circle counterclockwise and the dismount is completed by flanking back over the horse as in a double leg circle. As the left hand thrusts off the pommel, however, it pushes backward as well as upward and does not regrasp. This institutes a 90° turn to the left (5) so that the performer drops to a stand with his right side toward the horse (6).

TEACHING TECHNIQUES. This stunt is a combination of the kehre-out and the double leg circle and if they have both been learned other intermediary steps are unnecessary.

V. ADVANCED ROUTINE

This routine will not be described from start to finish as the others have in the book. For the complete routine the reader must refer to the abbreviated routine description, page 380. This technique is being used for sake of brevity as only four new stunts are included. The rest of the exercise is composed primarily of double leg circles as the rules specify. It includes scissors in both directions, the forward scissor three times in succession, to meet the requirements of the rules. There are, of course, the usual number of half leg circles necessary to get into, and out of, scissors. Two kehres, or double rears, have been included. Almost all advanced routines include two of these. The kehre-in is a little more difficult than the kehre-out that was included in the previous routine, but the principles of execution are the same. Double leg circles appear on the end of the horse in this exercise. These are more difficult than doubles in the center but are performed in the same way. The four new stunts in the routine are presented in the order in which they appear—a loop, a tromlet, a moore, and a loop to a rear dismount.

1. Loop (Fig. 9–26). This movement is not completely new as it is very similar to the elementary loop mount in Routine III, page

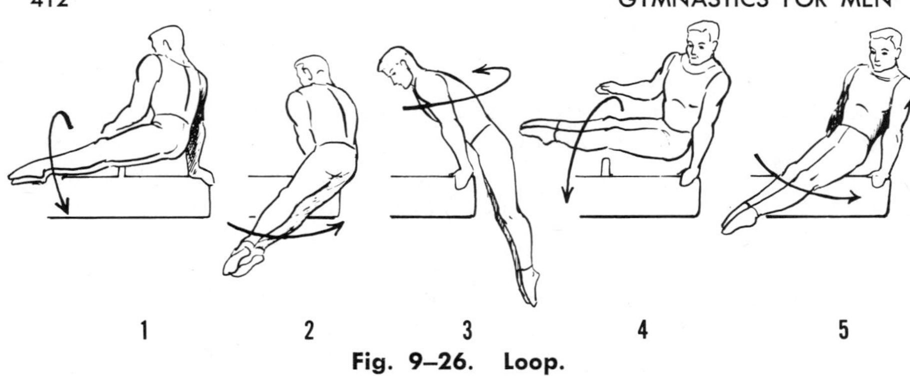

Fig. 9–26. Loop.

393. The loop in this routine follows a counterclockwise double leg circle. During this circle the right hand is replaced close to the end of the horse with the fingers curled over the far edge and only the palm on top. As the double leg circle is completed, the left hand thrusts off the pommel (1) and is also shifted to the end of the horse and placed in much the same position as the right hand but on the opposite side. The body turns to the left during the left hand shift and leans onto the right arm to compensate for the weight of the legs that are swung out to the side (2). As the legs circle around the end of the horse the feet drop considerably below the top section, the weight is centralized on both arms, and the shoulders are leaned directly forward over the horse. It helps some performers to keep their eyes on the near pommel during this part of the loop (3). As the legs swing around to the opposite side of the horse the weight is shifted almost completely to the left arm, the body turns to the left again, and the right arm thrusts off the end (4). As the legs pass over the pommel, the body is extended as for a normal double leg circle and the right hand grasps the pommel as soon as possible (5).

TEACHING TECHNIQUES. The best lead-up is the elementary loop mount. The buck, or the horse with the pommels removed, can be used for practice.

2. Tromlet (Fig. 9-27). The tromlet is a travel that starts usually from a double leg circle and ends usually with a double leg circle on the adjacent section of the horse. It does not involve a turn, as in a kehre, but faces the same direction throughout. In this routine the tromlet follows two counterclockwise double leg circles in the center and finishes with a double half leg circle on the right end. During the double leg circle that precedes the tromlet the right hand must be placed on the back side of the pommel leaving enough

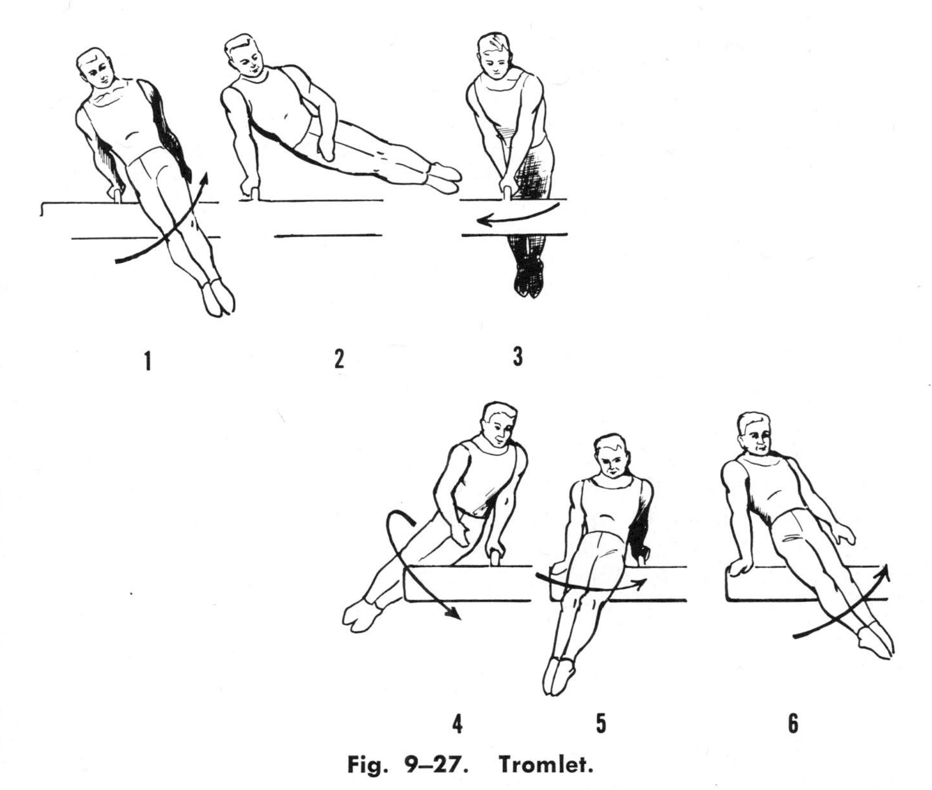

Fig. 9–27. Tromlet.

room on the front side for the left hand. As the legs flank backward over the left pommel, the left hand thrusts off (1) and transfers to the right pommel in front of the right hand (2). The weight has to be shifted to the right with this movement, but it is a bad mistake to transfer it too far. It should be shifted only to the pommel as the left hand is moved. No attempt should be made to shift the center of gravity all the way from the center to the end of the horse in one movement. The arms should be rigidly straight and the shoulders extended to make the position as tall as possible (3). As the body flanks forward over the end of the horse (4), it is extended as in a double leg circle (5) and the right arm is shifted to the end with the fingers turned to the side or maybe slightly backward. During the entire travel the shoulders should remain in line with the horse. The tromlet finishes in a rear support with the legs circling to the left (6).

TEACHING TECHNIQUES. The following stunts provide an excellent background for the tromlet.

1. The simple half leg circle travel.
2. A single leg circle travel from a front support. The hand change and timing for this skill is exactly the same as the tromlet but only one leg circles instead of two.
3. Start the tromlet as usual with both legs flanking backward over the horse but finish it with only the right leg circling forward over the end to a straddle support.
4. Start from a straddle support with the left leg forward so that only the left leg circles backward over the horse but finish with both legs flanking forward over the end to a rear support. This stunt is usually referred to as a simple tromlet.
5. Practice the complete tromlet but finish with a dismount rather than to a rear support.

3. Moore (Fig. 9–28). The moore, like the tromlet, is almost always preceded and followed by double leg circles. As the legs flank forward over the right pommel in the counterclockwise double leg circle prior to the moore, the right hand is replaced well forward on the pommel to provide enough room for the left hand beside it. The body should be extended a little more than usual on this circle to build up momentum for the moore. The flank backward over the horse should be done as usual. It is a bad mistake to start to turn too early as it will cause the body to fall way from the

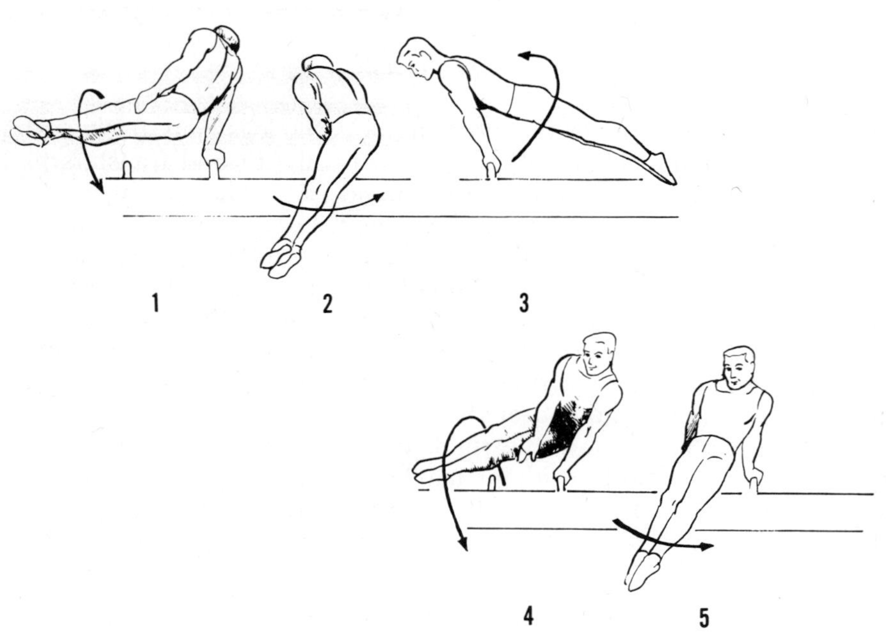

Fig. 9–28. Moore.

horse. Instead the shoulders should remain in line with the horse during the flank backward and should lean forward over the horse as in a regular double leg circle (1). This illustration is poor as the shoulders are twisting too early. As the double leg circle is completed, the body starts to turn to the left and the left hand is placed on the right pommel in an undergrip (2). In this position the center of gravity should be directly over the hands. This means the shoulders must lean well forward over the pommel. Some gymnasts like to look at, and concentrate on, the other pommel to aid in maintaining their balance. The body is almost straight, the arms are locked, the grip is very tight, and the shoulders are extended (3). Both hands press away from the pommel very vigorously and as the legs circle around to the other side of the horse the body is piked as in the double leg circle and the right hand is released (4). The legs flank forward over the far pommel, the body is extended, and the hips are rotated upward (5). The right hand grasps the pommel as soon as possible and the performer is all ready to continue with another double leg circle.

TEACHING TECHNIQUES. The simple moore has been included in a previous routine, pages 403–5. This is an excellent lead-up. Another technique is to straddle the legs so that they do not have to be lifted as high to clear the end of the horse but otherwise to execute the moore the same as usual. A third lead-up is to use the left hand on the far pommel during the first half of the moore to aid in maintaining the balance and then to quickly transfer it to the other pommel beside the right hand to complete the moore. Still another lead-up is to transfer the right hand to the opposite pommel before the legs flank over to finish the moore. This hand can be used to thrust off and assist during the flank. Some gymnasts prefer to use the regular hand and leg movements as they learn the stunt but to progress into it in another way. The first step in this method is to start the moore in the usual way but allow the legs to hit against the horse and then drop to the floor. The next step is to progress a little farther by completing the first half of the moore and then to drop to the floor on the far side of the horse. The third step is to complete the moore but as a dismount rather than to a rear support.

4. Loop to a Rear Dismount (Fig. 9–29). These two stunts are not completely new. The first half of the loop is identical to the one that started this routine, but it is not completed in the same way. The rear dismount is a familiar stunt, but this one requires a somewhat different technique. The dismount series in this routine

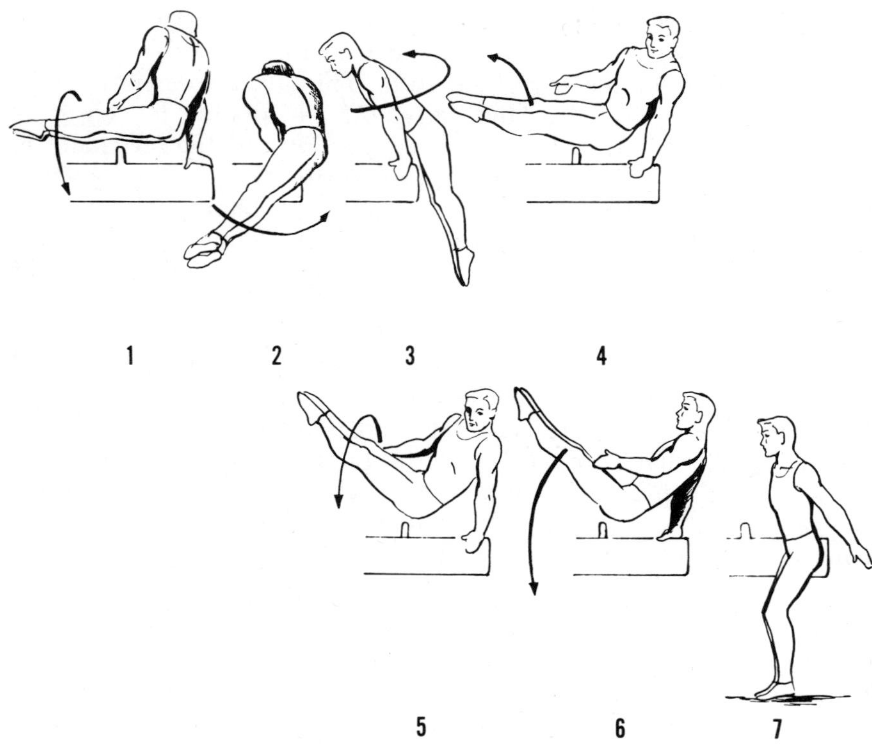

Fig. 9–29. Loop to a Rear Dismount.

is started with a kehre-out. A counterclockwise double half leg circle on the right end of the horse follows the kehre and positions the gymnast for the loop (1). As this double half leg circle is completed, the body turns to the left, the legs are swung out to the side, the weight is shifted almost completely onto the right hand, and the left hand is placed on the end of the horse with the right hand (2). The legs circle around the end of the horse with the feet considerably below the top section, the weight is equally distributed on both hands, and the shoulders lean well forward over the horse (3). Up to this point the loop has been the same as the previous one in the routine. For a more detailed description refer to page 411–12. As the legs swing around to the opposite side, the weight is shifted almost entirely onto the left hand and the right hand is taken off the horse (4). The rear dismount actually starts at this point. The legs are pumped vigorously upward and to the left over the top of the horse. The turn, which was going to the left, now reverses and starts to the right. This rotates the hips so they are facing upward. The shoulders are kept forward at this point by pressing backward on the end of the horse with the left hand. The toes are lifted as high as possible with the body in a tight pike (5). By this time the weight, which had been shifted almost entirely to the left hand earlier in the loop, is so far to the left of the horse that the balance cannot be maintained. At this point the left arm gives one last vigorous backward push as it is taken off the horse. This will tend to lift the toes a little higher. The right hand is then placed back on the end (6) as the legs are whipped downward from the high pike position to a landing with the right side to the horse (7).

TEACHING TECHNIQUES. The best way to practice the dismount is with a jump from a stand on the floor. The buck should be used. At first the jump can start from the right side of the horse when facing the end. As the gymnast becomes more proficient, he gradually moves farther and farther to the left around the end of the horse until he is jumping into almost a complete loop before the dismount.

10

Competition

GOVERNING ORGANIZATIONS

The Federation of International Gymnastics (F.I.G.) is the governing body for international gymnastics. The F.I.G. rules are used for the Olympic Games, World Championship, European Cup, Pan American Games, International Student Championship, and usually for other smaller international contests including dual meets between two nations.

There are many organizations in the United States that conduct gymnastic competition. The Amateur Athletic Union of the United States (A.A.U.) is the official representative of the F.I.G. and as such selects teams or individuals that compete for the United States in most international competitions. It also conducts a national senior and junior meet for both men and women. Approximately fifty A.A.U. associations (districts) conduct meets throughout the country at novice, junior, and senior levels. The A.A.U. has recently started an age-level gymnastic program similar to the age-level swimming program that has proved so successful.

The United States Gymnastic Federation was founded in 1962. It is an organization of other national organizations and coordinates effort between them. Unfortunately, the A.A.U. has not become a member and there has developed considerable friction between these two groups. The U.S.G.F. has received the support of most of the organizations that are interested in gymnastics and most of the coaches in the country. High schools and colleges, which are responsible for a very high percentage of our gymnastic competition, have been the backbone of this recently developed federation. The U.S.G.F. conducts national meets for both men and women at two levels, the elite and the class A divisions. The eight districts, established by the U.S.G.F., have not been very active as yet but plans are to have district meets at four levels of ability, adding classes B and C to the two above. In 1965 the U.S.G.F. introduced an excellent outline for an age-level program but as yet this has not been put into operation on a wide scale.

The National Collegiate Athletic Association (N.C.A.A.) has probably been the most active United States organization in the sport of gymnastics. For years it has conducted a national meet for men. Athletic conferences throughout the country, comprised of N.C.A.A. member institutions, also conduct gymnastic championship meets and many dual meets.

For many years isolated areas such as Philadelphia, Minneapolis, and Los Angeles have had excellent high school gymnastic programs. Since 1955 the movement has spread until almost every state now has an active high school program under the control of its state high school athletic association.

Other organizations that have conducted both national and district gymnastic competitions for their members are the American Turners, the Slovak Gymnastic Sokol, and the Y.M.C.A.

RULES

It is recommended that all teachers and coaches obtain a rule book each year and keep up to date. The most important part of the rules is the F.I.G. Code of Points. This, especially, should be in the library of all gymnastic enthusiasts. It tells better than anything else what a gymnast must learn and do to become a top performer. Refer to the bibliography for the source of rule books and the code of points.

Gymnastic competition is of two general types:

1. The dual meet (sometime triangular or quadrangular) in which the prime purpose is to determine a team champion. Determining the individual event winners and all-round winner is secondary.
2. The tournament, or championship meet, in which a team champion, an individual all-round champion, and individual event champions are determined.

F.I.G. OR INTERNATIONAL RULES

International teams are composed of six individuals and all six members compete in the six events that are included in international competition. In each event the lowest score is dropped and the five best scores are totaled to give the team score in that event. This means the maximum team score in an event is 50 points and the maximum score for the entire meet is 300 points (6×50). This method of determining a team champion uses the judges' scores directly in determining the team scores. An example is given below:

Competitor	Floor Ex.	Side H.	Rings	Long H.	Parallels	Horiz. Bar.	All-round
Endo	9.5	9.5	9.5	9.5	9.6	9.7	57.4
Hayata	9.3	9.3	9.7	9.4	~~9.3~~	9.4	56.4
Mitsukuri	9.3	9.3	~~9.3~~	9.3	9.3	9.4	55.9
Yamashita	~~9.2~~	9.4	9.4	9.7	9.4	~~9.3~~	56.4
Ono	9.3	~~9.1~~	9.5	9.3	9.3	9.6	56.1
Tsurumi	9.4	9.6	9.5	~~8.8~~	9.3	9.6	56.2
EVENT SCORE	46.8	47.1	47.7	47.2	46.9	47.7	

Team Score 283.4

NOTE: You can not obtain the team score by adding the all-round scores but must add the totals for each event, from which one score has been dropped. The scores that have been dropped for team purposes are still included in the individuals all-round score.

In dual meets (or triangular, or quadrangular) the two (or three or four) teams compete in one event at a time in the order listed above. Competitors on the teams involved are alternated in each event. In dual meets teams also alternate in being up first in events. A rotational system is used if more than two teams are involved.

In large tournaments six events are held at a time. Six teams are assigned, as team units, to each of the six events. After all six team members have competed in the event to which their team was assigned, the teams are rotated to the next event. This procedure is followed until the six teams have competed in all six events. If there are more than six teams in the tournament, another six teams are assigned and compete in the same way. If some participating groups do not enter a full six-man team, the individuals from these groups are combined into units of approximately six to facilitate the organization of the meet. These combined units do not, of course, compete as a team for a team score. The individuals within the units compete only for individual event or all-round championships.

In most big tournaments both a compulsory and an optional exercise are used. The compulsory exercises are pre-established by a committee. The compulsory competition is held on one day, the optional competition on the next, and then the two scores are totaled

University of Washington News Service photo

Charlie Denny Performing a Back Lever on the Rings. Charlie was the University of Washington's first national gymnastic champion. He won the A.A.U. flying ring title in 1962, the last year it was included as a gymnastic event. Notice the old style gymnastic pants with the stripe down the side. These have gone completely out of style in recent years.

to determine the all-round and team champions. Individual event winners are usually determined on a third day of competition by having the top six performers in each event compete again. Their third score is added to the average of the first two days' scores. Usually a dual meet between two countries lasts one day and only an optional exercise is used. If compulsory exercises are included, the meet is held on two days with the winners being determined by totaling the two scores.

COLLEGE RULES

American organizations have been slow to adopt international rules (except for the Code of Points), but in 1965 the N.C.A.A. established rules for use starting in the 1966 season that are very similar to the international rules. This lead will probably be followed by other organizations. Prior to 1966 the college rules were very similar to those used by the high schools, which are presented later.

The order of events for college competition is floor exercise, side horse, trampoline, horizontal bar, long horse, parallel bars, and rings. The trampoline is added to the six international events and is included into the team score but not included into the individual all-round.

In college dual meets a team is limited to a maximum of four men in each event. One man must be designated as an all-round contestant. This rule is to encourage the college coach to develop all-round performers. The all-round man may also enter the trampoline event if he wishes. One other contestant may be entered in an unlimited number of events. All other team members are limited to a maximum of three events. This rule discourages small teams. Its purpose is to give an opportunity for participation to more individuals.

In college championship meets five men may be entered in each individual event and three men in the all-round. Other limitations are the same as for a dual meet.

In dual meets one event is held at a time and competitors from the two teams are alternated. The principle of determining the team winner is the same as for international competition. In each event the lowest of the four scores for each team is dropped and the three best scores are totaled to give the team score in that event. This means the maximum team score in each event is 30 points and the maximum score in the meet is 210 points (7×30).

The N.C.A.A. district and championship meets follow international meet organization in theory, but the system is quite complicated and will not be presented here.

Only optional exercises are used in college competition for both dual meets and tournaments. Tournaments usually last two days with the team and all-round champions being determined on the first day. Individual event champions are determined on a second day of competition by having the top eight performers in each event compete again. The second day's score is added to the first to obtain the final score.

HIGH SCHOOL RULES

There is no such thing as official national high school rules, but the National High School Gymnastic Coaches Association does include a "Manual of Rules and Suggestions for Conducting District and State Final Gymnastic Meets" in their Handbook. Many states have a set of rules that have been adopted by the state high school athletic association or by the coaches association within the state. These differ from state to state but are generally patterned after the N.C.A.A. rules that were used until 1964. The following summary is, therefore, primarily a digest of the 1964 college rules.

Eight events are usually included in high school competition—the six international events plus tumbling and trampoline. Some states also include the rope climb but it has been dropped in the majority.

A team may enter only three men in each event in dual meets and five men in each event in tournaments. In dual meets the individual receiving the highest score from the judges in each event receives six points for his team. The second place man receives four points, the third three points, and so forth down to fifth place. In tournaments ten places are scored with first place receiving eleven points, second—nine points, third—eight points and so forth down to one point for tenth place. Competitors on the teams involved are alternated in both dual meets and tournaments. In dual meets one event is held at a time, in tournaments two events. Compulsory exercises are not used. Most tournaments involve only one day but occasionally a second day is scheduled for competition between the top ten men in each event. In two-day meets the two scores are added to determine event winners and also to determine the placings for team scores. The all-round competition, however, is completed on the first day.

A.A.U. RULES

All A.A.U. meets are of the tournament type. No provision is made in the rules for dual meets. Eight events are included—the six international events plus tumbling and trampoline—with the order of events left up to the meet committee. In championship meets both compulsory and optional exercises are used for the six international events and the trampoline. The compulsory work is held on the first day, the optional on the second day, and the event finals on the third day. Only the top six individuals compete on the final day in each event. Tumbling does not have a compulsory exercise. The top six individuals in this event also compete on the final day. Teams are not limited in total number or in the number they may enter in an event. The order of competition in each event is by draw out of a hat, but no competitor is required to perform first in more than one event. In the international events team points are awarded to the top six competitors in each event on the following basis: seven points for first place, five points for second place, four points for third place, three points for fourth place, two points for fifth place, and one point for sixth place. In the special events, tumbling and trampoline, the top six finishers also receive team points, but they are reduced by half from the international event scoring (3½, 2½, 2, 1½, 1, ½).

U.S.G.F. RULES

Almost all U.S.G.F. meets are of the tournament type. Eight events are included for men—the six international events plus tumbling and trampoline. For national meets both a compulsory and optional exercise are used for all eight events. The U.S.G.F. was the first large national organization to incorporate compulsory exercises for tumbling and trampoline. The national meet is a three-day competition with compulsory work on the first day, optional on the second, and the finals on the third day. The six top men in each event enter the finals. No provision is made for team competition in the U.S.G.F. rules. Whether this will be incorporated in the future is not known. The U.S.G.F. rule book is incomplete at the present time

Opening ceremonies of the 1962 National A.A.U. Championship for men and women. The meet was held in the Seattle Arena on the World's Fair Grounds. Note the balance beam, men's parallel bars, trampoline, and two floor exercise areas. Judges, score flashers, scorekeepers, and other officials are in position to start the first two events—the balance beam and the parallel bars.

in other respects as well as regarding team competition. As the organization grows, their rules will undoubtedly be expanded.

DIGEST OF F.I.G. CODE OF POINTS

The F.I.G. Code of Points form the basis for judging most gymnastic competition in the United States. This code applies to the actual evaluation of a competitor's performance.

Article One—Purpose and Motive of the Code of Points

The code of points was created with the aim of assuring an objective and uniform assessment of gymnastic exercises at the international level. It also provides valuable information for gymnasts and coaches to aid them in their preparation for competition.

Article Two—The Jury and Its Organization

The jury for each event is composed of five members; one judge-referee, and four other judges. In international competition an equal number of judges are chosen from participating countries.

Article Three—Judging

1. The judge-referee supervises the other four judges, calls them together when consultations are needed, and determines whether the spread between the middle two scores is too great. He scores all exercises himself in case his score is needed as an aid in securing agreement between judges. He may replace any judge who is not performing his duties according to regulations. He is responsible for the administrative aspects of the judging process.
2. All exercises are scored from 0 to 10 points in tenths of a point by the four scoring judges. The competitor's score is determined by dividing the middle two scores by two.
3. The difference between the two middle scores must not exceed:

   .2 if their average is 9.50 or more
   .3 if their average is between 8.50 and 9.45
   .5 if their average is between 7.00 and 8.45
   1.0 if their average is below 7.00

   If the difference exceeds these limits a consultation must be held to obtain agreement. In situations of this kind it follows that the two extreme scores are also incorrect.. The judge-referee should point this out to the four judges so that judging will proceed more accurately.
4. In order to obtain a common starting point the judges consult for the first and second exercises of the day. If the scores drift apart during the day, the judge-referee has the right to request other consultations. In finals consultations will not take place.

Article Four—Uniforms

A team must be uniformly dressed. On parallel bars, horizontal bar, rings, and side horse all gymnasts shall wear long pants with socks and shoes, or socks only. For floor exercise and vaulting the gymnast may wear long pants with socks and shoes, or socks only; or, he may perform in shorts without socks or shoes. The uniform may differ from one to another in these two events providing the color is the same. In all events a shirt must be worn.

Article Five—Composition of Exercises

1. *Parallel Bars.* Swinging, flight, strength, and holds with swing and flight predominating. Must contain one strength part and one B part in which both hands release the bars momentarily. Not more than three held positions.
2. *Horizontal Bar.* Exclusively swinging movements without stops, with giant swing turns and variations, and with high value connecting movements.
3. *Side Horse.* Exclusively swinging movements with no stops, single and double leg circles, scissors forward and backward of which one must be executed at least twice in succession. Double leg circles must predominate and all three sections of the horse must be used.
4. *Rings.* Swing, strength, and holds without swinging of the rings. At least two handstands, one executed with strength and one with swing through the hanging position. One difficult held position must be included besides the handstands.
5. *Floor Exercise.* A harmonious and rhythmic composition alternating elements of suppleness, strength, balance, and agility with kips, jumps, and tumbling movements. The competitor must move in different directions and avoid: repetitions, connecting movements and poses that are too easy, and excessive running steps. The duration of the exercise is 50 to 70 seconds. The area is 12 x 12 meters.
6. *Long Horse.* The type, difficulty, execution, and value of the vaults are included in Article Eight.

Article Six—Judging of Execution

A. Special Provisions for Compulsory Exercises

1. On parallel bars, horizontal bar, side horse, and rings a compulsory exercise may be repeated if done poorly. The gymnast is obliged to inform the jury of his intentions to repeat by raising his hand as soon as he dismounts so that the first attempt will not be judged. The repetition takes place after a reasonable rest and only the second trial counts.
2. On the long horse two vaults are executed but only the best one counts.
3. Floor exercise can not be repeated.
4. The compulsory exercise contains three to four B parts besides the necessary A parts. Its value is only 9.2 to 9.4 by optional difficulty standards but nevertheless is awarded full combination and difficulty rating and is scored out of 10.0 points. In order to facilitate judging each compulsory exercise is divided into parts and each part is assigned a point value.
5. The judge must be sure that the exercise is performed according to the printed text. Deductions for execution contrary to the text will be as follows:

a. If movements are not performed, the total value awarded to the part is deducted. If the omission facilitates the execution of the part preceding or following, an extra deduction of up to 1.0 can be made.
b. Movements not prescribed (including extra swings) are penalized .3 to .5 for each movement. If the movement facilitates the execution of the part that precedes or follows, an extra deduction of .1 to .5 may be made.

B. Imperfect Execution of Compulsory and Optional Exercises
1. Deductions are made for both execution faults and faults of technical order.
2. General faults of execution and the deduction each time they occur are:
   a. Bad position of the feet, legs, arms, head, and body .1 to .3
   b. Touching the horse, the bars, the pommels, the uprights, the base of the apparatus, the floor, or the ropes with the legs, buttocks or any part of the body in which this is not called for in the proper execution of a movement .2 to .5
   c. Stops during an exercise taking into account the difficulty of the part preceding .3 to .7.
   A pronounced interruption .5 to .7
3. Faults of technical order and the deduction each time they occur are:
   a. Walking in a handstand .1 each step .1 to .5
   b. Several attempts at a skill .2 to .5
   c. Interruption in raising to a handstand .1 to .3
   d. Swinging movements executed with strength or strength movements executed with swing .1 to .3
   e. Duration of holds should be 2 seconds on parallel bars and floor exercises and 3 seconds on rings

   Holds too short:
   On parallel bars and floor exercise only 1 second .2
   On rings only 2 seconds .2
   On rings only 1 second .4
   Holding positions too long, especially if they are not difficult, may be considered a fault in combination.

   f. On rings:
   Bent arms in a handstand *or* touching ropes .2 to .3
   Bent arms *and* touching ropes .3 to .5
   Bent arms in any cross or lever .1 to .5
   Too much swing of the ropes .1 to .3
   Falling from a handstand .3 to .5

   g. Floor exercise:
   Lack of balance and precarious stands .1 to .5
   Lack of harmony, rhythm, or suppleness for individual skills .2
   Lack of harmony, rhythm, or suppleness during the entire exercise up to 1.0

   h. Side horse:
   Lack of freedom in double leg circles .1 to .3
   Scissors without raising the hips .1 to .3

i. In general:
Horizontal supports, suspensions, "L" supports, too high or too low; poor scales; handstands not perpendicular or with shoulders forward; regrasping the bars late after a somersault or stutz on the parallel bars; moving from one movement to another too rapidly; etc. .1 to .3

4. Landings
Deductions for an exercise that does not begin or end in a perfect stand are:
   a. Small step or hop or bad posture .1 to .2
   b. Several steps or hops, or touching the floor with the hands without real support, or very bad posture .2 to .3
   c. Sitting or kneeling down, or falling on the back, or supporting weight on the floor with the hands .3 to .5
   d. Undesirable behavior before or after the exercise .1 to .3
5. Falling from the apparatus or touching the floor
   a. If a gymnast drops to the floor, he can continue his exercise immediately or at the latest after 30 seconds. During the 30 seconds the gymnast has freedom of movement. If he does not continue in 30 seconds he is scored on the basis of movements executed. The judge-referee should notify the gymnast or coach after 10, 20, and 30 seconds.
   b. Interruption on the side horse and parallel bars by touching the floor with the feet without releasing the equipment .8
   c. Interruption by a complete release, then continuing within 30 seconds 1.0
   d. Ripped uniforms, unwound wrist bands, ripped hand guards, or wounds can not influence the stipulations concerning interruptions.
6. Assistance to the gymnast
   a. So as to prevent accidents a spotter is permitted by the horizontal bar, parallel bars, rings, and long horse. The penalty for touching is .1 for a slight touch to 1.0 for assistance to stop a fall. In compulsory exercises the deduction should be equivalent to the value of the part in which assistance is given.
   b. On the side horse and floor exercise a spotter is not permitted.
   c. On the horizontal bar and rings the gymnast can receive assistance to jump onto the apparatus.
   d. In no case can the coach, or any other person, talk to the gymnast while he is competing.

Article Seven—Scoring Optional Exercises

A. General Rules
   1. Two important elements of scoring must be added to *execution* for optional exercises, these are *difficulty* and *combination*. These two items represent the value of the exercise.
   2. The optional exercise can not be repeated except for the long horse where two trials are allowed.
   3. The optional exercises for the four apparatus and for floor exercise are rated from 0 to 10 points with deductions by tenths of a point and full points. The ten points are divided as follows:

Value of the exercise—Difficulty		3.40
	Combination	1.60
Execution		5.00
Total		10.00

4. On parallel bars a reuther board may be used for mounting.

B. Difficulty

1. To obtain the maximum score on the four apparatus and floor exercise the routine must be composed of at least:

   Six parts of A difficulty (least difficult)
   Four parts of B difficulty (medium difficulty)
   One part of C difficulty (superior difficulty)

2. In the finals of competitions such as the World Games and the Olympic Games exercises must include at least six A parts, four B parts, and two C parts.
3. Deductions for missing parts are as follows: A parts—.20, B parts—.40, C parts—.60. If a C part is replaced by a B part, the difficulty score will only be decreased by .20.
4. An extra C part can replace a B part and an extra B part can replace an A part.
5. When exercises are very difficult to rate because of many major faults, the 3.40 points for difficulty are disregarded and the competitor is scored a maximum of 7.5 points for three quarters of an exercise, a maximum of 5.0 points for half of an exercise, and a maximum of 2.5 points for one quarter of an exercise.
6. The exercise must correspond to the capabilities of the gymnast because in artistic gymnastics the competitor must show he is master of his body and that he can complete his exercise with grace, ease, and sureness.

C. Combination

1. The exercise must be composed of parts proper for the apparatus, according to Article Five.
2. Each exercise must end with an effective dismount corresponding to the rest of the exercise in regard to value.
3. The essential parts must be connected with elegance and without extra swings. Excessive repetitions and parts too easy in relation to the standard of difficulty must be avoided.
4. The composition of the optional exercise must differ clearly from the compulsory. Including similar parts does not necessarily constitute a fault if movements before and after are different.
5. An exercise that presents great risks, originality, and different connecting parts will be less severely judged for small execution faults than the exercise that is lacking in these aspects.

D. Penalizing Combination

1. Combinations and movements of the wrong type	.1 to .3
2. Extra swings	.3 to .5
3. Dismount not corresponding to the difficulty of the rest of the exercise	.1 to .3
4. Parts without value or excessive repetition	.1 to .3
5. Resembling compulsory exercise	.1 to .5
6. Same dismount as the compulsory and with the same preceding part	.2

7. Over or under floor exercise time limit; two seconds or less .1; two to five seconds .2; five to nine seconds .3; more than nine seconds .5.
8. Going outside the floor exercise area each time: with one part of the body .1; with both feet or both hands .2; sitting, kneeling, or lying outside the area .3.
9. Maximum penalty for combination is 1.60.

Article Eight—Long Horse Vaulting

A. General Rules
1. The horse is placed lengthwise with the distance of the reuther board at the discretion of the gymnast.
2. All vaults must have a momentary support of one or two hands. The length of the run is optional but the running track must be at least 18 meters long.
3. The compulsory and the optional vaults can be executed twice and the best score obtained for each will count. The gymnast has the option of doing the same vault twice or two different vaults for his optional. Both vaults are performed one after the other.
4. The scoring of the vault begins when the board or the horse is touched. It ends when the gymnast is in a normal standing position. It is permissible to run around the board and horse without it counting as a trial but this may be done only twice. If this happens, a third and last trial will be given.
5. In the finals of the World Games, Olympic Games, or other similar competitions each finalist must execute two different vaults and may have two trials for each. The final score is obtained by adding the scores of the best two different vaults and dividing by two. This score is averaged with the competitor's previous score obtained during the first two days.

B. Judging Long Horse Vaulting
Judging long horse vaulting is divided into four factors: difficulty of the optional vault or interpretation of the compulsory vault; position of one or both hands; flight before and after hand contact; and technical execution and interpretation.

C. Difficulty and Form of Vaults
1. The vaults must conform to the illustrations provided for each of the nineteen listed vaults. (Note: Most of these are included in Chapter 4 of this text.)
2. Vaults not included in the table of difficulty must be evaluated by comparing them with similar vaults that are included. In order to encourage execution of vaults of greater difficulty than those included in the table small faults in these will be less severely penalized.

D. Position of the Hands and Zones of Support
The length of the horse is divided into five zones from one end to the other and in the following order: 400 mm.; 200 mm.; 400 mm.; 200 mm.; and 400 mm. The zones are marked by white lines 1 cm. wide so that the exterior edge of the line delimits the zone. To obtain maximum credit for the vault the hand or hands must be placed clearly in either of the two end zones. Should any part of the hand extend beyond the end zone a penalty of 1.0 point per zone will be incurred. (Refer to page 110 in Chapter 4 for an illustration.)

E. Pre-flight and After-flight
The maximum of ten points will be awarded only if, at the time of hand contact, the angle between the line of the body and the top of the horse is at least 30°. (This applies only to certain far end vaults.) The maximum will be 9.5 for a horizontal support and 9.0 if the feet are not higher than the top of the horse. (Refer to page 110 in Chapter 4 for an illustration.) Vaults must have high and long after-flights according to the illustrations for each vault. For vaults with near end hand placement the pre-flight and after-flight must correspond to the illustrations.

F. Penalizing Execution
For practical reasons this section includes deductions for execution, placement of hands, difficulty, and for pre-flight and after-flight.

1.	Body angle at time of hand contact less than 30°	.1 to 1.0
2.	Flight too low and short after hand contact	.1 to .5
3.	When, at the landing the gymnast is not at a distance from the horse corresponding to the illustration	.1 to .5
4.	Too much flexion of the body before landing	.1 to .5
5.	Bad direction of the vault	.1 to .5
6.	Placement of the hands in either of the 200-mm. zones	1.0
7.	Placement of the hands in the 400-mm. center zone	2.0
8.	Momentary bad position of the feet, legs, body, or head	.1 to .3
9.	If the faults in No. 8 are committed during the entire vault	.4 to 1.0
10.	Touching the horse with the feet, legs, knees, or body	.2 to .5
	For serious cases	.6 to 1.0
11.	Arms bent during a handspring or a Yamashita	.1 to 1.0
12.	Knees bent during a hecht	.1 to 1.0
13.	The landings after the vaults are judged on the same basis as for the other events	.1 to .5
14.	For vaults of great difficulty with a high and long after-flight the landing deduction may be reduced by	.1 to .2

G. Organization of the Jury for Long Horse Vaulting
1. Two judges shall place themselves so that they can observe the vault head on and they should concentrate on the trajectory. The other two concentrate on the first phase of the vault.
2. The two judges assigned to check the placement of the hands place themselves on either side of the horse.
3. The judge-referee places himself on a diagonal to the front of the horse so that he can observe the vault in its entirety.
4. In order to expedite judging the competitor must announce to the jury the type of vault he will execute.

H. Form and Technical Execution of the Vaults
(Note: This section includes the illustrations, the description, and the difficulty rating of each vault. It is a very lengthy section and because almost all of this material has been included in Chapter 4 it will not be repeated here.)

DIFFICULTY TABLE OF A, B, AND C PARTS

In conjunction with the F.I.G. Code of Points there is a table for each event that lists many of the A, B, and C stunts that are commonly incorporated into gymnastic exercises. The list is too lengthy to be included in this text. Coaches and teachers should have one of them available for reference. The list is included in the U.S.G.F. rule book or in the F.I.G. Code of Points published by the A.A.U. of the United States. Refer to the bibliography for these references.

Some general remarks regarding A, B, and C parts will be included in this chapter.

The "A" parts are the basic movements of an exercise such as a kip, hip circle, giant swing, scissor, and handspring. They are the easiest parts of the exercise. In some cases parts are too easy to be classified as an A part unless a series or combination is included. An example of this would be a half leg circle on the side horse.

A "B" part is a stunt of average difficulty, or one more difficult than an A part. Combining two A parts may result in a B part. The difficulty that arises from the combination is the determining factor.

The "C" part is a skill of superior difficulty and must be more difficult than B parts. C parts often result from a combination of A and B, or B and B parts.

Generally a stunt recognized as an A, B, or C part counts only once within an exercise but it may count twice, or even more, if the movement that precedes or follows is of a different nature.

HOW TO JUDGE

The first step in good judging is to get a rule book and study it carefully. The second step is diligent practice. These are requirements for becoming proficient in any activity—study and practice. The practice does not have to occur in a competitive situation but may be obtained by evaluating performances at any team practice session at which complete exercises are being performed. Judging performances recorded on film is another way to get practice.

The digest of the F.I.G. Code of Points in this chapter gives all the information that is necessary for a judge but does not indicate how to apply it. There are many techniques that are used. Some judges use a mechanical "counter" or "clicker" in one hand and "clicking off" the number of deductions in tenths of a point as they occur. Others use their fingers to count B and C moves or to add up deductions. Some record B and C moves and/or technical requirements on a work pad as they occur and add execution deductions in their head. Many areas in the United States are experimenting with two, or even three, sets of judges. One set of judges scores difficulty, another set combination, and a third set execution. If just two sets are used, one group scores both combination and difficulty.

Many systems of judging have been developed. The only one that will be explained in this chapter is the "Approved Method of Judging Men's Gymnastics" established by the F.I.G. Technical Committee in 1964. The following is a digest of this method as presented by Tom Maloney in the 1965–66 A.A.U. Gymnastic Guide and Handbook. Mr. Maloney, former coach at the U. S. Military Academy and Olympic Team Coach, is now one of the leading judges both in the United States and internationally.

F.I.G. APPROVED METHOD OF JUDGING MEN'S GYMNASTICS

The judge must first be alert and give complete concentration to the routine being executed.

As the gymnast performs the judge must first count the number of B and C parts. These may be recorded on a scoring pad without taking the eyes off the gymnast. At the finish of the exercise the first step is for the judge to count the number of B's and C's and award a difficulty rating. If the gymnast included one C part, four B parts, and six A parts the judge can immediately give the full difficulty value of 10.0 to this routine. If he had no C part, four B parts, and six A parts there would be a deduction of .6 for the missing C part and the exercise would be given a difficulty value of 9.4. If another gymnast's exercise has five B parts, six A parts, but no C part it would be subject to a .2 deduction only, and would receive a difficulty value of 9.8.

Item number two, combination, is now considered. The first point is, did the exercise meet with the requirements for that particular event? If, for example, on the rings the gymnast did not have a press to a handstand this would mean a deduction of .3 for failure to meet one of the event requirements. Or, if he did not have one hold of pronounced difficulty he would receive an additional .1 to .3 deduction. It is interesting to remember that an exercise composed of eleven C parts, if it lacks an event requirement, is subject to a .1 to .3 deduction. Deductions must be made for other combination faults such as extra swings, a poor dismount, parts without value, and abusive repetitions. The total of these deductions is subtracted from the difficulty value awarded to the exercise to give an exercise value considering both difficulty and combination.

For example, let us consider that a gymnast has just finished an exercise with one C, three B, and six A parts. The one missing B part calls for a deduction of .4 and gives a difficulty value of 9.6. If this gymnast omitted an event requirement, a .3 deduction, and had an extra swing, determined to be a .5 deduction, a total of .8 must be deducted for combination. This brings the value of the exercise down to 8.8. All judges should be able to agree on a common score for difficulty and combination if the system is being used correctly.

The third item, execution, can now be considered. Actually, faults in execution can be divided into technical errors and errors in form. Technical errors refer to poor execution of gymnastic movements, or to movements not performed to their highest potential. For example, scissors too low, double leg circles lacking amplitude, bent arms in a cross, handstands overarched and poor "L" positions. Errors in form are poor positions of the feet, legs, body, or head. It is very possible that judges will differ on the degree of the fault, that is, whether the fault should bring a .1 or .2 deduction. Differences like this are very acceptable as long as they do not bring about a spread in scores greater than the range considered acceptable in the Code of Points.

As the gymnast performs, the judge keeps a running total of the deductions in his head. At the end of the exercise this total can be recorded on the scoring pad. After deductions are made for difficulty and combination, execution deductions can be subtracted from the value given to the exercise to give the gymnast's score.

This system requires that the judges remain alert and concentrate at all times, but the judge is more likely to give the gymnast the score he rightfully earns with this system than with any other. At first it seems too complicated, but it is sound and thorough and has been developed by a group of gymnastic experts with many years of judging experience.

A device that could revolutionize gymnastic judging has recently been developed by Chet Phillips, former coach at the United States Naval Academy. It is a very simple and inexpensive "stick" called a Scorstik. A judge can keep a count of his deductions on this scorstik by moving his thumb and first finger along a series of notches on the stick.

HOW TO KEEP SCORE

Score-keeping does not involve great mathematical ability, but it does require concentration and the ability to work speedily and accurately. The author is a firm believer that two individuals should be assigned to every phase of score-keeping and that they should work independently and then, after completing each process, check to see if they have the same results. This eliminates almost all chance of error. If this procedure is followed, the only real chance of error is in "flashing the score" as this is the only process done individually. If the judges are instructed to take the time to visually check their score flasher's boards this process can also be kept free of error. At the end of the meet each judge's score sheet can be checked very rapidly against his column on the scorekeeper's sheet as an extra check for accuracy.

In a dual meet two scorekeepers can handle all the processes of score-keeping but, for a larger meet, two or more individuals must be assigned to keep the individual event score, two to keep the all-round and two to keep team score. If the results are to be duplicated, extra helpers may be assigned to copy the results onto the ditto master after the scorekeepers are sure their work is accurate. If these individuals stay just one step behind the scorekeepers, the ditto can be ready to go a few seconds after each event ends.

Whether one or many individuals are used, the steps in scorekeeping are the same and are as follows:

1. Copy the four judges' scores on the official score sheet being careful to keep them in the correct column, that is, judge number one in column one, and so forth.

2. Cross out the highest score and the lowest score, add the middle two scores and divide by two. Example: ~~8.8~~, 8.6, ~~8.3~~, 8.5–17.1–8.55. For the long horse, in which two vaults are scored, only the highest total of the middle two scores is divided by two to give the competitor's final score.

3. If both a compulsory and an optional exercise have been performed in the meet, the two scores obtained are added together for the composite score. This same procedure would apply if two scores are received in a preliminary and final session of a meet even though an optional exercise was performed in both sessions. If it is a three-day meet with a compulsory, an optional, and then another final optional, the compulsory and first optional scores are added and divided by two and then the second optional score is added to this composite score.

4. After an event is completed the place winners are determined and marked on the score sheet. The number of place winners that have to be indicated will differ for different meets. It will range from three to as many as ten.

5. After an event is completed the scores are transferred to the team score sheet. This will involve one of two procedures.

   a. *International method*—The total of the scores obtained by the top five performers on the team is transferred to the team score sheet. In the college adaptation of this method the total of the scores obtained by the top three performers on the team is transferred to the team score sheet. A running score may be obtained after each event.

b. *Traditional U.S. method*—The number of team points awarded to the various places from first to fifth in a dual meet, or first to sixth in other meets, or first to tenth in still other meets are indicated beside the performer's name on the event score sheet. If there is a tie, the points for the two positions are added together and divided by two so that the tying individuals receive an equal number of team points. A tie for a position eliminates the next position, for example, if there is a tie for third place there will be no fourth place awarded. The next man will be fifth. These points are then totaled for each team and transferred to the team score sheet. A running score may be obtained after each event.

6. When an event has been completed, the scores obtained by competitors competing in the all-round event are transferred from the event score sheet to the all-round score sheet. A running score can be kept for each all-round performer so that this can be announced periodically.

7. At the end of the meet the final all-round scores and team scores are obtained by totaling the event scores. The scorekeeper must see that at least one copy of every score sheet (there will be two if all scorekeeping has been done in pairs) gets to the meet director. One copy is usually given to the announcer after each event.

PLANNING GYMNASTIC TOURNAMENTS

In a gymnastic tournament any number of teams or unattached individual competitors can compete. Careful planning is necessary to have a successful meet. This is also true for swimming, track or any other sport in which there are a number of different events. It is no more difficult to run a gymnastic tournament than a meet in one of these other sports.

The following steps in planning for a meet are presented as a guide. This list includes all the steps necessary for a large championship meet in which many teams and competitors come from out of town. It is hoped that the length of the list is not disconcerting. Many items can be overlooked for an intramural meet or even an interschool meet with a limited number of participants from the local area.

ITEMS TO CONSIDER

1. Form a games committee and select a meet director. An energetic teacher or coach can serve as a one-man games committee as well as the meet director if he wishes.

2. Select a date and time for the meet. Check to see that the date does not conflict with other activities. Reserve facilities.

3. Apply for a sanction from the A.A.U. or the U.S.G.F. if the meet is an open meet. This is not necessary if competitors are limited to those attending school and the meet is held in one of the participating schools.

4. Establish rules for the meet. It is always wise to make known to all coaches and competitors that unless otherwise stated the official rules of the A.A.U., U.S.G.F., N.C.A.A., or state high school athletic association will govern the meet. The latest rule book should be used. In case a question or protest arises the meet director can then refer to the official source. For almost every meet there are rules that have to be modified and special regulations that have to be established, such as:

a. Who is eligible to compete?
b. How many levels of competition are to be held? Will all compete together or will they be divided by ability (beginners, intermediates, and advanced) or by school grades?
c. What events will be held? Is the all-round event to be included? Because of lack of equipment or lack of performers certain events are sometimes not held.
d. Are required, or optional, or both required and optional exercises to be used? (See item 7 for further information.)
e. Will it be a single-session or two-session meet? What will be the order of events and time schedule of events?
f. How many boys may enter from each team? How many from one team may enter each event? Neither the A.A.U. nor the U.S.G.F. rules limit the number on a team or the number in an event from a single team.
g. How many events may an individual enter?
h. How many places are to be scored and how will team points be awarded?
i. Are awards to be presented? If so, they should be ordered well in advance. Awards should be inexpensive and of the symbolic type.
j. Is an entry fee to be charged? It has become customary to charge a small entry fee for most meets to cover the cost of awards and incidental expenses. An entry fee usually insures that the competitor will actually show up for competition. A knowledge of the number of participants facilitates planning and organization.
k. Is there to be an entry deadline? A deadline at least a day before the meet enables the meet director to make last minute plans, to draw for order of competition, and to prepare score sheets in advance.

5. Appoint committees. If the meet is small this is not necessary, as the meet director can, and often does, handle all details himself.

For a large meet, committees are usually established for several or all of the following: publicity, financing, equipment, housing of competitors, awards, duplication of results, program, judges, scorekeepers, score flashers, and ushers.

6. Distribute the information bulletin and entry blanks to prospective competitors and coaches. This should be mailed to other schools or organizations several weeks in advance. For an intramural meet, posting pertinent information and a sign-up sheet on bulletin boards might be all that is necessary. Two example information bulletins and two example entry blanks are included in the Appendix, pages 453–56. One of these, in each case, is suitable for an intramural meet, the other for a larger meet.

7. Distribute required exercises. If required exercises are to be used, they should be made available several weeks in advance. Usually exercises for large championship meets are available several months, or even as much as a year, in advance. These should be mailed out with an announcement of the coming meet, or if they are for an intramural meet they should be posted on the bulletin board in the gymnasium. Required exercises should always be tried out before adopting them. Usually revisions are necessary, as a routine that looks good on paper is not always practical. Advantages of required exercises are:

a. They provide an example for the gymnast. This is especially valuable for a beginning gymnast.
b. They set a standard for the meet. Students unable to learn the required exercises are eliminated.
c. They stimulate interest by providing a goal.
d. They are disciplinary in nature as competitors are forced to learn new skills or perform old skills in a particular way. Even the advanced gymnast is often forced to learn a skill that he has neglected.
e. They are easier to judge than optional exercises because difficulty and technical value do not have to be considered.

The main disadvantage of required exercises is that they force competitors to follow a pattern and allow no place for initiative, originality, and the presentation of the gymnasts' best and most difficult skills. If time permits, a combination of the two types of exercises can be used. If time does not permit, required exercises are best for the inexperienced gymnast, while optional exercises are best for the experienced gymnast.

8. Publicize the meet by using the usual mediums in the school, in the entire community, or throughout a wider area depending on the nature of the meet.

9. Make arrangements to house competitors if necessary. Meets

that involve overnight stays should ordinarily be avoided for school teams.

10. Invite local dignitaries such as the principal, superintendent, and community leaders.

11. Plan the awards ceremony. Awards can be presented after each event, at special times throughout the meet, or at the end of the meet. Presenting awards periodically throughout the meet is probably the best method. Arrange for a "queen" or other dignitary to present the awards. A victory stand should be used, but the awards ceremony should not be overly emphasized so that winning seems more important than the recreational and physiological values of participation. An added feature sometimes incorporated is to have photos taken of event winners for presentation to them at a later date.

12. Provide enough equipment for an adequate warmup for all events. A duplicate set of equipment in an adjacent gymnasium is desirable. A policy that is now generally being followed is to forbid warmups on the floor of competition after the meet starts. If a certain piece of equipment was not available prior to the meet, an exception is made to this policy. Gymnasts should be instructed to be on the gym floor at least 45 minutes before the meet in order to warm up for all events.

13. Arrange for lockers, shower facilities, and towels. Provide a checking service for valuables.

14. Arrange for the necessary number of officials and other workers.

a. *Judges*—The rules call for four scoring judges, a superior judge, and an extra judge for certain events. For a small meet this number can be reduced without affecting the success of the meet. For a large meet in which more than one event is held at a time a second set of judges has to be provided. Mail special instructions to judges and/or hold a briefing or instructional session prior to the meet. Have their pay checks ready in advance so that they can be paid immediately after the meet.

b. *Scorekeepers*—It is wise to have two scorekeepers who work independently and then check to see if they have obtained the same results. In this way mistakes are almost eliminated. If more than one event is held at a time, a second set of scorekeepers has to be provided. If an all-round score, or team score, is being kept, two more scorekeepers should be assigned to these tasks. For a large meet a head scorekeeper should be appointed to coordinate the work and collect and safeguard all score sheets. Example score sheets are included in the Appendix, pages 457–59.

c. *Announcers*—If only one event is held at a time, one announcer can handle a meet very satisfactorily. A public address system should be used for opening remarks, announcing each event, presentation of awards, calling competitors for competition, reading judges' scores, and any special announcements. If two events are held at a time, two announcers may be used, although one experienced announcer can handle the work.

d. *Score flashers*—The work of the judges is made easier if each judge is provided with an assistant to flash his score to the scorekeepers. Flash cards can be made out of paper or cloth. Two pads with numbers from 1 to 10 tacked side by side on a piece of plywood enable the score flasher to flash any number from .1 to 10.0. Another common method of flashing scores is to use small slates and chalk. Another less common method in the United States is to have a clerk collect the judges scores on four slips of paper and take them to the scorekeepers.

e. *Floor manager and equipment men*—There is always a certain amount of equipment moving or adjusting necessary just prior to, during, and after the meet. Depending on the size of the meet a crew of two to six individuals who are familiar with the equipment is needed. Appoint one as floor manager and brief him in detail before the meet starts.

f. *Medical attendant*—A doctor, nurse, trainer, or person qualified in first-aid is a desirable official to have on call for any athletic contest. The common first-aid materials should be available.

g. *Pushers*—"Pusher" is the name given to an individual who moves among the competitors and alerts them as their turn to compete approaches. These officials greatly speed up a meet by seeing that gymnasts are ready with sweat clothing off, hand guards on, and chalk applied.

h. *Marshals*—As in track and field, keeping the field of competition clear of unauthorized individuals is a problem. Marshals should be provided with an arm band or badge to identify them.

i. *Other personnel*—Ticket sellers, ushers, program distributors, photographers, locker room attendants, parking lot attendants, refreshment stand personnel, etc., might be necessary for some meets.

15. Decide on event order and the number of events to be held at a time. This should be done well ahead of time, if possible, so that the information can be released in the information bulletin. Sometimes this cannot be done until the number of entries is known. If the information has not been released previously, or included in the program, it should be posted in several places for the benefit of competitors.

16. Diagram the placement of equipment on the floor and plan for the movement of equipment during the meet. Be sure to measure and mark the floor exercise area prior to the meet.

17. Have programs printed. The program should be planned and outlined well in advance. It is desirable to leave the actual printing of the program as late as possible in order to include information that is usually not available until just before the meet. Some of the usual items included in a gymnastic program are: the meet committee; officials; acknowledgments; time schedule of events; list of competitors with their numbers and team affiliation; order of competition for each event; informative information such as how gymnasts are judged, digest of rules, and how exercises are composed in each event; and a blank score sheet so that spectators can keep score.

18. Plan the opening ceremony. Include a march in of competitors, necessary introductions, the National Anthem, etc.

19. Prepare score sheets and announcer's sheet. As soon as the entry deadline has passed, the order of competition can be drawn and score sheets prepared. It is desirable to have this information in the program, but if this is not possible the order of competition should be posted in several places so that competitors can refer to it. It is desirable, but not essential, that each judge have an order of competition list on which to write and record his score.

20. Provide the following list of equipment besides the necessary gymnastic equipment: public address system; gymnastic chalk and resin for hands and feet; chalk receptacles; dry towels to wipe off equipment; wet towels for competitors' feet; competitors' numbers; fine sandpaper to rub caked chalk off the equipment; record player or tape recorder for background music; stop watch to time floor exercise and tumbling; wrenches and tape measure to use in adjusting equipment; pencils, scratch pads, and clip boards for judges and scorekeepers; flash cards or slates, chalk, and erasers; chairs for judges, score flashers, and scorekeepers; tables for the superior judge and scorekeepers for each event; a table for the head scorekeeper (isolated from all the hustle and bustle of the meet); a duplicating machine; the awards and an award platform.

21. Provide seating for competitors, officials, and the press, and a rest area away from the competition for competitors.

22. Have results duplicated. In recent years it has been common practice to provide copies of the results for newspapers, coaches, and competitors. With a little planning this can be done within a few minutes after each event is over. There are a number of methods that can be used. If only a few copies are needed, the scorekeepers can keep carbon copies of their work. If more copies are needed, as each event is concluded the results can be quickly typed on a ditto sheet. A more efficient method to use, if many copies of the results are needed, is to prepare the ditto masters ahead of time. A

few blank copies can then be run off in advance so that judges can have these on which to work, some can be posted for competitors, and the scorekeepers can use these as work sheets. It is possible for the scorekeepers to keep score on the ditto master so that immediately upon conclusion of the event the results can be duplicated. The disadvantage of this method is the possibility of the scorekeepers making errors on the ditto master. For this reason it is best for them to keep score on work sheets and then quickly transfer the results to the ditto master after their work has been checked.

23. Arrange for gate passes for competitors, officials, and guests or prepare a gate list.

24. Report results to local papers, radios, and TV stations.

25. Mail results to interested parties.

26. Arrange to have the facilities cleaned and equipment put away.

27. Prepare a financial statement.

PLANNING DUAL GYMNASTIC MEETS

(NOTE: The suggestions below also apply to triangular or quadrangular meets.)

Dual meets are very easy to plan and conduct in comparison with the gymnastic tournament. All competitors are under the supervision of the two coaches. If the visiting team is from out of town, the coach usually makes his own travel and housing arrangements. Dual meets are practically always one-session meets with one event held at a time so that only one set of officials is needed. There are usually no awards and no entry fees. There is no need to mail out information sheets or entry blanks. A letter or phone call to the opposing coach to establish procedures and regulations is all that is necessary.

ITEMS TO CONSIDER

1. Select a date and time for the meet. Avoid conflicts if possible. Arrange for use of facilities.

2. Select a meet director. The host coach almost always serves as meet director.

3. Establish rules for the meet. Some decision will have to be made by the two coaches regarding most of the items listed under item 4 in the previous section "Planning Gymnastic Tournaments." It is wise to agree that unless otherwise decided the latest rules of the N.C.A.A. or state high school athletic association will apply. In

dual meets there is usually just one level of competition with three or four competitors from each team in each event. Teams alternate competitors in each event and in being first "up" in each event. Required exercises are usually not used in dual meets, but there is no reason why they could not be used. It has been recommended previously that required exercises are desirable for inexperienced gymnasts.

4. Publicize the meet.

5. Invite school administrative personnel.

6. Provide for warmups prior to the meet. Warmups are usually not permitted on the floor after a dual meet has started.

7. Provide locker room facilities for the visiting team.

8. Arrange for the required number of officials and other workers. All of the same officials, in reduced numbers, are needed for a dual meet as an invitational tournament (except pushers). Refer to item 14 under "Planning Gymnastic Tournaments."

9. Diagram placement of equipment on the floor and plan for the movement of equipment during the meet. Be sure to measure and mark the floor exercise area before the meet.

10. Have programs printed. If the opposing team's entries can be obtained in advance for each event, this adds to the value of the program.

11. Prepare score sheets. These should be prepared in advance with the host team's entries included. The visiting coach can make his entries just prior to the meet as the competitors are warming up. Example score sheets are included in the Appendix, pages 457–59.

12. Provide for all necessary miscellaneous equipment as well as the gymnastic apparatus. This list is the same as for "Gymnastic Tournaments" except that competitors' numbers, awards, and the award platform are not needed.

13. Provide a copy of the results for the visiting coach. Results do not have to be duplicated. If two scorekeepers are used, as mentioned previously, and each scorekeeper keeps a carbon copy of his own work, there will be a set of results available for each coach plus two extra copies for newspapers.

PLANNING INTRAMURAL COMPETITION

Intramural competition can be either the dual meet or tournament type. There is no need to include a special intramural section in this book as the steps already listed for either a dual meet or tournament can be followed in conducting competition within a school. Many of the items can be bypassed, however, in organizing an intramural meet. Judging and team scoring can be modified in a number of ways. It is certainly not necessary to have four scoring judges as specified by the rules.

CONDUCTING GYMNASTIC MEETS

No matter how carefully you plan in advance for a gymnastic meet it will not run smoothly unless the key personnel are efficient in the performance of their duties. Three individuals are vital to the running of a meet once it starts. They are the superior judge, the announcer, and the floor manager. The meet director may assume one of these positions on the day of the meet, but as he is usually also the host coach he should be left free to be with his team. Actually, an experienced announcer can also act as floor manager by giving directions to the appropriate personnel over the public address system. This method is used by the author for intramural meets but is not recommended for larger, more important competition.

The superior judge, the announcer, and the floor manager all need to possess considerable gymnastic knowledge. Do not select an announcer only because of a good voice or a floor manager only because of a strong back. The superior judge must see that the judges work effectively and quickly. He must keep the length of conferences to a minimum. He must move the officials quickly from one event to another. His duties require leadership ability as well as gymnastic knowledge. The announcer is responsible for the efficient operation of the meet. He must keep it moving and fill in with interesting material if it drags unavoidably at any time. The floor manager is primarily responsible for setting up the equipment and moving it during the meet. Besides this, however, he takes care of any unusual or unforeseen situations that might arise. He needs a crew of two or more strong young men to work with him (the number depends on the size of the meet).

ANNOUNCER'S OUTLINE

1. During the pre-meet warmup the announcer should review his material and check on pronunciation of names. He may also operate the record player. Lively band music provides the best atmosphere.

2. About 10 minutes before the scheduled start of the meet the announcer asks competitors to stop warming up and to clear the floor.

3. He then starts the opening ceremony. In a dual meet this is quite simple. He welcomes spectators and contestants; introduces the judges, who walk out on the floor as they are introduced; introduces the visiting team, then the home team (individuals stand as their names are read); introduces the coaches; and makes other necessary preliminary remarks. Often the win-loss record of each team is given. The method of scoring competitors and awarding team points may be included; however, it is probably best to insert this information in a dead spot a little later in the meet. As the coaches are introduced, the home captain and home coach usually walk over and shake hands with the visiting coach and captain. The announcer then asks everyone to stand for the National Anthem. In a large tournament the opening ceremony is more complicated. The announcer usually has to direct a march-in of competitors and introduce a dignitary for the welcoming address. However, the competitors are not introduced individually and if many judges are involved usually only the superior judges are introduced (and the Meet Director).

NOTE: From this point on, it will be assumed that one event is being held at a time. If two or more are held at a time two announcers might be needed. This will complicate the procedure but will not change it in principle.

4. The competition is now ready to start. It is common practice at some schools for the announcer to read a brief outline of the rules and requirements for each event before it starts. At other schools, so as not to prolong the meet, this information is inserted between performances in the event. The announcer calls the first competitor "up" and alerts the next competitor by using the term "on deck." Sometimes a third competitor is alerted by calling his name, followed by "in the hole." After the first competitor is finished and scored by the judges (the judges give their score to their score flasher so that she can have her flash board ready), the announcer asks for "scores, please." The score flashers flash their scores simultaneously to the scoring table. As the scorekeepers copy the scores, the announcer reads them. Judges should be assigned a number and the announcer should always read the scores in order from judge one to judge four. An experienced announcer can also come up with the average of the middle two scores immediately and give this without any hesitation. The scorekeepers should not rely on the announcer but should copy the scores visually to ensure accuracy. After the scores are read, the score flashers slowly turn their boards, in unison, so that spectators can see the scores. Sometimes the superior judge, who has to check the scores to see if they are within the required

range, also has a score flasher to flash the competitor's final score. If this procedure is used, the announcer can read the average score. The announcer then calls the gymnast "up" who had been "on deck" and alerts the next one or two competitors. This procedure is followed until all competitors have performed. Immediately after the last man in the event has competed, the results of the event should be given. This can be done if the scorekeepers have determined a tentative placing prior to the last man. Usually three to five places are announced. The announcer should start with the third (or fifth) man and progress in reverse order to the winner. The scores for each man may or may not be read. By this time the scorekeepers should have a running score for the meet so that this can be announced before proceeding to the next event.

5. This same procedure listed in item 4 is followed for each event to be contested.

6. At the end of the meet the results of the last event and the final team score are announced as usual. The all-round places should also be announced. As well as this the spectators should be reminded of the next home meet.

FLOOR MANAGER'S OUTLINE

This material comes largely from a "Guide for Competitions," written by Glen Wilson and published by the U.S.G.F. Wilson's book contains detailed information about all phases of conducting gymnastic competitions.

1. Prior to the meet the floor manager must:

   a. Set up equipment an hour and a half before the starting time of the meet allowing at least one hour for warm-ups.
   b. Run through the equipment checklist to make sure that all items have been provided.
   c. Show visiting teams to their dressing rooms and provide them with towels and programs. He should also explain the opening ceremony and inform them where their bench will be located on the floor.

2. As soon as the announcer asks for the floor to be cleared just prior to the meet, the floor manager must:

   a. Supervise any necessary shift in equipment.
   b. Supervise the dust mopping of the floor exercise area.
   c. Move some chalk receptacles to the team benches.
   d. Place a damp towel by one corner of the floor exercise area.
   e. Dust judges' and score flashers' chairs and rearrange them if they have been moved during warm-ups.

3. During the meet there are many things that the floor manager must do. Some are standard procedure, others are unforeseen duties and do not appear below.

a. Make any adjustment to equipment for the next event while the preceding event is taking place.
b. Shift judges' and score flashers' chairs after each event. Use two sets of chairs so that one set is always ready for the following event.
c. Sand the side horse pommels, horizontal bar, or parallel bars if competitors request it.
d. Help competitors adjust equipment (width and height of parallel bars especially).
e. Provide a wet towel for the competitors to wipe their feet on in the long horse event; also a dry towel for the hand zone judge to use.
f. Remove equipment from the floor as each event is completed. Mats should be left until after the meet as these do not block the spectators' view and the moving of them might interfere with the meet.

4. After the meet the floor manager must:

a. Supervise the removal of any equipment that remains on the floor.
b. Assist in getting results to visiting coaches, teams, and reporters who have attended. He might also assist in telephoning results to radio, television, and newspapers not represented at the meet.

ORGANIZING TEAM PRACTICE SESSIONS

There are hundreds of exhibition teams and gymnastic clubs in the schools across our country but still very few competitive teams in relation to the number of teams in many other sports. The suggestions made here apply especially to practice sessions for competitive teams. It is hoped that with the tremendous upsurge in gymnastics, in a few years there will be many more competitive teams with active coaches.

Until recently most coaches have not held organized practice sessions. A team workout usually consisted of an informal period with team members wandering from one event to another. The coach, and maybe some of the better performers, would help first here, and then there, in a haphazard fashion. Gymnastic coaches have recently adopted the methods of coaches of other sports who are forced to get the most out of their players in order to compete successfully. The way to develop top teams in gymnastics is to have organized, scientifically planned practice sessions just as in other sports.

Practice sessions should be planned for a week at a time. Each

University of Washington Work Out Schedule – October 1-March 31

		Monday	Tuesday	Wednesday	Thursday	10/1- Fri. 11/15	11/15- Fri. 1/1	1/1- Fri. 3/31
Group 1 Varsity All Round A	3:30 3:45 4:30 5:15 6:00	--- Floor Exercise Side Horse Long Horse ---	---WARM UP & Horizontal Bar Parallel Bars Rings ---STRENGTH	STRETCHING--- Long Horse Floor Exercise Side Horse WORK OUT---	--- Rings Horizontal Bars Parallel Bars ---	--- Three Weakest Events ---	--- All Six Events ---	--- Little or No Work– Individual's Choice
Group 2 Varsity All Round B	3:30 3:45 4:30 5:15 6:00	--- Long Horse Floor Exercise Side Horse ---	---WARM UP & Rings Horizontal Bar Parallel Bars ---STRENGTH	STRETCHING--- Side Horse Long Horse Floor Exercise WORK OUT---	--- Parallel Bars Rings Horizontal Bar ---	--- Three Weakest Events ---	--- All Six Events ---	--- Little or No Work– Individual's Choice
Group 3 Freshmen All Round	3:30 3:45 4:30 5:15 6:00	--- Side Horse Long Horse Floor Exercise ---	---WARM UP & Parallel Bars Rings Horizontal Bar ---STRENGTH	STRETCHING--- Floor Exercise Side Horse Long Hose WORK OUT---	--- Horizontal Bar Parallel Bars Rings ---	--- Three Weakest Events ---	--- All Six Events ---	--- Little or No Work– Individual's Choice

Group 4 Varsity Trampoline	3:30 3:45 4:45 5:45	Trampoline	WARM UP & Trampoline STRENGTH	STRETCHING Trampoline WORK OUT	Trampoline	Tramp. Tramp.	Tramp. Tramp.	Little or No work– Individual's Choice
Group 5 Freshmen Trampoline	3:30 3:45 4:45 5:45	Trampoline	WARM UP & Trampoline STRENGTH	STRETCHING Trampoline WORK OUT	Trampoline	Tramp. Tramp.	Tramp. Tramp.	Little or No Work– Individual's Choice

Specialists–Work with the appropriate group when it is working on your events and by yourself the rest of the time.

Trampolinists–Work at least one other event every day. When not assigned to the trampoline go to an event of your choice.

All Varsity–Starting November 15 you will be expected to demonstrate two complete competitive exercises in each event Monday through Thursday. As soon as the exercises have been demonstrated to the satisfaction of the coach, you may work on unlearned stunts. Also, every Friday starting November 15 you will be expected to demonstrate three competitive exercises on all six events except for the side horse on which five must be performed.

All Freshman–The above will apply to freshman starting December 15 instead of November 15.

University of Washington Work-out Schedule– April 1 to September 30 (3:30-6:00 April, May, and June; 7:00-9:30 July, August, September)		
Monday	Wednesday	Friday
1. Warm-up and stretching 2. Events for the day Floor Exercise Side Horse Long Horse Horizontal Bar Trampoline 3. Strength work-out	1. Warm-up and stretching 2. Events for the day Parallel Bars Rings Floor Exercise Side Horse Trampoline 3. Strength work-out	1. Warm-up and stretching 2. Events for the day Long Horse Horizontal Bar Parallel Bars Rings Trampoline 3. Strength work-out

Specialists–If your events are not scheduled, work other events and try to develop proficiency in them.
Trampolinists–Work an hour and a half on the trampoline then try to develop proficiency in another event.
All-round–Work at least three of the events scheduled for the day.
Everyone–Concentrate on learning new skills that can be used in competition next year.

Seattle Y.M.C.A. Pre-season Work-out Schedule

Mon. 6:30 – 9:30	Wed. 6:30 – 9:30	Fri. 6:30 – 9:30	Sat. 1:00 – 5:00
Work on compulsory exercises all six events	Work on optional exercises all six events	Work on weaknesses in either compulsory or optional exercises	Demonstration of complete compulsory and optional exercises in all six events

week prior to the start of the season of competition is organized in much the same way. Once competition starts, a new weekly plan is put into effect and this remains somewhat standard throughout the season. After the season is over another plan is used in preparation for the next season. If required exercises are a part of the competition, this factor greatly affects the practice sessions and a different type of plan is needed.

Gymnasts can be divided into two groups—the all-round performers and the specialists. The largest group of specialists is the group that specializes in trampoline and tumbling. If a boy specializes in one or more all-round events, he can devote his whole time to the practice of these events working with a group part of the time and on his own part of the time. Those who combine tumbling and trampoline as a specialty can divide their time between these two events each workout session.

As most gymnasts today want to become all-round performers, practice sessions are usually planned with this in mind. The all-round performers should be assigned to a piece of equipment with boys of their own ability for a specified length of time. A variation of this might be when one or two advanced boys are assigned to help with groups of less ability during some practice sessions. At the end of the time limit, groups shift to another piece of equipment and work on that for a specified period of time. If considerable time is available, the all-round performers cover all events each day; if less time is available, they work three events one day and the other three the next day.

The daily schedule can follow a number of patterns. Some examples of these are given on pages 448–50.

Appendix

University of Washington—Intramural Gymnastics

INFORMATION BULLETIN

General Information

1. Teams may enter as many men as they wish in the qualifying meet.
2. There will be required exercises for the qualifying meet. These are available in the intramural office.
3. Optional exercises only in the final meet.
4. The eight top performers in each event in the qualifying meet will advance into the final meet.
5. Contestants may enter a maximum of four events.
6. Unless otherwise stated, the Official Rules of the A.A.U. of the U.S. will apply. Copies are on reserve in the physical education office.
7. The team championship shall be awarded to the organization scoring the highest number of points in the final meet. There must be at least two contestants scoring points for a team. Points shall be scored as follows: 7 points for first, 5 for second, 4 for third, 3 for fourth, 2 for fifth, and 1 for sixth place.

Events

1. Floor exercise
2. Side horse
3. Rings
4. Long horse vault
5. Parallel bars
6. Horizontal bar
7. Tumbling
8. Trampoline
9. Rope climb
10. Hand walk for distance

Coaching

Coaching will be available at the following times starting January 4.

Monday, Tuesday, Thursday, and Friday	4:00–5:30 P.M.
Wednesday	7:30–9:30 P.M.

Entries Must Be in the Intramural Office by Monday, February 22

Those wishing to participate must indicate the events they wish to enter on individual entry blanks by February 22nd.

Qualifying Meet—Wednesday, February 24, 7:00 P.M., Intramural Gym

The first eight places in each event will be eligible for the finals.

Final Meet—Wednesday, March 10, 7:00 P.M., Intramural Gym

INFORMATION BULLETIN

Pacific Northwest A.A.U. Gymnastic Championship
Friday and Saturday March 19 and 20, 19—
Issaquah Senior High School

Rules and Regulations

1. The rules governing this meet will be the official rules of the A.A.U. of the United States.
2. Competitors can not compete in the same event in two divisions. The exception to this would be a competitor forced into a higher class because he has won the event in the division below, but who is still competing in the all-round in the lower division.
3. The entry fee for novice men, junior men, novice women, and junior women is $1.00; senior men and women $2.00.
4. No entries will be accepted after 5:00 P.M. Monday, March 15. Entries will not be accepted unless accompanied by entry fee.
5. Gymnasts from outside the Pacific Northwest Association of the A.A.U. must furnish travel permits.

Events

Women	*Men*
Floor exercise	Floor exercise
Balance team	Side Horse
Side Horse Vault	Rings
Uneven Parallel bars	Long Horse vault
All-round	Parallel bars
Tumbling	Horizontal bars
Trampoline	All-round
	Tumbling
	Trampoline

Time Schedule

Women

Novice		
Compulsory	9:00 A.M.	Sat.
Optional	2:00 P.M.	Sat.
Junior		
Compulsory	9:00 A.M.	Sat.
Optional	2:00 P.M.	Sat.
Senior		
Compulsory	7:30 P.M.	Fri.
Optional	7:30 P.M.	Sat.

Men

Novice		
Compulsory	9:00 A.M.	Sat.
Optional	2:00 P.M.	Sat.
Junior		
Compulsory	9:00 A.M.	Sat.
Optional	2:00 P.M.	Sat.
Senior		
Compulsory	7:30 P.M.	Fri.
Optional	7:30 P.M.	Sat.

General Information

1. Nissen-Medart equipment meeting all F.I.G. requirements will be used. A floor exercise pad, 60-foot tumbling mat, and Goliath trampolines will be available.
2. A map giving directions to Issaquah High School is enclosed.
3. Those wishing to be billeted with an Issaquah family should fill out the enclosed form and return it immediately.

4. A copy of the required exercises is enclosed. Others can be obtained on request.
5. The Issaquah High School gym will be available for practice on Wednesday and Thursday evenings from 7:30 to 9:30 for those who arrive early.
6. Regulation A.A.U. Championship Medals will be awarded to the first three place winners in each event. Ribbons will be awarded to fourth, fifth, and sixth place.
7. Contestants and coaches should report to the contestants' table in the gym lobby to pick up their official envelope containing their numbers, gate passes, programs, and other general information. Travel permits must be presented at this time.
8. Please send publicity releases with photos as soon as possible to the meet director.
9. Meals will be provided, for a small charge, in the school cafeteria on Friday evening, Saturday noon, and Saturday evening.
10. Meetings: Judges—Gym, Friday 4:00 P.M.
    Technical Committee—Gym, Friday 6:00 P.M.
    Coaches and Pacific Northwest Gymnastic Committee—Cafeteria, Saturday 12:00 Noon; lunch will be served.
11. Additional information may be obtained by writing to the meet director: Mr. Charlie Denny, Issaquah Senior High School, Issaquah, Washington.

UNIVERSITY OF WASHINGTON
DEPARTMENT OF INTRAMURAL SPORTS

GYMNASTIC ENTRY BLANK

Date________________ 19____

I wish to enter the following events (check):

Floor exercise________________ Horizontal bar________________

Side horse________________ Tumbling________________

Rings________________ Trampoline________________

Long horse vault________________ Rope climb________________

Parallel bars________________ Hand walk for distance________

Name________________________ Organization________________________

Address________________________ Phone________________________

Pacific Northwest A.A.U. Gymnastic Championship

OFFICIAL ENTRY BLANK

Entries close Monday, March 15, 19—

Men

EVENTS	Novice	Junior	Senior
Floor Exercise			
Side Horse			
Long Horse Vault			
Horizontal Bar			
Rings			
All-Round			
Tumbling			
Trampoline			
Parallel Bars			

Women

EVENTS	Novice	Junior	Senior
Floor Exercise			
Balance Beam			
Side Horse Vault			
Uneven Parallel Bars			
All-Round			
Tumbling			
Trampoline			

Place an X opposite the events you wish to enter and in the division in which you wish to participate.

Entry fees must accompany entry blanks. Novice men, junior men, novice women, and junior women $1.00. Senior men and women $2.00.

Release: I hereby for myself, my heirs, and executors waive and release any and all rights and claims for damages that I may have at any time against the A.A.U. or Issaquah High School, or their agents and representatives, for any injuries or damages that may be suffered by me in connection with my association, or entry in, the above meet at Issaquah High School, March 19 and 20, 19___.

Signature ____________________

If contestant is under 21 years of age

Signature of parent or Guardian ____________________

Please Print

Contestant's Name ____________________ Age __________

Street Address ____________________ City __________

Team Affiliation ____________________ A.A.U. card no. __________

Meet information may be obtained by writing to the Meet Director:
Mr. Charlie Denny, Issaquah Senior High School, Issaquah, Washington.

EVENT SCORE SHEET

MEET ______________________ JUDGES 1. ______________________

LOCATION ______________________ 2. ______________________

DATE ______________________ 3. ______________________

4. ______________________

EVENT ______________________ SUPERIOR ______________________

Name	Team	Judges 1	2	3	4	Total Middle 2	Ave.	Prelim. Score	Combined Score	Place	Team Score

NOTE: 1. For most meets that only involve one session the two columns "preliminary score" and "combined score" will not be used.

2. This score sheet can be converted to one for the long horse by using two lines for each competitor. The scores of the first vault are entered on the top line and those for the second vault on the one immediately below. The middle two scores of both vaults must be totaled, but only the highest total needs to be averaged.

3. If the international system of team scoring is being used, the last column "team score" does not have to be used as the "average" column is also the team score.

4. If there is both a compulsory and an optional exercise in the meet, or for that matter in any meet in which there are two sessions, two lines may be used for each competitor—the first for the compulsory and the second for the optional. The preliminary score column will not have to be used in this case.

ALL-ROUND SCORE SHEET

Meet ________________ Location ________________ Date ________________

NAME																	
TEAM																	
Floor Exercise	Event score																
	Running score																
Side Horse	Event score																
	Running score																
Rings	Event score																
	Running score																
Long Horse Vault	Event score																
	Running score																
Parallel Bars	Event score																
	Running score																
Horizontal Bar	Event score																
	Running score																
TOTAL																	
PLACE																	
TEAM SCORE																	

TEAM SCORE SHEET

TEAM																	
Floor Exercise	Event score																
	Running score																
Side Horse	Event score																
	Running score																
Rings	Event score																
	Running score																
Long Horse Vault	Event score																
	Running score																
Parallel Bars	Event score																
	Running score																
Horizontal Bar	Event score																
	Running score																
All-Round	Event score																
	Running score																
Trampoline	Event score																
	Running score																
Tumbling	Event score																
	Running score																
FINAL SCORE																	
PLACE																	

Glossary

A.A.U.—Amateur Athletic Union of the United States.

AAHPER—American Association for Health, Physical Education and Recreation.

All-Round—An event in which the winner is determined by totaling the scores received in the following six events: floor exercise, side horse, long horse vault, rings, parallel bars, and horizontal bar.

"A" Parts—A difficulty rating for gymnastic stunts. It refers to stunts or movements that are relatively easy to perform.

Arch (Layout, Hollow Back)—A position in which the body is curved, like an arc of a circle, with the hips forward and the upper trunk and legs extended.

Baroni (Brani, Brandy)—A name given to a special type of a half-twisting front somersault with the body in a pike position.

Backward—A direction of movement in which the back of the head and back lead the movement (there are a few exceptions).

Beat Board—A short inclined takeoff board used for vaulting and mounting the parallel bars.

Bed of the Trampoline—A term used to refer to the woven nylon or canvas surface of the trampoline on which the performer bounces.

"B" Parts—A difficulty rating for gymnastic stunts. It refers to stunts or movements that are somewhere in the middle of the difficulty scale.

Breadth Axis—An imaginary line drawn laterally through the body from shoulder to shoulder.

Break—A point in an exercise at which a gymnast makes a mistake or has an unintentional pause.

Cast—A term used to describe movements in which the body is first piked and then extended upward and away from the point of grasp in either a forward or backward direction.

Center of Gravity—The center of the distribution of body weight. The point of balance.

Circle—A movement in which the body, or sometimes a part of the body, such as the legs, travels completely around a point of support.

Code of Points—The Code of Points refers to a document, prepared by the F.I.G., which specifies how a competitive gymnastic exercise is to be composed and evaluated.

Cody—A name given to a somersault on the trampoline that is executed from a front drop landing.

Compulsory Exercise (Prescribed Exercise, Required Exercise)—The term used to refer to a competitive gymnastic exercise that every competitor must perform.

Continuity—A term used to refer to the smoothness or flowing quality of a routine or series. A series is said to possess continuity if it is not interrupted by undesirable pauses, stops, or extra movements.

"C" PARTS—A difficulty rating for gymnastic stunts. It refers to stunts or movements that are of a great or superior difficulty.

CROSS POSITION—A position in which the breadth axis of the performer is perpendicular to the long axis of the apparatus.

CROUP—The right end of the side horse if the gymnast is standing facing the center section. Also the near end of the long horse as the vaulter approaches.

CUT—A movement in which one or both legs swing between the hand or hands and a piece of equipment. In a cut-on the performer starts on the floor and ends on the equipment. In a cut-off the performer dismounts during the cut.

DISLOCATE—A movement in which the body, while suspended from a fixed point by the hands, makes a complete circle or revolution, rotating around the shoulder joint, in a backward direction.

DISMOUNT—A stunt used by the performer to get off the apparatus. In a competitive exercise a dismount is the last stunt, or short series of stunts in the exercise. The last series of a floor exercise routine is sometimes referred to as the dismount.

DOUBLE LEG CIRCLE—A circle in which both legs move as a unit around the point of support.

EXERCISE (ROUTINE)—A planned series of stunts that a gymnast performs in every event except vaulting.

FEINT—A movement that is started but not completed.

F.I.G.—Federation of International Gymnastics. This organization governs and makes rules for international competition.

FLANK—A term used to describe a movement, stunt, or position in which the side of the body is toward the apparatus.

FLIP—A common term for somersault.

FORWARD—A direction of movement in which the face and chest lead the movement (there are exceptions).

FRONT (FRONTWAYS)—Two terms used to describe a movement, stunt, or position in which the front of the body is facing the apparatus.

GRIP (GRASP)—Two terms that refer to the handhold that the gymnast has on the apparatus. They are classified as: regular (ordinary, over, front); reverse (under); cross; mixed (combined); rotated (eagle); or false (high). Refer to the introduction of the horizontal chapter for an illustration of all of these except the false grip. The false grip is illustrated on page 269 of Chapter 7.

GOLIATH TRAMPOLINE (JUMBO)—Two terms used for a trampoline that is larger than the usual size used in schools (common frame size—9 x 15; goliath frame size—10 x 17).

HANG—A position in which the center of gravity, and usually the entire body, is below the point of support. The point of support is usually the hands but is sometimes the knees, the feet, the elbows, or the arms.

HOLD—The term "hold" refers to a stationary position in a gymnastic exercise of at least two seconds on the parallel bars and in floor exercise and of at least three seconds on the rings. The length of time is specified by the rules.

HOP—A spring into the air with a takeoff from one foot and a landing on the same foot.

HURDLE—The last step in an approach run prior to a two foot take-off. Usually refers to vaulting.

INTERNATIONAL EVENTS (OLYMPIC)—The events included in all international gymnastic competition, including the Olympic games. There are six of them —floor exercise, side horse, rings, long horse vault, parallel bars, and horizontal bar.

JUMP—A spring into the air with a takeoff from both feet.

KILLING THE BOUNCE—A term used when the bounce on the trampoline is suddenly stopped so that the feet remain in contact with the bed. It is accomplished by flexing the knees rapidly as the feet contact the bed.

KIP (UPSTART)—A movement from a hang to a support in which the body pikes and then rapidly extends.

"L"—A position in which the legs are forward in a horizontal plane so that they form a right angle with the trunk. The correct term is a half-lever.

LEAP—A spring into the air, taking off from one foot and landing on the other.

LEFT CIRCLE—A leg circle on the side horse that moves in a counterclockwise direction.

LEVER—A position in which the body is held horizontal to the floor. If the legs only are horizontal, the position is called a half-lever.

LONGITUDINAL AXIS—An imaginary line running from the top of the head through the center of the body to the soles of the feet.

LUNGE—A standing position in which the legs are apart with one knee bent and the other straight. This term also refers to the "movement" from a vertical standing position to the position described.

MAGNESIUM CARBONATE—The chalk that a gymnast uses on his hands to soak up perspiration and minimize slipping.

MOUNT—A stunt used by the performer to get on the apparatus. In a competitive exercise it is the term used for the first stunt or short series of stunts. The first series in floor exercise is sometimes referred to as a mount.

N.C.A.A.—National Collegiate Athletic Association. This is one of the organizations that controls men's intercollegiate athletics.

NECK—The left end of the side horse if the gymnast is standing facing the center section. Also the far end of the long horse as the vaulter approaches.

OPTIONAL EXERCISE (VOLUNTARY EXERCISE)—The term used to refer to a gymnastic exercise that is composed by the individual from stunts of his own choice.

PART—A term used to refer to the stunts or movements into which a complete gymnastic exercise is divided. Parts are classified as A (easy), B (difficult), or C (extremely difficult).

PIKE—A position in which the body is flexed at the waist with the legs straight. In most pike positions the trunk and legs form approximately a right angle. It is called an open pike if the legs are only slightly flexed and a tight pike if the legs are considerably flexed.

PIROUETTE—A movement around the longitudinal axis of the body with the body in a vertical position, either upright or inverted, throughout the turn.

PIVOT—A smooth turn left or right on the balls of one or both feet.

POMMEL HORSE—The name used for the side horse in many foreign countries.

PRESS—A movement into a head or hand balance that involves a shifting of body weight and a slow, steady muscular action rather than a kick-up or a swing-up.

REAR (REARWAYS)—Two terms used to describe a movement, stunt, or position in which the rear of the body is toward the apparatus.

REBOUND TUMBLING—A term used for stunts done on the trampoline.

REUTHER BOARD—The official takeoff board used in vaulting and sometimes other gymnastic events. The reuther board was developed in Germany and is of very recent origin.

RIGHT CIRCLE—A leg circle on the side horse that moves in a clockwise direction.

RIP (OR TEAR)—A patch of skin on the hands that has torn loose from the flesh below.

ROLL—A circling movement in which the body remains in contact with, and the body weight is supported by, the mat or equipment during the entire movement. The back is usually rounded and the legs tucked or piked during the roll.

ROUTINE (EXERCISE)—A planned continuous series of stunts performed in every event in gymnastic competition except vaulting.

SADDLE—The center section of the side horse between the two pommels.

SCALE—A one-leg balance in which the other leg is raised backward and the trunk lowered forward to a position approximately horizontal to the floor.

SEAT—A position in which most of the weight is supported by the thighs or buttocks. Seats are usually described according to the relationship of the body to the apparatus. Examples—cross seat, straddle seat, side seat, inner or outer seats.

SIDE POSITION—A position in which the breadth axis of the gymnast is parallel to the long axis of the apparatus. This is a rather confusing term as it has no connection to the side of the body. The gymnast is usually facing toward or away from the equipment in a side position.

SINGLE LEG CIRCLE—Refers to a circle in which one leg moves around the point of support.

SOMERSAULT (SOMI, FLIP)—A complete circling motion of the body in the air, usually from feet to feet, during which no other part of the body comes in contact with the mat or apparatus.

SPECIAL EVENTS—A term used to classify the tumbling, trampoline, and sometimes other events that are not all-round or international events.

SPLIT—A position in which the legs are in a straight line and at right angles to the trunk. Usually one leg is directly forward and one directly backward.

SPOTTING—The term used to refer to the proper positioning of an individual who assists a gymnast in the performance of a stunt. Spotting is also commonly used to refer to the actual "act of assisting" and the person providing the assistance is called the "spotter."

SPRING—A complete circling motion of the body in the air, usually from feet to feet, in which the hands, head, neck, or shoulders contact the mat or apparatus during the movement.

STAND—A position on the floor or apparatus in which the entire body is above the point of support. The point of support is usually the feet but can be the knees, hands, head, forearms, or shoulders.

STRADDLE—A position in which the legs are spread wide apart.

SUPPORT (REST)—A position in which the weight is supported wholly or partially by the hands with the shoulders above the point of grasp and the center of gravity below the shoulders.

SWING—A movement in which the body describes a circle, or an arc of a circle, while in a hang or support position.

SWING-UP—A smooth circling movement in which the gymnast changes from a hang to a support.

TOUR JETÉ—A leap off of one foot with a half-turn in the air to a landing on the other foot.

TRAVEL—A term given to stunts that bring about movement from one part of the equipment to another.

TUCK—A position in which the head is forward with the chin close to the chest, the back is rounded, and the knees are drawn up to the chest.

TWIST—A turn left or right around one's longitudinal axis.

UPRISE—A movement from a hang to a support, at the end of a forward or backward swing, in which the head remains above the center of gravity.

VAULT—A jump or leap over a piece of apparatus in which one or both hands touch the apparatus during the movement.

WALK-OUT OR STEP-OUT—A landing on one foot at a time. The second foot is placed in front of the first one as in a walking step.

WHIP-BACK—A type of back somersault that involves a fast whipping action of the body from a pike into an arch and then back to a pike.

Bibliography

Amateur Athletic Union of the United States. *Official 1965–66 Gymnastics Guide and Handbook.* New York. 133 pages. This guide is published every two years. It contains rules for men and women; international, national, and district meet summaries; inspirational and informative reports and articles; and compulsory exercises for men and women.

———. F.I.G. Code of Points. New York. 72 pages. Contains the A, B, C, Table of Difficulty as well as the Code of Points.

BAILEY, JAMES A. *Gymnastics in the Schools.* Boston: Allyn & Bacon, Inc., 1965. 297 pages. A very complete book covering history; values; teaching principles; equipment; public relations; stunts for the elementary school, junior high school, senior high school, and college students; exhibitions; and competition.

BURNS, TED. *Tumbling Techniques Illustrated.* New York: The Ronald Press Co., 1957. 96 pages. This text is for both men and women. It includes single tumbling stunts for beginners, intermediates, and advanced performers.

DAVIDGE, BERNICE, and QUINN, WM. J. *Elementary Tumbling and Stunts.* Langstaff, Ontario: David G. Smith, 1957.

DECARLO, TOM. *Handbook of Progressive Gymnastics.* New York: Prentice-Hall, Inc., 1963. 240 pages. Contains teaching techniques; safety suggestions; nomenclature; beginning, novice, intermediate, junior, advanced, and senior skills; promotion of a varsity gymnastic team; and a history of gymnastics.

FARKAS, JAMES. *Age Group Gymnastic Workbook.* Tucson, Arizona: United States Gymnastic Federation, 1964. 90 pages. Contains abbreviated descriptions and stick figures of suggested skills and routines for six age groups, both boys and girls. It also includes information about competition and U.S.G.F. awards and materials.

FISCHER, HUGO, SHAWBOLD, DEAN, and WOHLFORD, PAUL. *Individual and Dual Stunts.* Minneapolis: Burgess Publishing Co., 1950.

FREY, HAROLD J., and KEENEY, CHARLES J. *Elementary Gymnastic Apparatus Skills Illustrated.* New York: The Ronald Press Co., 1964. 144 pages. Includes descriptions and photographs for elementary skills in four events—parallel bars, horizontal bar, side horse, and rings. Also includes information on planning, organizing, teaching, and competitive gymnastics.

GRISWOLD, LARRY. *Trampoline Tumbling.* St. Louis, Mo.: Business Collaborators, Inc., 1958. 120 pages. This book has chapters on history, notes for instructors, body mechanics, fundamental bounces, basic exercises, simple demonstrations, advanced exercises, suggested routines, group tumbling, exhibitions, competition. It is illustrated with drawings.

HARRIS, RICH. *Physical Education and Rebound Tumbling.* Cedar Rapids, Iowa: Barnes Publishing Co., 1961. 48 pages. This pamphlet includes information on values, safety, equipment, class organization, basic instruction, lesson plans, and where to obtain reference materials. It is illustrated with photos and drawings.

———. *Safety and Rebound Tumbling.* Cedar Rapids, Iowa: Barnes Publishing Co., 1960. 21 pages. This pamphlet contains chapters on safety in schools, safety in recreation, mechanics of safety, and rules for safety. It is illustrated with photographs.

———. *Introducing Gymnastics.* Napa, Calif.: Physical Education Aids, 1964. 78 pages. An excellent book for the elementary school teacher who has no background in gymnastics. It is a complete outline for young children and has large wall charts to go with the book.

KEENEY, CHUCK. *Trampolining Illustrated.* New York: The Ronald Press Co., 1961. 160 pages. Keeney presents fifty trampoline stunts ranging from the simplest to the most difficult. The book is illustrated with photos.

KUNZLE, G. C., and THOMAS, B. J. *Olympic Gymnastics—Volume I—Free Standing Exercises.* London: James Barrie Books Ltd., 1956. 87 pages. Contains limited information on the floor exercise event.

———. *Olympic Gymnastics—Volume 2—Horizontal Bar.* London: James Barrie Books Ltd., 1957. 269 pages. An excellent source for beginning, intermediate, and advanced horizontal bar skills. Contains many instructional photographs.

———. *Olympic Gymnastics—Volume 3—Pommel Horse.* London: Barrie & Rockliff, 1960. 184 pages. An excellent source for beginning, intermediate, and advanced skills on the side horse. It has photos and illustrations.

———. *Olympic Gymnastics—Volume 4—Parallel Bars.* London: Barrie & Rockliff, 1964. 416 pages. An excellent source for beginning, intermediate, and advanced skills. Has a large number of instructional illustrations and photos.

LADUE, FRANK, and NORMAN, JIM. *Two Seconds of Freedom.* Cedar Rapids, Iowa: Nissen Trampoline Co., 1960. 167 pages. This text explains and illustrates with photographs a great number of trampoline stunts from beginning to advanced.

LAPORTE, WILLIAM R., and RENNER, AL G. *The Tumbler's Manual.* New York: Prentice-Hall, Inc., 1944.

LOKEN, NEWTON C. ("How to Improve Series"). *Beginning Tumbling and Balancing,* 1951; *Advanced Tumbling and Balancing,* 1958. Chicago, Ill.: The Athletic Institute. These are very small pamphlets. The title of each indicates the content. They are illustrated with photographs.

———. *Complete Book of Gymnastics.* Englewood Cliffs, N.J.: Prentice-Hall, Inc., 1959. 212 pages. This text has a chapter on every men's and women's gymnastic event as well as special activities such as balancing, calisthenics, rope, and springboard trampoline. It also has chapters on history, values, and gymnastic exhibitions. Stunts are illustrated with photographs.

MCCLOW, L. L. *Tumbling Illustrated.* New York: The Ronald Press Co., 1931. 212 pages. This book explains and illustrates with stick figures a great number of single, double, and group tumbling and balancing stunts. It is an excellent source for those looking for many novelty stunts suitable for exhibitions as well as class use.

Modern Gymnast. Santa Monica, Calif. This is a magazine devoted entirely to the sport of gymnastics and is published monthly. It contains many photographs, reports on meets and clinics, and informative articles for both men and women. It also contains lists of sources for gymnastic films, equipment, uniforms, and books.

National Collegiate Athletic Association. *Gymnastics Rules 1966.* New York: The National Collegiate Athletic Bureau. Contains the official N.C.A.A. gymnastic rules. Published annually.

National High School Gymnastic Coaches Association. *Handbook.* Cedar Rapids, Iowa: Nissen Co., 1965. 40 pages. Contains the constitution of the organization, suggested rules for high schools, gymnastic meet check list, reports from districts, a list of state coaches' and judges' associations, a list of members with their addresses, and a list of college coaches with their addresses.

PRICE, HARTLEY D., *et al. Gymnastics and Tumbling.* New York: The Ronald Press Co., 1950. 472 pages. This was formerly the book published by the United States Navy. It contains information on history, values, equipment, safety, principles of teaching, warm-up and conditioning, nomenclature, and instructional material on a great variety of gymnastic activities such as ropes, balancing, and pyramid building as well as the competitive events.

RUFF, WESLEY K. *Gymnastics—Beginner to Competitor.* Dubuque, Iowa: Wm. C. Brown Co., 1959. 204 pages. Contains primarily beginning and intermediate skills on all the competitive events plus rope climb and balancing. Also includes competitive suggestions and sample forms.

RYSER, OTTO E. *A Teacher's Manual for Tumbling and Apparatus Stunts.* Dubuque, Iowa: Wm. C. Brown Co., 1961. 193 pages. Contains suggestions on organization for teaching gymnastics. Has chapters on simple stunts, tumbling, balancing, pyramids, apparatus stunts, and sample demonstrations.

SZYPULA, GEORGE. *Tumbling and Balancing for All.* Dubuque, Iowa: W. C. Brown Co., 1957. 161 pages. Contains information on spotting, class conduct, as well as descriptions of single and double tumbling and balancing stunts. There are also sections on advanced competitive tumbling routines and officiating. It is illustrated with photographs.

TAKEMOTO, MASAO, and HAMADA, SEIICHI. Tokyo: Ban-Yu Shuppan Co., 1960. (U. S. Distributor—Frank Endo, Los Angeles, Calif.). 359 pages. Written in Japanese but with thousands of excellent photos and illustrations. Includes the six international events.

United States Gymnastic Federation. *U.S.G.F. Rules 1965–66.* Tucson, Ariz.: United States Gymnastic Federation. Contains the U.S.G.F. rules and regulations, compulsory routines, F.I.G. Code of Points, Table of difficulty (A, B, C parts) and past U.S.G.F. meet results.

U. S. Gymnast Magazine. Tucson, Arizona. This magazine publishes only gymnastic material. It contains reports from four district reporters from the West, Midwest, Mid-East, and East as well as informative articles, meet results, and instructional material with sequence photos.

WEST, WILBUR D. *The Gymnast's Manual.* New York: Prentice-Hall, Inc., 1946. 326 pages. Contains primarily beginning and intermediate skills on the side horse, long horse, parallel bars, horizontal bar, still rings, and flying rings.

WILSON, GLENN. *Guide for Competitions.* Tucson, Ariz., United States Gymnastic Federation, 1965. 25 pages. Contains a check list for dual and championship meets, announcing procedure, floor manager's duties, floor plans, program organization, example score forms, and other general information for competitions.

Index